# Succeeding in Graduate School

## The Career Guide for Psychology Students

# Succeeding in Graduate School

## The Career Guide for Psychology Students

*Edited by*

**Steven Walfish**
*Bay Psychiatric Center*

**Allen K. Hess**
*Auburn University at Montgomery*

2001

LAWRENCE ERLBAUM ASSOCIATES, PUBLISHERS
Mahwah, New Jersey                                         London

Lawrence Erlbaum Associates, Inc., Publishers
10 Industrial Avenue
Mahwah, NJ  07430

Cover design by Kathryn Houghtaling Lacey

**Library of Congress Cataloging-in-Publication Data**

Succeeding in graduate school : a career guide for psychology students /
  edited by Steven Walfish, Allen K. Hess.
    p.  cm.
Includes bibliographical references and index.
ISBN 0-8058-3613-6 (cloth : alk. paper)
ISBN 0-8058-3614-4 (pbk. : alk. paper)
1. Psychology—Study and teaching (Graduate)  I. Walfish, Steven.
  II. Hess, Allen K., 1945–
BF77 .S83  2001
150'.71'1 —dc21                                          00-067760
                                                              CIP

Books published by Lawrence Erlbaum Associates are printed on
acid-free paper, and their bindings are chosen for strength and durability.

Printed in the United States of America
10   9   8   7   6   5   4   3   2   1

# Contents

# II. Mastering the Personal and Political Dynamics of Graduate School

# III. Learning Career Skills

# IV. The Internship

# V. Becoming a Professional

# Preface

We want you to succeed. That is our goal and, it is the goal that each of the authors kept in mind in developing their chapters.

## HISTORY OF THIS BOOK

Telling you about the birth of this book will help you benefit from our labor of love. The idea for this book came to the first editor (Steve Walfish) and Gerry Sumprer as they were driving to a party to celebrate the completion of their predoctoral internship: "If we had only known at the beginning of graduate school what we knew at the end of it, life would have gone much more smoothly." This thought led to a question: Where could students obtain information about the realities of graduate education? Most either "work in the dark" or find out bits and pieces from other students and helpful faculty. Although both are important sources, they are constrained by personal bias and limited experience. Students seeking experts opinions are generally out of luck. Surveys and empirical studies suggest that students are left to their own devices.

Students are not the only ones to face problems. Conscientious faculty members advising undergraduate and graduate students face a conflict. On one hand, they want to provide their advisees with complete and practical information; on the other hand, they are handicapped by numerous and time-consuming demands. Gerry and Steve saw the need for a single source that could provide guidance to bridge the gulf between the type of knowledge needed to succeed in psychology undergraduate programs and that needed to succeed in psychology graduate school and careers. They decided to edit a volume on this topic and assembled excellent chapter authors and submitted the competed manuscript to their publisher.

During the years that followed, Gerry had to withdraw to meet other obligations, and Allen Hess joined the effort to bring the project to fruition, with the help of Larry Erlbaum and Susan Milmoe. The original concepts of the book were updated to make one suitable for the 21st century.

Our view of the graduate school experience can best be summed up in a line from a Charles Dickens novel: "It was the best of times, it was the worst of times." Our goal is for you to utilize this as a resource to help you succeed in developing the career that is optimal for you in psychology, and to increase the proportion of "the best of times" and decrease the proportion of "the worst of times."

## ORGANIZATION

The first section of this book focuses on understanding what *opportunities* are available for a *career in psychology* and on helping students make *educational choices* that are right for them.

Academic course work is rigorous in most graduate programs, at both the master's and doctoral level. The second section of this book focuses on *emotional aspects of the training process* that can have an impact on students' ability to achieve their educational and professional goals.

Advanced study in psychology involves *mastery of a core set of knowledge and values* and *development of specific skills* in order to deepen our understanding of human behavior and to improve life for individuals, organizations, and communities. The third section of this book focuses on skills that may serve as the foundation for professional activities as a psychologist.

A major component in skill and professional identity development of the doctoral graduate student in applied psychology is the *full-year internship*. This book's fourth section focuses on issues related to applying for and obtaining an internship, as well as making optimal use of this experience for professional development.

Upon graduation, the new degree recipient sets out into the world to apply his or her skills in research, teaching, and applied practice. The final section of this book focuses on important *issues related to being a new professional*: how to become licensed for independent practice, how to reach out in a community, and how to sustain a satisfying and productive career.

## ACKNOWLEDGMENTS

### Steve's Turn

There are a number of people who I would like to thank, some directly related to this project and others who have influenced my development as a person and as a professional psychologist. As this is my first book, what follows may resemble an Academy Award acceptance speech. First, I recognize Gerry Sumprer as my friend and initial partner in the development of this project. Only his overriding emphasis on being a good parent precluded his being a full partner in seeing this book through to fruition. Second, I thank Larry Erlbaum and Susan Milmoe for seeing value in this book and for their desire to help students through the written word. Third, I thank the authors who contributed their time and expertise. They did so out of a genuine desire to being helpful to students and to increase the likelihood of success in graduate school and beyond. Fourth, we thank Carolyn Long for her addendum to the Perlman chapter, pointing out licensing developments for the master degree-holder.

I thank my parents for helping to instill in me a combination of a strong work ethic and a compassion for people. I thank Laurie Kirkpatrick for the positive influence that she has had on my life. I thank Steven Tulkin and Jack Tapp, my undergraduate advisors, who introduced me to the value of research and the need to have fun while working hard. They instilled in me a confidence that I could achieve and contribute to this field. Bill Kinder, David Stenmark, and Tony Broskowski, my mentors in graduate school and postdoctoral training, helped to shape my professional identity and taught me to pay attention to the details, the big picture, and how to get things accomplished. To this day I continue to learn from them and they are among my closest friends.

I thank the students and postdoctoral residents I have worked with, including Peter AuBuchon, Mark Brooks, Amy Clark, Dale Coovert, Julie Hotard, Julie Polifka Kantor, Keith Kaufman, Renelle Massey, Jerry O'Toole, Steve Shealy, Sue Shealy, Jennine Moritz Sherrill, and Paula Whitaker. They have made me a better psychologist. Colleagues, supervisors, and professional practice partners over the years were always willing to share their ideas and expertise with me. These have included Fran Brennan, Ed Brown, Jane Brownstone, Colleen Clark, Bob Fink, Ellis Gesten, Maryanne Godfrey, Eric Goplerud, Andy Krone, David McConnell, Ron Oliver, Dean Rosen, Alan Saunders, John Schinka, Saul Shiffman, and Bob Smith. They have made me a better psychologist.

I cannot thank Allen Hess enough for a number of things. Early on he believed in this project and was willing to contribute two chapters. He resurrected this project, secured a reputable publisher, and brought to it a contemporary focus. He improved my writing skills and editing skills tremendously. As a substantial bonus during this process, we have developed a working relationship and a friendship that will last well beyond the publication of this book.

Finally, I thank my wife Mary O'Horo. She knows how important this book has been to me over the past nineteen years and has always been a source of support and encouragement.

## Allen's Turn

We hope you benefit from the efforts of our chapter authors. We are interested in what you find useful, puzzling, unclear, or missing in the following pages, and we are interested in your graduate school experiences and in your professional adventures. We would like to know your opinions about the book, and about your experiences, both the triumphant and the tragic. We may be contacted at psychpubs@aol.com. Best of wishes on your ventures.

| | |
|---|---|
| —*Steven Walfish* | —*Allen K. Hess* |
| *Seattle, Washington* | *Montgomery, Alabama* |

# Contributors

Madonna G. Constantine, Department of Counseling and Clinical Psychology, Columbia University.

M. Harry Daniels, Department of Counselor Education, University of Florida.

Joseph A. Denicola, Psychological Services Center, Los Gatos, California.

Bruce R. Fretz, Department of Psychology, University of Maryland.

Cynthia T. Furze, Psychological Services Center, Los Gatos, California.

David S. Glenwick, Department of Psychology, Fordham University.

Eric N. Goplerud, Department of Substance Abuse and Mental Health Administration, Rockville, Maryland.

Sami Gulgoz, Department of Psychology, Koc University, Istanbul, Turkey.

Terry B. Gutkin, Department of Psychology, University of Nebraska at Lincoln.

Mitchell M. Handelsman, Department of Psychology, University of Colorado at Denver.

Allen K. Hess, Department of Psychology, Auburn University at Montgomery.

A. Dirk Hightower, The Children's Institute and Department of Clinical and Social Psychology, University of Rochester.

Carolen A. Hope, Department of Medical Psychology, Oregon Health Sciences University.

W. Gregory Keilin, Counseling and Mental Health Center, University of Texas at Austin.

Bill N. Kinder, Department of Psychology, University of South Florida.

James H. Korn, Department of Psychology, Saint Louis University.

Raymond P. Lorion, Psychology in Education Division, Graduate School of Education, University of Pennsylvania.

Rodney L. Lowman, College of Organizational Studies, Alliant University.

James S. MacDonall, Department of Psychology, Fordham University.

Roy P. Martin, Department of Educational Psychology, Research and Measurement, University of Georgia.

Renelle Massey, Independent Practice, Atlanta, Georgia.

Daniel K. Mroczek, Department of Psychology, Fordham University.

Raymond S. Nickerson, Department of Psychology, Tufts University.

James M. O'Neil, Department of Family Studies, University of Connecticut.

Baron Perlman, Department of Psychology, University of Wisconsin at Oshkosh.

Dixie J. Pederson, Perspectives Counseling Center, Lafayette, Indiana.

Donald R. Peterson, Graduate School of Applied Psychology, Rutgers University.

Anita L. Saunders, Department of Psychology, University of Nebraska at Lincoln.

William I. Sauser, Jr., School of Business, Auburn University.

Gerard F. Sumprer, Independent Practice, El Cajon, California.

Steven Walfish, Bay Psychiatric Center, Everett, Washington.

Mark E. Ware, Department of Psychology, Creighton University.

Arthur N. Wiens, Department of Medical Psychology, Oregon Health Sciences University.

Lawrence S. Wrightsman, Department of Psychology, University of Kansas.

# I

Considering Career and Degree
Options in Psychology

# 1

# Choosing a Career in Psychology

*Steven Walfish*

*Allen K. Hess*

In the mid 1970s psychology was the most popular major on U.S. campuses. Students hoped to "change the world," and psychology was a favored path toward that goal. However, cultural changes led to the rise of other majors. In the 1980s business became the most popular major. Levine and Levine (1992) suggested that political tenor of the times relates to the way problems are defined in our society. Under conservative administrations, individuals are viewed as the cause of their own problems, it is assumed that they must help themselves out of their difficulties. Under liberal administrations, environmental approaches and social safety nets are seen as the way to improve the human condition.

Today psychology is once again among the most popular majors at colleges and universities. Murray (1996) pointed to a rise in the numbers of psychology majors of almost 50% and compared this to a growth of 18% in education and only 6% in business majors. One psychologist she interviewed indicated that he saw no reason for this pace to slow down before 2010 or 2020. Another opined that the influence of the media has increased awareness that major social problems are fundamentally related to human behavior, and that psychological science may help people, through research and practice.

Murray (1996) also noted that many of the new psychology majors are women. Kohout and Williams (1999) reported that more than two-thirds of the doctorates in psychology in 1997 were awarded to women. This proportion contrasts with figures of 15% in 1950 and 25% in 1970, respectively. Similarly, there has been an exponential increase in the proportion of ethnic minorities who entered the field from the 1970s to the late 1990s. The impact that such demographic changes will have on the profession is unclear at this time, but there is no doubt that the profession will evolve to incorporate the characteristics and values of these previously under represented groups.

## WHY CHOOSE PSYCHOLOGY?

Murphy and Halgin (1995) explored motivations and career experiences of practicing clinical psychologists. Compared to a sample of social psychologists, clinical psychologists were more likely to have experienced personal distress in their families of origin, and had a stronger desire to resolve personal problems. However, the magnitude of the differences between these two groups was small, and the career choice of psychotherapist did not appear to be centrally related to this problematic history. Murphy and Halgin suggested that the view of the therapist as "bearer of psychic wounds" has been exaggerated and applied only to a small minority of their sample. They found the two groups comparable in levels of altruism and the pursuit of personal growth through their work. Radeke and Mahoney (2000) compared the impact of type of work on the personal lives of psychologists employed as psychotherapists and those employed as researchers. Compared to researchers, therapists were found to experience higher levels of anxiety, depression, and emotional exhaustion. However, therapists were more likely than researchers to feel that their work had a positive impact on their personal lives. Specifically, they believed that their work made them a better person, and increased their self-awareness and capacity to enjoy life.

Mahoney (1991) suggested that "psychotherapists derive their greatest satisfaction not from income or from status but from helping people change, from developing deeper understanding about human nature, and from experiencing both intimacy and involvement in the process" (p. 370). Mahoney viewed the practice of psychotherapy as a "privilege of participation."

People want to have meaningful lives and select careers accordingly. Some may want to help people solve their problems; some to change organizations to function more effectively and humanely; and some to improve the communities in which we all live. Others may be of a more scientific bent and want to study basic principles underlying human functioning. These are lofty goals that converge in the careers of psychologists. Some thinking through of career goals can be shown in a conversation between a student and a psychologist: The student planned to study for a doctoral degree in clinical psychology in order to help people change their personality defects and to learn more adaptive ways of relating to the world. Although she expected to earn a decent salary, her altruism was undeniable. But, to benefit an appreciable segment of the population, the route for her to travel might not have been to practice one-to-one psychotherapy. More efficient pathways might include working in a large corporation as a director of personnel and human resources, earning a law degree and mounting class-action lawsuits on behalf of consumers, or choosing the life of a politician and enacting legislation by which lives of thousands may be improved.

There are a number of ways to help others and serve humanity. Lloyd (1998) and Buskist and Sherbourne (1996) discussed options for psychology-related career areas. These include agency/community counseling, school counseling, art therapy, marital and family therapy, special education, and social work. In addition, medical anthropology, public health, rehabilitation counseling, addictions counseling, and mental health counseling offer opportunities to spend one's professional time in prosocial activities. Although many in these fields function in a way similar to a psychologist (e.g., performs individual therapy or couples therapy, doing program planning and evaluation), there are critically important differences between them and psychologists. Psychology provides a conceptual foundation for all the activities in which psychologists engage. The choice of psychology as a career involves core values and a particular view of the world as expressed in the course curriculum in a typical psychology program. This wide perspective can even be seen in Hess's (1996) advice on careers in the narrower discipline of forensic psychology:

> A forensic psychologist is first and foremost a psychologist. There is no substitute for a core of courses consisting of the history and philosophy of psychology; the ethical, professional and legal issues psychologists face; research design and data analysis; psychometrics; and the basic processes (including personality, developmental and social psychology, learning-cognition, and the biological areas of psychology). Anything less than a core and basic processes approach would leave the student less than a psychologist. Anything less would not allow for the generation, development, and transfer of psychological knowledge. (p. 243)

The perspectives of other helping professionals may be similar in some respects to those of psychologists, but their basic theories and approaches to studying human behavior are different. Students should become familiar with these other specialties (perhaps by visiting the web sites of groups such as the American Association for Counseling and Development, the American Psychiatric Association, the American Sociological Association, the National Mental Health Association, the National Association of Social Workers, and the American Public Health Association) and consider whether they would prefer to be psychologists, studying core areas described by Hess, or to pursue another career path serving others.

The most flexible of the degrees other than psychology that have been mentioned here for those wanting a career in human services that closely parallels those of clinical, counseling psychology, and school psychology is the master's in social work (MSW). (The doctorate in social work [DSW] better fits students preferring a career in teaching and research.) In terms of direct service work, individuals receiving an MSW can do any type of work that is available to those receiving a doctorate in psychology, with the exception of psychological testing. They can do clinical work in an agency, and most states allow a person with an MSW to have an independent practice. There are a few insurance companies that will not reimburse MSWs for their services, but these are clearly a minority. Managed care companies also embrace competent MSWs because they are often reimbursed at lower rates than those paid to psychologists (which in turn are lower than those paid to psychiatrists). Master's-level degrees in counseling can also provide flexible career opportunities. If not licensed, however, individuals with these degrees will not be able to work in independent practice (unless practicing under another professional's license) but will be able to be employed in a variety of community agencies and government programs. See the chapter by Fretz in Section V. More information about the master's level training programs can be found at the web site of the American Counseling Association (counseling.org). One interesting document at counseling.org/resources/pc_sw.htm highlights key similarities and differences of degrees in mental health counseling (and its subspecialties: community counseling, gerontological counseling, marriage and family counseling) compared with a degree in social work.

## GRADUATE TRAINING IN PSYCHOLOGY

*Graduate Study in Psychology* (1998), published by the American Psychological Association (APA, 1998), is the single best source for information concerning master's level and doctoral programs in psychology. A glance at the index of this book can overwhelm and confuse the reader. Programs by area of study are listed, and the universities offering each degree are provided under a general heading. There are 128 different headings! Table 1.1 may help orient the reader.

It is important that students research prospective programs closely because what clinical psychology is at University A may be different from what it is at University B; what social psychology is at University C may be different from what it is at University D; and so forth. Differences can be found in number of faculty in the specialty area, number of courses offered, supervision available, and practicum placements. Titles can be especially misleading within general categories (e.g., clinical) with a specialty emphasis (e.g., clinical/community, clinical/ health). David Stenmark and the first author once reviewed materials from programs with the label *clinical/community psychology* in APA-accredited clinical psychology programs. There were vast differences among them. At some universities the program included five or six faculty members who were doing community work. There was a specific course sequence, and practicum placements were available to students. At other universities the program included only one or two faculty members who were doing community research. There were only one or two courses, and students worked on faculty research projects. The prospective student should also be aware that a specialty emphasis can change over time at a particular university, with faculty turnover changes in faculty interests, and reductions in grants available for research and training. For example, at one stage psychologists placed great emphasis on the importance of community-based work and were successful in obtaining substantial federal funding. Currently, behavioral medicine receives a lot of attention and financial support. The point is that programs evolve with new advances in the field and when the federal government and foundations offering grant support set new priorities. Students should make sure they look beyond a program title and search for the substance in the area in which they wish to become trained.

Woods (1987) and Buskist and Sherbourne (1996) outlined the major fields in psychology and offered descriptions of the primary focus of each. They presented more detailed information about each, but briefly stated by Woods the fields are:

*Clinical psychology*—assesses and treats people with problems. These may range from predictable crises that people experience in life to less common and more serious conditions such as major depression and schizophrenia.

*Community psychology*—is concerned with the behavior in natural settings with larger groups of people and the prevention of problems before they develop into significant psychological difficulties.

*Counseling psychology*—attempts to improve normal human functioning across the life span by helping people solve problems, make decisions, and cope with the stressors of everyday life.

*Developmental psychology*—studies of human development across the life span, from newborn to the aged.

*Educational psychology*—studies how people learn; designs the methods and materials used to educate people of all ages.

*Environmental psychology*—is concerned with the relations between psychological processes and physical environments.

**TABLE 1.1**

Programs Offered by Area of Study, Listed in *Graduate Study in Psychology:*
1998–1999 (APA, 1998)

| | | |
|---|---|---|
| Adolescence and Youth | AIDS Intervention/Research | Adult Development |
| Applied | Applied Developmental | Applied Social |
| Art Therapy | Behavior Therapy | Behavioral Analysis |
| Behavioral Genetics | Behavioral Neuroscience | Behavioral Medicine |
| Behavioral Science | Behavioral Science—Applied | Child Development |
| Child Psychopathology | Clinical | Clinical Assessment |
| Clinical—Child | Clinical—Community | Clinical—School |
| Clinical—Respecialization | Clinical Neuropsychology | Cognitive |
| College Counseling | College Teaching | Community |
| Community—Clinical | Community—Rural | Community—School |
| Community Rehabilitation | Comparative | Conditioning |
| Computer Applications | Consulting | Consumer |
| Counseling | Counseling & Guidance | Ecological |
| Counseling—Coll. & Universities | Counseling—Elem. School | Educational |
| Counseling—Marriage & Family | Counseling Psychology | Engineering |
| Counseling—Secondary School | Counseling—Vocational | Environmental |
| Developmental Psychobiology | Developmental | Forensic |
| Developmental—Exceptional | Early Childhood Education | General |
| Educational Administration | Educational Measurement | Group Therapy |
| Educational Research & Eval. | Experimental—General | Human Factors |
| Experimental— Animal Behavior | Exp.—Psychopathology | Human Relations |
| Health Psychology | History & Systems | Human Services |
| Human Development | Human Services Admin. | Humanistic |
| Industrial/Organizational | Law and Psychology | Learning |
| Learning Disabilities | Learning—Animal | Learning—Human |
| Life-Span Development | Marriage & Family Therapy | Marriage & Family |
| Medical Psychology | Mental Health | Mathematical |
| Mental Retardation | Minority Mental Health | Neuropsychology |
| Neuroscience | Organizational | Parent Education |
| Pastoral Counseling | Pediatric Psychology | Personality |
| Personnel & Guidance | Phenomenological | Physiological |
| Primate Behavior | Professional | Psychobiology |
| Program Evaluation | Psycholinguistics | Psychometrics |

*continued on next page*

**TABLE 1.1**  (*continued*)

| | | |
|---|---|---|
| Psychological Assessment | Psychology of Women | Psychopharmacology |
| Psychotherapy & Psychoanalysis | Public Policy | Quantitative |
| Quantitative Methods | Reading | Rehabilitation |
| Research Methodology | School Psychometry | School |
| Sensation & Perception | Sociocultural Perspectives | Social |
| Special Education | Sports | Statistics |
| Substance Abuse | Supervision | Animal Cognition |
| Clinical Mental Health Counseling | Evolutionary/Sociobiology | Doctoral Preparation |
| Individual Differences | Learning & Instructional | |

*Experimental psychology*—conducts research on basic human processes including learning, sensation, perception, memory, language, communication, and the physiological processes underlying behavior,

*Industrial/organizational psychology*—is concerned with the relationship between people and the workplace.

*Psychobiology*—investigates the relationship between physical systems (including the brain) and behavior.

*Psychometrics and quantitative psychology*—is concerned with the methods and techniques used in acquiring and applying psychological knowledge, such as psychological testing or statistical analysis.

*Rehabilitation psychology*—is concerned with people who have suffered a physical deprivation or loss and their adjustment to these challenges.

*School psychology*—is concerned with the intellectual, educational, social, and emotional development in children within the school setting.

*Social psychology*—studies how people interact with each other and how they are affected by their social environments.

Buskist and Sherbourne (1996) mentioned other specialty areas, including:

*Behavioral analysis*—studies of the relation between behavior and consequences.

*Cognitive psychology*—studies thinking, perceiving, imagining, and remembering.

*Evolutionary psychology*—studies the adaptive nature of behavior, especially how inherited dispositions have evolved and how they aid organisms in surviving.

*Forensic psychology*—applies psychological principles and theories to the law and justice system, especially as they pertain to criminal behavior and crime solving.

*Human factors/engineering psychology*—studies how humans behave when working with machines; seeks to improve efficiency.

*Personality psychology*—studies behavior patterns of individuals that remain stable for prolonged periods of time.

*Physiological psychology and neuroscience*—studies of the relationships among genetics, the brain, the nervous system, the endocrine system, and behavior.

*Psychopharmacology*—studies the behavioral effects of drugs in humans and animals.

*Sport psychology*—studies of how psychological factors affect athletic performance.

The American Psychological Association (APA) consists of 53 different divisions reflecting the diverse interests of its members and the diverse areas of study they have chosen. A list of these divisions may be found at the APA web site (apa.org). Some are narrowly focused and consist primarily of individuals who share similar background and training: for example, Division 39, Psychoanalysis. Others are wider ranging: For example, Division 7, Developmental Psychology, may include clinical psychologists interested in behavior problems of childhood, experimental psychologists interested in how children develop language, social psychologists interested in the development of friendships in childhood, and school and educational psychologists interested in how children learn in a school setting. Many of these Divisions have their own web sites and journals. Explore these in order to learn more about subspecialty areas of study within psychology.

## CAREER FLEXIBILITY

Sternberg (1997) noted the flexibility of a career in psychology, where can switch, often fairly easily and with a minimum of adjustment, from one track to another. Once a basic set of skills is learned (e.g., statistics and research methodology, psychotherapy, assessment), it can be applied to a new area of study or intervention if a concerted effort is made to learn the content of the area. The APA Science Directorate lists skills that may be obtained during graduate study in psychology at the web site apa.org/science/skills.html. The specific subset of skills are listed at this site merits further exploration, but it is also worth noting the general array of skills graduate students may acquire through a selection of courses and practicum experiences: (a) information gathering and reporting skills, (b) general analysis and synthesis skills, (c) project planning skills, (d) problem definition skills, (e) the understanding that people may have different perspectives, (f) methodological skills, and (g) statistical and inferential skills.

The APA Research Office offers a rich amount of data related to the employment status of psychologists at the APA web site (apa.org). The student interested in a career as a psychologist can utilize this for learning more about education and work possibilities. In terms of employment settings of APA members (not necessarily reflective of all psychologists, as not all psychologist belong to this organization), universities and colleges are where the largest proportion (34%) of doctoral-level psychologists earn their living. Those who are self-employed make up 17%, working in independent practice. The largest numbers of doctorates are awarded in the health service provider subfields of clinical, counseling, and school (70%), with the largest percentage of these being awarded in clinical. The remaining doctorates are earned in a variety of research fields. Among those earning doctorates in research fields, 50% are employed in academic positions. The rest apply their skills outside the university environment, with 11% employed in government positions, 6% in private nonprofit organizations, 14% self-employed, and 19% employed by private for-profit organizations.

The largest proportion (77%) of master's degree recipients in psychology are employed in organized human service settings such as hospitals, community mental health centers, and substance abuse treatment centers. The next largest group is those employed in elementary and secondary school settings. Limitations on the independent practice of psychology by state legislatures most likely account for the large difference between employment settings of master's- and doctoral-level recipients.

To summarize, students wanting to pursue a career that involves improving the lives of others through basic and applied research, direct clinical service, and/or community intervention should consider psychology. However, they must first decide that whether want to be psychologists, rather than social workers, addictions or mental health counselors, or other helping professionals. If psychology is chosen, the flexibility and diversity described by Sternberg (1997) can allow for a rewarding and prosocial career. The U.S. Department of Labor publishes descriptive and predictive data on all professions. On its web site at stats.bls.gov/oco/ocos056.htm it indicates that employment for psychologists is expected to grow through 2008. The majority of psychologists have found well-paid jobs, pursue personally satisfying goals, and would choose the same career path if they had the choice anew (Norcross, Karg, & Prochaska, 1997). We offer the following chapters to help you make optimal career choices and to help you succeed in your career journey.

## REFERENCES

American Psychological Association (1998). *Graduate study in psychology: 1998–1999*. Washington, DC: American Psychological Association.

Buskist, W., & Sherbourne, T. (1996). *Preparing for graduate study in psychology: 101 Questions and answers*. Needham Heights, MA: Allyn and Bacon.

Hess, A. (1996) The past, present, and future of forensic psychology. *Criminal Justice and Behavior, 23*, 236–250.

Kohout, J., & Williams, S. (1999, November) Far more psychology degrees are going to women. *APA Monitor*, (p. 10).

Levine, M., & Levine, A. (1992). *Helping children: A social history*. New York: Oxford University Press.

Lloyd, M. (1998, February 10). *Master's- and doctoral-level careers in psychology and related areas*. [Online]. www.gasou.edu/psychweb/careers/masters.htm

Mahoney, M. (1991). *Human changes processes: The scientific foundations of psychotherapy*. New York: Basic Books.

Murphy, R., & Halgin, R. (1995). Influences on the career choice of psychotherapists. *Professional Psychology: Research and Practice, 26*, 422–426.

Murray, B. (1996, February) Psychology remains top college major. *APA Monitor*, pp. 1, 42.

Norcross, J., Karg, R., & Prochaska, J. (1997). Clinical psychologists in the1990's: II. *Clinical Psychologist, 50*, 4–11.

Radeke, J., & Mahoney, M. (2000). Comparing the personal lives of psychotherapists and research psychologists. *Professional Psychology: Research and Practice, 31*, 82–84.

Sternberg, R. (1997). *Career paths in psychology*. Washington, DC: American Psychological Association.

Woods, P. (1987). *Is psychology the major for you?* Washington, DC: American Psychological Association.

# 2

# Pursuing a Career with a Bachelor's Degree in Psychology

*Mark E. Ware*

Given the title of this book, the title and contents of this chapter may seem anomalous. Nevertheless, the editors recognized that many psychology students would be well served by information about viable alternatives to graduate education.

Sometimes I have tried to imagine what takes place when undergraduates, bursting with excitement, approach their parents, friends, and faculty with the significant life decision of majoring in psychology. To assist me in that effort, I conducted a survey (Ware, 1991) of 225 students from one private and one public university, asking if they had ever heard the following statement: "You can't get a job with a psychology major." More than one third of the freshmen and sophomores and more than 80% of the juniors and seniors reported that they had heard such a statement. As many as 50% of the students reported that they had heard both faculty and students say that you could not get a job with a psychology major. Although some students received support and encouragement, many were challenged, discouraged, and ridiculed. Swanson and Tokar (1991) found that students cited family and friends among the most frequent barriers to choosing a major or career and provided results consistent with my observations. The data also indicated that lack of information and lack of capability were the only barriers that students identified more frequently than family and friends.

The problem seems quite clear. Many students hear that they are pursuing a degree that has no future and report that they possess limited skills. The purpose of this chapter is to provide students with information and strategies that correct these gross misrepresentations and facilitate pursuit of employment with a bachelor's degree in psychology.

# SELF

## Values

In response to the belief that their degree in psychology makes them unemployable, many students adamantly proclaim, "I'll do anything!" To challenge that response, I give students the following exercise. It uses four positions that writers cite as offering the greatest number of openings for the foreseeable future: Using a scale from one (*most likely*) to five (*least likely*), rate the occupations of computer programmer, janitor, secretary, and systems analyst in terms of how much you would you like to pursue these careers.

If you are similar to psychology students I asked, you gave these occupations less favorable ratings (i.e., 4's and 5's). Why do you suspect that the ratings were not favorable? For at least two of the positions (janitor and secretary), college students were not attracted because of the positions' salary and status. However, more frequent reasons for the low ratings for all four jobs emphasized lack of helping others ("Not really benefitting anyone"), meager social contact ("I want to be interacting with people on a regular basis"), nature of the task ("I do not want to clean, it is dirty"), and insufficient challenge ("Would not be able to work in a high pace, exciting environment").

One conclusion from these findings is that despite the strong assertion that "I will take anything!," students discriminate among positions and use a strongly held set of values as the basis for their discrimination. The discovery that one's values underlie career decision making prompts one to ask what other factors may contribute to such decisions.

Because employers hire people primarily because they need problems solved and tasks performed, you can infer that knowledge about your skills should help you find occupations in which you can be satisfied and successful. Skills developed in college can contribute to career success. Although some educational programs are "vocationally" or skill specific, such as nursing, engineering, and accounting, liberal arts programs that include a major in psychology emphasize generalized or *transferable* skills. Transferable skills are those that a person can use in a variety of settings, including work environments. Because students often have difficulty identifying and articulating their academic (liberal arts) skills, I asked them to describe experiences that illustrated transferable skills. Appendix A lists student-generated activities that correspond to skills most often identified as transferable to the work world. Examine that list and refer to it later in this chapter when reading the section about preparing resumés.

Some students have difficulty relating their class experiences to work activities. The contents of Table 2.1 may help make that connection.

Experimental Psychology (or Research Methods) is among the most frequently offered psychology courses (Perlman & McCann, 1999). I assume that you will have completed that course before you graduate. Can you identify at least five skills you acquired from that course? Try it!

Having difficulty? If so, you are similar to most psychology majors. I asked Experimental Psychology teachers to identify what students could have learned from their course. Appendix B contains a list of the variety of skills that you could have acquired (e.g., communication skills, skills as a team member, and human relations skills). Examine and refer to the list later in the chapter when reading about resume preparation.

Appendix B also reveals that Experimental Psychology may be a source for acquiring invaluable skills that can be particularly helpful for pursuing employment following gradua-

## TABLE 2.1
### Illustrations of Writing, Speaking, and Research Experiences and Work-Related Applications

| In College | On the Job |
| --- | --- |
| **Writing Skills** | |
| Term papers and essay tests | Writing reports, briefs, and proposals |
| Laboratory reports | Composing letters and memos |
| Notebooks and journals | Keeping clear and accurate records |
| **Speaking Skills** | |
| Speeches and presentations | Making presentations to peers and clients |
| Study groups | Working with members of the public and answering their questions |
| Participating in class discussions | Persuading, negotiating, and selling |
| **Research Skills** | |
| Library and laboratory research | Planning and decision making |
| Independent studies | Developing ideas and brainstorming |
| Literature reviews | Gathering, analyzing, and interpreting data |

Note. Adapted from "Liberal Arts Skills at Work," *Career Currents* (the career planning and placement newsletter of Hanover College), November 1994.

tion. Widespread anecdotal evidence informs us that psychology alumni frequently cite Experimental Psychology as the course most useful to them in their current position. I bet you never would have guessed that!

Psychology students often ask their instructors and advisers, "How do I get a job?" or "How do I get into graduate school?" The chapter by Kinder and Walfish in this volume answers the second question. I address the first one, but before I do, I want to point out that pursuing a career is not a one-time event but rather a developmental process.

## Development

In one of the few studies that examined psychology alumni's career development in employment, Titley (1978) asked alumni to identify the jobs they held 1, 5, and 10 years after graduation. Titley assigned jobs to one of three levels depending on the entry-level requirements, including amount of formal education and work experience. The percent of students in the lowest entry-level group dramatically decreased and the percent in the highest entry level group increased 5 to 10 years after graduation. His findings clearly indicated upward mobility in employment over time. Thus, you should not think that your first job will be your last one, but rather that your first job is simply a stepping stone to the next job, and the next job, and so forth. A second implication is that undergraduate education alone may not prepare you for your desired positions; education and experience may be necessary ingredients. I encourage you to think about your career pursuit as a *process* rather than a *product*.

Just as you realize that your values and skills have evolved during your teens and early twenties, you can expect that they will change by your thirties and forties. A reasonable hypothesis is that what attracted you to the first job will change. Moreover, because of volatility in the work world, particularly during the last decade, one cannot expect that the job market will remain static. Indeed, most experts predict that you can expect to change jobs, on average, once every 7 years. Entry-level employment is a first step into the world of work, not an end.

## WORLD OF WORK

### Careers for the Liberally Educated

In the previous section, I described some factors (i.e., values and skills) that can give meaningful and instructive direction to students' selection of an occupational or career path. Many students believe that the work world is organized according to academic majors. They can point to examples such as accounting, elementary education, engineering, and nursing, but many careers do not require specific majors. The following titles describe only a few of the positions that liberally educated students, including psychology majors, can obtain regardless of major: advertising, banking, fashion, government, human resources, investments, management, marketing research, nonprofit associations, public relations, publishing, real estate, retailing, and social service.

### Careers for Psychology Alumni

Additionally, numerous positions exist for students possessing the skills associated with a psychology major. Table 2.2 lists employers and areas of work in which psychology alumni can find opportunities for employment.

More direct evidence for the employability of psychology graduates exists in the results of several studies that examined the occupational pursuits of psychology alumni (Davis, 1979; Lunneborg, 1974; Titley, 1978; Ware & Meyer, 1981; Woods, 1979). Schools varied geographically and included large public and small private institutions.

Rather than simply listing all of the positions that psychology alumni pursued, I selected about three dozen occupations and organized them using Holland's model (1985). In brief, Holland proposed a typology in which he identified people and work environments as belonging to combinations of six categories, called *realistic*, *investigative*, *artistic*, *social*, *enterprising*, and *conventional*.

One advantage of Holland's model is that it can promote career exploration within career paths or clusters, which include many occupational alternatives, rather than suggest that there is only "one best job for me." In Table 2.3 is a sample of positions using Holland's *social* and *enterprising* categories, because large numbers of psychology alumni pursue careers in the human/social services and business environments.

Should you want to take Holland's Self-Directed Search inventory, contact your school's counseling center or career services office and complete the inventory at no cost. For less than $10, you can take the inventory online at http://www.self-directed-search.com. You can complete other self-assessments online by accessing one or more of the sites listed at http://www.creighton.edu/~mapoma/careers.html#self. Finally, you can find a particularly thorough approach at http://www.adm.uwaterloo.ca/infocecs/CRC/manual-home.html.

## TABLE 2.2
### Employers and Areas for Those With a Bachelor's Degree in Psychology

| Employers | Areas |
|---|---|
| Federal government departments of Health and Human Services, Veterans' Administration, and Justice | **Human services** |
| State government departments of human services, mental health, and mental retardation, psychiatric hospitals, community mental health centers, facilities for the mentally retarded, and probation/parole departments | Counseling, advocacy, human health services |
| Local government: senior citizens' centers | |
| Nonprofit organizations such as United Way, Goodwill Industries, Boys and Girls Clubs, and YWCA/YMCA | |
| Human resources (personnel) departments of companies | **Human resources** |
| Government personnel agencies and departments | |
| Employment agencies | Employment recruitment, labor relations, compensation and benefits |
| Public relations and advertising firms | **Public relations** |
| Companies with in-house public relations departments | |
| Trade associations | Research, programming, fundraising, writing and editing, special events, media placement, public speaking |
| Federal, state, and local government | |
| Colleges and universities | |
| Nonprofit organizations | |
| All major retail firms including pharmaceuticals, specialty, variety, and department store chains | **Retail and sales** |
| Wholesalers, manufacturers, insurance companies, and real estate companies | |
| Advertising agencies | **Advertising** |
| Companies with in-house advertising agencies or departments | |
| | Creative, media, account services, or research |
| Federal, state, and local governments | **Community relations** |
| National headquarters and local branches of nonprofit organizations | |
| Market research firms | **Market research** |
| Market research departments of consumer goods manufacturing firms | |
| Public and private schools | **Teaching** |
| Federal, state, or local government | **Program development** |
| Headquarters and branches of nonprofit organizations | |
| Federal, state, and local government | **Administration** |
| National headquarters and local branches of nonprofit organizations | |
| Federal government, especially Department of Health and Human Services and National Institute of Education | **Research** |
| National headquarters of nonprofit organizations | |

*Note.* Adapted from "Psychology: What Can I Do With This Degree?", available from the University of Tennessee Career Services Office.

**Table 2.3**

Occupational Pursuits of Bachelor-Level Psychology Alumni in Two of Holland's Categories

| Social | Enterprising |
|---|---|
| Residential youth counselor, case evaluator/social worker, admissions counselor, probation officer, program manager, counselor, resident adviser, surgical orderly, parent training research coordinator, bartender, quality assurance agent, recreation aide, nurse, recreation assistant, rehabilitation adviser, fast foods manager, executive director (e.g., YMCA), occupational therapist, quality inspector | Store manager, marketing representative, loan officer, insurance underwriting supervisor, personnel representative, small business owner, legal technician (e.g., FBI), sales, warehouse manager, transportation director, congressional aide, manager, sales service coordinator |

Widespread statements about unemployment for psychology alumni are simply inconsistent with the data (McGovern & Carr, 1989). In fact, the data indicate that psychology alumni are found in all six of Holland's categories. The myth about lack of employment prospects may be based on lack of information, a single salient incident, fear, or some combination of those and other variables. More comprehensive information about thousands of jobs, required education, job outlook, earnings information, and more is available online. The site for the *Occupational Outlook Handbook* is http://stats.bls.gov/ocohome.htm.

**Income**

Because students frequently ask about the income level they can expect to earn, I include relevant data in this part of the chapter. Data from a report by the National Association of Colleges and Employers (1999) supported a conclusion from the alumni surveys about the versatility of the major and offered additional data about the salary offers made to psychology majors. The September issue, reproduced in Appendix C, reported that campus recruiters made over 400 job offers to psychology majors with a median income of $26,030. This figure is consistent with those for other liberal arts majors. Because this figure and those in Appendix C will change over time, you should ask your school's career services office for current data.

Employers making the greatest number of offers were in education, social services, consulting services, merchandising, health services, and local/state government The results from these and other studies conclusively demonstrated that students can find employment with bachelor's degrees in psychology and that the majority of students will likely find themselves employed in positions associated with Holland's social (education and social services) or enterprising (business) settings. The findings also support a conclusion that, collectively, psychology alumni demonstrate versatility and adaptability in pursuing employment following graduation. Unemployment has remained at less than 5% for the last decade (McGovern & Carr, 1989).

## IMPLEMENTATION STRATEGIES

Having decided on a career path, each person is confronted with a question that can arouse great amounts of anxiety: "How do I go about finding a job?" One of the most valuable discoveries you can make is that an effective job search employs a system of time-proven, investigative techniques that enhance the likelihood of acquiring the first and subsequent positions. In Table 2.4 are several hints that successful psychology alumni suggested. Let those comments be your guide.

In the remainder of this section, I describe some important facets of a job search: (a) networking, (b) preparing resumés, and (c) interviewing. You can find more thorough discussion about each of these topics in the numerous career-oriented books available in libraries and commercial bookstores. The following online site provides additional information about the job search: http://www.adm.uwaterloo.ca/infocecs/CRC/manual/jobworksearch.html.

### Networking

At the outset, you should know that 75 to 90% of all available positions are never advertised. Thus, the *hidden job market* offers the greatest opportunity for employment but is also the least visible. At the same time, prospective employers face difficulties finding suitable employees from among the hundreds of thousands of available individuals. Networking can bring job seekers and employers together.

Networking is indispensable for gaining access to the hidden job market, and it helps to solve employers' problems in finding appropriate people. Remember: If you do not find the employer, the employer will not find you.

Many students think that they are at a hopeless disadvantage because they do not know anyone who can help. Fortunately, there are several *simple strategies* for networking. Here are seven of them.

*Personal Contacts.*    The most informal approach consists of talking to individuals from each of the following groups: relatives (including your parents; sometimes even they can surprise you!), friends, past and present employers, representatives from organizations for whom you have done volunteer work, and teachers. Ask individuals from each group to identify one or more persons with whom you might talk about a career in your areas of greatest interest. You should be able to develop a list of at least a dozen contacts from among those sources.

### TABLE 2.4
Psychology Alumni's Suggestions for Job Seekers

Start thinking about what you will put on a resumé and about the job search before your senior year.

Learn to become an articulate and persuasive writer and speaker.

Develop interpersonal skills. If you are shy, do everything you can to overcome your shyness.

Choose electives that will increase your strengths and strengthen your weaknesses. Don't choose electives just because they are easy or offered at a convenient time.

Good jobs are a result of hard work, persistence, and planning. Don't expect a good job to fall into your lap after graduation.

***Phone Book.***    The Yellow Pages of the phone book contain a listing of virtually all employers inside and outside of the immediate area. Public, college, and university libraries usually contain phone books from numerous cities. Contacting a company or institution and asking to speak to an individual who works at the type of position in which you are interested is a remarkably simple process, as described in the next paragraph.

***Information Interviews.***    When you speak with the targeted individual, indicate your name and the name of the college or university at which you are a student. Then say, "I am not applying for a job, but I am interested in talking to you because I am considering your profession as a career for me." The worst that can happen is that the person you talk to will say "No."

Be prepared with times at which you would be available and say, for example, "Would you be available some time Wednesday morning or would Thursday afternoon be better?" Do not say that "any time will do" unless you are available eight hours a day, five days a week. Figler (1988) provided a more detailed description of this technique in chapter 9 of his book and offered guidance for conducting such an interview.

Toward the conclusion of the interview, be certain to ask, "With whom would you recommend that I talk to find out even more about this profession?" Thus, each contact can be the source for additional contacts.

Finally, within 24 hours after each interview, send a short, hand-written thank-you note to the interviewee expressing your appreciation for the time and information that he or she provided. This procedure will also provide practice for the job interview described later in this chapter.

***Career Services Office or Career and Academic Planning Office (CO).***    An indispensable source for contacts is your college or university CO. The CO personnel possess an extensive resource library and a variety of services, including assistance in preparing resumes and scheduling interviews with prospective employers. Services are free to students. The best strategy is to contact the CO *early* during your senior year. To obtain one's most preferred type of position, 6 to 9 months of lead time is not excessive.

***Newspapers.***    Daily newspapers are another source for contacts. One word of caution. Avoid "blind" advertisements (i.e., those that do not identify the name of the employer). Frequently, such positions are particularly unattractive. In addition, be cautious about advertisements that sound to good to be true. As a wise person once said, "If it sounds too good to be true, then ...."

***Employment Agencies.***    One tempting source of contacts is an employment agency. Keep in mind that employment agencies have no corner on access to the job market. They often get their leads the same way you can, such as personal contacts and newspapers. In addition, employment agencies are profit-making organizations whose first interest is their own, not necessarily yours. Finally, before signing any contract, *closely* read all the material in any contract. Preferably have someone more knowledgeable than yourself (e.g., parents, family attorney) review and evaluate the contract.

***Electronic Databases.***    The site http://www.creighton.edu/~mapoma/careers.html-#job lists several online sites with searchable databases for job positions throughout the United States. Table 2.5 contains descriptions and addresses for four widely known databases. A link

**TABLE 2.5**

Online Sites with Databases Containing Available Positions

| Description | URL |
|---|---|
| Career Mosaic. Various databases are available to identify openings, post resumés at no charge, review employers' profiles, and more. | http://www.careermosaic.com/ |
| CareerPath.Com. Look for jobs in the classified ads from approximately 75 major U.S. newspapers. You can search by geographic area, job category or keyword. Click on "Find Jobs by Newspaper." Use of this database is free but you must register. | http://new.careerpathcom/ |
| JobTrak. This site partners with over 500 college and university career centers nationwide to provide position listings for students and alumni of those institutions. | http://wwwjobtrak.com/ |
| Monster Board. Offers access to over 50,000 openings, employer profiles, and an on-line resumé service. This is a very large and comprehensive site. | http://content.monster.com/ |

for nonprofit organizations, http://www.creighton.edu/~mapoma/careers.html#nonprofit, also contains several promising leads.

## Resumé

In some cases, the resumé may be the only contact you have with a prospective employer, and it is often the employer's only physical reminder of you after an interview. Thus, preparation of a resumé justifies serious effort.

The objective of a resumé is to describe briefly your goals, educational and employment experience, and interests. The resumé should reflect your aspirations for a career.

You may plan for more than one occupational goal. If the goals are similar, one resumé should suffice. If the goals are quite different, then you might decide to prepare two or more resumés that emphasize the type of position you are seeking.

Table 2.6 summarizes guidelines for preparing a resumé. Once you have produced a draft resumé, ask your adviser or the CO personnel for constructive feedback. The CO personnel can also identify sources for having your resumé professionally prepared, including formatting and reproduction.

Resumés do not follow a single format. Your primary objective should be to describe yourself in the most effective manner possible. Appendix D contains two illustrations. In the Experience section of each, note the use of active verbs to describe transferable skills. Recall what Table 2.6 said about referring to Appendixes A and B for additional examples of such skills.

The following online site provides links to several electronic sources for preparing *resumés*: http://www.creighton.edu/~mapoma/careers.html#resume. Specific sites offering

### TABLE 2.6
#### Guidelines for a Resumé

People do not read resumés; they skim them. Use margins and spacing that make skimming easy. Limit resumés to one or two pages. Think of your resumé more as a piece of advertising than a comprehensive data sheet.

Use action verbs. Do not use the verb "to be." Instead of "I did ... I was ... I am ... " use verbs such as initiated, created, developed, supervised, managed, instructed, counseled, negotiated, and maintained.

Emphasize skills, especially those that transfer from one situation to another (e.g., those listed in Appendixes A and B). The fact that you coordinated a student organization leads one to expect that you could coordinate other things.

Expound on your relevant experiences; condense jobs or experiences that are not directly related. This means that you slant your resumé to the type of job you are seeking. For example, if you are applying for a child care counseling job, devote more space to your experience as a camp counselor. If you are applying for a job as a manager trainee, condense the counseling activity and emphasize your organizational and supervisory ability.

help in preparing resumés and cover letters are http://www.adm.uwaterloo.ca/infocecs/CRC/ manual/resumes.html and http://www.adm.uwaterloo.ca/infocecs/CRCmanual/letters.html, respectively.

### Interview

Screening applicants is the purpose for most initial employment interviews. Individuals are not usually offered positions on the basis of an initial interview. The employer's objective is to decide whether individuals show sufficient promise to invest the time for closer scrutiny. Thus, the initial interview is one step in acquiring a position.

Initial interviews can last from 10 to 60 minutes. During that time, the interviewer describes the company or organization and the available position. The interviewer also attempts to acquire an impression about the applicant. Interviewers will probably forget details, but they will retain impressions. Thus, one of your objectives is to generate a most favorable first impression. Career personnel report that the following factors are among the most important personal qualities that prospective employers desire: (a) communication skills, (b) expressed goals, and (c) personality.

*Communication Skills.*    Effective communication is a skill like other skills; it improves with practice. Simulated interviews provide excellent practice, particularly when you answer types of question that employers ask most frequently. Table 2.7 contains a sample of such questions. I strongly recommend practicing answers to those questions and getting knowledgeable feedback.

*Goals.*    When investigators asked employers to identify reasons why they rejected students, the single most frequent reply was because of "ill-defined goals." In short, if a person does not know what he or she wants to do, then the prospective employer would rather not have the person "find" himself or herself on the employer's time.

*Personality.*   Personality is a global term probably referring to how well the interviewer likes you. The only advice is to be yourself and avoid artificial roles or actions. Expect at least a moderate amount of anxiety before and during interviews; interviewers expect and accept such nervousness.

Preparation for the interview should also include a study of the literature that each of the interviewers makes available. Additional information about companies and organizations is usually available on web sites and in the reference section of libraries. Ask a reference librarian for assistance in locating appropriate sources. Ignorance about the employer contributes markedly to an unfavorable impression because it shows a lack of interest in the company or organization and a lack of preparation for the interview.

Questions generated from specific knowledge about the company or organization elicit favorable impressions. Many students are surprised that they should be prepared to ask employers questions. Typical questions you might ask are: (a) What are the opportunities for advancement? (b) What opportunities are there for professional development? (c) What are some highlights about the community in which I would live? (d) How does the employer evaluate performance to determine promotions? You should *not* ask questions about the employer or the position that you could have answered by reviewing the employer's printed materials. Check the following online site for additional information about job interviews: http://www.adm.uwaterloo.ca/infocecs/CRC/manual/jobworldinterview.html.

The manner in which you dress for the interview reflects your degree of adult socialization and how well you would "fit" with an employer. Dress also expresses the amount of genuine interest you have in acquiring the position. A rule of thumb is to check the attire worn by individuals depicted in the employer-supplied literature.

### TABLE 2.7
#### Typical Questions that Interviewers Ask

**General questions**

Tell me about yourself.
Why do you want to work for us?
How do you spend your spare time?
What are your strengths and weaknesses?
What are your short-term goals? Long-term?
How do you think you can make a contribution to our organization?

**Questions regarding education**

What college courses did you like the most? Least? Why?
In what extracurricular activities did you participate? Why?
What did you gain or learn from your part-time job experience?
Do you think your grades are a good indication of your academic abilities? Explain.
Why did you attend your college or university? How do you assess your educational experience?
Why did you major in psychology? [Do not say, "Because I'm interested in people." Explain *why* and *how* you are interested in people.]

The following advice is important: "No interview is complete until you have sent the interviewer a thank-you note." In addition to being courteous, such a procedure provides another way to enhance your impression and keep your name in the interviewer's mind.

To evaluate your interview effectiveness, how many interviews will you have to do? Some authorities recommend that you plan to undertake at least five interviews. If you have not detected some favorable reactions by the fifth interview, then reevaluate your strategies and modify them accordingly. Do not hesitate to contact your CO personnel or your adviser.

As many as 30 interviews, including those both on and off campus, is realistic to achieve a mutually satisfactory match for you and a prospective employer. Anyone can get a job with fewer interviews, but to get one that you particularly want may require greater effort. Lunneborg and Wilson (1982) discovered that job satisfaction was directly related to the length and method of job search. They found that graduates were more satisfied with positions after long periods of searching and use of self-initiated interviews. Begin the process early in your senior year. Findings from this and other studies indicate several variables contribute to job satisfaction. That students were psychology majors was only indirectly related to satisfaction. How they pursued the job search and what they did were more important than the major per se.

Simply because you decide to seek employment immediately following graduation does not prevent you from pursuing graduate education in the future. Do not be surprised if you pick up this book and read additional chapters in a year or two. Many employers provide financial support to employees who develop job-related skills by attending graduate school. Moreover, experience in the world of work can help identify and clarify career goals that will require graduate education.

More thorough treatment of all of the topics in this chapter can be located in numerous career-oriented books in libraries and commercial bookstores. Thorough preparation and dedicated effort can pay large career dividends. Oh, and by the way, good luck in your career pursuits!

## REFERENCES

Davis, J. R. (1979). Where did they all go? A job survey of BA graduates. In P. J. Woods (Ed.), *The psychology major: Training and employment strategies* (pp. 110–114). Washington, DC: American Psychological Association.

Figler, H. (1988). *The complete-job-search handbook* (Revised and expanded ed.). New York: Holt, Rinehart and Winston.

Holland, J. L. (1985). *Making vocational choices: A theory of vocational, personality and work environments*. Englewood Cliffs, NJ: Prentice-Hall.

Lunneborg, P. W. (1974). Can college graduates in psychology find employment in their field? *Vocational Guidance Quarterly, 23*, 159–166.

Lunneborg, P. W., & Wilson, V. M. (1982). Job satisfaction correlates for college graduates in psychology. *Teaching of Psychology, 9*, 199–201.

McGovern, T. V., & Carr, K. F. (1989). Carving out the niche: A review of alumni surveys on undergraduate psychology majors. *Teaching of Psychology, 16,* 52–57.

National Association of Colleges and Employers. (1999, September). *Salary survey*. Bethlehem, PA: Author.

Perlman, B., & McCann, L. I. (1999). The most frequently listed courses in the undergraduate psychology curriculum. *Teaching of Psychology, 26, 177–182*.

Swanson, J. L., & Tokar, D. M. (1991). College students' perceptions of barriers to career development. *Journal of Vocational Behavior, 38*, 92–106.

Titley, R. W. (1978). Whatever happened to the class of '67? *American Psychologist, 33,* 1094–1098.

Ware, M. E. (1991, August). *"You're majoring in what? What can you do with psychology?"* Presented at the G. Stanley Hall Lecture Series, American Psychological Association, San Francisco, CA.

Ware, M. E., & Meyer, A. E. (1981). Career versatility of the psychology major A survey of graduates. *Teaching of Psychology, 8,* 12–15.

Woods, P. J. (1979). Employment following two different undergraduate programs in psychology. In P. J. Woods (Ed.), *The psychology major: Training and employment strategies* (pp. 120–125). Washington, DC: American Psychological Association.

# APPENDIX A

## Work-Related Transferable Skills with Student-Generated Examples

| Skills Employers Seek | Student Products and Experiences |
|---|---|
| **Communication Skills** | |
| Writing | Wrote essays for scholarships while applying for colleges and graduate schools |
| | Prepared a research article and submitted it for publication |
| | Wrote research papers and two experimental research projects |
| Speaking | Presented a speech to a group of students on a retreat |
| | Explained the strengths of our university to parents and prospective students |
| | Discussed research project in small groups, explained the project to our participants, and talked to the professor about our findings |
| **Cognitive skills** | |
| Coping with deadline pressure | Prepared manuscripts in advance of deadlines |
| | Completed reports on time when they were vital to patient treatment |
| | Refined an experiment to execute our study with a limited number of participants |
| | Evaluated new ways to solve daily problems (e.g., getting candle wax out of carpet with hot iron) |
| Research | Wrote numerous manuscripts that required gathering information from a variety of sources |
| | Conducted a job search and made contacts with people, asking them about the nature of their work |
| Planning | Scheduled study time in preparation for several major tests |
| | Balanced homework, classes, extracurricular time, and time for myself |
| | Balanced when to study and when to write papers |
| **Social skills** | |
| Human relations | Dealt with older patients, sick children, and families as a hospital volunteer |
| | Worked as a physical therapy aid to maximize quality of care and minimize waste of time |
| | Mediated between my roommates to ensure that tasks (e.g., paying bills) were completed |
| | Resolved differences between players and coaches |
| Negotiating/arbitrating/organizing/ managing/coordinating | Organized a benefit concert |
| | Organized workers for an Appalachian Habitat for Humanity project |
| | Coordinated dates, space, exhibitors, advertisers, and nurses for health fair |
| Supervising | Monitored and directed the members of a team in my capacity as captain |
| | Ensured that personnel in training attended required clinics and completed research projects and manuscripts |
| | Monitored a research project and gave directions |

# APPENDIX B

## Instructor-Identified Skills Available from Experimental Psychology (Research Method) Course

### Communication skills

Speak in a clear, concise, and persuasive manner

Defend ideas in a clear, objective, and non-dogmatic manner

Write coherent and well-organized essays

Write a technical, detailed manuscript (e.g., a research project)

Write a manuscript in APA style

Use computers to produce reports

### Skills as team member

Work well on a team as leader or follower

Develop rapport at group level and stimulate enthusiasm

Recognize and use skills and ideas of others

Give demonstrations and lead discussions

Adapt readily to organizational rules and procedures

### Human relations skills

Perceptive listening ability

Sensitive to the needs of a wide variety of people

Tolerant of values and attitudes different from mine

Work with children, adolescents, adults, and/or families

Conduct interviews

Assist others in personal development

Use library resources or personal contacts to find information to solve
problem or answer a question

### Skills for data collection, analysis, and retrieval

Collect, record, organize, analyze, or interpret empirical data

Select and compute statistical tests and interpret their results

Perform data analysis and statistical tests

Use computers to store, organize, or analyze data

Use computers to retrieve information from library sources

Use printed references to retrieve information from library sources

### Cognitive skills

Read printed material thoroughly

Assimilate large amounts of information

Understand, evaluate, or generalize from research findings

Identify, define, investigate, or solve problems

Think logically, critically, and creatively

### Laboratory research skills

Recognize assumptions and make logical inferences

Formulate hypotheses

Recruit research participants and treat them in an ethical manner

Make and record behavioral observations

Design and conduct a survey

Design and conduct an experimental or quasi-experimental study

Create understandable graphs and tables

# APPENDIX C

## Positions and Salaries Offered to Psychology Majors

| Arranged by Number of Offers | | | Arranged by Starting Salaries | | |
|---|---|---|---|---|---|
| Employer | No. of Offers | Average Salary | Employer | No. of Offers | Average Salary |
| Education | 65 | 24,953 | Pharmaceuticals | 1 | 45,000 |
| Social services | 55 | 21,124 | Metals and metal products | 1 | 42,000 |
| Consulting services | 35 | 36,991 | Consulting services | 35 | 36,991 |
| Merchandising | 32 | 27,623 | Real estate | 1 | 36,000 |
| Health services | 24 | 22,514 | Food and beverage | 3 | 34,067 |
| Local/state government | 23 | 24,855 | Computer software/data processing | 12 | 33,813 |
| Finance | 22 | 32,186 | Public accounting | 2 | 33,500 |
| Insurance | 16 | 28,307 | Finance | 22 | 32,186 |
| Hospitals | 15 | 20,533 | Automotive and mechanical | 7 | 31,357 |
| Computer software/data processing | 12 | 33,813 | Textiles and apparel | 2 | 31,000 |
| Personnel supply services | 11 | 28,659 | Banking (commercial) | 8 | 30,108 |
| Other service employers | 11 | 26,409 | Protective services | 1 | 30,000 |
| Communication services | 10 | 26,030* | Electrical and electronics | 1 | 30,000 |
| Hospitality | 9 | 20,659 | Paper and wood products | 2 | 30,000 |
| Banking (commercial) | 8 | 30,108 | Advertising | 6 | 29,500 |
| Research organizations | 8 | 29,488 | Research organizations | 8 | 29,488 |
| Computers and business equipment | 8 | 29,370 | Computers and business equipment | 8 | 29,370 |
| Federal government | 8 | 26,126 | Banking (investment) | 2 | 29,000 |
| Automotive and mechanical | 7 | 31,357 | Personnel supply services | 11 | 28,659 |
| Advertising | 6 | 29,500 | Insurance | 16 | 28,307 |
| Transportation | 6 | 23,308 | Building materials and construction | 5 | 27,780 |

| Industry | n | Salary | | Industry | n | Salary |
|---|---|---|---|---|---|---|
| Building materials and construction | 5 | 27,780 | | Merchandising | 32 | 27,623 |
| Legal services | 4 | 27,413 | | Legal services | 4 | 27,413 |
| Food and beverage | 3 | 34,067 | | Environmental/waste management | 1 | 27,000 |
| Other nonprofit employers | 3 | 20,187 | | Widely diversified | 1 | 27,000 |
| Membership/religious | 3 | 18,933 | | Other service employers | 11 | 26,409 |
| Public accounting | 2 | 33,500 | | Federal government | 8 | 26,126 |
| Textiles and apparel | 2 | 31,000 | | Communication services | 10 | 26,030* |
| Paper and wood products | 2 | 30,000 | | Chemicals and allied products | 1 | 25,000 |
| Banking (investment) | 2 | 29,000 | | Education | 65 | 24,953 |
| Printing | 2 | 24,500 | | Local/state government | 23 | 24,855 |
| Pharmaceuticals | 1 | 45,000 | | Printing | 2 | 24,500 |
| Metals and metal products | 1 | 42,000 | | Transportation | 6 | 23,308 |
| Real estate | 1 | 36,000 | | Health services | 24 | 22,514 |
| Protective services | 1 | 30,000 | | Engineering/surveying | 1 | 22,000 |
| Electrical and electronics | 1 | 30,000 | | Packaging and allied products | 1 | 21,300 |
| Environmental/waste management | 1 | 27,000 | | Social services | 55 | 21,124 |
| Widely diversified | 1 | 27,000 | | Hospitality | 9 | 20,659 |
| Chemicals and allied products | 1 | 25,000 | | Hospitals | 15 | 20,533 |
| Engineering/surveying | 1 | 22,000 | | Other nonprofit employers | 3 | 20,187 |
| Packaging and allied products | 1 | 21,300 | | Membership/religious | 3 | 18,933 |

**Total offers 429**

*Median salary 26,030

*Note.* From National Association of Colleges and Employers (1999), with permission.

27

# Paula A. Dostel

| **PRESENT ADDRESS** | **PERMANENT ADDRESS** |
|---|---|
| 1357 Palms Dormitory | 786 West 42nd Place |
| Creighton University | Chicago, IL 60609 |
| Omaha, NE 68178 | (312) 555-4973 |
| (402) 555-6393 | |

**PROFESSIONAL OBJECTIVE:**

Use my teaching, communication, and organizational skills in a human services or business setting

**EDUCATION:**

Bachelor of Arts, Psychology
Creighton University, May 2000

**WORK EXPERIENCE:**

1999 – Present

- guided students in understanding course material
- evaluated performance and developed effective study programs
- counseled students
- completed reports evaluating the program and recommended improvements

Student Support Services, Omaha, NE

Summers
1998 & 1999

- supervised and cared for three children
- coordinated educational and social activities
- Sunrise Gardens, Chicago, IL

Winter
1998 - 1999

- documented and organized invoices

Paul's Packing Co., Chicago, IL

Summers
1996 & 1997

- compiled and organized patient files
- gathered research pertaining to cardiology field
- documented and verified department purchase orders
- computed information relevant to department research

University of Chicago, Chicago, IL

**HONORS AND ACTIVITIES:**

- developed and organized Christmas food drive for low-income homebound in Chicago
- taught mentally and physically handicapped children
- published poetry in American Poetry Anthology
- Dean's Honor Roll

**REFERENCES:**  Furnished upon request

# Robert M. Summers

| PRESENT ADDRESS | PERMANENT ADDRESS |
|---|---|
| 4791 South 88th Plaza, #11 | 1154 Pine |
| Omaha, NE 68127 | Atlantic, IA 50022 |
| (402) 555-9181 | (712) 555-1647 |

**Professional Objective:** Acquire a professional training and personnel position

**Education:** Creighton University, Omaha, NE
BA Psychology. Graduation August, 1999
12 hours of business-related courses

Learned leadership skills, delegating power techniques, and communication skills at leadership conference, Creighton University

**Experience:**

Aug. 1998 to Present

**Assistant Manager, The Founders' Grill,**
Fine dining, seafood specialties, Omaha, NE
managed staff of 15 persons
monitored liquor control, cost, and ordering
promoted staff team spirit
managed banquet facilities (85–250 people), and room
 service for an 89 room hotel
trained new employees

January 1998 to May 1998

**Intern position, Jobs Inc.,** Omaha, NE
conducted a comprehensive job seeking skills workshop,
facilitated discussion in small groups of 5–15 people,
documented and maintained records of participants
communicated client progress to Department of Social
 Services

May 1996 to August 1998

**Building Supervisor, Kiewit Fitness Center,**
Creighton University, Omaha, NE
managed building during evening and weekend hours
supervised (5-7) student staff
enforced policies and resolved conflicts

**Activities, Interests:** Delta Delta Fraternity, Psychology Club, biking, tennis, reading, weight lifting

**Geographic Preference:** Open

**References:** Furnished upon request

# 3

## Choosing the Master's Degree in Psychology

*Baron Perlman*

Almost 150 departments in the United States and Canada offer the master's degree in psychology as a terminal degree (APA, 1999). Students interested in an advanced degree in psychology and employment in the field after graduation need to decide if this terminal degree fits their needs.

### OVERVIEW

Although master's and doctoral programs in psychology share some similarities, one of the biggest dissimilarities is the time needed to complete the degree. Generally the master's takes 2 years, whereas a PhD or PsyD requires 4 or 5 years of study and an additional year of internship in some applied subdisciplines (the next chapter provides information about these two types of doctoral degrees). Master's programs can vary in the breath and depth of what you learn, but a good master's program can be as demanding—and as rewarding—as doctoral study.

My experience, supported by independent research, indicates that there are many opportunities for bright, energetic, skilled people with a master's of arts (MA) or science (MS) in psychology. Geography can influence these opportunities, with employment requirements varying widely from state to state, and even within states.

This chapter discusses four areas pertinent to the master's degree: (a) the strengths and weaknesses of the degree; (b) educational opportunities for undergraduate majors and nonmajors; (c) admission standards for master's programs; and (d) professional concerns such as employment, supervision, and licensing/certification.

My goal is to provide practical information. A better understanding of the master's degree will help you make a better decision about continuing in school or seeking employment. While the bachelor's program is typically a broad-based one, graduate study requires a narrow, more focused curriculum. Graduate school can be exciting, but it is also time consuming and rigorous. You'll be more likely to succeed if you have a clear understanding of your motivation and some idea of what to expect.

## STRENGTHS AND LIMITATIONS OF THE MASTER'S DEGREE IN PSYCHOLOGY

Students usually apply to master's programs in psychology for one of two reasons: They have enjoyed psychology as undergraduates and want to further their knowledge, and/or they are seeking a job that requires a graduate degree (but not necessarily a doctorate). Master's and doctoral degrees are different career options. As you learn about the differences and how they affect your career options, the choice between a master's degree and a PhD or PsyD will become clearer.

My first recommendation is: *Choose the career and graduate education that makes the most sense to you.* Study your alternatives. You may decide to opt for a terminal master's degree and seek employment, or a terminal master's with the option to go on to doctoral work. On the other hand, you may decide you want to work toward a doctoral degree from the start. Capable, motivated students who know that the work and responsibilities they want require a doctoral degree, and are willing to make the 4- to 5-year commitment, should seek admission to doctoral programs.

Many departments offering a terminal master' s program of study do not offer a doctorate, recognizing that the master's degree is the appropriate and recognized degree for some areas in psychology. For example, elementary and secondary schools recognize the master's as the appropriate degree for their counselors and psychologists. Likewise, a master's in industrial/organizational (I/O) psychology allows graduates to work in personnel, training, and organizational development. A recognized terminal master's degree (e.g., counseling, education, I/O) allows recognition as a professional. The master's experimental degree is often aimed at preparing students for doctoral admission, but the private sector also employs graduates with this degree.

Many students are interested in working in clinical psychology with a master's degree, but there is controversy about practicing at this level. Psychologists, state licensing boards, and the health care industry often view the doctorate as the appropriate degree for clinical work. Anyone wishing to be a clinician should learn about the career at both the master's and doctoral level. Some students may be pleased with master's clinical work; others may seriously consider admission to an American Psychological Association (APA) accredited doctoral program.

### Opportunities Outside Psychology

Many excellent master's degree choices exist outside of psychology. The master's of social work (MSW) degree may be the finest mental health/human service degree offered nationally. Certain emphases in business administration (MBA) programs are similar to some I/O curricula. Departments other than psychology may offer master's degrees in school psychology, physical therapy, and counseling. Innovative interdisciplinary programs in health, sports, rehabilitation, geriatrics and other areas are appearing. Other alternatives are discussed in Fretz's chapter on licensing and credentialing in Section V of this book.

Students must do their homework. Many students I have advised have negative attitudes toward social work even though they know little about the value of this degree and the quality of training in many MSW programs. Students are well advised to make graduate school, career, and employment decisions based on facts, not biases.

## Good Reasons for Choosing Master's Programs

Master's programs offer many advantages and some disadvantages. One advantage is that the master's degree allows a choice of options for employment.

*Proper Level.*    Some mature, realistic students recognize a master's education as the proper level for their interests and abilities. Some of my greatest joys as a teacher have come from working with students who had no aspirations to a doctorate. They worked hard, were pleased to be getting a graduate education, grew professionally and personally, and became responsible, competent mental health professionals.

*The Nature of the Education.*    Master's programs can provide an excellent education. Compared to doctoral programs, they can provide smaller, more individualized classes, practicum placements, and instruction. Some students find large universities intimidating, and good master's programs are often found in smaller institutions.

*Insurance Policy.*    Many competent students apply to doctoral programs each year, and some are not accepted. Some of these individuals apply to master's programs as backups. Enrolled in good master's programs, these students can raise their Graduate Record Exam (GRE) scores, gain additional academic, research (e.g., completing a thesis and conducting other research), and practical experience, and secure letters of recommendation from graduate faculty. Enrollment in a master's program demonstrates motivation for advanced study and personal maturity. A well-conceived and well-executed master's thesis also aids in subsequent doctoral applications.

A word of caution: *If you do not want a master's program, do not waste your time and resources or those of the faculty.* Some of my most unpleasant teaching experiences occurred with students in our master's program who were angry about being rejected for a doctoral program.

*Is This What I Want to Learn About?*    Some students want to study developmental psychology, others want to learn more advanced laboratory skills, and still others want to be clinicians. For students unsure of their ultimate goals, a master's program may be the ideal way to test their interests and commitments to a career or to doctoral study.

*Prelude to Doctoral Study.*    Students who obtain a master's degree in psychology are not precluded from admittance to doctoral programs (Bonifazi, Crespy, & Rieker, 1997; Perlman & Dehart, 1985; Quereshi & Kuchan, 1988). A master's degree can be an asset in gaining admission to doctoral study by improving a student's strength in desirable admission criteria.

Eighty-one percent of doctoral counseling programs, 74% of doctoral school programs, and 67% of clinical PhD and 64% of clinical PsyD programs surveyed (Bonifazi et al., 1997) stated it would be beneficial for applicants to have a completed master's thesis, but there was no consensus among programs on what courses, activities, or other criteria make master's students attractive for admission. For any student, master's or not, Graduate Record Exam scores, undergraduate grade point average (GPA), recommendations, and research involvement are important admission criteria. A master's education can improve three of the four (students' undergraduate GPAs remain constant once they graduate).

Many students leaving the clinical program in which I worked moved directly to a doctoral program in counseling, I/O, developmental or social psychology, or some PsyD clinical programs. Students who applied for admission to an APA-accredited clinical doctoral were rarely admitted without additional work experience, usually 2 to 4 years. When they then applied to doctoral programs with this experience on their resumés, 86% (24 out of 28) gained acceptance (Perlman & Dehart, 1985); 17 (61%) had been denied admission before master's training.

Some professional schools of psychology offering the PsyD degree prefer students with master's degrees. They have demonstrated the ability to do graduate-level academic work, usually have practical experience in the field, and because they are often older and more mature than recent college graduates, they may have more to offer their clients and the graduate faculty working with them.

*Nonpsychology Majors*      These students may have good grade point averages, good GRE scores, and good work and/or volunteer experiences. In a master's program, these students can obtain the necessary background and better their chances of finding work or going on for doctoral study in the area.

*Take Less of My Life to Educate Me.*      Four or 5 years in graduate school can seem like eternity. Some undergraduates are simply burned out and cannot face another 4 years in school. Adults returning to school may not have the time to devote to a doctoral program. A master's allows students to get an education and then move on to a job in less time than a doctoral program.

*Foreign Students.*      Some foreign students cannot gain admission to a doctoral program because of limited language skills. A master's program may admit and educate these students, preparing them for doctoral study or giving them skills they can utilize when they return to their home countries.

*Geography.*      Some students have family responsibilities, jobs, or other valid reasons for needing stay close to where they now live and work. An in-state institution may offer these students the only viable alternative for graduate school, and master's programs may then need to be considered.

## Poor Reasons for Choosing a Master's Program

*I Want to Do Something and Here I Am.*      Some applicants simply want to change jobs, either voluntarily or because of layoffs or downsizing. Some find that the academic world protects them from the reality of having to find work, so they want to extend their stay. Such individuals have little understanding of the work and commitment needed for an advanced degree. They apply because it is the path of least resistance; their chances for success are slim.

*I Want to Make More Money.*     "I'm in it for the money" is a common statement faculty hear from students. They've heard that a master's in I/O, for example, can lead to a good paying job. If money is the primary motivation, students are likely to lack the commitment and motivation to do well in a graduate education.

*Reluctance to Move.*     Some students opt to do their graduate work at the same school they attended as undergraduates, even if they can gain admission to a higher quality program elsewhere. Or they limit their choices for graduate work to schools near their homes when competitive for higher quality programs elsewhere. A word of advice: *If you want a high quality graduate education, be prepared to go where it is offered.*

## Master's Program Opportunities

The 1998–1999 APA *Graduate Study in Psychology (APA, 1999)* lists 148 departments offering a terminal master's degree. The most frequently listed applied emphases are clinical (n = 66), counseling (n = 48), I/O (n = 36), and school psychology (n = 30). This is comparable to the 67 departments listed as offering clinical training in the 1976–1977 guide, but down from the 97 programs listed in 1982–1983. Ten departments offered an applied emphasis, often clinical. Additional professional schools offering the PsyD degree, some psychology departments moving from master's to doctoral degree status, and changes in health care have contributed to the decline in master's clinical training.

Some subspecialties in psychology offer more opportunity for admission than others. For example, the most common degree listed in the 1998–1999 *Graduate Study in Psychology* was general—experimental or general psychology (n = 79). Only three programs offer terminal master's degrees in neuroscience; two programs offer health psychology, one biopsychology, and one psychopharmacology. Few graduate programs exist to meet students' interests in these areas.

## Learning About Alternatives

Two questions will help you learn about graduate school opportunities both in and out of psychology. Always ask faculty members, supervisors at a volunteer placement, and peers who else you should talk with about your graduate school and work plans. And when you meet with these people, again ask them who else you should talk with. Second, when you talk with individuals about your graduate school plans, ask them if there are additional issues and questions you should have raised.

Make good decisions based on your abilities and interests. For example, if you struggle and do not believe you can earn a passing grade in statistics courses, perhaps an MSW program makes more sense than a master's psychology program with two semesters of graduate-level statistics. Know what is available.

# ADMISSIONS

Applicants to graduate psychology programs need constructive guidance from friends, faculty, professionals in the field, and directors of programs to which they apply. Read some of the materials in the recommended reading section at the end of this chapter. The APA directory of graduate programs lists extensive information about master's and doctoral programs, including number of students admitted and their characteristics (e.g., average GPA and GRE scores). You have a variety of options open to you and should explore these before you complete your applications. You will make better decisions and save time and money.

Each program has its own criteria for judging applicants. Typically, admission to doctoral programs is highly competitive. GRE scores and GPAs must be extremely high, and the student must be active in the science of psychology (publishing in jury reviewed forums) and must show a high activity index (volunteer work, campus extracurriculars). With many applicants for few openings, faculty choose to work with the most qualified. Many of the same criteria are utilized in master's program admissions, although cutoff points are not as severe. Keep in mind that different programs apply different admission criteria. A clinical program may look for volunteer or work experience; an I/O program will typically require high GRE scores and research abilities. Let me use the program in which I worked, and more specifically its clinical emphasis, as an example of admissions standards.

GPA was important, with 3.2 to 3.5 being desirable, but was not required to be considered competitive. Students gained admission with less than a 3.0 (B) average when other data indicated they had the potential to become competent, master's-educated psychologists. For example, nontraditional students were highly valued for their maturity, motivation, and life experience, and were often accepted with a somewhat lower GPA.

The GRE was required. Again, students were admitted with low scores, sometimes even below the 500 average, if an interview indicated they had potential. This may not be true of other clinical programs, and in some subdiscipline areas such as I/O, GRE scores may be a critical admission criterion. Letters of recommendation were important. Because past behavior is often an indicator of future behavior, admission committee members were interested in what the writers of these letters had to say about a candidate's past performance in an academic and/or work setting.

Other considerations also came into play. A personal statement of intent about why a student wanted advanced training in clinical psychology (one to two pages long) was required. Admission committee members were interested not only in how well thought out such statements were, but also in how well they were written. Graduate education in psychology entails endless hours teaching students to communicate orally and in writing, and students who communicate poorly when they apply may not have skills perceived as crucial to success in the field. Published or prior research carried medium weight (other master's programs, especially in experimental psychology or I/O, may be much more interested in these skills). In our program, students had to attend full-time. Although program literature stated schooling was full-time, many applicants assumed they could enroll as part-time students.

Work or volunteer experience in the field was important. Students with such a background demonstrated motivation to learn firsthand about their future career, and the more experience students brought to the program, the better use they made of coursework and practicum experiences. Finally, students were interviewed either by telephone or in person. Faculty wanted to get to know students and to discover how articulate they were. Questions revolved around reasons for wanting to attend graduate school, volunteer or work experience, and the strengths and relative weaknesses each student would bring to graduate training.

### Students Denied Admission

Students most likely to be denied admission fell into three categories. The first group consisted of students who desired an education in areas outside the program. The fit between such student interests and the curriculum was poor, and to admit such students was a disservice to them.

A second group of students had application materials that were weak both across the board and in comparison with other applicants. GPAs and GRE scores were relatively low, they had no volunteer or work experience, and their statements of intent were poorly written.

The third group consisted of students who displayed strengths in some but not all areas (GPA, GRE scores, letters of recommendation) and also were perceived as difficult to train or as having limited potential to work as master's-level clinicians. More specifically, such students were described in letters of recommendation or perceived by clinical faculty during interviews as immature, belligerent, hostile, or having poor interpersonal skills. Some students were unlikeable individuals with whom clinical faculty did not want to spend time, and whom they were reluctant to trust with clients in professional situations. Students with a high sense of entitlement (e.g., narcissistic, not wanting to work hard) were turned down.

Students' personalities are a factor that needs to be considered in many programs, although other reasons (e.g., "it was a difficult decision and the program had many qualified applicants for a limited number of openings") are given for denied admission. For example, although I/O psychology may demand greater quantitative skills than clinical, I/O graduates work closely with others in organizations, often in teams, and excellent interpersonal skills are necessary.

Applicants perceived as having the potential to learn and grow in their graduate education are desirable. Thus, for many experimental programs students who want to help faculty in the laboratory, are enthusiastic when asked to do research to learn different methodologies, and have a strong spirit of cooperation are much more likely to be admitted than peers with equal academic credentials and a weak spirit of cooperation.

## PROFESSIONAL ISSUES

There is a series of professional issues students need to be aware of if they want to obtain a terminal master's degree in an applied area. These issues are most relevant to those entering the helping professions because of national and state regulations of health coverage and providers.

For applied psychologists, a master's degree has historically been respected, although debate continues over master's clinical training. A master's degree need not be a truncated doctorate or a consolation prize, and a competent professional psychologist can be trained in two years. Many departments of psychology and doctoral psychologists are committed to master's-level education. More philosophically, societal needs exist for service providers at the master's level, who are willing to work with others, with salaries or job responsibilities that may not interest those with doctorates.

## Employment

Employment opportunities exist for those who hold a master's degree in psychology. A master's degree with experimental training gives a person advanced skills in research and use of statistics, and more generally in analytical reasoning and critical thinking. Jobs exist in a wide variety of public- and private-sector organizations and companies for people who are literate and can read and write critically, problem solve, analyze data, do research, and use computers and software programs.

The master's degrees in school counseling and school psychology are a logical stepping stone to specific types of jobs, and starting salaries are usually adequate. Holders of a master's degree in I/O training often find positions in corporate personnel or training departments and may earn a salary equal to or slightly below the faculty who trained them, with the potential to earn substantially more in the future. Specific, technical tool sets (e.g., job analysis, development of the validity of tests, employee opinion survey work) and practical experience lead to better employment opportunities for these master's I/O psychologists.

## The Clinical Master's Degree

The controversy around this degree mostly concerns terminal master's programs training students in clinical skills. Because school and counseling degrees and the MSW are well established, state certification rules and regulations usually recognize such master's-level professionals. I/O psychologists typically work in organizations where no certification is necessary.

*The Title Psychologist.*     The APA has defined a *psychologist* as someone with a doctorate, the only person who can use the title *psychologist* and practice independently. States differ in how they treat master's-level psychologists, but in 48 states a doctoral degree is required for psychology licensing (Sleek, 1995). Your title may be determined by the state in which you work.

*Master's Degree Viewed as a Consolation Prize.*     The APA has studied the issues involved in a terminal master's degree in clinical psychology since the late 1940s and early 1950s when master's degrees were often regarded as a consolation prize for those who could not stand the rigors of doctoral preparation. To some extent this attitude still exists today. Additionally, there are concerns that master's-level people are filling positions that would ordinarily go to doctorate psychologists.

*Employment.*     Descriptions of clinical master's programs testify to some fairly intensive and broad-based training. The skills learned and demonstrated in these programs can be applied in a variety of work settings. The responsibilities of the master's-level clinical psychologist appear to be those of a professional journeyman—counseling, psychotherapy, consultation, some psychodiagnostic testing, perhaps program evaluation and research, and administrative work. These clinicians work throughout the country in a variety of applied, service-delivery settings such as mental or general hospitals, outpatient clinics, and in private practice engaged in professional clinical activities, primarily psychotherapy (Perlman, 1985a). These responsibilities are congruent with the length, depth, and type of training offered by most terminal clinical master's programs. But is someone trained like this suitable for certain positions and can the person function with professional competence? A qualified "yes" seems appropriate (Perlman, 1990; Perlman & Lane, 1981; Richert & Fulkerson, 1987).

Most master's clinicians find their work and careers satisfying (Perlman, 1985b). Their roles and responsibilities continue to provide challenge and variety, they remain committed to the occupation and profession, their salaries rise commensurate with experience, and they report being respected and valued members in the organizations in which they work. They work within the mainstream of mental health service. It may take 2 years or longer to obtain an outpatient position. Because of both (a) the work experiences insurance companies demand (e.g., 3000 supervised hours in Wisconsin) before they will reimburse for an outpatient therapist's work and (b) state certification rules, employment may begin in an inpatient hospital or other setting to develop one's credentials. Then more and different employment opportunities are often available.

Objections to master's training are communicated infrequently to these clinicians by other professionals in human services. Much of the discourse and debate about master's training seems to lie within organized psychology and has little apparent effect on those working in the field except as it influences licensing and certification at the state level.

*Licensing or Certification.*    This is necessary to hold a title, to have credentials validated, and to be eligible for reimbursement by insurance companies. Some states have a mechanism for master's mental health graduates' certification. If you know you will be seeking a job in a certain state, learn the number of hours of direct client work and other criteria for certification and/or licensing. For example, in Wisconsin a person with master's-level clinical psychology training cannot easily become certified, making it difficult to offer services in an agency and be reimbursed by third-party payment. Those with a MSW or master's of counseling degree are much more easily state certified in Wisconsin.

*Supervision.*    The APA has adopted a recommendation for supervision of master's-level persons, and it is a sound policy. Anyone seeking employment in direct client work must receive supervision by someone who meets the state's criteria (e.g., licensed doctoral psychologist).

Be informed. My advice to people interested in an applied terminal master's education, especially in a clinical program, is: Go into such training with your eyes open. Talk with program faculty about the job placement of program graduates and about state regulations for licensing or certification of master's clinical psychologists. A sound knowledge of this side of professional practice will serve you well in the decisions you make.

Since 1990, progress has been made in promoting the master's degree and in obtaining certification/licensure for people with master's degrees. The Council of Applied Masters Programs in Psychology (CAMPP) has established training standards, and the Master's Program Accreditation Council (MPAC) is currently active in accrediting master's programs in psychology. Such accreditation is important in establishing competency-based training that protects the consumers of psychological services. As you apply to various schools, consider inquiring about whether the program is accredited or has plans to apply for such accreditation.

Much of the progress in relation to the master's degree has been accomplished through the efforts of the North American Association of Masters in Psychology (NAMP), headquartered in Norman, OK. Their web site address is www.nampwebsite.org. Founded by Dr. Logan

Wright, a past president of the American Psychological Association, NAMP continues to work cooperatively with state organizations to further the causes of those with master's degrees in psychology. Psychology is regulated by some agency, usually a board, in each state. In some states, use of modified titles such as *psychological examiner* or *psychological technician* is permitted. In some states, people trained at the master's level may be licensed under a different title, perhaps as a counselor or as a behavioral practitioner. In West Virginia and Alaska, you may use the title *psychologist* once you have passed the board's requirements. Because of such variation, you must check with the governing body in the state in which you wish to work to determine the exact requirements and privileges available to you in that state. Progress is being made and should continue in getting more recognition of the training that master's level people have obtained and in getting certification/licensure for them.

## The Essentials

Master's programs in psychology provide a viable option, and for some students they are the education leading to the career of choice. Students considering advanced education in psychology are urged to think and learn about the following:

- What it is they want to do , and why.
- What types of graduate programs allow for these career choices.
- A decision between master's or doctoral education.
- Sound knowledge of the admission criteria of master's programs.
- Advice on the process of gaining admission.
- Some knowledge of professional issues if they are seeking applied master's training.

The information provided in this chapter should aid individuals wanting more knowledge about the master's degree in psychology and should help in these considerations.

## REFERENCES

American Psychological Association. (1999). *The 1998 with 1999 addendum graduate study in psychology.* Washington, DC: Author.

Bonifazi, D. Z., Crespy, S. D., & Rieker, P. (1997). Value of a master's degree for gaining admission to doctoral programs in psychology. *Teaching of Psychology, 24,* 176–182.

Keith-Spiegel, P. (1991). *The complete guide to graduate school admission: Psychology and related fields.* Hillsdale, NJ: Lawrence Erlbaum Associates.

Perlman, B. (1985a). A national survey of APA-affiliated master's-level clinicians: Description and comparison. *Professional Psychology, 16,* 553–564.

Perlman, B. (1985b). Training and career issues of APA-affiliated master's-level clinicians. *Professional Psychology, 16,* 753–767.

Perlman, B. (1990, June). *Our plate is full: The state of applied master's psychology.* Invited keynote address presented at the 1990 National Conference for Applied Master's-Level Programs in Psychology, Norman, OK.

Perlman, B., & Dehart, P. (1985). The master's-level clinician: Application and admission to doctoral programs. *Teaching of Psychology, 15,* 67–71.

Perlman, B., & Lane, R. (1981). The clinical master's degree. *Teaching of Psychology*, *8*, 72–77.

Quereshi, M. Y., & Kuchan, A. M. (1988). The master's degree in clinical psychology: Longitudinal program evaluation. *Professional Psychology: Research and Practice, 19*, 594–599.

Richert, A. J., & Fulkerson, F. E. (1987). Master's-level training and employment in community mental health. *Professional Psychology: Research and Practice, 18*, 479–480.

## RECOMMENDED READING

American Psychological Association. (1994). *Getting in: A step-by-step plan for gaining admission to graduate school in psychology.* Washington, DC: Author.

Buskist, W., & Mixon, A. (1998). *Allyn & Bacon guide to master's programs in psychology and counseling psychology.* Boston: Allyn & Bacon.

Buskist, W., & Sherburne, T. R. (1996). *Preparing for graduate study in psychology.* Boston: Allyn & Bacon.

Fretz, B. R., & Stang, D. J. (1987). *Preparing for graduate study in psychology: Not for seniors only!* Washington, DC: American Psychological Association.

Sayette, M. A., Mayne, T. J., & Norcross, J. C. (1998). *Insider's guide to graduate programs in clinical and counseling psychology: 1998/1999 Edition.* New York: Guilford.

Sleek, S. (1995, January). Managed care sharpens master's-degree debate. *APA Monitor*, pp. 8–9.

Society for Industrial and Organizational Psychology, Inc. (1998). *Graduate training programs in industrial–organizational psychology and related fields.* Bowling Green, OH: Author.

Stevens, J., Yock, T., & Perlman, B. (1979). A comparison between master's clinical training and professional responsibilities in community mental health centers. *Professional Psychology, 10*, 20–27.

www.apa.org/ed/gradschool/ (a site for undergraduate students who plan to pursue an advanced psychology degree).

## RECENT DEVELOPMENTS AND TRENDS

**Carolyn K. Long**

Since 1990, progress has been made in promoting the master's degree and in obtaining certification/licensure for people with master's degrees. The Council of Applied Masters Programs in Psychology (CAMPP) has established training standards, and the Master's Program Accreditation Council (MPAC) is currently active in accrediting master's programs in psychology. Such accreditation is important in establishing competency-based training that protects the consumers of psychological services. As you apply to various schools, consider inquiring about whether the program is accredited or has plans to apply for such accreditation.

Much of the progress in relation to the master's degree has been accomplished through the efforts of the North American Association of Masters in Psychology (NAMP), headquartered in Norman, OK. Their web site address is www.nampwebsite.org. Founded by Dr. Logan Wright, a past president of the American Psychological Association, NAMP continues to work cooperatively with state organizations ro further the causes of those with master's degrees in psychology. Psychology is regulated by some agency, usually a board, in each state. In some states, use of modified titles such as *psychological examiner* or *psychological techni-*

*cian* is permitted. In some states, people trained at the master's level may be licensed under a different title, perhaps as a counselor or as a behavioral practitioner. In West Virginia and Alaska, you may use the title *psychologist* once you have passed the board's requirements. Because of such variation, you must check with the governing body in the state in which you wish to work to determine the exact requirements and privileges available to you in that state. Progress is being made and should continue in getting more recognition of the training that master's level people have obtained and in getting certification/licensure for them.

# 4

# Choosing the PhD

*Arthur N. Wiens*
*Carolen A. Hope*

This chapter was written on the eve of a new millennium, and it is almost inescapable that we would want to look back at least to the last 50 or 100 of the past thousand years and anticipate what lies ahead. The first author has been "in psychology" for the past 50 years; the second is starting her professional career in psychology in the year 2000. Our perspectives on time and psychology are different. Looking back 50 years, it is clear that the clinical psychology of 2000 is not the same as the clinical psychology of 1950: "All life is change." Personally, we are reminded that the passage of time is inexorable and that the changes that come with such passage cannot be turned back. Professionally, we note that the activities of psychologists have changed markedly over the past 50 years. Change may be accelerating with technological advances and the globalization of psychology and all of society. Although students now applying for graduate study in psychology may find it hard to realize, the field of psychology will change during their graduate study and will continue to change during their careers as psychologists.

We believe that every psychologist has a fascinating story to tell about how his or her career in psychology evolved over time. Educators in our psychology graduate programs should let students know that career shifts are the norm for psychologists across a professional lifetime, and should help them develop basic knowledge and generic skills that will help them make such shifts. For a student to think after graduation about the first job is too short a time perspective. Examination of the curricula vitae of most career psychologists provide ample evidence of multiple shifts in career focus. The following vignette is written in the first person because it is a personal history of the first author's own career evolution.

I worked at the Topeka State Hospital (TSH) from 1949 to 1953 with a bachelor's and master's degree in psychology. I had aspirations to advance in the state mental health system and realized that I had to obtain my doctorate in psychology. In the process of doing that my wife (a nurse-educator) and I accepted positions at the Oregon State Hospital. My doctoral dissertation was focused on the psychological effects of Thorazine, a psychoactive medication that was being introduced at that time. While at the hospital I also participated in the development of a psychology internship program and became interested in education and training in psychology.

I mention these two activities because they turned out to be major factors/motivations in my career shifts. By 1961 it was evident that the use of psychoactive medications and changing attitudes in society toward the mentally ill were going to have a major impact on the hospital and, in turn, on my career. In fact, the hospital was downsized from a census high of about 3600 patients to a low at one point of about 300 patients. It became a very different institution than it had been in the past. My interest in education and training grew, and I was fortunate to be offered a position at the Oregon Health Sciences University (OHSU). Interestingly, the funding for my position at OHSU came from a research grant and I became an active researcher for a number of years. Then National Institute of Mental Health (NIMH) research funding shifted, so again a career change was inevitable. Fortunately, my salary funding had been shifted to "hard money," and when I was also awarded tenure it became possible to settle into a longer term commitment to education and training in psychology and the diverse activities of a school of medicine faculty career. As I have reflected on my career shifts, it has been evident to me that some of the shifts were responses to external factors and some were responsive to personal changes and motivations that evolve over a lifetime. Many individuals look forward to new directions in mid career.

## CHANGE IS A CONSTANT

From a perspective of fifty years as a psychologist, the fact that all life (and psychology) is change becomes very real. From the perspective of a student impatiently preparing for a career in psychology, life may often appear to be static and it might even seem that psychology is an established and stable body of facts. Furthermore, if one could master the facts one would be established as a psychologist into the future. That is not the case: Learning must be lifelong; a function of doctoral education is learning how to learn.

From the perspective of the discipline of psychology, Peterson (1991) stated a conclusion with which we agree. He wrote, "In its modesty, the scientist-practitioner concept has enormous power. It acknowledges that the conceptual, methodological, and substantive bases for the practice of psychology forever need improving, and an unending flow of research is required to bring that improvement about" (p. 423). We think that it is incumbent on a professional psychologist not only to know about, but also contribute to, an ever-accumulating body of knowledge in psychology. This includes knowledge about cognitive psychology, brain imaging, brain–behavior relationships, test reliability and validity, and the influence of mood, motivation, and various demographic factors (e.g., age, gender, education, culture) on the assessment procedures used in practice. This body of knowledge ought to continually enhance our interpretation of performance on existing tests and drive the evolution/development of the next generation of assessment instruments and procedures. Our assertion is that the scientist-practitioner model of graduate education and training, which we discuss next, is essential to support the flow of research needed in the ever-changing discipline of psychology.

## DOCTORAL DEGREES IN PROFESSIONAL PSYCHOLOGY

As stated in the current APA *Guidelines and Principles for Accreditation of Programs in Professional Psychology*:

> Science and practice are not opposing poles; rather, together they equally contribute to excellence in training in professional psychology. Therefore, education and training in preparation for entry-level practice as a psychologist would be based on the existing and evolving body of general knowledge and methods in the science and practice of psychology. (APA, Committee on Accreditation, 1996, p. 3)

Although most psychologists agree on the importance of science and practice training in the doctoral education of professional psychologists, they have not been of one mind about how this should be accomplished.

The "Boulder model" (Raimy, 1950) was a formal statement of training needs in clinical psychology and provided for equal provision of extensive training in psychology research and the applications of that research to eventual practice. This model of training has been known for the last 50 years as the *scientist-practitioner* model. A second model, a two-track, practice-research doctor of psychology (PsyD)–doctor of philosophy (PhD) educational system, was proposed by the "Clark Committee" (APA, Committee on the Scientific and Professional Aims of Psychology, 1967). Donald R. Peterson established the first professional PsyD degree program at the University of Illinois, in 1968, to be able to graduate more psychologists for practice than were being graduated by the university's PhD program in clinical psychology. This PsyD model of training has been known since 1968 as the *practitioner-scholar* model. More recently, the establishment of the Academy of Psychological Clinical Science, a group of training programs with a strong commitment to the scientific aspects of clinical psychology, in essence defined a third model of training: the *clinical scientist*. In this model, programs provide training in the production of scientific research on clinical problems and its application (Academy of Psychological Clinical Science, 1997). We discuss each of these training models and then also discuss why each of us chose a PhD "scientist-practitioner" degree program for our own graduate study. For the first author the choice was simple: There was no other model in 1950.

### Scientist-Practitioner Model

The prospective graduate student seeking to be informed about the history and development of clinical psychology, and much of professional psychology, can benefit by reading *Clinical Psychology Since 1917: Science, Practice, and Organization* (Routh, 1994). Routh described contributions of individuals and conference reports to the development of the scientist-practitioner model. He asserted that David Shakow led the way in establishing modern clinical psychology training. Dr. Shakow's own training was at Harvard University. It was followed by an extensive period working at Worcester State Hospital. His PhD dissertation was based on experimental studies of mental patients there. His early career became the paradigm for clinical psychology doctoral programs: 2 years of basic academic training, a third-year internship in a psychiatric setting, and finally a fourth-year dissertation on real clinical problems. Carl Rogers, who was the president of the APA at the time, appointed David Shakow as chair of its

Committee on Training in Clinical Psychology. The committee issued what became known as the Shakow Report (APA, Committee on Training Clinical Psychology, 1947), which the Boulder Conference subsequently endorsed. In other words, Shakow was responsible, more than any other person, for the Boulder model of the clinical psychologist as a scientist-practitioner (Routh, 1994, p. 123). The Conference on Graduate Education in Clinical Psychology was held at the University of Colorado, Boulder, in August 1949. The conference was sponsored by the National Institute of Mental Health and was attended by approximately 70 participants (Raimy, 1950).

The didactic and scientific part of the training was already well understood by graduate schools. The introduction of experiential training (practica and internships) and permission for students to do research on clinical topics was new. Routh pointed out that the Boulder model may be seen as a historic synthesis between the goals of academicians and clinicians. It let universities accept Veterans Administration (VA) and NIMH training funds to support clinical students, but at the same time permitted them to continue with the research training they preferred to do. This kept the laboratories running but also supported the students while they began to acquire clinically relevant knowledge and skills. The first accreditation criteria developed for clinical programs required that the university psychology department have in place a full-time specialized clinical staff and offer graduate training in tests and measurement, therapy, and counseling; supervised practicum facilities were also mandated. Minimum practicum facilities for a university were a psychiatric facility (typically VA), a child clinic, and at least one other site. In 1947 only 18 universities met all of the APA Accreditation Committee's criteria. With these criteria, however, clinical psychology became better defined and, ideally, clinical psychologists could be described as persons with a doctoral degree from an APA-approved graduate program, a predoctoral internship, and a license to practice in a particular state or province.

Of course, it was not long before second thoughts began to register. One of them was that psychology was making a mistake by using psychiatry as a clinical role model. Another was that graduates did not do research or publish beyond their doctoral dissertation, and a third was that psychologists were second-guessing their career choice. There were also some major university faculties that felt that clinical training funds were distorting their preferred academic emphasis. For example, the University of Chicago, and Stanford, eschewing APA accreditation as clinical psychology training programs, were willing to train experimental psychopathologists or clinical scientists, but would not offer the more standardized clinical curriculum, practicum training, and internships necessary for an APA-approved program. However, as we noted, the Boulder model, is the foundation from which clinical psychology training programs developed. It has been a strong foundation, and many of the changes and developments we have seen in clinical psychology are attributable to the psychologists who were trained in accordance with this model.

Psychologists seek to improve their services; to develop new services for unmet needs; to evaluate the effectiveness of their services; and to ask the questions and perform the research needed to respond to these issues. Although the expectation has never been fully realized, it seems to us that the scientist-practitioner model of education (the PhD) is, by design, most likely to produce psychologists able to meet these demands. There are many instances in the history of psychology in which theory and experimentation led to ideas for clinical practice. Evaluation of clinical practice led to assessment of its efficiency and to ideas for improved techniques. As these ideas became available for further theory building and experimentation, the whole reciprocal cycle began again. Scientist-practitioners assume that behavior is lawful and subject to experimentation, and this assumption gives them an important scientific advantage in the health care arena. The graduate student in psychology will learn about important contributions to patient care that have been made by such experimental psychologists as Neal Miller, Richard Lazarus, and Ronald Melzack. For example, Miller pioneered the application of learning theory to behavioral therapies such as biofeedback and the use of chemical and electrical stimulation to analyze the brain's mechanisms of behavior, homeostasis, and reinforcement. His career, now spanning more than half a century, exemplifies ingenuity, perseverance, integrity, and humanitarian goals. Miller was also the first psychologist to receive the National Medal of Science. Social psychologists David Glass, Howard Leventhal, and Gary Schwartz made valuable contributions. Schwartz, for example, is known particularly for his work in biofeedback, largely based on the work of Miller. Many clinical/counseling/community psychologists are well known for their research and contributions to the scientific/professional literature in psychology. Generic education in psychology has served these psychologists, the profession of psychology, and society at large well.

The special quality of psychology as a profession was discussed by Copeland and Brown (Brown, 1980). They seem in some respects to have been prophetic. Bert Brown, a former director of NIMH, stated:

> Psychology, as a profession, has inherent in it a very strong scientific base about the nature of the human mind. If it splits into practitioners, doctors of psychology who do not necessarily have training into the nature of science, the nature of scientific methods, some training in doing research, it will become just another competing profession in the human problems arena along with social work, nursing, marriage and family counseling and a host of other professions. Then, psychologists would not necessarily be better or different from those professions as opposed to being right now almost first among equals because it has the scientific-professional components even as it moves into that human suffering field.... If they do make the choice to move toward the doctor of psychology, towards the practitioner group ... it is not necessarily a bad thing, but it will be changing the nature of the profession itself.... If it maintains a core science component even as it trains in clinical care, group dynamics, individual and family therapy and the like, then it has opportunities in the general health area which will make it a respected collegial component of the general health arena. (pp. 19–20)

## Practitioner-Scholar

One of the most noteworthy developments in the history of American psychology has been its emerging identity as a profession as well as a science. Routh (1994) made the interesting observation that physicians and lawyers existed long before medical schools and law schools developed. He noted that the traditional method of training in these professions was through apprenticeship to a practitioner. Psychology reversed this sequence in that it was an academic discipline first and practice came later. Routh noted that the stirrings of practice have been present, however, for about 60 years. As early as 1938, A. T. Poffenberger suggested the possibility of a new type of professional degree (PhD) for clinical psychologists. Harvard University appointed a commission in 1947 to consider the place of psychology in an ideal university, and the commission concluded that there should be two types of training in psychology, one the traditional scientist, a PhD, and the other a new type of professional with a new degree, the PsyD or doctor of psychology (Routh, 1994, p. 131). Harvard faculty rejected the commission's plan.

We noted earlier that Donald R. Peterson, who was a director of clinical training, established the first professional PsyD degree program at the University of Illinois. The PsyD students were to have class work as rigorous as that of their fellow students who were working for a PhD, but instead of doing research-based dissertations, they spent more time in practicum work and submitted a final document focusing more on a clinical demonstration project instead. Peterson (1991) said that his experiences as a professor and consultant to a state department of mental health had convinced him that it was possible to do a better job of training practitioners and that it was his responsibility as a clinical training director to do so. However, the Illinois program was soon discontinued when it did not maintain the support of the university faculty.

Just as Peterson perceived a public need for more mental health practitioners in Illinois, so did psychologists in California. Peterson (1991) wrote, "In the community of practitioners, would-be educators lay waiting to form their own schools if the universities failed to meet the demand" (p. 424). Under the leadership of Nicholas Cummings, with the cooperation of many members of the California Psychological Association (CPA), the California School of Professional Psychology (CSPP) was founded in 1969 with campuses in Los Angeles, Berkeley/Alameda, San Diego, and Fresno. Some of the supporting CPA members served in the new programs without pay, and faculty were expected to maintain practices in psychology. Faculty were part-time and were hired on contracts; that is, there were no full-time or tenured faculty (and still are not). Clinicians, rather than research scientists, were the role models for students. Judith Albino, President of CSPP, testifying before the U.S. House of Representatives Appropriations Committee (April 1999), described CSPP as graduating more than half of the psychologists educated in California and nearly 20% of the psychologists educated in the United States. She expressed a goal of sharing the abundance of CSPP psychologists and characterized them as persons with psychological expertise; experienced caregivers, supervisors, and teachers; and graduate students eager to learn and to practice.

Other professional practitioner programs then developed. Some were free-standing like the CSPP programs, others were in universities, and some were programs "without walls." Most of the programs were self-supporting and have relied heavily on student revenues and donated faculty time; some were established to be income-producing enterprises.

Education and training in psychology have become big business. On March 8, 1999, the American Schools of Professional Psychology began to be publicly traded on Wall Street as part of the Argosy Education Group, a Class A common stock with 2,000,000 shares under the symbol ARGY on the NASDAQ National Market. The following comments are from the company's web page (www.argosyeducation.com):

Argosy was founded in 1975, when the Company's Chairman, Michael C. Markovitz, Ph.D., recognized a demand for a non-research oriented professional school that would educate and prepare students for careers as clinical psychology practitioners. To address this demand, Argosy started the Illinois School of Professional Psychology in Chicago, Illinois, in 1976. The continuing demand for high quality, practitioner-focused psychology postgraduate education led Argosy to expand the renamed American Schools of Professional Psychology to seven campuses located across the United

States.... Three of the campuses of ASPP—Chicago, Georgia, Minnesota—have achieved American Psychological Association ("APA") accreditation for their doctoral programs in clinical psychology. ASPP's net tuition revenue has grown from $7.1 million for fiscal 1993 to $15.8 million for fiscal 1997, representing a compound annual growth of approximately 22%. In 1999 the number of ASPP programs grew to a total of nine.

We noted earlier that in 1947 only 18 universities met all of the APA Accreditation Committee's criteria for accreditation. In 1950 there were 36 accredited programs. In 1999 the APA Accreditation Committee listed 321 accredited programs offering doctoral degrees in applied psychology. The estimated number of students enrolled in psychology graduate programs in 1999 is 64,300 students; this is the membership of the American Psychological Association of Graduate Students (APAGS). In the new millennium we will see whether the public need for professional psychologists has been met. There is some suggestion that the demand for psychologists may diminish. The U.S. Bureau of Labor Statistics (1999) reported that the employment of psychologists was expected to *grow more slowly than the average* for all occupations through the year 2006. Interpreting the key phrase leads to a projected 0 to 9% growth. The report suggests that psychologists with extensive training in quantitative research methods and computer science skills featured in PhD programs may have a competitive edge over applicants without this background.

## Clinical Scientist

Although the practitioner-scholar model of training has been popular, in the past three decades there has been a group of psychologists that has been dedicated to the development of a science of clinical psychology. The Section for the Development of Clinical Psychology as an Experimental-Behavioral Science/Section for a Science of Clinical Psychology was organized in 1965. Organizationally, this group (first chaired by Leonard Krasner) has been a section of the Division of Clinical Psychology of the American Psychological Association. Its name has been changed to Society for a Science of Clinical Psychology, but it is still Section III of Division 12 of the APA.

The Academy of Psychological Clinical Science grew out of a conference on Clinical Science in the 21st Century, hosted by Indiana University–Bloomington in April 1994. Prominent scientists representing 35 graduate training programs in clinical or health psychology were invited to attend the conference; 25 programs were represented. The aim of the conference was to analyze the changing landscape in scientific clinical/health psychology and to chart a course for advancing the interests of clinical science. The Academy of Psychological Clinical Science (APCS) is described on its web page (http:w3.arizona.edu/psych/apcs/apcs.html) as an alliance of leading, scientifically oriented, doctoral training programs in clinical and health psychology in the United States and Canada. Academy membership is open to doctoral programs with strong commitments to, and established records of, successful clinical science training. The academy held its inaugural meeting in New York City, July 1–2, 1995. As stated on its web pages:

> The Academy's broad mission is to advance clinical science. "Clinical science" is defined as a psychological science directed at the promotion of adaptive functioning; at the assessment, understanding, amelioration, and prevention of human problems in behavior, affect, cognition or health; and at the application of knowledge in ways consis-

tent with scientific evidence. The Academy's emphasis on the term "science" under-scores its commitment to empirical approaches to evaluating the validity and utility of testable hypotheses and to advancing knowledge by this method.

Richard M. McFall has been a visible spokesman for the academy, and his "Manifesto for a Science of Clinical Psychology" (McFall, 1991) probably gave direction to the establishment of the Academy. He sketched four important issues to be considered. First, he suggested that the Boulder model of scientist-practitioner is confusing and misleading. If the scientist and practitioner are synonymous, then the hyphenated term is redundant. If the scientist and practitioner are either competing or complementary components, then the training is not as unified as is the goal of training clinical scientists. Second, scientific training should not be concerned with preparing students for any particular job placements. Graduate programs should not be trade schools. Scientists are not necessarily academics, and persons working in applied settings are not necessarily nonscientists. Well-trained clinical scientists might function in any number of contexts—from the laboratory, to the clinic, to the administrator's office (p. 84). McFall felt that faculty should stop worrying about the particular jobs their students would take and focus instead on training all students to think and function as scientists in every aspect and setting of their professional lives. Third, he suggested that the hallmarks of good scientific training are rigor, independence, scholarship, flexibility in critical thinking, and success in problem solving. Fourth, for a clinical psychology with integrity, scientific training must be integrated across settings and tasks. McFall was concerned that currently many graduate students were taught to think rigorously in the laboratory and classroom while being encouraged to check their critical skills at the door of clinical settings. For unified scientific training in clinical psychology, students' practical experiences must be integrated with their scholarly, conceptual, and research experiences.

The practitioner-scholar and the clinical-scientist models appear to us to be extremes in emphasis in scientific education and training in clinical psychology. Here is a brief history of a recent graduate student and her choice of the scientist-practitioner model in training, written by the second author.

## MY CASE FOR THE PhD

In 1994, when I began the application process for my graduate studies in clinical psychology, I knew that I would pursue a PhD, because I wanted the strong foundation in science that this degree provides. There were several reasons for this choice. First, I was interested in studying the ways in which research and practice are (or are not) integrated by practitioners within the field of psychology. I spent several years as a public school teacher and had become interested in this area as I observed how educators tried to bring the science of learning into their classrooms. A PhD appeared to offer the research tools I would need to investigate this problem.

Another reason for choosing a PhD program involved the level of legitimacy given to this degree. The PhD is still commonly accepted as the scholarly degree within the university setting, although there is little agreement that it is the only scholarly degree. Still, I imagined working as an educator in some capacity, and knew that a PhD would serve me in this regard. I knew I would be more competitive if I had engaged in research and had published.

The dissertation process would familiarize me with independent research, and this would help me to clarify my thoughts about seeking an academic career. In addition, an ability to conduct research, especially outcome research, might influence reimbursement as the pressure for demonstrating treatment efficacy increases. I also hoped that a Ph.D. would give me the greatest employment latitude. There appeared to be uncertainty regarding the roles or "territories" associated with the various practitioners, such as those in social work and marriage and family therapy, and I contended that with my chosen degree, I would be flexible in a changing job market.

Finally, as the call to "positive psychology" suggests, psychologists are being called upon to expand and revision the discipline. I hoped to add to a growing knowledge base about such areas as creating healthy lifestyles and healthy aging. I looked for a degree and program that would affirm the individual, that could address both the values of the individual and society, and that would be receptive to areas, such as spirituality, not traditionally associated with psychology.

Many factors were involved in my choice to pursue a PhD. The discipline seemed fragmented and uncertain, and I sought training that would allow me to be flexible enough to meet a changing employment landscape. I wanted to pursue my research interests, optimize my potential for an academic career, and contribute to a renewed vision of the discipline.

This chapter emphasizes that society at large, including psychology, changes constantly. To remain viable, our discipline must have constant input of new knowledge based on both basic science research and clinical practice. To us, the scientist-practitioner model of graduate education and training is the most likely to prepare the future clinical psychologist for the new millennium.

## REFERENCES

Academy of Psychological Clinical Science. (1997). APCS home page [Online]. Available: http://w3.arizona.edu/-psch/apcs/apcs.html

American Psychological Association, Committee on Accreditation. (1996). *Guidelines and principles for accreditation of programs in professional psychology.* Washington, DC: American Psychological Association.

American Psychological Association, Committee on Training Clinical Psychology. (1947). Recommended graduate training programs in clinical psychology. *American Psychologist, 2,* 539–558.

American Psychological Association, Committee on Scientific and Professional Aims of Psychology. (1967). The scientific and professional aims of psychology. *American Psychologist, 22,* 49–76.

Brown, B. (1980). The rise or decline of psychology as a health service profession: An interview with Bert Brown by Bruce Copeland. *Clinical Psychologist, 33,* 18–20.

McFall, R. M. (1991). Manifesto for a science of clinical psychology. *Clinical Psychologist, 44,* 75–88.

Peterson, D. R. (1991). Connection and disconnection of research and practice in the education of professional psychologists. *American Psychologist, 46,* 422–429.

Raimy, V. C. (1950). *Training in clinical psychology.* Englewood Cliffs, NJ: Prentice Hall.

Routh, D. K. (1994). *Clinical psychology since 1917: Science, practice, and organization.* New York: Plenum Press.

U.S. Bureau of Labor Statistics. (1999). *Occupational outlook handbook home page. Choosing the PhD.* [On-line]. Choosing the PhD. *http://stats.bls.gov/oco/ocosO56.htm*

# 5

# Choosing the PsyD

## *Donald R. Peterson*

Doctor of psychology (PsyD) programs are based on a few straightforward ideas. The pursuits of science and professional practice are related but not identical. People who intend to practice professional psychology should be trained to practice professional psychology. People who are qualified to practice professional psychology should hold a doctoral credential that certifies preparation for practice in professional psychology.

More than 50 programs that embody these ideas are now in operation in the United States. The programs differ somewhat in regard to specialties and theoretical emphases, but they all show several characteristics in common.

First, the objectives of the programs are expressly *professional*. Students are not expected to believe that the best way to prepare for a professional career is to do research. They are trained for practice. When they complete their doctoral studies, they are given a professional degree. As the MD degree certifies preparation for practice in medicine, the PsyD degree certifies preparation for practice in psychology.

Second, professional work and training for practice are *valued* by the faculty and administrators in charge of the program. Professional work is different from research, but no less noble. An explicitly professional program, symbolized and concluded by award of the PsyD degree, means that the faculty who run the program and the administrators who support it value professional work for its own sake, not as a servant to science.

Third, the programs are based in *disciplined* knowledge. Professional psychology is not an intuitive art. It is not a set of disembodied practices learned solely through experience. Professional psychology is the systematic application of psychological knowledge to the study and solution of human problems. The conceptions, methods, and facts of psychology are the foundations of practice.

Fourth, the programs are *comprehensive* in scope. They are not devoted merely to individual assessment and psychotherapy. At their broadest, they extend from the biopsychology of the brain and other organ systems, through the individual psychology of thought, feeling, and action, through the interpersonal psychology of families and other groups, to the psychology of organizations and communities. They include some skill training in assessment and change at all those levels, although the differing interests of students and the practical impossibility of attaining full breadth and depth within a limited period of graduate study require some specialization.

Fifth, supervised *practice* is emphasized in teaching. Direct, "hands-on" experience is introduced early and continued through all the years of graduate study, not deferred until the internship nor supplanted by dissertation research.

Last, doctor of psychology programs are dedicated to *self-renewal*. The field is constantly changing. The profession practiced today is different from the profession 10 years ago. The profession will be different again 10 years from now. At the least, responsible professionals must be prepared to keep up with the changes. They must examine new conceptions, absorb new findings, and acquire new techniques as these appear. In their own ways, they may contribute theories, knowledge, and procedures that advance the profession, although it is as unrealistic to expect every practicing psychologist to contribute significantly to traditional research in psychology as it is to expect all physicians to make important contributions to medical science.

## WHY CAN'T ALL THIS BE DONE IN A PhD PROGRAM?

In some ways it can, but rarely is. Students in scientist-practitioner programs are expected not only to become effective practitioners but productive scholars as well. Research methods and dissertation research are emphasized. This is appropriate for students with strong interests in research, but inappropriate for those who are solely interested in the practice of psychology. The system encourages hypocrisy. Regardless of genuine intent, students are forced to claim that they are impassioned by science in order to gain admission to most PhD programs. Once enrolled, they must profess enthusiasm for research to gain the favor of faculty. Emphasis on research in a time-limited program requires less emphasis on training for practice. If predoctoral education is limited to 4 or 5 years, something has to give. Comprehensive. carefully supervised training for practice and thorough training for research cannot both be accomplished in the time allowed. In research-oriented programs, the professional training of students is often slighted.

## BUT STILL, WHY A NEW DEGREE?

Why not construct a program in professional psychology and give a PhD at the end of it? In a few places this is done, but never in universities where traditional standards for award of the PhD (significant, independent contribution to knowledge) are firmly upheld. Official policies that govern higher education in America are clear on this matter. The following statement was issued by the Council of Graduate Studies in the United States (1969), was subsequently endorsed by the Association of Graduate Schools in the Association of American Universities, and has been enforced with increasing stringency by authorities responsible for the accreditation of educational institutions in the United States.

The *Doctor of Philosophy* (Ph.D.) degree, first awarded in the United States in 1861, has become the mark of highest achievement in preparation for creative scholarship and research, often in association with a career in teaching at a university or college. The Doctor of Philosophy shall be open as a research degree in all fields of learning, pure and applied.

The *Professional Doctor's* degree should be the highest university award given in a particular field in recognition of completion of academic preparation for professional practice, e.g., the Doctor of Medicine (MD), Doctor of Dental Surgery (DDS), Doctor of Veterinary Medicine (DVM). (p. 2)

In most universities, award of the PhD degree is controlled by a graduate college, designed to uphold high standards of scholarship. Most graduate colleges adhere closely to the principle that the PhD be employed as an emblem of independent scholarly accomplishment. If the PhD is used in a program for professional psychologists in a university with a strong traditional graduate college, research is inevitably valued more than practice, and these values pervade all PhD programs: in selection and promotion of faculty, in the requirements of curricula, and in other conditions to be met before the PhD is granted.

Beyond the need to preserve the distinctive academic identities of researchers and practitioners, however, lies an even more compelling reason for use of a professional degree in psychology. People seeking the services of professionals need to know what kinds of knowledge and skills different professionals profess. One takes a sick child to an MD and a sick kitten to a DVM because each professional has a different form of expertise to offer. One hundred years ago, there was widespread public ignorance about degrees in the health disciplines, and many an ailing person was treated by a "horse doctor." Now, however, the distinction between MD and DVM degrees is well understood. Public understanding could only be attained because each professional discipline used the name of its own field in the degree title. The public could be assured of the professional preparation of the bearer of the degree within, and only within, the boundaries of each field.

The PhD can never serve to certify professional competence in any one discipline because it is used as a general credential of scholarly accomplishment over all the arts and sciences. A PhD, standing alone, means only that the bearer has met PhD-level standards of scholarly accomplishment in the institution that awarded the degree. Psychology, chemistry, mathematics, French literature—any field at all might be represented. Psychology does not control the PhD, and never can. A profession, to be a profession, must control its credentials. The only way a doctoral degree can ever be employed as a specific credential of professional preparation in psychology is to use the name of the discipline in the title of the degree. For medicine, doctor of medicine. For psychology, doctor of psychology.

## COMMON CONCERNS ABOUT THE PsyD DEGREE

Students sometimes hear academic advisors tell them that the professional doctorate lacks the scholarly quality of the PhD. Those who object to the PsyD perceive in it risks of groundless practice, separation from science, and an undisciplined proliferation of arcane arts and mechanical techniques. In some of the early practitioner programs, especially those that formed outside universities, there probably was truth to this claim. However, accusations of poor scholarship were never valid in the best university-based programs and are false today in programs that adhere to standards developed by the National Council of Schools and Programs of Professional Psychology (Peterson, 1997, Peterson, Peterson, Abrams, & Stricker, 1997). PsyD programs are not intended to prepare students for lifelong careers in the conduct of theory-driven, group-based research. That is what the PhD programs are for. PsyD programs are intended instead to produce "scientific practitioners" whose professional actions are grounded in the most reliable knowledge available and conducted in the most rigorous way that practical conditions allow.

The core of effective practice is disciplined inquiry (Peterson, 1991, 1997). The role of the practitioner in providing assistance to clients is that of local scientist (Stricker & Trierweiler, 1995; Trierweiler & Stricker, 1998) bringing the most powerful available conceptions, the most illuminating methods of inquiry, and the most effective methods of change to the benefit of each case at hand. For many reasons, the simplifications and controls that are necessary and feasible in formal scientific research can rarely be exercised in practice. Still, the practitioner is cognizant of pertinent research, and the professional studies themselves—the assessments, interventions, and evaluations that constitute most of the daily activities of practitioners—are designed to provide the carefully collected, critically examined data on which informed decisions and constructive actions can be based. Throughout training, every case becomes an exercise in disciplined inquiry.

Nearly all PsyD programs require a dissertation in which some form of disciplined inquiry is pursued in depth. Scholarly inquiry is seen as a form of practice, not as an end in itself. PsyD dissertations address the kinds of issues that practitioners encounter throughout their careers. Methods are chosen or designed to suit each problem, rather than defining "scientific method" beforehand and then searching for a problem that suits the method. Types of projects include case studies, theoretical analyses, community needs analyses, and program evaluations, as well as the group-based experiments and field studies that are the norm in research-oriented programs.

A second concern about the PsyD degree is that it is less prestigious than the PhD. Within the academic culture itself, the mystically elevated status of the PhD cannot be denied. As Paul Meehl once said, some academics view the PhD as "some kind of sacred thing rather like the ecclesiastical conferring of holy orders" (Meehl, 1971, p. 54). Given the presence if not the prevalence of this view in the academic world as well as the functional necessity of rigorous training for the conduct of sound research, the PhD offers an advantage over any professional degree for those seeking careers of scholarship in major research universities. Doctors of psychology have not been excluded from university faculties. In fact, a substantial number have accepted faculty positions in universities and medical schools. Their training and experience are especially valued on the faculties of PsyD programs in universities and free-standing professional schools, much as MDs are valued on the faculties of medical schools. Students whose main interests fall toward research rather than practice, however, would be foolish not to elect one of the many PhD programs available to them. Those are the students for whom the PhD programs are suitably designed.

Outside the academic culture, the value of the PhD is not so clear. Among the general public, confusion still prevails. Many people do not distinguish accurately between psychiatrists and psychologists, let alone psychologists with PhD and PsyD degrees. Clients seeking psychological help are likely to be reassured to know that they are seeing a doctor, but according to the reports of practicing PsyDs hardly anyone inquires further. Those who do are usually pleased to learn that they are seeing a doctor of psychology whose training emphasized preparation for practice. As PsyD programs have matured and large numbers of psychologists with PsyD degrees entered the field, the initial strangeness of the degree has worn off and acceptance has increased. An article in the APA's *Monitor of Psychology* noted that some 9000 PsyDs had been awarded by 1999, and quoted a prominent psychologist who received the PsyD degree in 1976 as saying, "In the beginning the PsyD was a leap of faith. Now it is an accepted practitioner degree. You see it everywhere" (Murray, 2000, p. 52).

The school with which I am most familiar, at Rutgers University, graduated more than 500 doctors of psychology during its first 25 years of operation. All are employed, and many have earned distinction as witnessed by numerous public and professional honors, prize-winning publications, and election to prominent positions in the discipline, including presidency of the APA. In a recent address to alumni, Sandra Harris, dean of the school, remarked on this record and at the same time described accurately the range of activities in which graduates have been engaged.

> You do us proud with your service to the public and in the private domain. You are working in schools, mental health centers, not for profit agencies, corporations and private practice. You work in prisons, daycare centers, state hospitals, public schools, and universities. You treat people with AIDS, the mentally retarded, people with autism, people with chronic mental illness. You deal with violence, suicide, teen pregnancy and other problems of our contemporary schools. You consult with corporations to help them become more humane and productive places in which to work. You provide leadership on the local and national level. You write books, give talks, testify before legislative hearings, publish papers. You do it all and justify our existence (Harris, 1999, pp. 3–4)

Ultimately, the prestige of the PsyD degree will depend on the performance of those who have earned it. Unfortunately, not all PsyD programs enjoy the advantages of a strong university, standards for admission and graduation are not always as strict as they should be for the benefit of students and the public, and performances of graduates of some institutions are unimpressive. The records of graduates of the best programs are second to none, however, and standards for all programs, as developed and endorsed by member institutions of the National Council of Schools and Programs of Professional Psychology (Peterson et al., 1997), are rigorous and comprehensive.

## FINDING THE RIGHT PRACTITIONER PROGRAM

Many research-oriented scientist-practitioner programs discourage students who are interested in careers emphasizing practice from applying for admission. Unless practice-minded hopefuls are willing to lie about their intentions and maintain the deception throughout graduate study, it is unwise to consider application to these programs, no matter how prestigious a PhD from a famous university may seem.

Many other scientist-practitioner programs claim to offer balanced preparation for practice and research. Some programs actually do so, and no doubt the directors of all the programs are sincere, but the discrepancies between catalogue descriptions and the programs as actually experienced by students are sometimes extreme. Here are some clues that can help you to identify programs whose faculty and administrators genuinely value professional service and are likely to give training for practice the time and attention required.

- Do faculty members speak of practice almost entirely as an arena for research or as a valuable activity in its own right? Score –5 in the former case; +5 in the latter case.
- What kinds of practice, if any, do the faculty do? Score –5 if hardly any of them practice, +5 if all or nearly all are engaged in some form of practice.
- At promotion time, is the amount and quality of professional service considered, along with research and teaching, in evaluating faculty contributions? Score +10 if it is; –10 if research is really the only thing that matters.
- When students are chatting in the lounge, do they talk about the cases they are seeing and the service projects they have undertaken or almost entirely about traditional forms of research? Score +5 if you hear considerable talk about cases and service projects, +10 if you hear enthusiastic discussion of apparently effective professional innovations, and –10 if all you hear is talk about research.
- Do faculty seem to regard graduates who go into practice as educational failures? Score –10.
- Do faculty speak with pride of a graduate who has designed and managed an evidently successful public service program but never published any formal research? Score +10.
- If someone you love needed psychological help, would you send him or her to a graduate of the program? Score +20 if you would; -20 if you would not.

If the total falls on the negative side. you may be visiting one of the finest research programs in the country, but you are looking at a poor choice for education in the practice of psychology.

For talented students seeking the very best available preparation for the practice of psychology, a strong practitioner program would seem to be the best choice, but separating strong from weak programs is difficult. All programs claim excellence. Not all of them have it. When you are considering investments of several years and many thousands of dollars in doctoral education, you need to be wary. Accreditation by the APA is a sign that the program has met minimal standards. Discrimination of excellent from less-than-excellent programs above that level, however, requires more refined scrutiny.

One useful index of quality is the ratio of students selected for admission to the total number applying for admission. In the strongest PsyD programs, as in the best PhD programs, competition is keen. In general, the harder it is to get into a program. the better it is likely to be.

A second useful index of quality is the ratio of students to faculty. These ratios vary widely, from around 7:1 in the best staffed programs to much higher proportions in programs that need to admit large numbers of students to maintain their budgets. In general, the larger the number of faculty relative to the number of students, the better is the program.

Other aspects of programs, such as qualifications of faculty, career records of graduates, and satisfaction of alumni and students currently enrolled, are more difficult to quantify, but are equally important and need to be appraised in qualitative ways. There is no substitute for visits to the short list of institutions that gain your most serious consideration. By going to each campus, looking things over, and talking to students and faculty on the scene, you can get a feel of the place that may be as reliable a guide as any in deciding which program to choose.

There will never be a shortage of human problems on our planet. As soon as one disturbing condition appears to be corrected, another rises to take its place. I see no reason to doubt that there will always be a need for competent professional psychologists, PsyD and PhD, to bring the best available knowledge to bear on the troubles and opportunities of the human experience.

Not long before I wrote this statement, I had the pleasure of talking with Thomas Reid, the first graduate of the first PsyD program in the country, and George Allen, a PhD classmate whose program I also directed. Each of my students had gone on to a distinguished career, Reid as a practitioner and Allen as a university professor. For nearly 2 hours, we discussed the work lives they had experienced, pertinence of the training each had received to the work they wound up doing, and a wide range of other topics related to preparation for careers in the profession and science of psychology. A condensed version of our conversation has been published (Peterson, Reid, & Allen, 1999) and may be of interest to others pondering the choices Reid and Allen faced some 30 years ago. Here is how our meeting ended.

Peterson:   … We're winding down. I'd like to have a go around on one final question. If any of your children were approaching the time for career choice and said, "I'm thinking about going into psychology," what would you tell them? Tom?

Reid:   I think the first thing I would tell them is that it would be a good idea to have some conversations about what you think psychology is, what it is that attracts you.

Peterson:   Learn more about it before you commit yourself.

Reid:   Right. I'm happy to have a conversation with you about what I think psychology is, but my guess is that if you talk to people from several different perspectives about what they think psychology is and what it offers, their views may or may not correspond with your imagined fantasy of what it is. You need to be thinking about a broader definition of psychology than you probably have at the moment.

Peterson:   Well, George's principle—anything worth doing is worth evaluating—holds also for a person entering the field. First thing they have to do is get the best anticipatory picture they can of the field, as it looks now and as it appears to be moving, before they decide to spend their lives in it. What are your thoughts, George?

Allen:   I would took at my child and ask, "Can my child think critically and act compassionately?"

Peterson:   Beautiful.

Allen:   And, if both of those ingredients are present I would be encouraging. If either ingredient was not present, I would be discouraging.

Peterson:   I've said that students need to have their heads screwed on right and their hearts in the right place, but you've said it better. They need a capacity for and an interest in critical analysis of human problems—really getting to the heart and truth of things—and at the same time a genuine compassionate concern for their fellow human beings. With both of those, I would say yes. Without either of those, I would say no.

Reid:     Amen, brothers.

# REFERENCES

Council of Graduate Schools in the United States. (1969). *The nature and naming of graduate and professional degree programs* [Policy statement]. Washington, DC: Author.

Harris, S. A. (1999). *Remarks at the GSAPP 25th Anniversary.* Rutgers University, New Brunswick, NJ. Unpublished paper.

Meehl, P. E. (1971). A scientific, scholarly non-research doctorate for clinical practitioners. In R. R. Holt (Ed.), *New horizons for psychotherapy* (pp. 37–81). New York: International Universities Press.

Murray, B. (2000, January). The degree that almost wasn't: The PsyD comes of age. *Monitor of Psychology*, pp. 52–54.

Peterson, D. R. (1991). Connection and disconnection of research and practice in the education of professional psychologists. *American Psychologist, 46*, 422–429.

Peterson, D. R. (1997). *Educating Professional psychologists: History and guiding conception.* Washington, DC: APA Books.

Peterson, D. R., Reid, T. A., & Allen, G. J. (1999). Reflections on training: Donald Peterson talks with the first PsyD and a PhD classmate. *Professional Psychology: Research and Practice, 30*, 74–82.

Peterson, R. L., Peterson, D. R., Abrams, J. C., & Stricker, G. (1997). The National Council of Schools and Programs of Professional Psychology educational model. *Professional Psychology: Research and Practice, 28,* 373–386.

Stricker, G., & Trierweiler, S. J. (1995). The local clinical scientist: A bridge between science and practice. *American Psychologist, 50*, 995–1002.

Trierweiler, S. J., & Stricker, G. (1998). *The scientific practice of professional psychology.* New York: Plenum Press.

# 6

## Perspectives on Applying to Graduate School

*Bill N. Kinder*

*Steven Walfish*

Applying to graduate school is a long, arduous process involving numerous decisions and much tedious work, often with no information (or mixed information) from others regarding what direction to pursue next. In addition, it can be expensive, given fees necessary for applications, the GRE test, and transcripts, not to mention travel for interviews and long-distance telephone calls. This chapter is intended as a guide to make this a less confusing, more efficient, and hopefully more successful process. As we are limited in space to a chapter, we only stress the most important concepts. For a more in-depth look at the entire application process, consult the excellent texts by Keith-Spiegel and Wiederman (2000) and Mayne, Norcross, and Sayette (2000) and *Getting In*, published by the APA (1997).

Before you begin these Herculean tasks, however, you must make the most critical decision of them all: "Do I really want to go to graduate school in psychology?"

### INITIAL CONSIDERATIONS

The decision to attend graduate school will be among the most important ones you will make during your life. In addition to the questions of your ability to commit yourself to an inordinate amount of hard work, there are other considerations:

1. Are you willing to relocate?
2. Are you willing to live in relative poverty for several years?

3. If you are married or partnered, are all the members of your family willing to subject themselves to the poverty and other stressors of living with a stressed graduate student?

## COURSEWORK AT THE GRADUATE LEVEL

The academic demands will be exponentially different from those you have experienced as an undergraduate. Most students are surprised (and often overwhelmed) simply by the *amount* of work that is required in the average graduate program. Although graduate students usually take a fewer number of courses per semester than they did as undergraduates, the amount of work expected per course is significantly greater. Most first-year graduate students find that one course covers as much material as several undergraduate courses.

In addition to the quantity, many students are also surprised at the *quality* of work expected at the graduate level. In graduate school there are "no easy courses." Rather, some courses are "not quite as difficult as others."

The level of performance expected is also different at the graduate level. The grade of C is considered failing. The type of performance to earn a grade of A or B is quite different. On exams, for example, you will not simply report facts memorized from your readings; you will have to critically analyze and meaningfully integrate all these memorized bits of data.

In addition to these rigors of direct coursework, students will be expected to participate in other learning activities. If you are seeking an applied type of degree (e.g., clinical, counseling, school), practicum work will be associated with many of your courses. For a course in psychological assessment you will probably also be assigned to a practicum setting to learn firsthand to administer, score, interpret, and write a report related to the test you are learning in the classroom. Such a placement may easily take 10 hours of time per week in addition to other work required for the course.

Most students (outside of professional schools) are routinely involved in research throughout their graduate training. The major pieces of research are the master's thesis and the doctoral dissertation. Both are typically required during training for the PhD. In addition, most professors expect their students to be involved in ongoing research projects related to their area of interest. For those interested in academic careers these experiences are crucial in developing a career path. At the doctoral level some schools may also have comprehensive examinations as a hurdle to jump after the end of the second or third year. Other schools may substitute a major review of the literature, written in the form of a *Psychological Bulletin* or *Clinical Psychology Review* paper.

In return for some financial support, you will probably be required to do some additional work such as being a teaching assistant or a research assistant. This can easily consume 15 to 20 hours per week of your time.

Considering all these expectations as a whole, it is easy to understand how the average graduate student, at the PhD level, must spend 60 to 70 hours per week in activities directly related to graduate training.

## CHOOSING WHERE TO APPLY

Once you are committed to pursuing graduate training, it is important to carefully consider to which programs you will apply. Programs should first be evaluated on their ability to fulfill your needs and goals, and then on their likelihood of viewing you as an eligible and desirable applicant.

The first step should be to obtain a copy of *Graduate Study in Psychology*, published by the APA (1998) and available directly (www.apa.org). This book lists every program that offers any type of graduate training in psychology in the United States and Canada. A wealth of descriptive information is provided in summary form on each training program, including the specific areas of specialization offered. For students interested in clinical and counseling psychology we would also suggest the book by Mayne et al. (2000).

***Type of Program.***    It will be necessary to distinguish among various specialty categories of the types of training programs (e.g., clinical, counseling, school, developmental, community, industrial/organizational, experimental) to be pursued. This choice will primarily be determined by your specific career goals. An excellent overview of these areas is presented in *Getting In* (APA, 1997). The next choice concerns the level of degree you are seeking: MA/MS versus PhD versus PsyD. We suggest that you consult the chapters by Perlman, Peterson, and Wiens and Hope all in this section, for further discussion of these issues.

***Evaluating Specific Programs.***    Next, gather information on the various training programs. *Graduate Study in Psychology* provides basic information, but we suggest you use this publication as a preliminary reference guide. Most programs have written information available on request (a postcard will suffice). In addition, many have this information available on their home page on the World Wide Web. Asking a program to send you a description of their training program is not a commitment to applying to that university. Schools vary in the size of faculty, training facilities available, average Graduate Record Examination (GRE) scores and grade point average (GPA) of students admitted, and tuition (especially at the professional school level). Seek out as much information as possible to gain a broad perspective on the types of training opportunities that are available. Become an "informed shopper." By reviewing this information you may also be able to estimate your chances of gaining acceptance to the program. From each school, find out how many applications are received each year, how many students are accepted, and the mean GRE scores and GPAs of those accepted into the program. Also compare the number of students accepted to the number of degrees awarded to give you an estimate of your chances of receiving the degree after being accepted. For example, based on information from *Graduate Study in Psychology*, we see that a randomly chosen PsyD program enrolled 36 students of the 209 that had applied, a relatively high rate. However, that year only 21 people were granted the PsyD from that school. Assuming enrollment was consistent over the 4 years, this would indicate that 41% did not successfully complete the program. This is important information. In addition, try to ascertain the average length of time it takes students to complete their degrees. At some institutions this can be an extraordinarily long period of time.

You also may want to consider asking faculty members and current graduate students about possible places to apply. They may have firsthand knowledge of what program might be a good match for you in terms of types of training available and faculty members available as research advisors.

## IMPROVING PROBABILITIES FOR ACCEPTANCE

Your chances for being accepted into a graduate training program can be improved by strengthening your application and by wisely choosing where to apply. Several studies have examined variables related to acceptance to graduate school. Although traditional indexes such as undergraduate GPA, GRE scores, and letters of recommendation remain important criteria (Keith-Spiegel, Tobachnick, & Spiegel, 1994; Rem, Oren, & Childrey, 1987; Sternberg & Williams, 1997), other criteria appear increasingly important. Keith-Spiegel et al. (1994) noted that research experience, "good match" factors between student and program, and writing skills (usually viewed from the personal statement from the application) are significant factors in acceptance to a PhD program. Other factors that have been noted are computer skills, paid or volunteer human service (Eddy, Lloyd, & Lubin, 1987), and ratings obtained by personal interviews (Nevid & Gildea, 1984).

Lawson (1995) and Norcross, Hanych, and Terranova (1996) provided summary data from the 1993 and 1994 editions of *Graduate Study in Psychology* regarding acceptance data into graduate programs. Essentially what do these findings tell us? First, gaining acceptance into a graduate training program in psychology is competitive. Second, this competition is even greater at the doctoral level than at the master's level. Third, the most competitive area is clinical psychology at both the doctoral and master's level (as an aside, the acceptance rate is much higher at professional schools in applied psychology than those found for traditional PhD programs). Fourth, for students who do not have the outstanding grades and GRE scores required for acceptance into a doctoral program, serious consideration should be given to application to master's programs. Consult Perlman's chapter in this section for specific issues related to this topic. Finally, although these data are not presented to overwhelm prospective applicants, in terms of the high standards generally required by training programs, they are meant to reinforce the need to prepare oneself as much as possible prior to making application. In addition, these data may allow a realistic appraisal of your credentials in order to apply to programs for which you have reasonable chances of obtaining acceptance.

*Academic Work.*    Clearly, if students want to make themselves attractive to a graduate program, they should first demonstrate that they have the capability for doing outstanding academic work. The applicant's grades in undergraduate coursework are considered the best estimate of this capability. Most schools consider a "B" average to be the bare minimum; most students at the doctoral level have grades that are substantially higher. With the realization that students may have difficulties adjusting when they first come to college, many admissions committees examine the student's GPA separately and minimize the grades from the first 2 years. In addition, they also tend to view the applicant's GPA in psychology courses separately. Therefore, the serious applicant should make a special effort to get high grades in these courses.

In addition to grades, admission committees often take a special look at the type of courses taken as an undergraduate. An exclusive focus in the social sciences may not be seen as favorably as a well-rounded background in the physical sciences, mathematics, and the humanities, as well as the social sciences. A background in mathematics and sciences also prepares the student for many of the quantitative tasks required in graduate school.

***The GRE.***    One factor heavily weighted by admission committees in screening the large number of applicants for a relatively low number of positions is the GRE. There are three sections on the GRE—verbal, math, and analytical—with the first two areas emphasized more. Scoring high on this exam is important. Prospective applicants should assess their abilities in the verbal and mathematical areas and determine if there is anything that can be done to improve their skills. We suggest that you purchase one of the commercially available GRE study guides (soft-cover book or software program) and take a practice exam months or even a year before you plan on taking this exam. This will give you an idea as to the nature of the questions and the format of the test. Use this as a diagnostic tool to assess your abilities, your competitiveness for admission to graduate school, and areas that need further improvement. There are commercially available GRE study courses that offer practice in taking this type of test, a working knowledge of the format on the test, familiarity in the types of questions asked, and practice working under "test conditions." However, it should also be noted that taking such courses has not been consistently associated with admission decisions. Some students to take the GREs twice. If you are not satisfied with your test scores, by all means take the exam a second time. However, please note that admission committees are likely to take the average of two scores, so you should not take the test "on a lark" before you adequately prepare, just to see how you will score.

Students should also consider taking specific classes as undergraduates that will increase their skills in these content areas. Vocabulary courses can help with the verbal section. Mathematics courses can help with the quantitative section. Logic courses can help with the analytical section. If you are test anxious, and this interferes with your ability to perform well on standardized tests, consider consulting the college counseling center to see if they have a program that targets this problem area.

In addition to the general section of the GRE, most schools require the GRE Advanced Test in Psychology. This is a specialized exam that focuses on the basic content areas in the psychology. We encourage you to purchase a study guide to become familiar with the types of questions and as a self-assessment. Even if you are applying to programs in clinical psychology, please note that this test covers all of the general content areas of psychology (e.g., experimental, social, physiological, perception, etc.). For this reason, we suggest that you take a wide variety of psychology courses as an undergraduate even though your interest may be more focused. In addition, in preparing for this exam we would suggest that you read and study at least two recent textbooks on "introduction to psychology."

***Practical Experience.***    This is experience relevant to the social service area and could take the form of either a paid part-time job or volunteer work. Such experience is crucial for those applying to professional school programs. One form it might take is work on a crisis hotline. In this setting students are often taught basic listening and counseling intervention skills during an intensive training program. This is invaluable. After the training program, volunteers are given the opportunity to work with "real-world clients" over the telephone. Most large cities have these hotlines, and many universities have their own to deal with student-oriented problems. You may also volunteer to serve at community mental health centers, state hospitals, state schools for the mentally retarded, family service centers, and runaway shelters.

Perhaps the best situation for the student considering applying to graduate school is to be directly supervised by, and work with, a professional psychologist on a specific project. There are many advantages to this including the opportunity to: (a) observe the roles and functions of a psychologist in an professional setting; (b) have a role model outside of academic areas; and (c) have a person who will be writing a letter of recommendation on your behalf for graduate school.

***Research Experience.***     This is crucial for those applying to PhD programs. The prospective applicant should keep in mind that faculty members who will be evaluating their applications value research a great deal. They will be looking for students who can make contributions to their research teams and research programs. Applicants who have research experience will have a competitive advantage over those who are a complete novice. Along these lines we would make the following recommendations:

> Take classes that will enhance your research skills. These include statistics, research methods, advanced statistics, and computer science. Learn the computer packages that most psychologists utilize in their research (e.g., SPSS, SAS). Students who can step right in and take responsibility for data analysis activities are highly valued by faculty members and will also have a competitive advantage for obtaining a paid research assistantship.

> Volunteer with at least one, and preferably two, professors to help out on their research team. This will give you firsthand experience in learning how a research project is carried out. It is best to choose a professor who is actively publishing and well known so their letter of recommendation may carry more weight. Begin this research no later than the start of your junior year.

> Become intensely interested in a research area of one of these professors. Conduct a literature review of the area, participate in research meetings, and work with graduate students who are completing theses and dissertations. If possible, conduct a research project that you have conceptualized and refined under the supervision of this professor. Many schools have honors programs or independent study courses that encourage research projects by undergraduates. Such research projects are often *publishable* in professional journals or may be presented at professional meetings. Having a publication on your application will look impressive.

## PREPARING THE APPLICATION

Once you have worked so hard at becoming an attractive candidate, you will want to make sure your application package accurately reflects this effort. The application process involves mostly tedious, time-consuming, and often repetitive tasks. The general goals are efficiency, accuracy, and effectiveness in promoting the product— you!

Organize carefully the requirements for applying to each program of interest, keeping in mind these will vary from program to program. Notice especially which requirements may take longer to complete. Transcripts are notoriously troublesome. Keep in mind that you will need official copies for each application, and allow plenty of time for bureaucratic processing (and mistakes). The same holds true for GRE scores. Letters of recommendation must be secured in advance. Professors do not like being asked to complete these at the last moment. Please remember that you are probably not the only student requesting such a letter of this professor.

Never forget that it is *your* personal responsibility to assure that the programs receive all of the required materials well in advance of the deadline. This will require constant monitoring of the progress of all the materials. It does not matter which computer broke down, which faculty member should have remembered to write your letter, or what dog ate your demographic information sheet. With the high ratio of applicants to positions available, a certain degree of screening takes place just because some materials are not received by the stated deadline. Most schools simply do not consider these applications, even though the applicant's credentials may be competitive. The point should be clear: Do not "screen yourself out" by neglecting to make sure that all of the required materials arrive on time.

Be sure all materials are sent to the correct address. This may sound simple, but problems can and do arise in this respect. Some schools have graduate programs in clinical and counseling psychology. However, one may be housed in a department of psychology and the other in a school of education. Some programs require that all materials be sent to a central location, such as the office of graduate admissions. Others require that they be sent to a specific program or a particular person within that program. Some even require a mixture of some materials going to the specific department and another going to the admissions office. Check this carefully.

Be aware that copies of transcripts and GRE scores must be sent directly from the source. Photocopies that you have made will not suffice. However, you may want to include such copies in your application packet with a note indicating that originals have been requested. We suggest that the applicant keep a separate file for each program with a checklist for all of the required materials and deadlines.

***Materials Required for the Application.***    Several different types of materials will be required for your application to be complete. All schools will require GRE scores, transcripts, and letters of recommendation. Almost every school will also require some type of personal statement in which you will be asked to describe in more detail your previous experiences, discuss your present career goals, and perhaps explain why the particular institution meets your specific needs. Some schools will require responses to much more in-depth and personal questions, especially professional schools that are interested in training clinicians. Finally, a growing number of schools are relying heavily on information obtained during an interview. Typically such schools will have completed their initial screening and have a list of the "top" 25 to 50 applicants. These students will then be invited (usually at their own expense) to come to the campus for an interview.

***Letters of Recommendation.***    These are among the most important sources of information used in determining admission into a graduate program. A good letter will contain information regarding your potential for successfully completing graduate-level work. These letters can be especially pivotal if there is some weakness in your other application materials. For example, if you have mediocre GRE scores but an otherwise stellar undergraduate record, the person writing your letter can state that based on personal experiences with you, GRE scores are not likely to be good predictors of your potential. Given the weight assigned to these letters by most admission committees, there are some steps that you can take to assure that you obtain the strongest letters possible.

Remember that the members of the admissions committee will be reading these letters specifically seeking information regarding your potential to successfully complete the rigorous coursework and research required in a graduate program. Therefore, persons who are qualified to make this judgment should write the letters. Such people will have completed a similar program themselves. If they teach in a graduate program, they will be in an even better position to make these judgments and they will also have more credibility with the committee. Thus, the letters that will be valued most will be those written by psychology professors.

Another potential source of letters is psychologists who have supervised any experience you may have had in an applied setting. This supervisor will be able to comment on your potential to do applied work, such as work with clients, responsiveness to supervision, and ability to relate to other treatment team members.

The value placed on any letter, however, will vary depending on the orientation of the programs to which you apply, and your choice of emphasis of who to ask to write on your behalf should vary accordingly. It is also important to ask the writer of the letter if it is going to be a positive recommendation (Range et al., 1991). If not positive, consider asking someone else to write on your behalf. You should chat with the person who is writing the letter to see how comfortable the person is in endorsing you for the prospective programs.

An equally important factor to be considered is the type of person you should *not* ask to write a letter of recommendation. Letters from persons who are not in a position to validly determine your potential for graduate school success are usually not highly valued by admissions committees. One exception, however, might be if the person writing the letter is describing some of your applied experiences rather than attempting to speak specifically about your academic potential. *Do not* request a letter of recommendation from friends, neighbors, relatives, clergy, attorneys, or former supervisors of your work in settings that had nothing to do with psychology.

Avoid requesting letters from "influential" people you may know such as judges or your representative in congress. Such letters are often viewed by selection committees as subtle attempts at political influence; they may have a negative impact.

In general, all letters (or perhaps all but one) should come from your psychology professors. If you choose to request one letter from someone else, a psychologist who has supervised some of your applied experience is generally a good choice. One other good choice is to request a letter from a nonpsychologist professor who taught you in one or more difficult courses in areas such as mathematics, computer science, or the basic sciences.

*The Personal Statement.*     Most programs will require some type of personal statement as part of the application materials. There is considerable variability in the form and content of these statements, and care should be taken to tailor each of them to the specific requirements and interests of each institution. There are several important factors that should be considered in writing a personal statement that will have a maximal impact.

Do your homework on the programs to which you have chosen to apply. Carefully read the brochures, catalogues, and web pages of each program. Tailor your writing to its general philosophy of training and its unique emphasis. Highlight your interests and career goals as they best match the program to which you are applying. It is important to mention a specific faculty member with whom you would like to work.

The Ph.D. is first and foremost a *research* degree, and your research experiences and interests should be clearly stated. Career goals such as private practice or working in applied settings should be downplayed. If on the other hand the program is more applied in nature (e.g., many MA/MS programs and all professional schools), your interests in these areas should be emphasized.

Emphasize those positive aspects of your application, such as (a) the variety of psychology courses that you have taken, (b) your broad-based undergraduate background, and (c) special skills or training that you have that will be of interest to the faculty, for example, computer skills for research programs, or counseling skills for applied programs.

If there is an obvious weakness in your application, concisely explain the reasons for the weakness. A common example is a lower GPA due to not adjusting well to college the first year or two. The student should then point out his or her much higher GPA of the last 2 years.

Equally important to consider are the types of information that *should not* be included. A detailed biography (unless required) will be of little use to most admission committees. Do not emphasize interests or goals that are incongruent with the program's stated orientation. Similar consideration should be given to not describing your own personal therapy experiences (unless required and viewed as relevant) and the problems that led you to seek counseling.

It is important to remember that the admissions committee will be reading your personal statement as part of an effort to determine your potential to successfully complete graduate work. After it is composed, read it carefully. Make sure it is concise (maximum of two single-spaced pages) and that the grammar is correct. It is a good practice to have your advisor review it for you before it is submitted. In many ways this piece of the application material is viewed as a "rule-out, not a rule-in." That is, a strong personal statement may not get you accepted into graduate school all on its own. However, a weak personal statement may override an otherwise strong application with high GRE scores, excellent grades, outstanding letters of recommendation, and publications.

## MAKING A CHOICE

Gaining admission to an advanced training program in psychology is competitive. However, if you are an outstanding candidate there is a high likelihood of acceptance by more than one program. Then comes the difficult decision of choosing among the various options that are available.

Perhaps the best way to facilitate an informed choice is to visit, if you have not already interviewed there, the programs where you have been accepted. Although this may be expensive we suggest that it is well worth the investment of time, energy, and resources. Remember this will be your home for several years and will have a major impact on the shaping of your career as a psychologist.

*Financial Support.*    One issue to consider is economic. In PhD programs, most programs do support their students through some type of teaching or research assistantship. This is rare at freestanding professional school programs. When you receive an acceptance letter or telephone call, ask what type, if any, of funding will be made available to you if you choose to enroll in the training program. Relevant questions in this regard include:

1. What is the amount of the stipend being offered?
2. How long is it for—first year only, or does it cover 3 or 4 years?
3. What is my obligation in terms of teaching, research, or other activity in exchange for the financial aid?
4. Does the offer also include a waiver of tuition?

Graduate school is an emotionally demanding endeavor. The student should realize that the extra burden of not being financially secure or always "being strapped" would only add to the stress of an already stressful situation. We also would add that students entering professional schools with extremely high tuition might also be taking on a substantial amount of debt. This should be part of the equation in making a final choice.

*The Atmosphere.*    A study of 201 first-year clinical psychology students cited "the emotional atmosphere of the program" as the third most important reason for choosing a program to attend, after reputation of the program and clinical supervision available (Walfish, Stenmark, Shealy, & Shealy, 1989). We suggest that you carefully assess the more subjective aspects of the program, such as the nature and quality of the interactions with faculty, other students, and degree of competitiveness. Suggestions for specific questions you can ask faculty and students are presented in Tables 6.1 and 6.2. When you evaluate the answers, keep in mind your own individual style and needs, and how well someone like you will function in each particular atmosphere.

*The Geographical Setting.*    Keep in mind that your decision may involve choosing a town that will be "your home" for anywhere from 2 to 5 years. Again, assess your own tastes and needs. Ask yourself:

1. Would I be happier in an urban or a rural setting?
2. Do I want to live in a warm or a cool climate?
3. Is this a university commuter school or one with many on-campus activities?
4. How far away from home is the setting, as I may want to visit during my breaks?

**TABLE 6.1**
Suggested Questions for Faculty

What are the courses I will be required to take?

What elective courses will be available to me, both in and outside of the department?

What research projects are currently being conducted by faculty members?

What types of practicum placements are available for applied training?

Are undergraduate students available to serve as research assistants on thesis and dissertation projects?

Is it possible to teach an undergraduate course as a graduate student?

What types of internship settings have previous students been able to obtain?

If the program is at the MA/MS level, what happens to graduates of the program? Do they go on to doctoral programs? What types of jobs are they able to obtain?

If the program is at the doctoral level, what happens to graduates of the program? Do they go on to faculty positions? What other types of jobs are they able to obtain?

What is the average length of time that it takes a student in the program to obtain the degree?

How many students during the past 3 years have been terminated from the training program? What were the circumstances?

How are advisor–advisee relationships determined? With whom will I be working? If for some reason this does not work out, may I switch to another advisor?

## TABLE 6.2
### Suggested Questions for Students

Do students and faculty have good relationships with each other?

Do professors take an adequate interest in students, both professionally and personally?

Are faculty available for consultation an adequate amount of time or are they "unreachable"?

What is the quality of the teaching?

Is there ample opportunity to learn applied skills?

Is there ample opportunity to conduct research that I am interested in?

What is the quality of the supervision of applied work? Research supervision?

Is the environment competitive?

What is the nature of the work load?

Do students have a role in shaping departmental policy with regards to training philosophy? Do students serve on committees with faculty, and if so, are they given "real" versus "token" power?

What type of town is this to live in?

Are the stipends enough to live on?

How do most of the graduate students spend their free time?

However, keep in mind that you will only be in this setting for a relatively brief time. Too often students choose ill-fitting programs because they like the location. Keep in mind your long-term goals, and apply to all programs that help you reach these goals, regardless of location.

***The Best-Fit Solution.*** The only "right" choice is that program that best suits *you,* the program most conducive to *your* successful completion of training (please remember that not everyone finishes), and the program most likely to facilitate the fulfillment of *your* career goals. It is imperative that you choose a program where you will feel most comfortable "living." This is especially important as significant percentages of students receiving degrees in clinical and community psychology have reported "no or "not sure" whether, "given a chance to lives their lives over again," they would choose to attend the same graduate training program (Walfish, Moritz & Stenmark, 1991; Walfish, Polifka, & Stenmark, 1984). Assess your career goals and your personality style carefully. If you want to engage primarily in clinical practice after receiving your degree, determine if the development of clinical skills is given adequate coverage in the training curriculum. If you want to work in the community, attempt to identify the adequacy of training opportunities for developing these skills in terms of faculty available as role models and available practicum placements. If you want a career in academia, assess the quality of the research programs of the professors and determine what percentage of former students were able to obtain academic positions upon graduation. We are suggesting that you choose not to be a student who goes to a training program and complains, "I came here to learn to be a therapist and all they have me do is research."

Finally, at some point in time (typically 2 weeks after you have been officially accepted) you will have to make a final choice. Many schools may try to pressure you into making a decision before you are ready to do so (if you decline they want to offer the slot to another qualified applicant before the other candidate accepts elsewhere). Although you should not needlessly delay the final decision, do not feel as if you have to make a decision before the agreed-on deadline. Once you have made your choice, first telephone the appropriate faculty member and inform him or her of your choice. Then quickly follow up this call with an acceptance letter to this individual. Then contact the other programs that have accepted you, thank them for the offer, and inform them that you have chosen to attend another program. Although they may be disappointed with your choice, they will be grateful so they may quickly offer the position to another applicant. Once you have accepted the offer in writing, you should honor that commitment. Changing your mind after accepting an offer and accepting at another program instead is considered by many to be unethical behavior.

We have tried to convey the message that applying to graduate school is a time consuming and complex process. Before the applications are made, students will have to have gained experiences and credentials that make them stand out in a situation in which gaining acceptance is competitive. Carefully assess your career goals, do well in classes and on the GRE, participate in both research and applied endeavors, and carefully prepare and monitor your application. Following these suggestions will not assure your acceptance into an advanced training program. However, we suggest that following these guidelines will greatly enhance your chances. Good luck!

## ACKNOWLEDGMENT

The authors thank Thomas Brandon and Allen Hess for their comments on an earlier version of this chapter. Their wisdom and guidance helped to make it stronger.

## REFERENCES

American Psychological Association. (1997). *Getting in: A step-by step plan for gaining admission to graduate school in psychology.* Washington, DC: Author.

American Psychological Association. (1998). *Graduate study in psychology.* Washington, DC: Author.

Eddy, B., Lloyd, P., & Lubin, B. (1987). Enhancing the application to doctoral professional programs: Suggestions from a national survey. *Teaching of Psychology, 14*, 160–163.

Keith-Spiegel, P., & Wiederman, M. (2000). *The complete guide to graduate school admission: Psychology, counseling and related professions.* Mahwah, NJ: Lawrence Erlbaum Associates.

Keith-Spiegel, P., Tobachnick, B., & Spiegel, G. (1994) When demand exceeds supply: Second-order criteria used by graduate selection committees. *Teaching of Psychology, 21*, 79–81.

Lawson, T. (1995). Gaining admission into graduate programs in psychology: An update. *Teaching of Psychology, 22*, 225–227.

Mayne, T., Norcross, J., & Sayette, M. (2000). *An insider's guide to graduate programs in clinical and counseling psychology.* New York: Guilford.

Nevid, J., & Gildea, T. (1984). The admissions process in clinical training: The role of the personal interview. *Professional Psychology: Research and Practice, 15*, 18–25.

Norcross, J., Hanych, J., & Terranova, R. (1996). Graduate study in psychology: 1992–1993. *American Psychologist, 51*, 631–643.

Range, L., Menyhert, A., Walsh, M., Hardin, K., Ellis, J., & Craddick, R. (1991). Letters of recommendation: Perspectives, recommendations, and ethics. *Professional Psychology: Research and Practice, 22*, 389–392.

Rem, R., Oren, E., & Childrey, G. (1987). Selection of graduate students in clinical Psychology: Use of cutoff scores and interviews. *Professional Psychology: Research and Practice, 18*, 485–488.

Sternberg, R., & Williams, W. (1997). Does the graduate record examination predict meaningful success in the graduate training of psychologists? *American Psychologist, 52*, 630–641.

Walfish, S., Moritz, J., & Stenmark, D. (1991). A longitudinal study of the career satisfaction of clinical psychologists. *Professional Psychology: Research and Practice, 22*, 253–255.

Walfish, S., Polifka, J., & Stenmark, D. (1984). An evaluation of skill acquisition in community psychology training. *American Journal of Community Psychology, 12*, 165– 174.

Walfish, S., Stenmark, D., Shealy, J. S., & Shealy, S. (1989). Reasons why applicants select clinical psychology graduate programs. *Professional Psychology: Research and Practice, 20*, 350–354.

# II

# Mastering the Personal and Political Dynamics of Graduate School

# 7

# The Politics of Graduate Programs

*Gerard F. Sumprer*

*Steven Walfish*

When the second author entered graduate school, he did not have financial aid. During the first quarter he made a conscious attempt to do well in the class taught by the director of clinical training. Indeed, he scored at the top of the class and was then rewarded with an assistantship by the director to work on his research project 20 hours per week. He had been exhausted by the first quarter's work and faced an additional 20 hour per week responsibility. He decided, for the sake of his own physical and mental health, to take one course fewer during the second quarter. Because two of the three courses were part of sequences (e.g., statistics, assessment) he chose to not take the third course, Theories of Personality, which appeared as though it could be taken the next year. This seemed to be a healthy and reasonable decision. Unfortunately, the director of clinical training taught the Theories of Personality course. When the student informed the professor that he would be taking the course the following year, the second author was told, "If you have withdrawn from this course and are not enrolled by tomorrow I will be unhappy. Please know there are plenty of people who would like your slot in graduate school." Naturally, he enrolled the next day.

Consider this story of a colleague. After completing the first year of his doctoral studies he received an excellent evaluation regarding his progress in the program. However, he was told that he was an anxious person and he went into therapy to address this problem. At the end of the next semester, just 6 months later, he was told that he was going to be asked to leave the program after he received his master's degree. This was despite the fact that he had passed all of his courses and had received favorable evaluations from his practicum supervisors. There were two or three professors who just did not like him and did not think he would be a good therapist. He had always wanted to be a doctoral-level psychologist. Rather than just live with

77

this sentence handed down by the faculty he decided to consult with a prominent attorney. The attorney informed him of his rights and gave counsel on how he should proceed. The attorney also consulted with the attorney who represented the university. In a calm, mature, tactful, and straightforward manner the student addressed the issues with the chair of the department of psychology and the director of clinical training. He did not directly threaten to file a civil suit. However, the student made it clear by his actions that if he was not able to resolve the issue with the faculty in a reasonable manner, he was protecting his interests and considering legal action. There was one faculty member who was willing to stand up for him and became his major professor. The decision to terminate the student from the program was reversed. He successfully completed the program and now has a full private practice in a major city. It is not known what impact the attorney had in this process although it was clear that he did give wise counsel, made an initial inquiry to the university, and was willing to be an advocate for the student if the decision was not reversed.

Finally, consider the experience of another colleague who is now chair of a department of psychology. He described sitting through his own bizarre master's thesis defense while a graduate student. His advisor and coadvisor argued for 30 minutes about a single word. When the student spoke up, both professors verbally attacked him! At that point in time he shut up, realizing that the issue was not the word, but who would rule the roost. The rest of the defense was anticlimactic.

## THE RISE AND FALL OF IDEALISM

Most students who enter graduate school have the expectation that they are beginning a period in their lives, that will result in the development of their competence as professional psychologists. The general belief is that faculty, as teachers, role models, and mentors, will impart the necessary basic knowledge and skills.

However, graduate education entails much more than learning the knowledge and skills of one's profession. Unless trainees realize this, they will have a difficult, if not impossible, time during their tenure as graduate students. It is easy for the idealistic new student to be enchanted at the beginning of graduate school. Expectations of embarking on a new career, possibly moving to a new city, establishing a new peer group, and training with an illustrious faculty all contribute to this excitement. However, the excitement quickly fades and soon graduate students are wondering if they will even survive the emotionally draining process. As Mahoney (1976) eloquently elaborated in response to this initial idealism: "Graduate life is seldom a bed of roses. It is more often imbued with confusion, anxiety, and a paranoia, which is occasionally reinforced by the quirks and injustices of the mysterious 'system'" (p. 41).

Graduate school is fraught with stress and life change. Dixon (1973) offered a description of graduate education as a process in which the "more able people manage to survive rather than thrive" (p. 61). Most graduate students are extremely intelligent and highly motivated. However, these are "necessary but not sufficient" characteristics for ensuring success in the graduate school environment.

The purpose of this chapter is to elaborate on the "politics" that graduate students will most likely encounter during the course of their training. By the term *politics* we are referring to those intangible factors, interpersonal likes and dislikes, that may impede the future psychologist's development and the attainment of an advanced degree. That is, receiving your union card and being allowed into the profession requires more than obtaining good grades in the classroom, publishing papers, and demonstrating professional competence in applied settings. It is important to understand the players involved and the social setting in which one is being trained. Such an understanding and acceptance of these issues may mean the difference between relatively smooth sailing through a program and a terribly noxious experience, in which hurdles to be jumped are constantly placed in front of the trainee. In such cases, graduate students experience poor relationships with faculty members and most often become angry and depressed individuals. Under such conditions, progress through the program is slowed down. In extreme cases students are asked to leave the training program or will more often voluntarily choose to leave, feeling that they cannot put up with this any more. It is our hope, an idealistic one we admit, that armed with the knowledge of the realities of graduate education, students in training will be able to maximize all that is positive about the experience and mitigate much of the noxious. In the spirit of Mahoney's (1976) chapter "Rites of Passage: Selected Absurdities in Graduate Training," we elaborate on some of the "initiation rites" that are usually encountered in surviving the process of graduate education. As did Mahoney, we do not contend that the scenarios we describe are universal, but rather they are representative of the "milieu" of current training programs. There are universities where the politics that negatively impact students are either nonexistent or minimal. However, it is our contention that this will be the exception rather than the rule.

Students must first and foremost realize that, like many powerless groups in society, that they have a limited, if almost nonexistent, power base! This realization may lead to feelings of anger, confusion, self-doubt, paranoia, and apathy, similar to "learned helplessness" (Seligman, 1975). We believe it is essential that students understand the concept of powerlessness and its consequent effects if they are to avoid many of the pitfalls and frustrations inherent in such a situation.

After elaborating on these concepts, we report anecdotal data gathered from informal interviews conducted with psychologists. These respondents were asked to reflect on the "politics" of their graduate school experience and to offer, in hindsight, practical suggestions for dealing with the issues. It was apparent from their reflections that students must learn to deal with political reality if they are to maximize their learning experience (and maintain their mental health). On the other side of the coin, their unrealistic expectations of the graduate training experience may contribute to the difficulty of obtaining an advanced degree.

As long as the political conflicts are not overwhelming and deleterious, learning to deal with the politics of the training environment can serve as a beneficial training experience. Generally all work environments are political, so graduate students can begin mastery of political skills in graduate school. For the sake of balance, we do not want to create the faulty impression that all power is bad. In the right hands, and when used appropriately, judiciously, and to the benefit of the trainee, the exertion of power by faculty can be helpful in preparing the trainee for unknown future events. As an example, the first author's department chair used his power to "invite" graduate students to take more than the minimal number of courses required to earn the doctorate—(a route they had shunned) for fear that some state licensing boards would not accept a particular course as meeting their requirements. The available substitute (a course the first author did not want to take but did under pressure) saved him from years of delay in gaining licensure. In retrospect he says, "Thank you, chair with power."

However, faculty are imperfect human beings, and organizations in which psychology programs are housed are imperfect as well. It is the negative consequences resulting from the utilization of power by imperfect human beings and organizations that the authors accept as reality and seek to address in this chapter.

## THE CONCEPT OF POWER

Graduate students should have a clear understanding of the extent of their power base. It is extremely limited and in some cases virtually nonexistent. Before we elaborate on this contention further, let us first examine the definition of power. *The Oxford English Dictionary* offers the following descriptors:

1. Ability to act or affect something; to act upon a person or thing.

2. Ability to act or affect something strongly; might; vigor; force of character.

3. Possession of control or command over others; domination; control; influence; authority.

Pruitt (1976), a social psychologist, defined power as the capacity to influence another party's behavior in a desired direction. From these definitions it should be clear, in the graduate student–faculty hierarchy, that the former are in a "one-down" power position compared to the latter. For the most part, students have little ability to influence behavior, have limited individual "force," and possess virtually no command, control, domination, nor authority over faculty's behavior. Finally, and somewhat ironically, the faculty are sometimes viewed as "the enemy," armed with grades, stipends, evaluations, comprehensive examinations, letters of recommendation, and final approval of theses and dissertations as "ammunition" to be used when necessary in the heat of battle to "keep the troops in line."

Mahoney (1976) contended that the ambience of many graduate programs appears to be diametrically opposite to that recommended by educational researchers:

> The unfortunate atmosphere of all too many graduate programs is one which encourages anxiety, confusion and insecurity on the part of the student.... Financially, socially and psychologically, the graduate student is forced to sacrifice many of his "inalienable" rights.... In my opinion, this atmosphere is not only a travesty of scientific apprenticeship, but also an affront to the dignity and sensitivity of the student ... one can hardly expect new paths to be blazed by those who have been immobilized by an enforced lack of confidence. (pp. 59–60)

What are the effects of being educated in such environments? Clearly, faculty are perceived as having control of the major reinforcers in the graduate school environment. Just as Gurin and Gurin (1976) suggested that the poor, through past experience or social learning, may develop a feeling of powerlessness so may graduate students. Sue and Zane (1980) argued that although individuals who have power can affect outcomes, those who are powerless will find that outcomes are independent of their actions. They pointed out that laboratory research findings concerning learned helplessness demonstrate the importance of having control, or perceptions of control, over one's life. Sue and Zane (1980) suggested that where individuals in a particular community lack control, psychological well-being and the psychological sense of community (i.e., the student–faculty environment) may be diminished. It is their contention that where events are unpredictable (e.g., changes in requirements, having a moody major professor), an increase in helplessness will occur.

What are the effects of helplessness? Sue and Zane (1980) cited studies in which subjects exhibit carelessness, difficulty in problem solving, and diminished prosocial behavior. They proposed that lack of faith in the "system" may also be the result of helplessness. Depression, alienation, and apathy are also other commonly described consequences (Strickland & Janoff-Bulman, 1980). These factors debilitate the learning process.

How does all of this relate to the student in training? In some institutions, students do have some power to shape their curriculum and combat seeming injustices. However, as we mentioned previously, we contend that few programs allow much power to students. Many graduate students report the "symptoms" of helplessness—depression, alienation, apathy, pessimism, and lack of faith in the system. In case you believe that this phenomenon is solely found in psychology we would direct you to read an investigative account of a prominent laboratory in the Department of Chemistry at Harvard University in which two students committed suicide (Hall, 1998). We quote from the suicide note from a brilliant graduate student:

> This event could have been avoided. Professors here have too much power over the lives of their grad students.... We need a committee to monitor each graduate student's progress and provide protection for graduate students from abusive research advisors. (p. 121)

Similarly, a recent review of the literature suggested that anxiety and depression were common among law students (Dammeyer & Nunez, 1999).

For the sake of psychological health, we strongly advise that students accept the conditions of powerlessness as reality and the status quo. Indeed, short of a systems and values overhaul of how graduate students are trained in psychology, any attempts at fighting small, individual battles will result in little change in the system (where the problem actually lies) and in added frustration and helplessness on the part of the student. When the second author was a second-year graduate student he considered taking a leave of absence to do specialized therapy training. He felt that he had become detached from his feelings and that it would be helpful to regroup and to resume graduate school a year later. One of his advisors, who understood the training environment, then told him: "When you are in graduate school you do not want to be in touch with your feelings. If you were you'd be angry all of the time."

He chose not to take the time off but rather to move quickly through the program. However, he is acutely aware that repression and denial are his primary defense mechanisms, and in the instance of being a powerless student these served him well.

Exacerbating this kind of problem is the type of person who enters graduate training in psychology. Celani (1976) opined:

> There is one personality factor of the obsessive graduate student that is not adaptive for the role of student-apprentice. This is the desire for dominance, control, and power and conversely an aversion for acting in a submissive manner. (p. 4)

We recommend that students should realize that the "system" will long outlive their tenure as graduate students (as it has that of many generations before them). The sooner students accept the fact of their limited power, the sooner they can better cope with the deleterious effects of this condition. Evidence for this lies in the reformulation of the learned helplessness model by Abramson, Seligman, and Teasdale (1978). The initial model proposed by Seligman (1975) did not specify the conditions that would determine the generality and chronicity of helplessness. Thus, Abramson et al. incorporated the work of attribution theorists to better predict the conditions in which an individual would feel helpless and subsequently suffer the consequences of such a situation (e.g., depression). In reference to this model, Sue and Zane (1980) suggested that the cognitions (beliefs or attributions) invoked about the situation will have a mediating effect as to whether or not helplessness will occur in a powerless situation. In the Abramson et al. (1978) reformulation, attributions about a situation (e.g., being a powerless student) can be placed on three dimensions: (a) internal–external; (b) stable–unstable, and (c) global–specific. If the difficulties of the situation can be attributed to external factors induced rather than to an internal characteristic of the student (e.g., "This is a crazy system" vs. "I must be inadequate"), to be unstable (or time-limited) rather than stable ("Yes, this first year is difficult" vs. "It will take me 10 years to finish"), and specific rather than global ("I'm having trouble with this aspect of the statistics course" vs. "I can't master graduate school"), helplessness is less likely to occur. How the student views the situation or sets expectations as to the way things should be will help mitigate against some of the deleterious effects of being in a situation of dependence and powerlessness.

In his brief but elucidating piece, Celani (1976) described the transformation from neophyte to advanced graduate student. From having one's own opinion early on advanced graduate students learned to role-play and display behavior that was accepted and reinforced by the faculty because independent thinking and challenging the status quo were severely punished. (As an aside, we recall one professor telling a student, "Mr. Smith, when we want your opinion, I'll tell you what it is.") Celani described:

> The message was clear, (a) suggestions for reform from the bottom were dangerous, if not suicidal, and (b) it was preferable to be a compromised insider than an uncompromised outsider.... All forms of overt challenge ceased. Secret student meetings were held so that even the most hostile students became proficient at mouthing the orthodox catechism with the proper affect and enthusiasm. Naturally, there was considerable skepticism on the part of the faculty at this sudden widespread conversion; however, after several months of continuous student role playing the faculty began to believe that the students had finally "caught on," which, paradoxically, we had. (pp. 4, 7)

The authors hope these conceptualizations of the graduate-school environment, the role of the student, and the "politics" of training in psychology will be helpful to the reader. Students interested in learning more about power issues faced by faculty in departments of psychology should read the work of Salancik (1987). An understanding of these issues will allow the student to develop appropriate coping strategies to deal with current issues and, in the best of worlds, prevent future problems that would interfere with the attainment of the advanced degree. Next, we present "survival strategies" for graduate students, gathered in interviews from psychologists reflecting back on their own training experiences. Five key areas in training are explored: (a) choosing a training program; (b) expectations of faculty; (c) choosing an advisor; (d) doing the dissertation, and (e) supervision on counseling/therapy.

## Choosing a Training Program

In a study examining the reasons why clinical psychology graduate students chose their particular program to attend, the "emotional atmosphere of the program" was ranked as the third most important factor after reputation of the program and amount of clinical supervision available (Walfish, Stenmark, Shealy, & Shealy, 1989). The most emotionally intense statements given by the psychologists we interviewed concerned the "atmosphere" of the training program. This atmosphere was seen as being either supportive or competitive. Two specific examples illustrate the differences. The senior author of this chapter remembered his first week in a doctoral program in which the program chairman addressed the new students with the department's philosophy. Simply put, the faculty felt that they had done their screening of students during the selection process for the program. The job of the faculty, now that the students had been selected, was to aid them in obtaining their degrees. Students were expected to cooperate and help one another in their common goal of obtaining their doctorate. That expectation was met with students cooperating and helping one another through hard times.

On the other side of the coin was another training program where the faculty openly stated that, poor students were to be "weeded out" in the following year and openly published a ranking of the students. Needless to say, the program was the epitome of competition, with students developing a "cutthroat" philosophy. Manifestations of such a philosophy were the mysterious disappearance of required readings from the library, students attempting to make other students "look like fools" for asking questions in class and chronic "one-upmanship."

Most of the psychologists interviewed believed that the faculty set the atmosphere for the program in two ways. The first was by acting as if their primary duty was screening students out of the program. The second was by modeling a critical and sarcastic attitude that the students emulated. Celani (1976) suggested that this is especially true for advanced graduate students who were ready to "join the club" and took their turn at harming the more junior and/or less able students.

Unfortunately, those interviewed by the authors did not believe that the student could obtain a realistic perspective by reading the printed information provided by the department. They recommended that anyone considering entering a particular program talk to students presently in the program. In a review of the primary information source regarding graduate school, APA's *Graduate Study in Psychology*, Halonen and Young (1999) argued:

> Although the text is extremely thorough in capturing quantitative descriptors, prospective graduate students would benefit from some qualitative analysis as well. The quantitative data only hint at the kind of climate each graduate program maintains.... Prospective students would be helped in their application decisions if the graduate program descriptions captured the climate of the graduate program. Some graduate programs are fiercely competitive; others strive for a more nurturing environment.... Perhaps graduate programs could be encouraged to evaluate this feature based on alumni or even current students' ratings. (p. 234)

Unfortunately, Mahoney (1976) suggested that the competitive atmosphere may be the most prevalent. We add our pessimism in predicting that programs will not conduct such evaluations, and will not make them public if they are unfavorable in any way.

We concur with the advice of Halonen and Young (1999) that students choose those programs in which they are most likely to thrive, even if the programs do not have the highest ranking in reputation. In this regard we encourage a great deal of introspection on the part of the student. Do not choose to enter a prestigious program or to work with a prestigious professor if it is only going to leave you "prestigiously miserable." Understand the emotional atmosphere of the program and do not expect it to change. Acceptance may help reduce the anger, frustration, and depression that often result from the learned helplessness described earlier. It is the astute clinician, teacher, organizational consultant, and applied researcher who can assess the climate and politics of a setting. Apply these same rules when choosing a program to attend, and understand how they may influence your behavior and adaptability while a graduate student.

The second most prevalent issue raised by the interviewed psychologists concerned the orientation of the program. This relates to the scientist-practitioner model. Most graduate programs in clinical and counseling psychology adhere to the APA's training model for psychologists, which advocates that a psychologist have skills to do both research and therapy or counseling. PsyD programs typically place more of an emphasis on the latter than the former, and it is just the opposite with PhD programs. However, although PhD programs may publicly state (e.g., brochures, catalogues) that they follow the scientist-practitioner model, most of the interviewees viewed their programs to be biased in one direction or the other in primary emphasis. Most reported that their programs emphasized research and the scientist role. This follows in that the biggest factor used in hiring and promoting faculty is the number of publications that they have (Mahoney, 1976). Obviously, if research is what the faculty members are highly rewarded for, then conducting research is going to be the activity on which they will want most of their own and their students' energy spent. In fact, some of the interviewees reported having little contact with clients while in the program. Some stated that they were told that they would receive most of their clinical skills on their internship. Other programs were reported as emphasizing development of assessment and therapy or counseling skills and initiating students into having client contact in the early stages of the program. Depending on what the student's career goals are (researcher or practitioner), satisfaction with the program selected will be affected by the program's orientation. Again the interviewees felt the best source of information about the program's emphasis was students already enrolled in the program.

The lesson for the student enrolled in a PhD program who wants to do applied clinical work in a private practice setting is simple: Do not ever tell this to faculty members. Understand that faculty members want to produce students who will follow in their footsteps, emulate their behavior, and support their research goals. Of course there are exceptions to this rule, but for the most part faculty members view the choice of a nonacademic life as a rejection of them and their values. The facts that there are not enough academic positions for the number of doctorates awarded and that academic life has been described as being less than idyllic (Boice & Myers, 1987) are immaterial. The fastest way for students to go to the bottom of the rung is to admit to their major professor that they want to spend most of their professional life (a) helping people through direct service and (b) earning an excellent living. This is despite the fact that resolution 8.9 from the National Conference on Graduate Education in Psychology (APA, 1987) dictated that faculty members should respect a career choice of practitioner by their students. The preceding statements should not be construed as implying that private practitioners should not be well trained in research methodology or statistics. Without such knowledge and skills, they could not competently maintain their therapy and assessment skills.

## Expectations of Faculty

The faculty are probably the most important aspect of any program. They teach, evaluate, reward and punish, and serve as role models for students. How students relate to the faculty greatly affects how they will enjoy several years of their life and the quality of their training. Of particular interest is the fact that a large number of psychologists interviewed believed that a lot of their dissatisfaction with faculty was due to their own unrealistic expectations of them. The most common problem was not seeing faculty members as human beings with limitations. Quite naturally, when students enter a program they are under a considerable amount of stress. They are meeting a great number of new people, both faculty and students, all of whom the student would like to impress. This is especially so with the faculty members, who are perceived as having power over the students, as well as already being in a role the student aspires to achieve. Adding to the stress is the fact that most of the students are going to be trying to impress the faculty within areas where they are only neophytes such as research and therapy or counseling. Naturally when under stress in a new environment, especially if it is a competitive one, with new people, anyone would have a tendency to seek someone on whom to become dependent on and to idolize. Quite understandably, students have a tendency to turn to faculty members. The problem arises when the student clings to an all-knowing, all-wonderful image, rather than the truth that faculty are human beings who may have their own problems and limitations. Let us look at some examples to get a better understanding of this: "I expected the faculty, who were therapists, to be perfect in every way, to be self-actualized and all understanding. They weren't." "I don't know why but I just assumed that the professors' lives would revolve around my needs and concerns because they were so important to me." "I remember being really shocked when I saw a faculty member get angry and tell another faculty member where to get off. It just didn't fit my ideal image of a psychologist—what I wanted to become."

It is a normal tendency to idealize someone on whom you feel a need to depend under stress. Naturally you want a perfect person to depend on because it makes you feel secure, especially if you doubt your own abilities and feel vulnerable. Also quite naturally, faculty probably do not try to stop this false expectation. Who would not like to be seen as perfect by others? However, this expectation is never met, and the next step reported by students is disillusionment, anger, and fear. From one of our respondents came the comment: "How dare the faculty not be perfect! What am I going to do? I'm being taught and evaluated, especially evaluated, by people with faults." When this occurs, life is no longer secure. The next step is to overreact against the faculty members, and to harp on their limitations and to ignore the strengths from which the student can benefit. This may especially be the case given the prevalence of what we call "the paradox of faculty perfection." That is, they are the first to admit that they are not perfect but the last to admit they ever made a mistake!

Most of the psychologists interviewed reported neither enjoying nor gaining from the false expectations they had of the faculty nor the natural consequences they experienced when their expectations were unfulfilled. Rather, the best learning experiences were reported when the faculty were perceived as human beings with faults, who happened to have more knowledge or expertise in an area than the student and therefore could be someone from whom to learn. For another account of the same process from the faculty point of view, as well as a good theoretical understanding of this process, see Hess and Sauser's chapter in this section. For a better understanding of what it is like to be a faculty member, essentially a view from the other side, we recommend reading Zanna and Darley's (1987) *The Compleat Academic*.

Here are some recommendations made by the psychologists we interviewed on how to deal with issues related to faculty expectations:

1. Stay away from programs with competitive atmospheres, especially between faculty members. This seems to exacerbate the problem. Henry Kissinger once said, "The reason academic politics are so vicious is because the stakes are so low." Students are typically the fodder that gets caught in the crossfire.

2. Stay away from faculty who act as if they want to be seen as perfect. This is especially true for students who want to be independent and have a rebellious streak in them.

3. Try to go into the program with a mindset that nobody, faculty or student, is perfect. Realize that each faculty member has something to offer, but none have everything to offer.

4. Talk with advanced students about your expectations. They can help you get a better perspective, for example, trusted faculty, grading, emphasis placed on training students.

5. On an internal level, if you have high expectations from the faculty, reflect on why this is the case for you. Perhaps some of these needs could be met elsewhere, such as through friends, family, a therapist, or other mentors outside of the immediate faculty.

## Choosing an Advisor

In general, an advisor is a faculty member who aids the student in planning courses, supervises the thesis and dissertation, and helps the student through difficult times, be they academic or personal. Finding a mentor is an important pursuit (see O'Neil and Wrightsman's chapter in this section for a more complete discussion of this topic). However, each program has different role expectations for advisors, so this definition may not apply everywhere. Also, some departments do not allow a student to choose his or her advisor. They also differ on when a student may make that choice. But with these qualifications in mind, the following suggestions are given for the student to consider in choosing an advisor:

1. Some advisors are helpful in obtaining good internships and/or employment for their advisees if the advisee has earned their respect, and others are not. Therefore assess your career goals carefully and choose an advisor who will help you obtain these goals.

2. Some advisors put time and effort into the advisor–advisee relationship. Others see this role as a waste of their time. Keep your individual needs or preferences in mind when selecting or being matched with an advisor so a good fit is made.

3. Most advisors want students who are interested in their area of research. Remember, most faculty jobs and promotions are based mainly on research productivity. As described by Hall (1998), "Mentoring is not the reason faculty get tenure at major research institutions. Science is what they're hired for and science is what they're admired for."

4. Some advisors are committed to so many projects (e.g., research, writing a book, workshops, consultation, private practice, etc.) that even if they want to, they cannot give you the time you may need.

5. Most advisors want an advisee who can demonstrate independent thought, reliability, and forethought. However, remember that too much independent thought or behavior may be punished.

6. Some advisors understand the political undertones in a department and can educate the student as to the unwritten rules that exist. Others are idealistic or unaware of the factors that can affect a graduate student.

7. All advisors want an advisee who makes their time and effort seem worthwhile by at least being pleasant but also, more desirably, by being someone of whom the advisor can be proud because of the advisee's performance and behavior.

8. The best source to obtain information on what each faculty member is like as an advisor is, once again, more advanced graduate students, especially the current advisees of the professor in question.

9. The best source for finding out what is expected of you as an advisee (it's a two-way street!) is your potential advisor. Seeking an open and frank discussion of one another's expectations saves a lot of misunderstanding down the road. Do not assume you know what your advisor wants from you or that he or she is aware of your expectations. Discuss these with the advisor. Then be prepared to be somewhat disappointed that your advisor does not meet all of your expectations. Life is not perfect. Even an advisor cannot meet all of your needs; there are other faculty with other strengths to draw on.

## Doing the Dissertation

The large number of people that are described as ABDs (All But Dissertation) attest to the difficulty of this typically last hurdle to obtaining a doctorate. It seems to be a particularly difficult hurdle for applied psychologists, whose usual rationalization is that they are not interested in research but just "want to help people." It is the belief of the authors that research and the ability to comprehend its utility in applied work, as well as its limitations, are essential to the effective practicing psychologist, even for those in private practice. For those readers who plan for a career in academia, the dissertation is an essential training ground. However, most students, on graduation, will probably spend little time actively involved in research and view the dissertation as an obstacle in their way to the doctorate. This latter attitude itself is probably the biggest obstacle in finishing one's dissertation, because it gives the student a half-hearted attitude to face the many trials and tribulations that one must go through to complete the process. For the practicing clinician, a complete understanding of how research is conducted, including its assets and limitations, in relation to the practice of these skills is essential. Being actively involved in a research project gives the student a wealth of information that is extremely difficult, if not impossible, to ascertain from mere reading on the subject. An example of this is the first author's understanding of the difficulty in measuring anxiety obtained through his dissertation as well as the important difference between research that is statistically significant and the amount of variance it accounts for (i.e., its clinical significance).

Whether or not the reader agrees with this position, the fact remains that if you are in a doctoral program you will have to complete a dissertation. Martin's chapter in Section II gives an excellent guide for completing a thesis and dissertation. We provide here a few simple guidelines related to us related to political issues of completing the thesis and dissertation.

1.  Pick a major advisor who will have time for you, is interested in what you are doing, can be assertive with other faculty, and can be depended on if difficulties arise between committee members. Remember, as a student you will have little power in inducing faculty members to be responsive to your needs (e.g., attempting to coordinate schedules of five people for a proposal defense meeting, use of students in their classes as subjects for the study). A strong faculty advisor can help with some of these issues.

2.  Get involved in research with faculty as early as possible. There are several benefits to this strategy. You will be able to find an area of interest before you begin to think of an actual dissertation topic. If the faculty member you become involved with helps you learn about the area being researched, you will probably be on a good start for the massive literature review you will be conducting for your dissertation. You will also learn a great deal about research skills, including statistical analysis, so that you do not make all the common mistakes that will just add to the stress of completing a dissertation.

3.  Pick a committee that can work together. To have a committee with members who dislike one another or do not agree on basic issues will lead to a tennis match, with you and your dissertation being the tennis ball being beaten back and forth. Although conflict may exist among the faculty members, it is essential to understand that there is only one big loser in these situations, the student.

4.  Keep all committee members updated on your progress and seek advice from them as you progress through your research project, not just before the defense. Remember, they are evaluating your dissertation. Do not attempt to surprise them in your final written product with some innovative way of obtaining subjects or analyzing data. Often there are flaws in such innovation that may not be foreseen by the student. When faculty members approve a proposal for an experiment they expect it to be followed, and the proposal approval serves as a contract between the student and the committee. If this contract is violated, most likely the student will be placed in an uncomfortable situation and experience negative consequences (e.g., delays in graduation, negative reputation).

5.  Expect to do revisions of both the proposed experiment and the written product. If you go into a committee meeting with the expectation of complete approval, you will be setting yourself up for disappointment. Do not insist that things be a certain way in terms of either how your experiment is conducted or how the manuscript is written. Do not think, suggest, imply, or even "ooze" the possibility that you have the "best" solution to a problem, even if you actually do. Find a way to tactfully present your dissenting ideas but never imply that they do not know the best way of doing things. It helps if you realize in advance that faculty have to initially approve your experiment, it has to be defended before them, and the final manuscript will have to be signed by them for you to receive your degree. They hold all of the cards (e.g., they have power and we suggest you react accordingly) and they will "smell blood" if you present yourself as knowing more than they do. There is plenty of time after you graduate to take your own deck and play solitaire with your own future re-

search program. If you have no interest in doing further research and view this as the only chance to do a research project, all the more reason to "do it their way." For these individuals, the final signed, sealed, and delivered dissertation is only a stop along the way to obtaining the "union card" necessary to pursue one's career goals.

6. Remember, you are learning about research and mistakes are to be expected. If mistakes are made, do not attempt to cover them up, slide them by, or otherwise escape responsibility. Faculty members may be disappointed or angry with you for the mistake that was made, especially if you have not been updating them along the way. However, they may be ready to call in the firing squad if they find out that you are trying to cover something up.

## Supervision on Counseling/Therapy

Nowhere else do students report feeling that their ego is more on the line than when they are being supervised in their assessment and counseling/therapy skills. And why wouldn't this be the case, considering that the psychologist-to-be is finally being confronted with the extremely difficult task worked on for so long—helping other people. It is therefore probably no coincidence that students are most defensive when they are being supervised. In this section we address some of the emotional reactions that the interviewed psychologists related, so you can judge and address your own emotional reaction better. (Hess's chapter, Learning Psychology, in Section III gives an excellent presentation of the stages of supervision and what students should expect during the learning process.)

In addition to the issues related to being a neophyte therapist once again, please remember that faculty members and supervisors typically follow this variation of the "Golden Rule": Those who hold the gold, rule! Judgments as to who is going to become a good therapist and who is not are subjective. Despite laying claim to being scientists, faculty members usually base their conclusions about a student's therapeutic ability on a hunch or "gut feeling." Consider the following, presented by Anker (1984):

> Recently, I had an opportunity to learn of a former student of mine who left the graduate program after several years, under great fire from most faculty in the department. Although, as a matter of principle, I did not feel the student should have to leave, I eventually encouraged him to go because it was a practical matter, given the fact that attitudes of the faculty were so set against him. The student completed his PhD at another clinical program and now, I have learned, has a successful practice, and is highly regarded by clinical and academic peers in his community.... For some reason, perhaps because we are clinicians, we may be so much aware of the "less than perfect" characteristics of our students that we tend to make dire predictions about how they will, after all, eventually turn out. When decisions to terminate must be made on bases other than academic failure, as I believe they must on occasion, I confess to having no good rules or principles. Like all such matters, patience, kindness, and as much prudence as you can muster in such circumstances.... However, I suggest the exercise of great caution in pursuing this course. (p. 113)

The initial reaction to beginning their therapy training most commonly reported by those interviewed was fear and self-doubt. This is understandable because helping other people is a difficult task. It is also stressful when the client is looking at the student with this "you're the doctor; help me" look, while at the same time the student knows that the videotape is rolling or the interaction is being observed and evaluated in some manner. To exacerbate the problem, the student has been hearing or watching tapes of Carl Rogers, Albert Ellis, Fritz Perls, or some other well-known therapists, as they exhibit their "greatest moments" in counseling. This is combined with faculty contentions about how to do all the "right things" in therapy, thus making a student feel completely inadequate. Rarely does the student hear about all the mistakes that are made in therapy by everyone: great and not-so-great therapists. Further, in some cases it may have been a long time since the supervising faculty member has actually seen a client and he or she may be out of touch with doing therapy on a regular basis. Of all the psychologists interviewed, only one stated that his first supervisor discussed with him his own initial reactions to therapy and some of his biggest blunders. The student's reaction was one of relief. Most of the psychologists stated they would have enjoyed that type of information.

The other major point, which is highly related to what we just described, is that most of the psychologists had an assumption that they should be perfect therapists from the start. With that assumption, one can only get worse and not better. Based on these two observations, the recommendation would be twofold:

1. Openly discuss your fears with your supervisor and solicit initial reactions to mistakes made while he or she was a beginning therapist. Hopefully your supervisor will be open enough to share these with you.

2. Constantly remind yourself that you are a therapist in training and are supposed to make mistakes. The odds are that this will result in you being you less defensive and more open to admitting to mistakes. This is the first and most important step in learning about helping others.

One of the problems noted by several of the psychologists was their reaction to having their supervisor begin to treat them as clients by probing into their feelings and personal thoughts. Quite often, supervisors do attempt to help their students become better therapists by attempting to bring out personal conflicts that may be hindering the student from helping a client. This is a necessary skill, which students will have to learn and be able to do on their own if they are to become effective clinicians. For example, a therapist who is going through a divorce who sees a client who is considering a divorce must be aware of his or her own biases in order to avoid leading the client in a direction in conflict with the client's values and preferences. This is not an easy task, and one may need help initially (from one's supervisor) to develop the skill of internal questioning. In fact, a student initiating such self-probing questions about such a bias is highly regarded by most supervisors. However, the fault-admitting process is a far cry from the other roles the student plays in graduate school, and most feel uneasy about the situation. This may be especially threatening as the student is disclosing these faults or mistakes to the same person who is also evaluating them. The best way to deal with this problem is to openly discuss it with the supervisor. One also has to be clear that there is a distinction between supervision and therapy, although as already alluded to, there is sometimes a fine line between the two. In choosing a therapy supervisor (if the choice is yours to be made), be clear about this from the beginning with your supervisor. An expectation may exist that students need this type of supervision, even though they may have no interest in being a "quasi-client" of the faculty member. In a reasonable situation, students could decline such an arrangement if they were uncomfortable. However, not all training requirements are reasonable. If you have no choice then you have to adopt the role that is expected in the training climate. As mentioned earlier, by Celani (1976) found that students learned to role-play and display behavior that was accepted and reinforced by the faculty because independent thinking and challenging the status quo were severely punished.

Finally, when a student favors one particular theoretical orientation to counseling and has an advisor who favors another, there are usually some conflicts. Some supervisors are open to different orientations; others are not. The same is true for students. Most of the psychologists interviewed believed that students could only benefit from learning about other approaches to therapy. Most found that only after a long period from when the student has obtained the degree does the person, as a professional psychologist, find the approach (usually a combination of several different orientations) that fits his or her personality and is effective for the client population with which the professional is working. Usually when you ask a supervisor to supervise you with an orientation that is different from his or her usual style, it is similar to asking a football coach known for his rushing game to coach you on passing. This is not an effective learning situation, and it is unclear why the supervisor would agree to such an arrangement. In short, the reader should try to ascertain what a supervisor has to offer and whether or not these are skills the student would like in a therapeutic repertoire. Do not try to talk the supervisor out of his or her orientation and demonstrate to them why your ideas are better. Even if supervisors are wrong and utilize procedures that have no documented benefit (e.g., we have known supervisors who interpreted the Bender–Gestalt as a projective test), try to learn what the professors have to offer, and reject what is not useful at a later date.

## ABUSE OF POWER

Please recall the early portions of this chapter where we focused on the fact that students have little power. In departments of psychology where professors are the gatekeepers for entry into the profession, a vastly disproportionate amount of power is in their hands. Individually most faculty members are nice, reasonable, and likable people. However, there is something about the dynamics of the group that inclines them to be prone to abuse the power of their faculty status. The dynamics are similar to those in the well-known prison study conducted at Stanford University (Haney & Zimbardo, 1998). In this experiment, undergraduate college students took either the role of prisoner or that of guard. The experiment had to be stopped prematurely because of the danger that emerged. Haney and Zimbardo (1998) suggested that their study represented an experimental demonstration of the extraordinary power of institutional environments to influence those who passed through them. Unfortunately, students are usually the losers in academic politics. Put another way, "Politics rolls downhill."

Departments of psychology and the American Psychological Association do give "lip service" to the need to treat students with dignity and respect. Resolutions passed at the National Conference on Graduate Education in Psychology (APA, 1987) attest to this being a paramount responsibility:

> Within graduate programs, quality assurance standards should be established and maintained with respect to the quality of academic life for students and faculty. In order to promote quality of academic life, psychologists should act with due regards

for the needs, special competencies, and obligations of their colleagues and students. (p. 1075)

The resolutions adopted by the conference are definitive in stating that the responsibility for providing appropriate socialization experiences resides with individual faculty, programs, departments, and schools, and the national APA organization. Faculty are key to the process because they are in close contact with students and are directly involved in issues of work relationships, supervision, complex role relationships, grievances, and so on and because they are the main role models for students and are the conveyers of norms, values, and beliefs of the discipline. (p. 1081)

Grievance procedures that recognize the status and power differences between faculty and students should be established within each department or school to resolve conflicts. A departmental ombudsman is another effective means to protect the rights of graduate students and faculty members. (p. 1082)

It is inspiring to read these resolutions drafted by a distinguished panel of academics and APA staff. Unfortunately, when it comes down to individual situations, we believe, as our colleague Allen Hess says, "Guidelines like this are carved in Jello." They do not have to be followed. If they were, students would have a different experience in their training.

In general, we do not believe that faculty members police themselves well. If they did, there would be no instances of faculty having sexual relationships with graduate students, of professors claiming first authorship of a publication for which graduate students rightfully deserved that honor and credit, of students painting the house or cutting the lawn of their major professor, and of students discharged from a graduate program without cause. In an important paper, Biaggio, Duffy, and Staffelbach (1998) presented obstacles to addressing professional misconduct by practicing psychologists. These reasons generalize well for psychology faculty and include: (a) loyalty to colleagues and institutions (e.g., "I can't turn in my colleague"); (b) personal costs or repercussions (e.g., whistle-blowers usually receive painful backlash); and (c) a misunderstanding or lack of information about ethics or conduct (e.g., "This is how graduate students have always been treated. In fact this is how I was treated.").

The question then becomes: What's a student to do? We urge students to become acutely aware of the politics that exist in their training site. They must then respond in a manner that reduces the likelihood that they will get caught up in political battles. We have known colleagues who were described as "low-key" or "faded into the woodwork" while in graduate school. Although they were not considered the "stars of the program," they had minimal disruption and upheaval in their lives, received their doctorates, and went on to have productive careers. The interpersonal role-playing skills described by Celani (1976) served them well in achieving their long-term goal of obtaining the doctorate.

If a student does get caught in a political battle, or feels abused in some manner, we suggest following departmental guidelines that have been developed for resolving such conflicts. Most likely this means attempting to resolve the issue directly with the individual faculty member. If this does not work, the next step may be to go to the director of the program or the chair of the department to try to enlist help. Please understand that these people are unlikely to take your side unless there is a blatant abuse of power that can be documented, preferably with witnesses. Further, understand if you become a whistle-blower, you are likely to experience a backlash and viewed as a disgruntled, inadequate student.

If the abuses become unbearable, or if a student is threatened with termination from the training program, as a last resort we strongly recommend considering consultation with an attorney regarding student rights. It is our contention that most departments of psychology treat the world as their own little fiefdom, where rules of due process, employment law, discrimination, or harassment do not apply. However, just because one is a student does not mean that one's civil rights are sacrificed. Although no body of scientific literature exists to demonstrate who will be a good (or even adequate) psychologist, students are often terminated from programs on the grounds of not having what it takes to be a good clinician. Note the example at the beginning of this chapter of the student who was asked to leave the program for this reason. After consulting with an attorney and following his counsel, the student was reinstated and went on to be a successful clinician.

Although we do not advocate the filing of frivolous civil lawsuits, or threatening people with "I'll call my attorney," we do believe, as an extreme last resort, that students can consider this as an option. Individuals who go through civil lawsuits understand that it is a long, tedious, and often gut-wrenching process. There is a case on record in which the student successfully sued a Department of Psychology for wrongfully being terminated from her graduate studies. From the *Daily Record* (6/10/96 and found at http://www.fac.org/legal/fawatch/lw61896.htm), we quote:

> A jury awarded a former university psychology graduate student $600,000 in damages for her termination from the clinical/community psychology program. The defendant-professors claimed she was terminated for "poor professional judgment and lack of professional responsibility." However, the jury found her explanation more credible, finding that she was terminated after she spoke out against racist and sexist actions on the part of certain faculty members. Her attorney stated: "The verdict really stands up for the First Amendment. It's a verdict for all students who push the edges of the status quo."

It should be pointed out that this is an extremely large award, and we do not advocate this as a method to "get rich quick." This is especially the case after considering attorney fees, court costs, and the emotional turmoil associated with the tort system. However, graduate students, like the rest of the citizenry, do not abdicate their civil rights when they agree to pursue an advanced degree.

In balance, graduate education can be exciting and rewarding, and can lead to a great deal of personal growth. Working with clients and finding out that you have the skills to help people change their lives for the better, analyzing data from your research and discovering that the results will help advance an area of study, and making a presentation at a regional convention and being well received can all be exhilarating. Relationships with your classmates may develop into strong friendships for life, similar to those bonds forged by veterans who fought in battle together overseas or by individuals who have survived a natural disaster together.

This chapter has highlighted some of the political aspects of the graduate training process—that is, those aspects of the experience not traditionally considered as part of the learning process necessary to become a professional psychologist. Celani (1982) pointed out, "There is a potential, because of the loose structure and large interpersonal component, to succeed or fail independently of the academic curriculum." By changing one's expectations and understanding the lack of a meaningful power base, we believe students can avoid many of the pitfalls and much of the disillusion that often accompanies the pursuit of an advanced graduate degree in psychology.

## ACKNOWLEDGMENT

The authors thank Allen Hess for his excellent feedback on an earlier version of this chapter.

## REFERENCES

Abramson, L., Seligman, M., & Teasdale, J. (1978). Learned helplessness in humans. Critique and reformulation. *Journal of Abnormal Psychology, 87*, 49–4.

American Psychological Association. (1987). Resolutions approved by the National Conference on Graduate Education in Psychology. *American Psychologist, 42*, 1070–1085.

Anker, J. (1984). A profile of training in clinical psychology. In T. Peake & R. Archer (Eds.), *Clinical training in psychotherapy* (pp. 105–116). New York: Haworth Press.

Biaggio, M., Duffy, R., & Staffelbach, D. (1998). Obstacles to overcoming professional misconduct. *Clinical Psychology Review, 18*, 273–285.

Boice, R., & Myers, P. (1987). Which setting is happier, academe or private practice? *Professional psychology: Research and practice, 18*, 526–529.

Celani, D. (1976). The acquisition of interpersonal role playing skills as a consequence of the graduate experience in clinical psychology. *Clinical Psychologist, 29*, 4–7.

Celani, D. (1982). A family model as applied to the graduate experience. *Vermont Psychologist, 7*, 9–14.

Dammeyer, M., & Nunez, N. (1999). Anxiety and depression among law students: Current knowledge and future directions. *Law and Human Behavior, 23*, 55–73.

Dixon, B. (1973). *What is science for?* New York: Harper & Row.

Gurin, G., & Gurin, P. (1976). Expectancy theory in the study of poverty. *Journal of Social Issues, 26*, 83–104.

Hall, S. (1998, November 29). Lethal chemistry at Harvard. *New York Times Magazine,* pp. 120–128.

Halonen, J., & Young, R. (1999). Is that all there is? *Contemporary Psychology, 44*, 233–235.

Haney, L., & Zimbardo, P. (1998). The past and future of U.S. prison policy: Twenty-five years after the Stanford prison experiment. *American Psychologist, 53*, 709–727.

Mahoney, M. (1976). *Scientist as subject.* Cambridge, MA: Ballinger.

Pruitt, D. (1976). Power and bargaining. In B. Seidenberg & H. Snodowsky (Eds.), *Social psychology: An introduction* (pp. 343–375). New York: Free Press.

Salancik, G. (1987). Power and politics in academic departments. In M. Zanna & J. Darley (Eds.), *The compleat academic* (pp. 61–84). Mahwah, NJ: Lawrence Erlbaum Associates.

Seligman, M. (1975). *Helplessness: On depression, development and death.* San Francisco: Freeman.

Strickland, B., & Janoff-Bulman, R. (1980). Expectancies and attributions: Implications for community mental health. In M. Gibbs, J. Lachmeyer, & J. Sigal (Eds.), *Community psychology: Theoretical and empirical approaches* (pp. 97–119). New York: Gardiner.

Sue, S., & Zane, N. (1980). Learned helplessness theory and community psychology. In M. Gibbs, J. Lachmeyer, & J. Sigal (Eds.), *Community psychology: Theoretical and empirical approaches* (pp. 121–143). New York: Gardiner.

Walfish, S., Stenmark, D., Shealy, J. S., & Shealy, S. (1989). Reasons why applicants select clinical psychology graduate programs. *Professional Psychology: Research and Practice, 20*, 350–354.

Zanna, M., & Darley, J. (1987). *The compleat academic.* Mahwah, NJ: Lawrence Erlbaum Associates.

# 8

# Students and Faculty:
# The Growth of Relationships

*Allen K. Hess*

*William I. Sauser, Jr.*

Perhaps no experience can lead to a greater understanding of someone than to know that person's perspective—and few roles are as hard to understand for a student as the role of professor. The graduate student–professor relationship can be characterized as an "up–down" relationship, in which one person is a subordinate and the other a "superior" or superordinate. Each appears at times to perceive the other as more mythical than real. This chapter describes the characteristics of the relationship, beginning with the myths or initial expectations the parties bring to the relationship, which are illustrated by actual case examples. Definitions of the roles both parties enact are followed by a brief description of the student–major professor relationship (dealt with in detail by O'Neil and Wrightsman in their chapter later in this section). Effective and ineffective student behaviors are then presented with the intention of guiding the student to a more enriching graduate school experience. The chapter concludes with a discussion of "mentoring" as an integrating developmental concept.

## MYTHS AND MORALS REGARDING INITIAL EXPECTATIONS

### The Myth of Unlimited Faculty Time

Among the many expectations students bring to graduate school is the belief that faculty time is virtually unlimited and flexible. Appointments are seen as merely a "one-down" maneuver whereby faculty show students how important faculty are. However, manuscript writing and revision, manuscript reviewing, grant writing, preparing for and attending university and departmental committee meetings, working with professional societies and state licensing boards, developing practicum and assistantship positions, reviewing theses and dissertations, and planning syllabi and curricula are demands on professors' time that often are unrecognized by students. Only the 5 to 12 hours per week in class contact hours and the few standing and scheduled office hours are observed by most new students. Thus they are not aware that faculty members have much of their time committed to the "low-profile" maintenance activities just listed. The following case illustrates the problems that can result from an acceptance of the myth of unlimited faculty time. (The cases are composites, which, while actual, are altered enough to obscure identifying features of the persons described.)

*Case A.* A colleague of ours received a research proposal at 1:00 p.m. for a meeting to be held at 3:00 p.m. that same day. The meeting time had not been revealed to the committee members by the student before 1:00 p.m. that day. Furthermore, the chair of the committee had not laid eyes on the proposal before, nor had she known of the meeting beforehand. She was extremely embarrassed when an irate committee member called her to complain. Because the committee members had not been given sufficient time to prepare, the meeting was unproductive, and the student's research project was considerably delayed.

*Moral.* Faculty time needs to be scheduled. Proposals and arrangements for thesis and dissertation meetings must be approved by one's committee chair in advance. Whenever possible, at least 1 to 2 weeks of lead time should be given for faculty to read proposals. Although this example concerns research proposal meetings, the principle should be generalized to other student–faculty meetings.

## The Myth of Faculty Omniscience

Because most faculty members possess doctoral degrees, it is often assumed by students that they are omniscient. Thus graduate students sometimes fail to provide faculty with important information, acting on the belief that faculty are fully informed on all topics. This assumption can lead to trouble, as the following case illustrates.

*Case B.* Ben avoided his faculty advisor during a trying personal crisis. When it became evident that Ben was about to drop out of school, his advisor called him in for a talk. Ben was surprised when he found out that the advisor, although recognizing that Ben was upset, did not know that Ben had fallen for a campus beauty queen. Ben had unsuccessfully courted her and accumulated a large emotional and financial debt while bankrupting his study time. Ben assumed that his advisor knew of this torrid—although unilateral—romance, because many students and a few faculty were aware of his troubles.

Ben was counseled about setting priorities (getting work done on time, being aware of the "games" played in his relationship), and personal counseling was suggested to deal with his absorption in the affair. Fortunately, Ben responded well to this advice and his performance in graduate school improved.

*Moral.* You need to select a faculty advisor carefully, with the feeling that the faculty member can be trusted. This feeling can range from relying on the professor to prepare you academically (e.g., teaching necessary research skills, suggesting courses to be taken, and guiding you to appropriate practicum experiences) to trusting him or her regarding personal development issues (such as feeling prepared to do psychotherapy) and providing feedback on how your style comes across to others.

## The Myth of Fixed Student Aims

One set of assumptions faculty may have is that the goals a student expresses on entering graduate school remain fixed throughout that student's educational program. The student may initially express an interest in research or perhaps state an interest in securing the doctorate merely as a license to go into private practice. In fact, such assumptions are often mistaken when first made, or soon become inaccurate due to shifting student interests. Graduate school is a setting that should be used by the student to experience various aspects of both theories and professional activities. A student may have gained experience in research as an undergraduate or expressed such interest to enhance the chances of getting into graduate school. A professor, assuming strong internalized interests, may wind up in conflict over the student's dilatory and "irresponsible" behavior in completing research tasks. In fact, the student's aims could have simply shifted as diverse interests were developed. Professors often lose track of the developmental nature of the rich and sometimes overwhelming set of experiences graduate school provides. They might even feel betrayed when a student's interests shift from laboratory research on phobias, for example, to the career goal of using one's degree to help formulate public policy concerning workplace safety. Students need to understand professors' assumptions and expectations, tactfully clarifying them when necessary and even switching major professors when adjustments by both parties cannot be achieved.

*Case C.* David entered graduate school wanting to be a practicing clinician. He resisted involving himself in research. Faculty views of him as a potential researcher were initially strong but ebbed after a year of fruitless efforts to involve him in research other than standard thesis requirements. However, David's career goals shifted after publishing a few manuscripts as a result of his assistantship and getting his expenses partially sponsored to present papers at conventions. Faculty members continued to see him as wishing to be a practicing clinician, although he had shifted toward a clinical research career goal. When a valued research assistantship position became available David was not considered for it, because he had not made his change of interests known to the faculty.

*Moral.* Graduate school is an intensive learning setting offering exposure to a variety of experiences. It is not surprising that students—typically young adults—may have ephemeral career goals. Faculty need to recognize this, but can do so only when students are directly involved with them and inform faculty about their changing interests.

## ROLES OF STUDENTS AND FACULTY

Role theory can shed some light on the kinds of conflicts that can arise between students and faculty, as typified in the cases just described. Students tend to be more successful when their role expectations match those of their professors (Descutner & Thelen, 1989) and when role conflicts are minimized. Role conflicts can arise from three basic sources: intrarole conflict, interrole–intrapersonal conflict, and interrole–interpersonal conflict.

## Intrarole Conflict

The first type of conflict occurs when a role—for example, that of student—makes multiple demands on the role incumbent. The "good student" may have several assignments competing for a limited amount of time. Due to the ambiguity of the student role and the ambiguity of the evaluation processes in graduate school, it is hard for students to gauge how best to invest their time. Is it equally important to complete the assignments for professors A and B, or will B take the assignment a bit late so the student can do the kind of quality work that professor A demands? These time management problems can be troublesome for students, as the faculty survey we present later illustrates. Managing intrarole conflict needs to be mastered.

Faculty, too, have considerable intrarole conflict. Suffice it to say that they produce a complex product, a professional scientific psychologist, the quality of which is grossly and ambiguously measured, by a process that is shrouded in uncertainties and bereft of validation. Thus faculty may find frustration inherent in completing the ostensibly simple task of producing an educated person.

## Interrole–Intrapersonal Conflict

This type of conflict is, in a sense, a variation of the first one. Essentially, the role of graduate student incorporates a number of subsidiary roles. In addition, several roles may compete with the graduate student role.

The student is called on to be a student, a teacher, a researcher, a clinician, and in some cases an undergraduate advisor. Performance in each of these roles is subject to faculty evaluations. In the case of competing roles, the student may be a son or daughter, a spouse, a parent, a diabetic, a Scout leader, a tenant, a would-be basketball star, or a marathon runner. These roles each demand time, and tension results when the demands conflict.

Interestingly, students too often see their professors as faculty only, and are not sensitive to other aspects of professors' lives. At the supermarket, the student encountering a faculty member may be surprised because the role of shopper may be incongruent with the image of a faculty member as a mythical figure. The same competing roles that students face also confront the faculty. The experiential anguish of a faculty member in the fifth year of a tenure-track position, with impending promotion and tenure votes, easily matches the student's angst before dissertation orals.

Students and faculty often lose sight of the other's complex roles. Faculty can forget the student's anxieties; in some of the more sadistic cases, faculty may even have internalized an aggressive role, with the "trial-by-fire," "I had it rough so you must be roughened up to be a member of my club" approach. A century of learning theory and research supports the dictum that we learn best by positive reinforcement. Yet well-published, well-known and experienced professors continue to wield the punishment stick as if it were a job perquisite. To counteract this loss of sensitivity, the first author enrolls in a course every year or two, in part to continue skill development but more to stay in touch with how it feels to be on the other side of the lectern. (Statistics, art, and guitar classes help keep him humble!) Perhaps knowledge of each other's position is a particular form of empathy. It can certainly foster communication and cooperation between faculty and students.

## Interrole-Interpersonal Conflict

The third type of conflict refers to the nature of dynamics or tensions inherent in the graduate student–professor relationship. One person is examiner, the other examined. One demands work, the other reacts and often resists. One grants assistantships and work assignments, writes letters of recommendations, signs off on theses, dissertations, and clinical reports, and controls other reward structures; the other intensely feels the need for these experiences and rewards. One controls the gates to the promised land of the doctorate; the other may be a needed research laborer and disciple for disseminating a cherished theory. One is a source of information, inspiration, and frustration regarding research, financial aid, clinical skills, and career counseling; the other is a neophyte needing guidance and support. These dualities lead to tension and provoke reactions of dependence, disillusionment, rebellion, and collaboration—a process outlined later in the section on developmental stages of the graduate student–faculty relationship.

When you realize the multiple roles of faculty, you can better sense the various ways that faculty can serve you. Nonetheless, if you determine that a faculty advisor or major professor is not serving your interests, you should discuss your concerns about the relationship. This confrontation may be difficult for you. If the advisor is unable to discuss the relationship in a nondefensive and nonthreatening way, then you need to consider discussing the mismatching of you and the professor with the department chair or program director to effect a switch to another advisor. Also, the dean, department head, and program head need to know if there is a faculty member who has difficulties with a number of students. After all, if faculty members do not wish to help students, they are in the wrong line of work. There are consequences for you that should be considered carefully in confronting a poorly functioning advising relationship, but failing to confront the relationship can be devastating to your graduate career.

The question, then, is how to relate to faculty so as to get your legitimate needs met. Some faculty are more helpful in some ways than in other ways (Cesa & Fraser, 1989; Cronan-Hillix, Gensheimer, Cronan-Hillix, & Davidson, 1986); do not expect to get most or all needs met by a single professor. Broaching a topic (e.g. financial aid) with a faculty member allows you to evaluate the professor's helpfulness in a particular domain. If a faculty member fails to provide help with emotional, research, clinical, career planning, job market, or other problems, you are well advised to question why you are working with that professor. On the other hand, the key word here is *help*. As shown in the survey presented later, various student requests are seen as manipulative, dependent, and irresponsible. Judgment is required to determine which are legitimate requests and which faculty would be most appropriate sources of support. This judgment is shrouded with a number of concerns and is not simple. Consider which faculty members seem to "fit" best with your abilities and personality style. Which faculty seem to move student-peers with similar qualities toward their goals? By the time you have been in the program for a few terms, you should have had exposure to various faculty members in class, seminars, colloquia, in research team meetings, or informal settings. These encounters should serve as a basis for you to determine "fit" with the faculty.

# DEVELOPMENTAL STAGES OF THE GRADUATE STUDENT–FACULTY RELATIONSHIP

Drawing on the work of Bennis and Shepard (1956), Reid (1965) proposed a developmental theory of small group functioning and leadership. We now consider the implications of Reid's theory for an understanding of the graduate student–faculty relationship (Hess, 1987). Basically, Reid's theory suggests that the relationship progresses through four stages much like those in the child–parent relationship: dependence, disillusionment, rebellion, and collaboration.

## Dependence

When beginning a program, the new graduate student typically has strong dependency feelings. Graduate school, although new and exciting, differs enough from undergraduate work to produce uncertainty about which courses to take, which topics to research, and how to interact with faculty members. During this period the typical student expects a lot of guidance from the faculty. Indeed, it is during this period that many graduate students operate as though the myths of unlimited faculty time and knowledge are actually true. Some faculty members enjoy perpetuating these myths, thus extending the period of initial dependence. However, most professors expect their students to make at least some decisions on coursework and research topics on their own. Rather than guiding their students every step of the way, some professors demand that their students take much of the responsibility for their own graduate education, but nonetheless reserve veto rights if they disagree with a student's choices.

We would be remiss if we did not mention Celani's (1976) trenchant article. He described the initial graduate year as one in which the student needs to act "hyperadequately." This seems contradictory—being dependent and hyperadequate—and results in a "double-bind" conflict that can impair the student. The deceitful or sadistic advisor acknowledges the conflict as if sympathetic but then torques up the intensity of the conflict. The naive or conflict-avoidant advisor simply does not deal with the student's conflicts. The student should then either work with supportive faculty in addition to his or her advisor, or switch advisors. There are good advisors who can help the student negotiate conflicts so there is no reason for the student to remain with sadistic, deceitful, naive, or conflict-avoidant and nonsupportive faculty.

During undergraduate education a student can hide in larger classes and by not closely interacting with faculty. However, graduate training involves close faculty–student interactions. Professors pursuing grants, a publication career, and high citation rankings (their works cited by others) can demand adulation that takes the form of the student acting as if "sitting at the feet of Giants," hearing Olympian pronouncements. Celani (1976) describes the resulting "role playing" extorted from attentive graduate students. The student thinks of graduate school as a place of learning and questioning. However, Celani described a chilling and all too common incident characterizing some graduate schools:

> A brash and impulsive student directly challenged the wisdom of the department's prelim test policy during an open meeting. An ominous silence fell over the room as the chairman formally called upon each faculty member, by title, and asked him to speak on the issue. On cue, each solemnly spoke about his concerns with the steadily-lowering quality of student performance,... some spoke about the ever-increasing size of the applicant pool ... [and] ... the need to concentrate faculty effort on students who really

*wanted* to be in graduate school to learn. The original question remained unanswered and waves of anxiety wafted through the students. Anxiety replaced bravado. The student was moved to speak again but this time he mentioned how his previous statements might have been in error and based on his ineptitude and inexperience. The graduate students adapted more facilely to the role-playing prescribed by the meeting. Subsequently students developed dormant interests. A professor with photographic interests found himself cornered in the darkroom by several first year students with their Leica cameras; the faculty pool player found a few budding first year hustlers; and one faculty who casually mentioned clearing some wooded area in his yard found several former city boys metamorphosized into neophyte Paul Bunyans. (Celani, 1976, p. 4)

Graduate students are faced with the pressures to emulate role models, which in many cases leads to learning skills essential to becoming excellent psychologists. They also may have to learn obsequiousness, which may take a tremendous toll on one's self-regard.

### Disillusionment

Faced with the hard reality that the earlier described myths of unlimited faculty time and of faculty omniscience are untrue, many graduate students go through a period of disillusionment. They question the faculty's competence, the program's quality, their decision to attend graduate school, and even their own sanity (Sauser, 1999)! They experience the feelings of inadequacy, frustration, strain, and hostility that often accompany unanticipated freedom and its associated demands for responsible behavior. It is no wonder that Reid (1965) characterized the work typically produced during this period as uncreative and nonrewarding. "Discussion tends to be disjointed and unsatisfying; morale is low; communication is difficult" (p. 329). Some students resign from graduate school during this difficult period; most survive it, although bearing scar tissue, and move on to the next stage.

### Rebellion

The typical reaction of the graduate student who survives the period of disillusionment is to resolve, "I'll make it on my own." Faced with the perception of faculty as uncaring and incompetent, the student decides to make things happen, to take control. Reid (1965) characterized behavior during this period as "almost manic" (p. 329), and suggested that advice from faculty members is often ignored during this phase. The student by now has firmly rejected the myths of unlimited faculty time and knowledge and indeed may have begun to believe that the faculty members possess no time or knowledge! The graduate student fixated in this stage typically goes about setting up his or her own plan of study, research proposal, and practicum experience with little to no regard for faculty input or feedback. Students run the risk of getting into trouble during this stage; because they may violate rules and norms they may elicit sanctions from their professors. Reid suggested that, fortunately, most students eventually run out of steam during this stage, and choose to stop fighting against their professors. During his third year, one student took three courses, taught three courses, published three journal articles, passed the doctoral written examinations, held three part-time jobs, and even managed to sleep 4 hours per night. At the end of the semester, he indulged in "Morita therapy," remaining in bed for several days in silence. Subsequently he modulated his activities, began to feel competent and independent, then moved to the fourth stage. Secure in their independence, successful students move into the fourth stage.

### Collaboration

Reid (1965) compared this final, mature stage of the graduate student–faculty relationship with the pleasurable feelings experienced by adults who, after making it on their own, are now able to interact with their parents on an equal footing. This period, according to Reid (1965), "has the greatest potentiality for creative and constructive work" (p. 330). Students in this stage are able to accept and take advantage of the faculty's knowledge and expertise, while drawing on their own strengths. During this phase, according to Reid, "ideas are weighed more carefully than before and honesty is more common. Discussion tends to be on a deeper, more personal level, and morale is high. Smooth functioning and a high rate of productivity are often the result" (p. 330).

Celani's view was less sanguine. He wrote of "joining the club," of "survivors [of the first three stages being] ... no longer ridiculed or criticized for their opinions, particularly in areas that they had researched." If Celani was describing a simple rite of passage, the description was innocent. But he seemed to describe the internalization by the new PhD of the same sadistic bent suffered during the person's own graduate career when he wrote of a "sense of excitement and anticipation that the cycle would begin anew—but now it was our turn!" (p. 7). Students need to be careful to avoid falling victim to such professors described by Celani and to avoid internalizing and transmitting this pathogenic attitude.

Reid recognized, as do we, that there are tremendous individual differences in progression through these stages. Some students may skip certain stages altogether; others may become fixated in an unproductive stage and never reach the point of collaboration. For some students the progression is irregular—they may move back and forth through the stages over time. Our point in presenting this developmental perspective is to foster some understanding of the typical progression of relations between graduate students and faculty. Although a few professors may enjoy working with dependent, disillusioned, or rebellious students, by far the majority prefer students in the collaborative stage! Given an understanding of this typical developmental sequence, we hope you will minimize the time you spend in the first three stages and strive to acquire a mature, collaborative style of interacting with your professors.

### A Situational Model

Hershey and Blanchard (1988) provided a *situational leadership* model that major professors might find useful as they seek to guide their students through these stages toward maturity. Their model, based on varying levels of guidance and support necessary for each stage of maturation, has some useful implications for consideration when working with graduate students in the four stages of growth described above.

For students in the least mature of Hershey and Blanchard's four stages—those who are less able and who are unwilling or insecure—they suggested a "telling" approach: Provide specific instructions and closely supervise performance. As students become more confident, the professor shifts to a "selling" style, explaining decisions and providing opportunity for clarification. As ability increases to match confidence, the "participating" style—sharing ideas and facilitating decision making—becomes most appropriate. Those mature students who are both fully able and confident (and thus ready to prove themselves at the dissertation stage) are ready for a "delegating" style of leadership from the major professor. At this point, the professor may choose to turn over to the mature student responsibility for decisions and implementation. This is the level of maturity expected of those students who are ready to graduate with their doctoral diplomas in hand.

The stage models we are presenting are helpful heuristic guides but not inevitable determined sequences. A student may be more advanced in one set of skills than another. He or she may be facile in research yet in need of hand-holding in psychodiagnostic work, or vice versa. Moreover we suggest continual "pulse-taking" because students experience ebbs and flows as they mature and as they progress though graduate school and beyond.

Our readers might wish to gauge their own levels of maturity using Reid's (1965) and Hershey and Blanchard's (1988) stages, then determine whether the professor's style of leadership is optimal for that stage. Reflection on the style displayed by the professor can also provide insight regarding the professor's view of the level of maturity of the student! Ideally, there would be a match between perceptions held by the student and the professor; a mismatch will likely produce discomfort in the relationship.

## WHAT TO DO AND WHAT NOT TO DO

Now that we have presented some theory regarding graduate student–faculty relationships, we would like to discuss the results of an empirical study we conducted for this chapter. In order to find out the student behaviors that impress faculty members—either positively or negatively—we surveyed 17 graduate faculty.[1] Our brief, open-ended questionnaire contained just two items.

1. What actions should a graduate student take in order to gain favor with you? What actions typify the good graduate student from your point of view?

2. What actions on the part of the graduate student would cause him or her to lose favor with you? What actions typify the poor graduate student from your viewpoint?

Our content analysis of the responses revealed a number of common themes. These themes and some of the behaviors are displayed in Tables 8.1 and 8.2. It is difficult to behave "perfectly" in graduate school, and there may be differences among programs in how faculty evaluate student behavior. Nonetheless, we present these behaviors so graduate students can evaluate their own behavior and perhaps anticipate the effect of their behavior on faculty. The behaviors in Table 8.1 will most likely have a positive effect; the student interested in minimizing faculty disapproval will attend to Table 8.2.

Although our study is limited in terms of the subject sample, it is striking how the general findings are confirmed by the results of other studies. Bloom and Bell (1979) informally sur-

[1]We wish to acknowledge our faculty colleagues in the Department of Psychology and the Department of Counselor Education at Auburn University who completed our brief survey questionnaire: Phil Benson, Joe Buckhalt, Barry Burkhart, Keith Byrd, Bob Felner, Sam Green, Mal Gynther, Verne Irvine, Crystal Kelley, Phil Lewis, Gene Meadows, John Moracco, Randy Pipes, Janet Proctor, and Warren Valine.

## TABLE 8.1
### If You Want to Impress the Faculty ...

1. Do actively participate in class, prepare for class, get to class on time, look alert, ask questions, show that you have thought about the material; take personal responsibility for making the class a good one.

2. Do demonstrate initiative and independence; establish and accomplish personal goals; make suggestions for self-improvement; take responsibility for your progress through the program; actively seek knowledge; demonstrate the attitude, "I'm here to gain all I can."

3. Do develop professional commitment; present papers at conferences; attend conventions; join professional organizations; be aware of professional issues.

4. Do produce high-quality work; go beyond the minimal requirements; work for knowledge attainment rather than simply for grades; read books and articles beyond those assigned; maintain professional standards on assistantship assignments.

5. Do use time well; complete tasks on or ahead of schedule; be on time and prepared for meetings; call ahead if you will be late or cannot keep an appointment; make appointments in advance; notify the professor when you must miss class or leave early.

6. Do communicate frequently, openly, and honestly; keep your professors informed regarding your progress; visit professors periodically; talk to professors outside of class; come to professors privately with complaints; openly disagree when necessary; give honest feedback about issues without personalizing, flattering, or blaming.

7. Do develop a learning relationship with professors; show interest and knowledge in the professor's research areas; be available to help with the professor's research and professional activities; show interest in the professor as a person.

8. Do demonstrate a breadth of intellectual interests; show respect for other professions and disciplines; consider the philosophical foundations of your own theoretical orientation; nurture an attitude of intellectual curiosity.

9. Do assess your own strengths and weaknesses and seek help when appropriate; maintain a reflective, studious, open-minded attitude; be open to career options; seek and use advice from professors.

10. Do develop technical skills; learn how to write well; know how to use the computer; express yourself well orally and in writing; produce publishable papers.

11. Do have an active interest in research; engage in designing and carrying out research projects; apply your knowledge in research activities; identify researchable questions; apply research findings in your practical work.

12. Do develop interpersonal skills and sensitivity; be polite, respectful, and sincere; treat support staff well; consider the feelings of others; dress appropriately; have a sense of humor.

13. Do become a good departmental citizen; attend colloquia; participate in departmental committees; volunteer for special assignments.

veyed 40 colleagues throughout the United States in order to define the behaviors distinguishing "superstar" psychology graduate students from their less notable counterparts. Five qualities emerged: (a) visibility—being physically present in the department, often after working hours; (b) hard working—the faculty actually saw them working hard; (c) reflection of program values—evidence of research and scholarly excellence, intellectual curiosity, and

## TABLE 8.2
### Unless You Want to Get into Trouble in Graduate School ...

1. Do not whine and complain. Do not present excuses for poor performance, for not taking a course, for not completing assignments, or for not knowing administrative deadlines and procedures; do not blame others; do not whine about workloads.

2. Do not be superficial in your knowledge or scholarship. Do not engage in research without proper background and literature review; do not ignore professional organizations and journals; do not use only secondary sources in papers, nor have weak bibliographies; do not disparage academic and scholastic standards.

3. Do not be evasive. Do not deny or avoid feedback; do not be defensive or unwilling to listen; do not engage in indirect communications, particularly with students and faculty about other students and faculty.

4. Do not be narrow, inflexible, or intolerant. Do not display lack of interest in the scientific and theoretical bases of psychology; do not avoid research or show contempt for experimentation; do not show interest only in private practice; do not be arrogant, dogmatic, or disrespectful regarding other professionals; do not convey the impression you believe other disciplines to be of inferior status.

5. Do not foment trouble. Do not be manipulative, phony, insincere, flattering, or obnoxious; do not gossip or belittle others; do not play faculty or students against each other; do not be insensitive with students, clients, or faculty; do not crusade for causes or subvert classes to gripe sessions; do not personalize or monopolize discussions; do not display ingratitude; do not get into fights with faculty.

6. Do not try to get by with the minimum in class; do not appear bored or lazy in class by asking no questions, failing to prepare, or making no effort to participate; do not display nonverbal cues of disinterest, such as yawning, sleeping, or reading a newspaper in class; do not make bad grades.

7. Do not avoid work; do not miss deadlines or turn in work that is incomplete; do not avoid your share of work on team assignments; do not choose courses on the basis of convenience only; do not avoid demanding courses.

8. Do not avoid faculty; do not go into hiding or act as if the professor will "bite" you; do not be unavailable when you are needed; do not make major decisions about your graduate training without consulting faculty.

9. Do not be unethical; do not engage in improper involvement with clients or students; do not cheat, plagiarize, lie, or be abusive of drugs or alcohol; do not engage in sexual activities that will adversely affect your professional functioning.

10. Do not waste time; do not miss appointments, come late, miss class, frequently reschedule appointments, or come to appointments unprepared; do not over commit time to inessential projects; do not schedule appointments that conflict with classes or other obligations.

11. Do not abuse book lending privileges; do not borrow too many books, nor fail to care for and promptly return books; do not mark in others' books.

12. Do not be overly demanding of the faculty; do not expect unreasonably quick reviews of theses, dissertations, or proposals; do not call at home unless you have been given permission or you have an emergency; do not make "last minute" demands.

13. Do not write poorly; do not use poor grammar; do not fail to proofread carefully.

breadth of interests; (d) professor attachment—working closely with one or two faculty members; and (e) the W factor—making faculty feel worthwhile and rewarded. Distinguishing the W factor from ingratiation is important for the student's self esteem and genuineness in the relationship. The W factor refers to interest in the faculty member as a person and the merits of that individual's work; ingratiation has as its primary focus the securing of favor, whether or not such favor is merited.

Robertson and Molloy (1981) used the Kelly repertory grid procedure to define the constructs used by two British tutors—a physicist and an engineer—in working with postgraduate students. The tutors used terms such as "gets on with others," "self-starter," "tries to impress," "socially cooperative," "willing to disagree," "brilliant," "can make choices," "can make (explicit) assumptions," "can analyze and synthesize," "can produce," "concentrates on aims, outcomes, solutions," "broad grasp of situations," "persistent," and "uses what is useful to solve problems" to describe effective students. The complete list of 19 bipolar constructs (p. 168) is consistent with our results and the list that Shakow (1947, 1969) presented.

Shakow (1947) listed 15 qualities important in selecting clinical students. These qualities are reflected in our survey. Shakow's (1969) list included: (a) superior resourcefulness and versatility; (b) "fresh and insatiable" curiosity; (c) "self-learner"; (d) interest in persons as individuals rather than as material for manipulation—a regard for the integrity of other persons; (e) insight into own personality characteristics and a sense of humor; (f) sensitivity to complexities of motivation; (g) tolerance, "unarrogance"; (h) ability to adopt a "therapeutic" attitude, ability to establish warm and effective relationships with others; (i) industry, methodical work habits and ability to tolerate pressure; (j) acceptance of responsibility; (k) tact and cooperativeness; (l) integrity, self-control, and stability; (m) discriminating sense of ethical values; (n) breadth of cultural background—"educated man"; and (o) deep interest in psychology, especially in its clinical aspects (p. 101).

The substance of the studies just presented should be clear to the reader.[2] It is useful at this point to take a broader perspective, and again view the student in relation to the faculty. Goplerud (1980) found that frequent faculty contacts in the first 10 weeks of the first-year student's program led to fewer intensely stressful events, fewer emotional and physical health problems, and greater general satisfaction on the part of students. Cumulative stress was reduced as faculty influence, number of faculty role models, and quality of relationship with the faculty advisor increased. The greater the number of role models, and the larger the amount of faculty influence, the fewer physical and emotional problems the students suffered. Goplerud pointed to the rewards and the feedback the faculty can offer as the key elements in stress reduction.

Hartnett (1976) asserted that respect and acceptance of the students by the faculty, and the degree of friendship and collegiality, rather than unapproachable one-up versus one-down-ness, is quite likely the most salient feature of the productive and favorable graduate school climate. Walfish, Stenmark, Shealy, and Shealy (1989) affirmed that the emotional atmosphere of a particular program plays an important part in student success and satisfaction. Key components of a healthy culture for success include shared activities, communica-

---

[2] These qualities resonate with the type of attributes that will help the assistant professor gain promotion and tenure, and, indeed, are virtues that will ensure success at every level and stage of one's career. It might be helpful for us all to reread this section every few years of our career.

tions about attitudes and values, mutual respect and concern, and acknowledgment of and responsiveness to individual differences. These are words that all programs subscribe to on paper, but are the behaviors and the emotional tone experienced by the students and faculty faithful to these admirable goals?

It should be noted that our results, along with those of the other studies just described, generally served to confirm our theoretical views. The "good" behaviors are those that would be associated with collaboration, the mature stage of the graduate student–faculty relationship described earlier. The unfavorable behaviors often typify dependence, disillusionment, or rebellion. Many of the negative behaviors can be recognized as reflecting a belief in the myths of unlimited faculty time and faculty omniscience.

## EFFECTIVE MENTORING

Having examined student myths about faculty, a role-conflict analysis, a developmental stage model, and specific behavioral "do's and don'ts" gathered in our survey and paralleling others' work, we conclude with the integrating concept of *mentoring*. This currently fashionable idea (Willis & Diebold, 1997) has some relevance to Reid's collaboration stage. The mentor serves as one's teacher, sponsor, advisor (Levinson, 1978), and as coach, trainer, role model, and developer of talent (Schein, 1978). Moreover, mentors provide knowledge, advice, challenge, and support in helping neophytes pursue full member status in some aspect of life such as career, social, or personal (Cronan-Hillix et al., 1986; Wrightsman, 1981). The relationship is characterized by mutuality, comprehensiveness, and congruence, which derive from role complement, respect, trust, consistency, informality, informational openness, optimal level of intimacy, frequent interaction, and "a larger perspective" (Wrightsman, 1981).

Actions that an effective mentor might take to prepare a student for an oral defense were discussed by Kuhlenschmidt (1992). Likewise, Taylor (1992) provided a practical approach for mentoring graduate students to improve their seminar presentations, whereas Blanton (1983) and Dillon and Malott (1981) examined effective mentoring in the supervision of theses and dissertations. Ethical issues in mentoring were addressed by Kitchener (1992), and Atkinson, Neville, and Casas (1991) and Bogat and Redner (1985) explored the effectiveness of mentorship with ethnic minorities and women, respectively, in their professional development as psychologists.

Green and McDade (1991) pointed out that mentoring, "whether informal or part of a planned effort" (p. 216), can be an excellent leadership development tool in educational environments. They noted:

> A mentor supports a protégé in a variety of ways: serving as sponsor and advocate, showing the more junior person the ropes and explaining the system, providing career counseling, and helping to develop a sense of confidence and competence. Good mentors provide feedback and actively coach the protégé, pointing out mistakes and suggesting improvements. (p. 216)

In our opinion, this mentor–protégé relationship characterizes the ideal student–faculty relationship (Carifio & Hess, 1987), one that results in interpersonal respect, professionalism, collegiality, and role fulfillment (O'Neil, 1981).

Beans (1999) suggested that informal mentor relationships are more enjoyable, support-ive, and accepted than structured mentoring. The faculty and students need to sift through to find the match that provides "good chemistry." Those informally mentored find they are visi-ble and have standing in the department, are buffered from adversity, are sponsored for ad-vancement, and earn more money than those formally mentored. However, there are gender differences that show men to benefit from both formal and informal mentoring, whereas women do not gain as much from formal mentoring. In a forced mentoring situation, the stu-dent might feel the weight of paternalism, the imposition of one more task and one more task-master, and another burden in a faculty–student (mis)match. Then, too, the mentor might not be ready for the student's progress and transitions and might feel unappreciated for the mentoring efforts. For successful mentoring, these factors need to be taken into consideration in appraising the mentoring relationship.

In a larger sense, the more that faculty and students follow the "do's and don't's" of Tables 8.1 and 8.2, the more each can be successfully involved in the fulfillment of the mid and early adulthood stages, respectively—and the more they can believe in each other, share dreams, and create space for each other to realize their dreams (Clawson, 1980).

## ACKNOWLEDGMENT

We thank Joe Buckhalt, Martin Diebold, Sid Hall, Kathryn D. Hess, and Rebecca and Rick Moffett for their comments on earlier drafts of this chapter.

## REFERENCES

Atkinson, D. R., Neville, H., & Casas, A. (1991). The mentorship of ethnic minorities in profes-sional psychology. *Professional Psychology: Research and Practice, 22,* 336–338.

Beans, B. (1999, November). Proteges want mentors "sympatico," not paternal. *American Psycho-logical Association Monitor, 30,* 35.

Bennis, W., & Shepard, H. (1956). A theory of group development. *Human Relations, 9,* 415–437.

Blanton, J. S. (1983). Midwifing the dissertation. *Teaching of Psychology, 10,* 74–77.

Bloom, L., & Bell, P. (1979). Making it in graduate school: Some reflections about the superstars. *Teaching of Psychology, 6,* 231–232.

Bogat, G. A., & Redner, R. L. (1985). How mentoring affects the professional development of women in psychology. *Professional Psychology: Research and Practice, 16,* 851–859.

Carifio, M. S., & Hess, A. K. (1987). Who is the ideal supervisor? *Professional Psychology: Re-search and Practice, 18,* 244–250.

Celani, D. P. (1976). The acquisition of interpersonal role playing skills as a consequence of the graduate experience in clinical psychology. *Clinical Psychologist, 9,* 4–5.

Cesa, I. L., & Fraser, S. C. (1989). A method for encouraging the development of good men-tor-protégé relationships. *Teaching of Psychology, 16,* 125–128.

Clawson, J. G. (1980). Mentoring in managerial careers. In C. B. Derr (Ed.), *Work, family and the career: New frontiers in theory and research* (pp. 144–165). New York: Praeger.

Cronan-Hillix, T., Gensheimer, L. K., Cronan-Hillix, W. A., & Davidson, W. S. (1986). Students' views of mentors in psychology graduate training. *Teaching of Psychology, 13,* 123–127.

Descutner, C. J., & Thelen, M. H. (1989). Graduate student and faculty perspectives about gradu-ate school. *Teaching of Psychology, 16,* 58–61.

Dillon, M. J., & Malott, R. W. (1981). Supervising masters theses and doctoral dissertations. *Teaching of Psychology, 8*, 195–202.

Goplerud, E. N. (1980). Social support and stress during the first year of graduate school. *Professional Psychology, 11*, 283–290.

Green, M. F., & McDade, S. A. (1991). *Investing in higher education: A handbook of leadership development.* Washington, DC: American Council on Education.

Hartnett, R. T. (1976). Environments for advanced learning. In J. Katz & R. T. Hartnett (Eds.), *Scholars in the making* (pp. 49–84). Cambridge, MA: Ballinger.

Hershey, P., & Blanchard, K. H. (1988). *Management of organizational behavior.* Englewood Cliffs, NJ: Prentice Hall.

Hess, A. K. (1987). Psychotherapy supervision: Stages, Buber, and a theory of relationship. *Professional Psychology: Research and Practice, 18*, 251–259.

Kitchener, K. S. (1992). Psychologist as teacher and mentor: Affirming ethical values throughout the curriculum. *Professional Psychology: Research and Practice, 23*, 190–195.

Kuhlenschmidt, S. L. (1992). Teaching students to manage the oral defense. *Teaching of Psychology, 19*, 86–90.

Levinson, D. (1978). *The seasons of a man's life.* New York: Knopf.

O'Neil, J. (1981, August). *Conceptual and operational definitions of mentoring.* Paper presented at the meeting of the American Psychological Association, Los Angeles.

Reid, C. H. (1965). The authority cycle in small group development. *Adult Leadership, 13*, 308–310, 329–331.

Robertson, I., & Molloy, L. (1981). An investigation of the constructs used by tutors to assess postgraduate students. *Studies in Higher Education, 6*, 163–168.

Sauser, W. I., Jr. (1999). Staying sane in an ever-changing world. In R. R. Sims & J. G. Veres, III (Eds.), *Keys to employee success in coming decades.* Westport, CT: Quorum.

Schein, E. (1978). *Career dynamics: Matching individual and organizational needs.* Reading, MA: Addison-Wesley.

Shakow, D. (1947). Recommended graduate training program in clinical psychology. *American Psychologist, 2*, 539–558.

Shakow, D. (1969). *Clinical psychology as science and profession: A forty year odyssey.* Chicago: Aldine.

Taylor, P. (1992). Improving graduate student seminar presentations through training. *Teaching of Psychology, 19*, 236–238.

Walfish, S., Stenmark, D., Shealy, J. S., & Shealy, S. E. (1989). Reasons why applicants select clinical psychology graduate programs. *Professional Psychology: Research and Practice, 20*, 350–354.

Willis, F. N., & Diebold, C. T. (1997). Producing mentors in psychology. *Teaching of Psychology, 24*, 15–21.

Wrightsman, L. S. (1981, August). *Research methodologies for assessing mentoring.* Paper presented at the meeting of the American Psychological Association, Los Angeles.

# 9

## The Mentoring Relationship in Psychology Training Programs

*James M. O'Neil*

*Lawrence S. Wrightsman*

Janice Hudgins has just arrived at the state university, to begin her doctoral work in clinical psychology. As she sits in the hallway awaiting her first interview with her assigned major professor, she feels hot and sweaty. Is it because of the early September lingering heat? Or is it her apprehension over meeting the person who will guide her work and training for possibly the next four or five years? The wait is mercifully short, and Professor Willetson ushers her into his cramped office. After sitting down, he scrutinizes her carefully and says, "My, what's a pretty girl like you doing, taking on the task of getting a PhD in clinical?" Janice Hudgins's first thought— which she successfully struggles to keep to herself—is, "God, is this the way professors behave in graduate school?"

Meanwhile, in a different university in a different state, Professor Steven Barretmeyer has just met one of the new graduate students in counseling psychology, Ted Havens. Although the student knows little about Professor Barretmeyer except that he has published several articles in attribution theory, the professor has studied Mr. Havens's credentials carefully. Without any of the usual preliminaries (such as "Settled into town?" or "How do you like the university?"), Professor Barretmeyer begins firing nonstop questions at the student about his past training and competence: "I see you had two courses in statistics as an undergraduate. Do you know anything about linear regression models?" "How are your programming skills? Have you used SPSS or Biomed?" Ted Havens is thinking, "Gee, this fellow sees me as his research assistant, not as a student. He's putting a lot of pressure on me. I wonder if I can do it?"

At a third university, the conversation between a new doctoral student—this one in school psychology—and his faculty advisor progressed further, in a leisurely fashion. In contrast to the previous examples, Professor Galesberg has been quite relaxed and interested in the student's well-being. But now the conversation has seemingly reached an impasse. The student has candidly revealed his lack of any well-defined professional interests; in fact, he's not even sure he knows what school psychology is, and he has no idea of what courses he wants or needs to take. Professor Galesberg is becoming increasingly uncomfortable, as he thinks, "Why do I always get the students who have to be told? I do a better job of supervising students who know what they want and how to get it. This guy acts like a freshman. Boy, am I going to have to spend a lot of extra time with him!"

These three examples are fictitious (and not all professors show the reactions that these did!). Still, we believe that incidents similar to these take place between professors and new graduate students at the beginning of each academic year. Mentoring of some type is inevitable, and many interactions are positive and mutually beneficial, but not all are. Each of these examples reflects a different kind of obstacle to a successful relationship between a faculty advisor or supervisor (henceforth called a *mentor*) and the student advisee (henceforth called a *mentee*).

One goal of this chapter is to identify some factors that contribute to a good mentoring relationship. There are also parameters and correlates by which the quality of the relationship can be assessed; there are related tasks that can be described. A second goal is to raise the consciousness of all of us—authors and readers, mentees and mentors—about a process that all of us have for too long taken for granted. At the end of the chapter we provide recommendations for improving the mentoring relationship in psychology training programs.

Just because some form of mentoring happens when professor and student are cast together, we do not assume that it is a simple process. In fact, we propose a "source-of-variance" model to explain effectiveness; that is, the quality of the mentoring process is determined by a number of factors, including (a) the role of the mentor, (b) the role of the mentee, (c) the personality, abilities, and needs of the particular persons who fill these roles, and (d) various situational and environmental factors, ranging from physical ones (e.g., a faculty office shared with three colleagues) to psychological ones (e.g., attitudes of professors or a program that is encouraging or demeaning towards students). Not only do these many factors contribute to the vast differences in mentoring outcomes, but also the mentoring relationship is a complex one because it must change over time. We realize that the needs and activities at the entry period differ from those after the mentor and mentee have spent considerable time working together.

A mentor is much more than an academic advisor. The mentor's values represent idealized norms that can have considerable influence on how mentees see themselves and the profession. Mentees have various emotional responses to their mentors, including admiration, awe, fear, and idolization. Experiences with mentors can be impactful and remembered for many years. The mentor's power and influence on the mentee approximates the intensity that parents and children have with each other.

Students entering graduate programs in psychology need to recognize the importance of having a mentor to aid in their personal and professional development. In a study of recent clinical psychologists doctorates, 94% of the graduates reported having a mentor as important to them (Clark, Harden, & Johnson, 2000). Students who participate in positive mentoring relationships are more likely to find satisfaction in their careers and to increase their professional skills and competencies (Baugh, Lankau, & Scandura, 1996; Jacobi, 1991). Additionally, mentors can be very helpful to students in negotiating the often-byzantine politics of a graduate department and graduate school (see chapter by Sumprer and Walfish in this section) as well as in completing theses and dissertations (see chapter by Martin in Section III). And the mentoring relationship often continues far after graduate school; young professional people need advice as they make decisions about professional choices and opportunities.

But some mentoring relationships can produce stress, conflict, and pain for either the mentee, the mentor, or both. Issues of competition, power, and control may emerge (Fagenson, 1992) and remain unresolved, souring the relationship between two caring people. We hope that by identifying some potential problems, this chapter can improve the quality of your mentoring relationship, whether you are mentee or mentor—or both.

## A CONCEPTION OF MENTORING: SOURCES OF VARIANCE IN MENTORING RELATIONSHIPS

But what is mentoring? Although we offered a definition earlier, let us consider mentoring in more detail. We propose that mentoring exists when a professional person serves as a resource, sponsor, and transitional figure for another person (usually, but not necessarily younger) who is entering that same profession. Effective mentors provide mentees with knowledge, advice, challenge, and support, as mentees pursue the acquisition of professional competence and identity. The mentor welcomes the less experienced person into that profession and represents the values, skills, and success that the neophyte professional person intends to acquire someday.

We have divided the multiple sources of variance in mentoring relationships into factors, parameters, correlates, and tasks. Four factors that underlie mentoring relate to role, personality, situational–environmental, and diversity variables. Other sources of variance, which may emerge later, include the parameters of mutuality, comprehensiveness, congruence, and diversity sensitivity. Additionally, six correlates of mentoring have been identified and include power, control, competition, interpersonal respect, professionalism–collegiality, and role fulfillment. Meanwhile, as these different variables come into play, mentoring relationships must deal with six different tasks, including: (a) making the critical entry decision, (b) building trust, (c) taking risks, (d) teaching skills, (e) learning professional standards, and (f) dissolving or changing the relationship. The four factors and parameters and the six correlates and tasks represent multiple sources of variance and the major concepts to be discussed in this chapter.

## FACTORS IN THE MENTORING RELATIONSHIP

### Role Factors

Role factors in mentoring are the assumed characteristics of the relationship, including role definitions, functions, and flexibilities. In mentoring relationships, both mentor and mentee are in roles; thus there are some general role definitions and specific functions for each. *Role definitions* are statements of understanding about the nature of the role relationship, whereas the *role functions* are the behaviors expected of the individual holding that role. It is important for mentors and mentees to discuss role definitions and functions in order to establish the purposes and to identify the dimensions of their relationships. Table 9.1 summarizes our literature review of the role definitions and specific functions of mentors and enumerates 14 role definitions and 25 role functions of mentors.

**TABLE 9.1**

Role Definitions and Specific Role Functions of Mentors
in Their Interpersonal and Role Relationships

| Role Definitions | Specific Role Functions |
| --- | --- |
| Teacher | Stimulating ideas |
| Coach | Giving information |
| Trainer | Gatekeeping for the organization and profession |
| Sponsor | "Opening doors" (having connections) |
| Leader | Providing opportunities to learn |
| Advisor | Enlarging mentee's perspective |
| Role model or exemplar | Believing in the mentee |
| Confidant | Helping mentee define newly emerging self |
| Friend | Helping mentee fight inner battles; conquer inner fears, doubts, and obstacles |
| Healer | Helping mentee integrate father–son/father–daughter polarity or mother–son/mother–daughter polarity |
| Consultant | Discussing and clarifying mentee's personal–professional dreams |
| Host or guide | Listening without distorting |
| Transitional figure | Acting as a sounding board |
| Counsel and Moral Supporter | Reflecting feelings |
| | Summarizing content |
| | Helping clarify mentee's values |
| | Helping in decision making |
| | Helping the mentee in acting on decision |
| | Helping the mentee evaluate the results of the action |
| | Having awareness of the teachable moment and using it |
| | Assessing state of mentee's knowledge |
| | Helping mentee set goals for life and career |
| | Assessing what the mentee can realistically achieve |
| | Identifying resources for mentee's learning and growth |
| | Completing evaluations of learning and competencies |
| | Providing professional visibility |
| | Providing sponsorship for internships, jobs, and grants |
| | Providing protection from organizational politics |

Much less has been written about the mentee's role definition and functions. Yet graduate students are expected to carry out assigned tasks, to establish and clarify professional interests, skills, and identifications, and to develop courses of action so as to achieve these goals. Clearly, the role definition of mentees focuses on their activities as learners. Student role functions include any behavior that will maximize learning and promote personal and professional growth. Learning from the mentor implies being influenced by the mentor's feedback, knowledge, and experience. Additionally, other role functions include successfully completing the academic courses and requirements for the degree. Mentees can also function as a resource for mentors by helping them in their research and other professional activities. Sometimes mentees will serve as a sounding board for the mentor's beliefs and research ideas. In these ways, mentees provide collegial support for the mentor's professional activities.

What strikes us is the extreme latitude in behaviors within these mentor–mentee role definitions and functions. Clearly a specification of expected role behavior is not enough of an explanation for why a particular mentoring relationship "works" and another does not. Yes, you may say, every individual is unique, and hence every relationship between mentor and mentee is thus bound to be unique, and it is true that every mentoring relationship will have some unique role definitions and functions. But we believe that there are some general aspects of a role that lead to more successful outcomes.

One of these is role flexibility, or the ability to respond or adapt to different situations in a role relationship. In the third introductory vignette, we find Professor Galesberg and the student at a stalemate. Professor Galesberg is going to have to show some role flexibility of his own if the mentoring relationship is to prosper. But the student may need to change his role expectations also. Novice graduate students often enter their new role not knowing that the department expects more self-directed and assertive behavior than that typical of an undergraduate. We advise entering students to "case the joint," to talk to advanced students about how the system operates. Some graduate programs thoughtfully provide a designated advanced student for each incoming student, not only to help in finding a place to live but also to disseminate role expectations and institutional norms.

## Personality Factors

One reason that behaviors fluctuate so much within the agreed boundaries of role expectations is the collection of personalities and needs of the two persons involved. In identifying the sources of variance we can never disregard the personality traits, the attitudes, and the habits of the mentor and mentee. Congruence with respect to degree of interpersonal distance is an important determinant of comfort in the relationship, but each participant needs to recognize that interpersonal flexibility will increase the probability that mutual trust will emerge in the relationship.

## Gender Roles

Of all the many individual differences in roles and personality factors that contribute to the mentoring process, we want to single out gender roles for special attention, because of their importance and potential negative impact (Gilbert & Rossman, 1992). Clark et al. (2000) found that 11% of those with recent doctorates in clinical psychology reported gender concerns related to their mentors. Women reported significantly more than men.

The way that we are socialized in this society to "act like a man" or "act like a woman" can result in gender role conflicts. Gender role conflict is a psychological state in which socialized gender roles have negative consequences for the person or others (O'Neil, Good, & Holmes, 1995; O'Neil, Helms, Gable, David, & Wrightsman, 1986). Gender role conflict occurs when rigid, sexist, or restrictive gender roles result in personal restriction, devaluation, or violation of others or self. The ultimate outcome of this kind of conflict is a restriction of human potential of the person or the restriction of someone else's potential.

Gender role conflict and sexism can be real problems in the mentoring relationship. The very first vignette in this chapter, although its sexism is crude and blatant, represents a response more frequent than desired. The vast majority of mentors in psychology are men, and in recent years, women have accounted for approximately half of the entering graduate student class.

To the extent that gender role conflict and sexism perfuse male–female relationships, the large numbers of male faculty and female students compel us to examine gender role issues (Gilbert & Rossman, 1992). Hence mentees who are women may have a special problem in finding effective mentors to facilitate their personal and professional development (see Bogat & Redner, 1985; Bolton, 1980; George & Kummerow, 1981; Gilbert & Rossman, 1992; Kahnweiler & Johnson, 1980; LaFrance, 1981; Mokros, Erkut, & Spichiger, 1981). The following can serve as guidelines in evaluating the quality of those mentoring relationships that involve both sexes:

1. How do the participants' beliefs (or stereotypes) about masculinity–femininity, men–women, and achievement–relationships affect the interactions between them?

2. Does sexism intrude on the goals, the tasks, and the interpersonal actions of the mentoring relationship?

3. Are there situational factors in the environment that are sexist or gender-restrictive and hence affect the possibility of constructive mentoring?

Levinson, Darrow, Klein, Levinson, and McKee (1978) provided a stimulating analysis of the ways that gender role adherence may affect men's potential for mentoring. He proposes that most men are socialized to view masculinity and femininity as extreme polarities. In contrast, in order to be effective mentors, men must be able to recognize and overcome the artificiality of these masculine and feminine polarities. Additionally, males who have integrated the masculine–feminine polarity increase the quality of their mentoring relationships with female mentees. They can approach women mentees as human beings rather than as sex objects or as stereotyped manifestations of femininity. The male mentor can come to respect the possibly different views of personal and professional development of the mentee, and appreciate her as a person without being defensive or exploiting her.

Gender role conflict and sexism may also occur in other mentor–mentee dyads including male mentor/male mentee, female mentor/female mentee, and female mentor/male mentee. Moreover, sexism represents only one form of bias, discrimination, and oppression that can impact mentoring relationships. Racism, classism, ethnocentrism, homophobism, and ageism represent other biases that can do harm in mentoring relationships. We explore this further when we discuss sensitivity to diversity in a later section.

Potential gender role conflict and sexism in the mentoring relationship raise questions about how students should handle problems with mentors. Students should know that they do not have to endure sexist and restrictive situations. Tactful confrontation, consciousness raising, and sometimes termination of the relationship may be necessary. They are encouraged to obtain advice and consultation from others when dealing with a sexist or gender-restrictive mentoring situation.

### Situational–Environmental Factors

We should not neglect situational–environmental qualities that contribute to the effectiveness of the mentoring relationship. Even the best intentions and mature perspectives may be wasted if, for example, the mentor has heavy administrative duties that prevent spending time and energy on an individual mentee. Also, at some institutions, a professor may have a large number of graduate advisees—as many as 20 or 30—thus preventing the development of the relationship with each.

These are examples of situational factors—that is, events, conditions, norms, or structures that are beyond the two participants' roles or personalities but that can affect the kind, depth, and quality of mentoring. Such factors include: (a) office space and privacy; (b) department norms, including support for mentoring and also departmental atmosphere (e.g., collegial vs. conflict and "infighting"); (c) resources available (library, computer time, laboratory space and equipment, subject pool); (d) other job duties that erode on available time, thus limiting contact; and (e) other situational demands on the mentor's and mentee's personal lives.

These situational–environmental factors can be important in developing an environment where mentoring can be a positive experience for both the mentor and mentee. Students can assess how situational–environmental factors may affect mentoring possibilities by interviewing advanced students and visiting the academic department before accepting an admission offer.

## PARAMETERS OF MENTORING

We build on Clawson's (1980) analysis to propose four parameters of mentoring: mutuality, comprehensiveness, congruence, and sensitivity to diversity. Mentors and mentees who are aware of the parameters will have an active vocabulary to describe the dimensions of their relationship. Higher degrees of mutuality, comprehensiveness, congruence, and sensitivity to diversity as described next will produce more functional mentoring; lower degrees will produce more dysfunctional mentoring.

### Mutuality

Clawson (1980) defined mutuality as the respect, trust, and affection that mentors and mentees have for each other. Some mentors and mentees show no respect for each other; some possess this reciprocal sharing of feelings and values (or bilateral mutuality); in other pairs, one participant may reflect respect and affection whereas the other does not. Mutuality implies that each person will develop trust, positive regard, and sensitivity to the rights and requests of the other person. Each person attempts to share personally and professionally, and there is a mutual giving and receiving. When mutuality is present, role definitions and functions are understood and comfortably integrated into the relationship.

## Comprehensiveness

Some mentoring relationships are quite limited in regard to their depth and breadth. The mentor's influence on the mentee may be quite restricted. On the other hand, a comprehensive mentoring relationship involves influence on both career and personal development. For us, comprehensiveness implies that both the mentor and mentee will desire to develop as many aspects of the role of the professional and interpersonal relationships as possible. Comprehensive mentoring relationships have more than superficial meaning; affection, risk taking, challenge, and confrontation become active parts of the relationship.

## Congruence

Although comprehensiveness deals with the breadth of the relationship, congruence means the matching of the mentor and mentee's needs, values, and goals. Research has shown that mentor–mentee similarity can be an important predictor of mentor's functions (Burke, McKeen, & McKenna, 1993). Congruence is achieved when the mentor and mentee attempt to understand how their personal, professional, and role relationships interact with each other. The relationship is sustained even with multiple roles and potential role conflicts. That is, when professional differences in values or attitudes are expressed, they can be accommodated because both individuals recognize the overall importance of the special intimacy they have developed.

Incongruence may occur because of conflicting personality styles, unclear role definitions, limited interpersonal or role flexibility, gender role conflict, or lack of mutual professional interest. When possible, the degrees of incongruence should be discussed, particularly as they relate to the overall functioning of the relationship. Many times these discussions can result in acceptance and mutual respect for each person's individual differences. Other times the discussions will result in decisions to terminate or redefine the relationship. Students may wish to discuss incongruent mentoring relationships with objective, and trustworthy, third parties or a departmental or university "ombudsman" before approaching their mentor.

## Sensitivity to Diversity

There is a growing interest in mentoring and diversity experiences related to sex and gender roles (Gilbert & Rossman, 1992), sexual orientation (Lark & Croteau, 1998), and race/ethnicity (Atkinson, Neville, & Casas, 1991). Sensitivity to diversity is the capacity to understand and respect human differences. Diversity sensitivity reflects the degree to which mentors and mentees can discuss differences and constructively use them to enhance their relationship. This parameter of mentoring is essential for mutual acceptance and trust in the relationship. Sensitivity to diversity also includes heightened consciousness about how discrimination and oppression can be personally internalized and how this may affect the mentoring relationship. When mentors and mentee have experienced sexism, racism, classism, homophobism, ethnocentrism, ageism, or any other oppression, it can affect the trust and openness in the mentoring relationship. Insensitivity occurs when there is limited awareness of how diversity can affect the mentoring relationship. Furthermore, insensitivity occurs when stereotypic biases and discrimination enter the relationship and negatively affect or restrict the interpersonal dynamics between the mentor and mentee. Sensitivity to diversity means being able to respect, accept, and celebrate differences, thereby deepening the mentoring bond.

## THE CORRELATES OF MENTORING

The correlates of mentoring define more specific criteria and properties to evaluate student–faculty relationships. The correlates define, in interpersonal terms, what actually transpires between mentors and mentees in their interpersonal and role relationships. The correlates are more behaviorally descriptive of mentoring dynamics than the parameters and provide another way to analyze sources of variance in mentoring. The six correlates of mentoring relationships include interpersonal respect, professionalism–collegiality, role fulfillment, power, control, and competition issues.

Interpersonal respect, professionalism and collegiality, and role fulfillment are considered functional correlates. When interpersonal respect exists there is honesty, trust, and recognition that each person has human limitations. There is sensitivity to feelings and thoughts, as well as the monitoring of power, control, and competition dynamics in the relationship. Professionalism and collegiality exist when there are mutual commitments to professional collaboration, sharing resources, and interpersonal professional support. There is mutual cooperation, challenge, and commitment to advancing the profession through individual and collective work. Role fulfillment occurs when interpersonal and role flexibility facilitate understanding of role definitions and the completion of role functions. Both the mentor and mentee are committed to insuring that each person meets their role responsibilities.

Power, control, and competition issues are considered dysfunctional correlates and can produce conflict in mentoring relationships. *Power* implies obtaining authority, influence, or ascendancy over another to demonstrate personal worth. Power plays can take many forms, but usually they relate to using fear, threats, and making unilateral decisions. *Control* is an outcome of power that implies regulating, restraining, and having others or situations under one's command. Situations in which negative control is operating will produce tension in the relationship and decrease interpersonal openness. Each person may resist the other's influence, and inflexibility may inhibit the learning process. *Competition* is striving against others to gain power and control or comparing self with others to establish one's superiority. This can produce intellectual one-upmanship and personal devaluation of others that are antithetical to constructive mentoring relationships.

Table 9.2 details the specific behaviors that typify the six correlates. These specific behaviors represent a comprehensive description of the sources of variance in mentoring relationships. We take the position that individuals can choose to develop the functional or dysfunctional correlates and therefore determine the degree that the parameters of mentoring are actualized. Students and faculty members can use the correlates and the descriptions in Table 9.2 as a checklist to evaluate the quality of their mentoring relationships.

## TASKS IN THE MENTORING RELATIONSHIPS

The preceding analysis may imply a static quality to the mentoring relationship. Not so; rather, it must constantly change in order to remain effective. When we think about the central tasks of the mentoring process, we see this even more clearly. The mentoring tasks are those

TABLE 9.2
Correlates of Mentoring and Their Behavioral Descriptions

**Interpersonal Respect**

Mentors and Mentees

Are honest and direct

Demonstrate interpersonal flexibility

Are empathic and supportive

Are self-disclosing

Have reciprocal sharing of feelings, thoughts, and values

Demonstrate trust of the other person

Demonstrate vulnerability

Monitor power, control, and competition dynamics

Demonstrate sensitivity to human limitations

Demonstrate sensitivity to diversity

Monitor sexist, racist, classist, ageist, ethnocentric, or homophobic behavior

Recognize transference and countertransference issues

**Professionalism and Collegiality**

Mentors and Mentees

Are intellectually open

Are committed to sharing knowledge and resources

Give challenges to each other

Recognize each other's accomplishments

Experience a mutuality of learning

Set or discuss expectancies for excellence

Provide opportunities of personal–professional growth

Care about each other's career development and advancement

Are confidential in the relationships

Discuss the personal–professional dreams

Work as a team

Stimulate each other's creativity

Work toward contributing to the profession

Overcome or integrate political problems in setting

Encourage risk taking

Negotiate authorship to mutual research projects

Demonstrate role flexibility

Discuss the political realities of setting in a professional way

**Role Fulfillment**

Mentors

Model competent and professional behavior

Communicate academic requirements

Communicate criteria and successful performance

Complete academic and administrative paperwork

Guide and monitor students' academic progress

Communicate role definitions and functions

Help students set educational–career goals

Assess students' strengths and weaknesses

Supervise research and scholarly work

Communicate professional standards

Sponsor student during evaluations
Identify resources for students
Provide discriminating feedback to students
Help student develop professional identity
Discuss the job-seeking process
Sponsor student for employment
Provide support during job adjustment
Respond to students' emotional reactions

Mentees
Are open to faculty influence
Understand role definitions and functions
Fulfill course requirements on schedule
Communicate strengths and weaknesses
Communicate about academic progress
Use resources available
Demonstrate competence
Take on professional roles and demeanor
Seek advice on important decisions
Set educational and professional goals
Respond to mentor's personal and professional reactions

**Power**
Mentors and mentees
Make unilateral decisions
Use threat or fear in the relationship
Are overly authoritarian or submissive
Communicate indirectly and through personal "put–downs"
Are overly critical of the other person
Act sexist, racist, classist, ethnocentric, or homophobic
Are unavailable or distant
Abuse personal or confidential information
Sexualize the relationship

**Control**
Mentors and mentees
Express intellectual rigidity
Do not give positive or negative feedback constructively
Demonstrate interpersonal role inflexibility
Are unwilling to compromise
Encourage overdependence in the relationship
Resist influence of other person
Delay academic program of study

**Competition**
Mentor and mentees
Play intellectual one-upmanship
Show needs to be superior
Devalue other students and faculty
Compare other students and faculty to other students and faculty

critical activities that define the working relationship. They include: (a) making the critical entry decision, (b) building mutual trust, (c) taking risks, (d) teaching skills, (e) learning professional standards, and (f) dissolving or changing of the relationship.

## Making the Critical Entry Decision

The first critical decision for the mentor and the mentee asks whether they have the potential for an effective relationship together. Little has been written about how entry is experienced and how critical decisions are made. Finding a mentor can be difficult for some students. In one study, almost 30% of the students couldn't find a mentor (Clark et al., 2000). From the social psychological literature, personal qualities such as physical attractiveness, intelligence, sense of humor, and extroversion—found to be related to attraction, generally—are certainly relevant to the mentoring relationship developing. But some period of mutual testing may be necessary once an assessment is made that these conditions are met.

Graduate programs differ with respect to the pairing of advisees and advisors. Many assign new students to an advisor without consulting the student. Although such assignments are theoretically provisional, they often have a tendency to become fixed and permanent, for some students are reluctant to request a shift in advisor assignment out of fear of recriminations. At other schools, new students are encouraged to interview different faculty members and then ask one of them to serve as an advisor.

Generally, during the entry stage the relationship begins as a formal one, relying on the role relationship as the dominant focus of interaction. Conversation topics are either oriented to the two participants' roles, or focused on superficial personal aspects. However, some potential mentors and mentees are able to move easily and quickly to a more informal interaction style that utilizes an interpersonal relationship as well as a role relationship.

## Building of Mutual Trust

Once entry is established and some commitment is made to work together, the mentoring task shifts to one of a gradual and reciprocal development of confidence, self-disclosure, and reliance on the other. Trust emerges as a result of personal and professional disclosures between the mentor and mentee. The mutuality and depth of these disclosures determine the kind and quality of the intimacy. Highly intimate disclosure might include revelations about the person's felt strengths, weaknesses, vulnerabilities, and dreams in respect to both professional and personal areas. However, self-disclosures can be excessive, especially if they are expressed by one participant but not the other. The reciprocal nature of self-disclosure is crucial. There is often a struggle to find the right balance for the optimal level of growth and learning.

## Taking Risks

Both mentors and mentees take professional and personal chances that could result in either personal and professional loss or gain for each of them. The risks facing students relate to competence, professional acceptance, and career development. By entering a demanding academic program, their intellectual skills and professional competencies come under scrutiny and are assessed frequently and often rigorously. Students incur risk as they prepare assignments, write papers, participate in practicum courses, and take examinations that measure their knowledge and judgment. Sometimes, they incur additional risks because the institution has established some quota system, so that only a certain percentage of students get A's, or are allowed to continue in the program, regardless of the quality of the entering class. With these evaluations, fear of failure can become rampant.

Students can also take risks by challenging the conventional practices of the academic system or, specifically, the mentor's ideas of the relationship with the mentee. Mentors can facilitate risk taking by understanding the psychological causes of a student's need to question authority.

Mentors also face risks in mentoring. Bad advice from them can lead to failures and disappointments for the mentee; conscientious mentors identify with their students and share these feelings. There is an investment of one's selfhood in one's mentees; if they fail, then one's credibility and reputation for expertise may suffer in the eyes of the one's colleagues. Additionally, mentors also risk by disclosing their feelings and vulnerabilities to mentees, only to be rejected (devalued) by them after these disclosures have been made.

## Teaching Skills

Central to the mentor's role is that of teacher. In fact, the mentor's broadly based perspectives, experiences, and knowledge comprise much of his or her attractiveness for potential mentees. Although the teaching function is not entirely reciprocal, it is not entirely one-sided either. Mentees are able to contribute to the mentor's knowledge; they also bring energy and excitement about new ideas and perhaps a different viewpoint on old ones.

Educators have discussed how mentors can effectively teach skills to mentees (Brown & DeCoster, 1982; Knox, 1974; Lester & Johnson, 1981). This crucial activity can emanate either from the professional role relationship or from the informal interpersonal relationship. Some forms of learning (particularly academic coursework) are best disseminated through the formal role functions. Other forms of learning, not as directly tied to course content, are more easily taught through informal dialogue. Students can promote informal dialogues by encouraging student–faculty interactions at departmental colloquia, social events, and even over an occasional lunch.

According to observers of the process (Knox, 1974; Lester & Johnson, 1981), the teaching process provides the mentor with four vantage points to enhance the mentee's learning. Mentoring as a teaching process includes: (a) assessing students' knowledge base, (b) helping students establish learning and career goals, (c) identifying resources and opportunities for the student, and (d) evaluating the learning process.

## Learning Professional Standards

Every profession has its own standards and values in both practice and conduct. These may be transmitted through formal courses (on methods or on ethics), but mentors often bear much of this responsibility, too. In order for mentors to set professional standards for mentees, it is necessary for mentors to have developed a set of standards for themselves. These are usually developed from the formal training they had received from their own mentor, their professional experiences, and their institutions or the professional expectations about the quality of academic and professional work.

Professional standards may become more focused during completion of a master's thesis or dissertation research. At these points, the mentor's and mentee's individual standards interact through the generating and completing of research and professional writing. Mentors are expected to be responsible for ensuring that high professional standards are met and that ethical guidelines are followed.

As a matter of fact, mentors' professional standards are being tested and clarified as their students complete and defend master's theses and doctoral dissertations. Colleagues may note that the mentor's standards and competence are revealed in a more public way when the mentor's student's work is examined by a committee. By implication, the faculty member may be found wanting (or feel he or she has been let down) when the student's work is not satisfactory.

Transmission of professional standards also becomes important during the mentee's search for a job. Again, the mentor's competency is reflected in the contributions, manner, and values of his or her student. If the student is accepted by peers, it serves as a validation of the mentor's efforts to be a good trainer of others. On the other hand, the mentee requires sponsorship and endorsement for his development to continue. The job search is a process that leads to inevitable changes in the mentoring relationship, as mentees ask their mentors, in effect: What do you really think of me?

### Dissolving or Changing the Relationship

The final task of mentoring reflects the changing or ending of the relationship. This can be a difficult and emotional experience for both mentor and mentee. Clark et al. (2000) found that 17% of recently graduated students in clinical psychology reporting termination of mentoring to be difficult. The most crucial point is that the relationship has to change. Mentees have to test their skills as independent professional persons in order to fully manage the next developmental task in their adult lives. Some mentees cannot wait to break away. But others continue to cling to their mentor and need to be nudged (or even shoved) to go out on their own. Either way, the mentor's relationship to the mentee must change. Some mentees may feel that their mentors are abandoning them or have not adequately prepared them for the job search or the job entry process. Some mentors may feel that their mentee's independence is a sign of ingratitude for the many long hours of professional attention and commitment.

Negotiation about ownership of ideas and research projects may be part of the changing relationship. Conflict over these shared efforts may mask the real issue—the pain felt as a result of necessary changes in the relationship. Awareness of this phenomenon is helpful if the pair is to avoid irremediable conflict and misunderstanding.

## SUMMARY, IMPLICATIONS, AND RECOMMENDATIONS

It is impossible to "mass produce" mentoring relationships. Mentoring effectiveness depends on faculty members' training philosophies and students' expectations of their training programs. Mentoring is both a curricular and professional issue that needs more discussion between faculty and students in psychology. At the risk of over generalization, we offer the following recommendations to increase the quality of mentoring in psychology programs:

1. Students applying to graduate school should assess each department's philosophy of training and values about mentoring. Additionally, students should ask whether recent graduates have received mentoring and how this has affected them personally and professionally.

2. Students and faculty should discuss how the parameters of mentoring can positively affect their relationships. Clearly, mutuality, comprehensiveness, and sensitivity to diversity can increase congruence and the overall depth, breadth, and quality of the relationship.

3. Faculty should offer students more mutual and comprehensive mentoring relationships. This could include greater sharing of personal experiences, mutual expectations, and role definitions. Also, faculty can increase mutuality and comprehensiveness by taking more active interest in mentees' opinions, perspectives, and their emerging career development.

4. Students should realize that they can be central in initiating mentoring relationships. One study of graduate students in psychology found that the inability to find a satisfactory mentor was the predominant reason for not having one (Cronan-Hillix, Gensheimer, & Cronan-Hillix, 1986). Students can have considerable effect by being available to faculty and demonstrating collegial and professional behaviors. Additionally, students should recognize that mentors need to be supported in their mentoring efforts. They can support mentors by donating research time or providing intellectual stimulation and help with research projects.

5. Students should be sensitive to the professional demands on the mentor's time and energy. Students should recognize that mentoring is an expensive process in terms of faculty time and the institution's overall educational mission. Mentees can increase mentoring efficiency by meeting with faculty members for serious discussions focused on personal and professional development. More superficial topics are best saved for more leisure discussions at purely social functions. Overall, the mentoring process can be facilitated by individuals who are informed, prepared, and have positive personalities.

6. Mentors and mentees should acknowledge how past or present parental, supervisory, and love relationships may affect their specific mentoring dynamics (e.g., transference–countertransference issues)

7. Mentors and mentees should recognize problems, role conflicts and strains that emerge in their relationship. Both parties should recognize that these conflicts are a natural part of a complicated process and hence allow time to discuss these conflicts as they emerge. It is important that problems and conflicts be discussed professionally without fear of recriminations. This is particularly important given that ethical problems in mentoring have been recently reported (Clark et al., 2000). Ethical guidelines have been suggested for mentoring and are worth review by both mentors and mentees (Johnson & Nelson, 1999).

8. Mentors and mentees should admit their vulnerability in taking risks with each other. Both individuals need to be sensitive to the risks taken by the other during the mentoring process. Risk taking, mutual evaluation, and supervisory processes can stimulate inse-

curities and fears for both the mentor and mentee. Under these circumstances, both individuals should realize that sensitivity and expert communication skills are essential.

9. Mentors need to help mentees express their personal feelings about their graduate school experiences and their thoughts about becoming a professional. Mentees will need help defining their emerging self and the mentor can assist by listening, confronting, and labeling the mentee's inner battles, doubts, and fears. Helping students with these issues can revitalize mentoring and foster a special kind of intimacy in the relationship.

10. Mentees should realize that the mentor will need to be in control of the learning process at times for growth to be realized. This means that the mentee will need to give up some control and be influenced by the mentor. We recommend that mentors utilize this control humanely and with sensitivity.

11. Mentors and mentees should monitor a number of environmental factors together. Power, control, and competition issues between different faculty members within a department and sometimes between students can destroy environments where mentoring might otherwise flourish.

12. Socialized and negative stereotypes of masculinity and femininity should be monitored. Gender role conflict in mentoring should be identified and discussed constructively. Furthermore, sensitivity to diversity issues should be a high priority for both mentor and mentee.

13. Mentors and mentees should complete research on the mentoring factors, parameters, correlates, and tasks described in this chapter. One study has found empirical evidence for the parameters of mutuality and comprehensiveness in mentoring relationships (Busch, 1985). Much more research is needed, using a variety of research methodologies (Wrightsman, 1981), if we are to understand the complexity of mentoring in psychology training programs.

14. Mentees who have grown because of their mentor's help should personally acknowledge and thank them for their contribution to their life. Likewise, mentors should share their own growth with their past mentees. We need to start dialogues with each other about our mentoring experiences. These kinds of discussions can bring us closer to each other and provide more information about this special relationship. In an age of increased academic competition and guarded collegiality, we believe that mentoring could be an important concept for improving professional training in psychology and the relationships between students and faculty.

## REFERENCES

Atkinson, D. R., Neville, H., & Casas, A. (1991). The mentoring of ethnic minorities in professional psychology. *Professional Psychology: Research and Practice, 22*, 4, 336–338.

Baugh, S. G., Lankau, M. L., & Scandura, T. A. (1996). An investigation of the effects of protégé gender on responses to mentoring. *Journal of Vocational Behavior, 49*, 309–323.

Bogat, G. A., & Redner, R. L. (1985). How mentoring affects the professional development of women in psychology. *Professional Psychology: Research & Practice, 16*, 6, 851–859.

Bolton, E. B. (1980). A conceptual analysis of the mentor relationship in the career development of women. *Adult Education, 30*, 195–207.

Brown, R. D., & DeCoster, D. A. (1982). *Mentoring-Transcript Systems for promoting student growth. New directions for student services*, Number 19. San Francisco: Jossey-Bass.

Burke, R. J., McKeen, C. A., & McKenna , C.(1993). Correlates of mentoring in organizations: The mentor's perspective. *Psychological Reports, 72*, 883–896.

Busch, J. W. (1985). Mentoring in graduate schools of education. *American Educational Research Journal, 22*, 257–265.

Clarke, R. A., Harden, S. L., & Johnson, W. B. (2000). Mentor relationship in clinical psychology doctoral training: Results of a national survey. *Teaching of Psychology, 27*, 262–268.

Clawson, J. G. (1980). Mentoring in managerial careers. In C. B. Dear (Ed.), *Work, family and the career: New frontiers in the theory and research* (pp.144–165). New York: Praeger.

Cronan-Hillix, T., Gensheimer, L. K., & Cronan-Hillix, W. A. (1986). Students' views of mentors in psychology graduate training . *Teaching of Psychology, 13*(3), 123–127.

Fagenson, E. A. (1992). Mentoring who needs it? A comparison of protégés' and nonprotégés' needs for power, achievement, affiliation, and autonomy. *Journal of Vocational Behavior, 41*, 48–60.

George, P., & Kummerow, J. (1981). Mentoring for career women. *Training/HRD, 18*, 44–49.

Gilbert, L. A. & Rossman, K. M. (1992). Gender and mentoring process for women: Implications for professional development. *Professional Psychology: Research and Practice, 23*, 232–238.

Jacobi, M. (1991). Mentoring and undergraduate success: A literature review. *Review of Educational Research, 61*, 505–532.

Johnson, W. B., & Nelson, N. (1999). Mentor–protégé relationships in graduate training: Some ethical concerns. *Ethics & Behavior, 9*(3), 189–210.

Kahnweiler, J. B., & Johnson, P. L. (1980). A midlife developmental profile of the returning women student. *Journal of College Student Personnel, 21*, 414–419.

Knox, A. B. (1974). *Adult development and learning.* San Francisco: Jossey-Bass.

LaFrance, M. (1981, August). Women and the mentoring process: Problems, paradoxes, and prospects. In J. M. O'Neil & L.S. Wrightsman (Chairs), *Mentoring: Psychological, personal, and career development implications.* Symposium conducted at the American Psychological Association Annual Convention, Los Angeles.

Lark, J. S., & Croteau, J. M. (1998). Lesbian, gay, bisexual doctoral students' mentoring relationships with faculty in counseling psychology: A qualitative study. *Counseling Psychologist, 26*(5), 754–776.

Lester, V., & Johnson, C. (1981). The learning dialogue: Mentoring. In J. Fried (Ed.), Education for student development (pp.49–56). *New Directions for Student Services*, No. 15, San Francisco: Jossey-Bass.

Levinson, D. J., Darrow, C. L., Klein, E. B., Levinson, M. H.,& McKee, B. (1978). *The seasons of a man's life.* New York: Alfred A. Knopf.

Mokros, J. R., Erkut, S., & Spichiger, L. (1981). Mentoring and being mentored: Sex related patterns among college professors. Working paper no. 68. Wellesley, MA: Wellesley College Center for Research on Women.

O'Neil, J. M., Good, G. E., & Holmes, S. E. (1995). Fifteen years of theory and research on men's gender role conflict: New paradigms for empirical research. In R. Levant & W. Pollack (Eds.), *A new psychology of men* (pp.164–206). New York: Basic Books.

O'Neil, J. M., Helms, B., Gable, R., David, L., & Wrightsman, L. (1986). Gender Role Conflict Scale (GRCS): College men's fear of femininity. *Sex Roles, 14*, 335–350.

Wrightsman, L. S. (1981, August). Research methodologies for assessing mentoring. In J. M. O'Neil & L. S. Wrightsman (Chairs) *Mentoring: Psychological, personal, and career development implications.* Symposium conducted at the American Psychological Association Convention, Los Angeles.

# 10

# Stress and Stress Mastery in Graduate School

*Eric N. Goplerud*

Entering graduate school marks the beginning of a period of frequent stressful life changes for most students. Some of these changes are episodic and correspond to major academic role transitions—for example the first few months following entrance to graduate school, preparation for comprehensive examinations, such points in the dissertation process as proposal defense and oral dissertation defense, the first months of an internship (especially after a geographical relocation), and beginning work as a new professional. Other stressful life changes occur more randomly. Some are associated with the graduate school environment, while others are not (e.g., death of loved ones, being a crime victim, having a health problem). Levine and Perkins (1997), in a chapter titled "Life Is a Soap Opera," found the occurrence of critical life events to be the rule rather than the exception. One study found that during the first 6 months of graduate studies, students reported an average of 3.9 stressful life events (Goplerud, 1978).

This chapter examines aspects of stress that may be especially relevant to students in graduate psychology training. First, specific stressors of graduate training are examined. Second, organizational and role contributions to the production of stress are discussed, related to "job" and working conditions of graduate training programs. Third, a theoretical analysis of the processes involved in stress mastery with the primary role that social support plays in the successful resolution of stress reactions is presented. Finally, strategies for dealing with stress during graduate training, including the need to gain a perspective, to become informed, and to manage anxiety, are highlighted.

## STRESS AND GRADUATE SCHOOL

Three types of stressful situations were reported by one group of graduate students in their first year of study: (a) events wholly unrelated to graduate life, such as, being robbed or the death of a close friend; (b) events specifically related to school, such as, exam week or deadlines for term papers; and (c) confidence/competence stresses, such as, doubts about one's commitment to a field of study, or anxiety about fitting into the graduate program (Goplerud, 1980). Two-fifths of the events reported by first year students were unrelated to their graduate school program.

Stressful life changes are common. Over half of a sample of graduate students administered the Social Readjustment Rating Scale (SRRS), a standard stressful event instrument that assesses the number and intensity of events experienced, reported more than 300 life change units in the previous year (Goplerud, 1977). Research has demonstrated that the likelihood of future illness increases when a person experiences a high number of these life change units within a relatively brief time period (Montat & Lazarus, 1991).

It should not be surprising, then, that graduate students frequently seek help for medical and emotional problems. Halleck (1976) reported that, following freshmen, graduate students had the highest rate of student health and counseling services use at the two university health systems that he studied. Because a significant percentage of individuals who begin graduate training in psychology with the intention of earning a doctorate do not persist long enough to actually earn the degree (American Psychological Association, 1998), the potential impact of stress on graduate students should be taken seriously.

Cahir and Morris (1991) developed the Psychology Student Stress Questionnaire utilizing 133 graduate students from one university as their subject pool. Utilizing multivariate statistics, these researchers were able to identify seven separate factors. These included: (a) problems with time constraints; (b) difficulty with feedback from specific faculty; (c) financial constraints; (d) trouble getting help from faculty; (e) limited emotional support from friends; (f) difficulty with feedback with regard to status in the department; and (g) stress from lack of input in program decisions. Given that the sample was from one particular academic department, it is important that there was an attempt to replicate this study at another setting by Keim, Fuller, and Day (1996). These authors found the factors of time and financial constraints and the difficulty with feedback with regard to status in the department to be replicated from the original Cahir and Morris (1991) study. A separate factor emerged in this study related to demands of courses.

Kuyken, Peters, Power, and Lavender (1998) suggest that clinical graduate students face many challenges during their training. These include learning to manage a variety of professional roles, coping with the demands of both academic and personally and professionally demanding clinical work, and changing clinical placements on a regular basis. These authors view these challenges as being demanding on relationships and responsibilities both at work and at home. Although they were not specifically targeting psychology students, Mallinckrodt and Leong (1992) found female graduate students to experience greater role strain than their male counterparts. They suggest this finding may be due to less support for their multiple roles and greater concern about balancing academic and family demands. Holzman, Searight, and Hughes (1996) completed a survey of clinical psychology students' involvement in psychotherapy. They found that although a large number of students enter therapy for the purpose of personal and professional growth, the data suggests that the possibility of coexisting clinical distress should not be ruled out. They also hypothesize that a trainee's psychological issues may be uncovered or exacerbated by the emotional demands of learning to practice psychotherapy.

## WORK FACTORS RELATED TO STRESS

Organizational factors and job roles may exert great stressors on individuals. Although "job" stress in graduate schools has not been systematically studied, there are several studies focusing on the roles students inhabit during critical transition points during their education (Baird, 1969; Goplerud, 1978, 1980; Hall, 1969; Mechanic, 1962). There are several factors that may increase graduate students' strain.

### Work Overload

Perrewe and Ganster (cf. McKee, Markham, & Scott, 1992) used the term *quantitative overload* to define a situation in which the amount of work exceeds what an individual can reasonably accomplish in a given period of time. French and Caplan (1973) described *qualitative overload* as working on tasks that demand high standards stretching beyond a worker's abilities or training. Particularly during major role transitions, graduate students work under high levels of both qualitative and quantitative work overload. Some graduate programs may use heavy workloads to "weed out" students who are not able to prioritize overwhelming assignments. With sharply reduced training funds available to support graduate students within their programs, many students will have to accept part- or full-time jobs in addition to their graduate school loads simply to survive financially. Work overload will increase correspondingly.

### Role in the Organization

Another major source of graduate student stress is associated with roles in the work setting. Role ambiguity exists when individuals have inadequate information about the work objectives of their role, and a lack of clarity about the expectations and evaluation criteria for judging their performance. Uncertainty in the work environment has been linked to both psychological and physical distress (Quick, Murphy, Hurrell, & Orman, 1992). Becker and his colleagues (Becker, Geer, Hughes, & Strauss, 1961) found that one of the most frequent and intense stressors that students complained about was the lack of clear performance criteria in the setting, and the absence of indicators to help them discriminate between critical and less important work assignments.

Baird (1969) conducted an extensive survey of role relations of graduate students. Responses from over 680 students on a questionnaire sampling their relations with faculty, others outside the graduate setting, general aspects of the role, and relations with other students were submitted to extensive factor analysis. Students' scores on his scales of role stress and psychological withdrawal were higher, and scores on morale were lower, when demands of faculty appeared to be unclear or conflicting. Another project found that students who reported poor working relations with their major faculty advisor reported a greater number of intense stressors and a greater number of emotional and health problems than did students with close relations with faculty (Goplerud, 1980). Furthermore, those graduate students who interacted frequently with faculty during the first 10 weeks of graduate study experienced fewer health and emotional problems during their first year of graduate study, and reported that stressors experienced during the first year were less intense and persisted for shorter periods of time, than did students who infrequently met with faculty during the first weeks of graduate study. Presumably, feedback from faculty on the requirements of the setting and on students' performance within the setting helps buffer the organizational stresses of role ambiguity for those students who frequently interact with faculty.

## Role Conflict

Another source of potential job stress exists when conflicting job demands tear an individual in a particular work role. Lowman (1993) found role conflict to be implicated in burnout and worker stress.

Graduate students typically have several bosses, each of whom has considerable independent authority over the students' immediate and long-term careers. Faculty control most of the patent reinforcers in the graduate school milieu. They disburse grades, teaching and research assignments, financial rewards, and entrance into the professional job market. Faculty members provide day-to-day clues to students' performances and aptitudes for their chosen careers, and precipitate life crises for students through negative evaluations, examinations, and assignments. The collegial organization of graduate programs means that often there is not one clearly designated ultimate arbiter for a student. Rather, a student in graduate training will typically have at least several, if not many, faculty members who are in authority positions, and whose demands may conflict. Furthermore, research has suggested that role conflict may affect women more than male graduate students due to multiple role demands (Mallinckrodt, Leong, & Kralj, 1989).

## Participation

Participation in decision making plays a role in the stress experienced by members of organizations. From their review of the literature, Murphy, Hurrell, and Quick (1992) concluded that low worker control is a risk factor for developing occupational health problems. Further, they found higher levels of worker control to be associated with high levels of job satisfaction, commitment, and motivation, as well as low levels of physical complaints.

Opportunities for participation in major decisions affecting students' lives vary from program to program, as well as within program components. In my study of first-year graduate students, only 14% strongly agreed with the statement "I think that graduate students here have a major impact on decisions that really concern them." More than two-thirds disagreed with that statement (Goplerud, 1978). Just under half reported that they did not feel that graduate students were treated as mature adults. Cahir and Morris (1991) found one factor related to psychology student stress to result from lack of input in program decisions. Although faculty–student relationships are structurally unequal, it is likely that there are some means by which students can gain greater control or feeling of participation into their work setting. For example, graduate students at several of the largest and most prestigious universities have formed unions, which negotiate with the university administration over wages, workload, health insurance, and working conditions. Within individual departments and program areas, students have banded together to gain representation and input into such decisions as those about curricula, course workloads, and incoming student selection. Finally, at the individual student level, frequent and collegial contact with faculty increased students' feelings of control and reduced perceptions of stress (Goplerud, 1980; Hartnett, 1976).

## STRESS MASTERY AND SOCIAL SUPPORT

Caplan (1981) proposed four aspects in mastering stress. In each aspect, social support may play a distinct part. The relevance of Caplan's stress mastery model for coping with graduate school stresses is briefly presented.

*Facet 1: Acquiring New Capabilities So That a Person Will Be Able to Operate More Effectively in Stressful Conditions.*    Although by definition, a stressful situation overwhelms individual's response capabilities, education and training may fortify a person's resilience before encountering stress. Goplerud (1978) found that students rated informal contacts with other graduate students, particularly those who had been in the program longer, as especially helpful to them in learning the norms and priorities of the graduate setting. Students reported that formal information channels, such as printed catalogs and program descriptions, and informal meetings, were of little help. At least one graduate psychology training program provides its entering students with a "mini-assessment center" in which students are presented with simulated graduate classes, examinations, and research and teaching assistant demands. Students are prepared through feedback and coaching for the actual graduate program that they will be entering (N. Reed, Personal Communication, 1982). In another paper (Goplerud, 1978), I described an orientation program for entering students which was developed and conducted by students who had been in that program for 2 or 3 years. Social interaction data indicate that the program was successful in increasing the amount of informal communication between students, and in better preparing entering students for the graduate work setting.

Students can also be trained to develop expectations of an increased range of discomforts that they will be able to tolerate, so that they will persevere through their program despite temporary distress. McLaughlin (1985) stressed the need for greater information about particular programs to be disseminated to students. Several students in my earlier study reported relief and some comfort when told by faculty or more senior students that the discomforts of writing papers and preparing class presentations, and the doubts they were feeling about being admitted into the program by mistake, were a typical part of the graduate student experience. It was also helpful that they were told that faculty and more senior students had similar experiences and survived the ordeal.

*Facet II: Acting Directly on the Source of Stress in Order to Reduce It and Its Consequences or to Find Ways to Physically Escape It.*    This facet involves goal-directed problem-solving behavior. Unfortunately, the intense emotional arousal and dysphoria associated with stress characteristically also erodes an individual's problem-solving abilities. Caplan (1981) cited numerous studies that show that under stress, people exhibit deficits in judgment, planning ability, capacity to implement plans, and ability to use feedback. Also, he reported that people under stress have lowered self-esteem, reduced expectations of personal success, and diminished capacities to use past successes and skills in effectively dealing with current problems.

Caplan pointed out that social supports can play crucial roles in overcoming these cognitive deficiencies. First, they serve as an auxiliary ego to recognize and point out to the stressed individuals when their cognitive effectiveness has been eroded by stress. Second, social supports can also help distressed persons improve their own data collection, and aid in evaluating the stressful situation and working out a sensible plan. A supportive network may assist an individual in implementing the plan, assess its consequences, and re-plan in line with feedback information. Supports can also remind the individual of past successes, and assure that discomforts are expected and can probably be tolerated. Kuyken et al. (1998) examined psychological adaptation in a sample of clinical psychology graduate students in Great Britian. They found the combination of emotional support from clinical supervisors and from a main confidant at home to predict much of the variance in positive adaptation.

Graduate students who are linked to supportive networks generally perform better academically than their socially isolated colleagues. Students linked to supportive networks experience less emotional and health distress during major academic role transitions (Goplerud, 1978, 1980) and show greater commitment to their field of study (Baird, 1969). A primary mechanism for this improved performance of socially supported students appears to be the instrumental roles played by peers. Peer networks help graduate students define standards for acceptable academic performance when faculty standards appear ambiguous or overwhelming; students also help one another to set priorities during high-demand periods, and they serve as conduits for sharing information, technical skills, and advice. This is consistent with Caplan's contention that the primary mechanism by which social networks assist in the mastery of stress is their contribution to improved cognitive problem solving. As an example related to students in clinical training, Kleepsies, Smith, and Becker (1990) noted the importance of support and guidance from a supervisor in helping interns deal with a client suicide.

***Facet III: Intrapsychic Behavior to Defend Against Dysphoric Emotional Arousal.***    People will seek relief from stress-induced anxiety and depression by using their customary defense mechanism as far as possible. Defenses most frequently used, according to Caplan (1981), are denial, selective inattention, and isolation (i.e., removal of the feeling from the attendant perception). The social environment may confirm and strengthen an individual's defenses, validating a perception that there is little or no threat, that the threat is unimportant, or that the individual has the capability to adequately handle it.

At times, support systems for graduate students do work in these ways to shore up defenses of students under stress. However, both Hall (1969) and Mechanic (1962) documented that strong groups of graduate students who are all under high-stress conditions (preparation for comprehensive examinations in both studies) that participate in a social network composed of graduate students may overwhelm the defenses of these same students, greatly elevating their anxiety and decreasing their abilities to adequately function. By transmitting others' anxiety, social networks may undermine some students' defenses. Isolation from other anxious students may be highly adaptive for at least some people.

Graduate students who progress well in their programs and those students who experience academic difficulties may have different styles for coping with stressful situations (Kjerulff & Wiggins, 1976). Students who, on the basis of their grades and ratings made by faculty, were completely handling the academic and environmental rigors of graduate school responded to all types of stressful situations with moderate levels of anxiety. Students who are progressing well do not tend to blame themselves or others when confronted by difficult situations. For these individuals, Kjerulff and Wiggins speculated that anxiety is channeled into constructive, problem-solving pathways. Students who are less competent react to stresses with a different coping style. These students reported that when confronted by an academic failure they become angry with themselves, react to interpersonal problems with anger directed at others, and react to ambiguous stresses in which fault is difficult to assign (e.g., getting insignificant results on one's master's thesis). Differences in coping styles may be factors contributing to the differences students experience in handling stresses.

*Facet IV: Intrapsychic Behavior to Come to Terms with the Event and Its Sequela by Internal Readjustment.* In many settings, particularly those associated with organized religions, social support has long been recognized as a key to facilitating the readjustment people make following severe stresses (Pargament, 1997). Supportive groups stimulate the distressed person at intervals to review the adjustment to the distressing event or situation, allowing feelings of grief and anger to emerge. The group assuages this pain by shared concern and by offering consolation and nurturance. It also helps overcome feelings of hopelessness and helplessness by emphasizing the supportive group's continuing links to the distressed person, and the continuity of that individual's identity through the distressing period (Caplan, 1981).

In mastering this facet of stress, graduate students may be influenced by supports in contradictory ways. Baird's (1969) study of role relations of graduate students clearly showed that commitment to graduate study and to one's major field is strongly affected by the quality and quantity of contacts with other graduate students. When students get involved with other students, they often make graduate school the basis of much of their activity and concern. Therefore, support networks composed of other graduate students may help individuals resolve their distress by emphasizing the student's continuing identity within that setting. On the other hand, ongoing contact with support systems outside the graduate school environment (e.g., spouse, family, nonacademic friends) presents the potential for severe role conflict, which may increase rather than decrease the difficulties of readjusting to stress. Baird (1969) found the extent to which a student uses others outside the university for comparison or reference to be inversely related to commitment to graduate study and to a student's desire to pursue an academic career after graduation.

## TACKLING STRESS

Although dealing with graduate school stressors is probably best done by groups of students and faculty familiar with their unique settings, there are many useful steps that students can undertake on their own. The following suggestions are derived from discussions with students and former students, and from the literature on stress management.

### Getting a Perspective

Identify your goals for attending graduate school. What is really important to you? When immediate stressors loom, it is easy to lose sight of your purposes for embarking on graduate studies. By identifying your goals and checking back during periods of stress, it is easier to concentrate on your own priorities, rather than becoming overwhelmed by the myriad hurdles pressing you.

Get rid of trivial obligations, which sidetrack you from your goals. If you know why you want the degree, and what you hope to do with it after you graduate, you can better assess which obligations to assume, and which to avoid. For example, training opportunities of all kinds are constantly available to students. A seminar on group processes is offered, out-of-town speakers are announced, a community agency contacts the department about its interest in program evaluation, a crisis center sends out a call for volunteers. Choosing which to pursue and which to pass up should be based on your goals, not on what training is next on the calendar.

Assess whether you hold beliefs about your performance that add unnecessarily to your stress level. Particularly unhealthy are beliefs that you should be thoroughly competent in all areas, that you should be respected and appreciated by nearly everyone important to you, or that you should not be hassled by the outside world while involved in training. Certainly it would be nice to be perfect, or to be loved by faculty, peers, and spouse alike, but is it worth all the added suffering you will heap on yourself to try to keep those beliefs in an imperfect world? Self-help books on cognitive therapy that are often suggested for clients may be equally helpful for graduate students (Burns, 1999; Ellis, 1994).

Become an expert on your stress indicators. Learn to identify your own signs that you are under stress and look for common elements that trip off your stress reaction. For some, stress indicators are physical, such as tension headaches, sleeplessness, and "butterflies" in their stomachs. For others, stress indicators are more behavioral or interpersonal, such as short temper, avoiding others, or working hard but getting nothing done. Stress indicators vary from person to person, and it is helpful to become an expert on your own early warning signs that stress is building up for yourself. Use your supports when you find your stress response to be clouding your thinking.

Consider personal therapy (especially if it is available free or at low cost) to assist you with clarifying goals and learning stress management techniques. Personal therapy can be a crucial factor in maximizing learning experiences for student therapists (Binder & Strupp, 1997) and as a source of social support (Holzman et al., 1996), and can also be used instrumentally to help you deal with stress.

Recognize that under stress you will act abnormally at times. You will neglect your spouse, friends, sex, sports, eating, and sleeping. More than 90% of the students in my study experienced periods of sleep difficulties. It is unlikely that your behavior under stress indicates a permanent character change.

Students entering doctoral programs in psychology frequently are among the brightest graduates of their undergraduate programs. In undergraduate school they have had high grades, special access to faculty, and an established support system. In graduate school, being good is the norm, and they may suffer from the change from being a big frog in a small pond to a not very large frog in a bigger pond. Baird (1969) found that under competitive situations, nearly all students reported distress. Again, it is important to look to your values. Is it important to you what you get from the training experience or what your standing is in the program may be?

Expect that life will continue while you are in graduate school, and be willing to adapt your plans and activities accordingly. Stressors, crises, and pleasant experiences will intrude from the outside world. It is probably impossible to put your life in stasis for 4 to 6 years until you finish training. Practice seeing your training within the broader context of your life plans.

There is always going to be more work than you can handle. See if you can treat academic work as a job, not as a special calling. Set work priorities, schedule work, and take the night off regularly.

Many people believe that at some point, perhaps when they get their doctorate, finish their internship, get certified, or at some other time, they will be an expert, and that they will finally be finished. Wrong! There is always more to learn, to practice, so see if you can't back off some of the self-imposed or situationally imposed pressure to be finished. The dissertation, for example, should be a good piece of work. If you start believing that it must be great, that it has to be the greatest thing that you will ever do, what does that leave for the rest of your life? If your goal is to become a competent psychologist (among other things), you have a lifetime to discover what that uniquely means for you.

## Becoming Informed

Get to know the rites of passage in your program. Identify the key transition points where you can anticipate stress. In this way, you can learn the characteristic demands of these key periods, the length of time involved, typical student reactions to these transitions, and techniques for mastering the stresses. For example, in the graduate program I studied, it was well known that most first-year students experienced a period of depression and self-doubt 2 to 3 months after beginning the program. Known as the "Thanksgiving Blues," this period was countered by prewarning entering students, and by planning several sybaritic Thanksgiving parties.

Identify your prime sources of information about program mores and requirements, and establish a network to get feedback on your performance. Faculty, older graduate students, department secretaries, and other members of your class are all primary sources. Establish contacts early in your academic career, and cultivate these contacts regularly to maintain a steady flow of information.

Develop and maintain regular working relations with one or more faculty members. Close faculty relations are key to establishing an advocate, a buffer to some faculty-imposed stresses, and a source of information on discriminating between important and unimportant uses of your time and energy. Selecting a faculty advocate is a critically important activity. Consult with other graduate students to see who would best fit your needs.

Develop and maintain some key informants among students who have been in the program for several years. They can provide guidance on pitfalls to avoid, the natural history of stressful events and stress reactions in the program (e.g., precomprehensive examination anxiety, important exams, places where other students have gotten stuck), information on dealing with faculty (selecting thesis and dissertation committee, good advisors, faculty or courses to avoid), and the environment (reasonable course loads and sequences, pacing one's own progress, reasonable reactions to unreasonable demands).

Assemble a support group. Many programs have formal groups for first-year students, which are useful for sharing information and for complaining about the program. Be careful about anxiety contagion during high-stress periods. Norton (1996) described the value in a social support group for the sole purpose of completing the dissertation. She found the experience to increase stress tolerance throughout the process, decrease feelings of anxiety, frustration, and isolation, and provide instrumental information about the nuts of bolts of completing the process. She also found the mutual accountability to result in a decrease in the tendency to procrastinate, which is a factor often related to a delay in the completion of the dissertation (Muszynski & Akamatsu, 1991). Consider developing such a group in your department.

Analyze your working environment for role conflict, role ambiguity, work overload, and other structural factors. Where possible, try to avoid getting into structural binds by identifying them ahead of time.

### Anxiety Management

When you begin to feel signs of stress, seek out others, especially other students, to gain some validation of your feelings. Others are probably feeling as miserable as you do. Feeling miserable is an integral part of the normal graduate school experience.

Monitor your stress level. When talking or interacting with others, monitor your own stress. If regular contact with a particular person makes you anxious, avoid that person. Limit stress-inducing contacts, especially in times of high external stress, and at those times keep the focus of interactions on instrumental tasks such as sharing information rather than on emotional discharge. For example, share lecture notes or outlines of readings before a big exam, but not your fears and anxiety about what life will be like if you do poorly on the exam.

Some people are stress carriers, either in general or for you in particular. By stress carriers, I mean that some people increase your level of anxiety or other symptoms of stress beyond useful levels without providing information or other help to offset the increased load of stress you get. Because over 80% of all out of class interactions during the day are with graduate students in the department, stress contagion is easy to get going (Goplerud, 1978).

## CONCLUSION

Stressful life changes are a natural, if often unpleasant, part of living. The time when students are in professional training is no exception. Keim et al. (1996) opined about the importance of becoming self-stress management experts, especially for those students working in applied fields. They suggested that learning self-awareness and stress reduction techniques would not only be helpful for the student in training but also for the clients they are attempting to help.

In this chapter, sources of stress for graduate students have been outlined, and suggestions have been made to help students better manage those stressors. Stress management is a relatively new area of interest for psychologists, and there have been few studies that look specifically at graduate school stress. Far more research needs to be conducted before the observations made in this chapter can be considered proven, and the suggestions on stress mastery are prescriptive. Comparative studies of graduate students and their age cohort not in graduate school are necessary to identify the specificity of job and working conditions stresses to the graduate environment. Also, the impact of a wide variety of stress management techniques (including those suggested in the last part of this chapter) has not been subjected to rigorous outcome assessment. It may be a challenge for current and prospective graduate students in psychology to scrutinize their working conditions systematically for stress-inducing factors, and for additional techniques for mastering the stresses found.

# REFERENCES

American Psychological Association. (1998). *1996–1997 Insert to Graduate Study.* Available from APA Research Office, 750 First St. NE, Washington, D.C. 20002–4242.

Baird, L. L. (1969) A study of the role relations of graduate students. *Journal of Educational Psychology, 60*, 15–21.

Becker, H. S., Geer, B., Hughes, E. C., & Strauss, A. L. (1961). *Boys in white: Student culture in medical school.* Chicago: University of Chicago Press.

Binder, J., & Strupp, H. H. (1997). Supervision of psychodynamic psycho therapies. In C. E. Watkins (Ed.), *Handbook of psychotherapy supervision* (pp. 44–62). New York: John Wiley.

Burns, D. (1999). *Feeling good: The new mood therapy.* New York: MorrowBooks.

Cahir, N., & Morris, R. (1991). The psychology student stress questionnaire. *Journal of Clinical Psychology, 47*, 414–417.

Caplan, G. (1981). Mastery of stress: Psychosocial aspects. *American Journal of Psychiatry, 138*, 413–420.

Ellis, A. (1994). *How to stubbornly refuse to make yourself miserable about anything.* New York: Carol Books.

French, J. R. P., & Caplan R. D. (1973). Organizational stress and individual strain. In A. J. Marrow (Ed.), *The failure of success* (pp. 30–66). New York: AMACOM.

Goplerud, E. N. (1977). *Thoughts on a model program for assessing and promoting competence.* Unpublished manuscript, SUNY at Buffalo.

Goplerud, E. N. (1978). *Social support and stress during the first year of graduate school.* Unpublished manuscript, SUNY at Buffalo.

Goplerud, E. N. (1980). Social support and stress during the first year of graduate school. *Professional Psychology, 11*, 283–289.

Hall, D. T. (1969). The impact of peer interaction during an academic role transition. *Sociology of Education, 42*, 118–140.

Halleck, S. L. (1976). Emotional problems of graduate students. In J. Katz & R. T. Hartnett (Eds.), *Scholars in the making* (pp. 161–176). Cambridge, MA: Ballinger.

Hartnett, R. T. (1976). Environments for advanced learning. In J. Katz & R. T. Hartnett (Eds.), *Scholars in the making* (pp. 49–84). Cambridge, MA: Ballinger.

Holzman, L., Searight, H. R., & Hughes, H. (1996). Clinical psychology graduate students and personal psychotherapy: Results of an exploratory study. *Professional Psychology: Research and Practice, 27*, 98–101.

Keim, J., Fuller, C., & Day, J. (1996, August). *Stress among psychology graduate students.* Paper presented at the Meetings of the American Psychological Association, Toronto, Canada.

Kjerulff, K., & Wiggins, N. H. (1976). Graduate student styles for coping with stressful situations. *Journal of Educational Psychology, 68*, 247–254.

Kleepsies, P., Smith, M., & Becker, B. (1990). Psychology interns as patient suicide survivors: Incidence, impact and recovery. *Professional Psychology: Research and Practice, 21*, 257–263.

Kuyken, W., Peters, E., Power, M., & Lavender, T. (1998). The psychological adaptation of psychologists in clinical training: The role of cognition, coping and social support. *Clinical Psychology and Psychotherapy, 5*, 238–252.

Levine, M., & Perkins, D. (1997). *Principles of community psychology* (2nd ed.). New York: Oxford Press.

Lowman, R. (1993). *Counseling and psychotherapy of work dysfunctions.* Washington, DC: American Psychological Association.

Mallinckrodt, B., & Leong, F. (1992). Social support in academic programs and family environments: Sex differences and role conflicts for graduate students. *Journal of Counseling and Development*, 1992, *70*, 716–723.

Mallinckrodt, B., Leong, F., & Kralj, M. (1989). Sex differences in graduate student life-change stress and stress symptoms. *Journal of College Student Development*, *30*, 332–338.

McKee, G., Markham, S., & Scott, K. (1992). Job stress and employee withdrawal from work. In J. Quick, L. Murphy, & J. Hurrell (Eds.), *Stress and well-being at work* (pp. 153–163). Washington, DC: American Psychological Association.

McLaughlin, M. (1985). Graduate school and families: Issues for academic departments and university mental health professionals. *Journal of College Student Personnel*, *26*, 488–491.

Mechanic, D. (1962). *Students under stress*. Glencoe, IL: The Free Press.

Montat, A., & Lazarus, R. (1991). *Stress and coping: An anthology* (3rd ed.). New York: Columbia University Press.

Murphy, L., Hurrell, J., & Quick, J. (1992). Work and well-being: Where do we go from here? In J. Quick, L. Murphy & J. Hurrell (Eds.) *Stress and well-being at work* (pp. 331–347). Washington, DC: American Psychological Association.

Muszynski, S., & Akamatsu, T. (1991). Delay in completion of doctoral dissertation in clinical psychology. *Professional Psychology: Research and Practice*, *22*, 119–123.

Norton, K. (1996, August). *Dissertation support group: Transitions from graduate student to practicing professional*. Paper presented at the Meetings of the American Psychological Association, New York.

Pargament, K. (1997). *The psychology of religion and coping: Theory, research, and practice*. New York: Guilford.

Quick, J., Murphy, R., Hurrell, J., & Orman, D. (1992). The value of work, the risk of distress, and the power of prevention. In J. Quick, L. Murphy, & J. Hurrell (Eds.), *Stress and well-being at work* (pp. 3–13). Washington, DC: American Psychological Association.

# 11

# Stresses and Strategies for Underrepresented Students: Gender, Sexual, and Racial Minorities

*Renelle Massey*

*Steven Walfish*

All graduate psychology students experience rigorous demands during the course of their training. However, certain groups of students may experience special conflicts and realities that can add more stress to the training experience. Women, racial minority and gay/lesbian/bisexual/transgendered (GLBT) students have additional issues that can make a demanding education regimen even more difficult. In this chapter the focus primarily is on these minorities, but we discuss other minority groups to a lesser extent. Minorities usually experience the same stresses in graduate school that they do in Western society at large. The overall intent of this chapter is to identify the stressors of being different from "the mainstream," thereby offering validation of the experience, and to identify ways to cope with the challenges that often accompany this status. The good news is that the issues are being acknowledged and there are growing resources and support to help with them.

## STRESSORS FOR MINORITY GROUPS

Stressors specific to minority groups range from identity and esteem issues to subtle prejudice and blatant discrimination. Briefly, the identity issues we are discussing involve such questions as: Where do I fit in this profession? How does my minority status affect me as a professional? Do I want to focus my professional work on issues related to my minority group? What do I have to offer the profession, especially as it pertains to my minority group? What can I offer my minority group that relates to psychology?

## STRATEGIES FOR COPING

There are a number of ways all minorities can seek both instrumental and emotional support for their professional training and identity development. Some of these approaches are discussed, and various resources are provided in this chapter. The strategies described stem from the personal experiences of the authors, their colleagues, their students, and their clients, as well as from research. As with any coping mechanism, you may need to make adaptations to fit your unique situation and use your best judgment in implementation.

Before we start with these strategies, we first look at the general issue of attitude. It is probably best to assume people will treat you fairly. Give them the benefit of the doubt. For example, if you are struggling to get time with a professor, recognize that professors are busy people. Making an appointment, organizing your questions well in advance, and expressing appreciation for their attention are helpful strategies in using your time with professors effectively. Do not read sexism, homophobia, and racism into situations too easily, but be willing to offer gentle, educative dialogue when prejudice, insensitivity, or ignorance is clearly present. Conversely, choose your associations with discretion, but not snobbery. This may seem obvious, but we have found psychologists sometimes can be overly analytical and judgmental of others. Treat all your classmates with respect, although you may be closer to some than to others. This advice holds true for department secretaries, members of other classes, and professors, even if they seem to be the object of others' jokes or derision. This behavior will earn you a reputation as a respectful and fair person, something we hope you value. Plus, you never know who will keep you informed about department comings-and-goings and help influence your career opportunities. Some people, for example, say secretaries really run an office. Also, everyone you encounter can teach you something, even if it is how you do not want to be. Having reviewed these general points, let us examine some specific stressors.

## STRESSORS FOR WOMEN

Despite the fact that women are a numerical majority in our culture, they are often in the minority in positions of authority. The lack of women elected as legislators or hired into upper management positions in the corporate world illustrates this point. Psychology is more gender-balanced than many professions, but pay and promotion inequities still exist. For example, in medical school settings, despite no differences in productivity or years of employment, male faculty members are better paid than their female counterparts (Black & Holden, 1998; William & Wedding, 1999). In academia, male professors are often predominant, sometimes bringing misogynistic biases and practices. We are aware of a situation in which one female student was told to sit in the back of the classroom when she was in graduate school, just as African-Americans were forced to sit in the back of buses decades ago. Because patriarchal systems often exist in academia, women may be challenged to find female role models who can help develop their professional identities.

Assuming an authority role or being in a competitive, achievement-oriented environment will be an adjustment for many women in clinical, academic, corporate, or other institutional settings. In a culture where women are often still not considered adequate leaders, women have to work harder to gain confidence about their knowledge, skills, and abilities. In reflecting on their own graduate training experience, McGowen and Hart (1990) noted:

> Male students were more self-assured and opinionated from the outset and were geared toward academic success.... In contrast, the women were more undecided about their goals and more likely to approach graduate school with questions about how to make course work personally relevant and consistent with a sense of themselves in relation to others ... Men's achievement was focused on objective measures. Women's achievement was embedded in an interpersonal context. (p.120)

Women may particularly need help embracing the belief that their way of doing or viewing something has value and is no less valid even though it is different from the methods men employ. Conversely, women may need to guard against pushing assertiveness into abuse, as some authority figures are prone to do, especially when they initially obtain power.

One issue women are likely to find easier to discuss with another woman is sexuality, such as how to deal with erotic transference and countertransference in clinical settings. Our profession's ethical standards commit us to avoiding dual relationships. So heterosexual women will need to address issues about how to work closely with male colleagues, supervisors, or professors without pursuing a consensual sexual relationship. A related problem women face more than men is sexual harassment, which is most likely to involve heterosexual men targeting (usually heterosexual) women.

## STRATEGIES FOR WOMEN

### Classmates

In the first year in graduate training, although women need to establish cooperative relationships with everyone in their admissions class, bonding with the other women is especially important. This group will be the main group you interact with early in training, and can be a foundation for support. Organized, but informal, get-togethers are a helpful idea. Most of you will have relocated and be scared about starting school and meeting people, so it's likely everyone will welcome this idea. One class that we are aware of started its own psychotherapy group, but we observed problems stemming from forced intimacy. However, suggesting a weekly dinner (pot-luck or at an affordable restaurant) can provide time to connect, gripe, laugh, and share struggles, fears, and solutions. This setting can also help you ascertain the level of trust and similarity in values you can have with your colleagues, which may help to form individual friendships. Agree to try these dinners for the first semester, and then evaluate if it would be helpful to continue. (Citing time demands may then be a socially acceptable way to back out of the dinners if you find them unpleasant). Through get-togethers, the first author's first-year graduate class began addressing each other as "Dr.," which was a nice way to start taking ourselves seriously as young professionals-to-be.

Do not make these gatherings just gossip-fests or times to gripe. Make sure they are aimed at professional development and problem-solving. You could even make it a point to preplan topics of discussion for each meeting or provide a platform to practice upcoming presentations. Aim to develop a vision of who you want to be as professionals. Talk about how you will deal with issues such as competing for jobs, negotiating salaries or charging clients, and balancing work and personal life. Relevant discussion topics include examining messages you receive(d) from your family, movies, teachers, and others about becoming a professional and specifically a psychologist. Also, what are your ideals and how can you start living up to them?

For other topics to consider, look to writings about and by women. We know you are swamped with reading, but you might add some feminist literature to your list by alternating discussion leaders who read a chapter each week. *Women's Reality* (1992) by Anne Wilson Schaef and Carol Pearson is great feminist thought regarding women's obstacles to valuing themselves. Juanita Williams' (1985) *Psychology of Women* is an excellent collection of writings on the same issues. There are also plenty of well-known authors, such as Betty Friedan, Gloria Steinem, Marilyn French, and psychology's own Carol Gilligan. You can look into professional journals that address such women's issues as assuming authority, taking yourself seriously, and more.

## Mentors

Students further advanced in your training program, as well as established professionals, can be mentors. Consider talking to students in more advanced classes as soon as possible. If there is not a buddy or mentor system set up already, propose that one be developed. Seek information from students that are respected. Find out:

- What are the qualities of the supervisors and professors.
- What elective courses are useful.
- Other ways to maximize your training experience.
- Who holds negative or affirming attitudes toward women.

## Sexuality

One particularly useful piece of information is whether any of the male (or female—less likely, but it happens) professors approach female students to engage in sexual relations. This may be in exchange for better grades or to develop an ongoing relationship. Students are more likely to share this information than a professor.

Avoid any such liaison, for grades or otherwise. You are building your professional reputation from day one of your training. A sexual relationship with a professor is a violation of our profession's ethical standards against having two types of relationships at the same time (i.e., dual-role relationships). Such relationships are inherently unbalanced in terms of power issues, and aspects of one role (e.g., love, or later anger) may compromise another role (e.g, integrity in grading, awarding assistantships, writing letters of recommendation). Some researchers have even found that women who have sexual relations with their professors are later more likely to do the same with psychotherapy clients (Pope, Levenson, & Schover, 1979). It is a dangerous trend and predatory practice that can hurt you and others, regardless of whether the poor boundaries started with the professor or were already there within the student. Besides, people will find out, even if you try to keep the relationship secret, and this discovery will likely damage your professional reputation (probably much more than that of the professor). You will have difficulty rebuilding your reputation after people learn of these types of lapses in your judgment. It is no different from developing a relationship with an employer. It is inappropriate and should be considered to be sexual harassment due to the inequality in power. The student is almost always the loser in this situation. We suggest adhering to the sage advice of one of our colleagues, who opines, "She who screws the boss, usually gets screwed!" This is borne out in data presented by Hammel, Olkin, and Taube (1996) who found that 2% of males had sexual contact with an educator during their graduate school years but this figure was 15% for females. These researchers concluded:

> Respondents were, in retrospect, more likely to view the sexual relationship as coercive, ethically problematic, and a hindrance to the working relationship.... The gender and age composition of these liaisons still reflects a great power differential. The modal relationship is between an older male professor and a younger female graduate student.

Talk about your attraction to a professor or supervisor with a trusted person, maybe someone not associated with your training program. Such a discussion can decrease the power and intensity of your secret.

Mintz, Rideout, and Bartels (1994) reported an alarming number of women experiencing sexual harassment from male faculty and supervisors during their graduate training. Schover, Levenson, and Pope (1983) elaborated on coping strategies at both the individual and organizational level for students who are sexually harassed by faculty members. We would suggest that if a professor makes one or two advances toward you that are indirect or uncertain, ignoring the advances may be enough to end the matter. However, if the supervisor or professor is more direct or persistent, be equally direct from the start, stating that you wish to keep your relationship strictly professional. This stance will be easier on you and will be clearer to the professor. Should the professor persist, document the actions, your responses and reactions, and the dates and settings of the events. Further, report the matter to the appropriate authorities up the chain of command over the offending professor or supervisor. The student can seek aid from administrative personnel or student advocates in the offices of the dean of students or human resources. It may be appropriate to file complaints with the state licensing board and any state or national psychology associations to which the professor belongs. The unfortunate reality is that sexual and other forms of harassment still occur, even in our profession, and students are an inviting target because they want to please professors in order to get good grades and letters of recommendation. Biaggio, Paget, and Chanoweth (1997) provided a model for ethically managing the inevitable dual relationships that can develop between students and faculty. They argued that a key aspect is fostering and maintaining an education and training climate that supports ethical relationships with students.

These steps may also be a useful approach to addressing issues of gender discrimination. An organization that specializes in all of these issues for women in work settings is "9 to 5" (800-522-0925). The American Civil Liberties Union (ACLU—your local chapter or 125 Broad Street, 18th Floor, New York, NY 10004 or www.aclu.org) may be another useful resource.

Sexuality is also an uncomfortable subject that may arise in the context of psychotherapy, testing, and other professional relationships in which you, not the professor, will be the authority figure. It is worth thinking about the issue in advance to have an idea about how you will address it when the occasion inevitably arises. The first author's first experience with a client expressing amorous feelings was on internship, and it was helpful to talk with a supervisor about the experience. Even though the issue had been discussed in theory in an ethics seminar, it was unnerving to have to handle it and set clear limits while dealing with the whole incident therapeutically. Although other students may give you support, it is most important to talk with a trusted supervisor who likely has more experience with the issues of attraction from or to a client. Pope, Keith-Spiegel, and Tabachnik (1986) reported that 55% of therapists surveyed reported no training or education about coping with sexual attraction to clients. If this is true in your program, be proactive and talk about this issue with a supervisor, so you can avoid these types of dual relationships as well.

### Professional Organizations

State and national professional organizations can provide opportunities for connecting with mentors, whom you may work with or speak with in several forums. The American Psychological Association (APA) Division 35 (www.apa.org/divisions/div35) focuses on women's issues, and many state, regional, and specialty area psychology associations have similar divisions. Also, the Association for Women in Psychology (AWP) has its own annual conference. Although going to these conferences can be costly for students whose money and time are tight, these organizations often give student discounts or work credits. Consider these expenditures as investments in your future. You will see many issues covered and observe differing ways of being a professional that you might otherwise not get a chance to witness. In addition, these professional organizations may be sources for scholarships and research grants.

### Coursework

Required term papers, your thesis, and your dissertation provide opportunities to pursue topics that may be of interest to you, including women's issues. For example, a woman interested in studying substance abuse may want to look more closely at how women's patterns of substance use differ from men's patterns. In many areas of the allied health professions, men—not women—have been studied or the two genders have been studied as if they have the same opportunities, biologies, attitudes, and feelings. Some savvy students even begin their publishing by focusing on a topic of interest, producing high-quality papers for classes, and then submitting them to journals for consideration for publication.

Create opportunities for more exposure to female professionals and various women's issues. Most programs have some room for choosing elective courses and a minor or subspecialty. Consider taking classes on women's issues, perhaps in other departments, if allowed. Another option is to design your own curriculum for an independent study, perhaps with a professor in another department. In some circumstances a student can have a professor from another department serve on thesis and dissertation committees, albeit as an extra member. Adjunct faculty may be particularly valuable, as they are likely to work mainly in an applied area of interest to you. They usually have fewer students, so they may have more time to spend with you, thereby maximizing variety in your coursework and mentoring.

## STRESSORS FOR GLBT PERSONS

Regrettably, it is easy to find examples of homophobia in our culture, such as the murder of Matthew Shepard or the ban on gays in the military. Sexual minorities still contend with legal discrimination. Many people do not realize that most states have no protection for sexual minorities in regard to jobs, housing, education, and other basic issues of living. A colleague of the authors was out as a gay man in his psychology training program, and his research topics were often gay related. He did not receive an internship offer when he first applied, despite being considered one of the best students in his graduate program. He applied again the next year, intentionally "downplaying" his interests in gay issues, and finally received an internship offer. Although racial, gender, and other minorities still face hidden and subtle discrimination, only sexual minorities still face legalized, blatant discrimination.

A more subtle form of prejudice that GLBT people face is "heterosexism," a concept not as widely known as homophobia. Briefly, heterosexism is the assumption that people are or should be heterosexual. When your Aunt Gertrude asks when you are going to marry a nice man or woman (i.e., person of the opposite sex), without even considering the possibility that you might not be heterosexual, you are experiencing heterosexism. Heterosexism in mental health fields is beginning to be researched, as well as "biphobia" (negative attitudes and feelings toward bisexuals). For example, Berkman and Zinberg (1997) found that 10% of social workers surveyed were homophobic, and a majority were heterosexist. Certainly graduate psychology students—homosexual and heterosexual—will encounter these forms of prejudice. Pilkington and Cantor (1996) presented data on perceived heterosexual bias in professional psychology training programs by detailing and categorizing examples regarding antilesbian, antigay, or heterosexually biased experiences during all aspects of the education and training process.

For a member of one of these sexual minority groups, graduate training and professional development may be particularly complicated if these issues coincide with the person's "coming out." This timing is often the case, as many people grasp more about their sexuality during their twenties, an age when many students are in graduate school. This "developmental collision" means that these sexual minority group members have less experience dealing with their minority status issues and integrating them into their overall personal development, much less into their professional identity.

Female and racial minorities usually have no choice about revealing their minority status. For the most part, their minority status is obvious, which makes selecting them as mentors for women and racial minority students an easier proposition. GLBT students may have to work harder to find mentors who are either GLBT or are supportive heterosexuals. Making that kind of match means that both the student and the mentor must have the courage to self-identify in their minority group. So the coming out process, both personally and professionally, calls for raising personal standards and embracing the risks inherent in that stance. The amount of help GLBT students can get in integrating their GLBT status with their professional identity will relate directly with the degree to which they openly address these issues with peers, professors, or anyone. Thus, these students face inherent risks of coming out just to work on how being GLBT interfaces with their professional lives.

GLBT issues and role models are largely hidden for most of us growing up—GLBT or otherwise. Thus, GLBT persons come out largely on their own, without the loving guidance of an adult or authority figure. The same isolated position may be replicated in the professional experience. Some professionals stay closeted because of stigmas associated with their minority status and legalized discrimination (e.g., no job protection). Liddle, Kunkel, Kick, and Hauenstein (1998) reported on the experiences of gay, lesbian, and bisexual psychology faculty. Although positive aspects were noted, "the picture that emerged was one that included issues of anxiety, isolation, and threat." Thus, GLBT students have to sort through whether or not to come out, to whom, how, and when. Whatever their choices in this regard, stigma and discrimination are issues for a GLBT person to resolve personally and professionally, hopefully in ways that are affirmative and empowering.

## STRATEGIES FOR GLBT PERSONS

In the name of ethical self-disclosure, we should mention that our bias is that being as out as you are comfortable being is the best overall strategy for every area of your life. Being out is good for your own mental and physical health, for progress for other GLBT people, for society as a whole, and for our profession in particular. For example, being out reduces all sorts of stresses, from spending energy trying to hide, to hoping not to be found out. Research findings suggest being more out decreases some heterosexist experiences (Waldo, 1999) and some privately held negative attitudes (Grack & Richman, 1996). We also recognize that coming out is an individual and personal process that continues throughout one's life and across all domains of thoughts, feelings, and actions. Although there are many rewards to being as out as you can be, there are also consequences, some serious or even fatal. So try to ensure you have the support needed to deal with possible consequences before taking actions that may have results you may not like.

Integrating this facet of yourself into your professional identity will be affected by the point you are at and what your goals are in the coming out process. The coming-out process ranges from just starting to recognize your homosexual feelings, to telling a few friends, to taking your partner to family gatherings, to being politically active, to bringing your partner to work or school functions. If you are early in your coming-out process, it is wise to educate yourself, garner social support, and clarify your personal values before you try to form your identity as a professional who happens to be GLBT. Obtaining the name of a GLBT-affirmative psychotherapist (e.g., from APA or your state psychology association) plus connecting with social, political or support groups may be useful if you are early in the process. You may find these groups listed in local GLBT newspapers, magazines, and some mainstream newspapers. Bookstores and Internet sites address GLBT issues. However, if you are further along in the coming-out process, you may be ready to take more advanced steps to integrate your personal issues into your professional identity, in addition to establishing a support network outside of your professional training.

There are several ways to handle the coming-out process as it affects personal and professional issues. Some people decide to remain highly closeted, and that is a valid choice, although it requires a lot of energy and has costs just like being out. Others try to establish themselves as good students or competent individuals before coming out. Another alternative is to come out first with people who are likely to be supportive and will not hurt you or your career. Simply being consistently out from the start with everyone (or almost everyone) you meet is another option.

### Classmates

If you have any classmates you think might be GLBT, start with them, if you find them trustworthy. Share impressions and information about the department atmosphere and how out you can safely be. If no one in your class is GLBT, look into whether or not your university or program has a group for GLBT students and/or faculty.

## Reading

Peers and GLBT bookstores can recommend books to educate yourself about GLBT issues from shame to equal rights and parenting to partnering. The number of books, journals, and websites dealing with these issues is growing astronomically. Nonprofessional books that cover a range of simpler issues are a good place to start. Then focus on issues of most interest to you, including professional literature. If a bookstore near you does not have titles, check some professional organizations identified later in this chapter, and major psychology book and journal publishers.

## Mentors

In choosing a mentor, GLBT and GLBT-affirmative faculty may both have advantages and disadvantages. Carefully think about the compatibility of any mentor with you and your needs. Sometimes only GLBT-friendly professors, or ones you are unsure about, may be available. In some cases, these faculty may be better mentors for you than GLBT professors. However, you are likely to want and benefit from having at least one GLBT faculty member among your mentors, if one is accessible.

Although there are exceptions our experience is that many psychologists in their fifties and older tend to be more "closeted," as is true for the overall GLBT population. We do not mean any disrespect to older colleagues who have faced more rigid and traumatic times in our culture and profession. Younger psychologists tend to be out more as society has become somewhat more accepting of sexual minorities over time, with more GLBT people coming out. These observations are made to offer ideas about where to look for your mentors. In general terms, younger psychologists may have higher expectations about being treated fairly and accept less discriminatory treatment, although plenty have still encountered it. Older psychologists may have more experience coping with discrimination, emotionally and otherwise. Older psychologists may also provide some sense of the significant history of discrimination faced by sexual minorities, including in psychology, and may know more about negotiating department politics. We offer GLBT students the following suggestions in choosing mentors:

- Mentors who are more out personally and professionally may help you expand your view of your own possibilities for being a psychologist who is GLBT. Even if you do not choose to be as out as these mentors, they can support you in your process of choosing how out to be—ideally without their own fears inhibiting you and without pressuring you to be like them.

- Find mentors who have integrated their GLBT status into their professional identity in a way that you want to emulate.

- Though these are just emerging, another possible resource is through your program's or university's GLBT alumni group.

- Seek GLBT-affirmative mentors. You can use informal means to see who fills the bill. Also, some programs have recently developed "Safe Space" indicators: Professors who are GLBT or GLBT-friendly put a pink triangle (a symbol from gay men persecuted during the Holocaust) on their doors. In some schools, professors complete a brief training course to obtain the pink triangle.

## Sexuality

Most of the same considerations discussed in the section for women apply here as well. Attraction may arise with supervisors, clients, and/or colleagues. Depending on the gender of the person and his or her sexuality, you may find it even more uncomfortable discussing these issues. It is wise and ethical to avoid these dual relationships and to discuss these issues with a trusted supervisor.

For psychotherapists, school psychologists, and psychologists in other settings, there may be questions about disclosing your sexuality. You can expect to be asked directly at some point, so it is worth thinking in advance about how you want to respond. Your solutions may differ depending on the circumstances (e.g., clients with poor vs. healthy boundaries). The way you respond may also be related to how you live your personal life. For example, if you are a political activist for GLBT rights, many of your clients will obviously already know your GLBT status, which may be to your advantage when you are establishing a clientele.

On the other side, we know of an instance in rural Florida in which it is considered to be "moral turpitude" to be a homosexual. A school counselor, not wanting to lose her job, remained "in the closet." In some situations, such as organizational psychology you may have more separation between your personal and professional life. The first author, practicing as a clinical psychologist, was forced to leave a group practice as she became increasingly out as an activist with occasional media exposure. The senior partners in the practice feared this would hurt the practice's earnings by scaring away conservative clientele. Clearly, psychologists are not excluded from narrow-minded and bigoted thinking as well as fear-based decision making.

## Professional Organizations

There are numerous professional organizations for GLBT psychologists, and many have student divisions. APA Division 44 has a large presence at the APA annual convention, even developing its own mini-convention and hospitality suite in recent years. Division 44 (Society for the Psychological Study of Lesbian, Gay, and Bisexual Issues; www.apa.org/divisions/div44) keeps its membership list confidential. An increasing number of state psychology organizations have GLBT divisions, and some are even taking steps to develop mentoring programs. If your state association or your university/program does not have a branch for GLBT students, you could consider starting one. This may seem ambitious, especially given your busy schedule. Yet it can be rewarding in terms of providing support for yourself and future students. It can also be a way to establish yourself in the area as a person dealing with GLBT issues and to network in ways that may aid your career. Psychology and other organizations dealing with GLBT issues increasingly offer financial support for students and research.

## Coursework

Similar principles apply as discussed previously for women. Courses focusing specifically on GLBT issues are even more rare than courses focusing on women's issues. Again, consider using other departments, adjunct faculty, and developing independent study courses to the fullest extent allowed. Bear in mind that doing your thesis or dissertation on GLBT issues may "out" you now and alert future internship interviewers and employers to your GLBT status when these projects appear on your curriculum vitae. The good news is that there are more people studying and working with these issues in established programs and institutions, so you may just open the door for pursuing career opportunities of interest to you. Nonetheless, the risk of adverse consequences due to being GLBT still remains.

### Internship and Practica Sites

If you want to work with GLBT clients or organizations, we suggest that you first become fairly advanced in your own coming-out process for the same reasons mentioned in seeking a mentor who is out. You may need to be even more creative with pursuing these training experiences. Do your homework in advance to see what is already approved that matches your interests. If nothing fits, see what local organization you can work with and draft a proposal, especially with the help of a faculty advocate. Then pursue formal channels to have your proposal accepted. Remember, you will be breaking new ground in this case and need to be as professional as possible to make a case for others who may follow after you.

If you feel you are discriminated against due to your sexual minority status, first try to get validation about your perception. If your perception is borne out, then get some social support from friends and/or family. Seek guidance from someone with authority who may understand and have been through the situation. Document the incident(s), and consider trying to have witnesses to the problem. Pilkington and Cantor (1996) indicated that the Committee on Lesbian, Gay, and Bisexual Concerns of the American Psychological Association of Graduate Students has developed a guide (Cantor, 1994) for dealing with bias and discrimination (as well as more general resources). Study the ethics of our profession and see if informally addressing the situation is appropriate and effective. If not, study your legal options, consulting an attorney, Lambda Legal Defense and Education Fund (212-809-8585), the ACLU, or other relevant organizations. Again, if you need to express complaints, verbal or written, you should go up the ladder of your training program and/or institution. It also may be appropriate to file complaints with APA, your state psychology association, or the state licensing board. However, do understand that making charges of discrimination will not be taken lightly, and those being charged will most likely fight back vigorously. The student should be emotionally prepared to wage such a battle before taking steps to higher levels.

## STRESSORS FOR RACIAL MINORITIES

Most people in graduate training settings would now view racial discrimination to be at least "politically incorrect" and inappropriate, if not unethical, unacceptable, and illegal. Nonetheless, Farrell and Jones (1988) objectively documented racism in higher education, and scales have been developed to assess more subtle and perceived racism (e.g., Landrine & Klonoff, 1996; McNeilly et al., 1996; Utsey & Ponterotto, 1996). An African American colleague trained in a psychology graduate program in the 1980s encountered a professor who was researching racial differences in intelligence. The professor was prejudiced in believing that African Americans were intellectually inferior to Caucasians, not wanting to believe that test score differences might be attributable to cultural, economic, and educational differences. Such an environment can not have beneficial effects on developing a positive professional identity that embraces one's racial difference from the Caucasian mainstream.

More subtle forms of racist attitudes and behaviors, conscious and unconscious, create stressors with physiological and psychological effects for their targets (Clark, Anderson, Clark, & Williams, 1999). Subtle racism may translate into feelings of inferiority or of being treated as "less than." Overly high or low expectations of a racial minority may also be present, leading to such problems as not being considered for certain positions or opportunities. Keith-Spiegel and Wiederman (2000) wrote:

> Ethnic minority students may also be concerned about the effects of social isolation and/or identity maintenance once enrolled in a graduate program, whether they will be perceived as "token" students who would not have been accepted had it not been for their ethnic status, and whether racism—albeit, perhaps, more subtly expressed—will continue to cloud their paths. (p. 26)

Similar to other groups, racial minorities may also struggle with internalizing negative views of society at large, which may contribute to intragroup racism. Particular pressures may exist from within your own racial group to succeed and become a model for your particular race. Conversely, you may be criticized by members of your own race for appearing to sell out to the mainstream Caucasian culture and abandoning the heritage of your specific racial background by pursuing higher education. Once again, Keith-Spiegel and Wiederman (2000) wrote:

> Not every minority group member is an expert on his or her own group, is similar to others with the same ethnic designation, is a civil rights activist or aspires to specialize in research on or service to, other minorities. Yet all of these depictions are often automatically assumed by others to exist. (pp. 26–27)

## STRATEGIES FOR RACIAL MINORITIES

Strategies for racial minorities to survive graduate school are similar to those for the other minority groups, although family or other social support may be even more important than for some other minority groups. Daniels and Crawford (1997) found academic success in psychology graduate training to be positively related to receiving financial aid, establishing a mentor relationship, and the development of friendships with other minority students. These factors seem to buffer the stressors that are encountered in graduate school and allow minority students to thrive.

### Classmates

Develop ties with any other students who are racial minorities in your department. You will need to assess over time if these are peers with whom you want significant associations. In reflecting on his first attending a conference on Asian American Training in Psychology, recent APA President Richard Suinn (1992) wrote, "It is hard for me to express in words the emotion of being in the presence of so many Asian Americans in one place, and all of them psychologists" (p. 15).

Taylor (1994) recalled that an important objective in developing the Minority Fellowship Program at APA was to develop a critical mass of ethnic minority students for the purpose of social support. Similarly, Taylor pointed to the need for a critical mass of ethnic minorities within the faculty ranks to serve as role models. Several publications have focused upon issues related to the recruitment and retention of ethnic minority graduates students and faculty. We would urge students and academic administrators interested in these issues to consult Hammond and Yung (1993), Myers, Wolford, Guzman, and Echemendia (1991), and Stricker et al. (1990). Hammond and Yung (1993) presented a specific list of retention support strategies, both academic and nonacademic, for ethnic minority graduate students. Also the APA Commission on Ethnic Minority Recruitment, Retention, and Training in Psychology has several useful publication on these matters.

In addition to looking for peer support within the department in which the student is receiving training, we also suggest looking more broadly to the entire institution. Although you already know the cultural advantages you enjoy being around your own racial group and celebrating that heritage, you can also benefit from ties with other racial groups. You will not only gain wider exposure to new cultures, but you may learn new mechanisms for coping with being a minority.

## Mentors

Psychology graduate programs have made efforts to retain professors who are racial minorities, but not with much success. Finding role models of your race may be difficult in your immediate department, but casting a wider net may yield better results. There may be faculty in related departments or even in a minority faculty group who would provide mentoring. Outside the university setting, there are such organizations as "100 Black Men" willing to provide mentoring and other community services. Other community support may be available from churches, the Urban League, the National Council of La Raza, and the National Association for the Advancement of Colored People (NAACP at www.naacp.org). Some of these role models obviously may not address psychology issues directly, but may have gone through a similar process of identity development within their own professions.

Gary, Childs-Jackson, Durham, and Lewis (1990) described a program at Rutgers University in which ethnic minority alumni have an ongoing committee to advise the graduate psychology program on training issues related to working with ethnic minority clients, as well as to "facilitate a supportive environment for ethnic minority students, and to recruit ethnic minority faculty and students" (p. 490). We suggest that this program most likely is an anomaly which merits replication at training programs across the country. We would encourage students to approach their training departments to initiate such programs at their individual universities

## Professional Organizations

As with the other minorities, there are numerous professional organizations that are useful resources. These resources may provide mentors and funding information. They may also include journals and research topics, as well as helpful reading for your racial minority group. APA Division 45, Society for the Psychological Study of Ethnic Minority Issues (750 First Street, NE, Washington, DC 20002; 202-336-6029), has parallel divisions in various state psychology organizations. There are more specialized racial minority organizations for psychologists such as the Association of Black Psychologists (PO Box 5599, Washington, DC 20040; 202-722-0808), the Asian American Psychological Association (3003 North Central Avenue, Suite 103-198, Phoenix, AZ 85012; 480-230-4257), the National Hispanic Psychological Association, and the Society of Indian Psychologists (listserv at maryc@ mail.couns.msu.edu; website in development).

### Coursework

Some programs or institutions have departments that specialize in or include studies of certain racial groups. Use these for electives or to create joint curriculum including two or more departments. Also, independent studies and research projects, including your thesis or dissertation, can address racial issues.

### Internship and Practica Sites

These may be valuable experiences in terms of hands-on work with populations of interest to you. Interview at these sites while listening to your "gut" about the atmosphere for racial minorities. Although subtle prejudice is rampant, decide if the prejudice is typical and workable or overwhelming. If there is not a site where you can work with your own racial group and you want to do so, you might create a program that involves outreach to your community. In many large cities there are Jewish, Hispanic, Asian American, and African American service centers that may serve as great training sites. However, be aware that you may be the one who must establish the contact between your training program and the agency. Do so with the appropriate administrative approvals during this process.

If you encounter discrimination, refer to the previous sections for some general guidelines. More specifically, you can also access such organizations as the NAACP, the ACLU, and the like for further advice and possibly legal representation. Before taking these steps, recall that problems can often be solved in less formal and less adversarial means than in official administrative or legal proceedings. Less formal steps also provide the benefit of being less emotionally and financially taxing to all parties.

## STRESSORS FOR OTHER MINORITY GROUPS

Less literature is available on other minority groups, such as students of a non-traditional age or with physical disabilities. Also, recall that there are many ways of being different or a minority in any culture or subculture. In some settings the mainstream may even become the minority. For example, many clinical psychology programs have cognitive-behavioral emphases, and some professors are "anti-spiritual," for lack of a better phrase. In such a setting, people of any faith may feel oppressed due to the power structure in the subculture of that psychology program. We know of one instance in which a Jewish student who observed the Sabbath was expected by her major professor to be in the laboratory on Friday nights. Although she was not forced to be there, it was clear to the student that the faculty member was upset with her and questioned her dedication to her training. Whatever the minority status, smaller minority groups than the others discussed face the specific challenge of finding support among fewer resources.

## STRATEGIES FOR OTHER MINORITY GROUPS

Whether your minority status is more obvious and "traditional," such as a physical disability, or less recognized, such as being older, younger, or spiritually minded, we encourage you to use the principles outlined in the preceding sections. This includes finding support with peers and professional role models where possible. Develop connections and support groups, informal and formal, with peers who share your minority experience. Create or organize coursework, curricula, and training sites that meet your needs and interests. Seek out professional organizations and their divisions that may address your minority status (e.g., APA Division 22 for Rehabilitation Psychology at www.apa.org/divisions/div22; Division 36 for Psychology of Religion at www.apa.org/about/division/div36.html; and Division 20 for Adult Development and Aging at www.iog.wayne.edu/APADIV20/APADIV20.HTM). These may also help you find educational and validating reading lists as well as funding opportunities. As you probably already know from your life experience, you can expect people to speak or act in inappropriate or ignorant ways at times. Often you can educate them, but you also need not be discouraged by others' lack of consciousness. Finally, be willing to lead the way and create groups or opportunities for yourself to figure out how to integrate your minority status into your professional identity.

## CONCLUSION

The bad news is that prejudice and discrimination are alive and continue in the world. The good news is that there is progress, such as a heightened awareness and many more resources for combating the ill effects of such ignorant and sometimes illegal behavior. Varied types of discrimination and prejudice create adverse psychological and physiological effects. There are active ways of coping through accessing mentors, resources, information, social support, and reading. More passive means of coping, such as internal cognitive reframing, prayer, and meditation, are also options. Expect that most people will try to treat you fairly. However, you may also have to educate some people who may speak or act hurtfully out of either ignorance or malice. Remember, people's attitudes change just by being exposed to a positive, living, breathing member of a minority group. Thanks to the work of those before them, most members of underrepresented groups can now create the career and professional identity that they want for themselves.

## REFERENCES

Berkman, C. S., & Zinberg, G. (1997). *Homophobia and heterosexism in social workers. Social Work*, 42, 319–332.

Biaggio, M., Duffy, R., & Staffelbach, D. (1997). Obstacles to addressing professional misconduct. *Clinical Psychology Review, 18*, 273–285.

Black, M., & Holden, E. W. (1998). The impact of gender on productivity and satisfaction among medical school psychologists. *Journal of Clinical Psychology in Medical Settings*, 5, 117–131.

Cantor, J. (1994). *APAGS guide to graduate school for lesbian, gay, and bisexual students*. Available from APAGS, 750 First Street NE, Washington, DC 20002–4242.

Clark, R., Anderson, N. B., Clark, V. R., & Williams, D. R. (1999). Racism as a stressor for African Americans: A biopsychosocial model. *American Psychologist, 54*, 805–816.

Daniels, D., & Crawford, I. (1997, August). *Predictors of academic success for minority graduate students*. Paper presented at the meetings of the American Psychological Association, Chicago.

Farrell, W. C., Jr., & Jones, C. K. (1988). Recent racial incident in higher education: A preliminary perspective. *Urban Review, 20*, 211–226.

Gary, J., Childs-Jackson, G., Durham, I., & Lewis, S. (1990). Role of an ethnic minority alumni advisory committee in training professional psychologists. *Professional Psychology: Research and Practice, 21*, 489–492.

Grack, C., & Richman, C.L. (1996). Reducing general and specific heterosexism through cooperative contact. *Journal Psychology & Human Sexuality, 8*, 59–68.

Hammel, G., Olkin, R., & Taube, D. (1996). Student-educator sex in clinical and counseling psychology doctoral training. *Professional Psychology, Research and Practice, 27*, 93–97.

Hammond, W. R., & Yung, B. (1993). Minority student recruitment and retention practices among schools of professional psychology: A national survey and analysis. *Professional Psychology: Research and Practice, 24*, 3–12.

Keith-Spiegel, P., & Wiederman, M. W. (2000). The complete guide to graduate school admission: Psychology, counseling, and related professions. Hillsdale, NJ: Lawrence Erlbaum Associates.

Landrine, H., & Klonnoff, E. A. (1996). The Schedule of Racist Events: A measure of racial discrimination and a study of its negative physical and mental health consequences. *Journal of Black Psychology, 22*, 144–168.

Liddle, B., Kunkel, M., Kick, S., & Hauenstein, A. (1998). The gay, lesbian, and bisexual faculty experience: A concept map. *Teaching of Psychology, 25*, 19–25.

McGowen, K. R., & Hart, L. (1990). Still different after all these years: Gender differences in professional identity formation. *Professional Psychology: Research and Practice, 21*, 118–123.

McNeilly, M. D., Anderson, N. B., Armstead, C. A., Clark, R., Corbett, M. O., Robinson, E. L., Pieper, C. F., & Lipisto, M. (1996). The Perceived Racism Scale: A multidimensional assessment of the perception of White racism among African Americans. *Racism and Health, Ethnicity and Disease, 6*, 154–166.

Mintz, L., Rideout, C., & Bartels, K. (1994). A national survey of interns' perceptions of their preparation for counseling women and of the atmosphere of their graduate education. *Professional Psychology Research and Practice, 25*, 221–227.

Myers, H., Wohlford, P., Guzman, P., & Echemendia, R. (Eds.). (1991). *Ethnic minority perspectives on clinical training and services in psychology*. Washington, DC: American Psychological Association.

Pilkington, N., & Cantor, J. (1996). Perceptions of heterosexual bias in professional psychology programs: A survey of graduate students. *Professional Psychology: Research and Practice, 27*, 604–612.

Pope, K. S., Keith-Spiegel, P., & Tabachnik, B. G. (1986). Sexual attraction to clients: The human therapist and the (sometimes) inhuman training system. *American Psychologist, 41*, 147–158.

Pope, K. S., Levenson, H., & Schover, L R. (1979). Sexual intimacy in psychology training: Results and implications of a national survey. *American Psychologist, 34*, 682–689.

Schaef, A. W., & Pearson, C. S. (1992). *Women's reality: An emerging female system in a white male society*. San Francisco: Harper.

Schover, L. R., Levenson, H., & Pope, K. S. (1983). Sexual relationships in psychology training: A brief comment on ethical guidelines and coping strategies. *Psychology of Women Quarterly, 7*, 282–285.

Stricker, G., Davis-Russell, E., Bourg, E., Duran, E., Hammond, W. R., McHolland, J., Polite, K., & Vaughn, B. (1990). *Toward ethnic diversification in psychology education and training*. Washington, DC: American Psychological Association.

Suinn, R. (1992). Reflections on minority developments: An Asian-American perspective. *Professional Psychology: Research and Practice, 23*, 14–17.

Taylor, D. (1994). The autobiography of a social psychologist: Scholarship, advocacy and leadership. In P. Keller (Ed.) *Academic paths: Career decisions and experiences of psychologists* (pp. 159–170). Hillsdale, NJ: Lawrence Erlbaum Associates.

Utsey, S. O., & Ponterotto, J. G. (1996). Development and validation of the Index of Race-Related Stress (IRRS). *Journal of Counseling Psychology, 43*, 490–501.

Waldo, C. R. (1999). Working in a majority context: A structural model of heterosexism as Minority Stress in the Workplace. *Journal of Counseling Psychology, 46*, 218–232.

Williams, J. (1985). *Psychology of women: Selected readings*. New York: Norton.

Williams, S., & Wedding, D. (1999). Employment characteristics and salaries of psychologists in United States medical schools: Past and current trends. *Journal of Clinical Psychology in Medical Settings*, 6, 221–238.

# 12

# Stresses and Strategies for International Students

*Sami Gulgoz*

Students from many countries apply to graduate schools in the United States. American universities have become the most popular choice for graduate work in most disciplines, and psychology is no exception (Bhagwati & Rao, 1996). Despite some restrictions on financial support for international students and the limits on income generation set by the Immigration and Naturalization Service (INS), the international student population in U.S. graduate schools has grown considerably in both psychology and other fields (National Science Board, 1996; Snyder & Hoffman, 2000; Syverson & Bagley, 1999). In this chapter, I describe the process of being a graduate student in the United States from the perspective of an international student. I had the chance to experience graduate school life in the United States from many perspectives. I have been an applicant and subsequently a graduate student; I have had contacts with many international students during graduate school; I was a faculty member in the United States a job in which the responsibilities included selecting graduate students; and finally, as a faculty member in Turkey, I have advised and helped students on their applications to U.S. programs.

A number of the topics covered here overlap with the rest of the chapters in this book. In this chapter, the focus is on the group of applicants who are not U.S. citizens, and I write with the assumption that they know little about life in the United States. Therefore, this chapter should be viewed as supplemental to the other chapters, aimed particularly at international students.

## CHOOSING A UNIVERSITY TO ATTEND

One of the relevant types of information in making your decision is the number of international students in a university. A university with a substantial number of international students will probably have specialized offices to serve their needs. Many international students feel they would like the company of at least some other students from their own countries, although on most campuses international students socialize with students from many countries, not necessarily their compatriots. A university with a good number of international students would be more conducive to adaptation, more likely to have a "critical mass" that increases the international student's comfort level.

A related factor is the location of the university. Universities in North America are located in large or small cities or even in university towns. In university towns, most of the activity revolves around the university and most of the inhabitants are in some way connected to it. Some universities are located in big cities where there are a number of other universities and many activities and events unrelated to campus life. The applicant must remember that graduate study represents a commitment of about 2 years for a master's degree and 4 or more years for a doctorate. Therefore, it is important to consider the city in which the university is located. The environment provided by the city is as important as the university environment.

International students should be able to continue their cultural and religious lifestyles at least to some extent in the new environment. The presence of other people who share their interests and beliefs, whether or not they are fellow international students, is helpful. Therefore, if applicants are practicing Buddhism, they may search for others who are doing so; if they are members of Amnesty International, they may try to learn whether there is a chapter of AI in the town. If going to the ballet and the opera every week is important, then the choices of universities may be limited to a few big cities. Needless to say, the applicant may decide to forego some preferences during graduate school and focus on studies instead, but valued cultural activities make for a richer life experience, and will keep student life from becoming stale and a "grind."

Some international students may have different diets than those readily available in North America. Even if a student may not mind changing eating habits and adjusting to American food, there will be times when ethnic food will be desirable. North American supermarkets are increasing their selection of food from around the world, but even so, less common ethnic foods are only available in major cities. Therefore, a search on the Internet to determine the availability of markets with ethnic food may contribute to making your decision.

Your choice of schools should include universities in which you are comfortable and in cities where you would adjust relatively easily. For each university on your list of possible choices, be sure there is an international community and look for support for at least some elements of your lifestyle.

## BEFORE YOU LEAVE HOME

When you receive an acceptance letter, you will experience elation. If you receive multiple acceptance letters, you have to make a decision regarding which university to attend. Once this is done, a number of tasks will have to be completed before leaving for North America.

First, prepare a checklist of things to be done before leaving your home country. The activities can be classified as things to be done in order to leave the home country, to arrive at the school, and to live in that town. There may be a set of necessary tasks before leaving your country. These may vary from country to country and according to your lifestyle. For example, there may be a set of bureaucratic paperwork for you to complete with the government, such as registering with the ministry of education or postponing your required military duty. You may want to leave a forwarding address for your mail and for various bills. You will want to finish tasks at work, school, and home, and notify your friends, colleagues, teachers, and employers about your venture.

Complete as many of the graduate school's requirements as you can in your home country. One typical example is to copy your undergraduate transcripts and degree and have them translated. Some institutions also request that their students have their credentials validated at the local embassy.

The set of tasks to do in order to arrive at the graduate school begins with the task of getting a student visa to enter North America. The U.S. embassies or the consulates will require a set of documents as well as a visa application form. The visa procedures may take a considerable amount of time, depending on your home country. Therefore, it is important to submit the visa application well ahead of time, although some embassies will not accept an application long before the travel date. Buying plane tickets early may enable price comparison as well as guaranteeing a seat. The visa department in the embassy may request a copy of your plane ticket, too, so photocopy the ticket for the embassy, for your family's reference, and in the event it gets misplaced and you need to obtain a duplicate from the airline. Finally, it is important to get instructions for the trip from the local airport to your US residence.

Preparing one's luggage for living in North America can be tricky. Because the airlines limit luggage to two pieces per person and because inexpensive shopping is more available in North America than many other countries, the list of items you take should be limited to basic necessities. For example, taking linen for the beds may be inappropriate because it is possible that your home country uses different standards in bed sizes and one cannot predict what size of bed will be available. Of course, you need to be sure that you take along prescription medication in sufficient quantities to tide you over until you can secure a physician in your new locale. Be sure to take along documentation or prescriptions for the medication, too.

Probably one of the most crucial preparations is the psychological preparation to separate from family, friends, and a set of habits, especially if you have not separated from home for extended periods. It's a good idea to jointly decide about ways of keeping in touch with each other, to overcome the anxiety of separation.

## WHERE TO LIVE

Finding a residence may be the most important task in easing the transition for you. Fortunately, many universities have offices serving the residential needs of the students, and the Internet provides access to rental information in many towns. The critical decisions to make are residence on campus versus off campus, and shared versus single dwelling. Finances may dictate some of your choices. However, if there is a choice, the advantage for the first year will be to live in campus residences so that there are chances to establish social ties and to learn the culture. Whether you share the residence with another person is a personal choice. If your native language is not English, sharing a room with a native speaker may be beneficial. However, you should find a graduate student as a roommate, because lifestyles of undergraduate and graduate students in North American campuses are different. Undergraduate students are noisier and they are more inclined to partying than graduate students are. Indeed, if there is such a choice, you may prefer to stay at an on-campus residence strictly for graduate students.

When choosing residences, be sure to consider whether costs ancillary to rent are included. Some rents include the utilities, meaning that you will not need to pay separately for electricity, gas, water, and garbage pickup. Telephone bills are your responsibility even when the utilities are included in the rent. If the utilities are not included in the rent, you will have to pay separately for them, but generally water service and garbage pickup are still included in the rent. It might be useful to seek some advance information about the cost of utilities in your new city.

If the graduate school is providing financial assistance, you are not likely to receive any funds until the end of the first month. Therefore, you must be prepared to pay for your initial costs. In the initial costs of school, books, and other purchases, you may be required to pay deposits to your residence, the utility companies, and the telephone company. Another area to think about is transportation from your residence to the school. It is wise to learn how to drive. Even if you will live in a city where there is adequate public transportation (which is the case in a small number of cities), the driver's license is the most important form of U.S. identity. To obtain a license, you need some basic driving skills, because you will have to take a driving test.

## THE FIRST YEAR

Typically the first year at your new school is the most difficult one. Beyond the first year, patterns emerge and you get used to the environment. Therefore, let's focus on the issues of adjustment that will appear the first year.

### Initial Cultural Adjustment

There are many international students who thought of going back home in the first few days of being in North America. Most of these students have not had any assistance in their initial adjustment because they did not know of anybody who could assist them or because the university did not have an orientation for them. The adjustment happens for the majority of international students in a short time. In fact, once you have found social support from friends or from the university, or both, you may decide you would like to remain in North America after your graduate work (Johnson, 1998; Ries & Thurgood, 1993). But for your first arrival, contacting the international office, a student association of your home country, or your advisor before you arrive may provide you with the initial support necessary for a smooth transition.

There are a number of tasks that need to be handled in the first few days of arrival at graduate school. One of them is getting a driver's license if you are prepared to do so. However, in the United States, getting a driver's license is possible only after having a social security number. A social security number is a number that each person in the United States needs to have for most serious transactions, including opening a bank account, getting a driver's license, getting paid, and sometimes for obtaining a telephone, opening an account with utility companies, and many others. Therefore, it is critical that you get a social security number from the local social security office soon after arrival.

The initial days should be spent learning the neighborhood area, the university, and the particular program. A few people can be particularly helpful to you in the initial adjustment period. They include people from your home country, your faculty advisor, and other graduate students who have been working with the faculty advisor. These individuals can be contacted before arrival to school by requesting contact information from the international student office and the departmental graduate coordinator.

### Language and Culture

Comprehending spoken language can be a problem for many international students for whom English is a second language. Even if you have a high TOEFL score and have mastered the language, you may have problems when listening to English spoken in a somewhat different accent. Moreover, the vocabulary of the daily language, the slang, and the topics of conversation may not be familiar to you, contributing to the inability to comprehend a conversation fully. There are some steps to take to overcome these difficulties. First of all, try to socialize with native speakers, especially with the people from your new local community. Friendship with the people of your community will teach you much of the local culture. Second, choose a native speaker as a roommate, if possible. A third important step is to buy a television and watch whatever everybody else is watching, in addition to local news. In time, you will form your own preferences and will stop watching certain programs or channels while continuing to watch others. Many international students have reported picking up the colloquial English from TV situation comedies. Also, you can benefit from reading the local newspaper on a daily basis.

It is important at first that you explore new experiences and participate in different types of activities. You do not have to like all the activities or force yourself to continue to do these activities, but try them out. Participation in social and cultural life will facilitate your adaptation and improve your command of the language.

### Relationships and Social Life

Every culture defines acceptable and offensive relationships among people. Of course, these vary from one culture to another. Because differences are often subtle, strains in relationships due to cultural and linguistic sources can be frustrating. Graduate students in psychology can appreciate such differences and consider them as learning experiences toward an understanding of human relations from a cross-cultural perspective. Personally experiencing such differences may add to their understanding and contribute to their perspective in the sociocultural sources of human behavior.

An important source of frustration for many international students studying in North America is that people know so little about their countries. Americans are notorious for having little knowledge about other countries in the world. Don't let this disappoint or frustrate you. Actually, this situation may be an advantage for some. If people do not know much about a country, and prejudices they may harbor about its citizens are more easily overcome. Cultural differences appear most clearly when people from different cultures live together, but may be overcome by increased contact between people, although such fundamental preferences as the smells of food may remain unaltered. Therefore, sharing a residence with a person from another culture can be problematic in such areas as food odors and personal hygiene. You can deal with these differences by talking openly about expectations and trying to improve your tolerance and understanding, as well as your roommate's.

### Missing Home and Visiting Home

Shortly after arrival at the new environment, an international student may start missing home and may plan a trip back there. Generally, such trips are costly both financially and in terms of valuable time. You will get used to being homesick in time. It is wiser to stay in graduate school and continue the process of adaptation, as well as concentrating on graduate work, which may involve both courses and research. The first time that will be convenient for a trip back home will be around the Christmas break at the end of December. The season between Thanksgiving Day and New Year's Day, from the last week in November to the first of January, is holiday season in the United States. It is a major component of the American culture, and experiencing this season can contribute considerably to your cultural adaptation process. It is a good time, too, to catch up on school assignments and papers.

American graduate schools are more like a job that continues through the summer. So you may need to modify your habit of taking the summers off. Summer is a time when research and other work will continue. You may have to take some courses during the summer as well. Therefore, you must consider summer as a time when work continues, although you are able to take a couple of weeks of vacation.

## ACADEMIC LIFE IN THE FIRST YEAR

Success in graduate school is primarily determined by a student's performance in academic life, even though adaptation to the new environment is important (Espenshade & Rodriguez, 1997). The first year in graduate school generally entails taking a predetermined set of courses in the program area. Besides the courses, there may be the responsibilities of assistantship and research. However, the most critical person in the graduate student's life is the advisor/major professor.

### Advisor/Major Professor

A major professor or an advisor is a faculty member who will oversee your program of studies, research, and thesis or dissertation. Many times, the advisor may be able to assign assistantships to his or her students. Generally, faculty members who have agreed to work with international graduate students are more open to cultural differences. However, some faculty might not value training an international student as they would value working with a native student. In many universities your advisor may be assigned before your arrival to the graduate school, whereas in others you choose an advisor once you begin your studies. Most institutions allow students to change advisors before thesis work is under way. It would be wise for you to collect some information about your advisor and decide whether to stay with this advisor or change. If you have already done the research regarding a good fit between you and the advisor during the application process and have contacted your advisor in advance, then there will no need to change unless you discover a mismatch.

The relationship between a graduate student and an advisor is a significant one that will continue to have an impact long after you receive your degree. The cultural habits of the international student may restrict such a relationship. It is important to overcome those habits and form a relationship that will be mutually beneficial. Mutual benefit is one of the key expectations in a relationship between a graduate student and an advisor in the academic environment of the United States. The advisor expects the student to learn and start working rapidly, to help and be useful in research or other types of projects. The graduate student should expect to learn as an apprentice and contribute to the work of the advisor.

Students from many cultures will be in the habit of putting a respectful distance between themselves and their advisors. This is not the case among most American faculty and students. Even though there is still a mutually respectful relationship, this does not reveal itself as a distance between the two. The students may refer to their professors by their first names, socialize together, and talk to their advisors in the same way they would talk with their friends. For some international students, this is difficult to accept, let alone practice. If that is the case for you, you may decide to relate to the professor in a way that lets you feel comfortable, and this should not prevent you from benefitting from the relationship.

You may have arrived at the graduate school with bright ideas for projects. When you share these ideas with your advisor, the advisor may not sound as enthusiastic about your ideas. There may be several reasons. It is possible that what is a bright idea for you has already been done or is irrelevant in the context of current theory and research. It is also possible that the idea is a good one but is not part of your advisor's agenda. Your advisor might value his or her own project program and want to devote attention to this program and not divert to another project. When this is the case, you are better advised to get involved in the advisor's projects and postpone your own.

The *principle of reciprocity* is important in the American culture. Any favor done to a person creates an expectation for the other person to reciprocate. This is true in a student's relationship with the advisor as much as in social life. Some international students perceive the professor through a cultural lens revealing the professor as a person whose job is to serve the student. This perception may lead to some resentment from the professor because no favor is returned by the student. Recognizing this cultural perspective may help avoid culturally caused conflicts.

## Courses

The classroom environment in North America is substantially more relaxed than in many other countries. It is acceptable to drink coffee or a soft drink during the lecture; students ask questions easily; and student participation in class discussions is expected. At the same time, being in class on time and meeting the deadlines for assignments and projects are important. Many professors use humor in the classroom. Humor is a culturally defined matter as well. An international student may not understand the humor, may be intimidated by it, or may find it insulting because of cultural differences in definition of humor. Many students get offended or discouraged by their professors' remarks even when the remarks are well intentioned. Again, openness is an important quality in dealing with such situations. If you find yourself in a situation where you are offended by the professor's humor, you may want to consult American students and learn the intention and meaning. Humor can take place with good intentions with no hurtful motivation, but cultural nuance can lend a sharp edge to a joke. Be aware of and charitable of humor's subtlety.

Plagiarism and cheating are serious offences, and all the academic institutions have severe penalties for them. The definition of cheating and plagiarism may vary according to one's culture. In the American culture, any borrowing of someone else's work without clear reference to whose work it was would be considered plagiarism. The international students must be aware of different types of behaviors that may be considered plagiarism or cheating. In some cultures, cooperating with a classmate in assignments would not be considered cheating. However, in the American culture, graduate students are expected to submit work done individually, regardless of whether it is an insignificant assignment or a major project.

In some universities, the environment is highly competitive, leading to aggressive behavior by the students. Such behavior may include a lack of cooperation, hiding information or notes, a tendency not to share material or knowledge important for all students, and even misleading peers. Not all students exhibit this kind of behavior, and international students who are uncomfortable in such environments can form a support group with students who do not enter into the frenzy of competitiveness. However, this should not become a form of laziness that leads to lower performance.

Success in coursework is important. In graduate school, a grade of B (on a 5-point scale of A, B, C, D, and F where A is 4 and F, is 0) is an average grade, and C is a low grade and considered failing. Major obstacles for the international student can be the speed of reading in English, and difficulty in understanding lectures. Those international students for whom English is a second language may find it difficult to keep up with the readings assigned by the faculty in each course. Despite variations in assigned readings across schools and courses, you must spend a large portion of your time on reading assignments. The real difficulty lies in the integration of information from various readings. Many international students spend so much time and energy in comprehending individual reading materials that information coming from different materials cannot be integrated. Real comprehension lies in the integration of information. Therefore, you should take notes while reading the material, and review all the notes after finishing readings on a particular topic.

Difficulty in comprehending lectures is generally more pronounced at first, and vanishes gradually. There are a few actions that you can take to overcome this difficulty. First, you can request some assistance from the professor. Second, with the permission of the instructor, you can tape-record the lecture so that you can fully concentrate on understanding what is being said without worrying about taking notes. Finally, you can ask a classmate if you can copy his or her notes. Some students with a more competitive spirit may decline your request, but it is generally possible to find people who are sympathetic to such a request, as long as you do not forget the principle of reciprocity.

## RESEARCH

Research is a major issue in graduate school, especially for doctoral students and master's degree students who wish to continue in a doctoral program later. International students who have been somewhat isolated from the mainstream research trends and issues may feel some research issues are irrelevant. However, generally the issues are dictated by the general research paradigm, and therefore they are not selected independently. Similarly, your main research topic choices may be limited to areas in which your advisor has interests.

Nevertheless, you should not feel limited to your advisor's research areas. It is quite acceptable to get involved in other faculty research projects if they, too, are interesting. However, set priorities before getting involved in too much. If your resources are divided among too many projects, then the likelihood for successful and timely completion of the projects is greatly reduced.

Research should be conducted within a program. You may not like a particular research project and may leave it after getting involved for a while. Graduate school is an appropriate place to try different research programs, but there should not be too many changes. You need to settle soon on a research program and concentrate your efforts on successfully completing a project in that research program.

## ASSISTANTSHIP

Because an assistantship is a job, the rules that are valid when one has a job operate for an assistantship as well. There are a certain number of hours that an assistant is expected to work. It is important to meet those expectations. Also, international students are generally in a more difficult position as teaching assistants. Just like native students, you may have difficulty predicting your role as you teach students during teaching assistantship, feeling that you are not really an instructor but not one of the students either. A good way to overcome this difficulty is to assume the role of instructor of the course. A second difficulty is language. International students will have to pass some kind of spoken English test, such as the Test of Spoken English, before they begin to serve as teaching assistants. However, even if you pass the spoken test with high scores, you may still have problems related to your accent. It has been frequently observed that students may blame the teaching assistants as an excuse for their own poor performance. A couple of strategies are useful. One strategy is to explain to the students that your accent is different and it will not change for quite a long time. The second strategy is to reserve and announce certain periods every week for students who had trouble understanding the lecture and who would like to meet individually with you. These efforts to reach out to students often mute criticism, are good opportunities to help students learn, and are good ways to learn more about North Americans.

Misunderstandings with students of the opposite sex can be a serious problem for the teaching assistant. Because of cultural differences, behaviors may be interpreted in different ways and may lead to trouble. For example, the tendency of Americans to smile at people has been interpreted as interest in dating by some members of other cultures. Similarly, Americans or other cultures may interpret an innocent bodily contact for one culture as sexual harassment. Behavior that is culturally unacceptable may lead to misunderstandings and penalties, and therefore teaching assistants must be cautious in their relationship with students.

The research assistantship is simpler. A research assistantship offers freedom from possible problems that may develop when teaching, and an opportunity to gain research experience. Yet this trade-off may not be a good one in the long run. Although graduate school coursework emphasizes the preparation of graduate students for research, there is usually no training in teaching, leaving the student ill prepared for future teaching positions. A teaching assistantship can be an important source of this preparation. It may prove valuable when a doctoral student completes school and is ready to take a teaching position.

# BEYOND THE FIRST YEAR

Most of the major difficulties that are particular to the international student will confront the student in the first year. After the first year, there are fewer problems. A few additional issues that emerge after the first year are related to writing and to learning psychotherapy.

## Papers, Thesis, and Dissertation

Being a graduate student entails plenty of writing. The American educational system emphasizes writing, and therefore most American students are proficient writers. Actually, a large number of students have taken typing lessons and have good keyboard skills. International students who are not used to writing much will go through a period of adjustment and additional fatigue (Angelova & Riazantseva, 1999). The first step in learning to write for American graduate schools is to learn the rules established by the American Psychological Association, which can be found in the *Publication Manual* (APA, 1994). Research and review papers have particular structures and formats. The professors in graduate school will expect the students to write according to that structure and format. A basic method to learn writing that way is to read many articles published in scientific journals in psychology, in addition to reading the APA *Publication Manual*. International students may also have difficulty writing papers that are free of grammatical errors and problems of expression. Fortunately, the word-processing programs on computers catch many errors, but they are not sufficient in dealing with problems of expression. For that, you may want to seek assistance from appropriate offices on campus or from sympathetic friends. Also, there are several good stylebooks available, and some are mentioned in Hess's chapter on psychological assessment in Section III of this book.

The most critical writing during the graduate school will be the thesis as the dissertation. The student must select a topic first. Often the experience of being an international student stimulates an interest in cross-cultural comparisons. Such comparisons are necessary and important. It is a pity that most research literature in psychology today is composed of research on American participants (Kagitcibasi & Poortinga, 2000).

When cross-cultural research is conducted, the results may cast doubts on some prior literature, as did the research that showed us that fundamental attribution error may not be so fundamental (Markus & Kitayama, 1991). However, engaging in cross-cultural research for thesis or dissertation may entail certain risks (Triandis & Brislin, 1984). For one, cross-cultural research is more expensive. You may spend considerable time and energy in finding funding for such research. Second, cross-cultural research takes more time and may cause lengthy delays in finishing the thesis or dissertation. Finally, cross-cultural research will not find as much support if it is not closely linked with a currently fashionable theory. On the other hand, cross-cultural research is gaining importance, and as businesses develop cross-nationally, there may be ample payoffs for the student who studies issues of interest to them.

## Therapy

Therapy is based on communication and empathy. Both of these processes are facilitated by a common cultural background or a thorough knowledge of the client's culture by the therapist.

Lack of familiarity with the American culture would be an impediment for an international student who intends to conduct therapy in the United States. However, recent literature indicates that cultural differences exist not only between people of different countries but also between people of different subcultures within a country. Cultural differences in therapy emerge on the basis of race, gender, national origin, and sexual orientation. Nevertheless, understanding such subcultural differences may be easier than relating to major cultural differences. For example, for some international students, sexual orientation as a subculture would be completely incomprehensible. Therefore, cultural adaptation and learning about the American culture are critical for an international student who plans to study and practice clinical psychology.

In addition, the international student should bear in mind and learn to be sensitive about cultural differences. Fortunately, there is a growing literature on the relationship between cultural differences and the therapeutic relationship (e.g., Fish, 1986; Hanson-Kahn & L'Abate, 1998; Jenkins, 1999; Singh, McKay, & Singh, 1998; Waldman, 1999).

In this chapter, I pointed out the challenges associated with being an international student when applying to a graduate program in North America. In that context, I suggested certain strategies that should be considered early in your thinking about your graduate career. There are specific difficulties involved in attending graduate school for an international student, particularly related to cultural adaptation and awareness of expectations. International students without much contact with the American educational system may be unaware of the demands and expectations of both the culture generally and the graduate programs specifically. Consequently, a lot of time might be wasted if students do not confront these questions as soon as possible.

Overall, being an international graduate student is a rewarding experience. A vast amount of learning takes place, and it does not happen only in the classrooms, laboratories, and therapy rooms; it also happens in interaction with members of other cultures. I hope you have as valuable on experience as mine and form the type of lifelong friendships I have found.

## REFERENCES

American Psychological Association. (1994). *Publication manual of the American Psychological Association*. Washington, DC: Author.

Angelova, M., & Riazantseva, A. (1999). "If you don't tell me, how can I know?": A case study of four international students learning to write the U.S. way. *Written Communication, 16,* 491–525.

Bhagwati, J., & Rao, M. (1996). The U.S. brain gain: At the expense of Blacks? *Challenge, 39,* 50–53.

Espenshade, T. J., & Rodrigues, G. (1997). Completing the Ph.D.: Comparative performance of U.S. and foreign students. *Social Science Quarterly, 78,* 593–605.

Fish, J. M. (1996). *Culture and therapy: An integrative approach*. Northvale, NJ: Jason Aronson.

Hanson-Kahn, P., & L'Abate, L. (1998). Cross-cultural couple therapy. In F. M. Dattilio (Ed.), *Case studies in couple and family therapy: Systemic and cognitive perspectives* (pp. 278–302). New York: Guilford Press.

Jenkins, Y. M. (1999). *Diversity in college settings: Directives for helping professionals*. New York: Routledge.

Johnson, J. M. (1998). *Statistical profiles of foreign doctoral recipients in science and engineering: Plans to stay in the United States* (NSF 99–304). Arlington, VA: National Science Foundation, Division of Science Resources Studies.

Kagitcibasi, C., & Poortinga, Y. H. (2000). Cross-cultural psychology. *Journal of Cross-Cultural Psychology, 31,* 129–147.

Markus, H., & Kitayama, S. (1991). Culture and self: Implications for cognition, emotion, and motivation. *Psychological Review, 98,* 224–253.

National Science Board. (1996). *Science & engineering indicators—1996* (NSB 96–21). Washington, DC: U.S. Government Printing Office.

Ries, P., & Thurgood, D. H. (1993). *Summary report 1991: Doctorate recipients from United States universities.* Washington, D.C.: National Academy Press.

Singh, N. N., McKay, J. D., & Singh, A. N. (1998). Culture and mental health: Nonverbal communication. *Journal of Child & Family Studies, 7,* 403–409.

Snyder, T., & Hoffman, C. (2000). *Digest of education statistics, 1999.* Washington, DC: National Center for Education Statistics.

Syverson, P. D., & Bagley, L. R. (1999). *Graduate enrollment and degrees: 1986 to 1997.* Washington, DC: Council of Graduate Schools, Office of Research and Information Services.

Triandis, H. C., & Brislin, R. W. (1984). Cross-cultural psychology. *American Psychologist, 39,* 1006.

Waldman, F. (1999). Violence or discipline? Working with multicultural court-ordered clients. *Journal of Marriage & Family Counseling, 25,* 503–515.

# 13

# Stresses and Strategies for Graduate Student Couples

*Dixie J. Pederson*

*M. Harry Daniels*

Beginning a graduate psychology program is a dramatic event that will substantially define the student's professional opportunities and influence most of the aspects of personal life. Graduate school invites personal growth and adaptability as the student encounters a variety of stresses. These stresses are many and sometimes severe for any student, married or single, involved or not with a partner in an intimate love relationship. Indeed, couple relationships have many stresses and difficulties inherent in themselves. When the stresses of being a couple are combined with the stresses of being a graduate student, the difficulties can become overwhelming. The stresses associated with professional training for couples are familiar to those who have completed their training; the intention of this chapter is to make prospective graduate students aware of some potential difficulties they and their partners may face during their tenure in graduate school.

Based on an assessment of the state of your relationship with a partner, you may decide to postpone entrance into graduate school or to not enter at all. Or, you may find yourself saying, "Given all the potential difficulties in establishing and maintaining a relationship at this time, do I really want to be involved in a love relationship while in graduate school?"

On the more optimistic side, prior awareness of potential difficulties may help partners to focus attention on the issues as they arise so that relatively minor difficulties do not escalate into major problems. In fact, some difficulties may be averted altogether. In addition, knowing that you are not the only couple to experience these stresses, you may experience a sense of universality or identification with your peers in the training program. This knowledge may allow you to recognize that the difficulties may be the result of external stresses and that they are probably transitory. Being able to say, "I know this won't last forever, " or "This is not necessarily something wrong with me or us," can reduce a couple's anxiety about the future and prevent difficulties from escalating into major problems.

This chapter is based on the results of a survey of 64 couples in which at least one partner had completed doctoral psychology training. Of these, 23 were no longer with the partner they had during the training program, whereas 41 couples had survived the training process intact. In addition, 27 individual graduate students were interviewed. Of these students, 14 remained involved in the relationship, but their partners were unavailable for interview, often because they lived in a different city. The others were not involved in a relationship at all. Participants were asked two questions:

1. Please describe the specific stresses in your relationship since you and/or your partner began the graduate training program in psychology. In what ways has being a couple either increased or decreased the stresses on you in the training experience?

2. Please describe specific strategies you used to deal with these stresses, and indicate how well you think they worked for you.

Four major topics emerged pertaining to managing the stresses of a graduate student couple and are discussed in this chapter. First we discuss issues germane to student couples involved in any advanced professional training and possible strategies for dealing with these issues. Second, we focus on issues specific to training for psychologists because the nature of their training as therapists may affect their relationship with a partner. Third, we address professional role issues for psychologists and how they may affect the couple relationship. These issues may have implications for the couple well beyond the completion of the training program and possibly for the remainder of the psychologists' career years. Fourth, we consider the special difficulties of the so-called "dual-career" couple. We included those couples in which the student has a spouse or partner who is also highly career oriented and currently involved in a career, and those couples in which both members are concurrently students, and make several comments about the special stresses for the dual-psychologist couple.

## GENERAL TRAINING ISSUES IN GRADUATE SCHOOL

Entrance into a graduate program can seriously disrupt one's lifestyle in a variety of ways. Graduate training usually necessitates relocation to the site of the training facility. Oftentimes the partner of the student is asked to subjugate personal and/or professional development, needs, and wishes for the sake of the student's educational development (Napier, 1999). The partner, as well as the student, may be required to relinquish a job and seek employment in the area of the graduate school site. The partner's new job may not be comparable to the previous one in terms of salary, working hours, or opportunity for promotion. Accrued seniority may be lost and the partner's own career development disrupted for the sake of the student's career.

By moving to the new location, the partner may sacrifice friendships and long-standing social ties as well. This situation may not change once the couple has settled into the new area. Scholastic pressures and time demands often result in a narrowing of social experience for both the student and the couple as a unit. The partner making these sacrifices may express some resentment toward the student, especially if the couple is experiencing difficulties in other aspects of their relationship. As one disgruntled, angry partner of a doctoral student expressed just prior to the eventual termination of a relationship:

> I feel like I have given up everything for his sake. I left a stable job that I enjoyed only to have to settle for a much less satisfying one with longer hours and less pay in a field I'm not even interested in. I gave up close friendships with lifelong friends to move to a state several hundred miles away from my family. After all of this, I expect a little extra attention and gratitude from him. But it seems like he has become more and more interested in his books and courses and less and less interested in me. I feel terribly cheated and used by the whole arrangement.

The intense academic and training pressures on the student often compete with couple involvement and time investment. Some students, however, still expect unilateral emotional replenishment. Inadequate and unsatisfactory sexual relationships are one of the common indicators of the stress related to training and to its related marital stress (Coombs, 1971; Nelson & Henry, 1978). Interestingly, unsatisfying work-role quality for either partner, more than the number of hours actually worked, is the primary cause of poor sexual relationships (Hyde, DeLamater, & Hewitt, 1998). One partner of a graduate student complained:

> I just don't get it. It seems like every time I'm interested in spending a quiet evening at home with her, maybe a little wine and conversation, maybe lovemaking later, she says she doesn't have the time. I have a really hard time accepting it when she says sex takes up too much time! But just let her get upset about something to do with one of her courses or professors, and all hell breaks loose if I'm not there with a listening ear, one hundred percent sympathetic to her. It all seems like a pretty lopsided arrangement to me.

In other cases, students who have become accustomed to recognition and success in professional training endeavors may have come to view themselves as infallible. The student's partner may become the unfortunate and inappropriate target of blame when such a student is confronted with the inevitable setbacks all students encounter (Perlow & Mullins, 1976). The student who is late with a thesis proposal, for example, may deny his or her own part in poor time management, blaming the partner for demanding too much time and attention.

Those partners who identify strongly with the student's involvement in the training program and commitment to the profession may also identify with, even experience simultaneously, the student's stressors and anxieties (Coombs & Boyle, 1971). One partner may experience confusion and guilt regarding the amount of time and attention he or she should expect from the student partner. The partner's own worry about how the relationship affects the student's academic performance may become a considerable stressor in and of itself. Thus, a cycle is created with academic stresses and concerns affecting the relationship, which in turn may be reflected in the students' educational achievement, again straining the relationship.

Some students report certain advantages to living apart from their partner during their training program. These students enjoy the ability to structure their time so that uninterrupted commitment can be given to their work during the week. Those weekend and holiday periods in which the couples are reunited can ostensibly be devoted entirely to the relationship. However, this on-again, off-again arrangement requires a considerable amount of adjusting and readjusting from being with an intimate partner at times to being alone most of the time. As one student described the situation:

> It was difficult for me to adjust to being with him for the first couple of days we were to-gether after a long separation. Then it was difficult to get used to being away from him when I returned to school. It felt like I was on an emotional roller coaster.... He finally joined me, and then we had to deal with his unemployment, underemployment, and lack of social support. He began to feel resentful and I felt guilty. He left to return to his job in another state and the relationship ended.

Sometimes the full negative impact on the relationship is not manifest until near the end of the training program, or shortly thereafter. If the partner is not simultaneously involved in an educational process, the increasing gap in educational levels may decrease the perceived commonality between them. The student's new professional status may result in feelings of inferiority on the part of the partner and feelings of superiority on the part of the student. After years of other relationship stresses, the couple may not survive this final outcome as an intact unit:

> When my husband and I were first married, we seemed to enjoy the same recreational activities and share common preferences in our choice of friends. He now expresses boredom with our old friends and doesn't seem interested in the activities we all shared together. I feel hurt and inferior when he finds the people I enjoy to be boring. I guess I'm just not sophisticated enough for him any more.

Adjustment to the gap in educational status may pose a special problem if the status of the woman in the relationship exceeds her partner's:

> My husband is a successful accountant with a bachelor's degree from a well-known university. The firm with which he is associated is well respected and his income will probably always be greater than mine. We discussed the potential status issues involved in my having a doctoral degree while he holds a bachelor's degree before I went back to school. The adjustment has still been a bit difficult at times; occasionally he winces a bit when new acquaintances call me "Doctor___." "Doctor and Mr." is an unusual combination even today.

Financial stress may be one of the most pervasive and limiting problems the couple may face. Tuition, books and supplies, lab fees, moving expenses, the cost of student housing, and other living expenses can be extremely expensive, depending on the particular school selected and its geographic location. Membership fees for professional organizations and expenses for attendance and/or participation in professional conferences and workshops can result in large expenditures. Travel expenses for trips to and from home during holiday periods may be a luxury some students cannot afford, so that family and friendship ties cannot be enjoyed for their potential support and comfort.

Many students resort to loans and other forms of financial aid to finance their way through school. Those students who do obtain loans are faced with making payments for several months or years following the completion of the degree. Therefore, the couple that has scrimped and saved for several years during the student's training still may not be able to immediately enjoy the financial rewards of their efforts upon graduation.

The extended educational period can also result in a phenomenon resembling an extension of the adolescent period of development for the couple. Resolution of certain developmental issues may be delayed for several years. Autonomy from parents, marriage, the beginning of a family, and developing social ties with the community as a family can be extremely difficult or impossible for the couple, given the financial and other constraints upon them (Newman & Newman, 1998).

## SPECIAL STRESSES FOR THERAPISTS-IN-TRAINING

One of the most common complaints of partners of student therapists is the student's unclear differentiation of the role of therapist from the role of partner in an intimate relationship. As new therapists begin to acquire skills in the observation of human behavior, they may carry the professional passive-observer role into personal relationships. The student therapist's partner may note marked changes in the student's behavior (Bellak, 1974) and be unsure of the reasons for and implications of these changes. Furthermore, students may develop a tendency to overanalyze their own domestic relationships as therapy skills are acquired (Gilberg, 1977). This situation may result in an uneven distribution of power in the relationship. Having no immediate access to knowledge about these observational and therapeutic skills, the student's partner may feel at a distinct disadvantage in conflict situations, especially if the student uses his new skills as a weapon. In the early stages of learning, the student's skills may be inadequate and interpretations inaccurate or incomplete, compounding the problem. Thus the partner is being asked to adapt to changes in the student that are difficult to understand, such as emotional shifts and attitudinal changes; the student may apply diagnostic, interpretative terminology to the partner's behavior (Halleck & Woods, 1962). This is clearly inappropriate and demeaning behavior.

Although imbalances of power and influence may be part and parcel of the couple's graduate experience, a more important issue is the couple's methods for coping with these imbalances. Coping styles vary between flexible and rigid, and the distinguishing feature is the degree to which couples have achieved a negotiated coping style (Stanfield, 1998). An extreme example of a rigid coping style that results in a disturbed relationship follows:

> When my husband started his training as a therapist, it seems like all the rules in our relationship changed. He acted as though he was the expert on everything about people and relationships. He behaved as though he thought that he was infallible and not to be questioned in his opinions about our relationship. I felt like I was more of a case study than a wife. If we disagreed about anything, he told me all about how relationships and people are supposed to be. Then he decided the problem was that I was neurotic, or compulsive, or paranoid. I didn't know enough about it all to defend myself. Finally, I would retaliate by saying that if he were such a good therapist, he should at least be able to have a decent marriage. After a while, it all seemed pretty hopeless to me, so I left.

In other cases the partners may not exchange hostilities, but the coping style is no less rigid. Some couples may begin to lose touch with one another, as the student therapist becomes involved in a personal growth process related to training as a therapist. The students may learn about the potential satisfaction that a relationship can offer and develop higher or idealized expectations of themselves and their relationships. Despite having been quite satisfied with the relationship initially, the student therapist may realize that the partner does not share the same knowledge or interest in personal and relationship improvement. The following report conveys the tragic tone of the situation:

> Within a few weeks after she started training I began to notice a difference in our relationship. At first she would come home and share her excitement in discovering things about herself. I was happy for her at first, but after a while I couldn't really understand some of the things she talked about. She began to talk to me less and less, and seemed to stop depending on me for emotional support. As her so-called "independence" grew, I felt useless and wondered if she needed me at all. Finally, in her mind it seemed to come down to her choosing between our relationship and her own personal growth, whatever that all meant. I lost her, and I still don't really understand why.

Alternatively, the student may become so concerned about keeping the relationship intact that career decisions are made to minimize the possibility of the relationship succumbing to the pressures of the profession. The student's partner may feel lonely and isolated because of the demands on the student's time. Further, the student may be unavailable during times when the partner is in need of emotional support. If the partner expresses a great deal of frustration to the student and the student places the maintenance of the relationship at a high priority, the student may make career choices intended to minimize this frustration in the future (Brohn & DuPlessis, 1966; Stanfield, 1998). A case in point would be the student's decision to forego a specialty involving a lot of emergency crisis interventions because of the demands on such a therapist's time after hours. If the student feels this decision requires undue sacrifice for the partner, the student may feel wistful or even resentful.

## PROFESSIONAL ROLE ISSUES

Unfortunately, many psychologists learn that the time and energy demands of graduate school may not lessen a great deal after completing the degree. As a professional, the psychologist may find that couple involvement continues to compete with professional responsibilities. It can be quite difficult for the psychologist who is a therapist to set and maintain boundaries for privacy in personal life. Phone calls in the middle of the night from distraught or demanding clients and emergency duties may become routine and expected. There is some professional socialization for therapists around the belief that the client is sacrosanct; thus, partners may express feelings of jealousy toward clients, as this vignette illustrates:

> I've always been one of the lucky ones. My clients don't seem to make as many night calls or suicide gestures as some of my colleagues report they experience. But they do seem to happen at the most inopportune times, like in the middle of a family gathering or a dinner party. The worst of all is when a client calls after my wife and I have finally gotten the kids to bed and we're making love. That certainly upsets and frustrates my wife, and I can't blame her. I've resigned myself to expecting a certain amount of that sort of thing, but she sometimes says she wonders how much I care about her if I leave her side to attend to a client. She thinks I should only talk to those who are really on the brink of suicide, like standing on the window ledge, ready to jump.

The therapist's work requires a high level of attention and involvement with clients. Therapy work is often quite emotionally depleting for the therapist, especially if it is full-time work, if the therapist is relatively inexperienced, or if it involves a great deal of crisis intervention or intensive, long-term work. The therapist may respond to this emotional depletion on the job with various forms of withdrawal at home. Withdrawal may be manifested as irritability or a lack of sensitivity to the problems and concerns of family members. The emotional fatigue may lead to emotional distancing in the form of the defensive use of therapeutic objectivity, that is, refusing to identify with the issues of family members, even those concerning the therapist's own behavior. Some therapists develop an inflated sense of self-importance as a result of the trust and responsibility accorded by clients and may fail to recognize their own human fallibilities and potential for error. This aura of analytical objectivity may be seen as threatening by friends and family, and they may withdraw in turn, fearing they will be analyzed and found lacking. A university professor who is involved in training therapists describes:

> I realized when I was working on my master's degree that I should avoid analyzing and diagnosing my friends. So I have always made an attempt to leave my role as a psychologist when I leave the office. Nevertheless, I notice that people seem a bit put off if I introduce myself as a psychologist. Lately, I've been introducing myself as a teacher or professor to avoid that initial anxious reaction. But I'm not entirely satisfied with that since I am proud of my professional identity. New acquaintances are not the only ones I have problems with. Some of my relatives have even asked me point-blank if I analyze them when my husband and I are visiting ... it sometimes makes things socially uncomfortable for my husband and me.

## THE DUAL-CAREER COUPLE

For purposes of this discussion, the "dual-career couple" will refer to those couples in which both partners place a high priority on a career or on career preparation. Dual-career couples are oriented toward the goals of creating and sustaining both an intimate relationship and successful careers for each partner. Historically, these two goals have been considered to be non-complementary. An increasing number of women and men are now actively pursuing a dual-career relationship. This change in orientation has been linked to three assumptions (Gilbert, Hallett, & Eldridge, 1994). First, there is economic equality between men and women; second, occupational and family systems are compatible; and third, the partners' self concepts as women and men allow for building a relationship that is characterized by role-sharing, mutuality, and interdependence. Without questioning the accuracy of these assumptions, it is clear that dual-career relationships can be fraught with a variety of problems that are brought on by unconscious defense mechanisms (Napier, 1999), social and cultural discourses that influence multiple role opportunities for women and men (Gilbert & Brownson, 1998), and the incumbent problems of the dual-career family lifestyle, such as issues of fairness, parenting and role conflict, and sources of support (Deutsch, 1999; Gilbert, 1994; Silberstein, 1992).

Of special interest for this chapter is the dual-psychologist couple, including those couples in which one or both partners are students or those couples in which one or both partners are professionals. There are both advantages and disadvantages to being part of dual-career or dual-psychologist couples, as for the couples described in this section. We will discuss the couples' perceptions relative to some of the specific issues affecting their functioning: (a) the couple as students, (b) job search and career mobility, and (c) household management and child care. It should be noted that some of the specific stresses and strategies included in this section apply also to single-career couples.

## The Couple as Students

The dual-student psychologist couple shares many common interests and experiences, which the couple may see as an advantage or disadvantage, depending on the impact on the relationship or one or both members' careers.

> My partner and I are doctoral students in the same program. Aside from all the personal attractions between us, I enjoy his ability to understand and accept my intense interests in the field of psychology and the stresses I experience in training. When I began work on my dissertation prospectus, he knew exactly why I was as anxious as I was. He understood about preliminary exams and the professor that everyone was afraid of. On the other hand, he knows why I was so thrilled when that internship acceptance call came, and he knows what it is like to have a therapeutic breakthrough with a difficult client after weeks of struggle. We can share the good times as well as the bad times in ways that I was never able to share with men who were not psychologists.

Others see the dual-psychologist arrangement as leading to too much contact or closeness at school or work:

> Sometimes I think it might be better if there were only one psychologist in the family. We are not overly demanding of one another's time or attention, but sometimes I wish I could have my own "turf" and have my home life and my school life separate. I am always aware of his presence and want to be considerate of him, so I don't feel I can really devote my full attention and energy to the department. If I'm talking to another student or a professor and he is there, I feel self-conscious, wondering about his opinion of me, too. I wish each of us had our own career fields, rather than it seeming like "our" career field. I would like clearer boundaries on where "I" begin and "we" end. We have to put limits on the amount of time we spend talking about psychology. We have found ourselves not being able to have a calm, relaxing breakfast without becoming involved in an extremely intense, abstract discussion about some esoteric issue in psychology. That kind of overload can become extremely exhausting. Sometimes I wish he were an artist or engineer, for example, so that we could have more conversations about topics completely unrelated to psychology.

If both partners undertake particularly demanding and stressful tasks at the same time, both may need extra support just when each is least likely to be able to offer it.

> My wife and I made the mistake of deciding that each of us would undertake the thesis requirement at the same time. The results were disastrous. We were both anxious at the same time about our committees accepting our thesis, and exhausted at the same time. We became irritable with one another because we were tired and stressed and at times were angry at one another because one wasn't getting the support they wanted from the other. We had more quarrels and arguments during that six-month period than we have had during the balance of our eight-year marriage. Most of the quarrels came down to "If you care so much for me, why are you not giving me more attention and support?" When it came time to consider dissertations, we agreed that we would work on them one at a time.

It meant that we spent an extra semester in school, but it also meant being less stressed during the process and less stressed when each of us went on internship. We made several decisions regarding strategies we would use before either of us began dissertations. We had an agreement to not make suggestions orally since oral communication requires the receiver's attention and involves at least a non-verbal reaction. My wife is especially skilled in research design and statistics. She left suggestions for me on 3 x 5 index cards with ideas for improvements in those areas. I left suggestions for improved wording of her literature review in the same way. We wanted the writer to be able to either accept or reject suggestions without feeling pressured. We also agreed on a "wouldn't it be neat" kind of suggestion format as opposed to a "this would be better if" or "this needs improvement" format. We also made deliberate plans to avoid taking on any additional stressors during this time. We decided not to have children until both of us had graduated and were employed. We canceled holiday periods with family, stressful events for both of us, and spent that time enjoying and renewing our relationship. No additional commitments were taken on, and we relieved ourselves as much as possible of those extra-curricular commitments that we had previously made. We reminded ourselves again and again, "this, too, shall pass." We complimented ourselves on our successes in coping and our support of one another. We focused on the belief that our relationship was growing stronger by taking on and meeting these challenges. We believed that if we could make it through two theses and two dissertations we could survive anything.

## Job Search and Career Mobility

Professional psychologists who are partners in a dual-career relationship may have difficulty finding suitable and satisfying employment. Although college and university administrators are increasingly adopting dual-career couple policies in order to recruit and retain faculty (Shoben, 1997; Wolf-Wendel, Twombly, & Rice, 1998, 1999), barriers to the creation and implementation of such policies still exist. Two partnered professionals seeking employment in the same area will be confronted with the "two-body problem," that is, the difficulty of finding two professional jobs in the same geographical location (NcNeil & Sher, 1998), especially if both partners have similar or identical degrees or specialties. Planning job search strategies can be a complex undertaking; it may involve intensive negotiation and revision of goals and plans, taking into consideration constraints that have pertinence for the couple and the employer.

Couples coordinating two careers can be considered in four categories (Butler & Paisley, 1980), with a high probability they will make one or more shifts between categories over time. Couples may work in the same specialty area in the same institution, in the same specialty in different institutions, in different specialties in the same institution, or in different specialties in different institutions. The couples in our sample appeared to follow trends similar to those in the Butler and Paisley group: If shifts were made in the career orientation pattern of the couple, they tended to be away from the category of sharing both specialty and institution.

Couples who differ in both specialty and institution cited the advantages of crossover intellectual stimulation, clear professional and personal boundaries, and mutual respect for one another's career accomplishments; these perceptions appear to parallel those expressed by students in training. In contrast, couples sharing both specialty and institution may choose to market themselves as a team on the job market. Some employers offer job-sharing opportunities, with each partner having a half-time appointment. A job-sharing arrangement can be an especially workable strategy for the couple that plans to establish a part-time or eventual full-time private practice. The equivalent of one salary in non-private-practice employment can provide relatively secure income, which can allow the couple to risk the uneven income of often-unpredictable client loads in private practice.

Recent studies about the hiring practices of the employers of dual-career couples (e.g., college and university administrators) have identified several emerging trends that will increase the employment opportunities of these individuals (Wolf-Wendel et al., 1998, 1999). Among the more important trends are the following: (a) Spousal or partner accommodation is an important issue facing most administrators, (b) research institutions are most likely to have a dual-career policy, and (c) dual-career policies are most likely to be applied when institutions are attempting to attract "hard-to-find" faculty members. Moreover, institutions may employ a variety of strategies to help the spouse or partner find work (Wolf-Wendel et al.,1998). The institution may actively assist the spouse or partner in finding a position by making contacts, distributing resumés, or paying for prearranged career assistance programs. Alternatively, the institution may elect to send information about job possibilities to the spouse or partner. Another strategy would be for the institution to hire the spouse or partner in a part-time, adjunct, or non-tenure-track position. The institution may create a share position in which both the initial hire and the spouse or partner share a single academic line, or the institution may find an administrative position for the trailing spouse. Finally, and least frequently, the institution may create a tenure-track position.

Among the barriers to the establishment of dual-career couple policies are concerns about departmental autonomy, worries about the quality of the "trailing" spouse or partner, the lack of adequate resources, and intradepartmental communication problems. Other barriers that have been frequently cited include institutional size, faculty resistance, problems with fairness and equity, and other legal reasons. However, many of these perceived barriers are problematic because there are no legal barriers to dual-career policies (Shoben, 1997). Nonetheless, administrators who opposed hiring couples cite disadvantages for both the department and the couple (Pingree, Butler, Paisley & Hawkins, 1978). The most frequently listed drawbacks for the department include: (a) the department's faculty evaluations being difficult, (b) the couple's marital and emotional problems upsetting the department, (c) the couple as a "voting bloc," exercising a disproportionate or adverse influence on departmental policies, and (d) the couple's dissatisfaction resulting in two vacancies at the same time. The most frequently perceived disadvantages to the couple are: (a) the department's effect on the couple's decisions and behavior, (b) the couple's personal competition and jealousy, (c) the couple's inability to maintain separate identities, and (d) the couple's social problems with others, such as resentment, quarrels, and so on. For example, if one spouse has a disagreement with a colleague, this can create tension or uneasiness between that colleague and the other spouse of the couple.

Several job search strategies were described by the couples, with each having its own set of advantages and limitations. One strategy was for both partners to search independently and consider those offers in which both partners received indications of positive interest. This strategy involved a timing problem; it was sometimes difficult to delay responding to a prospective employer's offer while waiting for the partner to receive word on the chances of securing a job in the area. Some couples narrowed their search to one particular geographic area or to a limited number of geographic areas, often for personal reasons; others chose to search nationwide. The former strategy limited the number of potential openings for which the partner could apply; the latter limited the couple's ability to investigate ahead of time the professional and social community in which the positions were located.

Couples also had varying strategies for deciding which offers to accept. Some chose the two positions that provided the best joint offer; others chose to locate where one partner received the best offer. The latter strategy sometimes included an agreement to alternate first choice positions between the two partners for future career moves. In other cases, one partner undertook an additional training assignment such as a postdoctoral internship while the other supported the couple financially. This additional training increased the job placement flexibility for the couple during the next job search. However, this strategy necessitated living apart and a commuting lifestyle for some couples. (Struik, 1974) Another strategy was to alternate so that only one partner worked at a time, while the other assumed part-time employment or full-time child care and home-management responsibilities.

Financial constraints and career development concerns were often cited as an important consideration in choosing a strategy. For some couples, accepting the first reasonable offer made to either partner was seen as necessary to manage basic financial needs such as rent, groceries and loan repayments. The other partner then either remained unemployed for a time or accepted employment outside of the career field. The latter two strategies can present serious difficulties in terms of meeting state licensure requirements. Because most states require 1 to 2 years of postdoctoral supervision in order to meet the requirements, the partner who works in another career area or remains unemployed will be at a disadvantage in the next job search process. One couple elected this option, however, and found it met their special needs quite well:

> When my husband finished his degree, he took a position as an outpatient therapist at a large mental health facility. I was writing my dissertation at the time, so he provided financial support for the two of us and moral support for me. I completed that task within the year, and our first child was born six weeks later. We decided that my being able to stay home with the child for the first year was a luxury we really could afford. During that same time period, my husband was doing part-time private practice work under the supervision of a licensed psychologist in a group practice. After our child was about a year old, I began to do some part-time work with that same group. We especially enjoy doing marriage therapy together, and seem to get quite a few referrals because we are a couple ourselves. Our eventual goal is to set up both of us in our own practice, which will necessitate my completing the supervision and licensure requirements of this state. We don't have as much money now as we might if both of us were working full-time, but this arrangement allows me to spend time with my child, which is a high priority for me during the early years of life.

It appears that colleges and universities are making serious efforts to address the "two-body" problem. According to Wolf-Wendel et al. (1999), dual-career couples should be aware of the following trends:

- There seems to be a high level of interest in policy solutions to this issue at the upper administrative level.

- A lot of the solutions to this issue rely on luck, timing, and flexibility.

- Not every couple can be accommodated as they might like. Institutions that work to accommodate dual-career couples constantly work to balance the needs of the institution with the needs of the individual.

- Variations in how faculty lines can be created and funded influences an institution's ability to accommodate dual-career couples.

- Institutions tend to minimize the problems associated with dual-career couples and instead focus on the positive.

## Household Management and Child Care

Managing the demands of home and family life can be time-consuming and emotionally draining, especially for two-career couples. Division of labor in these households tended to follow traditional sex-role lines, with one person (in heterosexual couples, the woman) primarily responsible for most tasks including cleaning, marketing, and child care (Deutsch, 1999; Gilbert, 1994; Gilbert & Brownson, 1998; Hammer, Allen, & Grigsby, 1997). This greater relative role strain was one reason cited for women's greater dissatisfaction in these relationships. Even the best-managed dual-career households become disorganized by relatively minor events, such as the illness of a child or babysitter, so that the family's routines disintegrate quickly.

In heterosexual couples these problems are usually seen as the responsibility of the female partner, so that she experiences additional role strain. Although the male partner may be willing to perform some household and child-care tasks, this may be seen as his performing tasks that are beyond his responsibility as a favor to his spouse. As this woman psychologist suggests, career equality may not imply equality for household and family responsibilities:

> I felt like I had to be a Superwoman if I was to have the right to insist on having my own career. I had to always have a perfectly cleaned house, have well-behaved, perfectly well-adjusted children, have a perfect, conflict-free marriage, be a career superstar, and be a perfect hostess. Of course, I was to always be cheerful and pleasant at all times. Overloaded with demands, I became stressed and irritable. My husband offered to "do some of the household tasks for me." I was glad for the relief from the pressure. Later I realized that he was assuming that all of the household tasks really were my responsibility, in spite of both of us having equal career responsibilities. Then I realized I was making the same assumption by my appreciation of his "helping me." Also, if the work is not done well, I am the one who feels guilty or inadequate because it is my "responsibility." Further, if the work is done well, I was appreciative of his "help," but I felt unappreciated by him because it was expected of me anyway. I was able to recognize that this was a result of our shared socialization, so that I did not feel angry, resentful, or blameful of my husband. Fortunately, he has shown a remarkable amount of openness and willingness to examine and change these attitudes and behaviors.

There are many excellent books available on the topic of time management for couples (e.g., Deutsch, 1999; Gilbert, 1993; Hertz, 1998). Some strategies mentioned as especially helpful by these couples can be given special attention here:

> Good communication skills were so important to us! We listened carefully and discussed the topics rationally and clearly, with a focus on our commitment to make things

the best they could be for us as a couple. We made a list of tasks that we both agreed had to be done. Then we each made a prioritized list of the tasks that each of us felt were important. We negotiated which of these items each of us just couldn't live without and which could be sacrificed if time was limited. We discussed who should assume responsibility for certain tasks. We developed a combination of strategies that we used to our mutual satisfaction, considering our individual temperaments and talents. I hate cooking and am not very good at it, but don't mind cleaning up. She's a great cook, but hates the cleanup. We both benefit; we both eat well and she doesn't have to clean. If one of us is especially perfectionist about a task, we choose to do it ourselves. We alternate doing tasks we both dislike on a weekly or monthly basis with whoever is responsible setting the standards. We consider the other's time demands to pressure at home if work demands are high. If we are both really pressured, we discuss the importance and urgency of tasks, focus on those that are both urgent and important first, and then prioritize the others. We agree that some tasks are much less important than work demands or time to relax. Flexibility is the key for us. We allow ourselves to divert from stereotypical male or female roles, but we don't feel compelled to avoid them. We also consider seasonal and social demands as well. I help more in the kitchen in the winter when the lawn doesn't need to be mowed, and I do more housecleaning during holiday periods when she spends more time cooking. Sometimes we trade tasks just because we are bored with the ones we have been doing. The main idea is to be supportive of one another, and demonstrate our commitment for a happy home and family life for the two of us.

Child-care responsibilities may also be a major demand on a couple. Children can affect the career plans of each partner. Planning for the couple as a family, each partner must consider their ability and willingness to meet the educational and developmental needs of the child. Many of our couples stressed that the birth of the first child had dramatic impact on the couple's lifestyle and ability to manage the demands of two careers, especially if one or both partners was in training. Many couples are now electing to delay the birth of the first child until the woman is in her early or mid thirties. There are advantages to choosing later parenting, including greater career and financial stability, greater opportunity for personal growth and exploration of each of the partners, and greater stability of the marital relationship (Hall & Hall, 1979).

Many couples also stressed the importance of establishing support systems outside of the relationship, including organized or semiorganized gatherings of couples to discuss their own experiences and strategies. Some meetings were mostly social in appearance, but the topics of conversation often drifted toward these common concerns. Some nonstudent partners indicated that some support groups especially established and designed for them had been very helpful in recognizing the universality of their experiences.

Not all of the problems of being a professional couple can be addressed here, nor can all the possible strategies for dealing with them be outlined. Perhaps this chapter will serve as a base from which to generate new ideas. In summary, the most important points of this chapter can be distilled into some suggestions for the graduate student couple:

- Be proactive in planning for stress. Don't let surprises sneak up on you, throwing the relationship into disequilibrium. Talk about what you expect to happen before it does, and plan strategies for coping.

- Be as aware as possible of both current and potential stressors affecting the relationship.

- Recognize the sources of stress; determine which can be changed and which can't.
- Be realistic and patient in selecting and implementing coping strategies. Change doesn't occur overnight.
- Recognize that not all stresses can be eliminated, but remember, "This, too, shall pass." There will come a time when the stresses and strains become a fading memory. Avoid taking on additional, unnecessary stressors.
- Establish and enjoy support outside of the relationship. Partners need a sense of their own separateness and independence, as well as a sense of interdependence in order to cooperate and negotiate through this process.
- Recognize the value of conflict and its resolution. The relationship is enhanced and strengthened when partners can confront and negotiate differences to increase mutual satisfaction.
- Identify the unique needs and vulnerabilities of each partner and the couple as a unit. This chapter has discussed many important considerations for student couples, but each couple is unique. Know yourselves. Recognize that you may have special needs that have not been addressed here. Take those needs into account in your long-term planning process. Develop plans for your particular concerns, using the strategies you know have worked well for you in the past.
- Recognize that each partner and the relationship itself are in a process of change. Realize that change is part of growth, a necessary process to the continued development of persons and relationships.
- Cherish one another. Be a team. Talk openly and lovingly about feelings and issues, being supportive, trustful, respectful, and tolerant of one another. Verbally reaffirm your commitment to the relationship often, especially during periods of high stress.
- Focus on your successes and the times you have coped well. Use these examples to support yourselves in the belief that you can successfully handle the pressures. It is important to see yourselves as capable of mastering the tasks you have chosen to undertake. These successes can strengthen you throughout life.

## REFERENCES

Bellak, L. (1974). Careers in psychotherapy. *Dynamische Psychiatrie*, *7*, 242–247.

Brohn, J., & DuPlessis, A. (1966). Wives of medical students: Their attitudes and adjustments. *Journal of Medical Education*, *41*, 381–385.

Butler, M., & Paisley, W. (1980). Coordinated-career couples: Convergence and divergence. In F. Pepitone-Rcakell (Ed.), *Dual-career couples*. Beverly Hills, CA: Sage.

Coombs, R. H. (1971). The medical marriage. In R. H. Coombs & C. E. Vincent (Eds.), *Psychological aspects of medical training*. Springfield. Charles C. Thomas.

Coombs, R. H., & Boyle, B. (1971). Marriage as a buffer against emotional stress in medical training. *California Mental Health Research Digest, 9*, 59–65.

Deutsch, F. M. (1999). *Halving it all: How equally shared parenting works*. Cambridge, MA: Harvard University Press.

Gilberg, A. L. (1977). Reflections of being a psychoanalyst. *American Journal of Psychoanalysis*, *37*, 83–84.

Gilbert, L. A. (1993). *Two careers/one family.* Newbury Park, CA: Sage.

Gilbert, L. A. (1994). Current perspectives on dual-career families. *Current Directions in Psychological Science, 3,* 101–105.

Gilbert, L.A. Brownson, C. (1998). Current perspectives on women's multiple roles. *Journal of Career Assessment, 6,* 433–448.

Gilbert, L. A,. Hallett, M., & Eldridge, N. S. (1994). Gender and dual-career families: Implications and applications for the career counseling of women. In Walsh, W. Bruce (Ed.) *Career counseling for women (Contemporary topics in vocational psychology).* Hillsdale, NJ: Lawrence Erlbaum Associates.

Hall, F. S., & Hall, D. T. (1979). *The two-career couple.* Reading MA: Addison-Wesley.

Halleck, S., & Woods, S. (1962). The emotional problems of psychiatric residents. *Psychiatry, 25,* 339–346.

Hammer, L B., Allen, E., & Grigsby, T. D. (1997). Work–family conflict in dual-earner couples: Within-individual and crossover effects of work and family. *Journal of Vocational Behavior, 50*(2), 185–203.

Hertz, R. (1998). *More equal than others: Women and men in dual-career marriages.* Berkeley: University of California Press.

Hyde, J. S., Delamater, J. D., & Hewitt, E. C. (1998). Sexuality and the dual earner couple: Multiple roles and sexual functioning. *Journal of Family Psychology, 12,* 354–368.

McNeil, L., & Sher, M. (1998). *Report on the Dual Career Couple Survey* [Online]. Available: http://www.physics.wm.edu/dualcareer.html.

Napier, A. Y. (1999). Experiential approaches to creating the intimate marriage. In J. Carlson, & L. Sperry (Eds.), *The intimate couple.* Philadelphia: Brunner/Mazel.

Nelson, E. G., & Henry, W. F. (1978). Psychosocial factors seen as problems by family practice residents and their spouses. *Journal of Family Practice, 6,* 581–589.

Newman, B. M. & Newman, P. R. (1998). *Development through life: A psychosocial approach.* Homewood, IL: Dorsey.

Perlow, A. & Mullins, S. (1976). Marital satisfaction as perceived by the medical student's spouse. *Journal of Medical Education, 51,* 721–734.

Pingree, S., Butler, M., Paisley, W., & Hawkins, R. (1978). Anti-nepotism's ghost: Attitudes of administrators toward hiring professional couples. *Psychology of Women Quarterly, 3,* 22–29.

Shoben, E. W. (1997). From anti-nepotism rules to programs for partners: Legal issues. In M. A. Ferber, & J. W. Loeb (Eds.), *Academic couples: Problems and promises.* Urbana: University of Illinois Press.

Silberstein, L. R. (1992). *Dual-career marriage: A system in transition.* Hillsdale, NJ: Lawrence Erlbaum Associates.

Stanfield, J. B. (1998). Couples coping with dual careers: A description of flexible and rigid coping styles. *Social Science Journal, 35*(1), 53–64.

Struik, R. (1974) The two-city problem. *Association for Women in Mathematics Newsletter, 4,* 8–11.

Wolf-Wendel, L., Twombly, S., & Rice, S. (1998, November). *Dual-career couples: How institutions of higher education are keeping them together.* Paper presented at the Association for the Study of Higher Education Annual Meeting, Miami, FL.

Wolf-Wendel, L., Twombly, S., & Rice, S. (1999). *Case studies of dual-career couple policies.* Paper presented at the Association for the Study of Higher Education Annual Meeting, San Antonio, TX.

# III

## Learning Career Skills

# 14

## Learning to Become Ethical

*Mitchell M. Handelsman*

J ust as it takes training and experience to become an *excellent* psychologist, it takes training and experience to become an *ethical* psychologist. The term *professional ethics* refers to decisions about right and wrong behaviors. We have all heard celebrated cases of unethical behavior: therapists who sleep with their clients and researchers who fudge their data. However, all professionals are faced with situations every day that may seem less extreme but are no less ethically charged. The purpose of this chapter is to present some of the themes that you will encounter throughout your career as a graduate student and a psychologist, and to give you some advance warning about the ethical traps inherent in your chosen profession. To get us started, consider the following case, from three perspectives. Picture this:

*Case 1a*. You are a professor in a university psychology department. At the department's end-of-semester party, one of the more attractive students in your graduate seminar strikes up a conversation with you. After several minutes your keen clinical intuition picks up a mutual attraction. You say to the student, "Listen, I've already turned the grades in, so don't take this the wrong way. But would you like to go out to dinner with me tomorrow night?"

*Case 1b*. You are a graduate student at the end-of-the-semester department party. In an effort to do that networking thing that you've heard is so important, you decide to mingle with as many people as you can. You approach the closest person, the rather demanding professor you just had for a course. After several minutes of amiable conversation you plan to excuse yourself to talk to others, but the professor says to you, "Listen, I've already turned the grades in, so don't take this the wrong way. But would you like to go out to dinner with me tomorrow night?" Struggling to pick your jaw up from the floor, you consider the consequences of accepting or refusing the professor's invitation. You remember that (a) there is a policy against faculty dating students over whom they have __ some authority, and (b) you will likely need this professor to write you a recommendation for an internship and/or a postdoctoral fellowship.

*Case 1c*. You are a graduate student who has just finished a grueling and highly successful semester, except that you are on the borderline between an A and a B from one of your more demanding professors. As it happens, at the end-of-semester party, you overhear that professor talking to another student in the class—an attractive student—and asking the student out to dinner. You know there is a department policy against dating students over whom professors have some authority. You consider your options: Should you turn the professor in to the department chair? Should you talk to the professor after grades are published? Should you confront the professor now and prevent the date and help both the student and the professor avoid big trouble?

The professor in this case engaged in unethical behavior: that is, behavior that is wrong or inappropriate given a professional role. Although Case 1 involved a professor with a student, the situation could also involve a therapist with a patient, a consultant with a client, a supervisor with an intern, or a researcher with a volunteer participant. Ethical decisions are part of the very nature of professional relationships.

At this point in your career you may identify with the students in Cases 1b and 1c, and you may feel that even when you become a professor you will never find yourself in the situation described in 1a. However, no matter how aware and compassionate you might be, being a knowledgeable and good person is not enough to avoid, prevent, or handle the ethical issues and dilemmas that you will face in a career in psychology. Ethical problems are faced by all professionals, not just those who are sociopathic, ill-trained, or mean. For example, consider the following:

*Case 2*. You are a therapist seeing a couple for marital therapy. One night the husband calls you to reschedule an appointment, and in passing tells you that he is having an affair, and "please don't tell my wife." What do you do? Do you uphold the husband's right to privacy, or do you act in the wife's best interests by disclosing information that will help her make important decisions about whether to stay in the marriage? If you keep the information secret, you risk harming the wife. If you disclose the information, you risk harming the husband, not to mention your income.

The solutions to ethical problems such as these are not obvious. And clearly this chapter is no substitute for a course in ethics, and a full awareness of the principles and standards involved (Bersoff, 1999; Kitchener, 2000; Koocher & Keith-Spiegel, 1998). However, after reading this chapter, I hope you will be more sensitive to the ethical dimensions and pitfalls of your work.

To begin, I outline four general guidelines that may be helpful in thinking about many ethical pitfalls. I then consider some specific problems and pitfalls that may arise at various times throughout your career. I end with some specific suggestions for avoiding pitfalls and staying ethical.

## GENERAL ETHICAL GUIDELINES

### Develop Ethical Reasoning Skills and Ethical Sensitivity

All professional behaviors, not just difficult decisions like those depicted in Case 2, have ethical dimensions. Such simple tasks as deciding how to describe our experience as a research assistant on a graduate school application, selecting research topics or lecture material, choosing to cancel office hours, and designing waiting rooms for therapy offices have ethical aspects. It is important to understand these ethical considerations and to think explicitly and carefully about them.

We might think that being ethical flows naturally from being a caring, intuitive person. These personality characteristics will clearly help. However, professional ethics can be quite different from our ordinary moral sense. Our options as professionals may seem artificially constrained if we do not understand the ethical dimensions of our work. For example, hugging somebody in distress is a commonly accepted means of expressing concern. Lending money to someone in need is certainly compatible with our everyday moral sense. But these behaviors take on vastly different meanings and effects when they occur in the context of psychotherapy; psychologists need to find more appropriate ways of helping.

An important part of ethical sensitivity is to know "the rules." Agency policies, as mentioned in Case 1, often prohibit certain types of activities. Professional organizations like the American Psychological Association (APA) have codes of ethics (APA, 1992), and all states regulate at least some of the practice of psychology. In addition to knowing these specific rules and guidelines, one must look at professional behavior in terms of more general ethical principles (Beauchamp & Childress, 1994; Kitchener, 2000). For example, in considering Case 2 you need to know that it is unethical according to the APA Code, and illegal according to all state laws, to violate confidentiality. However, the general ethical considerations also include autonomy (respect for people's rights to make their own decisions), nonmaleficence (not causing harm), beneficence (doing good), justice (treating people fairly), and fidelity (keeping one's word). The psychologist in Case 2 must weigh the rights of both spouses (justice), to minimize harm to each spouse (nonmaleficence) while providing some therapeutic benefit (beneficence) according to the wishes and privacy rights of each party (autonomy).

Many authors have presented models of ethical reasoning (e.g., Handelsman, 1998; Kitchener, 2000; Tymchuk, 1981) that help psychologists think through these complex ethical problems. All these decision-making procedures include understanding the facts of the case, applying ethical rules and principles, and anticipating the consequences of alternative courses of action. Clearly, the professor in Case 1 did not think of all the ramifications of a dinner invitation to a student. In Case 2 an ethically sensitive therapist would anticipate such situations and would do two things: first, develop a policy for how to handle information in marital therapy; and second, inform the clients at the beginning of treatment what the policies are so that the clients can make better decisions about their therapy (Haas, 1991).

In addition to knowledge of principles and ethical reasoning skills, ethical sensitivity includes an awareness of our own motivations and roles. The next three guidelines deal with such issues, which arise in virtually every professional decision we make.

## Be Aware of Your Motivations and the Interests Served by Being a Psychologist

Why do we do what we do as professionals? Students of psychology, perhaps more than those in other disciplines, should recognize that the answer to that question is always complex. The graduate school applicants' ubiquitous statement, "I want to help people," is only part of the story. We also enter the profession to make money, to be excellent at what we do, to be and feel powerful, to make others proud, and for a myriad of other reasons.

Most of these motivations are neither good nor bad—they are human. However, some predictable problems can arise, given their complexity. The first problem occurs when motivations conflict. Inherent in the private practice of psychotherapy, for example, is the conflict of interest between making money and helping clients. Consider this case:

> *Case 3*. You are a new therapist who has bought a new house and new car that are slightly beyond your means. You come to work in a brand new office with rent that is slightly higher than you can afford given your current case load. During an initial therapy session, a client tells you that she is anxious about the large inheritance she just received, and has begun having panic attacks. The client mentions that she had been in therapy before several years ago, but it did not help. You know that you have no experience with panic disorders, but you decide to see the client, and to charge double your usual fee. (This case is based on Case 4-1 in Handelsman, 1998.)

Situational factors, such as the financial pressure you feel in this case, may be different at different stages of your career. For example, as a student you may be well aware of the motivation to cheat on an important exam for good grades. However, it may be more difficult to imagine an intern falsifying information on a resumé to get a job, or a professor taking authorship away from a student or falsifying data so the professor is in a better position to get tenure. In a similar way, insurance fraud may seem totally incompatible with your value system now, but it may be a much more likely option when your children are old enough for college and you have payments due on a new vacation house.

Some motivations we have for our professional activities are simply inappropriate, in that they cannot be fulfilled and lead inevitably to poor consequences. The professor in Case 1 may have felt that having dinner with a student would help the student adjust to the new graduate school environment. However, the need to be that involved with the student's adjustment is inappropriate. Compassion that is not tempered by ethical considerations can lead to many unethical behaviors. In fact, inappropriate needs include the need to rescue, to solve other people's problems in unprofessional ways.

In a profession that places such a high premium on self-awareness and self-knowledge, it is hard to imagine how professionals can so easily mask their own inappropriate or neurotic needs by convincing themselves (and trying to convince others such as ethics committees and licensing boards) that their motivations were compassionate. Therapists in Case 3 may convince themselves, for example, that because the client's previous therapy was unsuccessful, what that client really needed was a nontraditional form of therapy, so that the therapist's lack of experience with panic disorders really didn't matter. The problem is that with compassion, but without understanding—and without applying—ethical principles including competence, nonmaleficence, and autonomy, therapists are prone to sloppiness, poor judgment, and unethical behavior. Also, many would agree that unexamined or conflicting motivations can get us into trouble. But even the perceptions of motivations can be problematic. Perceptions of psychologists are important because they influence feelings of trust, which are critical to much of what psychologists do. In Case 1, the professor's motivations may have been entirely innocent; however, the motivations of both the recipient of the invitation and the professor may be suspect from the point of view of the observing student. What may be seen by the participants as an innocent invitation may be perceived by others as the attempt to influence a grade unfairly, or an attempt to take advantage of a student's vulnerable position to fulfill some personal emotional need.

Other such inappropriate needs on the part of therapists include misogyny, narcissism, insecurity, and power. To the extent that professional training includes an exploration of our motivations, it may help prevent these needs from interfering in our work. However, our training may not help because it may engender two opposing types of feelings that may become pitfalls. First, rigorous graduate school experiences including constant evaluations during classes, theses, comprehensive exams, internships, and dissertations may increase our insecurity. Second, training may actually increase feelings of grandiosity or narcissism: Having successfully completed all these difficult tasks, we now believe we know everything!

## Exercise Power Carefully

By definition, professionals have expert knowledge in their field, and clients (e.g., students, patients) must trust that professionals will use that knowledge wisely. Expert knowledge and the vulnerabilities of clients create not only a power differential in professional relationships, but also opportunities for professionals to exploit their power for their own ends to the detriment of clients. In Case 1, we saw that the professor was clearly misusing power and may have been unaware of the potential to exploit the student. The fact that grades had been submitted did not diminish the ongoing power that the professor had over the student; for example, the professor may need to write letters of recommendation, serve on thesis committees, and fulfill other professional obligations. Therapists in Case 3 abuse their power by not referring the client to a competent therapist, by inflating fees, and in general by serving personal needs rather than those of the client.

Power, of course, is not always bad. Psychologists at times must exercise power. For example, they must tell students what courses to take, advise company executives to change their hiring practices for minority candidates, hospitalize psychotic individuals against their expressed desires, and temporarily deceive research participants about the true nature of a study. However, psychologists must always justify their use of power, and be sure that they are using their power in the interests of those with whom they work. In Case 2, if you have strong values against extramarital affairs you may decide to disclose the affair to the wife not because it would be best for the couple or for either party, but only because of your own values. This would be a misuse of power.

## Be Aware of the Boundaries of Your Professional Roles

*Boundaries* refer to the constraints on our behavior that occur when we assume professional roles. All professional roles have boundaries, or limits, which are defined by law, ethics, or simply good practice. At each point in our career, our quests for professional actualization (e.g., knowledge, influence, excellence, success), as well as personal actualization (e.g., interpersonal, sexual, emotional, financial), must always be assessed with reference to the limits of our professional roles. We must ask ourselves what it means to be a graduate student, intern, psychotherapist, researcher, or teacher. What behaviors are part of these roles, and what behaviors are not? For example, if we meet another person at a party, it is within the boundaries of the relationship to ask that person out for dinner. However, if we are in the role of therapist and meet another person, pursuing a romantic or sexual involvement is clearly outside the boundaries of the relationship.

Boundary crossings can be small and innocent: Bending the rules for a favorite student, coming late to an appointment, and disclosing a bit too much about one's personal life to a client may not be harmful. However, they can quickly develop into larger and more harmful crossings, which Gutheil and Gabbard (1993) called *boundary violations*. Violations would include behaviors that are considered unethical, such as breaching a client's confidentiality, or basing a student's grade on affection rather than academic merit.

One type of boundary violation is a *dual relationship*, in which a professional has two types of relationships with the same person. The most common types of dual relationships that wind up as complaints to ethics committees—or malpractice lawsuits—involve sexual contact with a client, which can be harmful (Pope, 1988; Pope & Bouhoutsos, 1986). But other types of dual relationships can be harmful as well: Doing therapy with a relative or close friend, dating a student, and having a supervisee clean our house are all examples of dual relationships that would be unethical.

Finally, judgments about what constitute boundary crossings or violations can be difficult. Accepting a key chain from a client upon termination of a long therapy experience is clearly different from accepting a new home sound system from a student before a dissertation defense. But what about accepting a rare book as a gift from a former graduate student who is applying to the department for a teaching job? Likewise, accepting an invitation to a client's wedding is certainly different from accepting an invitation to dinner and a movie (especially if it's *after* the wedding). But what about accepting tickets to a sporting event from a client? In order to make these judgments, psychologists must be ethically sensitive, aware of their motivations and values, judicious in their use of power, and aware and respectful of the boundaries of their professional roles.

## ETHICAL PITFALLS

You will face ethical decisions and dilemmas every day of your professional life. In this section I outline some ethical traps or pitfalls. With knowledge of such pitfalls you may be better able to see the warning signs and prevent the occurrence of, or ameliorate the effects of, ethically questionable behavior. No such list of pitfalls can be comprehensive and anticipate every conceivable situation, but I hope to give you at least a representative sample from which you can generalize.

I have organized this section of the chapter into particular pitfalls that may be most likely at certain times in your career. But don't be fooled: You may be advanced! You may face pitfalls early in your career that I have listed as occurring later. Most of these pitfalls can be salient at any point in one's career, especially when many psychologists are entering the profession as "nontraditional students" who have had other careers. At each stage, I consider issues in ethical reasoning, motivation, power, and boundary issues. And my examples are not hypothetical—they come from actual cases brought before ethics committees and state boards.

### Graduate School and Internships

Although most graduate programs now offer ethics training, such courses and workshops may not occur before students have begun their research and clinical activities and before students have been called on to apply ethical principles to these activities. Thus, a major pitfall during graduate training is simple ignorance of ethics and ethical reasoning. For example, when you see somebody commit a crime, your immediate impulse is to call the police. However, if a client tells you of a crime he committed, the principle of confidentiality prohibits you from reporting it (with only a few exceptions, such as child abuse). Thus, behaviors that were acceptable in previous kinds of relationships may not be acceptable now. Students may have difficulty with the transition between everyday, commonsense considerations and ethical ones. Some graduate students come from other professions in which the ethics codes are quite different. Although it may be tempting to think of unethical behavior being committed only by scoundrels, the fact is that good, caring people can easily find themselves in ethical predicaments.

Another type of pitfall concerns students' motivations. The good news about motivations at this stage is that they are strong and idealistic. But this is the bad news as well. The motivation to help or to achieve may outstrip a student's knowledge and lead to what we can call the "new toy" pitfall: Students develop new skills and want to use them all the time. They quickly gain skills in clinical work, research, consultation, and/or teaching. This huge jump in skills and knowledge in such a short time leads to two types of dangers. The first is using new skills ineffectively. For example, students may make interpretations to their psychotherapy clients that are ill-timed or simply inaccurate. This type of mistake can be exacerbated when, in their efforts to get good grades in their practicum classes, students are not as forthcoming as they need to be with their supervisors about the weak spots in their therapy.

The second danger of the new toy pitfall is using new skills inappropriately, with people with whom we do not have a professional relationship. The continuum here runs from being an insufferable bore at parties trying to teach everyone you meet about the intricate questions involved in your research, to recommending therapy to your brother-in-law so he will pay you the money he owes you, to actually "practicing" with your new WAIS–III on the children of your close friends. Having new toys is no fun unless other people know about them. One potential danger here is of violating confidentiality, which is one of the most common ethical pitfalls faced by psychologists (Haas, Malouf, & Meyerson, 1986; Pope & Vetter, 1992).

The power relationships at this time may be as complicated as they will ever be because of the "in-between" position in which students and interns find themselves. In some ways psychology graduate students have much power because they are acting as therapists, research collaborators, and teachers. However, graduate students are still students! They are evaluated on every aspect of their learning and performance. Sometimes it is hard for them to know how much power they have in relation to their professors, students, clients, and research subjects. Problems can arise from both overestimating and underestimating the power they have in each of these relationships.

The in-between power position of graduate students and interns makes it difficult to negotiate boundaries. Some relationships are clearly dual relationships, such as romantic encounters between faculty and students. But what appear to be dual relationships may simply be behaviors that are all within the boundaries of a single relationship, such as the professor who is a classroom teacher and also a research supervisor. Professionals must carefully consider the nature of the complex relationships in academia and internship agencies in order to make appropriate decisions about boundaries (Kitchener, 1988, 2000). Graduate students may learn important and lasting lessons about boundaries from watching their professors; unfortunately, professors are sometimes not the best role models (Branstetter & Handelsman, 2000; Keith-Spiegel, Wittig, Perkins, Balogh, & Whitley, 1993).

An important consequence of these complex power and boundary issues is the problem of whistle blowing, confronting professional misconduct among our colleagues. In their review of the literature, Biaggio, Duffy, and Staffelbach (1998) noted that psychologists are reluctant to report (blow the whistle on) colleagues who are engaging in unethical conduct. They reviewed the obstacles that psychologists face when addressing the misconduct of their equal-status colleagues, including issues of loyalty and the fear of negative repercussions. These issues are magnified in cases such as 1b and 1c, when students with little power notice unethical or questionable behavior among professors and others with so much more power. "Persons who are in positions subordinate to or under the influence of offending practitioners could be especially vulnerable to actual or feared consequences of confronting or reporting misconduct" (Biaggio et al., 1998, p. 277). These situations arise, at least on occasion, for many graduate students (Branstetter & Handelsman, 2000), and, again, the lessons learned may last a long time.

### Early Career

If students and interns can move beyond the "new toys" problem, and they acquire good training (in psychology and ethics), the first stage of their careers can be wonderful. They can experience large jumps in freedom, income, and self-confidence. The feelings of freedom from constant supervision and evaluation can be powerful. Unfortunately, they can lead to several pitfalls. First is a feeling of arrogance. Combined with the new toy pitfall, arrogance may lead new professionals to overgeneralize their skills and practice beyond the limits of their competence. For example, they may believe that they can do custody evaluations because they care about children (see APA, 1994), work with those from any ethnic group because they have good listening skills (see APA, 1991), or teach any course in the curriculum because they have a good presentation style. Second, the desire to put into practice what they have learned may lead new professionals to provide services when they are not wanted. Thus, a danger here may be paternalism: overriding clients' autonomy for beneficent reasons (Beauchamp & Childress, 1994).

Third, new professionals may overestimate their competence based simply on their education or licensure. After taking all the courses and exams, they may be tempted to say, "I am competent (and/or ethical) because I have a doctoral degree," or, "because I am licensed." This reasoning, unfortunately, is equivalent to concluding that you have money in the bank because you still have checks! Degrees and licenses are indicators of significant achievement, but they are not guarantees of ethical behavior (Handelsman, 1997). However good their training, psychologists will always be called on to see a wider range of clients, to teach new courses to different types of students, and/or to conduct research in new areas. As the scope of psychology is broadened and applied to more areas of expertise and more diverse populations, psychologists must continue their training throughout their professional careers to assure competence.

In fact, the potential for conflicts of interest may begin in earnest during the early stages of one's career. Although income may increase, so may financial pressures like those mentioned in Case 3. New professors may face new course preparations, reappointment and tenure pressures, and political intrigues at their institutions. Many new professionals have moved from far away, and their needs for companionship and other forms of emotional gratification are high. Agencies and insurance companies may also pressure psychologists to do more than they can. All these competing motivations and interests may make it difficult to think clearly about ethical issues.

Power increases exponentially at this time, and new professionals need to guard against exploiting students and clients. This exploitation may stem from misguided compassion, from arrogance, or from other sources. For example, some new professors may harbor feelings of vengefulness against the professors they had. It is hard to become aware of sentiments such as, "I suffered; now it's time to make others suffer they way I did." Sometimes new professors' attempts to establish and maintain high standards can mask a misuse of power.

As shown already, conflicts of interest and misuses of power can lead to boundary violations. Such violations may be likely at this stage because there is usually a small age difference between new psychologists and their students or many of their clients, and the pull to be "just one of the guys" can be strong. It is easy, then, to cross boundaries with clients and students at this stage.

## Midcareer (and Later)

Reaching midcareer does not let us off the hook in terms of ethical pitfalls. In a recent study in Colorado, psychotherapists who were found guilty of unprofessional behavior had been in practice an average of 15 years, the same length as a randomly selected comparison group of therapists who had never been complained against (Handelsman, 1997). Thus, having achieved a record of professional success does not guarantee immunity from unethical conduct. Why might midcareer psychologists get into trouble?

Ignorance is one answer to this question. We might think that ignorance would not be a problem after years of experience. But two types of ignorance emerge at this time that underscore the need for psychologists to continue their technical and ethical education. First, the life experiences of psychologists change how they work. For example, marital therapy may be done differently by a newly divorced therapist, and teaching development may change (not necessarily for the better) as a professor's own children grow up. Psychologists must be aware that new blind spots can develop due simply to growing and changing. Second, the field of psychology is constantly advancing. Psychologists cannot sit back and keep doing what they learned in graduate school; what was acceptable practice 10 years ago may be malpractice today.

One common correlate of unethical behavior is professional isolation. Therapists often move from working in agencies to private practice, and thereby reduce the contact they have with other professionals. Professors with tenure are usually not evaluated as often or as rigorously. Consultants may choose to work alone after years of being a member of a team. Isolation may make it easier for psychologists to take ethical chances without scrutiny, and may make it less likely that somebody will warn the psychologists about an ethical pitfall.

The effects of isolation can be exacerbated by some cognitive mistakes that midcareer professionals may be more likely to make. One such cognitive error is a misattribution of therapeutic effects: Early in their therapeutic careers, psychologists pretty much do what they learned in graduate school, and these therapeutic strategies work. Beginning therapists may be likely to attribute their success externally: "I did what they told me, so therapy was effective." After 10 to 15 years of practice, however, psychologists may start attributing their success to internal variables (personal attributes) rather than situational ones (accepted therapeutic practices): "My therapy is effective because I am a good therapist." At this point therapists may justify taking chances that may look like innovation but that are clearly unethical behaviors: "If I'm a good therapist, then my decision to date clients to teach them social skills, or to go to their birthday party to observe family dynamics, is good therapy."

Another dangerous attribution might be, "I'm ethical because I'm experienced." This is similar to the pitfalls described earlier regarding licensure and degree status, and may lead to a deemphasis of ethical reasoning. Professors may feel that their teaching ability is a matter of the charisma they developed or the awards they won, and they stop preparing as well as they used to (the "yellowed notes" pitfall). Therapists may stop listening for the uniqueness of each client or stop keeping adequate records. Also, after years of fighting for reimbursement from insurance companies (and often waiting for months to get those reimbursements), psychologists may feel that padding their bills may be acceptable because the insurance companies "owe" them.

Another cognitive mistake is that personal norms for success rates may become skewed. After having great success for years at practicing therapy, therapists often have difficulty maintaining the perspective that *all* therapists have similar success rates—most therapy with most therapists works for most people most of the time. Thus, for example, a client with borderline personality disorder comes to the therapist and says, "My last 10 therapists failed with me, but I know you will succeed." At this point, therapists may judge the chances of success at about 80%, which is their usual success rate. However, the true rate of therapeutic success with clients *who have failed 10 times before* is much closer to zero. Therapists may now want to demonstrate their prowess by trying techniques that have not been tried by previous therapists, such as visiting clients' homes, sending them flowers, attending their parties, or having them sit on the therapists' laps (remember, these are actual examples!). Notice that all of these unprofessional behaviors constitute boundary violations.

Situational pressures may be especially great during midcareer and influence the motivations of psychologists. As they achieve some professional success, psychologists might buy a second house, have three children in college, get divorced, and start feeling burned out just when they would like some professional recognition for their years of efforts. These pressures may show up initially as sloppiness: misplacing records, talking in a bit too much detail with others about their clients, taking cases they may not be competent to treat, spending too little—or too much—time with their students outside of class. These little slips can grow into serious ethical violations.

All of these pressures faced by psychologists, along with cognitive errors, increase the twin dangers of abuse of power and boundary violations. If psychologists feel that the force of their personality creates good outcomes, they may be more likely to use this power to serve their self-interest rather than client interests. And power at this stage is not only personal power but institutional power: Psychologists in midcareer are department chairs, program directors, supervisors, and board members. As psychologists move into being the "elders" of their professional community, they must resist the temptation of seeing themselves more in terms of making rules than following them.

## SOME STRATEGIES FOR STAYING ETHICAL

Difficult situations that call for sound ethical judgment occur frequently, and such judgments are difficult when we are in crisis mode. Therefore, I believe that many pitfalls can be avoided if professionals take some preventive measures. I present for your consideration several guidelines to help you develop good habits that will keep you from being an example that I can use in a later edition of this book. This is not a comprehensive list, but I trust that you will get the idea and add your own strategies over time.

### Develop Virtues

Certainly, knowing the rules is important; these rules include agency policies and ethical standards. But an exclusive focus on rules is incomplete. Jordan and Meara (1990) asserted that "achieving professional maturity and internalizing professional virtue are prerequisite to competent application of ethical principles" (p. 109). Don't just think about what to do or what not to do. Think about who you want to be as a professional (Meara, Schmidt, & Day, 1996).

I believe a central virtue to nurture in yourself is humility, which is similar to the Meara et al. notion of prudence. An attitude of humility encompasses the following types of beliefs:

- Our skills are limited, even as we attempt to develop areas of excellence.

- Our skills are not applicable to all clients, students, advisees, or supervisees.

- We cannot always do what is in our clients' or students' best interests.

- We cannot always fulfill our own interests.

- Therapy is not perfect, and is not good for everybody.

- We must always proceed with caution.

Another virtue discussed by Meara et al. (1996) is integrity, which refers to an articulated set of professional values that you are willing to actualize in practice, even in the face of competing pressures. Meara et al. (1996) also wrote about respectfulness toward individuals and communities with whom they work. These virtues do not replace principles and rules, but thinking about who we want to be can help us make good decisions and guide us when principles and rules are not enough to solve ethical dilemmas.

### Beware of Isolation

Psychologists who come up before ethics committees or state boards sometimes defend their unethical actions by saying they were being "creative" or "innovative." However, a dead give-away that this is not the case is that the psychologists did not mention these new innovative techniques to any of their colleagues. In fact, they did not even record their behavior in their own records. If you are not willing to share what you are doing with others, it is probably unethical at worst, or poor practice at best. You will be surprised how bad your judgment sounds when you try to justify it, out loud, in front of others. A better approach is to discuss your judgments with colleagues before the behavior occurs, rather than in front of an ethics committee after a complaint is filed against you. As mentioned earlier, the perceptions others have of our behavior are critical to our profession, and such discussions with colleagues help us judge objectively what those perceptions might be.

Do not fall into the trap of believing that once you are licensed, or tenured, you no longer need education, consultation, or supervision. Many psychologists avoid isolation by pursuing continuing education and by joining an ongoing consultation or supervision group in which they routinely discuss not only their success but their failures.

### Develop Explicit Ethical Policies and Do Not Make Exceptions

Many psychologists who have been punished for unethical behavior knew that they were taking risks, but made exceptions to their usual practice because the client was especially bright, or because they were facing some deadline or thought they would be OK "just this once." The more explicit the policies you have, the more likely it is that you will avoid this trap. For example, just as you will have policies about charging fees, you should have explicit policies about such issues as what you tell clients about your practice, authorship credit when publishing with students, accepting gifts or invitations, and confidentiality—not only with couples as in Case 2, but with all clients.

The process of formulating explicit policies gives you the opportunity to clarify your own values (Abeles, 1980) and to actualize the virtues that you have defined for yourself. It also allows you to share your thinking with others, thereby avoiding isolation.

Does having policies mean that you have no flexibility in how you practice your profession? Certainly not. Many exceptions and conditions can be built into policies. For example, a policy about accepting gifts may include different courses of action depending on such variables as the value of the gift and the cultural context in which the gift is offered. A policy about accepting invitations to social events may begin something like, "I will not accept invitations from students to social events, *unless* the event is a large, public, socially accepted event that is clearly part of academic life, such as a graduation party." After thinking carefully about your work and developing clear policies, you can be pretty sure that exceptions that you did not anticipate are likely to be boundary violations or other suspect activities. Before making such an exception you should at least seek consultation from a respected colleague.

### Incorporate Ethical Principles and Rules into Your Thinking

Avoid the temptation to justify all your actions and policies only by claiming therapeutic or educational benefit. Although pragmatic considerations are important, they are not enough. Be familiar with the APA Ethics Code (APA, 1992; Canter, Bennett, Jones, & Nagy, 1996; Nagy, 2000) and general ethical principles (Beauchamp & Childress, 1994), and do not wait for dilemmas or difficult situations to arise before assessing the ethical dimensions of your work.

### Stay in Touch with Yourself as Well as with Others

Being ethical does not guarantee staying ethical. As you grow and develop over time, you will need to continue to clarify your values. The answer to the question, "Why am I in this profession?" will change over time. That is OK. Not being aware of the change can lead to trouble. Indeed, in a survey of over 300 professional psychologists, Coster and Schwebel (1997) found that the most frequently cited component of "well-functioning" was self-awareness or self-monitoring.

Assume that you have blind spots, that those blind spots can change over time, and that you can work on them to reduce their negative effects. For example, some psychologists may have difficulty working with people of particular ages, cultural or religious affiliations, felony histories, and so forth. They may have difficulty with the financial aspects of their practices, or with the undergraduate courses they are obliged to teach. Working on these blind spots may take the form of careful thought and self-exploration, additional training, consultation, supervision, and/or your own therapy.

## Get a Life

This final advice is not as flippant as you might think. Psychology is a noble profession, but it may be dangerous to believe that actualizing our professional aspirations is enough. In speaking about therapy, Gutheil and Gabbard (1993) stated, "Trouble begins precisely when the therapist stops thinking of therapy as work" (p. 192). When we believe that our identity as human beings is dependent exclusively on the professional success we have, then the therapeutic or educational progress of each client and student becomes too important. At that point our motivation and judgment may be diminished and we become prime candidates for unethical behavior. Getting a life means putting your professional activities in perspective.

Obviously, our professional roles are the source of much satisfaction in our lives. However, they are not the only source of satisfaction, and some needs simply cannot be met by teaching, therapy, research, or consultation. Getting a life means being enough of a well-rounded human being that you can find ways to get your emotional (especially romantic and sexual) needs met outside the professional arena.

## Conclusion

In summary, learning to become ethical involves the same level of dedication and work as learning to become a good clinician, researcher, consultant, or teacher. Becoming ethical is more than good intentions and technical expertise. And staying ethical involves continuing to expand our ethical knowledge and skills.

## ACKNOWLEDGMENTS

This chapter benefitted greatly from the expert editorial input of Margie Krest and the professional and ethical wisdom of William Sobesky.

## REFERENCES

Abeles, N. (1980). Teaching ethical principles by means of values confrontation. *Psychotherapy: Theory, Research and Practice, 17,* 384–391.

American Psychological Association. (1991). *Guidelines for providers of psychological services to ethnic, linguistic, and culturally diverse populations.* Washington, DC: Author.

American Psychological Association. (1992). Ethical principles of psychologists and code of conduct. *American Psychologist, 47,* 1597–1611.

American Psychological Association. (1994). Guidelines for child custody evaluations in divorce proceedings. *American Psychologist, 49,* 677–680.

Beauchamp, T. L., & Childress, J. F. (1994). *Principles of biomedical ethics* (4th ed.). New York: Oxford University Press.

Bersoff, D. N. (1999). *Ethical conflicts in psychology* (2nd ed.). Washington, DC: American Psychological Association.

Biaggio, M., Duffy, R., & Staffelbach, D. F. (1998). Obstacles to addressing professional misconduct. *Clinical Psychology Review, 18,* 273–285.

Branstetter, S. A., & Handelsman, M. M. (2000). Graduate teaching assistants: Ethical training, beliefs, and practices. *Ethics & Behavior, 10,* 27–50.

Canter, M. B., Bennett, B. E., Jones, S. E., & Nagy, T. F. (1996). *Ethics for psychologists: A commentary on the APA Ethics Code.* Washington, DC: American Psychological Association.

Coster, J. S., & Schwebel, M. (1997). Well-functioning in professional psychologists. *Professional Psychology: Research and Practice, 28,* 5–13.

Gutheil, T. G., & Gabbard, G. O. (1993). The concept of boundaries in clinical practice: Theoretical and risk-management dimensions. *American Journal of Psychiatry, 150,* 188–196.

Haas, L. J. (1991). Hide and seek or show and tell? Emerging issues of informed consent. *Ethics & Behavior, 1,* 175–189.

Haas, L. J., Malouf, J. L., & Meyerson, N. H. (1986). Ethical dilemmas in psychological practice: Results of a national survey. *Professional Psychology: Research and Practice, 17,* 316–321.

Handelsman, M. M. (1997). *Colorado State Grievance Board sanctions.* Report available from the Colorado State Mental Health Boards, 1560 Broadway, Suite 1370, Denver, CO 80202.

Handelsman, M. M. (1998). Ethics and ethical reasoning. In S. Cullari (Ed.), *Foundations of clinical psychology* (pp. 80–111). Needham Heights, MA: Allyn & Bacon.

Jordan, A. E., & Meara, N. M. (1990). Ethics and the professional practice of psychology. *Professional Psychology: Research and Practice, 21,* 107–114.

Keith-Spiegel, P., Wittig, A. F., Perkins, D. V., Balogh, D. W., & Whitley, B. E., Jr. (1993). *The ethics of teaching: A casebook.* Muncie, IN: Ball State University.

Kitchener, K. S. (1988). Dual role relationships: What makes them so problematic? *Journal of Counseling and Development, 67,* 217–221.

Kitchener, K. S. (2000). *Foundations of ethical practice, research, and teaching in psychology.* Mahwah, NJ: Lawrence Erlbaum Associates.

Koocher, G. P., & Keith-Spiegel, P. (1998). *Ethics in psychology: Professional standards and cases).* New York: Oxford University Press.

Meara, N. M., Schmidt, L. D., & Day, J. D. (1996). Principles and virtues: A foundation for ethical decisions, policies, and character. *Counseling Psychologist, 24*(1), 4–77.

Nagy, T. F. (2000). *Ethics in plain English: An illustrative casebook for psychologists.* Washington, DC: American Psychological Association.

Pope, K. S. (1988). How clients are harmed by sexual contact with mental health professionals: The syndrome and its prevalence. *Journal of Counseling and Development, 67,* 222–226.

Pope, K. S., & Bouhoutsos, J. (1986). *Sexual intimacy between therapists and patients.* New York: Praeger.

Pope, K. S., & Vetter, V. (1992). Ethical dilemmas encountered by members of the American Psychological Association. *American Psychologist, 47,* 397–411.

Tymchuk, A. J. (1981). Ethical decision-making and psychological treatment. *Journal of Psychiatric Treatment and Evaluation, 3,* 507–513.

# 15

# Learning Research as a Lifelong Skill

*David S. Glenwick*

*Daniel K. Mroczek*

*James S. MacDonall*

Science, as Carl Sagan noted, "is a way of thinking much more than it is a body of knowledge. Its goal is to find out how the world works, to seek what regularities there may be, to penetrate to the connections of things" (1980, p. 15). This chapter focuses on learning to think about, and do, research for success in both graduate school and in one's later career, either as one's principal activity or as one component of one's work life. We begin by considering how one begins doing research as a graduate student. We then present five research tools—writing style, American Psychological Association publication style, statistical knowledge, computer skills, and information-accessing skills—that one should acquire during graduate school. Next, we discuss how research skills are influenced by the setting in which they are used, including laboratory, campus, community, or archive. Finally, we address the arts of obtaining grants, making convention presentations, publishing, networking, and securing postdoctoral training, arts that can be helpful in fostering a career in research.

## GETTING STARTED

In most graduate programs, the student is asked to come up with two questions about how the world works—which become the foci of a master's thesis or its equivalent (e.g., predoctoral research project) and a doctoral dissertation. Although students vary greatly in the research experience they bring to graduate school, most come with at least a minimal undergraduate or postundergraduate background, given (a) the competitiveness of graduate school admissions and (b) the use of research experience as one criterion for admission. The following remarks assume a typical situation in which the first-year student has participated in some previous research and may even have carried out a project (e.g., senior honors thesis) in which he or she was the primary researcher. Graduate school training seeks to build on this foundation.

In developing one's first graduate school research study, it is important to pick a topic that is manageable. This initial master's thesis type of project is intended mainly as a learning experience, although it may serve other goals (e.g., contributing to the scientific literature) as well. Therefore, it should be a study that one can carry out and complete in a reasonable period of time (e.g., within 1½–2 years). The research question asked needs to be of sufficient importance to be worth addressing, but not so large as to be unmanageable within that span of time. A long-term longitudinal study or a complex field intervention likely would be impractical for such a predissertation (or even dissertation) project. Although a laboratory or campus-based experiment may well prove feasible, correlational research, in which one explores how two or more constructs naturally "hang together," generally is easier to carry out than applied interventions in which one may spend years arranging the logistics of the project and awaiting outcome data.

There are several ways in which you can arrive at a topic. Based on your own life or work experience, you may come up with a question that piques your curiosity. Alternatively, reading a published study can cause you to arrive at a next logical question for research ("future directions," as authors are wont to say). You can then approach a faculty member who might have some interest in that topic.[1] The faculty member's task is to aid the student in operationalizing the question and in seeing that it is indeed manageable. If the first faculty member whom you approach is unable or unwilling to mentor you, do not be discouraged. Try someone else. If the idea is an interesting one, you will almost always find someone on the faculty who will support you.

Many students do not enter graduate school with a particular idea that they want to research. If this is the case, do not panic. Find out more about the faculty's research interests. Most departments have a brochure describing those interests; this provides a useful starting point. A number of departments have faculty make presentations to first-year graduate students, in which the faculty members lay out their recent, current, and prospective research interests and activities. Based on such written and oral presentations, you can then seek out a faculty member with whom you think you might wish to work.[2] You can discuss with that faculty member what he or she is researching or even what he or she is reading and might wish to research. Some faculty members (especially those with a research program, that is, a series of sequential studies lined up) have projects ready to hand to you; others can help you carve out your project from a larger, ongoing study that they are conducting; and still others will assist you in developing a project from scratch, based on your mutual interests and reading. Thus, the degree of originality and extent of collaboration required in the development of the research idea will vary depending on the particular situation.

In some departments, graduate students are restricted to working with faculty belonging to their particular program. Other departments permit the student to choose a mentor from

---

[1] This suggestion assumes a situation in which the student is free to choose a research mentor. In some programs, a student is admitted in part because his or her research interests, as expressed on application materials and interviews, fit a particular professor's interests.

[2] In some cases, the prospective student may have already begun doing this before or during the application process.

among all the members of the department, which obviously widens one's options. Find out which situation exists in your department and whether cross-fertilization, although technically allowed, is frowned upon or not by your program head. For some research projects, you may discover that having co-mentors possessing complementary strengths would strengthen the study, and you can assess the two faculty members' receptiveness to such an arrangement.

Selecting a mentor is an important decision, involving not just similarity of research interests. Although such similarity is certainly important, additional considerations should enter into the process. Look for someone with whom your personality and style mesh. If you know that you are a procrastinator, a mentor with a laissez-faire, laid-back approach might not be the best fit for you. You might do much better with someone who is going to provide you with frequent prompts and keep you on schedule. If you are a self-starter, who can take the ball and run with it, such external structuring may be less necessary. In any event, you need to select a mentor with whom you feel comfortable working and whom you would not be afraid to contact regarding even seemingly trivial questions. (Such apparently trivial questions, if glossed over, can sometimes result in major flaws being introduced into a study; prevention is preferable to after-the-fact, Band-Aid remediation or lamentation.) Additionally, the mentor should be someone who has the time to meet with you and to answer your questions either in person, by phone, or by e-mail. It is no windfall to be mentored by a luminary who is never available; in such cases an untenured assistant professor in need of students to mentor and who might be more willing to give of his or her time and energy would be a wiser choice of mentor. Similarly, the mentor should display responsible behavior, such as showing up for scheduled meetings, giving you timely feedback on drafts, and making whatever contacts are necessary to facilitate your project.

The mentor–student relationship is a marriage of sorts, and, like any marriage, the partners need to be compatible with one another if the partnership is to work. At the same time, marriage is not necessarily permanent. If you find that you are having difficulty in working with your mentor, due to lack of accessibility, a personality clash, or any other reason, attempt to talk with him or her about the problem. Should this prove fruitless, you can obtain a divorce and change mentors. However, you should do this in a responsible manner, informing your prospective new mentor about your history with the mentor whom you wish to leave and, once the break is made, letting the first mentor know what you are doing, in the most cordial and polite fashion possible. As a graduate student in your psychology department, you are a member of a community, and you want to maintain a positive reputation.

During the period in the 1950s and 1960s when Richard Daley was the mayor of Chicago, a frequently heard slogan around Election Day was, "Vote early and often." Similar advice would serve one well in doing research in graduate school. It is important to become involved in research activity as early as possible in one's graduate career (certainly by the second semester of one's first year) and to work steadily on one's project. This latter behavior is sometimes difficult to maintain because there are constantly more pressing deadlines for papers, exams, and the like, and one can seemingly always put one's research project on the back burner. This is a risky course of action. Unlike fine wine, research doesn't ripen with age; it simply becomes staler. The longer you delay completing the project (including the write-up), the harder it is to maintain your interest. Putting the study aside for weeks or months at a time is an inefficient way to work, as you must then spend time getting reacquainted with the study each time you return to it. What keeps students from finishing graduate school in a timely fashion is usually not courses or exams, which typically have built-in timetables, but the predoctoral and doctoral research projects, which are deceptively open-ended (until one starts receiving threatening letters from the graduate dean regarding such constraints as 10-year limits). Graduate school should be a transitional stage in your life, not a permanent career. Moving along on your research will do much to help ensure that this occurs.

Finally, in the rare moments of reflection that a graduate student has, it is interesting to think about how your choice of research topic relates to your own personality dynamics and life history. People may rationalize their selections of research questions as being grounded in "intellectual interest." However, in observing our own and our colleagues' and students' research over the years, we have been struck by how frequently such choices are based not purely on cognitive factors but also may involve (usually unconsciously) issues that are relevant to one's own personality and behavior. Thus, if you're studying social skills or impulsivity or chronic illness, consider its connection to your psychological functioning and life course and ponder what you can discover about yourself from having selected this topic.

## TOOLS OF THE TRADE

Although science is indeed primarily a way of thinking, there are certain behaviors and knowledge bases that facilitate its taking place, as well as helping the student move from thought to action. In this section we consider five of these: (a) writing style, (b) American Psychological Association (APA) publication style, (c) statistical proficiency, (d) computer and software skills, and (e) information technology and library skills.

### Writing Style

Many laypersons think of science as consisting of the actual carrying out of the study. In reality, when the study has been run, it is only partially completed, as it still needs to be communicated to the rest of the world. You may have conducted a truly well-designed, meaningful project, but if you cannot effectively convey in writing what you did (method), why you did it (introduction/literature review), what you found (results), and what it means (discussion), it is as if the study never occurred. Thus, it is crucial to be able to present your research in clear, expository prose. As one of our graduate school mentors was fond of exhorting, tongue-in-cheek, "Eschew obfuscation." Ideally, students learn how to write effectively in the years before graduate school. Unfortunately, however, we are finding this to be less and less true. Having a lucid prose style—as well as mastery of such mainstays as grammar, syntax, punctuation, and spelling—helps you get your message across. Additionally, a well-written paper predisposes the reader to take the content seriously. If a paper contains many grammatical errors or has thorny prose that is difficult to wade through, many readers simply will not bother. If the writer does not seem to care, why should the reader? Good writing is crucial at all phases of a project—in preparing a proposal for a mentor or a funding agency; in describing the study for a department or university ethics committee; and in preparing a final report, be it for your thesis or dissertation committee, for a granting agency, or for publication or convention submission. Know thyself. If writing is an area that is challenging for you or for which you feel ill-prepared, seek assistance early on, either from a professional or peer consultant or from written sources, such as the American Psychological Association *Publication Manual* (1994), Strunk and White's *The Elements of Style* (1999), and Zinsser's *On Writing Well* (1985).

## American Psychological Association (APA) Publication Style

One of your first purchases upon entering graduate school undoubtedly should be the APA *Publication Manual,* currently in its fourth edition (1994). Peruse it soon thereafter to get a sense of its contents. Throughout your graduate career, you will or should be referring to it frequently, as it is the style bible not just for research articles but for almost all course papers you will be writing. Although it contains useful suggestions regarding writing style, it is more crucial as a guide to the nuts-and-bolts mechanics of preparing a paper in psychology (e.g., the sections of a research report, capitalization, punctuation). Although you need not memorize all of its more than 300 pages, being on fairly intimate terms with it and at least knowing where to locate something in it will facilitate your academic writing. Some of its precepts may seem maddeningly arbitrary (e.g., when to express numbers in figures vs. in words), but these are the rules of the game that the profession has adopted. As a new entrant to the field, you will profit from mastering them.

## Statistical Proficiency

Few people enter into doctoral studies in psychology for the express purpose of learning statistics. Budding psychometricians and quantitative psychologists excepted, many who undertake graduate work in our field view their statistics classes with fear, and some consider them a nuisance. Yet statistical training is one of the most important aspects of doctoral-level work in psychology. An undergraduate course or two in statistics is fine if you are ultimately going to become only a consumer of research, but for those who enroll in doctoral programs, the expectation is that you will become both a consumer and a producer of research. To produce research in psychology, statistical competence is required. To this end, graduate students should take this facet of training seriously, yet not approach it with terror as so many do.

Further, proficiency in statistics leads to another desirable graduate school goal—finishing the dissertation. There is an association between statistical competence and getting a dissertation project successfully proposed, executed, and analyzed. Too often, graduate students in psychology bog down when the time arrives for data analysis. However, doctoral candidates who are fluent in statistics are typically able to better manage the data analysis process, and get analyses done more speedily, than those whose ability is lacking.

Building statistical competence ideally is achieved through a sequence of courses that includes instruction in analysis of variance (ANOVA), regression analysis, and multivariate statistics. After this grounding, one may take higher level classes in such areas as structural equation modeling, time-series analysis, and hierarchical linear modeling. In addition, hands-on work is strongly recommended. It is one thing to learn about statistics in class, and another to perform data analysis using real information. Fundamentally, psychologists use applied statistics, and you should try to get your hands dirty doing applied statistics whenever possible in graduate school. Find a dataset and play with it. Output frequency tables and descriptive statistics. Run correlations and study the output. There is nothing like jumping right in and acquiring direct experience. However, it is important to first master statistical procedures by hand before delving too deeply into statistical software (a topic we cover in the next subsection). By doing so, you will not only understand the statistics themselves better, but also more fully appreciate the efficiency and speed of microprocessors. Finally, knowing statistics from a pencil-and-paper perspective will allow you to more easily detect errors on computer printouts.

It is not necessary to learn every type of statistic. Learn the statistics and analytical tools that are most relevant for your particular area. If your area uses primarily experimental designs, get a good grounding in the various types of ANOVA. If your area is developmental, make sure you learn the fundamentals of longitudinal design and how to properly analyze longitudinal data. You need not master all of the many types of data analysis, but it helps to have strong ability in the family of statistics you are likely to draw on the most for your dissertation and for the research you will conduct beyond graduate school.

### Computer and Software Skills

It is as important to gain mastery of computer software as it is to acquire statistical skills. Most people will obtain some computer skills as a by-product of procuring statistical expertise, but certain technological skills require additional efforts to learn. For most doctoral students, the most essential of these are word processing, spreadsheet work, and graphics skills, in that order. Word processing is by far the most important of these skills. Most students today will have acquired adequate word processing skills by the time they reach a doctoral program. Therefore, graduate school should be a time of honing your abilities with regard to a particular package (e.g., Microsoft Word). As you learn how to write journal articles and other research reports, and as you carry out your master's thesis and doctoral dissertation, word processing fluency will increase. The bottom line is that you should not worry too much about gaining word-processing skill, as circumstances likely will provide you with enough exposure to produce competence in this area.

This is not necessarily true, however, of skills involving spreadsheets and graphics software. Gaining proficiency with regard to these types of packages may take extra effort. Most of the major spreadsheet programs (e.g., Excel, Lotus) also are able to create graphs and tables of various sorts. Thus, if you learn one such package you will gain the ability to execute a number of important functions. Many students in experimental, quantitative, or neuroscience programs, though, will have to learn more specialized graphing software. Excel can create good graphs, but it is limited in its flexibility. For example, it is not easy to put multiple graphs on one page in Excel. For creation of publication-quality graphs and figures, packages such as SIGMAPLOT or ORIGIN are better than Excel.

Unlike word processing, Excel or SIGMAPLOT may not be required as part of a course. Nonetheless, because such software is vital for data entry and for making up tables, graphs, and figures, it is important to expose yourself to these packages. Often these programs have built-in tutorials that you can use as primers. Many universities also offer short courses of a day or less that teach students and faculty the basics of such software packages. Whichever way you choose to obtain your training, you will find that familiarity with spreadsheet and graphics programs will make life easier when the time arrives to enter data for your research projects and dissertation and when you create supporting tables and graphs.

Less important for some doctoral students but crucial for others are database management skills. Students will often be responsible for managing databases for their major professor or research group. In private-sector companies that conduct research or at large research universities where projects are often well funded by grants, professional full-time employees who have specialized training in database management frequently fill the role of data manager. At other institutions, but also in smaller projects at research universities, doctoral students often are charged with the task of managing data resources. Such duties involve data cleaning (i.e., fixing and correcting data entry and coding errors), creation of key variables (including scale construction), addition of new cases to the database, and, perhaps most importantly, documentation of the variables so that others can easily use them during data analysis. Some statistical software packages, such as SAS, have strong data management capabilities, allowing for data entry, management, and analysis all within one package. However, other software packages (e.g., Access) are commonly used to house and manage data. It is useful but not necessary to gain database skills in graduate school. Often a postdoctoral fellowship will provide such training. Nonetheless, familiarity with the fundamentals of database management can only make you more marketable and will certainly allow you to control the diverse aspects of your own research with greater ease.

Finally, depending on your particular concentration within psychology, you may be required to learn stand-alone specialized software packages that perform unique functions. For example, most psychometricians today must gain fluency in item response theory (IRT) programs such as BIMAIN or PARSCALE. Psychologists who estimate population parameters, such as accurate prevalence rates of psychiatric disorders in the United States, must create data weights to account for sampling bias with special bootstrapping packages such as SUDAAN. It is becoming more common for developmental, industrial-organizational, social-personality, and quantitative psychologists to acquire some training in the usage of structural equation modeling (SEM) software, such as LISREL, AMOS, or EQS (although some comprehensive statistical packages, like SAS, include SEM capabilities). Those who engage in the analysis of qualitative data are not immune to the need to learn specialized software. Content analysis of textual information, a favorite qualitative method, is rapidly going high-tech with such packages as NUDIST. Not all doctoral students in psychology will have to master stand-alone programs. However, many will, and it is good to find out early in one's graduate career if such proficiencies are expected.

## Information Technology and Library Skills

In days past, spending long hours poring over musty volumes in a quiet university library was a precondition for receiving your doctorate. The tradition of giving doctoral students their own carrels in the library was born from this necessity. Today, there is still a need to hit the stacks and deal with paper matter, but a large part of the gathering of research materials, especially journal articles and books, is more efficiently and effectively accomplished using computerized literature searches than by sifting through the contents of bookshelves. However, the last thing we would want to discourage is wandering through the library. Do not get completely dependent on automated searches, for there is much to be gained from taking a random walk through the psychology section of your university library. You undoubtedly will come across books that are enlightening and useful and that would not necessarily have turned up in your electronic inquests.

That said, you must become comfortable with doing computerized searches. PsycLit and PsycINFO searches are the most important for our field, but, depending on your specialization, you also might have to conduct regular inquiries into the medical, educational, sociological, or statistical literatures. For example, many doctoral students have to master Medline searches to effectively probe the medical or psychiatric literatures on a given topic.

Automated searches will save you time and energy and will unearth valuable and relevant articles that a traditional paper search would not have revealed. Get comfortable using a variety of keywords in hunting out a topic. Often, students will complain that they punched in one keyword and came up with only a small number of references. Variables in psychology often go by many names, and you must type in many related keywords to uncloak a larger collection of papers on that particular construct. Be persistent and find out the different names by which a variable is identified. By doing so, you will uncover a more full array of articles, chapters, and books on your topic of interest.

It is also becoming increasingly important to develop an ability to efficiently negotiate the Internet. There are many resources relevant to research on the Web. For example, many scales and inventories are located free of charge on the Internet, usually on professors' home pages. It is also frequently easier to purchase books and manuals via the Internet rather than through traditional means (and, for now, you avoid paying tax on such items when purchased online). Downloadable articles are becoming more common as well. All of the major APA journals place their current tables of contents on the APA web site and usually choose two or three articles from each issue as "featured articles" that are downloadable in full. This is an easy and cheap way to obtain recent and important papers.

Additionally, an ability to manipulate the Internet can lead to more informal sources of information that can help you in your research. By visiting the home pages of researchers whose work is central to your own, you are usually able to obtain their e-mail addresses. Although you should not inundate researchers you admire with long and frequent e-mails, if you have a question or two that cannot be answered by reading a person's published articles, it is often useful to drop an e-mail to that person and gain a bit of informal advice or information. Similarly, many listservs exist for particular interest groups within psychology. Often, doctoral students will post a question relevant to their dissertation on these listservs and get valuable responses from knowledgeable people around the world. For example, it is quite common to see postings from graduate students asking about existing measures of a given construct that they intend to assess for their master's or dissertation projects. Many students have gained a wealth of information by posting such requests on listservs.

Despite the abundance of knowledge available electronically, it is still important for students to begin subscribing to relevant scholarly journals. You will automatically receive subscriptions to certain journals when you join professional societies, but it is useful to get others as well. As these periodicals begin to flow in, graduate students often assume that they must be read cover to cover. Do not do this. Even the most specialized journals contain many articles that are not relevant to the specific research questions you are interested in answering. If you read the journals cover to cover, you will waste an enormous amount of time that could be put to more productive use, become frustrated, and lose your zest for reading journals. We recommend a three-tiered approach in tackling the issue of which articles to read. When you receive a periodical in the mail, immediately peruse the table of contents. If you see one or more papers that are directly relevant to your area of research, put the journal in a pile that contains articles you intend to read or skim soon—within a month or so. If you see an article that is relevant to a secondary area of your interest, or is of general interest to the whole field, place those journal issues in a second pile to be read or skimmed within the next few months. Finally, if a particular copy of a periodical holds no articles of primary or secondary relevance to your area, shelve it so that it becomes part of your personal archives. Years later you may pull out that issue out, but for now let it grace your bookcases.

## HOW THE SETTING INFLUENCES RESEARCH SKILLS

Good research is good research, and sound research skills are transportable across settings. The particular setting in which one conducts research and collects data, however, does influence the implementation of those skills, with different types of settings presenting different challenges and opportunities. In this section, we consider the impact of setting on research and suggest certain things that a researcher needs to keep in mind in these diverse environments. We first discuss laboratory and department-based research. This is followed by consideration of community-based and applied research and archival data.

### Laboratory Research

It is a truism to say that participants in laboratory research are either humans or nonhuman animals. Experimenters require specialized knowledge for conducting research with both types of participants. Working with human participants requires interpersonal skills, the ability to prepare clear written instructions, and the provision of appropriate feedback and debriefing. Working with animal participants requires knowledge of species' behavioral, physiological, and sensory characteristics; attention to their housing and feeding needs; animal-handling ability; and access to a consulting veterinarian. Investigators also need to know whether the species carries diseases infectious to humans. Often, depending on the species or the state in which the research is conducted, licenses or permits are required. Despite these challenges, the great advantage of laboratory research is the high degree of control the investigator has over the features of the environment, which results in high internal validity. Because of the opportunity for control, investigators must be vigilant in assuring that the control is maintained throughout the experiment. The longer the data collection period, the more difficult this becomes.

*Essential Laboratory Skills.*    Everything, including the advantages of laboratory research, comes at a price; laboratory research is expensive, time-consuming, and requires a variety of skills. The skills necessary to produce valid data in the laboratory are extremely varied. Most laboratory researchers make, modify, or repair their equipment and make extensive use of electronics, especially computers. Ideally you will have a technician who can do this work, but because ultimately you are responsible and because beginning investigators rarely have technicians, the more you know the better. You need to be skilled in the use of hand tools such as handsaws, hammers, and screwdrivers. Competence in the use of hand-held power tools also is useful. In addition, knowledge of basic electronic principles, integrated circuits, and the insides of computers is helpful, including the ability to read wiring diagrams, solder electronic components, and identify and replace integrated circuit chips. In addition, you should be comfortable opening and replacing parts of a computer. Most often, equipment fails for simple reasons. Knowing which cable connects which pieces of equipment can save the day's data. Frequently, the cause of equipment failure is that the equipment is not plugged in! Your skills do not need to be expert, but the more you have, the better.

*Computer-Programming Skills.*    Knowing how to write programs in various computer languages is essential. Computers often control all aspects of the experiment, collecting an abundance of data that need to be managed and analyzed. Typically, commercial programs for conducting experiments control the stimuli, and these collect and download the data to popular spreadsheet or statistical data analysis programs. Although computer programming is important, no recommendation can be made regarding which language to learn because the number of computer languages is large and growing. However, you can learn common programming techniques, which are used by many languages. Software packages for conducting experiments often provide prewritten routines for experimental control. However, we find that they never entirely suit our needs. Because of this limitation, the programs usually include a mini-language for one's own routines. These mini-languages rarely are a popular commercial language, but they always use common programming methods and concepts, such as do-loops, variables, constants, strings, double-precision numbers, indirect addressing, arrays, and if–then conditional branching. Because modern spreadsheets come with the capability for the user to write mini-programs, often called "macros," they provide a means of learning programming methods. If you are competent in one or two different languages or packages, these competencies likely will transfer to the specific package you will use in the future.

Finally, in multidisciplinary research, it is tempting to focus on one's own area of expertise and not learn the methods of one's collaborators. Different laboratories can provide experiences in different procedures and methods. For example, a research acquaintance of ours tells of how, although trained in traditional learning and conditioning methods, he gained invaluable insights while working for a year in a genetics laboratory learning recombinant technology.

## Campus-Based Human Research

Graduate students frequently collect data on participants who come from traditional participant pools drawn from introductory psychology classes. This is probably the most common form of campus-based human research. Occasionally, research questions demand surveys of the entire student body or recruitment from some special segment of the campus population. However, usage of the regulated human participant pool tends to be heavy among graduates students carrying out various types of projects.

Before you gather any data on campus, you must go through your departmental institutional review board (IRB) or ethics committee, or both. This is one of the most important parts of gearing up to collect data. You must ensure that human participants will be treated in an ethical manner and that appropriate informed consent and debriefing procedures are used. Often, these boards meet infrequently and have strict deadlines for submission of materials. These committees often require voluminous paperwork that you must provide well in advance. Logistically, you should think about the timing of these deadlines in relation to the data-collection schedule you have set for yourself.

## Community-Based and Applied Research

Many research questions require participants from segments of the population (e.g., schoolchildren, elderly persons, inpatients) that cannot be found on campus. Research in applied settings offers the chance to study real-world problems in their natural environment and to possibly contribute to their amelioration. In addition, it provides the potential for greater generalizability (i.e., external validity) than does the more artificial environment of the laboratory or psychology department. At the same time, there are several aspects of community-based research that need to be kept in mind if one is to successfully navigate such settings. First, the trade-off for potentially greater external validity (i.e., generalizability to the real world) is greater difficulty in achieving internal validity (i.e., experimental control) (Campbell & Stanley, 1966). The real world is often messy, and one will likely not be able to create a situation where all dimensions other than the variables of interest are held constant. Therefore, one needs to consider (a) which dimensions absolutely need to be controlled and (b) which dimensions cannot be controlled but need to be considered. For example, in mounting a substance abuse prevention program aimed at adolescents in a particular community, one may find that the population is ethnically and racially quite varied. Rather than experimentally controlling for ethnicity or race, one will probably be interested in how this variable influences the effect of the independent variable (your prevention program) on the dependent variable (use of drugs). Thus, one would want to gather data on the participants' ethnicity/race and then statistically examine possible interaction effects between ethnicity/race and your intervention.

Deciding what aspects of an applied setting to take into consideration requires sensitivity to the *context* of that setting. As Glenwick, Heller, Linney, and Pargament (1990) observed, "Neither the research process itself nor the subject of a research investigation occurs in a social vacuum. Contextual forces shape both the phenomena of interest and the process of studying those phenomena" (p. 77). One needs to understand such forces as the culture, social norms, and history of the setting in order to ask meaningful questions and gather appropriate data. Learning about community settings requires an investment of time, but the result is worth it in terms of the resulting gain in ecological validity, or the degree to which we can translate the results to real settings.

An additional challenge posed by applied research is that, unlike in the laboratory, where one is in charge of all or most aspects of the research, in the community the researcher is only one of many players. Thus, one needs to be able to enter into a *collaborative* relationship with these other players (e.g., the recipients of the intervention, the consumers of the research) if one is to be effective. In such a relationship, "there is a sharing of presuppositions, information, resources, results, and benefits," resulting in "more contextually relevant questions,… more sensitive research methods,… and improved data interpretation" (Glenwick et al., 1990, p. 79). Through this process, the seeming negative of the researcher not being in control can be turned into the positive of a richer, more meaningful investigation.

Applied research typically requires IRB approval not only from your university but also from the outside institution or agency involved. Sometimes you may be recruiting participants from the community to come onto campus for the data collection. Much of the research on children, for example, takes this form. In these cases the only IRB you will have to go through is your own, yet the logistics of conducting a study that recruits people from off campus will provide challenges of its own. Furthermore, such studies may be more expensive than those that use on-campus participants. Recruitment costs, including payment of participants, may require you to obtain funds from either internal or external sources to carry out the project. Even when off-campus participants are not required to come onto campus but are contacted via phone or mail for data collection, there will be costs. You will need to figure out a way to pay for phone time, postage, and copying.

### Archival Data

Over the past several decades, many different governmental, nonprofit, and for-profit entities have collected an almost unimaginable wealth of data on nearly every portion of society. Indeed, so much information has been collected that government agencies such as the National Science Foundation (NSF) and the National Institutes of Health (NIH) recently have encouraged scholars to write grants that fund only data analysis, with no new data collection. Obviously, such grants are highly cost-efficient.

Additionally, many NIH agencies now have explicit policies that grantees must make their data available for public use after a reasonable amount of time. The biomedical and social sciences now enjoy a situation where an abundance of data lies out there, waiting for analysis and interpretation. One of the most logical uses of these data involves graduate students. Graduate students need good data for their projects and theses but often do not have the money to pay for expensive data collection. Thus, the use of archived data makes sense. Although psychology has put a premium on firsthand data collection, this is slowly changing. Graduate students are being allowed to conduct projects that use archived data exclusively or partially. Indeed, data from some famous studies, such as the Terman sample of gifted children, are used regularly for fresh analyses by young investigators and seasoned scholars alike.

The two most prominent repositories containing archived datasets relevant for psychology are the ICPSR and the Murray Center. The former is an acronym for the Inter-University Consortium for Political and Social Research and is located at the University of Michigan. It contains thousands of different datasets and is by far the largest social science data archive in the world. The Murray Center is located at Harvard University and, although smaller, contains data that are much more relevant for psychology.

Archived data may not always fit your needs, but sometimes they will. Do not tailor your questions so that you can use public-use information, but be aware that many of the questions you are asking may be answerable through the thoughtful analysis of an archived dataset.

## GETTING GRANTS

Scholars, unless independently wealthy, always have had to seek out funds to help carry out their work. Often such funding comes from within a university. Some students and faculty can conduct most or all of their research using only what their institution has given them. Others need to look outside the university for support.

Depending on the type of institution in which you end up working as a full-fledged psychologist, there is a decent chance that you will need or choose to apply for funds at some point in your career. It may take the form of a small internal grant to do limited research or to hold a conference, or it may embody a multidisciplinary, multisite, multimillion-dollar project funded by one of the major agencies. Whatever the scope or size of a potential project, graduate students should begin learning how to write funding proposals at as early a stage as possible.

Many different types of entities make grants. Psychologists receive funding from foundations, nonprofit organizations, corporations, and local, state, and federal agencies. These sources are worth exploring, especially for finding funding for projects that are highly specialized or high risk in terms of likelihood of obtaining positive research results. However, many grants, and certainly most of the large ones, come from two key governmental organizations, the National Institutes of Health (NIH) and the National Science Foundation (NSF). Although other federal agencies, such as the National Institute of Justice (NIJ) and the Centers for Disease Control and Prevention (CDC), also make grants to psychologists, the amounts pale in comparison to those awarded by NSF and NIH.

It is worthwhile to browse the NIH (www.nih.gov) and NSF (www.nsf.gov) web sites early in your graduate school career, just to get an idea of the types of grants that are available and to learn which scientific topics currently enjoy funding priority. The NIH is a much larger entity than the NSF, and it helps to learn about the different components of that organization, as some frequently make grants to psychologists while others never do. The NIH comprises 25 different institutes and centers. However, only eight of these make regular grants to psychologists. These are the National Cancer Institute (NCI), the National Institute on Aging (NIA), the National Institute on Alcohol Abuse and Alcoholism (NIAAA), the National Institute of Mental Health (NIMH), the National Institute on Deafness and Communication Disorders (NIDCD), the National Institute on Child Health and Human Development (NICHD), the National Institute on Drug Abuse (NIDA), and the National Institute of Neurological Disorders and Stroke (NINDS). Try to learn about these institutes and their funding programs before you attempt to write a grant. We must caution that the only types of NIH grant that graduate students are generally qualified to submit are those that support postdoctoral work. NIH also has a small grant program (R03 grants) that new PhDs and other less experienced investigators are encouraged to submit before attempting a major proposal. Do not try to submit a major grant application while still in school. However, it helps to start learning about the types of funding proposals that you may submit in the future.

Additionally, it helps to make contact with program officers from one of these NIH institutes or from NSF. Get to know some of these officers at conferences and ask about what type of proposal you might submit for your first grant. Officers at NIH and NSF are generally quite good about reading the prospectus of potential grantees and giving advice about how to proceed with an application. Begin learning about this process while you are in graduate school and get to know the people in Washington, DC, who might be able to give valuable advice when you are finally ready and qualified to make your first independent submission. Additionally, it is useful to get to know the employees in your university's grants and contracts office. Such people are typically well informed about the grant procurement process and are usually willing to impart their knowledge to graduate students and faculty who wish to write grants of their own. Furthermore, try to learn grantsmanship from faculty who have been successful at securing grants and ask to read proposals that have been funded. As important, ask to read proposals that have been turned down, along with the critiques. This will give you an idea of what successful and unsuccessful applications look like, and why the latter were turned away. Most PhD-level psychologists do not get around to doing this legwork until after they have obtained their doctorates. By becoming educated about the rules, mores, and customs of the funding world while you are still in school, you will have put yourself ahead of the game.

Lastly, we offer the same advice as we did earlier in the section on acquiring statistical skills. Get your hands dirty and try your hand at an application. There is nothing like experience to demystify the process of applying for grants. Once you have done one, the procedures will not seem as mysterious. Even more importantly, you will have successfully brought a complicated project to completion and met a deadline. Regardless of whether or not you receive the award, the process of applying will increase your confidence. That alone is a valuable reward.

## CONVENTION PRESENTATIONS AND PUBLICATIONS

Having written whatever papers and passed whatever oral exams are associated with their department's predoctoral or doctoral research requirements, students often (and with a sigh of relief!) regard the project as finished. However, assuming that significant (in both the statistical and psychological senses) results have been obtained, the work is really only partially done. What yet remains is to communicate the findings to the larger scientific community. Presenting the study at a regional or (preferably) national conference or convention is typically a first step in this process. Although one may choose to skip this step and to submit the study directly for publication in a scholarly journal, convention presentations have several benefits. First, writing a convention abstract (typically 1,000 words or less in length) is less burdensome than preparing a manuscript for publication. Second, the time lag for convention presentations is usually shorter than that for publications, thereby enabling one to expeditiously get one's study in circulation. Third, travel is broadening, and convention presentations enable one to visit parts of the United States and sometimes other countries that one might otherwise not have the chance to do. Frequently, one's department, a professional organization, a grant, or the like can reimburse all or part of the expenses. Finally, presenting a paper or a poster facilitates networking with colleagues having similar interests (see the next section). One receives (sometimes helpful) feedback and (hopefully) positive reinforcement for one's work; is forced to discuss it in public (a useful skill to have); and develops professional connections that can result in job leads, offers to write a book chapter or an article for a special issue of a journal, opportunities to review manuscripts for journals, and, most important, the feeling of belonging to a community of scholars.

Despite these several positive aspects, a convention presentation, as a former professor of one of the authors used to say, is ultimately worth half a point (or less) compared to a publication (worth one point). That is because to become a permanent part of the scientific literature, the study needs to appear in a professional journal. Additionally, it is the publications on one's resumé, much more so than one's presentations, that are looked at by search committees when evaluating job candidates for academic positions. If your study has produced meaningful results, by all means attempt to publish it. Your mentor and other faculty can assist you in selecting an appropriate journal for your manuscript. Here are some suggestions that may be of use in navigating the sometimes tricky waters of the publication process:

1. Establish who will be included as coauthors of the manuscript and what the order of authorship will be. Resolving this early hopefully can prevent bruised feelings, misunderstandings, and later quarrels. However, "collaborators may need to reassess authorship credit and order if major changes are necessary in the course of the project (and its publica-

tion)" (APA, 1994, p. 295). The APA *Publication Manual* lays out guidelines that can be helpful in this respect.

2.  Try to publish in peer-reviewed journals; these are usually regarded with greater esteem by the professional community than are nonpeer-reviewed ones.

3.  Do not be too discouraged if your manuscript is rejected by the first (or even the second) journal to which you submit your study. First-tier journals have extremely high rejection rates (i.e., 85–90% or higher in some cases), and it is no disgrace to be published in a quality second-tier journal. If you believe in your study, and if it has a contribution to make, you will likely find an outlet for it.

4.  Manuscripts rarely are accepted "as is" by a journal editor. More common is a decision to conditionally accept your manuscript, contingent upon some changes being made by you, or (more commonly) an invitation to revise and resubmit your manuscript. One should receive such verdicts as encouraging and (unless the revision hurdles seem daunting and the probability of eventual acceptance low) proceed to attempt to modify the manuscript in accordance with the editor's recommendations. (These recommendations generally are accompanied by the comments of two or more reviewers, which the editor has taken into consideration in formulating his or her evaluation of the manuscript.)

The publication process can be frustrating and painful, but the arduousness is outweighed, in the end, by the gratification of seeing one's offspring (and one's name) in print and the feeling of accomplishment in contributing to the scientific literature.

## NETWORKING

Science is fundamentally a social enterprise. Undoubtedly, solitary work has its place, but the progress of research in most disciplines would grind to a halt if scientists stopped networking with one another. Networking foments the exchange of ideas and lets investigators know what others are working on. For graduate students, it serves these purposes and more. Networking can lead to research ideas and even the acquisition of datasets. It can lead to job interviews or offers and to publication opportunities. One of the authors made a contact at a conference that led to an impromptu interview and, a few weeks later, to a postdoctoral fellowship offer. Basically, people will choose familiar people over those they do not know. Thus, making yourself visible to others within your specialty will place you at an advantage.

Conference attendance provides the best entry into the networking process. Go to the social hours at conferences and introduce yourself to scholars working in your area. When scholars whose research is relevant to your own come to your campus to give a talk, make sure to be there and meet them. If your university is located in a large enough metropolitan area where there are other schools with programs of interest to you, it may be fruitful to seek out professors and graduate students at those other institutions. This will provide networking of a more local flavor, but that may well be as productive as conference-based regional or national networking.

Finally, do not discount networking among peers. Keep on good terms with your own colleagues in school and try to get to know graduate students with similar interests at other universities. In some ways, peer networking is more important than getting to know senior scholars. The reason for this is simple: In your career you will spend a much longer period of time with your peers than with more senior people, who will retire before you. Therefore, be kind to your same-cohort colleagues, for you will have to live with them for the full length of your career.

## POSTDOCTORAL TRAINING

There was a time when academic jobs were plentiful, and a true labor shortage plagued the nation's universities. This was more than 30 years ago, however, and today it is difficult to secure an academic position right out of graduate school. As a result, the research postdoctoral fellowship (referred to colloquially as a "postdoc") is fast becoming a prerequisite (or at least a plus) for obtaining an assistant professorship.

During a postdoc, you do nothing but research. You generally are prohibited from teaching and are given no service duties of any kind. This frees your time to focus on your research and to collaborate with a senior preceptor who acts as your advisor during the fellowship. It also provides many opportunities for networking and extra training.

The duration of a postdoc is usually 2 or 3 years, although we have seen them as short as 1 year or as long as 5 years. Official NIH-funded postdocs are not allowed to go beyond 3 years. You may stay on at your postdoctoral university beyond the official 3 years, but after that point you must be paid from separate funds, not from the designated NIH postdoctoral grants. As a postdoctoral fellow, you are between graduate students and assistant professors in both status and salary. You are paid a lot more than a graduate student but not as much as an assistant professor. However, doing a postdoc allows you to publish your dissertation, get a few other publications, perhaps submit your first grant, and receive extra training. Typically, you are encouraged to sit in on classes, which is an effective way of beefing up your statistical and technical abilities. Furthermore, doing nothing but research for 2 or 3 years makes you more seasoned and savvy. You are no longer a "greenhorn" after having completed a postdoc. Universities recognize this in their hiring of junior faculty, as someone who has finished a postdoc is a safer bet for them than is a young scholar fresh out of graduate school. In addition, postdocs have completed their dissertations. This is not always true of those who are hired right out of school. Finally, postdocs tend to have many more publications than those who are coming directly from graduate programs, and possibly even have a grant and contract history. All of these facts make universities more likely to hire someone who has done a postdoc than someone who has not. Thus, consider taking such a fellowship. It likely will prove to be an excellent career move.

## SOME FINAL THOUGHTS

Some readers of this chapter may be wondering about its relevance to them. For example, if you are planning on entering clinical practice following graduate school, why is it important to cultivate more than the most rudimentary research skills? Several responses come to mind. First, even if you do no further research after graduate school, your research competencies hopefully will have resulted in (a) the completion of two projects—predoctoral thesis and doctoral dissertation—in which you can take pride and (b) the ability to be a lifelong consumer and evaluator, if not a generator, of research. Second, even if you become mainly a practitioner, you may well find yourself in a situation where an employer (e.g., hospital or community mental health center) or organizational client needs to evaluate a program or obtain a data-based answer to a question (e.g., which clients, if any, are benefitting from a particular intervention?). Your value as an employee or consultant will be enhanced to the extent that you have pertinent research skills for the problem at hand. Finally, the authors can recall several students who began graduate school certain that they would become practitioners, but who discovered to their surprise that they really enjoyed research and ended up in full-time or primarily research positions. Fate and professional development can indeed work in strange and unforeseen ways! May you continue to be curious and ask questions about how the world works.

## REFERENCES

American Psychological Association. (1994). *Publication manual of the American Psychological Association* (4th ed.). Washington, DC: Author.

Campbell, D. T., & Stanley, J. C. (1966). *Experimental and quasi-experimental designs for research*. Chicago: Rand-McNally.

Glenwick, D. S., Heller, K., Linney, J. A., & Pargament, K. I. (1990). Models for adventuresome research in community psychology: Commonalities, dilemmas, and future directions. In P. Tolan, C. Keys, F. Chertok, & L. Jason (Eds.), *Researching community psychology: Issues of theory and methods* (pp. 76–87). Washington, DC: American Psychological Association.

Sagan, C. (1980). *Broca's brain: Reflections on the romance of science*. New York: Ballantine.

Strunk, W., & White, E. B. (1999). *The elements of style* (4th ed.). New York: Allyn & Bacon.

Zinsser, W. (1985). *On writing well* (3rd ed.). New York: Harper & Row.

# 16

# Developing Teaching Skills

*James H. Korn*

Teaching was exactly like sex for me—something you weren't supposed to talk about ... but that you were supposed to be able to do properly when the time came.
—(Jane Tompkins, 1990, p. 654)

**M**ost faculty in my generation had no preparation for teaching when we received our graduate education in the 1960s. Those of us who cared about teaching learned to do it by trial and error, and by watching others, which is about as far as I want to take the Tompkins metaphor. Unfortunately, the situation today as the century turns is not much different. There are some graduate programs that provide good preparation for a career in college teaching, but many other programs provide only superficial preparation or none at all. The model seems to be that one should sink, swim, or not even go near the water because research or clinical training is what really matters. The variability in the extent and quality of attention given to teaching in graduate programs has been documented in a recent survey (Meyers & Prieto, 2000), which suggests that in many departments students who care about teaching have to train themselves.

This chapter is intended primarily for graduate students and new faculty members for whom teaching will be a major part of their academic career. However, teaching is a generic activity that includes professional workshops and research presentations. Almost all of the ideas and skills that I discuss are part of any teaching activity in some form. My purpose is to provide some initial guidance to those who are searching for ways to help themselves become better teachers. Entire books have been written on specific aspects of teaching, so it is impossible in a few pages to tell you how to do any of these things. The best I can do is to provide some basic suggestions and point you toward sources and experiences that are likely to be helpful.

First, I offer a few words of inspiration and a warning. Teaching is a challenging and rewarding activity. You will be able to touch the lives of many students, and to observe them as they learn and change with your help. At the same time, you may never know that you have had this impact, and you will find that learning to teach is a life-long challenge; it does not get easier. Bill McKeachie (1999) has been teaching for more than 50 years and I heard him say that he still is learning about teaching and often finds new things to try in the classroom. Teaching is challenging, but it creates passion for one's work and adds meaning to the life of a teacher.

## A MODEL FOR TEACHING

Before discussing specific skills, I present a model for the development of teaching skills. If you are a beginning teacher who needs help right now, perhaps the last thing you think you need is an abstract model. My experience working with graduate students, however, has taught me that it helps to consider this fairly simple structure:

Philosophy > Objectives > Methods > Learning > Evaluation

Your philosophy of teaching and learning (explicit or implicit) determines the objectives you choose for your courses. These objectives lead to decisions about the most appropriate teaching methods and ways of assessing student learning. All of this should be evaluated and modified based on the data you obtain.

I can imagine that someone reading this chapter has been assigned to teach a section of a course and has had no preparation for teaching. This reader wants help right now in planning lectures for next week. There is no time to ponder one's philosophy of teaching, and the objectives are obvious; just give them facts. I assure this reader that neither teacher nor students will be greatly harmed if you skip ahead to look for hints to get you through the week ahead. In doing so, however, you will be making choices about objectives (giving facts vs. evaluating ideas), and these choices will be guided by your implicit philosophy, which at this point may simply be one of survival.

Your philosophy of teaching matters a great deal as you decide what to do to help students learn, so I urge you to take some time to think this through and write it down. Most philosophy statements are about two pages long, written in the first person, using nontechnical language. Yours may say something about your beliefs and values, your idea of teaching excellence or the ideal teacher, your style, and your view of how people learn. I hesitate to suggest any topics to include because this statement should be *your* philosophy in both content and style. I usually ask my students, without any instructions, to write their teaching philosophy. Just do it. After you have done so, reflect on it, then rewrite it and show it to others. Self-reflection and honest discussion are essential.

You might be tempted to view this task as an exercise in the creation of socially acceptable clichés. Avoid this temptation, and show your commitment to teaching and to students. Developing a philosophy of teaching is a good test of the scientist-practitioner model of graduate education because it allows us to apply our knowledge of learning, memory, and human relationships. After you have written a draft of your philosophy, put it aside while you plan your course and do your teaching. After a few weeks, return to what you wrote and see whether your teaching practices follow your beliefs. If not, one or the other should be changed.

## WHAT IS GOOD TEACHING?

Hundreds of articles and books have been written that attempt to answer this question. These include both empirical research studies (e.g., factor analyses of student ratings of teaching) and theoretical or inspirational essays. Lists of characteristics of good teachers and teaching range from three items to a dozen or more, but I think these six capture what most of us would include:

- Knowledge of the subject. You have to know what you are talking about, which means knowing the field of psychology in general, as well as your specialty area, and keeping up with new developments.

- Organization. The courses you teach and each of your classes should have a structure that can be made clear to students. This requires careful preparation, as you can see later in the section on the syllabus.

- Clarity. Your knowledge must be expressed in a way that students or your professional audience can understand. This includes not only your public speaking skills, but also use of examples, exercises, and technology aids.

- Enthusiasm. This characteristic often carries the most weight in factor analytic studies. Your excitement about your subject and about teaching helps to maintain student attention, and can be contagious.

- Rapport. This general category refers to your sensitivity to students' interests, concern with their learning, and your willingness to help them outside of class.

- Fairness. Students are concerned, as you also should be, about your impartiality in evaluation, the amount of work, and the quality of exams and other assignments.

If teaching is going to be an important part of your career, you will want to develop yourself in each of these areas. Your graduate program and continuing education should provide you with the knowledge base. I can simply urge you to appreciate the need for a broad education in areas of psychology beyond your specialty, such as the history of psychology. Being able to connect with students also involves interpersonal skills that you will not learn by reading this chapter, but that are essential for good teaching. In the remainder of this chapter I focus on activities of teaching that involve skills that you can learn and practice on your own.

## THE ACTIVITIES OF TEACHING

In each of the following sections I refer to various sources that provide more lengthy discussions of each topic. The two books that I find most useful are McKeachie's *Teaching Tips* (1999), now in its 10th edition, and Davis' *Tools for Teaching* (1993). "Tips" is more research based and has more discussion of theory, but still is quite practical. "Tools" is organized in many short sections, which, like a set of tools, can be taken out and used to fix specific problems. The American Psychological Society has published a helpful collection of short articles on a variety of teaching topics (Perlman, McCann, & McFadden, 1999). The best entry to Internet sources is the web page of the Society for the Teaching of Psychology, Division Two of the American Psychological Association: www.teachpsych.org. This includes links to the "Psychteacher" discussion list and to the Office of Teaching Resources in Psychology.

## Planning Your Course

The course syllabus is the description of your plan that shows students (and others who want to know about your teaching) what you hope to accomplish and the structure for achieving your objectives. It also is your promise to students about what will happen in the course and a description of the work that they will have to do. Any syllabus should include basic information about the course (especially your objectives) and the instructor, a list of textbooks and readings, a course schedule (especially dates of exams and when assignments are due), grading criteria, course policies (attendance, late or missed assignments, academic dishonesty), and available support services. See Altman and Cashin (1992) for a more detailed listing of syllabus items.

Many students will only pay attention to the assignments and dates of the exams, but will ignore the list of course objectives. The objectives are of great importance to the instructor, however, because they determine the kinds of assignments you have, the form and content of examinations, and the teaching methods you select. It is not easy to state clear objectives, that is, objectives that readily guide your decisions and can be evaluated, but Angelo and Cross (1993) and Grasha (1996) provided self-scoring inventories that can help you develop course objectives.

Forming a philosophy of teaching will help you make decisions about your objectives. For example, you may believe strongly that your role is to develop logical, critical thinkers. If so, at least one of your objectives should reflect this belief, and your syllabus should show where students would get to practice this and how you will evaluate this area. Another teacher may value the personal development of students, and that should then be reflected in the objectives and methods.

Perhaps the most common problem in lists of objectives is that they often are stated in terms of what the teacher will do, rather than what the student will learn. "To expose students to" something can be done if you simply tell them about it and show some pictures, but that usually is not what the teacher means by that objective. What the teacher really wants is to have students remember what they were "exposed to" by answering questions correctly on content-valid examinations. So be clear about your objectives by stating what you want students to learn and what they must do to demonstrate that learning. You can get very specific about this. For example, you could draw a matrix with the rows being individual test items or elements of assignments and the columns being your objectives. That would allow you to determine the extent to which you are assessing each of the objectives. This activity can be disappointing if you discover that you are assessing mostly knowledge of facts rather than critical thinking or some other higher level objective.

There are many other decisions to consider in designing your course, and these are discussed in the general sources given at the end of this chapter. For example, choosing a textbook can be a daunting task in courses where dozens of books may be available. However, it is the area of course policies where the beginning teacher is most likely to get in trouble, but where the syllabus can help to prevent problems. Your policies should be unambiguous, documentable, and enforceable. If you have an attendance policy, for example, you should specify a number of acceptable unexcused absences and what constitutes an acceptable excuse. Then you will have to take attendance every day and evaluate a creative variety of excuses. Think carefully about whether these clerical burdens are related to your course objectives. If not, why waste the time? Makeup exams create a related challenge. Students do get sick on exam days or have accidents, and grandparents really do die. You want to be sympathetic when there are true emergencies, but not be gullible in the face of good acting. I have discovered no perfect solution to this problem, but the point is to make your policy clear in advance in the syllabus and to be prepared to implement that policy.

## Lecturing

Good teachers do not simply stand and talk for an hour. We use the chalkboard and overheads, we ask and invite questions, we provide demonstrations, and we use a variety of other techniques to maintain interest. But talking is part of it, and it is the part that terrifies many beginning teachers. As a graduate student I was anxious when I had to teach a class, and I have spoken to excellent teachers who described their first experiences as "pathetic" and "awful." Somehow we survived and now even enjoy speaking in public. If that thought makes you anxious, consider these suggestions:

- Develop confidence with the knowledge that many award-winning teachers began with shaking knees and white knuckles, but overcame their fear. You will too.

- You probably will have a sympathetic audience. Students have similar fears and they appreciate it when they know you are trying, and you probably feel more nervous than you look.

- Learn what to do by observing good lecturers. Do what they do to the extent that it fits your personality.

- Practice by beginning with small steps (short "guest" lectures) in comfortable settings, like a small class of psychology majors who want to hear about your specialty.

- Learn to use relaxation techniques (e.g., Benson, 1975).

Once you gain confidence and can speak to a class with a manageable amount of overt nervousness, then you can pay attention to other important aspects of a good classroom presentation. The following list is a set of categories for observing teachers that I developed with Jeff Dyche based on research by Murray (1983). Be aware that all these categories are important, but do not try to work on them all at once. If you can be confident, organized, and clear, you will have made a good beginning.

- Speech: Not too fast, loud enough to be heard by all, expressive, and clear. Use notes for support, not as a script to be read.

- Nonverbal behavior: Use reasonable amounts of movement and gestures, make eye contact with students, and show enthusiasm. Become aware of any distracting habits or signs of nervousness that you may have.

- Explanation: Use lots of good examples; elaborate difficult ideas by rephrasing and explaining. Use visual aids. Become aware of when you are ambiguous or ramble.

- Organization: Have a clear structure for your class, and follow it flexibly; structure should not discourage student involvement. Make smooth transitions between topics, summarize periodically, and review major points.

- Interest: Your interest in the subject should be clear. Use good examples, including some from your own experience. Use humor appropriately. Stimulate discussion among students.

- Rapport: Address students by name, talk with them before and after class, and show respect for their ideas. Become aware of your students as individuals. On the first day of class, have students complete a "background questionnaire," in which you ask them about their hobbies, favorite TV programs, people they admire, and other things that can help you to communicate.

- Participation: As part of a lecture, participation means that students have a chance to ask questions and make comments. In large classes only a few students will do that, so use techniques that allow for greater involvement, such as e-mail questions or written questions handed in at the end of each class.

The skills involved in all these categories can be specified and practiced. As with other kinds of learning, the key is to get objective feedback on your performance. That feedback can come from your students, but it also is helpful to have a trained observer visit your class. You can ask a peer to do this, as long as the person is willing to give you an accurate description of what was observed. It might feel good, but is not at all helpful, to have a friend tell you what a great class you taught. What you really want to know are things like which of your examples did not work or when you left out an important point or inadvertently cut off a student's comment. So find a good observer, pick one or two categories to develop, ask the observer to pay attention to those things, and listen to the feedback. I also recommend the use of videotape. Although this can be intimidating for most of us, you can get used to it and it allows you to observe all areas of your presentation in successive viewings. For a more complete discussion of classroom presentation style and content, see Lowman (1995).

An effective presentation will include more than a well-organized, enthusiastic talk with good stories. You will hold attention better by using a variety of media. What we used to call "visual aids" is now called technology. This still includes the chalkboard, but Power Point has enhanced projectors, and the 8-mm film has been replaced by videotape. Some classrooms have consoles that integrate all these devices and allow projection of computer screens with reception of Internet web sites. Use these to embellish your lectures, but *be careful* because it may be tempting to devote large blocks of time to developing your technology at the expense of direct contact with your students or learning more about developments in psychology.

You do not need technology to include many effective demonstrations in your class presentations. The American Psychological Association publishes a series of "activities handbooks" for the teaching of psychology. One example of a simple demonstration that has worked many times for me is Ludy Benjamin's (1981) "an assignment to be forgotten," which requires only a chalkboard. In dramatic fashion, students are given a homework assignment. The instructor writes a three-digit number on the board, stares intently at it, and then says, "Your task is to forget that number." Most students fail the assignment (that is, they do remember the number) but learn some important things about memory. Often my end-of-semester course evaluations will refer to one of these simple demonstrations as among the most interesting aspects of the course.

A good teacher will develop the skill of turning lemons into lemonade by taking a demonstration that doesn't work, and making it a learning experience anyway. For example, there is a demonstration of the bystander effect, in which the teacher asks for help ("please get me a glass of water") in a class.[1] When this "works," no student responds to the request and all students experience the effect, which leads to discussion. But what if students do try to help? That can lead to an analysis of features of the situation that ran counter to the expected effect. The point is: When demonstrations do not work as planned, be prepared to use whatever did take place as an occasion for learning.

## Managing Discussions

"A discussion is an exchange of ideas where all members of the group have an opportunity to participate and are expected to do so to some degree" (Kramer & Korn, 1999, p. 99). Discussions are particularly effective in accomplishing several learning objectives, including integrating course content with personal experience, problem solving, and practicing critical thinking. The success of a discussion depends on every student being actively involved.

Here are some things that happen under the label of class discussion, but that usually do not accomplish the intended objectives: oral quizzes in which questions have specific answers; recitation, where smart students show what they know; pseudo-Socratic teaching, or "guess what I know"; and nonproductive arguments about "controversial issues." Most of these activities involve only a few of the students in a class and frustrate or bore the rest.

The most common form of discussion attempts to involve the entire class as a group, even when classes are large. In these discussions teachers ask questions, listen to students' responses, then summarize what they heard and give their own response to the question. That is an important teaching technique, and it is deceptively simple. However, teachers often encounter problems when using this technique. One problem is that teachers talk too much. In a study of discussion classes in a variety of disciplines, Nunn (1996) found that the median percent time of student participation was 2.3% and that the median number of students taking part at least once was 25.5%. That is, when teachers say they are having discussions, in most classes students do not talk much and most students do not talk at all.

Dividing a class into small groups of four to nine students will increase the proportion of students who talk and decrease the dominance of the instructor. That is good teaching if you agree that students learn more when they are involved actively. Managing small-group discussions involves specific skills that must be practiced, and problems that can be anticipated and prevented. These suggestions should help you begin to develop skill in discussion management:

- Create a supportive classroom climate by acknowledging and respecting students.

- Become an active listener. This is a skill you will want students to display in their discussions, so learn to model it for them by paraphrasing and summarizing what they say to you.

- Establish clear ground rules for discussions.

- Take time early in the semester to provide training in discussion skills.

---

[1] William Douglas Woody presented this demonstration at the Mid-American Conference on the Teaching of Psychology, Evansville, IN in October 1999. Doug now is at the University of Wisconsin, Eau Claire.

These suggestions should help you to prevent some of the most common problems associated with discussions, such as students who talk too much or not at all, and keeping the discussion on the topic. When I want to make extensive use of small-group discussion, I will devote one entire class period early in the semester to preparing students for participation. I do this by engaging the entire class in a discussion about what makes a good discussion. Students always mention all the important characteristics such as staying on the topic, being a good listener, respecting different views, and other characteristics that become our ground rules for that semester. They also realize that there will be more participation if we use small groups.

Is it really necessary to devote an entire class to training in discussion skills? Faculty are reluctant to give that much class time to working on a process because they have so much content to cover, but consider your objectives. If objectives like critical thinking and relating content to personal experience have high priority for you, then it is important that small-group discussions be used effectively, and most students need to learn and practice discussion skills.

One of the risks involved in using small-group discussions in your classes, especially on topics that are somewhat sensitive, is that discussion may lead to conflict. Effective use of ground rules should prevent this, but in a class with several assertive personalities, conflict may be hard to manage. Some individuals love a good argument, and can leave it with no hard feelings. Others, myself included, are conflict avoiders and feel quite uncomfortable when voices are raised and emotions run high. McKeachie (1999) gave some suggestions that will help to mediate most emotional discussions. For example, he recommended the two-column method: using the chalkboard to list points on both sides of an issue. In most classes, however, the risk of disruptive conflict is low, and there is much to be gained by involving students through discussion.

## Teaching Students to Think and Learn

I have heard teachers say that their job is to teach, and the students' job is to learn. However, I believe that in addition to creating the conditions for learning, a teacher is responsible for teaching students how to think and learn, and for providing support during the process. If you are reading this chapter, you have been unusually successful in our educational system, but it probably is difficult for you to say how you acquired the skills that you needed to survive in this system. Some of your teachers, intentionally or not, helped you with this, and now your task as a beginning teacher is to discover how to help others think and learn. The skills you need are those of an applied cognitive psychologist. The following suggestions have been gleaned primarily from McKeachie (1999).

- Get and keep students' attention. Varying your methods will do that, which means using demonstrations, discussion, questioning, debates, videos, role plays, and anything else you can find.

- Organization (the structure of knowledge) is important for learning. The teacher can provide structure, but it is better if students can do this themselves. Peter Gray (1993) provided an example of a structure that is idea based, using question maps and hierarchical review charts that are designed by students.

- Knowledge of results is essential. Help students see the progress they are making toward objectives. Short, ungraded assignments may be better than exams for accomplishing this goal.

- Active learning is better than passive learning. Focus more on what students do than on what you do.

- Meaningfulness helps recall. Students should form their own questions and state ideas in their own words.

- Take time to teach students how to learn by providing and modeling strategies, and helping them set learning goals.

Of all the active learning techniques available, I prefer those that involve writing. Writing to learn includes much more than term papers and essay exams. It relies heavily on brief writing exercises in class. The "one-minute paper" (Angelo & Cross, 1993) is a good example of this. After explaining some idea in a lecture, ask students to take a piece of paper and in about a minute write a brief summary of the idea. Then they exchange their written summary with another student. Discrepancy in understanding then becomes the basis for questions and discussion.

Exercises like this can be used in classes of any size. Writing increases the likelihood that students have thought about a question or issue. If you simply ask your class a question, then pause and wait for the usual hands to go up, students will learn that they do not have to do this hard thinking stuff. However, if you ask all students to write an answer, and then call on some, the effect is significantly different. Even in large classes most students will comply. Notice that the teacher does not have to read all this writing, although you may want to reinforce the importance of this work by collecting it occasionally, either anonymously or with names, and reading the responses as a way to assess students' understanding. A special issue of *Teaching of Psychology* (Nodine, 1990) addressed a variety of issues in writing to learn.

## Student Diversity

The increasing diversity of the students in our classes represents both a challenge and an opportunity for teachers. Our students are not only demographically diverse (age, gender, ethnicity, etc.), but also cognitively diverse, having different educational backgrounds and preferred ways of learning. Do not ignore the diversity among your students, but view it as an opportunity to enrich your classes. For example, most introductory psychology textbooks now recognize cultural and gender differences in psychological processes. Having a diverse student group allows you to find more relevant examples and occasions for sharing personal experiences.

Effective use of student diversity for learning requires that we recognize certain needs in all of our students. Based on her review of the literature on multicultural teaching, Nancy Chism (McKeachie, 1999, chapter 20) considered four messages:

- All students need to feel welcome by being included in conversations and activities, and by recognizing their different perspectives. Respect among students should be developed as a classroom norm.

- Treat students as individuals by looking beyond stereotypes; students are not token representatives of their various groups.

- Encourage full participation by recognizing differences in learning styles and using different teaching techniques. For example, some cultures value listening more than speaking.

- Treat students fairly, which is not the same as treating them equally. Visually impaired students, for example, are given assistance with reading examinations.

There are so many varieties of diversity that it is almost impossible to consider all the possibilities, but Chism presented some general ideas that can be applied to all students: Know your students, care about their needs, and be flexible in your teaching.

## Evaluation of Teaching

Eventually, someone is going to want to know how good a teacher you are. This may be someone who is considering whether to hire you, or who, having hired you, is thinking of giving you an increase in salary or granting you tenure. The people who are interested in your teaching will want some data. More importantly, as a dedicated teacher you are interested in your own improvement, so you want to know what is working well and what you should try to improve. If you are a creative, experimenting teacher, you will want data on the extent to which your innovations worked. These all are reasons to develop some evaluation skills.

You probably are most familiar with end-of-semester evaluations of courses and teachers, using student ratings. These often are used by administrators for making salary decisions and may be required for decisions about your promotion and tenure. Some colleges and universities have a form that all faculty members are required to use, but often each department has designed its own form. *If* the form has been designed well and *if* the evaluation is administered under controlled conditions, then student evaluations are reliable and valid. Hundreds of studies have been done that support that conclusion (Cashin, 1995). Notice that I emphasize the importance of a well-designed form, which means that there has been at least some rudimentary psychometric development, and of careful implementation of the evaluation. Students cannot rush through the evaluation on the day of the final, while the teacher is handing out cookies. See Cashin (1990) for a detailed discussion of these issues.

I always use student ratings but do not find them to be very useful for my own development. First, numbers tell me little about what I need to do to improve, so I ask students to write narrative responses. I always ask at least these two general questions: "What worked well?" and "What needs to be improved?" Then I ask questions about specific aspects of the course, especially areas where I made some changes. Second, I like to have students interact with each other about their evaluations, so in most classes I spend about 20 to 30 minutes having the students discuss their responses to my questions. A teaching assistant or colleague may manage this discussion. This allows students to consider the ideas of others and add them to their comments or to disagree with the ideas.

Evaluation done at the end of the semester helps me to improve my course the next time I offer it, but does not help the students in the current semester. For that reason I strongly suggest doing a narrative evaluation about one-third of the way through the semester, using only the general questions of what is working well and what needs to be improved. It is important to discuss the results with the students to show that you gave serious consideration to their ideas. Do not seek their opinions unless you are willing to make some changes, or you will lose credibility. You do not have to follow every suggestion, but be responsive to those that do not compromise your objectives and that come from a reasonable number of students.

Use multiple methods of evaluation, especially for areas where you are trying hardest to improve. For example, if I am concerned about the quality of discussions in my class, I will get student comments in writing, but also will invite an observer to chart the interactions and the content of the discussion during one or two classes.

Student learning ultimately is the criterion for your effectiveness as a teacher, so your evaluation toolbox should include measures of learning. Exams and other assignments should be designed to measure student achievement of your course objectives, so that student performance can be one indicator of your teaching effectiveness. Sometimes we would like to know what students have or have not learned on a particular day. Our intent is not to grade students, but to find out if the concept we were teaching was presented clearly or if some new exercise we used led to the expected learning. For this purpose, brief classroom assessments are helpful. Angelo and Cross (1993) published a handbook describing various assessments that are related to specific course objectives, including estimates of how much time it takes to plan, complete, and analyze these activities.

## EXPERIENCE

You now know a little about planning a course, presenting material (lecturing), managing discussions, facilitating student learning, and evaluating your teaching, and you have some other sources to go to for help. The next step is to put these things into practice. Seek opportunities to gain experience in situations where you can focus on just a few teaching skills, for example, by giving a "guest lecture" for someone. Approach this experience as a model for teaching an entire course: State your objectives for the class, select techniques that fit the objectives, and use a brief assessment to see how you did. Find a careful observer to give you feedback, then reflect on what worked well and what you might do differently next time. Do not try to do too much.

Some experience can be gained vicariously. "You can observe a lot by watching," as Yogi Berra said. Ask other teachers if you can visit their classes to see how they present ideas and involve students. Examine their syllabus and assignments. An excellent teacher once told me that he had "stolen from the best of them" to develop his own techniques. Visit classes in your imagination by thinking back to some of your teachers, and then apply the things that your best teachers did, while avoiding the mistakes of those who were less effective.

You may not have the good fortune to gain your first teaching experience in these safe, small steps. Many departments will assign graduate students to teach their own course as soon as they arrive on campus and with only a few days notice. If that happens, let this chapter be your lifeline and get a copy of *Teaching Tips* (McKeachie, 1999) as soon as possible. You also should try to find a teaching mentor, someone who loves teaching and will give you emotional support and specific advice. Even top-rated research departments should have one or two faculty like that, but it may be that you will have to seek support elsewhere. The larger community of teachers is amazingly generous, so do not hesitate to go online to find help.[2]

---

[2] You may contact me by e-mail: kornjh@slu.edu.

Be prepared to be both enlivened and humbled in your teaching, whatever form it may take. Parker Palmer (1997, p. 15) described the joyful moments in the classroom. "When my students and I discover uncharted territory to explore, when the pathway out of a thicket opens before us, when our experience is illuminated by the lightning-life of the mind—then teaching is the finest work I know." But there are also those hard days when "the classroom is so lifeless or painful or confused ... that my claim to be a teacher seems a transparent sham.... What a fool I was to imagine that I had mastered this occult art—harder to divine than tea leaves and impossible for mortals to do even passably well!" The challenge is worth it. Go for it!

## REFERENCES

Altman, H. B., & Cashin, W. E. (1992). *Writing a syllabus* (IDEA Paper No. 27).[3] Manhattan: Kansas State University Center for Faculty Evaluation and Development.

Angelo, T. A., & Cross, K. P. (1993). *Classroom assessment techniques: A handbook for college teachers* (2nd ed.). San Francisco: Jossey-Bass.

Benjamin, L. T., Jr. (1981). Meaning and memory: An assignment to be forgotten. In L. T. Benjamin, Jr., & K. D. Lowman, (Eds.), *Activities handbook for the teaching of psychology* (pp. 86–87). Washington, DC: American Psychological Association.

Benson, H. (1975). *The relaxation response.* New York: William Morrow.

Cashin, W. E. (1990). *Student ratings of teaching: Recommendations for use* (IDEA Paper No. 22). Manhattan: Kansas State University Center for Faculty Evaluation and Development.

Cashin, W. E. (1995). *Student ratings of teaching: The research revisited* (IDEA Paper No. 32). Manhattan: Kansas State University Center for Faculty Evaluation and Development.

Davis, B. G. (1993). *Tools for teaching.* San Francisco: Jossey-Bass.

Grasha, A. F. (1996). *Teaching with style.* Pittsburgh, PA: Alliance Publishers.

Gray, P. (1993). Engaging students' intellects: The immersion approach to critical thinking in psychology instruction. *Teaching of Psychology, 20,* 68–74.

Kramer, T. J., & Korn, J. H. (1999). Class discussions: Promoting participation and preventing problems. In B. Perlman, L. I. McCann, & S. H. McFadden (Eds.), *Lessons learned: Practical advice for the teaching of psychology* (pp. 99–104). Washington, DC: American Psychological Society.

Lowman, J. *Mastering the techniques of teaching* (2nd ed.). San Francisco: Jossey-Bass.

McKeachie, W. J. (1999). *Teaching tips: Strategies, research, and theory for college and university teachers* (10th ed.). Boston: Houghton Mifflin.

Meyers, S. A., & Prieto, L. R. (2000). Training in the teaching of psychology: What is done and examining the differences. *Teaching of Psychology, 27,* 258–261.

Murray, H. G. (1983). Low-inference classroom teaching behaviors and student ratings of college teaching effectiveness. *Journal of Educational Psychology, 75,* 138–149.

Nodine, B. F. (Ed.). (1990). Psychologists teach writing [special issue]. *Teaching of Psychology, 17(1).*

Nunn, C. E. (1996). Discussion in the college classroom: Triangulating observational and survey results. *Journal of Higher Education, 67,* 243–266.

Palmer, P. J. (1997, November/December). The heart of a teacher: Identity and integrity in college teaching. *Change,* pp. 15–21.

Perlman, B., McCann, L. I., & McFadden, S. H. (Eds.). (1999). *Lessons learned: Practical advice for the teaching of psychology.* Washington, DC: American Psychological Society.

Tompkins, J. (1990). Pedagogy of the distressed. *College English, 52,* 653–660.

---

[3] This series of IDEA papers contains many useful sources. For more information contact idea.ksu.edu

# 17

# Learning Psychological Testing and Assessment

*Allen K. Hess*

Psychological testing and assessment may be the most important set of skills that psychology students learn in their graduate school experience. In supporting this assertion, this chapter answers a set of questions: (a) why a budding psychologist should master assessment skills, (b) how one goes about learning testing, and (c) how testing fits into one's professional identity.

## WHY LEARN TESTING?

Historically, the earliest efforts by psychologists in the modern era concerned psychological measurement. Indeed, one can trace the history of psychology by following the development of mental testing. Decades before Wundt and James established the first psychology laboratories, Fechner and Weber sought to establish psychology on a scientific foundation when they developed methods to scale mental phenomena. Beginning in the 1840s, their study of psychophysics gave scientific respectability to our first efforts to study human skills, abilities, and traits. In the 1890s Galton measured various human factors that he fitted to the bell-shaped curve. His successful efforts served as the template for the efforts of Binet, Simon, and Henri in their development of the omnibus intelligence scales. The efforts of Yerkes and his colleagues resulted in the Army Alpha and Beta tests to assess intelligence on a mass scale to help with classifying troops needed for World War I. These accomplishments transformed the field. Instead of being seen as a specialty of philosophy, people began to see psychology as a scientific discipline having the potential to improve society by placing people in schools and jobs for which their skills are maximally suited.

There are several other compelling reasons for psychological testing constituting part of the core of graduate training and one's professional identity. When organizations need psychological services, their initial request often takes the form of a question involving human measurement. For example, many consultation relationships with educational, business, and forensic agencies are initiated by measurement questions. A school system typically wants children assessed; a business may want an assessment of executives for vice-president level positions or a fitness-for-duty evaluation of an employee who may have threatened coworkers. Prison systems need an increasing number of inmates assessed for mental status due to the decrease in community mental health facilities that has funneled former mental health patients into the prison system. A jail might need a psychologist to teach the correctional officers how to assess mental status and suicide likelihood. Usually testing serves as an entry point into these systems.

When executives and administrators gain confidence in the usefulness of psychologists, inevitably the psychologists are asked to serve as consultants on any number of questions that might arise while the psychologist is working with the organization. Industrial/organizational psychologists hired to plan and implement new programs in organizations include methods of assessment so they can both show the benefits and improve the quality of their services. For example, the psychologist might be involved by a school system in developing programs for children with learning or emotional disorders that have been assessed by the psychologist. This could involve grant writing and the gathering of data that may be publishable. In another case, an Air Force base sought a psychologist's help in reducing the potential for workplace violence. When the psychologist suggested that some pretest data be gathered so the baseline of violence experience and potential could be assessed and contrasted with posttest data, the military was enthusiastic and gained confidence in the consulting psychologist. It is common in the military and the government to seek to measure the effectiveness of every program. Thus they were reassured that they had chosen the right person for the job. Indeed, when any intervention is offered, be it conducting individual psychotherapy or setting up a shelter for battered women and children or developing a large-scale organizational program, the psychologist will benefit from gathering data.

In the current era, when health maintenance organizations are curtailing payments for psychotherapy, more clinical and counseling psychologists are finding an increasing portion of their practices centered around forensic concerns. Thus, child custody evaluations, parental fitness assessment, competency and insanity determinations, and disability evaluations may form an increasing part of their practice. Mastery of assessment skills enriches one's professional identity and provides intriguing insights into people. Finally, solving human problems through assessment can be fun.

## WHAT ARE PSYCHOLOGICAL TESTING AND ASSESSMENT?

Although these two terms have often been used synonymously, there are certain distinctions between the terms. *Testing* refers to both the technical mastery of psychometrics (e.g., item and test construction, and reliability and validity) and the administration and scoring of psychological instruments. *Assessment* refers to the more global process of understanding people in answering the referral questions that initiated the request for evaluation. Assessment involves selecting the appropriate measures to address the questions, and integrating the data gathered into a report. Assessment may include planning an intervention based on the test findings and seeing that the intervention is correctly implemented and is effective.

## HOW DO I LEARN TESTING AND ASSESSMENT?

### Mastering the Fundamentals

The first step in learning assessment is to become familiar with the basic concepts taught in a course on principles of psychological assessment. A testing course may be taken during the undergraduate years, but if the student has not done so, then reading one of the excellent texts on psychological testing can provide knowledge of the principles. Among the best of such textbooks are Anastasi and Urbiana's *Psychological Testing* (1997), Cohen and Swerdlik's *Psychological Testing and Assessment: An Introduction to Test and Measurement* (1999), and Gregory's *Psychological Testing: History, Principles, and Applications* (1996). The background provided by an undergraduate course or studying one of these texts is essential before taking graduate testing courses because such courses simply will not have enough time to cover prerequisite material.

An undergraduate testing course, or self-instructed reading from these textbooks, would cover the history, ethical concerns, and social context of testing. Then the student should learn about item and test construction, fundamental measurement and statistical concepts such as the averages, the standard error (and its forms such as the standard error of measurement, the standard error of differences, and the standard deviation), and correlation and regression coefficients. After the concepts of reliability and validity are covered, most texts will describe the constructs of intelligence, personality, abilities, vocational interests, neuropsychology, and the major test instruments in each area. The student should become familiar with two excellent resources; the *Buros' Mental Measurements Yearbooks* (www.unl.edu/buros) and *Test Critiques* (www.proedinc.com) which offer critical evaluations of most published psychological tests. Finally, the student should become familiar with the *Standards for Educational and Psychological Tests* (American Psychological Association, 1985), which is a guide for the test developer and the test user regarding the desirable qualities of a good test instrument and the types of inferences one can legitimately draw from test scores.

*Ethical Foundations.*     Ethical issues permeate assessment. Both the standards just mentioned and the American Psychological Association (APA) *Ethical Principles and Code of Conduct* (1992) guide psychologists in the ethical parameters in making valid use of test instruments and in interacting ethically with clients and agencies. Assessment activities immerse the psychologist in a host of ethical questions. These questions include: (a) the construction of measures, (b) the evaluation of the reliability and validity of instruments, (c) the selection of the appropriate tests for the particular client, (d) the people who are entitled to know about the test results and those who are not so entitled (see the Federal Educational Rights to Privacy Act regarding the safeguarding of student information and the exceptions to such privacy), (e) record keeping guidelines, (f) testing minority, disabled and other special groups, and (g) respecting the dignity and rights of the client. Two examples will illustrate the last point in concrete terms.

Is the psychologist placed in a position of ethical conflict when asked to assess death row inmates to see whether they are competent to appreciate the nature of the punishment? Consider whether the psychologist will have been an instrument in the carrying out of the death sentence. Does that comport with Principle 6 of the APA Ethical Principles of Psychologists, concerning the dignity and well-being of the client ? Consider the clinician who suspects that a child has been abused. What are the reporting statutes that may compel the assessor to break confidentiality and privilege? Does it matter whether the abuse is sexual, physical, or psychological? The competent assessment student must develop a sensitivity to such ethical issues.

## The First Graduate Course in Testing

A basic understanding of the principles of psychological testing provides the student with the prerequisite knowledge to learn about assessment. Typically graduate programs start with intelligence testing, then teach personality assessment, and then allow for specialization in such areas as child assessment, forensic assessment (conducting competence, insanity, child custody evaluations), neuropsychological assessment, or vocational testing. Once the student has mastered the basic knowledge about test construction, reliability, and validity, mastery of testing skills will require tremendous dedication.

The student must devote time to learn the details in test manuals that may run to hundreds of pages and to delve into the research literature that describes the characteristics of the tests. The student will learn how a test was developed, its applications and limitations, the reliability and validity of various subtests and indices, the administration procedures, scoring standards, principles of interpretation, and report-writing skills. The student's expenditure of time and energy will be similar to the demanding experimental laboratory courses on the undergraduate level or the research design and statistics courses on the graduate level. However, the demands of a good assessment course sequence are more than compensated for by the excitement of interacting with clinical cases and by learning these important skills that will serve students for their whole career. Even though graduate programs over the past decade have showed an increasing tendency to accept students with some human service experience (e. g., crisis telephone services, battered women shelters, or delinquency prevention and treatment programs), a rich assessment sequence will draw the student into a deeper and more professionally involving level of understanding and intervening with people than did the student's prior experiences.

## LEARNING INTELLIGENCE TESTING

Measuring intelligence is the bedrock of psychological assessment. Intelligence affects all questions one might be asked to assess, including those concerning personality, vocational, educational, and brain pathology. The student should become knowledgeable about the basic theories of intelligence and proficient with several types of intelligence tests. The intelligence course should cover the Stanford–Binet, the Wechsler tests (Wechsler Preschool and Primary Scales of Intelligence–Revised [WPPSI–R], Wechsler Intelligence Test for Children–Third Edition [WISC–III], and Wechsler Intelligence Scale for Adults–Third Edition [WAIS–III]), and several shorter and special purpose intelligence measures. Such special-purpose measures will allow the student to see how special populations such as amputees, the blind, or non-English-speaking or mute individuals may be assessed.

When learning the instruments, the student will be exposed to the theories underlying the test. For example, learning about Cohen's four-factor model of the Wechsler scales, Cattell's fluid and crystallized intelligence factors on the Stanford–Binet, and Porteus's theory of intelligence undergirding his mazes provides the basis for interpreting the respective tests. Often the test manual contains a brief overview of the theoretical foundation for the test and references for further reading about the theories.

The student is advised to study the manual before administering the test. In fact, I advise my students to memorize the administration procedures and the scoring standards, a daunting task but one that pays off both in the immediate course and for decades to come. If you do not know how to score an item, then the student will not know when certain criteria are reached and will misadminister the test. For example, on some of the Wechsler subtests, once a person misses a specified number of items in a row, the subtest is discontinued. If the student erroneously judges one or two items as missed and discontinues the subtest prematurely, the obtained score will not be precise and could result in misrepresenting the intelligence of the person being assessed.

As a student, I found my professors' demonstrations of how to test people to be inspiring. We could see that one needed to know the administration procedures and scoring standards while effectively managing the interpersonal relationship with the person being tested. As an instructor, I find the students gain a knowledge of technique and an appreciation of the joining of psychometrics with a clinical sense of the person being assessed that cannot be conveyed in a lecture or reading. Just as important, the student should be observed. I have found that many a procedural error and a sense of how the student manages people in a clinical setting cannot be detected by other means. Observations are time-consuming but indicate an investment by the instructor in the student's education and development. If your instructor does not model assessment, see if you can watch clinicians in nearby facilities or more advanced graduate students administer tests.

After observing an experienced assessor and mastering the administration procedures and scoring criteria, my students administer the instrument to each other. One of my colleagues provides sample protocols to be scored by his students. In either case, the student's scoring of the protocols is assessed to see that the scoring criteria and calculations of subtests, factors, and intelligence quotients have been mastered. As you can see, the mastery of testing involves careful attention to detail.

After learning the basics of administration, some courses will have the students practice administering tests and scoring protocols with volunteers from the undergraduate subject pool and from the community, particularly in the case of practicing child assessments. Remember sometimes people fail to show up on time, or show up at all. Some fail to bring their eyeglasses or some such other necessary item and testing may need to be rescheduled. Thus, the capable student will plan for these mishaps and stay ahead of schedule. Once you fall behind in the workload, catching up seems to require a Herculean effort. *Be sure to keep up with assignments.* Students should also be taught how to observe the behavior of the person tested. One of the great advantages of learning testing before psychotherapy is that the testing situation provides a standardized situation by which the student can see how people vary in response to the same demands. You will begin to build up norms of how people vary in confronting the challenges posed by the standardized testing situation. These observations and descriptions of the test scores not only form the basis for your first written clinical reports but also help you become more comfortable in the clinical setting, in preparation for psycho-therapy training and supervision.

The basic structure of report writing is introduced in the first graduate testing course. The student will learn how to present the basic information about the person being tested; where the referral question and tests administered are listed; how to report behavioral observations and test results; and how to pose basic interpretations in response to the referral questions.

## LEARNING PERSONALITY AND PSYCHOPATHOLOGY ASSESSMENT

Before learning personality assessment, the student should have completed a course in per-sonality theory and one in descriptive psychopathology at least at the undergraduate level. The personality course will familiarize students with a number of constructs or major con-cepts they will need when assessing personality and help them see how to structure a coherent picture of the whole human being.

The clinician will be unable to properly evaluate and diagnose without a course in abnor-mal psychology (also known as psychopathology or behavior pathology). Such a course typi-cally covers biological, social, and psychological sources of disorders and may assign a readings book that presents cases illustrating various disorders. Knowledge of personality and psychopathology will enable you to learn about tests of personality and psychopathology, and later will help you understand clinical cases, develop diagnoses, and propose useful rec-ommendations when writing reports.

The assessment of personalty and psychopathology is usually divided into objective and pro-jective assessment. Objective assessment involves such personality-psychopathology instru-ments as the Minnesota Multiphasic Personality Inventory (MMPI), the Millon instruments, and some "normal" instruments or measures that do not focus on abnormality, such as the Cali-fornia Psychological Inventory, the Jackson Personality Inventory, the Myer–Briggs Type Indi-cator, and the NEO-PI–R. Usually an objective personality assessment course will be devoted to the MMPI and will introduce the student to one or several of the other inventories.

### Objective Assessment

In mastering the MMPI, or any other of the inventories, you should learn the history of the in-strument. This helps in understanding what the creator of the instrument intended to measure and why the test has its particular structure. Then study the test's psychometric characteristics and the research literature concerning the test. This allows you to know to which questions the test is designed to answer. For example, when you are asked to diagnose psychosis, which in-strument would be best to help with the diagnosis, and would the literature support your choice if the decision were to be challenged as in a court case?

The student may find that the scientist-practitioner approach is the best way to learn per-sonality assessment. That is, the scientist would look at the empirical, nomothetic research lit-erature that tells about data collected from groups of people. The practitioner part of the scientist-practitioner model focuses on idiographic studies of individuals as found in case his-tories. When I learned personality assessment, I would read the literature concerning profiles and high point codes on the MMPI. For example, hunters who shot their hunting partners had elevated Scale 4 scores (Psychopathic deviate). This information helped me understand that people with high Scale 4 scores could be law-abiding but still impulsive and prone to cause harm. Reading such research helps refine one's understanding of personality inventory scales and indices. I complemented the research-based approach by reading the MMPI *Atlas* (Hathaway & Meehl, 1951).[1] This book contains a variety of code types (e.g., high Scale 1 and 2, high Scale 4 and 9) and a brief psychological profile of individuals with a particular code-type. Thus a student can read a variety of reports of people with an elevated Scale 4 in combination with other code types. The case reports give a sense of what it means when elevations on Scale 4 alone, on Scales 4 and 2, or on Scale 4 and 7 occur, so the student can learn how the trait scores interact. This combination of the scientist and practitioner model in learning testing gives the student more tools than using one approach to the exclusion of the other.

## Projective Assessment

The projective course usually features the Rorschach Inkblot Technique. In times past, students learned any one or more of a number of scoring and interpretations systems when learning the Rorschach. Over two decades, Exner (1993) synthesized the best components of the various systems and then produced a normative basis for the Rorschach. This allows the clinician to make interpretations that are soundly based on empirical foundations and does not preclude the clinician from making further clinical interpretations based on content or stylistic qualities of the inkblot responses. Although students learn the Exner scoring system from the workbook, interpretive depth is provided in Exner's *The Rorschach: A Comprehensive System, Volume 1, Basic Foundation* (1993). The student wishing to master the Exner system may go on to Exner's volume 2 (1991), which concerns interpretation, and volume 3 (Exner & Weiner, 1995) which is devoted to children and adolescent appraisal with the Rorschach. The Exner system is complex, comprehensive, and demanding. However, once the skills are mastered, the student will have a way of understanding and appraising people that will last a lifetime, yielding benefits that far outweigh the costs.

The projectives course may introduce the student to the Thematic Apperception Test (TAT) and to two types of minor projectives. These tests are called minor because of the time to take the test, the amount of information gathered, and the amount of interpretative material available for the examiner. One type consists of the incomplete sentence tests (a sentence stem such as "I feel _____" or "Most people _____" or "I get angry when _____" that the person then completes). A person *projects* or puts his or her own interpretation forward when completing the sentence stem. The other type of minor projective test, termed *graphic* methods, asks people to draw, usually a person, a tree, a house, a family, or some combination of these items. The drawings are then interpreted, usually with a psychodynamic orientation. As you can see, this is an immense amount of material to cover. Most courses either will not cover all the material, or more than one course will be offered to cover the material.

Again, with greater mastery of test administration procedures, the student can devote more attention to the client. The client may bring many expectations and feelings to the test setting. If you are busily managing test materials and scoring responses, you may miss nuances in the cli-

---

[1] While the *Atlas* is based on the first edition of the MMPI, most of the items were retained, and the scales seem to have similar content and interpretive value on the second edition of the MMPI. Although this resource is dated, students will still profit from the *Atlas*, which has not been matched since its publication.

ent's behavior that will compromise the most competently administered tests. Several examples illustrate this point. Pity the poor client who was so anxious throughout the Rorschach inkblot test but whose anxiety was not recognized by the examiner because of the examiner's own anxiety. After the testing session, the examiner realized the client was anxious and mentioned this observation to the client, asking whether this was typical of him. The client responded that he was told he was to take a "raw shock" test and he was awaiting the punishment. After disarming this harmful set, the examiner still used this information clinically. For example, was the client prone to such misinformation in the rest of his life, and was his sphere of information about general knowledge restricted? But the central lesson here is for the examiner to be sure before examining anyone that the examiner knows the set that the client brings to the setting.

When testing children, for example, I always ask what the child thinks we will be doing today. Many times I find the parent, guardian, or referral source may have told the child that he or she were going to get set straight by the psychologist because of various transgressions charged against the child; in short, we were portrayed as cops and punishing agents, which is hardly the best predisposition for the testing sessions. The examiner should explore the expectations that the examinee brings to the session and, after listening, correct the impressions when necessary without derogating the source of the misimpression.

At this point in the testing process the examiner might help the client establish a beneficial testing attitude. For example, when being examined on an intelligence test, the person should be told that there are some really easy items that almost everyone gets right and then there are some items that almost no one answers correctly, because intelligence tests are generally structured to measure a wide range of human abilities. When taking personality and psychopathology tests, we usually instruct clients that there are no right answers. The answers indicate one or another facet or part of their personality or how they see themselves and how others might see them. In this way the client is disabused of faulty attitudes and is encouraged to respond in a forthright fashion.

You should be aware of both the client's and your own feelings when learning testing. These feelings should be recognized and, if the classroom atmosphere welcomes such discussion, may be brought up in class. Otherwise, some peer sharing and individual supervision with a trusted faculty member or advisor may be helpful in using these feelings in developing a professional identity. The structure of the testing setting allows you to see the type of client responses that are usual and those that are unusual and pathognomonic, or signaling a disorder. Norms are easier to accumulate in structured testing setting than in the more amorphous psychotherapy setting. The last section of this chapter focus in more detail on personal and professional development.

## COMMUNICATING TEST RESULTS

The communication of clinical findings is all-important. No matter how fine an evaluation has been conducted, failure to clearly and completely transmit test findings will undo one's best professional efforts. Thus the testing curriculum should include considerable attention to reporting test results.

### The Oral Report

Communicating test results takes both oral and written forms. At the end of the test session, the client will want some feedback. If the test taker was instructed about the testing before it commenced, as mentioned in a earlier section, then the examiner is in better position to give feedback. Upon ending the testing, the examiner might want to first ask the person what the test taker what his impression was of the testing and of that person's own performance. That might provide rich clinical information as well as be a springboard to a discussion of the person's performance. The examiner might want to address any misinformation and might want to address self-condemning thoughts the client expresses. The examiner might provide an impression about the efforts expended by the person. The student might say, "you worked hard on this test, and I appreciate your efforts"; to the person who gave up easily, the student might say, "you seemed to be distracted or thrown off by some of the items—[pause] Did they surprise you?" These comments should be few, be descriptive, and be nonevaluative. Often these comments elicit material more meaningful than any test response.

The more advanced student might be able to give a general impression of the results, after supervisors have affirmed the student's ability to do so. The student-examiner should not give any scores. However, after the large expenditure of time and effort by most clients, they deserve some feedback and acknowledgment, even if in general terms. Make sure you understand what they heard and feel about the feedback before ending the session. Harm can be done by a client's misunderstanding of a term. Often a feedback session might be scheduled, by which time tests have been scored and some preliminary clinical interpretations have been deduced. By then the student should have benefitted from supervisory contacts and know what type of information the client would find useful. By carefully listening to the client processing the clinician's feedback, the clinician can correct any of the client's inferences that may not be on the mark. The feedback session also allows the clinician to gauge the client's ability to absorb information. Well-communicated results can begin and accelerate any remedial or therapeutic program in the client's future.

In many cases the client was referred by a third party who expects a report. Again, supervision might help the student in knowing who is entitled to the test findings and guiding the student in determining the level of sophistication applicable for a report to be sent to third parties.

The third party may be a parent or guardian, an allied mental health professional, an agency worker, a teacher, an employer, or a court. The report may determine the client's future. The most sophisticated psychological examination may be undone by a poorly communicated or incorrectly received report. In many cases, the oral report will be followed by a written report. In discussing the written report, I present a method for integrating the test data into a coherent portrait of the person who was tested.

## The Written Report

The written report typically has a uniform structure consisting of several sections. These include: (a) the block at the top of the report, (b) the referral questions and the referral source, (c) the list of tests and procedures used as the basis for the body of the report, (d) the behavioral observations, and (e) the body of the report, which includes an intelligence section, a personality and psychopathology section, and other sections that are responsive to the referral questions. For example, there might be a detailed report on neuropsychological functioning when the referral question concerns a closed head injury due to a motor vehicle accident or a physical altercation. Or there might be sections about competence, insanity, fitness to return to duty for employment, or parent custodial ability in a forensic report.

Finally there is usually a recommendations or disposition section and a signature block. Let us review these.

The heading block typically contains client information including the client's name and date of birth, the testing dates, the date of the report, the client's educational and employment level, and the referral source. Then the referral questions are listed. These are important because this information poses the questions and client's background for which the ensuing report will provide answers and potential interventions. The examiner should rarely take the referral question from a written form without calling the source to see what that person or agency really wants to find out. When the referral is standard, as when testing for intellectual capacity for entry to a special school, there is less of a need for direct discussion unless there are particular questions about the person to be tested. On the other hand, I have received seemingly simple or quite confusing referral questions that, if left unquestioned, would have led to poor evaluations. For example, one respected and well-read psychiatrist asked me, as the psychologist to test for "ocular schizophrenia." A phone call revealed that the psychiatrist had read about a schizophrenic condition brought on by ingestion of LSD-25, a hallucinogenic, hypothesized to work by way of disorienting coordination between a person's eyes. He wondered whether I could test for this mechanism, perhaps with the Rorschach, which is conceptualized as a perceptual-associative task by both Hermann Rorschach and John Exner. Noting the limitations of the literature in this regard, I proceeded with this novel referral to the psychiatrist's satisfaction. It is important to understand the referral question and not to make assumptions about it. The tests selected should logically follow from the referral questions and follow the referral questions.

We have referred to the behavioral observations section but have not discussed this important data source yet. We usually begin our testing course by having students make behavioral observations on a street corner for 10 minutes. In class we then discern which observations were truly observations and which were sets of inferences. We also demonstrate how rich a data source observations can be. We mention that German psychologists in the first third of this century used to have a client work on a set of problems, some easy, some hard, and some unsolvable. They would tell the clients to work away while the psychologists did some paperwork. Actually they were making detailed observations of the client and would later throw out the test results and base the report on the behavioral observations. Often, the way a person approaches a task and proceeds to illustrate attitudes and working style can be as informative as any test result. The next subsection describes noteworthy behavior that help frame the test results.

## The Clinical Matrix

Integrating behavioral observations, interview data, and test results can be both the most trying part of assessment and the most creative part of the process. We mentioned that the referral questions help determine the choice of tests used in a particular case, which is based on the assumption that tests measure particular traits, skills, and abilities. Integrating the findings using the clinical matrix is based on the assumption that the constructs measured can be manifested across the various tests. For example, intellectual skills can be measured by intelligence tests of course, but can be seen on the Rorschach and the TAT by the person's use of simple or sophisticated language in both the choice of words and the syntax. The conceptual levels can be assessed by noting the complexity of the percepts or stories. Similarly, on graphic or drawing methods the intellectual capabilities of the person can be measured (Harris, 1963).

When assessing personality, the examiner might see personality traits manifested across both personality and other test instruments. For example, impulsivity can be seen on the MMPI and Rorschach and also on intelligence tests and behavioral observations during the test sessions. A person who is impulsive and tends to disregard the rights of others may show flippancy when answering questions during an interview, show deficits on intelligence tests items requiring reflection and social appropriateness, produce certain MMPI profiles and Rorschach indicators of impulsivity, dash off drawings hastily, and complete sentence stems with little thought. When the student is faced with a profusion of data and needs a way to organize the data, the clinical matrix is one way to integrate the findings.

My students found that constructing a matrix is a helpful way to integrate the test findings. On the left-side of the page the examiner should list the instruments. Across the top of the page the examiner should list the major constructs or questions raised by the referral source. Then the examiner can write in the cells the test findings relevant to the particular column. When answering the referral questions, the examiner simply looks at the columns to see how the data weigh upon the question. For example, if asked about intelligence, the examiner can easily see how the test data converge to yield a clear picture across measures of the person's intelligence. The various measure may tap different types of intelligence such as mathematical, vocabulary, social, and speed of information-processing components.

If there are disparities between the tests, then the examiner can write about the different facets of intelligence and feel confident when, for example, verbal intelligence across measures shows consistency. When there is disparity within an intelligence facet—for example, verbal intelligence test results differ—this may provide the opportunity to further examine why the differences may have occurred. Perhaps two tasks are verbal but one is similar to a school situation, such as the WAIS—III Vocabulary subtest, whereas another may have been laden with emotional cues, such as the inkblot or TAT tasks. This could provide a finer grained analysis of the person. The clinical matrix provides a handy way to integrate findings for any of the referral questions and show cross-instrument consistency, or inconsistencies that merit further consideration and explication.

## Writing the Report

While many people feel they are gifted writers, psychology students are often disabused of this notion in no uncertain terms by their supervisors. Learning how to turn your findings into a meaningful report is a talent to be developed from the first behavioral observation in the first testing course. Attention should be paid to grammar and to cogent writing. When you are stuck with "writer's block," you may find it helpful to read a poem, short story, or other material that "flows" easily. Among my favorites is Dethier's *To Know a Fly* (1962), an account of an entomologist's discoveries while conducting biological research with an easily available subject pool. Choosing a favorite "page turner" can prime the pump. On questions of usage and style, the APA Publication Manual (1994), Baker's (1977) *The Practical Stylist*, and every discipline's favorite, Strunk and White's *Elements of Style* (1999), are the best guides for the psychology student and test report writer. Reading psychological test reports in the clinic or mental health center and in published case histories is useful, particularly if they were written by your supervisor or other students he or she supervised. Finally, Tallent's (1992) classic book *Psychological Report Writing*, is invaluable.

## WORKING WITH PEOPLE

So far, we have discussed the tests and the courses. Too often we psychologists become so busy with the research or testing activities, we forget that we work with people rather than subjects or participants and cases or profiles. This section is concerned with the development of the clinician's professional skills and personal development.

### Beginning to Learn Clinical Testing

Before you study an instrument, take each of the tests. This is the best way for you to experience the demands you will make on other people. The neophyte clinician will thus better understand the experience of furnishing a large list of definitions, then being told to play with puzzles under timed conditions but with no direct feedback, and then having to respond to the ambiguity of an inkblot card.

Taking the tests allows students to assemble their own dossiers, both to help learn about themselves and to see how the test registers their own personality traits. This may temper students' assessments of others when they see how the tests portray them.

The next step in gaining practical experience is to pair up with fellow students to practice administering the test items to each other. The partners can help by sharing feedback when a vocabulary word is mispronounced or an instruction given too fast or to slow. Then you should solicit volunteers across the age range in practicing test administration.[2] Be meticulous in scoring and rescoring the test responses and in the calculating of subtest, scale and index scores. You may team up with a peer to be doubly certain about scoring and calculations. Finally, you should administer the test to clinical samples, with the results not being used until you have gained proficiency.[3] You are well advised to begin a record of all tests administered, all reports written, all supervision sessions attended, and the types of patient contacts. When you apply for internships, you can then document an impressive and accurate record of clinical contacts. Internships favor experienced interns.

### Subjective Experiences of the Beginning Student

The student, too, will experience a variety of feelings when assessing clients. Feelings of power might be one kind. Your reaction to this feeling might be a shrinking from the awesome responsibility that testing brings, or might be the amplification of such power. These feelings are complicated by the client, who may ask for his or her scores and what they mean. This demand may be intensely felt by the student who has asked a person to devote several hours to a demanding probing of his or her mental life for the student's learning benefit, and for no evident benefit to the person. Yet students must tell testing participants beforehand that the student cannot report any scores because such scores will be inaccurate due to the fact that the student is learning and will make mistakes. What the student does owe the person is sincere

---

[2] The student should seek direction from the course instructor. Some instructors may have policies concerning practice volunteers, and some may have developed populations for students' practice testings.

[3] The student should be made aware of ethical consent forms, instructed about who constitutes the legal guardian in the case of child volunteers, and taught how to manage the pressures in not revealing test scores to practice volunteers.

appreciation and the hope that the testing experience was beneficial in helping the person know what psychological testing is like. As the student becomes more experienced and his or her scoring skills become more refined and accurate, then supervised feedback to the client will become appropriate.

The testing situation brings with it a number of demand characteristics that may draw on the student's personal dynamics. Once students gain enough mastery of the technical procedures of the testing instruments, they may begin to understand the more dynamic aspects of the assessment situation. Schafer (1954) described the voyeuristic, autocratic, oracular, and saintly aspects of the tester's role.

The testing situation has inherently voyeuristic aspects in that one peeps into another's interior without the reciprocal openness in a normal social situation. The stopwatch, testing materials, pencils, and notepad provide the examiner with distancing mechanisms. For the examiner who has not sufficiently understood the dynamics of hostility, the tests may well represent, to the patient with hostility problems, the instruments by which the examiner is peering, and perhaps piercing, into another person's emotional life. The client may feel exposed in the testing situation and to some degree is at the mercy of the tester's ability to balance compassion with the need to inquire in order to perform an informing examination.

The autocratic aspect refers to the examiner's control of the testing situation. The examiner tells the client what is needed, judges the adequacy of the response, and tells the client when to begin and when to stop each activity and how to proceed. Then the examiner asks why the client said or responded in the way that he or she did. The examiner needs to be aware of the controlling aspects of these demands and to be just as aware of the client's responses to this part of testing.

The oracular aspect refers to the momentous conclusions the examiner may be asked to give. For example, whether a child is admitted to a particularly prized school, whether custody is awarded to one or another parent, or whether a person should be treated therapeutically or incarcerated may hinge on the test findings and the examiner's conclusions. The beginning student may respond, according to Schafer (1954), by seeing "no response they cannot interpret, no contradiction they cannot resolve, no obscurity they cannot penetrate, no integration they cannot achieve" (p. 23). In others, the pull to be omniscient may be a real reaction to the wishes of the referral source and the client who is in pain, combined with the fantasy of the tester. Other students may beat a hasty retreat from this anxious position and find refuge in sticking to the facts as would Dragnet's Sergeant Friday, qualifying each interpretative statement in the report.

The saintly aspect of the tester's role refers to the tester doing his or her best to help the client: to do all one can for the client, to subdue one's needs and resentments to understand the client's life and feel the client's pain and anger. These feelings may spring from the referral source or the client and resonate with the tester's need system, which may have drawn that person to save others. Establishing rapport may be one positive outcome of saintly strivings, but saintliness may urge the tester to compromise the integrity of the testing standardization or slant interpretations in the report to "help" the client.

Each of these aspects of the testing situation interacting with the examiner's feelings has the potential to be adaptive (Schafer, 1954). As the tester grasps the psychological complexity of the testing situation with the interaction between the referral source, the client, the examiner, and the supervisor, the tester may develop insight, security, and a sense of competence as an assessor. The voyeuristic impulse can provide alertness and insight into the client's psychological dynamics; the autocratic position may allow the tester to see how the client handles power and powerlessness; the oracular aspect may motivate competence strivings in the student; and the saintliness of the student as tester may frame the objectivity of testing with the care and responsiveness we should expect in clinicians.

Recognition and processing of the emotional aspects of the client and the student may be a most useful tool in assessing the client, as well as in helping the student develop his or her personality and professional self. Such processing will provide the clinical student with the confidence to recognize, utilize, and manage the emotional ebb and flow of the testing session.

The testing setting allows the supervisor[4] and student to enter into exploration of the student's feelings or to focus more on the formal aspects of testing if the student feels too much threat to plunge into the supervisory aspect of processing feelings. For that reason, and because it is usually easier to make the transition from the more detailed and demanding testing setting to the unstructured psychotherapy experience, learning testing and assessment should precede the learning of psychotherapy. The student with a supervisor who is attuned to the emotional aspects of testing, who inspires security and trust in the student, and who can assess the student's readiness for grappling with personality dynamics while coping with the large amount of work involved in learning psychological assessment skills has a head start toward developing professional excellence, personal competence, and lifelong satisfaction in serving the welfare of others.

## ACKNOWLEDGMENT

I appreciate the careful editing of this chapter provided by Kathryn A. Hess, Tanya H. Hess, Steven G. LoBello, Steven Walfish, and Peter Zachar.

## REFERENCES

American Psychological Association. (1985). *Standards for educational and psychological testing*. Washington, DC: Author.

American Psychological Association. (1992). Ethical principles of psychologists and code of conduct. *American Psychologist, 47*, 1597–1611.

American Psychological Association. (1994). Publication manual of the American Psychological Association (4th ed.). Washington, DC: Author.

Anastasi, A., & Urbina, S. (1997). *Psychological testing* (7th ed.). Englewood Cliffs, NJ: Prentice Hall.

Baker, S. (1977). *The practical stylist* (4th ed.). New York: Harper & Row.

Cohen, R. J., & Swerdlik, M. E. (1999). *Psychological testing and assessment: An introduction to test and measurement* (4th ed.). Mountain View, CA: Mayfield.

Dethier, V. G. (1962). *To know a fly*. San Francisco: Holden-Day.

---

[4] In programs that discourage such personal explorations, the student may benefit from supervisory contact in a practicum setting where there may be more distance and less of a reporting line to the program. In such events, the supervision should be sanctioned by the program as in the case of practicum placements. The student should clarify what will be reported to the program and what will be held in confidence. The supervisory relationship is dealt with in greater detail in the next chapter, concerning learning psychotherapy.

Exner, J. E., Jr. (1991). *The Rorschach: A comprehensive system, Vol. 2, Interpretation* (2nd ed.). New York: Wiley & Sons.

Exner, J. E., Jr. (1993). *The Rorschach: A comprehensive system, Vol. 1, Basic foundations* (3rd ed.). New York: Wiley & Sons.

Exner, J. E., Jr., & Weiner, I. B. (1995). *The Rorschach: A comprehensive system, Vol. 3, Assessment of children and adolescents* (3rd ed.). New York: Wiley & Sons.

Gregory, R. J. (1996). *Psychological testing: History, principles, and applications, second edition.* Needham Heights, MA: Allyn and Bacon.

Harris, D. B. (1963). *Children's drawings as measures of intellectual maturity.* New York: Harcourt, Brace & World.

Hathaway, S. R., & Meehl, P. E. (1951). *An atlas for the clinical use of the MMPI.* Minneapolis: University of Minnesota Press.

Schafer, R. (1954). *Psychoanalytic interpretation in Rorschach testing.* New York: Grune & Stratton.

Strunk, W., Jr., & White, E. B. (1999). *The elements of style* (4th ed.). New York: Allyn & Bacon.

Tallent, N. (1992). *Psychological report writing* (4th ed.). Englewood Cliffs, NJ: Prentice Hall.

# 18

# Learning Psychotherapy[1]

### *Allen K. Hess*

Certain terms are "hyper-real" in the sense that people have a fixed and complex set of associations ranging far from the technical sense of the term. Thus, a person may think that Einstein's theory of relativity said everything is relative, when actually it says, "There are absolute things in the world but you must look deeply for them. The things that first present themselves to your notice are for the most part relative" (Eddington, 1958, p. 23). The term *psychologist* is hyper-real, or a richly elaborated stereotype. It immediately conjures up a set of associations that we learn quite early in life. For an older generation the image might be based on Montgomery Clift playing Freud, Kubrick's *Clockwork Orange*, or *The Bob Newhart Show*. More recently, Frasier, Billy Crystal in *Analyze This*, Dr. Malfi of *The Sopranos*, and even the Comedy Channel's *Dr. Katz, Therapist*, help form the hyper-reality of "the therapist." These stereotypes guide many to the study of clinical psychology, forming the image against which the student's experiences in graduate school will be measured.

---

[1]At one time *psychotherapy* and *counseling* were distinguished in that the former was intended for personality change, was of longer duration, was intended for more profound life questions of "patients," whereas counseling was an outgrowth of the guidance and counseling movement of a half century ago. As such, it was centered on youth and career guidance, and was later extended to career and marital crises of "clients." These crises were presumed to require short-term intervention, but once intervention began, it became obvious to professionals that the crises were eruptions of longer term problems. The crises may be amenable to short-term help, but change required longer-term psychotherapy. Because the distinctions between the terms *counseling* and *psychotherapy* have become blurred, and because the skilled professional in either case needs to know about the human change process, I use the term *psychotherapy* in the broader, inclusive sense, and use both *client* and *patient* and *clinical* and *counseling* indistinguishably.

I suppose students become interested in psychology for two reasons: curiosity about the varieties and sources of the human behavior they encounter, and the need to change or "cure" those they see as suffering from life's injustices and from internal emotional problems. The first year of graduate school can then jolt the student's expectations. Courses such as statistics, history and systems of psychology, learning, sensation and perception, and psychophysics seem unrelated to helping people. They are certainly far from learning the one-liners the media "shrinks" use to burst the clients' defenses and instantly solve problems that took decades to form.

Although a psychology graduate program may expose the students to clinical cases in the first year, most withhold such contact until a year or two later, and some provide scant clinical exposure at all, instead depending on the internship to provide clinical training. The student applying to graduate clinical psychology programs needs to be aware that some programs are hostile to clinical practice, with faculty members who pride themselves on being "informed skeptics." Such faculty do no clinical work and disparage the students' clinical interests. If you find yourself in such a program, you may seek faculty who are more balanced in their attitudes, seek another program, or go "underground" with your clinical interests. If you choose the last alternative, you may find excellent clinical supervision off-site at a practicum setting. There are other programs, more often located in professional schools, that give passing notice to research, instead devoting themselves to clinical teaching. The student who planned well and had the good fortune to arrive at a program following the Boulder model of scientist-practitioner (Raimy, 1950; Shakow, 1947) will delight in the struggle to integrate scientific reasoning with clinical artistry in becoming a clinical psychologist.[2] Although there may be variations in the pathways to the clinic, at some point the student will conduct psychotherapy.

The balance of this chapter provides a guide for the student embarking on the journey toward becoming a clinician. This guide takes the form of a three stage model describing the student's experiences as he or she learns psychotherapy skills.

## STAGE I: DEMYTHOLOGIZING PSYCHOTHERAPY

The new student faces psychotherapy with the global and undifferentiated "great booming buzzing confusion," characterizing unanchored experience described by William James (1890/1981, p. 462). Despite your experience with a battered women's shelter or crisis center hotline and some listening skills training, and even though you may have been selected for your ability to tolerate frustration and ambiguity, the anxieties of having the responsibility for a real clinical case can quickly erode your composure. From students who trust me (or are desperate for help), I frequently hear, "These people [directors of university and agency programs] are unreal. They gave me cases including a few folks who are suicidal. Don't they realize I sat in on only three cases on my practicum and they were at the student health center?" or "I have no idea

---

[2]For 30 years I have wondered why we provide applied psychology students with excellent training in the scientific method and statistical reasoning while depriving our experimental brethren of training in applied methods. It would seem that students of experimental psychology should take an assessment course and a clinical interviewing course. This training would not qualify the person to be a clinician but would allow better understanding and respect between psychologists as well as allowing experimental psychologists to better respond to people who ask for help by enabling such psychologists to make helpful referrals.

what to do in therapy. Sure I read a book or two but I am a green, green rookie. It is like painting-by-numbers for me to do therapy. I can follow a manual but do not know what I am doing."

The student's early and anxious attempts at psychotherapy are composed of snatches of technique picked up here and there. The techniques may be mandated by a program or supervisor's theoretical orientation, and may have come from a few assigned readings, from having watched an experienced clinician, or from the residue of the hyper-real experiences from the media. Whatever the source, these attempts usually feel hollow to the earnest student, and are either puzzling to the client or easily parried by the therapy-wise, chronic patient at the public clinic who may have "broken in" several other trainees over the years. It seems that the student's first cases are often those who are "good learning experiences," a euphemism for patients the rest of the staff finds untreatable or uninteresting, and to whom the student presumably can do little harm (Weiner & Kaplan, 1980).[3]

The themes of Stage I are demystifying psychotherapy, expressing fears, and growing from inadequacy to adequacy (Yogev, 1982). Among the demystifying processes are the simple mastering of the ability to enter an intimate professional relationship. The paradox is the pairing of the terms *intimate* and *professional*. The student begins to establish the boundaries that are special to psychotherapy. That is, the essence of psychotherapy is the ability to establish the asymmetrical relationship by which the therapist enters another person's world while maintaining a professional stance of withholding a reciprocal entry of the patient into the psychotherapist's world. In effect, the student begins to learn the asociality of psychotherapy. Several other mechanisms address the demystification and the adequacy issues.

Taking courses, readings, viewing and listening to audiovisual tapes of psychotherapy sessions, and attending psychotherapy sessions build competence. Course instruction and reading of theory and case histories provide the technical knowledge needed to understand how personality, psychopathology, and family and group dynamics result in the problem presented to the clinician, and how the clinician enters into the patient's life. Weiner (1998) and Zaro, Barach, Nedelman, and Drieblatt (1977) are superb guides for the beginning psychotherapist.

As the student learns from many professors about many theories and confronts varied clinical experiences, a number of dilemmas will challenge the reflective person. These include:

- Whether clinical psychology is a *science or an art*. Outcome research and third-party payers trying to wring dollars from "managed care" (an oxymoron itself) will see efficacy as the *leitmotif* of psychotherapy, whereas the caring clinician will see a human trying to mitigate life's uncertainties. Are scientific and artistic goals compatible?

- Whether effectiveness is a function of *technique or the use of the psychotherapist's self.*

- Whether the patient or the psychotherapist bears *responsibility for cure.*

- Whether the student will survive the *role confusion* of being one-up or superior when working with the patient and the next hour being one-down in the student role once more.

---

[3] Keep a file regarding each psychotherapy case assigned, the type of patient and psychotherapy, the number of sessions, and the number of hours in supervision because internships value experienced applicants. It is virtually impossible to reconstruct the number of psychotherapy hours, with which kind of cases, with how much supervision, after the fact. Thus, a contemporary recording system will benefit you immeasurably when you apply for internships and for clinical jobs.

- What *assumptions about humans* one harbors that affect the way one relates to people. Such assumptions include whether people operate as conscious or unconscious in motivation; whether historical, here-and-now, or teleological or goal-seeking orientations drive people; whether people are hedonic or altruistic; and whether future actions are determined or unfolding in nature.

- Whether *control of the clinical case* is the student psychotherapist's or the supervisor's when it comes to critical questions such as invoking the Tarasoff warning, violating the patient's privilege of confidentiality when the patient might be a threat to the life of a third party.

- *How to either adapt or develop a theory of choice to guide your work*, so you have an answer to the question, "What kind of a psychologist are you? I mean like a Freudian or behaviorist or what?" when asked by someone else or of yourself.

Students might find refuge in saying they are "eclectic" in theory. On the one hand, one can hardly be anything but eclectic if one learns from various theories and teachers. Pepper (1942) termed this "accidental eclecticism" because it signifies the state of growth on the way to theory development. However, Pepper saw "purposive eclecticism" as illegitimate. One can hardly be 83% cognitive-behavioral and 17% Gestalt, or 56% Freudian, 25% Rogerian, and 19% transactional analytic. One's theoretical assumptions must be based on one root metaphor. That is, what we understand as the nature of people, our metatheory, drives our theory, and our set of assumptions is unitary. For Rogers, people are like plants, needing nourishing conditions to actualize their innate potential. For Freud, people are the repositories of drives that are held in check by internalized social representations, resulting in behavior that is a compromise between internal forces. At their highest level, people operate through sublimation or having their drives serve society's interests. As students read, observe, and accept cases and participate in supervision, they will try on various theories to see how they fit and how they help make sense of the cases. Over time, through various courses, readings, and clinical experiences, including personal growth, one's root metaphor will emerge.

If the graduate program is not governed by one theory, students are exposed to various theories and models as a way of beginning to adapt a favored theory or develop their own models of human behavior. Or, the instructor or supervisor might be what Levenson (1982) termed Teutonic or authoritarian, insisting that the student be a clone. This approach by which the instructor has a formulation for every situation, sometimes fitting the patient's problem into the Promethean bed of the favored theory, may actually be comforting for the beginning student. "Painting by the numbers" allows the student to learn to handle paints and brushes. As psychotherapy proceeds, the student might allay fears based on false assumptions. For example, the careful and caring student might fear that the wrong word said at the wrong time might send the patient off the deep end, precipitating some mental breakdown as a slip of the hand might shatter a spun-glass sculpture.

## A Student's First Case

Psychotherapy supervision at this stage involves helping the student enter the case. First, a meeting reviewing the case files, including any history, testing, and other therapist's notes, is helpful in planning for the student's first meeting with the client. After the student's first session with the patient, I find it useful to have the student review the contour of the session and then select a part of the session for review. My strategy is to help the student relate the "map" or the learned theory and formulations with the "field" or actual events of the session. As good as a map or theory may be, the field or actual psychotherapy experience will never conform precisely to each other. How the supervisor handles the difference determines the essence of building the student or tearing the student apart.

The psychotoxic supervisor will play "gotcha" by pouncing on the student's "mistakes." One supervisor at a highly regarded university thinks a student therapist's interpretation should be no longer than 20 seconds. Dr. N. estimates how long a student talks when he is reviewing a tape with the student. He delights in extending his arms in front of him toward the student, with palms touching, and moving his arms with elbow locked in an upward and downward motion as if his arms were the beak of a duck, and then quacking in a loud voice for as long as the student is talking on the tape beyond the 20-second estimate. Mindless of common decency, he pays no heed to the American Psychological Association "Ethical Principles of Psychologists and Code of Conduct" (1992) guidance regarding the dignity, respect and well-being we need to afford people. At best the student becomes self-protective; at worst, he or she learns that horrible behavior is appropriate. Consider a different example.

A student was assigned by the director of clinical training to conduct group psychotherapy in a residential delinquent facility and only later was assigned to a faculty member for supervision when the director learned the facility would not provide psychotherapy supervision. The student came to her assigned faculty supervisor visibly shaken. She recounted how the youngsters sniped at each other, and how she then scolded one of the attackers and then told the group that she was there to help them. Group members countered by scolding each other for disrupting the session and then turned on the student, questioning her ability to help them and keep order. The session deteriorated further, leaving the student defeated and hopeless.

Supervision consisted of pointing out the frequency of this kind of behavior by delinquents, the unspoken goal of the student of keeping the youth orderly, and their use of her promise to help them as a weapon to attack her. The supervisor relaxed and laughed, asking whether the student thought that the delinquents had heard this before many times. The student said, "I suppose so." The supervisor asked whether she thought that the delinquents probably heard the promise of "help" as an attempt to control them. She agreed that it probably was an attempt to create order and her attempt to control the chaos. Rather than tell the student, "What did you expect? You set them up and failed to control the session," the supervisor laughed again, and said, "You are a bit ahead of your colleagues. They do not usually get this much material out of patients quite this early, nor do they feel as hopeless so quickly. In fact, a few insensitive ones fail to feel this sense of hopelessness at all nor bring it up in supervision. So let us see what is happening."

The supervisor took a situation the student knew and linked it to the events of the group sessions. He asked how order and a group climate are established in classrooms, and reflected on how it takes students years to learn such norms and teachers to learn how to develop classroom learning climates, how leadership develops in classes and groups, and how strategic and tactical interventions could be used. The student began to see how the concepts covered in her social psychology and group psychotherapy classes occurred in the group session. The supervisor and student role-played a few techniques so the student could make mistakes in a safe environment, and the supervisor assured the student that no harm had been done because the delinquents were all too familiar with chaos already. Buoyed with a new sense of direction and confidence, she countered a verbal assault the next session by gently asking the attacker what he was feeling, what he hoped to accomplish by his words, and how this helped or hurt the group. The group climate changed dramatically when the student kept her poise. At the-next supervision session, she asked for a few readings on group process. In this stage the student's experience changed from chaos to order, a sense of efficacy grew, supervision became an anticipated positive source of professional identity, and over the next several months the group became a positive influence in the student's and the delinquents' lives.

## STAGE II: SKILL DEVELOPMENT

The theme for this stage is dependence versus independence. Obviously these stages are useful, although fictional, conceptual conveniences, because the student just described already took the first steps toward independence. Movement toward independence of the supervisor for each step of psychotherapy accelerates in this stage. The student learns to articulate his or her experiences in psychotherapy with the theories and techniques learned in class; by reading and through discussions with peers and an experienced clinician in case conferences; or in informal exchanges. The student would do well to steep him- or herself in such classics as Freud (1963, 1965, 1977), Brenner (1973), Fenichel (1945), and Mitchell and Greenberg (1983) for psychoanalytic perspectives; Beck (1995), Clark and Fairburn (1997), Ellis (1963), Kelly (1955), Salkovskis (1996), and Wolpe and Lazarus (1966) for the cognitive and behaviorally inclined; and Barrett-Lennard (1998), May, Angel, and Ellenberger (1958), Rogers (1959), and Yalom (1989) for humanistic approaches. For the most widely used and comprehensive graduate text describing a range of psychotherapy theories by leading authorities, see Corsini and Wedding (2000).

Students should be fitting what they are reading to case phenomena, recognizing events in their cases, and finding literature that informs as to what is occurring. Supervision sessions might focus on general theoretical understanding and specific skills and techniques. In the case of the group psychotherapy with the delinquents, the therapist tried several structuring and trust-inducing activities she found in a book. She then reviewed the sessions in supervision to see whether her planning, timing, and implementation were optimal.

### Evaluation: The Patient, Psychotherapist, and Supervisor

When psychotherapy and its supervision begin, ground rules should be discussed between the student and supervisor. Who will evaluate whom and on what criteria needs to be clarified. Although we cannot review any particular situation here, we can describe the ways psychotherapists are viewed, so the student knows how he or she might be judged, the ways supervisors judge supervisees, and the ways students determine supervisor helpfulness.

*Psychotherapist Qualities.*     Veterans Administration patients saw good psychotherapists as honest, and positive in attitude, and poor ones as bossy, impatient, sarcastic, cruel, scared of patients, and uncomfortable with people (Hartledge & Sperr, 1980). Netzky, Davidson and Crunkleton (1982) found patients and professionals were concerned with such issues as whether the psychotherapist pays attention, shows respect, seems rushed, is encouraging when the patient needs support, uses understandable language, or is sexually seductive.

***Judging Supervisees.***   Swain (1981) found that supervisors viewed trainees along the following dimensions: (a) interest in the client and his or her welfare as a person rather than as a "case," (b) the degree of preparation for supervision (bringing tapes, reviewing notes), (c) cognitive and theoretical orientation and bringing it to bear on the case, (d) ability to explore own personality as it contributes to the psychotherapy interaction, (e) openness to supervisor's suggestions, (f) degree of development of clinical expertise and interpersonal skills, (g) boundary management (such as fee collection, appropriate self-disclosure, time management), and (h) ability to make decisions (when to bring up which topics with the patient).

***Judging Supervisors.***   Aldrich (1982) found that students saw their supervisors along the following dimensions: (a) defensiveness, or whether the supervisor is comfortable with students and their comments; (b) professionalism or whether the supervisor is s good role model; (c) experience as a clinician, enabling more skills to be taught to the student; (d) theoretical adeptness in helping the student to understand the case; (e) teaching ability; (f) appropriate concern about the student's life, not too intrusive but willing to explore issues when the student is distressed; (g) likeability and approachability; and (h) ability to motive and inspire.

These are evaluative dimensions to guide the student. Some ways in which the interactions in supervision may play out are described later, when we consider the growth of the psychotherapist's professional identity and personal skills.

## STAGE III: CENTERING THE PSYCHOTHERAPIST

The learning process of the student psychotherapist, who now enjoys a sense of competence from having mastered some skills and seeing a variety of patients, shifts focus toward establishing a "professional identity" or a "therapeutic personality." Supervision becomes more collegial. After hiding his or her values behind stereotypes in early clinical work, the student finds concerns broadening from the initial "how can I survive this session" stance, through a more strategic sense of relating patient themes over sessions to the treatment plan, to an examination of the therapeutic personality of the student psychotherapist. A summary of psychotherapy research (Kopta, Lueger, Saunders, & Howard, 1999) described client improvement attributable to nonspecific therapist effects, a charming euphemism for the professional skills and personality of the therapist. The therapeutic alliance is a key predictor of successful psychotherapy (Horvath & Greenberg, 1994). Luborsky et al. (1986) summarized four outcome studies and concluded that therapists differ from each other, that a therapist's case outcomes vary, and that success has more to do with the specific therapist than the type of psychotherapy. Finally, Wampold (1997) offered an analogy that makes sense. He said that when identifying the key factors in a basketball team's success, we would not examine man-to-man versus zone defenses or use of three-point versus two-point shots and ignore such variables as institutional support and the players' ability. Let us explore a bit about the therapeutic personality.

The learning process in Stage III involves changing from a dependence on theory and supervisory guidance in applying a theory-driven or manualized treatment to a growing sense of professional integrity and an internalized therapeutic personality. Hill, Charles, and Reed (1981) showed that 12 of 12 students studied reduced their anxieties over the 3 years of psychotherapy training. The students attributed the changes to supervision (10), client contact (8), and personal psychotherapy (4). Their views of their supervisors changed from omniscient beings to sources for consultation: they used fewer direct questions and more direct reinforcers with patients, changing from inquisitors to guides; and they shifted the complexity of their responses from high to low to moderate over the 3 years.

In the supervision with the delinquent group previously described, some of the student's own fears and experiences with controlling adults in her own life surfaced. These feelings affected the group psychotherapy, so they became the subject for several sessions. The student spoke about what effects the controlling adults had on her; how she must have come across in the first sessions of the group; how the experience had changed the youths and her; and what other psychotherapy experiences over the year had been affected by the supervision. As a gift to the supervisor, the student wrote a paper and insisted that the supervisor join with her on its development into a publishable article. The paper became a highly cited classic in its field; it served to further confirm the professional identity of the student, and to express gratitude to the supervisor.

***Supervision as Psychotherapy.***     The question of the appropriateness of doing psychotherapy on the student in the guise of supervision is crucial. Supervision is not and should not be psychotherapy. For resolutions of questions that might involve student impairment, the proper venues are psychotherapy with a professional unrelated to the training program, or remedial mechanisms designed in the annual student reviews that departments conduct. To do otherwise is to violate the possibility of students freely using psychotherapy without jeopardizing their graduate careers. If the graduate program can arrange for a student services center to provide free or low-cost psychotherapy for all the program's students, with the guarantee that the barrier between the center and the graduate program is inviolate, then the students might avail themselves of this valuable service.

Macran, Stiles, and Smith (1999) found through intensive qualitative interviewing that personal psychotherapy helped psychotherapists in three domains. The first domain was *orienting to the therapist*—to know their own strengths and weaknesses; to understand the power and process of disclosure and exploration in psychotherapy and to realize how difficult it may be for a patient to self-disclose; and to recognize that psychotherapists can be patients with occasions when they need care, when they need to prevent burnout, and when they need to understand boundary issues that may tug at them. Domain 2 concerns *orienting to the client*—giving the client space because the psychotherapist understood the pace that personal exploration might require, and holding back from jumping in to rescue the client or to provide answers. Macran et al. (1999) found Domain 3 to encompass *listening with the third ear*: parsing one's own feelings from the clients' feelings, working at deeper levels or entering the client's world, and judging the pace of psychotherapy.

Developing a psychotherapeutic personality or set of skills from which one can freely draw means the student develops the ability to be asocial in the relationship. That is, the psychotherapist can abstain from gratifying his or her needs and wishes as well as the patient's needs and wishes, if abstaining will benefit the patient. Thus the psychotherapist is able to "receive the patient's impulses without confirming of denying them so that the patient may become aware of the impulses himself ... [which] allows the patient to recognize the difference between what was anticipated and what is, giving perspective on his internal life" (Shapiro, 1999, p. 6). The ability to abstain allows for neutrality so that the psychotherapist can assume an attitude of listening to the patient's wishes, needs, and defenses without judging. This gives the patient space to find experiences that will lead the patient to solutions.

Traditionally, when psychotherapists reported feelings that were generated during a case, they met in supervision a tactful suggestion to take up the issue in their own psychotherapy. However, more contemporary views hold that countertransference may have facilitating as well as impeding effects on the psychotherapy. Freud originally wrote about interfering effects because of "romantic entanglements between Jung and his patient Sabina Spillrein, and Ferenczi and his patient Alma Palos, as well as Breuer's precipitous flight from his involvement with Bertha Pappenheim (Anna O.)" (Levine, 1996, p. 49). However, recent views (viz. Levine, 1996) take into account that psychotherapists are human and bring to the clinic their own experiences, proclivities, and peccadilloes. Reich (1951) declared that "Countertransference is a necessary prerequisite of analysis. If it does not exist, the necessary talent and interest are lacking," in effect affirming the psychotherapist as a functioning, empathic, and receptive being.

The student with the delinquent group had to suspend her need to control. She internalized the supervisor's smile and waited during the next session while the boys and girls acted chaotically. Then, in a gentle voice, she asked them whether they were interested in learning why they were assigned to group psychotherapy. The question was designed to pique their curiosity, and it did. She asked how they experienced the past few minutes and shared the fact that she had gotten little but an earache, and grinned. The residents looked at her as if they had not seen her before. She asked whether they knew of a better way to talk to each other. The responsibility placed on the youths to structure the group was new to them. Naturally, they knew the rules of civil discussion that had been imposed on them many times before, but they had never been asked to generate and agree to the rules. This ability to go beyond her needs, to trust herself and the youths, and to have faith in the fact that the supervisor was not interested in her mistakes but in her successes, allowed the group to flourish.[4]

## More on Distinguishing Psychotherapy from Supervision

There are several reasons why the psychotherapy and supervision become blurred for some. The supervisor may not understand supervision but be familiar with psychotherapy; and as Abraham Maslow said, when you only know how to use a hammer, you will treat the world as a nail. The processes of identifying human problems, figuring out fitting and timely interventions, tolerating anxieties, and understanding subtle and multichanneled communication are common to psychotherapy and supervision. Although the processes may be the same, there are two key distinctions. One concerns whether the student invites the supervisor into his or her emotional world for the purpose of clarifying the student's psychotherapeutic personality and not their personality in toto. The second indicator as to whether personal exploration of the student's psyche in supervision is legitimate is whether the focus has shifted from the impact of the student on the case to the student's personality (Hess, 1997).

There are psychotoxic supervisors who use the student to illegitimately gratify destructive needs. Dr. D prides himself on his reputation as his program's assassin. Either he is assigned his

---

[4] Some students may enter supervision at Stage II or Stage III with a particular supervisor. The student may find him- or herself back in Stage I when confronting new types of psychopathology or new types of clients, when working in new settings, or when trying out new techniques such that confusion sets in. This process can best be likened to a "spiral omnibus" where progress is made but some experiences and feelings are much like those experiences earlier in one's learning.

favorite students, who then turn supervision into a gabfest regarding the personalities of other students, or he is assigned those the other faculty members want to purge from the program. Given the amorphousness of psychotherapy and its supervision, he bores into the students' motivations and their psychopathological sources regarding any incident on the tapes of psychotherapy or that occur in supervision. Given his skill and the extreme asymmetry of power in the supervision, no student sent to him for assassination has escaped. The student who is a target needs to consult with a trusted faculty member as to what course of action to pursue.

Perhaps the reason for psychotoxic supervision may lie in the combination of: (a) insecure faculty members, (b) with no investment in teaching psychotherapy, (c) who are assigned a task on which they place little value, (d) for which they have no training, and (e) for which they receive no rewards toward tenure or promotion. One supervisor nationally known for his work in experiential psychotherapy sees as his mission to confuse any student who has begun to consolidate a conceptual framework of psychotherapy. Dr. M.'s students simply do not engage him if at all possible. Perhaps the best strategy is for the student to assume the attitude embodied in Elie Wiesel's (1972) advice: "Whether a source is blessed or not depends on the person drawing from it." I learned even from poor supervisors; in some cases I learned where my vulnerabilities lie, and how I should not supervise others.

The student who has experienced psychonoxious supervision may develop many adroit coping skills. One sensitive student came to me after experiencing several fault-finding supervisors. After discussing a troublesome case a few times, I asked him to bring an audiotape to supervision so I could get a sense of the case beyond his oral description. At the next session, he told me the clinic did not have a tape recorder that day but he would bring one the next week. At the following session he told me he brought the recorder but forgot the tape. I laughed and offered him my recorder and a new tape. He laughed and said that he was not that resistant. The following week he brought the tape and recorder to our meeting, plugged in the machine, fiddled with the tape and controls, set the machine to play, and sat back. We heard an unremitting stream of "white noise." As we looked at each other with puzzlement, his face cleared with an "aha" exclamation when he explained that he must have put the microphone on the clock radio in the office and recorded radio hum. He became deeply embarrassed and finally laughed when he realized that he would only get a benign grin from me and not a scold. From my own supervision with Jane Church, among other supervisors interested in my development and not in debasing me, I realized that students are brimming with self-evaluations, mostly of a corrective and even self-scolding nature.

Markus and Zajonc (1985) claimed it is impossible to view any act or object without making good/bad and pleasant/unpleasant judgments. Jarvis and Petty (1996) found humans are constantly evaluating and self-evaluating, which induces anxiety, and that "evaluation ... is assumed to be among the most pervasive and dominant human responses" (p. 172). Students, the products of structured and evaluative educational systems for most of their lives, are heavily laden with mental grade sets. Students are most in need of a supervisory environment that sees not mistakes but exploratory play (Aronson, 2000). In the words of Winnicott (1971), "Responsible persons must be available when children play; but this does not mean that the responsible person need enter into the children's playing" (p. 50).

Nurturing supervisors "perform with high levels of empathy, respect, genuineness, flexibility, concern, investment and openness. They are knowledgeable, experienced, and concrete [in guiding the student] ... using appropriate teaching, goal-setting, and feedback ... [and] appear to be supportive and non-critical individuals" (Carifio & Hess, 1987, p. 244). The fortunate student will have a supervisor who acts as if he or she lives by John Masefield's credo: "Once in a century a person may be ruined or made insufferable by praise. But surely once in a minute something generous dies for want of it."

## After All, Why Do We Want to be Clinical Psychologists?

There is an adage that when one becomes a teacher, one learns from students. The psychotherapy relationship is special in that it allows for "bridging" connections. Although "bonding" connections sustain us (bonding relationships are those with others who are like ourselves and with whom we interact either voluntarily or within an existing familial bond), the bridging relationships help us grow as human beings in special relationships that allow for intimacy between people who would otherwise never know each other. Thus psychotherapy offers the opportunity to interact with the profoundly mentally disordered, the retarded, those addicted to drugs, those who rent out their bodies for sexual favors, or those who appear to have all the privileges of life but experience internally driven despair. When we enter into the psychotherapeutic experience with them, we can begin to see beyond the diagnostic label or the face of the person and understand their character. The unfolding of a person's essence in a relationship, particularly one as focused as psychotherapy, is an awesome experience. The therapist can see the person's life as they experience it, beyond their physical, fiscal, and other objective features. Antonio, in Shakespeare's *Twelfth Night* realizes the transparency of facade and the importance of depth of character:

> *Antonio:*   But O how vile an idol proves this god!
> Thou hast, Sebastian, done good feature shame.
> In nature there's no blemish but the mind;
> None can be call'd deform'd but the unkind:
> Virtue is beauty but the beauteous-evil
> Are empty trunks o'erflourish'd by the devil.
> (Act III, Scene IV)

Bridging connections to the essence of the other allow us to connect across differences and find the truth in Sullivan's one-genus postulate: "We are all so much more human than otherwise."

## ACKNOWLEDGMENT

I am grateful to Jon Jensen for comments on an earlier version of this chapter, and to Kathryn D. Hess and Tanya H. Hess for comments on this version.

## REFERENCES

Aldrich, L. G. (1982). *Construction of mixed standard scales for the rating of psychotherapy supervisors.* Thesis, Auburn University, Auburn, AL.

American Psychological Association. (1992). Ethical principles of psychologists and code of conduct. *American Psychologist, 47,* 1597–1611.

Aronson, S. (2000). Analytic supervision: All work and no play? *Contemporary Psychoanalysis, 36,* 121–132.

Barrett-Lennard, G. T. (1998). *Carl Rogers's helping system: Journey and substance*. London: Sage.

Beck, J. S. (1995). *Cognitive therapy: Basics and beyond*. New York: Guilford Press.

Brenner, C. (1973). *An elementary textbook of psychoanalysis*. New York: International Universities Press.

Carifio, M. S., & Hess, A. K. (1987). Who is the ideal supervisor? *Professional Psychology, 18,* 244–250.

Clark, D. M., & Fairburn, C. G. (Eds.). (1997). *Science and practice of cognitive behaviour therapy*. New York: Oxford University Press.

Corsini, R. J., & Wedding, D. (2000). *Current psychotherapies* (6$^{th}$ ed.). Itasca, IL: F. E. Peacock.

Eddington, A. (1958). *The nature of the physical world*. Ann Arbor: University of Michigan Press.

Ellis, A. (1963). *Reason and emotion in psychotherapy*. New York: Lyle Stuart.

Fenichel, O. (1945). *The psychoanalytic theory of neurosis*. New York: Basic Books.

Freud, S. (1963). *A general introduction to psychoanalysis*. New York: Washington Square Press.

Freud, S. (1965). *The interpretation of dreams*. New York: Avon Books.

Freud, S. (1977). *Three case histories*. New York: Collier Books.

Hartledge, L. C., & Sperr, E. V. (1980). Patient preferences with regard to ideal therapist characteristics. *Journal of Clinical Psychology, 36,* 288–291.

Hess, A. K. (1997). Interpersonal psychotherapy supervision (pp. 63–83). In C. E. Watkins' (Ed.), *The handbook of psychotherapy supervision*. New York: John Wiley & Sons.

Hill, C. R., Charles, D., & Reed, K. G. (1981). A longitudinal analysis of changes in counseling skills during doctoral training in counseling psychology. *Journal of Counseling Psychology, 28,* 428–436.

Horvath, A. O., & Greenberg, L. S. (Eds.). (1994). *The working alliance: Theory, research and practice*. New York: Wiley & Sons.

James, W. (1981). *Principles of psychology*. Cambridge, MA: Harvard University Press. (Original work published 1890).

Jarvis, W. B. G., & Petty, R. G. (1996). The need to evaluate. *Journal of Personality and Social Psychology, 70,* 172–184.

Kelly, G. A. (1955). *The psychology of personal constructs*. New York: Norton.

Kopta, S. M., Lueger, R. J., Saunders, S. M., & Howard, K. I. (1999). Individual psychotherapy outcome and process research: Challenges leading to greater turmoil or a positive transition? *Annual Review of Psychology, 50,* 441–446.

Levenson, E. (1982). Follow the fox. *Contemporary Psychoanalysis, 18,* 1–15.

Levine, H. B. (1996). The capacity for countertransference. *Psychoanalytic Inquiry, 17,* 44–68.

Luborsky, L., Crits-Cristoph, P., McLellan, A. T., Woody, G., Piper, W., Liberman, B., Imber, S., & Pilkonis, P. (1986). Do therapists vary much in their success? *American Journal of Orthopsychiatry, 56,* 501–512.

Macran, S., Stiles, W. B., & Smith, J. A. (1999). How does personal therapy affect therapists' practice? *Journal of Counseling Psychology, 46,* 419–431.

Markus, H., & Zajonc, R. B. (1985). The cognitive perspective in social psychology. In G. Lindzey & E. Aronson (Eds.), *Handbook of social psychology* (Vol. 1, pp. 137–230). Hillsdale, NJ: Lawrence Erlbaum Associates.

May, R., Angel, E., & Ellenberger, H. F. (1958). *Existence*. New York: Basic Books.

Mitchell, S. A., & Greenberg, J. (1983). *Object relations and psychoanalytic theory*. Cambridge, MA: Harvard University Press.

Netzky, W., Davidson, J., & Crunkleton, A. (1982). Pertinent consumer issues in choosing a counseling professional. *Journal of Counseling Psychology, 29,* 406–413.

Pepper, S. C. (1942). *World hypotheses*. Berkeley: University of California Press.

Raimy, V. C. (Ed.). (1950). *Training in clinical psychology*. Englewood Cliffs, NJ: Prentice Hall.

Reich, A. (1951). On countertransference. *International Journal of Psychoanalysis, 32*, 25–31.

Rogers, C. R. (1959). A theory of therapy, personality and interpersonal relationships, as developed in the client centered framework. In S. Koch (Ed.) *Psychology: A study of a science, volume III. Formulations of the person and the social content* (pp. 184–256). New York: McGraw-Hill.

Salkovskis, P. M. (Ed.). (1996). *Frontiers of cognitive therapy.* New York: Guilford Press.

Shakow, D. (1947). Recommended graduate training programs in clinical psychology. *American Psychologist, 2*, 539–558.

Shapiro, E. R. (1999). Neutrality and abstinence. *Austen Riggs Center Review, 12*, 5–8.

Sullivan, H. S. (1953). *The interpersonal theory of psychiatry.* New York: W. W. Norton.

Swain, D. (1981). *Behaviorally anchored rating scale for recipients of psychotherapy supervision: Instrument construction.* Thesis, Auburn University, Auburn, AL.

Wampold, B. E. (1997). Methodological problems in identifying efficacious psychotherapist. *Psychotherapy Research, 7*, 21–43.

Weiner, I. B. (1998). *Principles of psychotherapy* (2nd ed.). New York: John Wiley & Sons.

Weiner, I. B., & Kaplan, R. G. (1980). From classroom to clinic: Supervising the first psychotherapy client. In A. K. Hess (Ed.), Psychotherapy supervision: Theory, research and practice. (pp. 41–50). New York: John Wiley.

Wiesel, E. (1972). *Souls on fire.* New York: Random House.

Winnicott, D. (1971). *Playing and reality.* London: Tavistock.

Wolpe, J., & Lazarus, A. A. (1966). *Behavior therapy techniques.* London: Pergamon.

Yalom, I. D. (1989). *Love's executioner and other tales of psychotherapy.* New York: Basic Books.

Yogev, S. (1982). An eclectic model of supervision: A developmental sequence for binning psychotherapy students. *Professional Psychology, 13*, 236–243.

Zaro, J. S., Barach, R., Nedelman, D. J., & Drieblatt, I. S. (1977). *A guide for beginning psychotherapists.* New York: Cambridge University Press.

# 19

# Learning Consultation Skills

*Rodney L. Lowman*

$C$*onsulting.* The images conjured up in starving psychology graduate students' minds by that word may include thoughts of riches and a pleasant and comfortable lifestyle fueled by the fires of sagaciously imparted expertise. The dream is of a professional lifestyle generating both respect and financial comfort—and derived from doing what one loves to do. This is not such a bad image. Such thoughts can sustain graduate student efforts through many a bad or self-questioning night. But like the fantasy-fueled dream of the pristine beach coast or the riches after rags, the anticipated view does not always match the reality. There are clearly many exciting and rewarding careers to have in psychological consulting in which it is possible both to make a good—and for some a *very* good—living and to make a positive contribution to the world. However consulting is not necessarily an easy or assuredly profitable career path. It is certainly the preferred scenario that the desire to consult matches the student's passions, preferences and talents.

Somewhere between the imagined riches of consulting and an anticipated future in the managed care graveyard lies the reality of psychological consulting. It is not an exaggeration to say that the nature and scope of clinical and counseling psychology are in the process of radical change. This change is mostly dictated by environmental factors on both the supply and the demand side. Increasingly, clinical/counseling psychologists are by necessity, if not by choice, forced to find new applications for their skills. Inevitably, perhaps, such psychologists have contemplated applying their clinical skills to business and industry. There are indeed substantial opportunities for the successful application of psychology to work organizations but there are also many pitfalls (see, Lowman, 1998a, 1988c). In this chapter I outline some of the types of consulting applications commonly found, including discussion of both the opportunities and the risks that go along with these uses of psychology.

*Consulting* does not mean much as a stand-alone word. It always implies an object one consults about something. In this chapter I, therefore, outline in some detail illustrative applications of psychology to business and industry.

## CONSULTING TO BUSINESS AND INDUSTRY

The largest area of interest today concerns consulting in the business world. This interest probably stems from the fact that the incomes derived are better, the area of practice less regulated, and the field in a rapidly expanding state rather than one that is leveling off or shrinking. In the case of business and industry, the consulting "objects" can, for the sake of discussion, roughly be grouped into three major domains, or levels: individual, group, and organizational/systemic (Lowman, 1998c). Each of these is briefly discussed.

### Individual-Level Organizational Consultations

These types of consultations for business and industry address workplace or career issues experienced by individual persons. These can include assessment of career and work issues (Lowman, 1991, 1993) such as the situations in which a person is trying to decide what job to do. There are three representative areas for consultation practice: career assessment/counseling, coaching, and work dysfunctions counseling.

*Career Assessment/Counseling.*     Determining the right career choice is an important issue for everyone who works. Often, perhaps most often, people fall into, if not the "right" career path, as least one that fits well enough. But when a career is not properly fitting, it can be the source of considerable unhappiness. A number of types of professionals and nonprofessionals provide career guidance. Psychologists are particularly well suited to providing assessment and counseling about career-related issues and consulting psychologists should be prepared to work with such issues. It is a curious reality that most individuals in clinical and industrial/organizational (I/O) psychology training programs receive little training in individually oriented career and work issues assessment and training. This limits their ability to provide effective training in these areas.

Consulting psychologists working with individuals on career issues need to know about the variables related to career choice and change such as occupational interests, abilities, and personality characteristics. Increasingly psychologists recognize that each of these areas, or domains, interacts with the others in a complex way, influencing the kinds of careers people are likely to find appealing (Ackerman, 1996; Ackerman & Heggestad, 1997; Carson, 1998a, 1998b; Holland, 1997; Lowman, 1991, 1997; Lowman & Carson, 2000). They also need to understand the individual in terms of how such variables interact with the environmental contexts in which the individual functions or may possibly function. For example, two individuals may, according to their interest–ability–personality profiles, both be well suited for careers in management. Still, the specific setting in which each will find career happiness (or at least avoid or minimize the effects of career unhappiness) will vary. Determining whether individual clients will be more satisfied and productive in a manufacturing or social service context is part of the process of contextualizing psychological knowledge and expertise. This is why it is important for the consulting psychologist to be trained in psychological principles and familiar with the cultural contexts and demands of a variety of different work settings.

*Coaching.*    Coaching has perhaps become to the current generation what "psychotherapy" was to previous ones. Just as psychotherapy became, for a time, an essential part of the culture, an almost expected way to cope with the age's anxieties and thought to be useful for a wide array of personal problems and issues, so, today, coaching is being advocated with the same zeal. It is viewed apparently as an antidote to a number of psychologically relevant problems and simply those problems that might be characterized as problems in living or working. Presumably some of the coaching frenzy derives from the fact that it may be easier for an executive or aspiring one to seek help, even if about personal problems, from a "coach" than from a psychotherapist. After all, basketball and football players, golfers, and even actors and actresses have coaches. The theme is the benevolent but tough-minded helper who can push one upward to ever-accelerating levels of performance. Therein lies the difference, at least in the consumer's mind, between coaching and psychotherapy. Coaching, even when touching on sensitive emotional issues such as the connection between anger at a boss and anger at a parent, is about work. What could be more socially desirable than getting better at one's work?

Coaching at its best is an amalgam of personal and occupational savvy applied with a sensitive touch to the needs of persons in occupational and organizational contexts. Kilburg (2000) demonstrated the dangers and the opportunities of coaching and helped differentiate when more psychological and more occupationally relevant approaches may be needed. For those who like the thought of working with others at the individual level but who are not particularly interested in psychopathology or clinical applications, coaching can be a nice application.

*Work Dysfunctions Counseling.*    If coaching is mostly about a particular method or process of intervention, work dysfunctions counseling more addresses content-specific areas of consulting. Lowman (1993) presented an initial attempt to articulate a taxonomy of work dysfunctions. The idea is that psychologists and others may need to consult with individuals in a way that is a cross between psychotherapy and coaching. For example, it may be necessary for a psychologist to differentiate whether clinically experienced depression derives from or tangentially or secondarily influences work. Either way, the client is depressed. However, the specific intervention may vary if the problems are the result of work issues rather than from what is going on in the rest of the client's life. For such assessments and interventions to be effective, psychologists need to understand both personal psychological dynamics and the world of work.

## Groups

Groups are one important social psychological fact of organizational life. They are important both because most of the world's work gets done in groups and because they can further or impede the organization's larger ambitions—or get in their way. Groups, naturally occurring and fabricated, occur in all organizations. They are the building blocks of organizations just as sentences are of paragraphs. Work groups can be functional or dysfunctional, and it was long ago demonstrated that manipulation of group parameters can make great changes in the working lives of employees (Roethlisberger & Dickson, 1939; see also Gottfredson, 1996).

Illustrative of the effective use of groups in organizations—and of how psychological consultants can use the group to further organizational and individual goals—is the Scanlon Plan (Frost, 1996). In this organizational development system approach a series of groups is created in which representatives are elected or appointed to represent their area of the organization to focus on how the organization can run more efficiently. When target objectives are met such that the product is produced for less money than had historically been the case, a portion of the cost savings is passed along to all members of the organization as a separate check, typically issued monthly. When there are no savings, there is no check so the monthly Scanlon check, or lack thereof, becomes a kind of report card for how well the organization is doing. Successful Scanlon companies such as Donnelly Mirrors, Herman Miller, Beth Israel Hospital, and Motorola show the substantial positive effects that such a program can have in organizational functioning. At the center of the intervention is the powerful recognition of the psychological impacts that groups can have on improving organizational behavior.

There are many other aspects of "groupness" with which consulting psychologists must deal. These include group conflict, intergroup dynamics (Alderfer, 1998), and the "group" issues associated with racial, ethnic, gender, and sexual identity group memberships (e.g., Alderfer & Tucker, 1996; Ferdman, 1999).

### Organizational/Systemic

The final level of organizational consulting that can be addressed by consultants is the organizational or systemic. Here, the organization as a whole is the client and the consultant's job is to help the client determine what ails the organization as a whole and devise appropriate intervention strategies.

Modern organizations by which much of the world's work gets done are complex entities, highly interactive with, and dependent on, their environment. Simple theories (such as bureaucracy theory; Weber, 1984/1864) do not go far to explain the vast array of types of organizations we now have. Theorists have long examined the organization as a whole (e.g., Katz & Kahn, 1978; March & Simon, 1958; Thompson, 1967). The usual theoretical orientation applied to studying organizations is open systems theory, whereas others have approached organizational change from the large system perspective (e.g., Mohrman & Mohrman, 1997). Organizations as systems for assessment and interventions are not individuals and individual-based models abstracted to macro systems without empirical and theoretical work do not generally fare well in helping us to understand or to change organizations.

## CORE COMPETENCIES IN CONSULTING TO ORGANIZATIONS

As a student begins to think about a career in organizational consulting psychology, it is worthwhile to consider the competencies that may be important in becoming a professional consultant. Research remains to be conducted to understand better and empirically what it takes to make a good consulting psychologist, but we can at least suggest (on the basis of consultants' experience) some of the personal characteristics and competencies that may be needed in doing this kind of work.

First and foremost, the psychologist must be a good psychologist. This means that core competencies in understanding psychological theory and empirical methodology are taken as givens. Psychologists who consult to organizations need to know the empirical, theoretical, and practice-based literature on all three levels (individual, group, and organizational) as it relates to organizational consulting. They need to have skills in sorting out whether a problem presenting to the consultant is what it appears to be and to differentiate problems whose parameters are misdiagnosed by clients. For example, it is not uncommon in consulting to organizations for the client organization to present with a proposed solution rather than a particular problem. For example, the client may approach the consultant with a request for team-building work or a participative management plan. It falls to the consultant to determine whether or not the intended solution addresses the underlying problem(s). When a psychologist is offered high fees to perform a particular intervention that seems not to be what the organization needs, it can be difficult to decline to provide the requested service.

What aspiring consulting psychologists often do not think about and should consider are nonpsychological competencies that are associated with many versions of organizational consulting. These competencies are discussed here.

***The Ability to Sell.***   Consultants, psychologists or otherwise, to organizations who cannot "sell" their services to organizational representatives had best find another line of work or a partner who sells well. It may seem odd to put this at the head of a list of core organizational consulting competencies, and certainly sales ability is no substitute for professional competence. However, it is so often an expected and critical component of consulting success that would-be consultants ought not to be able to pretend that someone else will be responsible for bringing in the business. Those who do not like the "rough-and-tumble" world of competitive environments and the reality of having to sell to have services to perform, might best consider other specializations in psychology.

***An Affinity for Working with "Normal" and Generally High-Powered Clients.***   Contrary to psychologists' sometimes naive and self-referential assumptions, executives in large organizations often can match them in brain power (general intellectual ability) and probably exceed their ability quickly to grasp the practical implications of data and ideas related to management. Consulting psychologists need to be comfortable working with normal persons who are bright, achievement oriented, and accustomed quickly to translating results into practice. Those who want things to be "perfect" before they can provide suggestions or outline the implications of preliminary research findings belong in other applications of psychology.

***Comfort with Group Contexts.***   Management is generally a "people" discipline and most managerial work gets done in groups. Psychologists uncomfortable with working with large groups of executives and decision makers, or in having their ideas critiqued in public settings will probably not last very long in organizational consulting.

***Proposals and Background Research.***   With some exceptions, consulting work generally takes place by proposals that are made to potential clients. In general, the consulting psychologist goes to the client, not the other way around, and the work is often delivered on the client's setting. Consulting psychologists often must do preliminary research on a company before making a proposal or meeting with a potential client. Consulting psychologists who wait for an initial discussion with a client or who rely on generic process skills will be at a disadvantage, especially with high-powered clients who expect the consultants to have done their homework and to be thoroughly knowledgeable about the client before they meet.

***Tolerance for Ambiguity and Long Waits.*** Consulting work often involves long waits between when business is proposed and when the work is contracted and actually done. When, finally, the client organization decides to proceed with a project, it is generally needed immediately. Corporate clients expect work output at a level that exceeds that of many other types of psychological applications.

There is another kind of ambiguity that is essential for success as a consultant. A person who has a high need for structure and personal control generally does not belong in consulting work. Psychological theories must be adapted to the needs of the client and the consultant. When in the field, the consultant must be expert at bridging theory and practice in a way that the client can work with and accept. Those who are rigid or staid will likely not do well over the long term.

***Travel, Travel, and More Travel.*** Travel is the norm in many, but not all, consulting applications. It is common for a consulting psychologist to be based, for example, in New York or Los Angeles, and have clients all over the United States and abroad. Getting on the plane on Sunday night and returning late Friday night, only to start the process all over again the next week, is not unusual. On the road, the consulting psychologist is expected to work at peak performance, often for 12- to 16-hour days without complaint, and to do what it takes to get the job done. In return, consultants are well paid, typically stay in top hotels, and often travel first class.

***An Ability to Function Simultaneously at Multiple Levels.*** The consultant must have or learn the ability to function on multiple levels. In interacting with a distressed executive the consultant must hear what is being said and understand it from the individual's perspectives and context, yet simultaneously see it from the larger group and organizational/systemic perspective. A newly laid off executive may need assistance in putting the event in the context of larger changes in the organization and the industry. Helping individual clients own up to their own share of responsibility while not being overly punitive toward themselves may be crucial. Conversely, organizations work with issues that often must be addressed conceptually and generically at the large system level. The ability to help key executives understand the impact of necessary difficult actions in human and individual terms may be a contribution the consulting psychologist is uniquely well suited to make.

***An Ability to Function Effectively in Teams.*** Even in science, but especially in organizational contexts, work is now done more often in teams than not. Those who work best on their own or whose personality makes it difficult for them to work in a non-self-focused way are likely to find organizational consulting to be an infelicitous match.

## THE TRAINING OF ORGANIZATIONAL CONSULTING PSYCHOLOGISTS

A complete issue of the major journal in consulting psychology was recently directed to "The Training and Development of Consulting Psychologists" (Garman & Hellkamp, 1998). Some of the common themes that seem called for in consulting psychology training include those discussed here.

*Assessment.*   Consulting psychologists benefit from understanding psychological assessment of individuals, groups, and organizations. They probably do not need to have clinical or counseling training in the sense of learning how to assess abnormal personality (although that training and skill set would not hurt), but should have supervised experience in using psychological tests with the normal population (e.g., in career assessment and counseling) and in assessing both functional and dysfunctional groups and organizations as a whole. There is no substitute for supervised experience in these areas and the more experience the better.

*Intervention Skills.*   Consulting psychologists need to be comfortable working on multiple levels of intervention. By the end of their training hopefully they will have had experience working intensely at all three levels (individual, group, and organizational) so they can perform at least minimally competent work at each of these levels. It is not particularly important that psychologists intent on consulting to organizations learn a specific set of skills or "techniques." Far more important are learning generic skills for matching interventions to well-assessed organizational issues. Techniques are fairly easily learned when the conceptual road map and generic skills are in place.

*Evaluation Research Skills.*   In the world of consulting there is often scant time or money expended to evaluate the effectiveness of particular interventions or applications. Consulting psychologists nevertheless need to be able to evaluate the effectiveness of their interventions. Of course a medical doctor does not evaluate the effectiveness of each application of a well-proven technique. Few physicians do any research or evaluation at all. What is needed by consulting psychologists is the ability to assess, independently of their own financial interests or personal gain, the extent to which a particular intervention is working or not and to make changes in the practices used when something is not working. As behavioral *scientists*, consulting psychologists also strive to help organizational clients understand the value of more systematic research of interventions. Sometimes, of course, the evaluation criterion is embedded: The presenting problem goes away or gets better or on assessment instruments used in a project clearly indicate improvement. What is important is that the *psychologist*-consultant not consider "the client keeps paying my fees" to be an adequate outcome measure.

*Training in Thinking Ethically While Practicing Complexly.*   Consulting psychologists work in "real time" with a myriad of complex issues and concerns. The psychologist will have many experiences in the workplace in which values and ethics are challenged. For example, is it ethical to own stock in a company with which one consults? What happens when the company president who hired the consultant turns out to be the problem? Who "owns" data generated in the course of an organizational consultation? What happens if data promised to be kept confidential are subsequently subpoenaed by a court for use in a law suit brought for wrongful discharge? The consulting psychologist in training clearly needs to be exposed to thinking about ethical issues in the context of actual practice experiences.

*Training in the Ability to Function Well Under Conditions of Ambiguity and Stress.*   Some psychologists are simply ill-suited to be consulting psychologists by virtue of their discomfort with ambiguity and their inability to function constantly under conditions of stress and change. Anyone in consulting psychology training needs to be exposed to real-world consulting applications such that they learn how they function under such conditions and how they can avoid adverse reactions in such contexts.

*Practica and Internships.*    Clearly, the discussions offered here imply that would-be consulting psychologists need lots of supervised experience in diverse situations so that they are able to feel confident in consulting roles. Atella and Figgatt (1998) identified many issues involved in obtaining practica training in consulting psychology.

## THE ETHICS OF ORGANIZATIONAL CONSULTING

Ethical issues in consulting psychology are increasingly complex (Gellerman, Frankel, & Ladenson, 1990; Lowman, 1998b). There are many levels of ethical complexity that need to be addressed when psychologists consult with individuals in organizational contexts or when the organization itself is the client. How, for example, does an organization "consent" to treatment or assessment? What happens when someone, let us say an employee whose input is critical to the success of a project, does not wish to participate in an intervention or assessment process? Can the consultant or organization insist on participation? What happens when sensitive information is obtained about the job performance of managers in the company and the good of the company may suggest a need to be terminated from employment?

Perhaps most noteworthy in this context is the issue of psychologists moving into consulting roles after having trained in other areas of psychology. What are the ethical implications of psychologists trained in clinical or counseling psychology who move without further training into organizational consulting? What about I/O psychologists who were never trained in individual work who are called on by their organization to do individual coaching or assessment? Psychology often cares more about such distinctions of training and supervised experience than does business and industry.

If these ethical issues strike you as interesting ones to sort through, then perhaps consulting psychology is the place for you to be. If, however, you cannot get spontaneously excited about using behavioral science techniques to attempt to improve organization's profit picture, and if you know in your heart that you really do not get excited about business or industry, then perhaps you need to consider other consulting applications of psychology such as those mentioned here, or other types of psychological consulting.

## TRAINING AND STANDARDS IN ORGANIZATIONAL CONSULTING PSYCHOLOGY

If the applications of psychology elaborated so far in this chapter are appealing to you, you need to consider the sources of training needed to help get yourself where you want to be. Traditional graduate school training programs in clinical psychology seldom train graduate students in organizational or occupational applications. Counseling psychology doctoral training programs do a better job than most of incorporating training in career assessment and counseling, an area in which substantive contributions have been made to the research literature. However, few counseling or clinical programs offer any courses in consulting psychology (Garman, Zlatoper, & Whiston, 1998). Industrial/organizational psychology generally trains its graduates well in statistical and methodological approaches to understanding behavior in organizations and increasingly incorporates applied training as well. However, few I/O psychology training programs offer any training at the individual level, such as in individual assessment or coaching.

A few programs are beginning to offer training specifically in consulting psychology at both the doctoral and postdoctoral levels. Because I am personally affiliated with some of these programs, I mention them and let the reader gather independent information about the programs. These include the doctoral program in consulting psychology at Alliant University (formerly the California School of Professional Psychology; www.cspp.edu) in San Diego, the organizational consulting PsyD program at Alliant University in San Francisco (www.cspp.edu), the organizational psychology program at Rutgers University (www.rutgers.edu), and programs such as the social-organizational psychology program at Columbia University Teacher's College (www.tc.columbia.edu). Programs in I/O psychology are also relevant. Programs in consulting psychology and related areas are starting to be listed online by Division 13 (Consulting Psychology) of APA (www.apa.org/divisions/div13).

## Standards for Training in Consulting Psychology

Currently, Division 13 of the American Psychological Association (www.apa.org/divisons/13) is preparing a set of guidelines on training at the doctoral and postdoctoral level in organizational consulting psychology. A draft of these guidelines may be read online (www.apa.org/divisions/div13/guidelines.html).

# OTHER TYPES OF PSYCHOLOGICAL CONSULTING

Space does not permit an extensive treatment of other types of consulting in which psychologists can engage. Generally, these areas require training in a substantive specialty area of psychology and consulting constitutes one application within a broader skill set. Here I briefly mention a few areas of application.

*School Consultation.*    School psychology is another area in which consultation takes place. Gutkin and Saunders (chap. 20, this volume) address this application of psychology in more detail, so only brief mention is made here. This type of consulting can interface between the medical models of consulting in which expert consultation services are sought and systemic/organizational consulting, in which the many forces impinging on an apparently individual problem (e.g., school, parents, legal authorities) are assembled and consulted to help solve or ameliorate problems. The focus for school consultation is typically schoolchildren. School consulting psychologists also need to understand the multiple levels of engagement discussed in this chapter and how expert consultation knowledge must be blended with an understanding of the process of consultation to the school as a system.

*Medical Consultation.*    Sometimes called psychiatric or medical psychological consultation (Caplan, 1995; Kush & Campo, 1998) or psychiatric liaison consultation (Rundell & Wise, 1996), this area addresses psychological consultation in the medical arena. In this type of consultation, there is typically a client who is hospitalized or seen in an outpatient clinic and the expert consultant is called in to help clarify, confirm, or to make a diagnosis or to make a recommendation about the preferred intervention(s).

In the case of medical problems, often the psychologist is brought in to help determine whether an apparent medical problem is in fact of psychogenic origin (e.g., pseudo seizures; Lowman & Richardson, 1987), whether there are psychological components deriving from a medical condition (e.g., depression secondary to the diagnosis of a serious medical condition such as multiple sclerosis), or whether psychological conditions are manifesting as physical ones (e.g., untreated depression masking as stomach disorders).

*Forensic Consultation.*    Psychologists play an ever-increasing role in consulting to attorneys and the judicial system on legal issues that overlap with psychological ones (Gottlieb, 2000; Hess & Weiner, 1999; Thomas & Howells, 1996). Types of consultation in the forensic area include child custody evaluations, helping to assess fitness to stand trial and competency at the time of a crime, jury selection, employment discrimination and fitness for duty, and violence and recidivism prediction (Brigham, 1999; Roesch, Hart, & Ogloff, 1999). As in many areas of psychological consultation, there are both art and science to the process of consulting, and knowledge from many specialty areas of psychology may be needed in order to be effective in these roles.

## WHERE TO FROM HERE?

If, in reading this chapter, you conclude that you at least want to know more about consulting or that you hope it will be your life's work, where can you go for further information? The reference list includes a number of relevant articles, book chapters, and books you may find helpful. A professor at your school might be consulting and able to discuss with you the rewards and limitations of this kind of work. Such faculty may be found in colleges of business, not just in psychology departments. Above all, consider joining Division 13 of the APA as a student member or attending one of its mid-winter "Consulting for Corporations" conferences. That membership will put you in touch with some of the key players in the world of consulting psychology.

## REFERENCES

Ackerman, P. L. (1996). A theory of adult intellectual development: Process, personality, interests, and knowledge. *Intelligence, 22,* 227–257.

Ackerman, P. L., & Heggestad, E. D. (1997). Intelligence, personality, and interests: Evidence for overlapping traits. *Psychological Bulletin, 121,* 219–245.

Alderfer, C. P. (1998). Group psychological consulting to organizations: A perspective on history. *Consulting Psychology Journal: Practice and Research, 50,* 67–77.

Alderfer, C. P., & Tucker, R. C. (1996). A field experiment for studying race relations embedded in organizations. *Journal of Organizational Behavior, 17,* 43–57.

Atella, M., & Figatt, J. E. (1998). Practica in consulting psychology: Working with the doctoral clinical programs. *Consulting Psychology Journal: Practice and Research*, 218–227.

Brigham, J. C. (1999). What is forensic psychology, anyway? *Law and Human Behavior, 23,* 273–298.

Caplan, G. (1995). Types of mental health consultation. *Journal of Educational and Psychological Consultation, 6,* 7–21.

Carson, A. D. (1998a). The integration of interests, aptitudes, and personality traits: A test of Lowman's matrix. *Journal of Career Assessment, 6,* 83–105.

Carson, A. D. (1998b). The relation of self-reported abilities to aptitude test scores: A replication and extension. *Journal of Vocational Behavior, 53*, 353–371.

Ferdman, B. M. (1999). The color and culture of gender in organizations: Attending to race and ethnicity. In G. N. Powell (Ed.), *Handbook of gender and work* (pp. 17–34). Thousand Oaks, CA: Sage.

Frost, C. F. (1996). *Changing forever: The well-kept secret of America's leading companies.* East Lansing: Michigan State University Press.

Garman, A. N., & Hellkamp, D. T. (1998). The training and development of consulting psychologists. Special issue, *Consulting Psychology Journal: Practice and Research, 50*, 203–270.

Garman, A., Zlatoper, K. W., & Whiston, D. L. (1998). Graduate training and consulting psychology: A content analysis of doctoral-level programs. *Consulting Psychology Journal: Practice and Research, 50*, 207–217.

Gellerman, W., Frankel, M. S., & Ladenson, R. F. (1990). *Values and ethics in organization and human systems development. Responding to dilemmas in professional life.* San Francisco: Jossey-Bass.

Gottfredson, G. D. (1996). The Hawthorne misunderstanding (and how to get the Hawthorne effect in action research). *Journal of Research in Crime and Delinquency, 33*, 28–48.

Gottlieb, M. C. (2000). Consulting and collaborating with attorneys. In F. W. Kaslow (Ed.), *Handbook of couple and family forensics: A sourcebook for mental health and legal professionals* (pp. 491–506). New York: Wiley.

Hess, A. K., & Weiner, I. B. (Eds.). (1999). *The handbook of forensic psychology* (2nd ed.). New York: Wiley.

Holland, J. L. (1997). *Making vocational choices: A theory of vocational personalities and work environments* (3rd ed.). Odessa, FL: Psychological Assessment Resources.

Katz, D., & Kahn, R. L. (1978). *The social psychology of organizations* (2nd ed.). New York: Wiley.

Kilburg, R. S. (2000). *Executive coaching: Developing managerial wisdom in a world of chaos.* Washington, DC: American Psychological Association.

Kush, S. A., & Campo, J. V. (1998). Consultation and liaison in the pediatric setting. In R. T. Ammerman & J. V. Campo (Eds.), *Handbook of pediatric psychology and psychiatry, Vol. 1: Psychological and psychiatric issues in the pediatric setting* (pp. 23–40). Boston: Allyn & Bacon.

Lowman, R. L. (1991). *The clinical practice of career assessment: Interests, abilities, and personality.* Washington, DC: American Psychological Association.

Lowman, R. L. (1993). The inter-domain model of career assessment and counseling. *Journal of Counseling and Development, 71*, 549–554.

Lowman, R. L. (1996). Dysfunctional work role behavior. In K. Murphy (Ed.), *Individual differences and behavior in organizations* (pp. 371–415). San Francisco: Jossey-Bass.

Lowman, R. L. (1997). Career assessment and psychological impairment: Integrating inter-domain and work dysfunctions theory. *Journal of Career Assessment, 5*, 213–224.

Lowman, R. L. (1998a). Consulting to organizations as if the individual mattered. *Consulting Psychology Journal: Practice and Research, 50*, 17–24.

Lowman, R. L. (Ed.). (1998b). *The ethical practice of psychology in organizations.* Washington, DC: American Psychological Association & Society of Industrial/Organizational Psychology.

Lowman, R. L. (1998c). New directions for graduate training in consulting psychology. *Consulting Psychology Journal: Practice and Research, 50*, 263–270.

Lowman, R. L., & Carson, A. D. (2000). Integrating assessment data into the delivery of career counseling services. In D. Luzzo (Ed.), *Career development of college students: Translating theory into practice* (pp. 121–136). Washington, DC: American Psychological Association.

Lowman, R. L., & Richardson, L. M. (1987). Pseudo epileptic seizures of psychogenic origin: A review of the literature. *Clinical Psychology Review, 7,* 363–387.

March, J. G., & Simon, H. A. (1958). *Organizations.* New York: Wiley.

Mohrman, S. A., & Mohrman, A. M., Jr. (1997). Fundamental organizational change as organizational learning: Creating team-based organizations. In W. A. Pasmore & R. W. Woodman (Eds.), *Research in organizational change and development, Vol. 10: An annual series featuring advances in theory, methodology, and research* (pp. 197–228). Greenwich, CT: JAI Press.

Roesch, R., Hart, S. D., & Ogloff, J. R. P. (Eds.). (1999). *Psychology and law: The state of the discipline Perspectives in law & psychology* (Vol. 10). New York: Kluwer Academic/Plenum Publishers.

Roethlisberger, F. J., & Dickson W. J. (1939). *Management and the worker.* Cambridge, MA: Harvard University Press.

Rundell, J. R., & Wise, M. G. (Eds.). (1996). *The American Psychiatric Press textbook of consultation–liaison psychiatry.* Washington, DC: American Psychiatric Press.

Thomas, P. B., & Howells, K. (1996). Professional and ethical challenges of forensic clinical psychology. *Psychiatry, Psychology and Law, 3,* 63–70.

Thompson, J. D. (1967). *Organizations in action.* New York: McGraw Hill.

Weber, M. (1984). *The theory of social and economic organization* (A. M. Henderson & T. Parsons, Trans.; T. Parsons, Ed.). New York: The Free Press. (Original work published 1864)

# 20

# Developing Essential Intervention and Prevention Skills for School Settings

*Terry B. Gutkin*

**Anita L. Saunders**

$\textbf{A}$s we enter the 21st century, it is becoming increasingly evident to growing numbers of psychologists and policymakers that schools are among the most important settings for the delivery of contemporary psychological services. Although not one of the venues traditionally attracting the most attention, schools are emerging as a vital component of our national mental health system. In contrast to hospitals, clinics, community mental health centers, and private practice offices, schools offer psychologists unique and powerful opportunities to address and affect an extensive range of meaningful psychological problems that currently afflict our society.

## SCHOOLS AS SITES FOR PSYCHOLOGICAL INTERVENTION AND PREVENTION: EXAMINING THE POTENTIAL

One factor attracting both practitioners and policymakers to school settings is the realization that prevention and early intervention are key elements to improving the quality of our nation's mental health (Meyers & Nastasi, 1999). Clearly, psychological dysfunction is best addressed when we are able to prevent its emergence (primary prevention) or at least identify early and intervene prior to the need for crisis management (secondary prevention). In general, it is going to be both substantially cheaper for society and less painful for our clients if we are able to address mental health problems by "nipping them in the bud."

Once our collective professional attention is directed toward prevention and early intervention, it is inevitable that children and youth emerge as a primary client group. Regardless of which school of thought serves as the foundation for one's professional practice, ranging from psychoanalysis through behaviorism (and virtually every theoretical position between these two extremes), it is clear that childhood and adolescent experiences have an enormous impact on the mental health of adults. We all know that in many ways, "the child is the father to the man." Consistent with this analysis, the American Psychological Association (APA) recently concluded, "the most serious and expensive health and social problems that afflict our nation today are caused in large part by behavior patterns established during youth" (APA, 1995, p. 3).

Given an increasing focus on young people as the target population for psychological services, psychologists will be (and are being) drawn inevitably toward our nation's schools. Just as Willie Sutton is reputed to have robbed banks because "that's where the money is," psychologists of the 21st century who are interested in serving children and youth will find themselves working more and more extensively in educational settings. This fundamental reality undergirds important policy directions being developed at the highest levels of our government. For example, in a joint statement issued by the Secretary of Education and the Secretary of Health and Human Services under the Clinton administration (Riley & Shalala, 1992), it was concluded that the health and mental health agendas of our nation are connected fundamentally and inextricably to the services we provide (or fail to provide) in schools.

Although schools may be unfamiliar territory for many psychologists, this setting does afford numerous and potent benefits. For one thing, schools are the only institution in our culture that can provide our profession with universal access to the population of interest. All children go to school. Not only do they attend school, but they also do so beginning at an early point in their lives (for handicapped children, preschool services are now available via federal programs from birth onward) and typically in an ongoing fashion for at least 12 years. During this extended period of school attendance, children and youth are available to school professionals for significant blocks of time (typically at least 6 hours per day, 5 days per week, 40 weeks per year) and during the most critical periods of human development. Beyond this, schools provide psychologists with a living laboratory for intervention. Rather than initiating therapeutic growth in artificial environments such as hospitals, clinics, and private practice offices and then having to struggle with generalizing behavioral, cognitive, and emotional changes to the natural environment, schools provide psychologists with an endless array of chances to make important changes in the "real worlds" in which children live on a day-to-day basis. Schools also give us unparalleled access to the significant others in a child's life (e.g., teachers, parents, peers, community leaders) who may have played a critical role in the genesis of existing or potential problems, and who almost always must be involved in intervention and/or prevention efforts.

## PROVIDING EFFECTIVE PSYCHOLOGICAL SERVICES IN SCHOOLS: SELECTED CRITICAL PERSPECTIVES AND COMPETENCIES

Although fundamental psychological principles and the laws of human behavior are, of course, invariant across institutional settings, it is nonetheless a truism that the manner in which psychological services must be delivered varies depending on the nature of the ecosystem within which services are being provided. Obviously, schools are neither hospitals, clinics, community mental health centers, nor private practice offices. They are inherently different in fundamental ways. These differences have a direct impact on the skills needed by psychologists working in school settings. Although space limitations preclude anything that even approaches a comprehensive review of these issues (see Reynolds & Gutkin, 1999, and Ysseldyke et al., 1997, for a more extensive treatment), the following discussion highlights what we perceive to be the most critical perspectives and competencies.

## Understanding School Culture

To function effectively in schools requires an understanding of this institution as a cultural ecosystem with its own set of powerful norms and organizational expectations (Sarason, 1971, 1995). An incalculable array of vital professional implications flows from this simple observation, only a few of which are detailed here.

In contrast to services in private practice, school-based psychological service delivery always takes place within an organizational context. School-based psychologists can rarely, if ever, intervene unilaterally on behalf of their clients. Treatment decisions are typically made within multidisciplinary team contexts that place professionals other than psychologists at the apex of the official power structure. Also relevant is the fact that these other professionals come almost exclusively from educational rather than mental health or medical backgrounds, which further sets schools apart from hospitals, clinics and other traditional mental health agencies. Succeeding in school environments requires skills far beyond those of determining how to best meet the needs of one's clients. Psychologists must also learn how to (a) work effectively within the decision-making structures that typify school environments (e.g., grade-level and subject-matter teams, prereferral intervention teams, multidisciplinary teams, individual educational plan [IEP] teams), and (b) communicate and negotiate effectively from a nonhierarchical position with professionals whose primary focus typically is educational rather than psychological.

Another central element of school culture is that most psychological interventions for children, whether they are targeted at academic, behavioral, or socioemotional outcomes, are implemented within a group structure. Although individual counseling and psychotherapy have been shown to be effective in schools (Prout & Prout, 1998), the "heart and soul" of school functioning typically centers around naturalistic group settings such as classrooms, resource rooms, libraries, playgrounds, hallways, lunchrooms, gymnasiums, after-school clubs, and athletic teams. This reality impacts the design of school-based psychological interventions in multiple and profound ways. It means that treatment plans not only must meet the needs of our clients, but they must also fit into the natural ecology of existing, prestructured group contexts (Lentz, Allen, & Ehrhardt, 1996; Martens & Witt, 1988). It is unlikely, for example, that teachers who rely entirely on large-group instruction are going to modify the nature of their teaching strategies based on a psychologist's recommendation to place a particular student into an individualized or small-group environment. The psychologist must design an intervention that will not only be effective for one's client, but will also fit easily into the school-based ecologies within which this student is embedded. This is often a significant challenge and requires that psychologists working in school settings be knowledgeable of the "universe of alternatives" (Sarason, 1971, p. 222) that are possible for accomplishing a particular therapeutic goal.

As a final example of school culture, it is interesting to note that most of the clients served by this institution (e.g., children and youth) are there involuntarily. Although there are doubtless many students who love being in school at any given moment, it is also true that few complain when holidays arrive and that most would "bolt for the door" at any given moment if given that option. Adding to this phenomenon is the fact that most students are quite impotent when it comes to setting the policies and procedures that control their lives while in their school building. In this way, most schools have characteristics in common with our armed forces when a draft was in effect, and with prisons. All of these institutions are working with constituents who are both involuntary and relatively powerless. As in a conscripted military or prison setting, it should thus come as no surprise that discipline problems are omnipresent. Survey after survey indicates that a primary concern for teachers and school personnel is classroom management and discipline (Merrett & Wheldall, 1993; Stickel, Satchwell, & Meyer, 1991). Rather than being a function of incompetent educators, this finding is more likely a reflection of an inescapable element of school culture in our society. Once again, the significance of this fact is far-reaching. Psychologists working in school settings must understand the psychology of classroom management and arrive for work prepared to cope with this complex set of issues.

In each of the examples just cited, the "bottom line" is that working in school settings requires that psychologists have knowledge and skills that extend beyond the psychology of individual children and youth. They must understand schools themselves as organizational and cultural systems.

### Taking an Ecological/Systems Perspective

Historically, psychologists have understood psychological dysfunction from the perspective of intrapsychic and intrapersonal dynamics and thus have focused primarily on the internal mental states of clients. Dubbed the "medical model," this orientation has led psychologists to search for solutions to presenting problems from a growing array of individually oriented psychopathological diagnoses (see the DSM–IV [American Psychiatric Association, 1994] for a comprehensive listing) and treatments options (e.g., individual psychotherapy, psychotropic medication). As implied in the discussion of "school culture," however, this perspective is likely to be too narrow when providing psychological services within school settings.

Specifically, potential and actual psychological problems for children and youth can rarely be understood solely by focusing on the "victim" (i.e., the identified problem child). This is particularly true in school settings, where multilayered and complex systemic forces are virtually (if not, literally) always among the factors contributing in some way to a client's symptomatology. Consider the following example pertaining to a common academic problem:

> When children have trouble learning to read,... this "dysfunction" is best understood as the product of multi-layered, proximal, distal, and interactive systems. Among these systems are (a) the individual children themselves (e.g., past life experiences, neurological deficits); (b) educational contexts (e.g., the curriculum employed by teachers, the pedagogical and behavior management skills of teachers, the interpersonal relationships between teachers and students, the organizational climate of the school); (c) prevailing social environments (e.g., the attitudes and behaviors of peers, classmates, and role models towards education in general and reading in particular); (d) family sys-

tems (e.g., values and expectations held by parents; whether parents read to and with their children, and model reading; the overall quality of home life); (e) local community variables (e.g., availability of adequate libraries; levels of school violence; prevalence of illegal drugs and guns; discriminatory attitudes and/or behaviors based on race, gender, handicaps, sexual orientation); (f) societal influences (e.g., national media and economic conditions; funding for remedial and preventive reading programs; city, state and federal legislative policies); and (g) the interactions among and across all of these systems. (Sheridan & Gutkin, 2000)

Of course, a parallel analysis could be developed for social-emotional (e.g., depression, anxiety) and behavioral (e.g., aggression) problems as well.

The central point is that school-based problems always take place within organizational systems, and thus environmentally contextualized analyses are essential (Apter & Conoley, 1984) if we are to diagnose the nature of presenting and potential client problems. The ecological model (Swartz & Martin, 1997) suggests that success in such endeavors will depend largely on our ability to grasp the relevant interactions between individual student characteristics and the environments within which they function. Our understanding must also encompass the mutual and reciprocal interactions that occur among environmental systems and subsystems (homes, classrooms, school district central offices, community agencies) above and beyond the specifics of individual students.

Given the importance of a systems orientation for diagnosis, it should come as no surprise that ecologically oriented thinking is also essential to the design of ameliorative and preventive interventions. It would be naive, for example, to think that problems commonly found in school settings could be remediated without attending to the salient environmental variables surrounding these problems. This is most obvious for academic dysfunction, in which alterations in curriculum, home and school motivational strategies, and teacher behaviors are likely to be needed if student achievement is to be enhanced. Social and behavioral problems, likewise, also require environmental intervention if they are to be treated successfully in school settings. Consider bullying as an example. Given that it is frequently maintained by the responses of those in the environment (e.g., unintentional reinforcement and insufficient punishment provided by teachers, parents, peer supporters, peer victims), it is unlikely that an effective intervention can be fashioned without meaningfully altering a number of environmental variables (Batsche, 1997).

As with the design of treatments for existing problems, an ecological perspective is essential when developing prevention programs. In fact, it is hard to see how prevention could be accomplished effectively in school settings without a substantial focus on an array of environmental manipulations. Whether it be the enhancement of academic performance, the reduction of substance abuse on campus, increases in inclusive programming for handicapped children, or the creation of a school climate that celebrates cultural diversity, it will be necessary to intervene with systemic variables that extend our professional reach far beyond the intrapsychic and internal dynamics of individual students.

### The "Paradox of School Psychology" and Centrality of Consultation Services

The ecological model and our reliance on understanding and intervening with environmental variables in school settings lead inexorably to the conclusion that school-based psychologists must be skillful at changing the behaviors of those adults who populate the worlds of our student clients (e.g., teachers, parents, school administrators). It is precisely these persons, not our student clients themselves, who control and have the power to change relevant environmental systems. Without their support, it seems doubtful that school-based psychologists could be successful at either remediation or preventive intervention (see Deno, 1975, for an interesting case illustration). Gutkin and Conoley (1990) referred to this as the "Paradox of School Psychology." That is, in order to serve children successfully in school settings, psychologists have to be competent first and foremost in working with adults.

The "Paradox of School Psychology" has sweeping implications for the practice of psychology in the schools and the professional competencies that are necessary to succeed in these settings. In particular, it has led many experts in this area to suggest that consultation with teachers, parents, and administrators must be a central job function (Ysseldyke et al., 1997). Rather than relying primarily on serving children directly through psychotherapy and counseling, psychologists are encouraged to provide service indirectly by consulting with the significant adults in children's lives. The "Paradox of School Psychology" suggests that the educational and mental health of our student clients will depend ultimately on the abilities of these adults to structure supportive environments at school and home, while functioning more effectively as parents and teachers. Although psychologists can provide short-term assistance through direct service to children, the long-term outcomes for our clients will typically depend more on the behaviors of those adults who are part of the natural ecologies that surround them.

To date, much has been written about school-based consultation services directed at impacting and changing the behavior of relevant adults as a means of improving the lives of children and youth (see Gutkin & Curtis, 1999, for a recent and extensive literature review). A growing body of empirical research has provided useful insights into the skills necessary to succeed in this role. Much of this knowledge has been captured in the work of Knoff, Hines, and Kromrey (1995), who created and refined the Consultant Effectiveness Scale. Their work suggests that effective school-based consultants are those with highly developed skills in the areas of interpersonal relationships with teachers and other relevant adults, problem solving, consultation processes and applications, and ethical practice.

Although functioning effectively with children and adolescents are obviously critical competencies for school-based psychologists, the "Paradox of School Psychology" suggests that these may often be less critical than the skills needed to work effectively with the adults who affect so strongly the lives of our nonadult clients. Psychologists entering school settings with the assumption that their ability to serve children will be mediated exclusively (or even primarily) by their abilities to work with children are in for a "rude awakening."

## Coping with and Supporting Cultural Diversity

America's schools are truly the crossroads of our nation. Every imaginable strength and weakness, ability and disability will at some point "show its face" in school settings. Psychologists functioning in these environments must thus be prepared to cope with the full range of human diversity and its many expressions. Although it is far beyond the scope of this chapter to address every aspect of this complex topic, the changing demographics of the nation make it is essential to attend, at least briefly, to issues of racial, ethnic, cultural, and linguistic diversity.

As we look forward to the future, it seems clear that children of color will be in the majority in many (or most) school settings in the not-too-distant future (Rogers et al., 1999). If we add to this the long-standing historical reality that ethnic minority children are referred to psychologists in numbers that far exceed their proportion of the population (Andrews, Wisniewski, & Mulick, 1997; Gottlieb, Gottlieb, & Trongone 1991), it seems inevitable that most school-based psychologists will spend much of their time working with an extensive array of culturally diverse students and families. To succeed in this environment, psychologists routinely will need access to a broad continuum of diverse cultural perspectives. To date, however, inadequate attention is being directed toward multiculturalism in our graduate training programs and scientific literature (Henning-Stout & Brown-Cheatham, 1999; Reynolds, 1999; Rogers, Ponterotto, Conoley, & Wiese, 1992). Making matters worse is the extremely narrow range of ethnic diversity among contemporary school-based practitioners (i.e., the overwhelming bulk come from the majority culture, Curtis & Zins, 1989; Fagan, 1993), creating the possibility that a diversity of cultural perspectives will not be available when needed for successful problem solving.

Fortunately, the American Psychological Association Division of School Psychology Task Force on Cross-Cultural School Psychology Competencies recently issued an extensive report addressing skill areas deemed to be essential for those providing psychological services to racially, ethnically, culturally, and linguistically diverse individuals in school settings (Rogers et al., 1999). It addresses the domains of legal and ethical issues; school culture, educational policy, and institutional advocacy; psychoeducational assessment; academic, therapeutic, and consultative interventions; working with interpreters; and research. For each of these domains, general statements of values and best practices are provided (e.g., "psychologists … are aware of the cultural values reflected in the curriculum, communication styles and instructional activities in the classroom and the potential facilitative or detrimental effects that these approaches may have on the learning of culturally diverse students," p. 253) along with extensive lists of specific multicultural competencies (e.g., "psychologists make a continuous effort to consider how the historical and cultural context of any given assessment instrument affects item content and test structure and potentially, test performance," p. 253). The Division of School Psychology Task Force report provides an invaluable "road map" for those functioning as psychologists in contemporary school settings.

Building on psychological theories relating to culture and to ethnic and racial identity, such as those by Helms (1990) and Sue and Sue (1990), Pederson and Ivey (1993) also identified areas of cultural competence that appear to be particularly critical. Three, in particular, emerge from their analyses: (a) cultural awareness, (b) cultural knowledge, and (c) cultural skills. Unlike the work of Rogers et al. (1999), which focused explicitly on schools, Pederson and Ivey developed their view of essential cultural competencies independent of any specific institutional settings. Nonetheless, psychologists working in schools would be wise to attend to the areas delineated by Pederson and Ivey, for they are directly relevant to school-based psychologists.

*Cultural awareness* involves identifying culturally learned assumptions in ourselves and others through an exploration of ethnic identities and cultural backgrounds. This element of Pederson and Ivey's (1993) work suggests that psychologists providing services in schools must understand both their own cultural heritage and those of their clients and other professional staff with whom they interact. *Cultural knowledge* entails increasing one's understanding of particular cultures. It requires psychologists to be able to identify how culture affects basic developmental events such as gender roles, childrearing, and social networks, to name but a few. Obviously, each of these is critical to child and adolescent emotional and educational health, both inside and outside school settings. Finally, *cultural skills* refers to the development and practical application of competencies grounded in appropriate awareness and knowledge. Among the most important of these skills are culturally appropriate interviewing techniques, evaluation of worldviews and level of acculturation, and cultural self-assessment. Interestingly, the emphasis here is not simply on the acquisition of specific and isolated skills, which practitioners frequently learn on a piecemeal basis with increasing years of experience. The point is to develop and maintain a broad awareness of the relevant cultural contexts for the populations with which one works.

With each passing year, the need for well-developed multicultural skills is going to increase. Although the future is usually hard to foretell with anything more than a modicum of accuracy, this prediction is a classic "no-brainer." School-based psychologists lacking refined multicultural competencies will, in the near to intermediate future, be unable to function effectively. Few challenges facing school-based psychologists are of a higher priority, particularly in light of how little most contemporary psychologists (both inside and outside school settings) know about these critical areas of practice.

### Additional Professional Practice Domains and Implications for Training

As suggested by the preceding analyses, the scope of competencies expected of school-based practitioners is expanding dramatically. Although the traditional skills associated with determining special education eligibility of referred students (e.g., assessment, diagnosis, intervention planning, knowledge of national and state special education law) remain critical, it is clear that these are no longer sufficient in and of themselves. As our nation's focus on education and children increases, the potential scope of school-based practice seems to grow exponentially with each passing year. For the purposes of communicating some of the highly diverse activities and professional foci for psychologists working in schools, we list in Table 20.1 a sampling of chapter topics from some of the leading contemporary volumes that delineate the scope of school psychological practice. Although far from exhaustive, this representative list highlights the breadth of contemporary psychological practice in school settings. Complementing and synthesizing this list are the 10 role domains constructed by Ysseldyke et al. (1997) for school-based psychological practice (Table 20.2).

Obviously, training programs hoping to prepare students for the full continuum of school-based psychological practice face a significant challenge. Whether emerging from the areas of school psychology, clinical child psychology, pediatric psychology, or other closely related fields, a wealth of theory building and practicum experiences will be necessary. As per the ecological/systems perspective suggested earlier in this chapter, psychologists will need to develop expertise in areas pertaining to: (a) individual children and youth (e.g., psychopathology, child development, wellness), (b) the systems surrounding children and youth (e.g., school, home, community), and (c) the interactions between individuals and relevant environmental systems. A restricted focus on any one of these areas (or a subset of roles within an area) will likely result in significant gaps of knowledge and competence that will serve school-based psychologists poorly.

## TABLE 20.1
Selected Chapters (Arranged Alphabetically) in Recent Volumes
Addressing School Psychological Practice

### *The Handbook of School Psychology* (3rd ed.)
### (Reynolds & Gutkin, 1999)

Assessing Educational Environments; Assessment of Infants, Toddlers, Preschoolers, and Their
Families; Behavior Analysis; Behavioral Assessment; Child Psychotherapy; Computers in Education;
Curriculum-Based and Performance-Based Assessment; Effective Schools; Effective Teaching;
Intelligence Testing; Intervention Techniques for Academic Performance Problems;
Neuropsychological Assessment; Personality Assessment; Primary Prevention; Program Planning and
Evaluation; Psychopharmacotherapy with School-Aged Children; School-Based Consultation;
Secondary Prevention; Systems Interventions; Working with Teams in Schools

### *Children's Needs II: Development, Problems, and Alternatives*
### (Bear, Minke, & Thomas, 1997)

Adolescent Eating Disorders; Adolescent Pregnancy; Adoption; Aggressive Behavior; Anger;
Anxiety; Attention-Deficit/Hyperactivity Disorder; Brain Injury; Bullying; Cheating; Child Sexual
Abuse; Conduct Disorders; Corporal Punishment; Creativity; Depressive Disorders; Divorce;
Encopresis and Enuresis; English as a Second Language; Ethnic and Racial Diversity; Family–School
Connection; Fears and Phobias; Fire Setting; Giftedness; Grief; Health Promotion; HIV and AIDS;
Homelessness; Homework; Inclusion/Mainstreaming; Learning Strategies; Life Satisfaction;
Loneliness in Childhood; Lying; Parenting; PhysicalAbuse; Play; Reading; School Dropout; School
Phobia; School Readiness; School Violence; Selective Mutism; Self-Concept; Sexual Interest and
Expression; Sexual Minority Youth; Single Parenting and Stepparenting; Sleep Problems; Social
Problem Solving Skills; Sociomoral Reasoning; Sports; Stealing; Stress; Substance Abuse; Suicidal
Ideation; Temper Tantrums; Tic Disorders

### *Best Practices in School Psychology—III*
### (Thomas & Grimes, 1995)

Alternatives to Ability Grouping; Applied Research; Assessing Environmental Factors; Assessment of
Adaptive Behavior; Autism; Bilingual Children; Building-Level Public Relations; Children With
Psychosis; Collaborative Problem Solving; Communicating With Parents; Conducting Needs
Assessments; Crisis Intervention; Culturally Different Families; Developing Local Norms; Evaluating
Educational Outcomes; Facilitating Intervention Adherence; Facilitating Team Functioning; Fostering
School/Community Relationships; Implementing Staff Development Programs; Individual
Counseling; Individualized Education Programs; Interviewing; Observation of Classroom Behavior;
Preschool Screening; School Discipline; School Reintegration; Serving as an Expert Witness; Social
Skills Training; Substance Abuse Prevention; Systems Influences on Children's Self-Concept;
Systems-Level Consultation and Organizational Change; Transition Services; Traumatic Brain Injury;
Vocational Assessment

Students wishing to prepare for a career oriented toward the delivery of psychological services in school settings should consider a number of crucial variables as they plan their educational future. At the undergraduate level it is important to include intensive study in the social
sciences, encompassing (but not limited to) both psychology and education. Given the inter-

## TABLE 20.2
Domains of School-Based Psychological Practice as Suggested by Ysseldyke et al. (1997)

1. Data-based decision making and accountability

2. Interpersonal communication, collaboration, and consultation

3. Effective instruction and development of cognitive/academic skills

4. Socialization and development of life competencies

5. Student diversity in development and learning

6. School structure, organization, and climate

7. Prevention, wellness promotion, and crisis intervention

8. Home/school/community collaboration

9. Research and program evaluation

10. Legal, ethical practice, and professional development

actions hypothesized by the ecological model between one's physiology and one's environment, a strong background in biology should also prove to be very helpful. Above and beyond formal coursework, however, undergraduates would be well advised to gain access to local schools where they can begin developing both practice and research skills. Shadowing school-based psychologists at work would be one viable mechanism for achieving these ends. Assisting faculty and graduate students engaged in school-based research and/or program evaluation projects would be another.

At the graduate level, students should be certain to select training programs that are school focused per se. As discussed earlier, simply learning to work effectively with children and adolescents does not, in and of itself, prepare psychologists sufficiently for practice and research careers in school settings. Stated simply, there is no substitute for supervised school-based experience (and lots of it)! It is also crucial that these experiences be developmental in nature. That is, students should begin early in graduate training to learn discrete but pivotal professional skills (e.g., conducting behavioral observations, administering curriculum-based and norm-referenced assessment measures, interviewing teachers and parents). With each passing year, these competencies should be employed in: (a) response to problems that are increasingly complex and multisystemic in nature, (b) contexts that require expanding circles of cross-disciplinary collaboration, and (c) a manner that progressively emphasizes the interrelationships among psychological theory, empirical research, and professional practice. Given the rapidly expanding roles of school-based psychologists, as summarized in Tables 20.1 and 20.2, graduate students should also give very serious consideration to developing particular areas of specialization and expertise (e.g., early childhood, prevention and wellness, program evaluation, home-school collaboration, consultation, health services, parent training). After deciding on a specific professional focus, it would be most sensible to select coursework, practica, internship, field-based supervisors, and research projects accordingly.

## OUTLOOK

As we move into the 21st century, schools are being viewed by many as the ideal setting within which a full spectrum of psychological and educational services can be provided to children, youth and their families.

> In the past decade a significant consensus has emerged in both national and state-level policy regarding children's health and mental health needs and services calling for the integration of social, psychological, and health services, that is, "one stop shopping," in school-based or school-linked sites. This consensus reflects the opinion of over twenty-five major reports from diverse public and private sources,... documenting the interrelatedness of children's health status and their educational experiences, and the need for customer-oriented, accessible services to children and their families. (Carlson, Paavola, & Talley, 1995, p. 184)

It is our prediction that these trends are going to continue and, in fact, accelerate. Training to function as a psychologist within school and educational environments is going to become more and more central to the professional practice of more and more psychologists. Shifts in service delivery models and training programs will be necessary if the field of psychology is to accommodate these changes in the ecology of contemporary service provision.

## REFERENCES

American Psychiatric Association. (1994). *Diagnostic and statistical manual of mental disorders* (4th ed.). Washington, DC: Author.

American Psychological Association. (1995). *School health: Psychology's role*. Washington, DC: Author.

Andrews, T. J., Wisniewski, J. J., & Mulick, J. A. (1997). Variables influencing teachers' decisions to refer children for school psychological assessment services. *Psychology in the Schools, 34*, 239–244.

Apter, S. J., & Conoley, J. C. (1984). *Childhood behavior disorders and emotional disturbance: An introduction to teaching troubled children*. Englewood Cliffs, NJ: Prentice Hall.

Batsche, G. M. (1997). Bullying. In G. G. Bear, K. M. Minke, & A. Thomas (Eds.), *Children's needs II: Development, problems and alternatives* (pp. 171–179). Bethesda, MD: National Association of School Psychologists.

Bear, G. G., Minke, K. M., & Thomas, A. (Eds.). (1997). *Children's needs II: Development, problems, and alternatives*. Bethesda, MD: National Association of School Psychologists.

Carlson, C., Paavola, J., & Talley, R. (1995). Historical, current, and future models of schools as health care delivery settings. *School Psychology Quarterly, 10*, 184–202.

Curtis, M. J., & Zins, J. E. (1989). Trends in training and accreditation. *School Psychology Review, 18*, 182–192.

Deno, S. (1975). Brad and Ms. E.: A consulting problem in which student behavior change is the focus. In C. A. Parker (Ed.), *Psychological consultation: Helping teachers meet special needs* (pp. 11–16). Reston, VA: Council for Exceptional Children.

Fagan, T. K. (1993). Separate but equal: School psychology's search for organizational identity. *Journal of School Psychology, 31*, 3–90.

Gottlieb, J., Gottlieb, B. W., & Trongone, S. (1991). Parent and teacher referrals for a psychoeducational evaluation. *Journal of Special Education, 25*, 155–167.

Gutkin, T. B., & Conoley, J. C. (1990). Reconceptualizing school psychology from a service delivery perspective: Implications for practice, training, and research. *Journal of School Psychology, 28*, 203–223.

Gutkin, T. B., & Curtis, M. J. (1999). School-based consultation theory and practice: The art and science of indirect service delivery. In C. R. Reynolds & T. B. Gutkin (Eds.), *The handbook of school psychology* (3rd ed.) (pp. 598–637). New York: Wiley.

Helms, J. E. (Ed.). (1990). *Black and White racial identity: Theory, research, and practice.* New York: Greenwood Press.

Henning-Stout, M., & Brown-Cheatham, M. (1999). School psychology in a diverse world: Considerations for practice, research, and training. In C. R. Reynolds & T. B. Gutkin (Eds.), *The handbook of school psychology* (3rd ed., pp. 1041–1055). New York: Wiley.

Knoff, H. M., Hines, C. V., & Kromrey, J. D. (1995). Finalizing the consultant effectiveness scale: An analysis and validation of the characteristics of effective consultation. *School Psychology Review, 24*, 480–496.

Lentz, F. E., Jr., Allen, S. J., & Ehrhardt, K. E. (1996). The conceptual elements of strong interventions in school settings. *School Psychology Quarterly, 11*, 118–136.

Martens, B. K., & Witt, J. C. (1988). Expanding the scope of behavioral consultation: A systems approach to classroom behavior change. *Professional School Psychology, 3*, 271–281.

Merrett, F., & Wheldall, K. (1993). How do teachers learn to manage classroom behaviour? A study of teachers' opinions about their initial training with special reference to classroom behaviour management. *Educational Studies, 19*, 91–106.

Meyers, J., & Nastasi, B. (1999). Primary prevention in school settings. In C. R. Reynolds & T. B. Gutkin (Eds.), *The handbook of school psychology* (3rd ed., pp. 764–799). New York: Wiley.

Pederson, P. B., & Ivey, A. (1993). *Culture-centered counseling and interviewing skills: A practical guide.* Westport, CT: Praeger.

Prout, S. M., & Prout, H. T. (1998). A meta-analysis of school-based studies of counseling and psychotherapy: An update. *Journal of School Psychology, 36*, 121–136.

Reynolds, A. (1999). Working with children and adolescents in the schools: Multicultural counseling implications. In R. Hernadez-Sheets & E. Hollins (Eds.), *Racial & ethnic identity in school practices: Aspects of human development* (pp. 213–229). Mahwah, NJ: Lawrence Erlbaum Associates.

Reynolds, C. R., & Gutkin, T. B. (Eds.). (1999). *The handbook of school psychology* (3rd ed.). New York: Wiley.

Riley, R. W., & Shalala, D. E. (1992). Joint statement on school health. *Journal of School Health, 64*(4), 135.

Rogers, M. R., Ingraham, C. L., Bursztyn, A., Cajigas-Segredo, N., Esquivel, G., Hess, R., Nahari, S. G., & Lopez, E. C. (1999). Providing psychological services to racially, ethnically, culturally, and linguistically diverse individuals in the schools. *School Psychology International, 20*, 243–264.

Rogers, M. R., Ponterotto, J. G., Conoley, J. C., & Wiese, M. J. (1992). Multicultural training in school psychology: A national survey. *School Psychology Review, 21*, 603–616.

Sarason, S. B. (1971). *The culture of the school and the problem of change.* Boston: Allyn & Bacon.

Sarason, S. B. (1995). *School change: The personal development of a point of view.* New York: Teachers College Press.

Sheridan, S. M., & Gutkin, T. B. (2000). The ecology of school psychology: Examining and changing our paradigm for the 21st century. School Psychology Review, 29, 485–502.

Stickel, S. A., Satchwell, K. M., & Meyer, E. C. (1991). The school counselor and discipline: A three-state survey. *School Counselor, 39*, 111–115.

Sue, D. W., & Sue, D. (1990). *Counseling the culturally different: Theory and practice* (2nd ed.). New York: Wiley.

Swartz, J. L., & Martin, W. E., Jr. (Eds.). (1997). *Applied ecological psychology for schools within communities: Assessment and intervention.* Mahwah, NJ: Lawrence Erlbaum Associates.

Thomas, A., & Grimes, J. (1995). *Best practices in school psychology—III.* Washington, DC: National Association of School Psychologists.

Ysseldyke, J., Dawson, P., Lehr, C., Reschly, D., Reynolds, M., & Telzrow, C. (1997). *School psychology: A blueprint for training and practice II.* Bethesda, MD: National Association of School Psychologists.

# 21

# Preparing for a Career in Psychology Outside the University

*Raymond S. Nickerson*

This chapter focuses on the question of how to use one's school years effectively to prepare for a career in psychology outside of academia. It is addressed primarily to students who are considering a career as something other than a clinical psychologist and in a setting such as industry or government. I limit my remarks to people preparing for a nonclinical career because I have no direct experience in the clinical area. Of course, much of the advice one might give to students who are preparing for a nonacademic, nonclinical career may pertain to those preparing for an academic or clinical career as well; if students in the latter categories find anything useful in the chapter, so much the better, but in making the following comments, I have primarily those in the former category in mind.

What I offer is personal opinion formed, for the most part, by my own experience as a researcher and manager outside the academic world. Perhaps I need to explain "for the most part." Most of my career as a psychologist was spent with two organizations—7 years with a U.S. Air Force research laboratory (in the Electronic Systems Division at Hanscom Field, Bedford, MA) and 25 years with Bolt Beranek and Newman Inc (BBN, a research and development company in Cambridge, MA). Although this work history pegs me as a nonacademic, I need to confess a feeling of greater affinity with the academic world than it might suggest. During several of the early years at BBN I taught classes at Tufts University and in industrial and government installations as part of my job. Throughout my career, I have participated in many of the activities that are common to academic life—reviewing journal manuscripts, editing books and journals, serving on PhD committees, reviewing grant or contract proposals for research organizations, and publishing research papers. I say this to make the point that, although I am accurately classified as a nonacademic, my view of the world may have more in common with that of an academic than would that of many psychologists who work in industry or in other contexts outside the university.

Although this book is addressed mainly to graduate students, some of the comments in this chapter pertain to undergraduate students as well, or even to students who are still looking ahead to their college days. I describe the skills, knowledge, attitudes, and habits that are important, in my view, in the workplace outside the university, or at least in the workplaces with which I am at all familiar. I hope to convince you that the acquisition of these capabilities and qualities should be a high priority objective of your education. Some of the components of the package take a long time to acquire, and the earlier in your educational experience you begin to work on them, the better.

## NONACADEMIC CAREERS IN PSYCHOLOGY

There are many opportunities for psychologists in the nonacademic world. As of the mid-1980s, only about one-third of all psychologists were employed by colleges and universities (Super & Super, 1988), and those who were in nonacademic positions were employed by hospitals and clinics (23%), in private clinical practice (18%), in public school systems (15%), in business and industry (4%), or in government positions (4%). Of the community of human-factors specialists, which is composed largely of people trained as experimental or industrial psychologists and who work primarily on applied problems, a large majority (85% to 90%) worked either for private industry or for the government (Van Cott & Huey, 1992).

Major industrial employers of psychologists include large corporations that build and sell consumer goods and services, developers of aerospace and defense systems, and research organizations. Government entities that employ psychologists in significant numbers in other than clinical roles include the Department of Defense and the various branches of the military, other departments of the executive branch that sponsor research involving people (e.g., the Department of Education, the Department of Health and Human Services, the Department of Transportation), and many of the regulatory and administrative agencies.

According to the survey reported by Van Cott and Huey (1992), six major areas accounted for about 83% of human-factors work: computers (22.3%), aerospace (21.6%), industrial processes (16.5%), health and safety (8.9%), communications (8.2%), and transportation (5.3%). Numerous other areas accounted for the remaining 17%. Regarding what psychologists in industry and government do on a day-to-day basis, a partial list would include research (mostly applied), design (of systems, devices and procedures), evaluation (of systems and devices for safety and usability), and personnel services (testing, counseling, placement, training, and development). More extensive representations of opportunities provided by the fields of applied experimental and engineering psychology, as I see them, may be found in Nickerson (1997, 1998, 1999).

Psychologists doing research in industrial or government organizations work on an extraordinarily diverse array of problems. They design and evaluate displays for use in airplane cockpits, on ship bridges, in power plant control rooms, and on personal computer interfaces; they help develop standards for the design of information displays for use in international contexts; they work on improving the safety of home appliances, toys, and children's furniture; they investigate potential applications of technology to education and training; they look for causes of risk-taking behavior of various types (smoking, driving while drinking, sun-baking); they try to understand the determinants of human error that often result in costly accidents (Chernobyl, Three Mile Island, Bophal, the Exxon Valdez); they study how people perform under extreme or stressful conditions (such as can be encountered in space flight, submarine duty, or arctic exploration)—and these are but a few of the ways in which researchers spend their time.

Many psychologists find their way into positions of management. Managers tend to be selected more on the basis of leadership abilities they have demonstrated in their job performance than on the basis of the area in which they received their academic training. Generally speaking, there are two types of management roles in industry: project management and line management. Project managers are selected to lead specific projects, or components of projects. Typically, this means leading a team that has been assembled for the purpose of accomplishing a specific goal. When the goal is accomplished—the project completed—the team may be disbanded and its members moved on to other assignments. People who have demonstrated their ability to lead projects effectively may move from one project-management position to another, or from project management into a line management position.

Line managers usually head an organizational component—department, division, corporate subsidiary—that is likely to have a longer life than a project. Often, line managers gain their initial managerial experience as project managers, and are appointed to their line positions only after having demonstrated their competence for the role. There are exceptions to all such rules, of course, but unless your parent owns the business, you cannot reasonably aspire to a position with significant managerial responsibility in industry until you have produced some fairly compelling evidence that you are likely to be able to discharge that responsibility effectively. Even if your parent owns the business, he or she may be unlikely to turn it, or a significant portion of it, over to the next generation in the absence of some demonstrated managerial competence in less-than-critical positions.

Again, generally speaking, effective managers have to have a variety of skills and knowledge, some of which can be learned in conventional courses, but some of which must be acquired, or sharpened, through out-of-class experiences. If you hope eventually to assume leadership or management roles in your profession, there is much you can do, both in class and out, during your student days that should help you to realize that goal.

## SOME SUGGESTIONS

There are several suggestions that I wish someone had made to me—and that I had followed—when I was a student. But before indicating what they are, two general points. First, there is much debate in the educational research literature regarding the relative importance of acquiring knowledge in conventional academic domains (mathematics, science, history, languages) and that of learning to think. I like to believe that this is not an either/or choice and have argued elsewhere (Nickerson, 1988) that the goal of education should be to produce people who are knowers, thinkers, and learners. Being well educated means having a lot of factual knowledge, being able to think well (reflectively and pragmatically), and being committed to continued learning. I hope this point of view is evident in what follows. Second, the quality of the teaching you encounter and of the other resources on which you draw during your school days can make the job of preparing for life after college easier or more difficult, but the task of learning is yours. In the final analysis, you are the one who is responsible for your education. You have the most to gain from ensuring that it is as good as it can be, and the most to lose from not doing so.

## Focus First on the Basics

It is perhaps a bit heretical, but when asked, I have recommended to undergraduates who intend to get a graduate degree in psychology that they not take a lot of psychology courses beyond an introductory course or two during their undergraduate days. There is plenty of opportunity to specialize in graduate school. What one wants from an undergraduate education is a *foundation* on which to build a profession. In my view, this means developing skill in the basics of communication (listening, reading, speaking, writing) as well as acquiring a fair amount of the kind of knowledge (history, literature, general science) that any well-educated individual might be assumed to have.

Make the mastery of English (or whatever your language of use is to be) a high priority in your education, and the earlier you recognize the importance of this, the better. The ability to express oneself clearly, both orally and in writing, is critical. Unhappily, many students get through college without acquiring an adequate grounding in basic communication skills. In my experience, the inability to write clear, grammatically correct, expository prose is exceedingly common among technically trained professionals, and it is a severe handicap; a surprising number of people complete a PhD program without learning how to express themselves well in writing. Limitations in this area become excruciatingly apparent when people are required to contribute to the writing of technical reports, proposals, letters, memos, or other documents essential to their work.

Learn how to speak to a group—to give talks that are not only comprehensible and informative, but also interesting. The ability to speak well before a group is likely to be an asset to almost anyone, but I think it especially important to one who anticipates a career as a psychologist in industry—it is a rare psychologist in industry who is not called on to speak to a group from time to time; many have to do it often. Skill in speaking not only works to the benefit of the speaker, but is much appreciated by listeners as well. A skillful speaker can make the most mundane of subjects interesting, and intrinsically fascinating topics can be made intolerably boring by an unskilled one.

Unquestionably, public speaking comes more easily to some people than to others, but I believe that, to a large extent, it is also an acquirable skill. And like any other complex skill, mastery of it requires study—learning of fundamental principles—and much practice. Competent coaching and critical feedback can be invaluable. The critical feedback is important because it is essential to skill development (if hard on the ego) to see and hear oneself as one appears and sounds to one's listeners. Without this kind of feedback it is much too easy to overestimate the importance of what one has to say and the clarity with which one says it. If your university offers instruction in public speaking, seriously consider availing yourself of it. Participation in a Toastmaster club may also be a suitable option. Finding a way to get a public speaking experience during school days, especially in situations that provide critical feedback, will pay handsome dividends in postschool life.

## Get a Solid Grounding in Science, Mathematics, and the Liberal Arts

I would argue for a solid grounding in science, math, and the liberal arts for almost anyone, irrespective of the field one is preparing to enter, because I believe that such a grounding is good preparation for any field, and, perhaps more importantly, that it can contribute immeasurably to one's ability to find life interesting and full. It is especially important, I believe, for anyone preparing for a career as a psychologist. Psychology is a science, and to understand it as such one must see how it relates to the other sciences and to scientific methods, many of which involve mathematics to a nontrivial degree.

An area of mathematics that deserves special attention from the psychology student is probability theory. One reason for emphasizing this is the critical role that statistics has played—and does play—in the evaluation of experimental data, from which most of our knowledge of psychology derives. Many researchers who routinely use statistical methods in their work do not have a deep understanding of the mathematical foundations of the methods they use. This is unfortunate and it impedes progress in the field. There is no easy way to acquire the deep understanding to which I refer, it requires study—a nontrivial amount of study—of the relevant mathematics, the primary component of which is probability theory. I do not have in mind, in this comment, the limited exposure to probability theory that one is likely to get in a typical textbook on statistical methods for psychologists, bur rather the kind of treatment one can expect in a course taught by a probabilist in a university mathematics department. It may be that relatively few psychology majors would be prepared to devote the time necessary to make this excursion into the world of mathematics (some may lack the elementary mathematical background that would make such an excursion feasible), but I believe that those who can devote the time to this pursuit, and do so, will find it time well spent.

There are other reasons for recommending some study of probability theory that apply to anyone who is seeking a broad and useful education. Probability theory is the area of mathematics that deals with uncertain situations—situations that are known only statistically or probabilistically. Many, if not most, of the important decisions that we find ourselves making throughout life must be made in the face of uncertainty about their outcomes, and an understanding of probability theory is useful in dealing with them. Such an understanding can be helpful too in assessing the plausibility of the various claims that one encounters from the media and elsewhere on a daily basis. Even a rudimentary familiarity with probability theory would provide a basis for dismissing as bogus many of the purported results of "scientific" comparisons between consumer products that are encountered in advertisements; a deeper understanding of probability theory gives one a rational means of distinguishing events that require a cause–effect explanation from those that could plausibly be attributed to chance.

I include a good grounding in the liberal arts as important to one's preparation for a career in psychology because one's grasp of the field would be limited indeed without an appreciation of the contributions of philosophy, literature, and the humanities generally to an understanding of human nature and human experience. The more compelling reason for emphasizing the liberal arts, however, is the belief that they are basic to any well-rounded education. When I recommend getting a good grounding in the liberal arts, I have in mind substantive demanding courses that require wide reading, research, critical thinking and writing on the part of the student. Any student who is serious about getting an education should avoid fluff courses like the plague.

## Get a Good Grasp of the Area in Which You Hope to Specialize

If you know that you want to work as a psychologist in a specific problem area—aviation, consumer products, medicine, highway safety, nuclear power plant design—you should try to get a reasonable grounding in that area, as well as in psychology. The chances are that you will find yourself collaborating with experts in the problem area and, although your job will be to bring psychological know-how to bear on the problem, your ability to communicate effectively and to command the respect of the domain specialists is likely to depend to a nontrivial degree on how well you can see and comprehend the problem from their point of view. Attempting to provide helpful advice to experts in the absence of a good grasp of the technical dimensions of a complex problem runs the risk of appearing (or being) naive and/or presumptuous. The *sine qua non* of an effective member of a problem-solving team is credibility with one's fellow team members, and there is no faster way to destroy it than to display a lack of understanding of the nature of the problem at hand.

I realize that one may not know as a student—at least not until late in one's student days—in precisely what problem area one would like eventually to work. Also, it often happens that people find themselves working in problem areas other than those for which they had prepared. In such cases, it is important to acknowledge one's lack of background—to not pretend to have knowledge one does not have—and to make a concerted effort to get the knowledge needed in order to make the contribution desired. The relatively high likelihood of sometimes finding oneself with a task for which one does not feel entirely adequately trained is one of the reasons for the next point regarding the importance of developing—during student days—good learning skills and a commitment to learning continuously on the job.

## Learn How to Learn and Make Learning a Lifelong Commitment

For some years now, the most striking characteristic of many job situations has been the rapidity with which their requirements change. That seems likely to remain true for the foreseeable future. Technology not only has been transforming the ways in which many tasks are performed, it has been—and is—making some tasks obsolete while creating others that could not have been performed a relatively short time ago. Rapid job obsolescence and the frequent need for retraining, largely due to advances in technology, are facts of life for increasing numbers of people in the workforce (Dentzer, 1989). One should think of one's college and graduate school experiences as steps (enormously important steps, but still only steps) in a lifelong learning process. There are many good reasons for taking this perspective beyond helping to ensure one's success at work, but the prospects of having to accommodate change in the workplace is a practical incentive of considerable weight. The person who views the acquisition of a degree, at any level, as the culmination of his or her education is destined for an unduly limited and perhaps stagnant career.

An effective way to prepare for rapidly changing job requirements is to do what one can to learn how to learn—to emerge from one's formal educational experience not only having learned quite a bit, but, more importantly, prepared and eager to learn a lot more. Ideas and suggestions regarding how to enhance one's ability to learn can be found in self-help books (Hartley, 1998; Kornhauser, 1924/1993; Race, 1992), and collections of reports and critical reviews of structured approaches to self-directed learning (O'Neil, 1978; Pintrich, 1995). Learning how to learn involves the development of self-discipline and good study habits. Learning requires study and study takes time. If not managed effectively, time has a way of evaporating, leaving no trace of accomplishment I personally believe strongly in the importance, for most of us, of establishing and adhering to—not slavishly, but conscientiously—a routine in which time is reserved for study on a regular basis.

An important aspect of learning how to learn is learning how to find information—to use information tools and resources effectively. At one time not long ago this meant learning to use indexes, almanacs, fact books, encyclopedias, and reference books of various sorts. Today, it means also being a competent user of electronic databases. An increasing variety of jobs require the use of computers and computer-based information resources. Of course, computer facilities have been becoming more and more widely used in schools at all levels, so most recent college graduates and certainly future graduates are likely to have had considerable experience as users of computer-based information resources by the time they graduate. But there are great differences in the efficiency and effectiveness with which people use this technology. It offers extraordinarily powerful tools for the performance of intellectually demanding tasks—information finding, composition, editing, mathematical computation and data analysis, illustration and figure drawing, among others. It offers also, however, a host of diversions, countless ways to kill time, and some dangers. It can be an enormous aid to one's productivity and contribute positively to the quality of one's work and life, but it can also be a time sink, and worse, if not managed skillfully and in a way that is consistent with one's basic values.

As we are constantly reminded, the Internet—and especially the access it provides to the World Wide Web—has rapidly become a major source of information of every conceivable kind. Learning to use this resource effectively and efficiently to constructive purposes is an increasingly important thing to do. The chances are good that you will use the Internet, either from necessity or preference, in your work after graduation, so the greater the mastery you gain of it (as distinct from it gaining mastery of you) as a student, the better.

## Discover Your Own Strengths and Weaknesses

We all have strengths and weaknesses. One who has an accurate perception of one's own is in a good position to exploit the former and to rectify or work around the latter. Justified confidence in one's abilities is an asset in the workplace, but believing oneself to have strengths one does not have can be the source of trouble. Confidence should be commensurate with ability, but it will not be so if one has a distorted view of what one can and cannot do.

Learn to estimate accurately how long it will take you to do specific tasks. People generally are not good at this. Underestimating task completion time—overestimating how much one can accomplish in a given time—appears to be a nearly universal human failing. There is good experimental evidence of this if own needs it (Buehler, Griffin, & Ross, 1994; Hayes-Roth & Hayes-Roth, 1979; Kidd, 1970), but I suspect that few of us need convincing that it is true of us individually. This is a failing that is worth considerable effort to correct if one aspires to work as a psychologist in a nonacademic setting. Deadlines are common in the industrial world, and missing them—especially after giving assurances of being able to meet them—can be costly.

I wish I could point to a tried-and-true approach to acquiring this skill, but I cannot. However, recognizing both the importance of making accurate estimates and the fact that people are generally not good at doing this is a step in the right direction. My suggestion is that you develop the habit of explicitly estimating how long it will take to complete specific nontrivial tasks and check to see how accurate those estimates turn out to be. I cannot guarantee that this will work perfectly, but all we know about the role of feedback in learning suggests it should.

## Develop Self-Management and Self-Evaluation Skills

In the final analysis, each of us is the one who has primary responsibility for his or her own education. Some schools are better than others; some teachers are better than others. But a motivated, disciplined student can learn from any environment, either with the help of effective mentors or despite the lack of them. Unquestionably, it is harder in the latter case, but universities have many resources on which the self-motivated student can draw. Learn how to budget time effectively, how to prioritize and to allocate your resources in a way that is consistent with those priorities, and how to evaluate your own performance and growth in objective terms. Self-management and self-evaluation skills will be especially useful in helping you continue to learn after graduation, the importance of which, because of the rapidity with which technology and job requirements are changing, has already been stressed.

## Learn Problem-Solving Skills

Being a good problem-solver in a specific domain requires knowing a lot about that domain. One cannot be a good solver of automotive problems unless one knows a lot about automobiles, and the same principle holds for electrical problems, plumbing problems, problems in nuclear physics, problems in biochemistry, and problems in psychology. There are, however, a number of approaches to problem solving that can be applied effectively more or less independently of domain. These approaches are sometimes referred to as problem-solving heuristic strategies, or simply heuristics. Examples include finding a way to represent a problem pictorially or graphically; breaking a problem down into manageable parts; finding a problem that is analogous to the one that has to be solved but that is simpler or that has a known solution; and rephrasing a problem by stating it in a more concrete or specific, or more abstract or general, or more extreme form. These and other heuristics are discussed in many books that offer help in improving one's own problem-solving skills (Adams, 1974; Bransford & Stein, 1984; Hayes, 1989; Schoenfeld, 1985; Whimbey & Lochhead, 1982; Wickelgren, 1974). One can find a variety of opinions in the literature on problem solving regarding the effectiveness of such heuristics. My own experience is that they can be quite useful; I believe that familiarizing oneself with them and practicing applying them is likely to prove to be a beneficial investment of time.

## Make Some Headway on Becoming an Interesting, Well-Educated Person

I say, "make some headway" because I believe that becoming an interesting, well-educated person is a lifelong process that, ideally, begins long before college days and continues indefinitely. For most people who attend college, however, undergraduate school provides an opportunity for broad intellectual development that is richer in possibilities than is anything they are likely to experience in later life. Failure to seize this opportunity is a tragedy.

I do not subscribe to the view that the main reason for getting a good education is because doing so increases one's options for employment or one's chances of making a lot of money. I believe that education has intrinsic rewards that are not measurable in monetary terms—that it enriches life in countless ways, whatever one does to make one's living. That being said, I want to argue too that a solid, broad education is an asset of great value in the workplace, and that broadly educated individuals are likely to have opportunities that would be less open to them if their knowledge and interests were more narrow and confined.

It is sometimes argued that one must make a choice between breadth and depth of learning. The idea is that one can be a generalist who knows a little about many things or a specialist who knows a lot about one thing, but that one cannot learn a lot about many things because there is simply not time enough to do so. The idea clearly has some merit; however, I believe that the dichotomy implied by the preceding sentence is a false one and that there are many possibilities between the extremes mentioned. A person of considerable achievement and for whom I have great respect once described his lifelong ambition as that of becoming "a jack of all trades and master of one." He was indeed a man of many talents and accomplishments in a variety of areas (scientific, artistic, and in the business world), but, as a scientist, he was keen to be at the cutting edge of his scientific specialty. What struck me especially about him was that he seemed to be genuinely interested in everything, and, perhaps for that reason, he was himself an exceptionally interesting person.

Probably most of us know people who are somewhat like this. My guess is that such people tend not only to do very well in life, but get a great deal of enjoyment in the process. For present purposes, the point I want to make is that having a broad education does not preclude being an expert in some area, and conversely it is not necessary that expertise be obtained at the expense of ignoring everything outside one's narrow domain of interest. The world of industry needs people who have both breadth and depth of learning.

## Learn How to Collaborate—to Work Well on a Team

Most jobs in industry require teamwork. Interpersonal skills generally are valuable assets in the workplace. Learning to collaborate effectively means learning to see and appreciate others' points of view (perspective-taking), to respect others' skills and contributions to collaborative efforts. Perspective-taking is not always easy, but it is a skill that can be developed if one is willing to work at it. By learning to appreciate others' points of view, I do not mean learning how to feign such appreciation, but learning how genuinely to understand and value what others bring to a collaborative effort Learn how to disagree agreeably—and not to aggravate—when disagreement is necessary. Learn how to negotiate and facilitate. Effective team members enhance the productivity of their teams and contribute positively to the continuing development of teammates in doing so. In industry, there is little room for abrasive *prima donnas*, no matter how technically competent they are; co-workers are simply not willing to put up with them. People who are able to motivate others and to help them do their best work are very important to corporations and to their colleagues as well.

Although one can get some idea from books of how important working well as a member of a team is considered to be (Rees, 1997), the skill is best acquired from experience. There should be many opportunities in school life to get such experience; but to improve one's collaborative skills one needs to pay attention to the feedback one gets from teammates. It is very easy to misjudge one's contribution to a team effort; research has shown, for example, that we tend to remember better our own contributions to a group effort than the contributions of other members of the group, and therefore are likely to exaggerate the relative size of our own contributions (Johnston, 1976; Ross & Sicoly, 1979). How well one performs as a team member is likely to be reflected fairly clearly in the reactions of one's teammates, however, so if one wants to get an objective view so as better to make improvements, one needs to attend carefully to those reactions.

## Learn What You Can About Employment Possibilities

I strongly urge that if you intend to make a career as a psychologist in industry, or if you are considering the possibility of doing so, you make every effort to familiarize yourself with the opportunities that exist and what those that appeal to you entail in the work world. This means going considerably beyond reading promotional brochures. It means taking the initiative and doing some digging. But the time and effort will have been well spent. Too many people discover, after taking a job and working at it for a while, that they do not enjoy what they are doing. This is unfortunate, the more so because in many cases the surprise could have been prevented with some investigation of the workplace during student days.

As you get near enough to the end of your formal training to begin thinking seriously about specific job situations, you may want to consult a variety of sources of information about employment opportunities for nonclinical psychologists outside the academic world such as Woods (1976, 1987, 1988), Super and Super (1988), Van Cott and Huey (1992) and Sternberg (1997). These publications contain information about career opportunities for psychologists outside the university, about what is needed by way of preparation for these careers, and pointers to sources of additional information. The most recent of these books, edited by Sternberg (1997), contains chapters on school psychology, consumer psychology, human factors and ergonomics, military psychology, counseling, and health psychology, among other topics.

Advertisements of position openings appear in the monthly *Human Factors and Ergonomics Society Bulletin*. Companies that employ psychologists often have brochures describing job opportunities that they will supply, perhaps along with other information, on request. (The companies that are sponsors of the Human Factors and Ergonomic Society, are listed on the back cover of *Human Factors and Ergonomics* and are good prospects from which to seek information.) The World Wide Web can be a major source of information while you are a student regarding various professional options you may be considering, and it can be useful in identifying specific job opportunities when you begin exploring them. Checking the recruiting booths at annual conferences of the American Psychological Association, the American Psychological Society and the Human Factors and Ergonomics Society is a good idea.

## Get Real-World Experience

Getting experience in the world of work while still a student is desirable for at least a couple of reasons. Experience in a job situation that is similar to one that you believe you might seek after graduation is especially useful because it is difficult to get an accurate understanding of what a particular work situation will be like simply by reading about it. Being in the situation, if only to observe others doing the kind of job you think you would like eventually to do, provides one with a firsthand understanding of how the work day goes. It is the best way to discover whether this is how you want to spend your work time after leaving school. Getting a part-time or temporary (e.g., summer) job in your field of interest is not always easy to do. In some fields, such jobs may be scarce and hard to land. If it is impossible to land a paying job, volunteer work may be a possibility.

The usefulness of job experience in your field of interest is obvious. Perhaps less obvious is the desirability of experience in job situations that have little to do with how you aspire to make a living after graduate school days. Broad work experience during your youth can be a primary source of some of the most valuable lessons you can learn in preparation for post-college life. By broad work experience, I mean to include experience in entry-level jobs and/or "unskilled labor" jobs that you would not necessarily choose to remain in indefinitely if you had a choice. In retrospect, I value my own experience in such jobs during high school and college days immensely. I firmly believe that one can learn lessons and acquire attitudes as a consequence of experience in the workplace that will prove to be invaluable in later life and that are difficult, perhaps impossible, to get from the classroom.

## Communicate with People Doing Work You Think You Would Like to Do

Gaining on-the-job experience may not be feasible. There are other ways to learn about what various jobs of potential interest entail. One is to communicate with people who are already doing those jobs. As a general rule, professors have not had extensive experience working in industry. This is not a criticism, just a statement of fact. It follows that much or their knowledge of industrial settings is necessarily secondhand. This is not to suggest that the knowledge they have is inaccurate, but only that it is bound to be limited; one who has not actually worked in a particular setting is not going to understand what it is like to do so as well as one who has had that experience. The academic world and the world of industry are rather different in many respects; if you really want to learn what specific industrial job situations are like, people who are currently in those situations are about as good a source of information as you are likely to find.

## Attend Conferences

There are several professional associations that many psychologists in industry join. Most notable among them in the United States are the American Psychological Association, the American Psychological Society, and the Human Factors and Ergonomics Society. All of these associations have student memberships. Each has an annual meeting that is well publicized in association literature (newsletters and journals) and encourages student participation. Some also have regional, local, or student chapters that sponsor events.

Affiliation with such an organization—and a local or student chapter of it—can provide a good source of information about what is currently happening in a field of interest and especially about job opportunities. The national associations typically publish information about job possibilities in their newsletters and provide opportunities for interviews with representatives of employers at their annual meetings. Annual meetings and conferences sponsored by these associations give one chances to learn, both by attending paper sessions and by interacting with individuals, about the kind of work currently being done in various research organizations within and outside the academy and about opportunities that are likely to exist in the future. They also represent excellent opportunities to get experience speaking before groups, composed of other than one's classmates, by participating in paper-presentation sessions.

## Read Informative Journals and Trade Magazines

Whatever your interests, there are probably a few professional journals and/or trade magazines that speak to them to one or another degree. Familiarize yourself with these journals and magazines, determine which (few) of them provide information that matches your interests well, and make it a habit to scan them when they arrive in the library. The mainstream journals that publish research in psychology and on specific topic areas within psychology—aviation psychology, psychology and law, health psychology, counseling, psychology and aging, educational psychology—are numerous. For articles that are expressly written more for general audiences than for specialists, and that will provide a good indication of research areas that are especially active at any given time, one should scan such publications as *American Psychologist*, *Psychological Science*, *Current Directions in Psychological Science*, *Educational Researcher*, and *Ergonomics in Design*.

## Consider Lifestyle Issues in Job Hunting

As a rule, psychologists do not do a lot of heavy lifting; there are exceptions, but in general they tend to have rather sedentary jobs. I mention this because, in my case, this was an issue that I had not anticipated. As a young person, I was physically active—more interested in sports than in scholastics, by far. The jobs I had while in high school and college were, in most cases, physically demanding jobs. I enjoyed physical work, took pride in it, and got a great deal of satisfaction from being in good physical condition. But I took all this for granted—gave it very little thought.

My first full-time job after graduating from college was as the athletic director and basketball coach for a small college. This was perfect for someone who enjoyed physical activity. This job did not last long; I had not quite finished my first year when I was notified by my draft board that the U.S. Army was desirous of my services for a couple of years. The Army was not where I would have elected to be, given a choice in the matter, but I was not given a choice, and it did provide opportunities for plenty of physical exercise.

Fast-forward a few years—completion of the Army tour of duty, graduate school, and a job as a research psychologist in a U.S. Air Force laboratory. The job was great—an opportunity to do research with some people who had been at it a long time and from whom I stood to learn much. I liked it a lot, but was not in it long before I had acquired 30 to 40 pounds that I did not need and had lost much of the feeling of physical well-being that I had taken for granted.

After a year or so of feeling not sick, but not really well, it began to dawn on me that my lifestyle had changed radically insofar as physical activity was concerned. I was getting far less regular exercise than I had habitually gotten before becoming a professional and I realized that this could be the reason for my sub-par feeling. I started then to jog regularly, took off the excess weight, and felt sufficiently better that for me jogging became a compulsion that I have indulged now for about 35 years.

The moral of this story is that life changes in many ways when one goes from being a student to being a full-time employee. Some of these changes are predictable; some may come as a surprise. It is good to try to minimize the surprises, I think.

## Put Your Formal Education in Perspective

A degree from a good school, high grades, some successful work experience; solid recommendations from professors, employers, and others, and a favorable impression by interviewers—such things will help you get a job. But they will not help you to keep it or to advance. Once in the door and on the payroll, performance is what matters. No one will remember, or care, that you got a 4.0 average and graduated at the top of your class from a prestigious school when it comes time to decide whether you are to get a raise, or a promotion, or whether you are to be retained when it is necessary to reduce the size of the staff. What will be remembered is how effective you have been in helping to get projects done well and on time. Another way to make the point is to say that credentials and evidence of performance in school will help one get a job, but what counts in keeping a job and moving ahead in a company is the knowledge, skills, attitudes, and work ethic that one displays on the job, day in and day out. In acquiring the credentials, one should not fail to get the knowledge and work habits they are assumed to represent.

## REFERENCES

Adams, J. L. (1974). *Conceptual blockbusting: A guide to better ideas*. San Francisco: Freeman.

Bransford, J. D., & Stein, B. S. (1984). *The ideal problem solver A Guide for improving thinking, learning, and creativity*. New York: Freeman.

Buehler, R., Griffin, D., & Ross, M. (1994). Exploring the "planning fallacy": Why people underestimate their task completion times. *Journal of Personality and Social Psychology*, *67*, 366–381.

Dentzer, S. (1989, November). The Maypo culture. *Business Month*. pp. 26–34.

Hartley, J. (1998). *Learning and studying: A research perspective*. New York: Routledge.

Hayes, J. R. (1989). *The complete problem solver* (2nd ed.). Hillsdale, NJ: Lawrence Erlbaum Associates.

Hayes-Roth, B., & Hayes-Roth, F. (1979). A cognitive model of planning. *Cognitive Science*, *3*, 275–310.

Johnston, W. A. (1976). An individual performance and self-evaluation in a simulated team. *Organizational Behavior and Human Performance*, *2*, 309–328.

Kidd, J. B. (1970). The utilization of subjective probabilities in production planning. *Acta Psychologica, 34*, 338–347.

Kornhauser, A. W. (1993). *How to study: Suggestions for high-school and college students* (3rd ed.; D. Mt Emerson, Rev.). Chicago: University of Chicago Press. (Original work published 1924)

Nickerson, R. S. (1988). Technology in education in 2020: Thinking about the not-distant future. In R. S. Nickerson & P. P. Zodhiates (Eds.), *Technology in education: Looking toward 2020* (pp. 1–9). Hillsdale, NJ: Lawrence Erlbaum Associates.

Nickerson, R. S. (1997). Designing for human use: Human-factors psychologists. In R. J. Stemberg (Ed.), *Career paths in psychology* (pp. 213–243). Washington, DC: American Psychological Association.

Nickerson, P. S. (1998). Applied experimental psychology. *Applied Psychology: An International Review, 47*, 155–173.

Nickerson, R. S. (1999). Engineering psychology and ergonomics. In P. Hancock (Ed.), *Human performance and ergonomics* (Vol. 17 of E. C. Carterette & M. Friedman [Eds.], *Handbook of perception and cognition*) (pp. 1–45). San Diego, CA: Academic Press.

O'Neil, H. F., Jr. (Ed.) (1978). *Learning strategies.* New York: Academic Press.

Pintrich, P. R. (1995). *Current issues in research on self-regulated learning.* Mahwah, NJ: Lawrence Erlbaum Associates.

Race, P. (1992). *500 Tips for students.* Oxford, UK: Blackwell.

Rees, F. (1997). *Teamwork from start to finish: Ten steps to results.* San Francisco: Pfeiffer.

Ross, M., & Sicoly, F. (1979). Egocentric biases in availability and attribution. *Journal of Personality and Social Psychology, 37*, 322–336.

Schoenfeld, A. (1985). *Mathematical problem solving.* New York: Academic Press.

Sternberg, R. J. (Ed.). (1997). *Career paths in psychology.* Washington, DC: American Psychological Association.

Super, C., & Super, D. (1988). Op*portunities in psychology careers.* Lincolnwood, IL: VGM Career Horizons.

Van Cott, H. P., & Huey, B. M. (1992). *Human factors specialists' education and utilization: Results of a survey.* Washington, DC: National Academy Press.

Whimbey, A., & Lochhead, J. (1982). *Problem solving and comprehension* (3rd ed.). Philadelphia: Franklin Institute Press.

Wickelgren, W. A. (1974). *How to solve problems.* San Francisco: W. H. Freeman.

Woods, P. J. (Ed.). (1976). *Career opportunities for psychologists: Expanding and emerging areas.* Washington, DC: American Psychological Association.

Woods, P. J. (Ed.). (1987). *Is psychology the major for you? Planning for your undergraduate years.* Washington, DC: American Psychological Association.

Woods, P. J. (Ed.). (1988). *Is psychology for them? A guide to undergraduate advising.* Washington, DC: American Psychological Association.

# 22

# Preparing and Defending Theses and Dissertations

*Roy P. Martin*

Graduate programs in the United States can be thought of as being on a continuum between two idealized models. In the first model, graduate education, particularly doctoral education, has as its primary purpose the training of research skills (Passmore, 1980). This training is designed to prepare scholars, with the university-based researcher/teacher as the prototypic product. In this model, the thesis or dissertation is considered to be the most important single aspect of the student's educational experience. Its successful completion is thought to demonstrate that the student has acquired the skills to function as an independent researcher. Finally, it is supposed to be of sufficient quality to add to the general body of knowledge in the content-area researched (Berelson, 1960).

Although this model of graduate education is dominant in most fields, it has been consistently challenged by critics who say it tends to remove students from the problems of the real world and their solutions. Many have proposed a second model that in its pure form looks much like contemporary medical education. The product of such an educational experience is conceptualized as a field-based professional who applies the basic knowledge of his or her field in an attempt to directly intervene in human problems. This model of graduate education emphasizes applied practitioner skills and knowledge; research training takes a clearly secondary position. In a prototypic program utilizing this model, no thesis or dissertation is required.

From the earliest days of graduate education in the United States there has been tension between these two models of training (Berelson, 1960). This tension is readily apparent in contemporary applied psychology (i.e., clinical, counseling, industrial/organizational, and school psychology) in the distinction between doctor of philosophy (PhD) and doctor of psychology

(PsyD) training. Applied training programs are often housed in psychology or educational psychology departments in which the majority of the faculty have basic research-teaching interests rather than practitioner interests. Many students in these programs are seeking high-level applied skills. During the 1960s and 1970s this tension resulted in the establishment of PsyD programs in which applied skills, not research skills, were considered primary. Many of these program retained research papers as one terminal academic exercise, some of which looked like a thesis; others required small projects directed at descriptions of applied projects.

However, many applied psychology programs did not take the PsyD route. They opted to retain what they perceived as the best aspects of both the scholar and the practitioner models of doctoral training. The dissertation in such a program takes on an important role and is the crowning achievement of the student's research training. However, it is thought to be no more important than, and must share time with, other training requirements like the internship.

Students in applied psychology PhD programs often feel unusual stress about the thesis and dissertation because they feel they have not been granted the same level of research practice as their academic peers in research-oriented programs (e.g., developmental psychology). Further, they worry that their work will be held to the same standards as that of their peers. Finally, all their practical work seems to interrupt the periods of concentrated time required for research.

For all these reasons, completion of a thesis or dissertation can be an especially stressful experience for students in applied psychology programs. The purpose of this chapter is to provide some hints or principles for such students that may be helpful in reducing the stress, and increasing the meaningfulness and enjoyment of doing research.

Before proceeding with these principles it is important to clarify the meaning of the words *thesis* and *dissertation* as used here. Historically, the label *thesis* was used to indicate the act of putting forth a hypothesis, and defending the hypothesis with relevant research. As used in current parlance, it is a research document that is very similar to the dissertation, although it is of perhaps a more limited scope. Further, the level of scholarship typically required of the writer of the thesis is less than that expected of the writer of a dissertation. In current usage, the thesis is most often thought of as the documentation of the terminal research project of a master's degree and the dissertation as the documentation of the terminal research project of the doctoral degree.

## PRINCIPLES TO GUIDE YOU

### Principle 1: You Don't Have to Do It Alone

A thesis or dissertation is not an independent effort. It is by necessity a collaborative effort between a faculty member and the student, with the student serving as principal investigator and project director. Consider for a moment the number of skills and types of knowledge that are required to appropriately complete an empirical research project.

1. Knowledge of the content area that is sufficient to make it possible to identify an important issue at the cutting edge of the field.

2. Knowledge of library facilities, electronic data searching methods, and library loan procedures to acquire the materials necessary to do a competent review of the theoretical writing and empirical research in a given area.

3. Ability to synthesize appropriate literature in order to isolate important issues, and critical questions that have not been addressed.

4. Judgment enabling the selection from these issues and questions of the most important to address.

5. Ability to develop a methodology that will address the important questions selected.

6. Ability to determine if the questions and methods selected can be addressed, given the time and budget that is available.

7. Knowledge and appropriate use of the ethical and legal protections required when studying humans and animals.

8. Ability to select and gain cooperation of human or animal participants.

9. Knowledge of, and skill in the use of, psychological measurement tools.

10. Ability to record data in such a way that appropriate data analysis techniques can be applied.

11. Knowledge of, and skill in the selection of, appropriate data analysis procedures.

12. Knowledge of, and skill in the use of, the computer for carrying out the data analysis.

13. Knowledge of the writing style of one's discipline.

14. Skill in the use of software packages that prepare text, tables, and figures.

15. Skill in managing one's own behavior in order to carry out a multistage project requiring consistent effort over long periods of time.

16. Skill in managing the behavior of others involved in the project.

Mature researchers realize that they cannot be experts in all of these functions. Most rely on colleagues and hired experts in the areas of research design, statistics, and measurement. Some many turn the actual data collection over to skilled technicians. Finally, to an extent that is often not appreciated by students, the mature researcher consults with colleagues on issues and questions in the content area of the research (e.g., child abuse). This is done to clarify points of theoretical or conceptual confusion, and to hear alternate points of view so that they may be taken into consideration in the planning and discussion of the project. The entire structure of the scientific enterprise is one in which a researcher builds on the work of others. Thus, the truly independent researcher is a myth.

If the most mature researchers seek the advice and skill of others at each step of a project, it is, of course, even more important for you as a student to do the same. Further, faculty do not expect students to do projects on their own. You are expected to seek the consultation and advice of your major professor and your committee at many important decision points in the process. They share responsibility for your project.

There is, of course, a difference between a dependent relationship and a consultative relationship. You should not expect your advisor to direct your behavior at each stage of the process. The process is one in which the student initiates interaction after careful preparation. Often a direct answer to a question is not given, but the issues surrounding the decision to be made by the student are discussed. There is a great difference between the student who asks, "What do I do now?" and the student who asks, "I think I need to do the following; what do you think?"

You should also not expect that your faculty advisor or committee will set up regular meetings to monitor progress on the project. Students preparing theses will need more help than those preparing dissertations. But in both cases, they assume the responsibility for initiating contact with faculty and structuring the work of the project. This transition is difficult for some students who are accustomed to typical classroom learning.

In summary, students doing theses or dissertations serve in the role of principal investigators. It is their task to control the pace of the project, initiate and coordinate contacts with others, and take responsibility for decisions made after careful consultation with others. In the best circumstances, faculty serve as technical advisors and involved colleagues, rather than evaluative superiors.

### Principle 2: Decisions About the Specific Topic to be Addressed Must be Made in Consultation with Your Major Professor

The thesis or dissertation project is designed to answer a specific question with a particular methodology. In order to be most productive, this question should not be one that has been addressed in the same way by previous researchers. Further, it should be a question that has practical and theoretical implications for your field of study. Thousands of questions can be asked; only a few are worth pursuing.

The best approach to topic selection is for students to describe to advisors the general areas of their interest. Then the advisor, or some other person with expertise, begins to describe some of the cutting-edge issues in that body of research. This process also involves at least an initial review of the relevant literatures. After some review and more discussion with experts, a determination is made as to the next step that can be taken to clarify the results already reported in the literature. In this way, the student is building on a solid foundation and avoiding all the wasted effort that can be spent in a blind alley that others have already walked down.

Finding a productive question to address is perhaps the best example of the principle that the student should not work independently. At no time during the process of preparing a major research effort is it more critical to utilize the expertise of others than at the time of topic selection. Graduate school typically does not prepare the student to understand a specific topic in sufficient detail to know where the leading edge of the research is located. But many faculty members spend their careers pursuing a few topics in one area of research. The advice and guidance of such active researchers is indispensable.

Some of the best student research projects are produced, and the most productive learning experiences occur, when a student is able to work with a faculty member as the faculty member pursues his or her program of research. In the physical sciences, or in psychology areas in which biological processes are studied, expensive experimental equipment is often essential to a project. It is typical in these circumstances for students to work directly on funded research with their advisors. The student, after becoming thoroughly familiar with the project and the procedures used, stakes out one question to investigate in which he will be the principal investigator. It has been my experience that the students who have the least trouble with their research are those who have previously served as research assistants. The student's research then becomes a natural extension of this work and is a natural consequence of this apprenticeship experience.

The preceding discussion does not suggest that when you are beginning to look for a research topic you should present yourself to a faculty member passively with no ideas of your own. If you have not worked closely with a faculty member prior to the time of topic selection, then more conversation and literature review will be necessary. I often schedule four or five meetings with a student over several months to help the person come to this type of decision. The following steps may be helpful.

1. Decide what specific areas in your field are of special interest to you.

2. Choose a topic that someone on your faculty is current actively pursuing.

3. Read some recent reviews in the area of your interest. All the social sciences and derivative applied fields (e.g., education) have journals specifically devoted to reviews, or that publish reviews along with empirical pieces (e.g., *Psychological Bulletin, Psychological Review, Clinical Psychological Review*).

4. Approach your advisor to talk about his or her current research program and issues that seem important in this line of research.

5. Consider the employment implications and future research opportunities of these topics. (You will spend a long time studying a topic and will at the termination of the project have accrued considerable expertise in the area. It is helpful if the area of your research is one with which you want to be identified in the future.)

6. Read several recent studies that address these issues.

7. Draft a brief sketch of a research question and possible methodology for investigating the question.

8. Submit the draft to your advisor.

9. Based on advisor and other expert opinion, redraft your idea in expanded form.

10. Continue to meet with your advisor with further drafts until an acceptable proposal is prepared.

Of the steps just outlined, students typically have the most difficulty submitting the first draft (Step 7). It is important not to be too compulsive about this draft; simply write down something. There will be time for editing and refining the idea as your knowledge of the area increases and your idea matures. At this point, beginning the process by getting something on paper is most important.

## Principle 3: The Originality of Your Idea May Not Be a Critical Factor

One issue that often concerns students regarding their thesis and dissertation topic is its originality. From one point of view this is a false issue; from another point of view, it is critical. Originality is a false issue in the sense that no two studies are ever exactly alike. If nothing else, the sample studied is different. If it is a replication of a study of the perceptual-motor performance of highly anxious second graders, the sample of anxious second graders cannot be identical to the first sample studied. Granting this trivial example, the issue of originality is also clouded by the fact that most useful research is carried out in a programmatic fashion in which highly related questions are studied repeatedly using similar methods. Even direct replication is often useful. Many researchers feel there is too little replication in the social sciences and that as a result generalizations are made from spurious results.

There are several ways in which originality, however, is a critical issue in topic selection. There are some areas of psychological research that have been studied extensively and have produced few important positive outcomes. As one example, the traditional investigation of the relationship between a global self-concept measure (measured through a self-report device) and measures of school performance is no longer worth doing. Hundreds of studies of this type have been done with only modest theoretical and practical advances. There are many other such topics. Unfortunately, there is a tendency for the initial idea for student research to be in a well-worn, overstudied area of research. The best insurance against wasting effort in such an area is to read recent reviews and to seek the advice of active researchers in the area. If no one on your faculty has an active research program in the area of your interest, then contact by phone or write to active researchers elsewhere. It is one of the joys of being a researcher to have students interested in your work, so most will try to be helpful. It is important when placing such calls to have specific questions in mind, and not to waste the expert's time with general guidance ("What do you think I should do next?").

Another way in which originality is important is that students will feel most involved in their research if they have contributed substantially to its design and the questions asked. Although it is important to consult others, in the end the topic selected should belong to you. In this way, your original ideas play a role in how the research was conceived and therefore its implications.

### Principle 4. Minimize Data Collection Time; Maximize Time Spent in Review, Theoretical Understanding, and Data Analysis

Many students design research that has an enormous time involvement in data collection. This sometimes occurs because their major professor wants to have some data collected or because the student is working on a granted project in which data collection is a primary aspect of the students work. Experience in data collection, in maintaining samples, in test administration, and in scoring are all-important. But most of the learning that takes place occurs early in the process. That is, after the 30th subject, the student is no longer learning much of importance and is simply serving a labor function. Because social science research often is costly in terms of labor, students may spend months in daily data collection from which they learn very little.

When you defend your project, at either the proposal stage or the final defense stage, techniques of data collection typically will play a small part. It is far more important to have a deep understanding a body of research, to develop theory, and to understand the implications of your research.

For all these reasons, during the past decade I have been fostering the use of intact databases for graduate student research. This approach is based on the observation that most faculty have data sets they have not fully explored. Further, there are a number of large and elaborate databases available at nominal fees from universities or governmental agencies. Thus, data are often readily available. Further, many of these data sets are of much higher quality than students could collect on their own. Most of the large data sets have web pages associated with them that will direct the potential user in the appropriate process to gain access to the data. Articles describing the research of another user of the database are often the best place to begin finding the relevant web page address and other pertinent information.

There are problems with this approach. First, the student may not feel ownership of the project. Second, the manner in which the data were collected may be opaque. Finally, the student may be tempted to write questions that simply look for relations between variables in the dataset, rather than address questions of theory or practical importance. Despite these shortcomings, the use of intact data sets may be helpful for some students, particularly if they use the time saved in data collection to master the literature involved to an extent that they can begin to make theoretical contributions to the literature as a result of their research.

## Principle 5: There are Many Considerations in Committee Selection, Not All of Which are Scholarly

The primary point made in this chapter has been that the dissertation is a project carried out by a student and a committee of faculty members. It is clear, following from this premise, that the selection of a committee is a step worthy of careful consideration.

In most graduate programs, students have the right to choose the members of their thesis or dissertation committees. In fact, this process begins much earlier, with the choice of a major professor. A major professor should be chosen who has interests that are similar to those of the student, and with whom the student feels comfortable working. If no such major professor can be found, the student has chosen the wrong program. Availability of an appropriate major professor should be a criterion for your selection of a graduate program.

Although I know of no institutions in which students are directly assigned major professors with no option of a change during their graduate program, there are many training programs in which major professors are initially assigned to the student to serve in the role of academic advisor. As the student begins to develop more precise research interests, he or she may be wise to change to another major professor.

The thesis or dissertation is a critical step in the education of the professional, and the successful completion of this step requires prolonged and mutually interested interaction between professor and student. If you have been working with an academic advisor who is not suitable (compared to the criteria for suitability described next), you should seek a change of advisors. This may be socially awkward, but is not usually as difficult as the student expects. Most faculty members have had the experience of a student wanting to change to another advisor and are willing to allow the student to make this choice.

Given that you must actively select a major professor and a thesis or dissertation committee, on what ground should your choices be made?

The first step in the process is the selection of a chairperson or major professor. The most obvious factor in this selection is your ability to work closely with this person. This relationship need not be a close one; in fact, if the student and chairperson are too close, their relationship may be detrimental to the efficient completion of the project. However, there must be a sense of mutual respect. There are wide individual differences in the style faculty members have when working with students. Some commit themselves to helping the student allocating considerable time from their schedule for this purpose. Others feel students will profit most if they work more independently. In this latter stance, advisors perceive themselves as agents of quality control, whereas in the former, the faculty member may perceive that he or she serves as a midwife to the birth of the dissertation idea and a consulting colleague for the remainder of the process. The best sources of information on the style of faculty member is classroom experience with him or her, reports from other students, and direct conversations to clarify expectations.

An equally critical factor in selection of a chairperson is that the person have some level of expertise in the topic area the student has selected to research. When faculty members are actively researching topics, their motivation to study those topic has already been made manifest in a clear way. Further, they will usually be more helpful to the student than a faculty member who has a casual interest in the project, because the outcome is important to them.

One mistake that some students make is to choose a thesis or dissertation chairperson on the grounds of national reputation alone. This is done in the hope that being associated with a major name in the field will open up career opportunities not otherwise attainable. Although this kind of gain may occur, some persons with national or international reputations are so busy with their own research work and with professional organizations that they have little time or interest in the student or the student's project. Being available for timely consultation is an essential characteristic of a chairperson.

Once the chairperson has been selected, the next step is the selection of the remainder of the committee. Several general rules seem pertinent to this process. A committee should be chosen with which both the student and the chairperson feel comfortable. Situations in which there are interpersonal difficulties between faculty members should be carefully avoided. In order to ensure that relations among all parties are comfortable, the opinion of the chairperson should be sought. A second rule is that in most cases the major content expert on the committee should be the chairperson. If this is not the case, there may be confusion about who is guiding the research. Similar difficulties can occur when two methodological experts are on the committee. These situations can result in a power struggle over points of theory or methodology, to the disadvantage of the student. Finally, other criteria utilized in selection of the chairperson are applicable to all committee members, in particular, having the time and interest to serve.

### Principle 6: Drafting the Proposal for the Project is Often the Most Difficult Phase of the Process

Through discussion with the chairperson, experts at other universities, and reading recent research, you cam narrow down your topic to an idea that seems manageable and appropriate. At this juncture, it is time to commit your ideas to paper.

A common mistake is to prepare a lengthy literature review and a detailed presentation of the experimental procedure for evaluation by the major professor, only to discover his or her perception of significant flaws in the design or even in the framing of the questions to be addressed. The student may become defensive and resentful of such suggestions, given the effort already expended. These negative feelings can damage the relationship between the student and the major professor for the remainder of the project.

The alternative problem also occurs. The student may discuss the project with the major professor and other experts for to long without creating a draft. Many major professors find this behavior wasteful of their time.

These problems can be avoided if a brief initial proposal is prepared early in the process. This proposal is then presented to the major professor and sometimes to committee members for their reaction before a final proposal is prepared. Its brevity reduces faculty reading time, and perhaps wasted student time and effort, while providing a concrete product for evaluation. This first draft maybe as short as five or six pages. It should contain the question(s) to be investigated, a brief rationale for the importance of the question, and a description of the proposed sample, measurement instruments, and procedure. Even if an element like the instrumentation cannot be included, such a first draft provides a first step from which the next step can be taken.

The brief draft of the proposal serves another important function for some students. For those who are fearful about writing, this draft begins the writing process in a relatively painless manner. It also provides the basic structure for the final proposal and much of the writing of the thesis or dissertation. Thus, the brief draft proposal is a flexible instrument that forms the foundation for the documentation of the research.

### Principle 7: The Purpose of the Oral Defense of the Proposal is to Obtain a Commitment of the Committee for This Research—Not Primarily a Personal Evaluation of the Abilities of the Candidate

In the process of completing the thesis or dissertation, the most important formal meeting is the prospectus defense. Contrary to student perception, it is not the final defense of the project. The proposal defense is a meeting required by almost all universities. At that point in your career, you seek the approval of your committee (the formal representatives of the entire faculty) for the research you want to do. Several simple pointers may help you gain maximal benefit from this important meeting.

First, if you have followed some of the suggestions made earlier with regard to communicating with your major professor, preparing drafts of the proposal and showing them to committee members, the process proceeds much more smoothly. If this is the first time the committee has heard about the project, and the major professor remains to be convinced about critical elements of the project, the meeting may be difficult. In this regard there is one pitfall to specifically avoid: Do not rush your major professor to schedule a committee meeting for the proposal defense. Some students, being particularly mindful of graduation deadlines or the need to complete the proposal before going on an internship experience, briefly chat with the major professor about their idea, and then prepare a proposal just in time for a previously scheduled meeting. This is a recipe for trouble. At the first sign of difficulties with the project, major professors will begin to distance themselves from the project. They may confess to the committee that they have not worked carefully with the student, but were willing to have the student attempt a defense if they wanted to try to go ahead with the meeting on short notice. At this point, the committee members may feel irritated with the major professor or the student, because they expected to review a carefully prepared and supervised document. The moral is, do not rush things. Make your major professor read and comment on your project. Adjust the project and the proposal until the major professor feels comfortable.

The best way to prepare for the prospectus oral, in addition to the points just made, is to attend the final defense of several fellow students. Sometimes university and department policy allows students to attend this prospectus defense (as well as the final defense), but others will not allow this. However, much can be learned from the final defense, and many students do not avail themselves of the opportunity. These meetings have a style of their own, and some students have imagined something quite different. One student of mine imagined that he would defend his prospectus in front of the entire college. When he found it he would do so in front of a committee of five people, he was somewhat disappointed! Some students think of these presentations as a public performance in the spirit of a lecture. In fact, they are typically more informal and interactive. Directly observing the process is an excellent way to learn what to expect.

### Principle 8: Most Students Who Do Not Receive Their Degrees Due to Failure to Complete the Thesis or Dissertation Do So Because They Have Failed to Allocate Sufficient Time to the Project

The vast majority of students who have difficulty with their dissertations are not failed by faculty. They simply cannot carry out the research as proposed in their prospectus. Two factors seem to be primary. First, many bright students have coped with assignments during their education through short-term bursts of energy and attention. For example, you may write your term paper during the week just prior to the due date. Some of the best and brightest can use such a procedure for almost all their work in graduate school. The thesis or dissertation is an exception. The project is large enough that activities must be planned, time must be systematically allocated, and effort distributed over months and sometimes years to successfully bring the project to completion. In my experience, a thesis takes about 9 months and a dissertation perhaps 18 to 24 months to complete, although the variation across students is large. This estimate assumes the student has other obligations and works on the project on a weekly basis, but perhaps not on a daily basis.

Many students simply have difficulty planning for such a project and realistically allocating time. This time must be actively allocated, not fit in between other pressing activities. When a student tells me he or she will write a prospectus or do data collection during the Thanksgiving and Christmas vacation, I know I will see a frustrated student and an inferior product in early January.

The second problem is that many students have so many competing time demands that a project of this type becomes impossible. If you are attempting to complete your dissertation while on a full-time internship, for example, you should know that most cannot accomplish this feat. The energy and time demands of internships are simply too great. In a similar fashion, if you take a full-time position in a school or clinic, particularly if you have family obligations, you place yourself at great risk of not completing your thesis or dissertation.

Part of the risk is being away from the university setting, in which the advisor can be easily contacted or library materials can be obtained. Research is an esoteric activity for most members of the society. Family and employers do not understand how it is done and how much time it takes. Thus, there are subtle pressures to attend to other matters. Most psychologists work in agencies that provide services directly to others. Service providers may allocate the student (on an internship or on a job) half a day per week for research to complete a dissertation. Half a day per week is simply not enough time. Further, even this time is often eroded by the immediate nature of service concerns.

## Principle 9: Alternative Formats for the Thesis and Dissertation are Becoming More Common and may be More Helpful to the Career of the Student

The traditional thesis or dissertation consists of five chapters: introduction (problem, purpose, hypotheses), review of the literature and statement of the problem and hypotheses, method (participants, instrumentation procedure), results, and discussion. Its form has been conventionalized by governing bodies in graduate education (Council of Graduate Schools, 1991). This format has been recently criticized on several grounds (Duke & Beck, 1999). The shortcomings include that the document is so large that it has limited dissemination, and that the exercise does not generalize to other writing that the student will do as a professional. Several critics of the traditional dissertation are suggesting that the final written product look more like a journal article. This would address both criticisms, in that the student could more easily publish the product and the style of writing would prepare the student for writing other professional pieces (Krathwohl, 1994). Some departments in which I have served on thesis and dissertation committees required two article-length papers: One is a systematic and publishable review of the literature, and the other is a report of the research. This procedure approximates some European models in which the PhD is awarded after the publication of a series of articles on a given topic.

Another issue that may affect many students is that the thesis or dissertation may be required in electronic form. This format has great utility to libraries and other repositories of scientific knowledge, due to the increasing volume of professional writing. The number of dissertations alone has increased substantially during recent years, from 9,733 (in all fields) in 1960–1961 to 44,446 in 1994–1995 (National Center for Education Statistics, 1997). Thus, if for no other reason, the volume of research writing by students may force new formats and new methods of delivery.

## Principle 10: The Final Defense of the Project is More About Learning to Present Your Ideas than About Passing or Failing

The defense of the completed project is in many ways of less importance than the defense of the proposal. Traditionally, the final defense was considered the major hurdle for the doctoral candidate. This defense is a direct descendent of the medieval European university practice of having a public ceremony in which the teaching ability of the doctoral candidate was judged prior to awarding of the title of doctor (Heiss, 1970). In the 19th century, this practice was modified; it became a defense of a theoretical position (a thesis), or a presentation of empirical findings. From the beginning of the 19th century to the present, European doctoral education consisted of a program of reading in one or more major areas under the guidance of a tutor-instructor. Formal evaluations of the student's progress were rare. The student was expected to write several papers on their theoretical ideas or demonstrating an empirical relationship, then to defend their idea (or thesis) in a public ceremony. In this system, the defense of the thesis or dissertation took on a "make-or-break" aspect, for it was the primary means of determining the achievement level of the student.

Several characteristics of contemporary graduate education in the United States have lessened the importance, or at least the all-or-nothing quality, of the final defense. First, students complete an elaborate series of experiences (a program of study) before beginning the dissertation phase of their education. Second, students are examined repeatedly at each stage of the process. Finally, the master's or doctoral candidate's research has been evaluated and sanctioned several times by each member of the dissertation committee. All these factors reduce the likelihood that a final oral examination will result in failure.

What then is the purpose of the final oral examination? There appear to be two. First, it allows the student the opportunity to practice the skills necessary to present research material to a forum of scholars, and provides the faculty with the opportunity to evaluate these skills. Second, it allows the student and faculty to engage in scholarly debate. In the busy lives of professors, this is one of the few times in which ideas can be discussed with their peers. It also helps to increase the general knowledge level of the faculty in areas in which they are not expert. In this regard, the student becomes the resident expert on the specifics of their research and educates the faculty, completing the life cycle of the student from learner to teacher.

Students often entertain misconceptions about the kinds of questions that are asked in such examinations. The most common mistake that is made is for students to concern themselves with preparing for questions about data analysis to the exclusion of more fundamental issues. This misplaced emphasis is a result of the way research skills are taught in most universities. Commonly, students take a series of statistics courses that exclusively form the basis of their research training. Issues of research design and measurement are often given less emphasis, and, unfortunately, the most critical aspects of research are often not taught at all. These aspects include isolation of an appropriate and meaningful problem, selecting the critical question to address that is most relevant to that problem, and fitting a design to these questions. These issues are given most attention in both the prospectus and the final examinations.

Consider a student who is concerned about the possible relationship between maternal cocaine use during pregnancy and the risk of attention deficit hyperactivity disorder (ADHD) in the child. The first and most important question to be asked by the committee is: "What makes you think there is a relationship between these behaviors?" This should be followed by the question, "If such a relationship does exist, what would be its theoretical and practical implications?" Through what mechanism or process is the maternal behavior related to the child's behavior? Are there multiple process?" Other questions might focus on the measurement necessary to make a diagnosis of ADHD, and specific procedures for obtaining data on maternal cocaine use. In my experience, issues like these that attempt to illuminate the logical connections between the problem, purpose, methods, and interpretation of the study consume 80% of the discussion during the defenses, with narrow statistical issues playing a minor part.

The thesis or dissertation is often the most difficult step in a doctoral program. It is difficult because it requires a large number of skills that students have been introduced to but have not mastered. It is particularly difficult for many students in applied psychology. Applied psychology students are often not as well prepared to conduct research as students in more research-oriented programs, simply because of the emphasis of their training. Further, students in applied programs have competing time pressures in the form of internships, which occur at about the same time in their program of study. For these reasons, it is important to understand the process and some typical pitfalls, so that this important learning process can be managed to maximize the quality of the experience and to allow for reaching the goal with the greatest efficiency.

## SUGGESTED READINGS

Cone, J., & Foster, S. (1993). *Dissertations and theses from start to finish: Psychology and related fields*. Washington, DC: American Psychological Association.

Martin, R. (1980). *Writing and defending a thesis or dissertation in psychology and education*. Springfield, IL: Charles C. Thomas.

Yates, B. (1980). *Doing the dissertation: The nuts and bolts of psychological research*. Springfield, IL: Charles C. Thomas.

## REFERENCES

American Psychological Association Research Office. (1999, November). Gender and graduate education. *APA Monitor*, p. 8.

Berelson, B. (1960). *Graduate education in the United States*. New York: McGraw-Hill.

Council of Graduate Schools in the U.S. (1991). *The role and nature of the doctoral dissertation*. Washington, DC: Author.

Duke, N. K., & Beck, S. W. (1999, April). Education should consider alternative formats for the dissertation. *Educational Researcher, 28*, 31–36.

Heiss, A. M. (1970). *Challenges to graduate schools*. San Francisco: Jossey-Bass, 1970.

Krathwohl, D. (1994). A slice of advice. *Educational Researcher, 23*, 29–32.

Passmore, J. (1980). The philosophy of graduate education. In M. W. K. Krankena (Ed.), *The philosophy and future of graduate education* (pp. 26–43). Ann Arbor: University of Michigan Press.

National Center for Educational Statistics. (1997). *Digest of educational statistics 1997*. Washington, DC: U.S. Department of Education/Office of Educational Research and Improvement.

# IV

## The Internship

# 23

# Applying to Professional Psychology Internship Programs

*W. Gregory Keilin*

*Madonna G. Constantine*

The predoctoral internship year in professional psychology is the capstone to graduate students' doctoral training experience. The internship generally integrates the theoretical and practical aspects of students' training, and requires of them a much greater level of responsibility and accountability. For many students, it is a time of great personal and professional growth, and a time during which their identity as a psychologist begins to solidify.

Finding the "right" internship can be both an exciting and challenging process. It is essential that the preparation for this experience begins early in students' graduate careers. The goal of this chapter is to help you successfully navigate the internship selection process, including: (a) finding an internship program that best meets your needs, (b) handling the application and interviewing procedures, (c) dealing with the computer match, and (d) making the transition from graduate school to internship.

## INTERNSHIP 101

The psychology internship is generally completed on either a 1-year, full-time or a 2-year, half-time basis. Completing a predoctoral internship is a required part of the doctoral degree program of most counseling, clinical, and school psychology programs. It is generally completed in an applied setting, such as a Veterans Administration Medical Center, psychiatric hospital, university counseling center, community mental health center, or other types of agencies that emphasize clinical practice.

Many psychology internship programs are accredited by the American Psychological Association (APA), which is the highest form of certification that a program can receive. Completing an APA-accredited internship means that students can be assured that future employers and licensing boards will consider their internship to be of high caliber. For example, certain jobs, such as at some federally funded hospitals, require the completion of an APA-accredited internship. Moreover, some state licensing boards may require students who complete a nonaccredited internship to demonstrate that the internship meets the boards' requirements for internship training (more information on licensing can be obtained from the Association of State and Provincial Psychology Boards, www.asppb.org).

Although it is generally preferable to complete an APA-accredited internship, it is not absolutely necessary to do so. In fact, each year some students choose to complete their internship at nonaccredited sites. However, students who complete a nonaccredited internship should be aware of the potential limitations on their future career and licensing options.

The Association of Psychology Postdoctoral and Internship Programs (APPIC) is an organization of predoctoral internship sites and postdoctoral programs in psychology and, although not an accrediting organization, does require its member programs to meet certain requirements and standards. Both APA-accredited and nonaccredited internship sites can be members of APPIC. APPIC oversees the predoctoral internship selection process, including the computer-based matching program (called the "APPIC Match") used to pair internship positions and applicants (Keilin, 1998).

## Internship Supply and Demand

As of this writing, there are not enough internship positions in psychology to accommodate the number of graduate students who apply for these positions each year. Although there are some recent indications that the situation may be improving (Keilin, Thorn, Rodolfa, Constantine, & Kaslow, 2000), this shortage remains a significant problem for the profession. Keilin et al. (2000) found that approximately 9% of students who participated in the 1998–1999 APPIC Match ultimately did not get placed at an internship site and were forced to reapply during the following year. This shortage of positions can add to the stress of what is already an anxiety-laden process. The good news is that the overwhelming majority of applicants do get placed each year, and that students do have some control in reducing the likelihood that they will be unplaced. In general, applicants run a greater risk of remaining unplaced if they: (a) apply to a relatively few number of sites, (b) apply to sites within a limited geographic area, particularly if that area is in high demand (e.g., New York City), or (c) apply only to sites that are considered "prestigious" or are highly competitive. Students seeking half-time positions may also find their options to be quite limited.

## PREPARATION

In theory, it is never too early for doctoral students to begin preparing for the predoctoral internship application process. You should generally begin organizing and planning for this process as early as the first year of your doctoral studies (Gloria, Castillo, Choi-Pearson, & Rangel, 1997; Mellott, Arden, & Cho, 1997).

An important first step for new graduate students is to establish mentoring relationships with selected faculty members. Developing such relationships early in your doctoral career provides you with a reliable and trustworthy source of advice, support, and guidance, and provides faculty members with valuable information about your interpersonal style and your clinical and professional development. In addition, these relationships are often cited as crucial to the internship selection process (Lopez & Draper, 1997), as they can provide the foundation for critical support throughout the process, and often lead to enthusiastic letters of recommendation that reflect an in-depth knowledge of students (Mellott et al., 1997; Mitchell, 1996).

Perhaps equally as important for new graduate students is to develop and maintain relationships with advanced students in the doctoral program. These advanced students can be invaluable sources of information and support, and are often more attuned to the realities and practicalities of the internship selection process than are faculty.

You should also keep accurate and detailed records of your practicum experiences, as the internship application process requires students to provide extensive documentation of their clinical work. Maintaining these records, starting with your first practicum experience, will make the internship application process far less cumbersome. With regard to each client, you should keep track of the type of intervention (e.g., individual, group, family, couples, assessment), client demographics (e.g., age, gender, ethnicity, sexual orientation, disability status), and the number of face-to-face contact hours. You also should record: (a) hours spent on activities related to client care, such as supervision, report writing, case notes, and consultation; (b) names of assessment instruments administered and interpreted, and the number of reports written; (c) the amount and type of supervision received (including individual, group, and peer consultation); and (d) the nature and amount of other psychological interventions performed (e.g., teaching, consultation, program development). You may wish to download the APPIC Application for Psychology Internship (AAPI) from the APPIC web site (www.appic.org) in order to see the variety of information that is currently required from internship applicants as well as the format in which it is to be reported (note that this standardized application is subject to change each year).

Other activities in which doctoral students may engage to increase their competitiveness in the internship selection process include: (a) joining professional organizations, (b) attending and presenting at professional conferences, and (c) seeking out varied clinical and other professional practice experiences (e.g., research). Obtaining training in specific professional practice competencies may also strengthen some candidates' internship applications. For example, some internship sites prefer interns with experience in managed health care issues (Constantine & Gloria, 1998) and multicultural diversity issues (Gloria et al., 1997). Some sites even value professional licensure or certification at the master's level (e.g., as a substance abuse counselor) in predoctoral internship applicants (Constantine & Gloria, 1998). Thus, it is important that internship candidates obtain the professional practice experiences that are relevant to the sites to which they are applying (Gloria et al., 1997; Lopez, Oehlert, & Moberly, 1996).

You should also make every effort to defend your dissertation prior to the beginning of the internship year. Not only will this make you more competitive in the internship application process, it will also greatly reduce the stress of your internship experience.

Applicants should also be aware that the internship selection process can be a costly endeavor. Expenses can easily total $1,000 and often considerably more (Oehlert, Lopez, & Sumerall, 1997). Travel to on-site interviews is usually the major expense, but you should also budget in such costs as obtaining transcripts, printing and copying, postage, telephone calls, child care, clothing for interviews, and lost wages.

During the internship application year, there are a variety of tasks to which candidates need to attend in preparing their application. A suggested timeline of activities for the application year is presented in the Appendix.

## Handling Stress

The predoctoral internship application process has been identified by both students and program directors as a stressful time in doctoral students' careers (Constantine & Keilin, 1996; Gloria & Robinson, 1994; Mellott et al., 1997; Oehlert et al., 1997). The stress experienced by many applicants seems to be linked to various factors that affect this process (Gloria et al., 1997). For example, factors such as students' (a) lack of knowledge about the predoctoral internship process (Gloria & Robinson, 1994; Lopez et al., 1996), (b) lack of emotional and organizational preparation (Mellott et al., 1997), (c) concern about not being matched to an internship site (Gloria et al., 1997), and (d) concern about dealing with possible violations of APPIC policies by internship training directors (Constantine & Keilin, 1996), may contribute to the stressors they experience. Moreover, increased competition for internship slots (Constantine, Keilin, Litwinowicz, & Romanus, 1997; Oehlert & Lopez, 1998), changes in managed health care that may decrease funding allocated toward internship training (Constantine & Gloria, 1998), and geographical limitations for some applicants (Gloria & Robinson, 1994; Oehlert & Lopez, 1998) may increase the stress that students experience in the process.

You can engage in a number of activities during the selection process in order to help reduce your level of stress:

- Get support from others. Seek out guidance from faculty members and other students throughout the selection process. Take advantage of any resources that may be offered by the graduate program (e.g., sample application materials, colloquia on the application process). Develop a "support group" with other internship applicants in the program (Albin, Adams, Walker, & Elwood, 2000). Open discussions about the emotional aspects of the selection process (e.g., anxiety, jealousy, competitiveness, anger) can be helpful in normalizing and reducing stress.

- Join e-mail lists that address internship-related issues, such as those sponsored by APPIC (Oehlert, Sumerall, & Lopez, 1998).

- Do not assume that internship selection is a one-way process, with sites as the interviewers and students as the interviewees. In fact, it is a reciprocal process, and students should take an active role in interviewing, selecting, and rejecting internship programs.

- Understand that rejection is a normal part of the process. In fact, many applicants are granted interviews at fewer than half of the sites to which they apply.

- Realistically anticipate the amount of work involved in applying and interviewing. Be sure to set aside sufficient time for these activities, particularly in the period from November through January.

## THE APPLICATION PROCESS

Identifying desirable internship sites can be a time-consuming experience and should begin no later than the summer prior to the selection process. APPIC publishes a comprehensive directory of internship programs in the United States and Canada. This directory lists almost all APA-accredited internship programs, as well as nonaccredited programs that are members of APPIC, and is currently available in both printed form and via the Internet at the APPIC web site. Many academic programs subscribe to the printed APPIC directory and make copies available to their students at no charge. Applicants may also ask faculty members, fellow students, and recent graduates from their program for information about internship sites that match applicants' interests.

All internship programs have a printed brochure and/or a web site describing their program and providing information about how to apply. Interested students should call or send a brief letter or postcard to sites, requesting a packet of materials. Most applicants review the materials of many more internship programs than they eventually apply to, and narrow down the list of sites based on how their interests and training goals fit with programs.

Choosing sites to apply to is generally based on a number of personal, professional, and practical considerations (Stewart & Stewart, 1996a). Stedman, Neff, Donahoe, Kopel, and Hays (1995) studied applicants' choices of desirable internship programs and found that the following eight variables were used to identify their top-ranked programs: (a) a "gut feeling" that the site is a good fit; (b) a program that has a good reputation; (c) a match between the applicant's interests and the program's training experiences; (d) amount and quality of supervision; (e) the breadth of the program's clientele; (f) high-quality training seminars; (g) the availability of specialized training opportunities; and (h) an interest in staying in the same geographic area after internship. Furthermore, Stewart and Stewart (1996a) encouraged applicants to consider a variety of personal and practical variables as well, such as internship stipend, location of the site, support network available, availability of employment for one's partner, and the "extent to which [internships] emphasize either provision of service to clients or training experiences of their interns" (p. 297). Applicants should also give some consideration to factors beyond the internship year (e.g., Where do you want to eventually live and practice? What opportunities are available in the area for post-doctoral employment? How does the internship experience fit with your career goals?).

In general, preparing internship applications involves conveying the breadth and depth of your skills and professional experiences to each program's selection committee (Mellott et al., 1997; Mitchell, 1996). Several years ago, APPIC developed a standardized application form (the "APPIC Application for Psychology Internship," or AAPI), with the goal of reducing the amount of work required of internship applicants in applying to multiple sites. The AAPI is designed to be completed on a personal computer, and may be downloaded from the APPIC web site (www.appic.org). Note that not all sites use the standardized application, and many sites request supplementary information (e.g., essay questions). Completing the AAPI can be quite time-consuming, as students are required to provide detailed accounts of their practicum experiences.

In addition to the application, most internship sites require several letters of recommendation. These letters are an extremely important part of the application (Gloria et al., 1997), and care should be taken in selecting individuals who will provide strong and enthusiastic recommendations. Having even one letter that is neutral or negative can severely impede your chances of success (Rodolfa et al., 1999). You should choose recommenders who know you well and are familiar with your work, and should ask them if they feel comfortable writing a positive letter. It is important to give these individuals plenty of advance notice for writing letters (a minimum of 4 to 6 weeks is advisable). You should provide recommenders with a list of the sites to which you are applying, along with the various application deadlines. It may also be helpful to provide recommenders with a copy of your vita, a summary of your work with them, and a list of any specific areas that you would like highlighted in the letters.

Most sites also require a vita and copies of graduate transcripts. Transcripts should be ordered well in advance, and may be less expensive if they are ordered in larger amounts rather than individually. Although many sites do not specifically require a cover letter, it is often a good idea to include one. In addition, you must have your academic training director complete a form certifying to internship sites that you are eligible to apply for internship. You should plan to complete your coursework, comprehensive examinations, and other requirements well in advance of the application process so that there are no delays in certifying your internship eligibility.

The literature is somewhat mixed with regard to the optimal number of sites to which internship candidates should apply (Stewart & Stewart, 1996b). For example, some researchers recommend no more than 10 applications (e.g., Mellott et al., 1997), and others suggest anywhere between 10 and 20 applications (e.g., Lopez & Draper, 1997). Keilin (2000), in a study of the 1998–1999 APPIC Match, found that applying to more than 15 sites did little to improve applicants' chances of being matched. For most people, applying to between 10 and 15 sites is a reasonable approach; applying to fewer can significantly reduce the chances of being matched to an internship site, and applying to more can make it substantially more difficult to devote sufficient time and energy to each site's application and interview.

Some of the more common mistakes made by internship applicants in the application process include:

- Sending out "generic" cover letters and essays. Instead, take the time to tailor your application materials to each particular site.

- Sending more information (e.g., testing reports, copies of manuscripts) than is requested by a site. Remember that most training programs tend to receive a large number of applications, and unsolicited material is generally viewed in a negative light. In this case, more is not necessary better.

- Sending several extra letters of recommendation (one extra letter is generally acceptable, but no more than that).

- Asking a prominent person for a recommendation, when that person does not know the applicant well. A strong letter from a person who is not well known is much better than a mediocre letter from a well-known individual.

- Failing to get feedback from faculty or other individuals about application materials, or failing to proofread and spell-check the materials.

- Applying to a site that appears to be a poor fit with the applicant's background, training, and experience (unless the cover letter and other application materials clearly explain as to why the site is actually a good fit). For example, (a) applying to a site that emphasizes working with children when an applicant's background is exclusively in working with adults, or (b) applying to a university counseling center setting when the applicant's personal statement describes a strong interest in working with a geriatric population. Internship Training Directors will often reject applicants if they appear to be a poor fit with the program, even if their applications are otherwise impressive.

## INTERVIEWS

Once internship applications have been submitted, the next step in the process is to begin preparing for interviews. Internship sites generally receive a large number of applications; thus, many will offer an interview to only a limited number of applicants. Many internship training directors will inform applicants (via telephone, postal mail, or e-mail) about whether or not they have been selected for an interview; however, students should contact a site directly if they have not heard anything from the site in a reasonable amount of time (e.g., 3 to 4 weeks after the application deadline). It is important to note that all contacts with a site are subject to evaluation; therefore, students should ensure that their interactions with various staff members and current interns are professional and respectful. Even interactions with secretarial staff, both positive and negative, can become a part of some sites' evaluation process.

Sites vary significantly in terms of how they conduct their interviews, with some requiring or preferring that students come to the site for an interview and others conducting interviews by telephone. Alternatively, some sites will offer one or more "open houses," in which applicants are invited to visit the site on selected dates. A few sites conduct on-site group interviews, in which a group of applicants is interviewed by one or more members of the training staff. Sites will generally disclose their interview policies and procedures in their application materials, but sometimes students will need to inquire directly in order to determine the site's requirements. In general, learning about individual sites' interviewing procedures will decrease anxiety and help students be prepared for interviews.

On-site interviews can be quite challenging due to the extensive time and energy required of the applicant along with the significant travel costs involved. Scheduling these interviews can sometimes be difficult, particularly when they are in different areas of the country. However, on-site interviews do provide you with an advantage over telephone interviews, in that you have the opportunity to see the site, meet the training staff and interns, and get to know the general geographic area. Of course, you may decide, for financial or other reasons, not to apply to sites that require on-site interviews.

In preparing for interviews, carefully review each site's brochure, web site, and other materials describing the internship. This will allow you to become familiar with the mission and goals of the agency, the training staff, the specific training opportunities available, and other aspects of the internship program. Taking the time to review this material will allow you to ask well-informed questions and provide you with the opportunity to communicate knowledge about, and sincere interest in, the program. Training staff are usually able to tell when an applicant has not reviewed the site's training materials, and this generally reflects negatively on the applicant.

Rodolfa et al. (1999) found that internship applicants should focus on presenting themselves in a professional yet personable manner, be prepared to articulate their clinical abilities, clearly express their training goals for the internship year, and display a familiarity with the training program. Furthermore, Lopez and Draper (1997) suggested that applicants participate in mock interviews with their peers or with faculty members in order to receive feedback about their interview behavior.

A number of researchers (e.g., Mellott et al., 1997; Stewart & Stewart, 1996a) have compiled samples of questions that interviewees may expect from internship sites. In general, such questions tend to address applicants' theoretical orientation, previous training experiences, interest in supervision, professional and personal strengths, and goals for the training year. Examples of questions that applicants may be asked on internship interviews include:

- What is your theoretical approach to counseling and psychotherapy?
- Present a case study utilizing your theoretical approach to counseling.
- What aspects of your personality most affect your work with clients?
- What types of clients are most difficult for you to work with? Why?
- What do you see as your strengths and areas for growth as a therapist?
- Describe an ethical dilemma and how you handled it.
- Describe your previous supervisory relationships and what you are expecting from supervision at your internship site.
- Discuss a difficult supervision experience, including how it was resolved.
- Describe your experiences as a supervisor. What is your approach to or theory of supervision?
- Why did you apply to this internship site?
- What are your goals for the internship year?
- If psychology did not exist as a field, what career would you have pursued instead?
- How do you deal with stress?
- What do you like to do in your spare time?

What do internship training directors look for in applicants? One of the most important factors for many training directors is the fit between applicants' training goals and the opportunities available at the training site (Rodolfa et al., 1999). Throughout the process, applicants should ensure that they communicate clearly to each internship site about how the program would meet their training needs. Other important variables that training directors use in assessing applicants include: (a) the amount of supervised clinical experience, (b) completion of course work, (c) quality of the interview, (d) APA accreditation status of the applicant's doctoral program, (e) completion of comprehensive examinations, (f) personal demeanor of the applicant, and (g) quality of letters of recommendation (Rodolfa et al., 1999).

Just as you will be asked about various aspects of your training and experience, you should be prepared to ask questions of internship site personnel. These questions should be designed to elicit information that will be useful to you in making decisions about which programs best fit your needs. It is also important that such questions reflect your knowledge about and active interest in the sites, and are not merely questions to which the answers may be found in the programs' materials. Examples of such questions include:

- How would previous interns at your training site describe your program's strengths and weaknesses?
- What is a typical work week for an intern at your site? How many hours does an intern typically work per week? How much time is spent in training and direct service activities?

- What types of training experiences, colloquia, and/or seminars are provided for interns?
- In what direction do you see your agency moving in the next year? In the next 5 years?
- Do you have any concerns about the stability of funding for your internship program?
- What types of jobs do your interns generally find after internship? What kind of support does the program provide interns during their job search processes?

Applicants should also attend to the more subtle aspects of the interview process. For example: Are you treated with courtesy and respect by the training staff? Are your phone calls returned promptly? How do staff appear to get along with each other and with the interns? How invested does the staff appear to be in the interns and the training program? How open is the training director to discussing the weaknesses of the program?

After completing the formal interviews, sites vary in terms of how much additional contact they will subsequently have with applicants. Some sites will not contact applicants again prior to the deadline for submission of ranking lists, and others may recontact applicants to ask or answer additional questions. Applicants may choose to send a thank-you note to each site after the interview. However, this should be done only as a courtesy, as thank-you notes will likely have little or no impact on how applicants are ultimately ranked by each site.

Applicants should not restrict their contact with a site to only the formal interview process. For example, talking to a current intern at each site is one of the best ways to learn about the internship, as current interns may be more candid about a site's true strengths and weaknesses. Or, during the process, applicants may have questions for the training director or another member of the training staff. Sites generally consider such contacts as an indication of applicants' interest in their program. However, applicants should remember that the training director and other staff members are generally dealing with the selection process on top of all of their other responsibilities, and thus excessive contacts could hurt applicants' chances (Albin et al., 2000).

## NAVIGATING THE COMPUTER MATCH

Beginning with the 1998–1999 selection process, APPIC adopted the use of a computer program to match prospective interns with internship sites (Keilin, 1998). The matching process is a significant improvement over the previous selection system, which encouraged unfair tactics and resulted in undue pressure and a high degree of stress on applicants. The APPIC Match is a fair and straightforward method of pairing applicants with internship programs. The Match gives equal weight to applicants' and sites' preferences, and is guaranteed to provide the best match possible for all participants.

The Match is currently administered by National Matching Services, Inc. (NMS), a company based in Toronto, Canada, that specializes in the administration of professional matching programs. The information contained in this section is accurate as of the 2000–2001 Match; however, changes and enhancements are made to the process each year. Thus, applicants should consult the latest materials on the Match to ensure that they have the most up-to-date information. These materials include the written materials from NMS, as well as information provided at the following web sites:

APPIC—http://www.appic.org/

National Matching Services—http://www.natmatch.com/psychint/

The information provided is both extensive and comprehensive, and applicants will find that most of their questions will be answered by reviewing these materials.

Here is a brief summary of the matching process: Upon completion of interviews, all applicants are required to submit to NMS a "Rank Order List," consisting of internship sites to which they would like to be matched in order of preference. Sites also submit Rank Order Lists of applicants to NMS. The computer then places applicants into positions based entirely on the preferences stated in the Rank Order Lists. Finally, applicants are notified of the sites to which they have been matched, and sites are provided with a list of applicants to whom they have been matched.

All APPIC-member internship sites are required to participate in the Match each year. Some nonmember sites also choose to participate in the Match, but many do not. Although internship applicants are not required to participate in the Match, most students will find it highly advantageous to do so. A student who does not participate in the Match can only be offered an internship position by (a) a site that is not participating in the Match, or (b) at the conclusion of the Match, by a participating site that has one or more positions left unfilled. Thus, in general, all students should participate in the Match except those who are seeking placement at sites that are not filling their positions through the Match.

## Match Registration

In order to register for the Match, applicants must request a registration packet directly from NMS, either via their web site or by submitting a request to the following address:

National Matching Services
595 Bay St., Suite 301, Box 29
Toronto, Ontario
Canada, M5G 2C2
Telephone: (416) 977-3431
Fax: (416) 977-5020

Applicants must pay a fee to participate in the Match, and must sign a contract indicating their willingness to abide by the rules of the Match. Once registered, each applicant is assigned a unique Match identification number that will be used by internship sites to identify and rank the applicant. Applicants are encouraged to register well before the registration deadline, in order to have their Match identification number available to provide to sites on internship applications.

## Match Policies

APPIC has developed a set of Match Policies that govern the behavior of all participants in the Match. Applicants should carefully read and familiarize themselves with these policies, as they are required to abide by them. Currently, the policies restrict the communication of ranking information between applicants and sites, although these restrictions are subject to revision in the future. The policies also emphasize the binding nature of the Match in that internship sites are required to accept the applicants to whom they are matched, and applicants are required to attend the internship to which they are matched.

The APPIC Standards and Review Committee (ASARC) investigates complaints from applicants, academic program directors, and internship training directors regarding violations of the Match Policies. The most common violations reported by applicants include a site pressuring applicants to share their rankings, or a site revealing its rankings of applicants (Keilin, 2000). Applicants are urged to report violations if other approaches to resolving the situation (e.g., discussing the situation directly with the internship training director; consulting with the student's academic training director and/or advisor) are unsuccessful, as this will help reduce the likelihood that future applicants will experience these difficulties.

## Constructing a Rank Order List

After completing the internship application and interview processes, the applicant's next step is to construct his or her Rank Order List. This List is considered confidential and must be submitted to NMS prior to the Rank Order List submission deadline.

In the Match, each internship site offers one or more "programs" or rotations (e.g., "General Internship," "Neuropsychology," "Geropsychology"), each of which is identified by a unique code number. Applicants should use these code numbers when constructing their Rank Order Lists to identify the specific programs to which they are interested in being matched. Applicants may rank as many or as few programs as they wish.

The design of the matching program dictates that applicants should always use their *true* preferences in constructing their Rank Order Lists. In other words, applicants should simply rank the internship programs in the order in which they are preferred, without regard for where they believe that they may have been ranked by the programs. Applicants should rank their most preferred program as their number one choice, followed by their next most-preferred program, and so on. When ranking sites, applicants should not take into consideration such things as a program's popularity, the number of positions offered by a program, how other applicants might rank a program, or how a program might rank other applicants. Doing so will ultimately hurt applicants because it will reduce the chances of getting the best possible match. If applicants simply rank programs in the order in which they prefer them, they are guaranteed of getting the best possible match.

Applicants should rank all programs to which they have applied and that they find acceptable. However, applicants may decide that a program is no longer acceptable to them; in this case, applicants should simply omit this program from their list, and they will not be matched to that program.

One special feature of the Match is that any two applicants who wish to coordinate their match placements (e.g., attempt to match to sites within the same geographic region) may participate in the Match as a "couple." Participating as a couple requires the use of special ranking procedures. More information on this option may be obtained from NMS.

## Receiving the Match Results

The results of the Match are released on a previously determined date known as "APPIC Match Day." On that date, applicants learn the name of the internship program to which they have been matched. Applicants should contact their new internship training director later on Match Day in order to acknowledge the match. Internship training directors will subsequently send applicants a written confirmation of their appointment.

Unfortunately, participation in the Match does not guarantee that all applicants will be successfully matched to an internship position. Learning that one has not been matched can be a serious disappointment, particularly after the great time, expense, and effort involved in applying and interviewing. APPIC operates a "clearinghouse" that allows internship programs with unfilled positions to publicize these positions to students who have not been matched. This clearinghouse begins operating on APPIC Match Day and remains available until the early summer. Other organizations in psychology, such as the Association of Counseling Center Training Agencies (ACCTA), also run post-Match Day clearinghouses. Unmatched applicants should also work closely with their academic training director to see if additional internship options can be identified or developed.

The APPIC Clearinghouse is much less organized than the matching process. It is essentially an electronic bulletin board where training directors post notices of unfilled positions. Each site determines its own procedure for submitting applications, conducting interviews, and making offers, and the amount of time between the initial posting of a vacant position and the filling of that position can range from several hours to many weeks. Thus, unmatched applicants should be prepared to act quickly; in fact, a recent study (Keilin et al., 2000) found that 40% of unfilled positions are filled within the first week after APPIC Match Day. In addition, relatively few positions at APA-accredited sites are generally available through the APPIC Clearinghouse, and thus unmatched applicants may be faced with the difficult choice between accepting a nonaccredited position and waiting until the following year to reapply.

## PREPARING FOR THE INTERNSHIP

The 4 to 6 months after Match Day is often a period of great transition and stress, particularly when students are moving to a new location to begin their internship. On one hand, it can be a time of excitement in anticipating the next stage of professional development and the various opportunities that lie ahead. This period can also be filled with stress, sadness, and apprehension (e.g., saying good-bye to friends and colleagues, wrapping up personal and academic obligations, moving to a different part of the country). Unfortunately, many new interns fail to anticipate the emotional turmoil that can accompany this period, and may not give themselves enough time to deal with these issues. While making arrangements to leave their academic programs, it is important that students take time to address the ending or changing of relationships that may be occurring with important people in their lives (Stewart & Stewart, 1996a), such as faculty members, other students in the program, friends, family, or others who have been a major part of their lives as graduate students.

Students who are leaving for internship with their dissertation unfinished should meet with their dissertation advisor in order to develop a timeline for completion. When constructing this timeline, it is important to consider the emotional energy involved in beginning and completing an internship. For example, some students make minimal progress on their dissertation during the first few months of their internship experience.

As students begin thinking about relocating, the internship training director and the site's current interns can be valuable sources of information and support. Students can learn a great deal from the current interns' relocation experiences (e.g., finding housing, locating day care for children), and the present interns can provide much information about the area's social and recreational activities. Many new interns travel to their internship sites in the late spring or early summer in order to secure housing, and this can be a great time to begin learning about the area and meeting the training staff.

It is also important for students to give themselves enough time to get settled in their new locations well before the first day of internship (Stewart & Stewart, 1996a). Although it may be tempting to delay the move until the last moment possible, this will ultimately add to the stress of the transition. Students who focus on taking care of themselves during this transition are likely to begin their internship year on a positive note.

## ACKNOWLEDGMENTS

We thank Mark Adams, Carla D. Hunter, and Sarah Walker for their assistance with this chapter.

## REFERENCES

Albin, D., Adams, M. A., Walker, S. J., & Elwood, B. (2000). The quest for an internship: Four students' perspective. *Professional Psychology: Research and Practice, 31*, 295–299.

Constantine, M. G., & Gloria, A. M. (1998). The impact of managed health care on predoctoral internship sites: A national survey. *Professional Psychology: Research and Practice, 29*, 195–199.

Constantine, M. G., & Keilin, W. G. (1996). Association of psychology postdoctoral and internship centers' guidelines and the internship selection process: A survey of applicants and academic and internship training directors. *Professional Psychology: Research and Practice, 27*, 308–314.

Constantine, M. G., Keilin, W. G., Litwinowicz, J., & Romanus, T. W. (1997). Post-notification day perceptions of unplaced internship applicants and their academic training directors: Recommendations for improving future internship selection processes. *Professional Psychology: Research and Practice, 28*, 387–392.

Gloria, A. M., Castillo, L. G., Choi-Pearson, C. P., & Rangel, D. K. (1997). Competitive internship candidates: A national survey of internship training directors. *The Counseling Psychologist, 25*, 453–472.

Gloria, A. M., & Robinson, S. E. (1994). The internship application process: A survey of program training directors and intern candidates. *The Counseling Psychologist, 22*, 474–488.

Keilin, W. G. (1998). Internship selection 30 years later: An overview of the APPIC Matching Program. *Professional Psychology: Research and Practice, 29*, 599–603.

Keilin, W. G. (2000). Internship selection in 1999: Was the Association of Psychology Postdoctoral and Internship Centers' match a success? *Professional Psychology: Research and Practice, 31*, 281–287.

Keilin, W. G., Thorn, B. E., Rodolfa, E. R., Constantine, M. G., & Kaslow, N. J. (2000). Examining the balance of internship supply and demand: 1999 Association of Psychology Postdoctoral and Internship Centers' match implications. *Professional Psychology: Research and Practice, 31*, 288–294.

Lopez, S. J., & Draper, K. (1997). Recent developments and more internship tips: A comment on Mellott, Arden, and Cho (1997). *Professional Psychology: Research and Practice, 28*, 496–498.

Lopez, S. J., Oehlert, M. E., & Moberly, R. L. (1996). Selection criteria for American Psychological Association-accredited internship programs: A survey of training directors. *Professional Psychology: Research and Practice, 27*, 518–520.

Mellott, R. N., Arden, I. A., & Cho, M. E. (1997). Preparing for internship: Tips for the prospective applicant. *Professional Psychology: Research and Practice, 28*, 190–196.

Mitchell, S. L. (1996). Getting a foot in the door: The written internship application. *Professional Psychology: Research and Practice, 27*, 90–92.

Oehlert, M. E., & Lopez, S. J. (1998). APA-accredited internships: An examination of the supply and demand issue. *Professional Psychology: Research and Practice, 29*, 189–194.

Oehlert, M. E., Lopez, S. J., & Sumerall, S. W. (1997). Internship application: Increased cost accompanies increased competitiveness. *Professional Psychology: Research and Practice, 28*, 595–596.

Oehlert, M. E., Sumerall, S., & Lopez, S. J. (1998). *Internship selection in professional psychology.* Springfield, IL: Charles C. Thomas.

Rodolfa, E. R., Vieille, R., Russell, P., Nijjer, S., Nguyen, D. Q., Mendoza, M., & Perrin, L. (1999). Internship selection: Inclusion and exclusion criteria. *Professional Psychology: Research and Practice, 30*, 415–419.

Stedman, J. M., Neff, J. A., Donahoe, C. P., Kopel, K., & Hays, J. R. (1995). Applicant characterization of the most desirable internship training program. *Professional Psychology: Research and Practice, 26*, 396–400.

Stewart, A. E., & Stewart, E. A. (1996a). Personal and practical considerations in selecting a psychology internship. *Professional Psychology: Research and Practice, 27*, 295–303.

Stewart, A. E., & Stewart, E. A. (1996b). A decision-making technique for choosing a psychology internship. *Professional Psychology: Research and Practice. 27*, 521–526.

# APPENDIX
## TIMELINE FOR THE INTERNSHIP APPLICATION YEAR

### July and August

1. Review the APPIC Directory and departmental internship files to identify potential internship sites. Get recommendations about potential sites from faculty, other students in the program, and other professionals.

2. Call or write internship sites for program brochures and application materials. Many sites now have this information on their web site.

### September

1. Register with National Matching Services, Inc., the company responsible for the operation of the APPIC Computer Match. Review the information about the Match, including policies and timelines.

2. Review internship brochures and descriptions to identify programs that meet your interests and training needs.

3. Download and begin working on the APPIC Application for Psychology Internship (AAPI).

4. Work on your vita, cover letters, and essay questions. Ask your advisor, another faculty member, or a colleague to review your vita and supplemental information and to give you feedback regarding aesthetics, organization, and clarity.

5. Identify and ask faculty members, clinical supervisors, and/or clinical staff for letters of recommendation.

## October to Early December

1. Finish the AAPI.

2. Request academic transcripts be sent to internship sites.

3. Follow up on letters of recommendation to ensure that they have been mailed.

4. Submit internship applications to sites. Deadline dates generally range from early November to early January.

5. Contact sites several days prior to the deadline date to ensure that your application file is complete. Missing application materials should be sent immediately.

6. Wait as patiently as possible to hear from sites.

## December to January

1. Practice answering interview questions. Participate in "mock interviews" with faculty and/or peers.

2. Schedule and participate in interviews with internship sites. Attempt to schedule on-site interviews with sufficient advance notice to obtain discounted air fares.

3. Spend time preparing for each interview. Review programs' brochures and the application materials that were sent, and compile a list of site-specific questions.

4. Keep notes about thoughts, feelings, and impressions after each interview. It may be useful to develop a preliminary site ranking list.

5. Do postinterview follow-up contacts, as necessary, to answer last-minute questions. Talk to sites' current interns about their experiences.

## Early February

1. Finalize site ranking list.

2. Submit site ranking list to National Matching Services, Inc., by the appropriate deadline.

3. Wait patiently for the release of the Match results.

# 24

# The Internship Year: The Transition from Student to New Professional

*Joseph A. Denicola*

*Cynthia T. Furze*

T he internship year, with its profound personal and professional implications for the development of the individual, marks the formal transition from student to beginning professional. During this year, the intern relinquishes the status of classroom student and begins to try out new roles as diagnostician, therapist, and consultant (Gold, Meltzer, & Sheff, 1982). However, these new roles may be accompanied by conflict. Trainees comes face to face with their own deficiencies and inexperience. Yet, at the same time, interns discover that their opinion about a particular client is regarded seriously, and may play an important role in treatment decisions (Shows, 1976).

In addition to the professional transitions that occur at this time, the internship year generally coincides with a major personal developmental passage. For most interns, the period that Levinson (1978) defined as "Entering the Adult World" comes to a close during the internship. The developmental tasks to be completed during this period are complex and have ramifications for the future of the trainee. Additionally, the clinical, institutional, and personal stresses created by the transition from graduate school to internship are emotionally complicated and can lead to a crisis (Solway, 1985).

This chapter focuses on the professional and personal transitions and practical concerns of the internship year. The emphasis is on ways in which you can shape the year to create a more gratifying internship experience. We suggest strategies for planning your internship and dealing with training, institutional, personal, and relationship issues. Finally, we address how best to make the internship experience a springboard for emergence as an autonomous professional.

# LAYING THE GROUNDWORK

Once an internship has been offered and accepted, a great weight of uncertainty is lifted. Actively preparing for the internship year can enhance the experience, minimize potential problems, and make the year much more rewarding.

## Preparation for Training

First, do some thinking about what you would like to accomplish professionally during the year. Conduct a self-assessment, and talk with your graduate school advisors and peers about strengths, weaknesses, and gaps in your training. Consider to what extent you want to spend your time filling in the gaps in your training or strengthening your skills in a specific area. Obtaining and reviewing psychology internship guidebooks can help prepare for the coming year (e.g., Baird, 1999; Zammit & Hull, 1995).

Second, find out as much as you can about the internship program that you have selected. The training brochure or manual is only a preliminary source of information about the program. Historically, there have been reports of misrepresentation, false statements, and inadequate facts in training program brochures (Foster, 1976; Kurtz, 1974; Snyder & Ray, 1972). It is helpful to clarify the expectations of the internship program beforehand by talking at length with the training director. Some important issues and questions to consider beforehand include: Does the internship program offer various training options or rotations? Do you have the opportunity to choose among different training settings such as inpatient, outpatient, family therapy, substance abuse, neuropsychological assessment, medical, and spinal cord injury? Are there training opportunities off site at affiliated institutions? What are the expectations and requirements of the internship program? For example, are you expected to complete certain core rotations? Are you required to attend specific workshops or educational presentations? What administrative responsibilities are assigned to interns? Can you obtain training in required areas before your internship so you can free up more time for other opportunities during the year? Can you obtain supervision from adjunct professionals outside the intern site? Foster (1976) outlined a representative sampling of other questions that the prospective intern should consider asking.

It can also be extremely helpful to speak with current and former interns, as well as potential supervisors. Of course, it is optimal to visit the site and interview people directly. However, due to practical, financial, and time limitations, a visit may not be possible. Alternately, telephone or e-mail interviews may allow you to ask relevant questions and make informed decisions about training options. If you know beforehand exactly to which programs you have been assigned within the internship, contact your future supervisors. Ask them about ways to prepare, recommended readings, and any expectations they might have of you as a trainee. Most training directors and potential supervisors will welcome your interest, and will see you as investing yourself in a proactive way into the program.

## Dissertation Blues

The status of your dissertation will have a major impact on your experience of the internship year. In interviews with Palo Alto Veterans Administration (VA) Medical Center interns, we have found that those who finished their dissertation during the internship often found themselves pressured and preoccupied. They were less involved in the training program and the social aspects of the internship year, and, not surprisingly, reported that they experienced great relief when the dissertation was completed. Interns who worked on the dissertation during the intern year *without* completing it reported that the work was demanding, and limited their experience. Some felt fatigued and demoralized, without a sense of relief.

We strongly recommend, if it is at all possible, that you complete your dissertation before leaving graduate school. Interns who did so consistently reported that the year was much more enjoyable. They were able to devote more time and energy to the internship training, and to preparing for their next professional position. Additionally, they had more time for elective clinical work, research, seminars, and other interests.

If you choose to work on your dissertation during your internship, make sure that you plan ahead. Interns have made the most of the situation by taking advantage of an available subject pool at the training site, utilizing research resources (e.g., computer time, library facilities, medical personnel), or working with experts in the field located at or near the internship site. Some internships will allow the trainees time to work on their dissertations. Clarify beforehand with the training director whether you will be able to integrate your dissertation into the internship hours, and in what ways. Make realistic decisions about what you want to accomplish, and plan accordingly.

## Logistics

Laying the groundwork for the internship also involves performing the practical tasks necessary to move to a new setting: moving, uprooting yourself from friends and perhaps family, finding a place to live, settling into the community, and establishing a new social network. Here again, planning can help smooth the transition. By talking with current and former interns, you can obtain a wealth of information about the cost of living, possible roommates, available housing, and convenient neighborhoods. Some of this information may be obtainable over the Internet on a web site for the city in question.

## TRAINING AND INSTITUTIONAL ISSUES

For many students, the predoctoral internship may be the most important career choice they make. Oehlert, Sumerall, and Lopez (1998) described the internship as "the capstone training experience in professional psychology." Yet several rarely addressed issues continue to have a major influence on the development of the psychology intern during the training year. These issues include the dissatisfaction of the internship staff with graduate school preparation for the intern year, breadth versus depth of training, and institutional politics.

**Filling in the Gaps**

A number of surveys have examined the adequacy of academic-clinical preparation for the psychology internship (Dana, Gilliam, & Dana, 1976; Petzel & Bemdt, 1980; Sheinberg & Keely, 1974; Sturgis, Verstegen, Randolph, & Garvin, 1980; Tipton, Watkins, & Ritz, 1991). Consistently, these studies have found that, according to internship directors and clinicians, graduate training is often remiss in providing students with basic clinical skills. Internship directors value clinical experience, strong training in personality assessment and psychopathology, and personal qualifications more than academic accomplishments (Petzel & Bemdt, 1980; Stedman, 1997; Tipton et al., 1991). Interns themselves reported feeling inadequately prepared in the areas of diagnostics, testing, psychopharmacology, bureaucratic issues, and neuropsychological assessment (Cole, Kolko, & Craddick, 1981). A number of studies have found directors of training to be critical of interns' preparation in assessment and psychotherapy (e.g., Malouf, Hass, & Farah, 1983; Sheinberg & Leventhal, 1981).

One study (Malouf et al., 1983) found that interns viewed themselves as having better initial clinical knowledge than ascribed to them by internship directors. The primary source of this discrepancy resides in the different expectations of the internship facility and graduate school, although, for the most part, it is the intern who is often left confused by conflicting feedback regarding competence and training needs (Rice & Gurman, 1973). Students have been reinforced at their universities for being adept at academic, statistical, and research skills, and searching for answers in books. Yet internship supervisors may express disappointment because of a lack of basic clinical knowledge and an unfamiliarity with psychological assessment or therapeutic techniques. Rice and Gurman (1973) reported that intern supervisors "generally desire to refine and enhance basic skills, not to inculcate them." Graduate students can better prepare for their internship by strengthening these skills through additional practicum assignments, seeking out supervision from practicing clinicians, and attending additional classes and workshops in assessment and therapy. It can also be helpful to seek out assessment and therapy experience in settings other than the university psychology clinic, to provide exposure to the wider range of therapeutic challenges posed by a varied population. The conventional clinical psychology internship setting is a medical center or psychiatric hospital, yet many interns have never been exposed to this setting and may experience apprehension or anxiety about working in a hospital (Heine, 1973; Shows, 1976). Seeking exposure to these settings during your university training, through preinternship practicums, clinical research, volunteer work, or extended site visiting, can help desensitize you and provide a framework for understanding how these systems function.

**Breadth Versus Depth**

The task of obtaining high-quality, in-depth training while also procuring the diversity of experience necessary to survive and adapt in a changing profession may be the most important issue in internship training (Rice & Gurman, 1973). At the same time, trainees are urged to both develop an area of specialization to help the distinguish themselves from the pack and obtain a breadth of experience. Some programs allow the student a considerable amount of flexibility in determining how they will spend their internship year. This may be particularly true among the larger internships (Tedesco, 1979). Students may find themselves faced with many attractive options and a finite amount of time. Early decisions about how to spend one's time during the intern year can have profound long-term ramifications on an intern's career.

How you decide to choose among training rotations influences your qualifications for subsequent job openings. On the one hand, the internship may seem like an ideal, and perhaps final, opportunity to explore new and different content areas under professional supervision. Professional curiosity compels some students to seek out multiple training opportunities in diverse settings. However, you only have 1 year. Thus, a choice of family therapy or neuropsychological assessment rotations, which provide attractive competencies, can be a springboard (or a constraint) that channels your career toward that specialty. On the other hand, some graduate students are extremely specialized by the time they approach their internship year and therefore seek out an internship site that provides an intensive experience in their area of expertise.

Most programs strive to allow the intern to pursue specialized interests while requiring a solid background in basic clinical skills. Furthermore, they recognize the individuality of the intern with respect to past training and current needs, while taking steps to insure that a minimum level of competence is achieved. Therefore, by virtue of prior training, some students will have more degrees of freedom in determining internship placements. There are no simple answers to the diversity versus specificity arguments, and each intern and training program will need to resolve this issue based on individual talents, deficits, training needs, desires, and intended career path.

## Developing a Professional Identity

Perhaps the most important function of the internship is to provide an opportunity for the trainee to practice in a professional capacity (Shows, 1976; Weiss, 1975). The intern is generally given the latitude to assume a great deal of autonomy and responsibility. Lamb, Baker, Jennings, and Yaffis (1982) identified three processes that occur during the time when the intern's identity is established. The trainee develops a realization of strengths and limitations, goes through a period of self-doubt and self-confrontation, and experiences an increased role differentiation. Rice and Gurman (1973) suggested that there are some training opportunities that the intern can seek out to enhance the transition to independent functioning. For example, they suggest working with psychological emergencies and major psychopathology, especially in their acute phases, and supervising other mental health professionals. These training experiences can further help the trainee develop a sense of self-efficacy. A primary component in the development of the intern is a growing awareness of how one's interpersonal style interacts with both the patients and staff. Although mastery of specific techniques and content areas is important, it is also paramount that interns learn about themselves as clinicians and as persons. Learning about your own style of relating can help you develop an awareness of how you influence and affect the individual patients and staff that you work with, as well as the system in which you function. The internship is a valuable opportunity to learn about and observe interpersonal process, and to understand your own role as a clinician and an individual.

Finally, working within a multidisciplinary setting can also contribute to the intern's developing sense of professional identity. Participating in a multidisciplinary treatment team can help developing psychologists clarify and define the limits and value of their own roles within the system. This is especially true for the student with little or no experience working with psychiatrists, physicians, teachers, social workers, nurses, and other health professionals. Relationships between disciplines in a health care system are complicated and even mercurial, particularly in times of shrinking resources. It is not unusual to find disciplines competing for limited funding, staff, space, and other resources. These "turf" battles can trickle down to the treatment setting where the intern is assigned. Furthermore, many interns arrive at the training site with an ingrained bias against physicians, psychiatrists, and the medical model (Shows, 1976). Optimally, the internship provides an opportunity to develop effective working partnerships with other health professionals and to recognize their unique contributions. This can be facilitated by demonstrating an interest in individuals from other disciplines, asking questions, discussing patients, collaborating on multidisciplinary projects or committees, and recognizing the contributions allied disciplines bring to understanding the patient.

### The Politics of Experience

Political conflicts are ubiquitous and can have a negative impact on the trainee, the intern class, and the system as a whole. Cole et al. (1981) found that interns reported that bureaucratic and political disputes were a major deficit of the internship experience. In that survey, most interns reported that they were surprised at the extent to which political conflicts detracted from the internship. Some of the political issues relevant to the internship program include the assignment of interns to particular supervisors, rotations, or programs, the availability of outside placements to the intern, and the assignment of the intern to two or more supervisors during one rotation. In addition, an intern's personal or interpersonal style can create an impact on a system, either positive or detrimental, that may have political ramifications. Interns are generally accorded a positive valence within any mental health system. They contribute hours of patient contact and bring new ideas and energy to the programs in which they work, and lend the setting the added status as a training program. For these and other reasons, interns may find themselves in the confusing role of having no "real" power, but a great deal of informal power within the system.

In addition to understanding and learning about the system, you should also be aware of how you have an impact on other individuals and groups. Insight into your own personal style and issues will ease your transition through this developmental phase, and can help you survive the politics of the institution. Assessment tools commonly used in organizational development, such as the Myer–Briggs Scale, can provide feedback about your interpersonal style. Interns have reported a need for training in the management of political and bureaucratic disputes (Cole et al., 1981). This is another instance during the internship where that training can occur on the job. It may be helpful to do some reading or take classes in management skills prior to or during the internship year.

The basics of working within any bureaucracy apply to the internship as well as other professional settings: Routinely obtain permission for any deviation of protocol, and avoid going over or around an immediate supervisor. If you are involved in a conflict, first attempt to work it out face to face with that individual. Finally, avoid speaking in a pejorative way about fellow interns, staff, or patients. Inevitably, what you say about another person will be repeated, probably out of context and twisted. It is also important when discussing even the most frustrating patients to be respectful. Many of these suggestions for coping with the politics of the system may seem simplistic, and in some cases are common sense, but the difficulty can be in implementing them. Human nature is fallible, and we often act in ways we later regret. Also, as a new and temporary member of an institution, avoidance may often seem the easiest path to take with conflicts. However, this is the time to learn and work through your role as a professional within an existing system. Seek assistance from your supervisors, internship director, and other social support systems if you do find yourself enmeshed in political conflict that detracts from your training or affects your personal well-being.

## PERSONAL AND RELATIONSHIP ISSUES

Many personal and relationship issues interact with, and help shape, the accelerated individual and professional development of the trainee. Most relationships formed during this year share two features: they are intense and time-limited. Significant personal and professional transitions are occurring at this time. The questioning, introspection, and self-disclosure that often characterize the development of new clinical skills can facilitate an intimacy with supervisors and fellow interns. This closeness may be comforting, especially if you are in a new setting, and geographically cut off from other important sources of social support. However, these feelings of intimacy may conflict with the awareness that the relationships are in many ways bounded by the end of your training period. Unlike graduate school, where you have three or four years to gradually develop and test out relationships, the internship is relatively brief. Each intern will approach and deal with these issues of closeness and intimacy in his or her own way. It is helpful to be cognizant of both the rich opportunities for relationships and the limits of the training year.

### Supervisory Relationships

Clearly, supervisory relationships are a pivotal facet of the internship experience. The role of the supervisor generally goes beyond the provision of guidance and feedback about clinical skills. The supervisor may act as a mentor, a friend, a colleague, a role model, and a general advisor in matters of career development and the internship experience (Hafner, 1973; Holroyd, 1973). Supervisory relationships have a major influence on the perceived quality of the internship year (Cole et al., 1981). Cole and his colleagues found only 5% of APA-approved site interns in their survey to be dissatisfied with the quality and quantity of their supervision, compared with 43% of interns polled at non-APA-approved sites. Interns who were dissatisfied with their training described poor quality and inadequate quantity of supervision as major deficits of the internship site.

Interns and supervisors bring many different hopes and fears into their relationship (Baird, 1999). It can be helpful early in the relationship to clarify expectations and to acknowledge fears. Among the expectations to be clarified at the outset of the supervisory relationship, Baird (1999) cited the frequency and timing of meetings, the content of the sessions, the theoretical orientation or techniques to be learned, how the intern will be evaluated, and the degree to which personal issues will be addressed in supervision. It is incumbent upon the intern to understand the responsibility of the supervisor to hold trainees to a high professional standard. Supervisors can and have been held legally liable for the actions of trainees (Harrar, VandeCreek, & Knapp, 1990).

Problems between interns and supervisors are not uncommon. Moskowitz and Rupert (1983) found three areas of conflicts in their survey of 158 interns: theoretical orientation, style of supervision, and personality issues. The intern's shift toward independence brings forth issues around evaluation, dependency, and assumption of professional responsibility within the supervisory relationship. Of course, these conflicts are not solely due to the intern's issues. Supervisors may have their own biases, and in the context of the supervisory relationship may be dealing with their own personal issues. In the Moskowitz and Rupert (1983) survey, when interns were unable to resolve conflicts with their supervisors they tended to seek support elsewhere, modify their behavior to conceal problems, or attempt to appear compliant with the supervisor. Resolution of supervisory conflicts can be an opportunity to enhance your own professional development. As in any system, first attempt to clarify and resolve the conflict with the supervisor before going to the director of the training program.

Finally, there are many ways in which supervisor–intern and therapist–patient relationships are alike. For example, they are both by definition unequal relationships in which one party is rendering a service (Biaggio, Paget, & Chenoweth, 1997). Thus, the ethical guidelines for dual relationships apply to supervisors and trainees. The most egregious violation of this boundary occurs when there is a sexual relationship between the intern and supervisor. Unfortunately, despite formal clarification in the 1992 American Psychological Association (APA) code of ethics (APA, 1992), sexual relationships between educators and students still occur with unsettling frequency, particularly in the case of female trainees (Hammel, Olkin, & Taube, 1996). Student participants, even those who viewed the relationships as neutral at the time, in retrospect viewed these relationships as coercive and harmful to their training (Hammel et al., 1996). Baird (1999) suggested that students who are harassed should file formal complaints with the training institution, as well as any licensing bodies, and professional organizations with which the supervisor is affiliated. Minimally, concerns about potentially exploitative practices or boundary violations should be discussed with the director of training or another trusted advisor.

## The Intern Class

Your fellow trainees, with their diversity of skills and backgrounds, are among the most memorable and rewarding elements in your internship year. Yet these relationships can be complicated by the often unspoken issue of competition. Your cohort group represents the eventual competition for jobs and can provide a new objective yardstick to measure your own professional development. As the year develops, interns may also be competing for the attention and approval of supervisors and colleagues, desirable training rotations, letters of recommendation, and job openings at the intern site. These issues of competition, if they are present, may be considered distasteful and be generally ignored, which can result in damage to group and individual morale. Awareness of your own competitive reactions is an essential first step in directing them in a positive way and learning more about yourself as a person and professional in relation to others. By anticipating that you will be meeting other interns whose abilities and experiences in certain areas will be better developed than yours, you may be able to welcome and learn from their strengths and become more aware of your own.

Your fellow interns can provide you with a major source of professional growth and personal enjoyment. They can be resources as you explore new content areas and theoretical perspectives. Seeking peer support and consultation about clinical issues during the internship will establish a precedent and make it easier to do so as an independent practitioner. Other interns can also share in the exploration of the social and recreational aspects of the training year.

## Personal Relationships

There are several strains of the internship year that differ from the general strains of graduate school in their influence on maintaining existing primary relationships or establishing new ones. Decisions about commitments, such as marriage, divorce, living together, and having children, are further complicated by the uncertainty of where you will be living in 12 months, and the growing awareness of your own issues with identity and autonomy. The internship occurs at a time in the life cycle when the trainee may be experiencing strong internal and external pressure to put down roots and establish a stable life structure. These factors have ramifications for the development of new relationships as well as established ones. Intimate relationships that are formed during the intern year have the unique strain of developing within a time limit of 12 months, during which both parties may be looking for jobs.

The internship year can severely test a preexisting long-term relationship, particularly if it has necessitated a geographic relocation. The intern's partner may be forced to move, leave social and family support, and defer career pursuits. Meanwhile, the intern may be unavailable due to time commitments of the training site and is also forming new professional and personal relationships that may not include partners, further increasing isolation for those who left friendships behind. It is easy to see how jealousies or resentments might build. Obviously, there are no clear-cut solutions to these dilemmas. Mutual awareness, loving concern, couples therapy, and structuring time for the relationship can help in the ultimate resolution of these potential difficulties.

## Taking Care of Yourself

It is all too easy, while surrounded by professional lures, to ignore your own personal growth and other facets of your life. During this time of professional challenge, questioning, and growth, it is important to retain and nurture the other aspects of your life that give you pleasure. These may include athletic, romantic, creative, or simply recreational pursuits. Find time for hiking, visiting galleries, historical sites, or whatever your location has to offer. Ask yourself, "What will I wish I would have done if I have to move away from here at the end of the year?" Write those things down, and structure some time to do them. Try to put aside time for introspection and self-assessment. Some internships provide a psychotherapy group for the intern class. The internship director may also provide a list of local psychotherapists who are willing to see interns at a reduced fee. Keeping a journal may also facilitate personal development and reflection, and may be a valuable chronicle of a time that slips by all too fast.

## A SPRINGBOARD INTO YOUR PROFESSIONAL LIFE

For some interns the end of the year marks a return to the university to complete the dissertation. For most, it culminates in postdoctoral employment (Kaslow & Rice, 1985). The final section of this chapter focuses on the transition of the trainee out of the internship setting and offers strategies to facilitate the process.

## Approaching the Internship with Your Professional Future in Mind

Even as you begin the internship, it is important to be mindful of your longer term goals. The internship can have a significant influence on the construction of your curriculum vitae, particularly if you discover an intriguing new career interest during the course of the year. If you are unable to obtain formal training in a new area of professional focus during the internship, try to create opportunities to establish your interest in some other way. For example, if you found an interest in the treatment of posttraumatic stress disorders (PTSD), you may be able to volunteer time at a rape crisis center, review existing cases and write a paper on PTSD, present an in-service, offer to establish a group treatment program with someone at your site who has experience in that area, or request that opportunities for treatment of a single case study be directed to you. These activities can help you test the strength of your newfound interest in an applied manner. In addition, by engaging in extracurricular activities of these sorts, you enhance your marketability to prospective employers and increase your contact with knowledgeable colleagues who can assist in your job search. However, as Plante (1996) advised, trends or hot topics in psychology are seductive and often ephemeral. Training in basic clinical skills should not be ignored for the sake of specialty training.

In recent years, managed health care has transformed the face of professional psychology. Yet in a survey of 311 internship sites, Constantine and Gloria (1998) found that overall managed health care had little effect on training. As a result, the intern may not develop essential management skills needed to function effectively in contemporary mental health settings. To perform in these settings, these authors suggest that individuals need to be able to work within a brief therapy model, have skills in documenting service delivery, and be able to competently relate to the managed health care entity. It may also be helpful to request speakers from the local psychological associations to address the intern group on these specific issues.

Similarly, Plante (1996) noted that advanced trainees are ill-informed about pragmatic aspects of professional practice such as managed health care, state licensing laws, and hospital admitting privileges. Few trainees have had experience in networking, marketing, and many of the business skills necessary for those providing psychological services. To remediate these deficits, it is helpful to regularly read the relevant professional publications, maintain collegial relationships with other professionals attentive to these issues, and join and actively participate in county, state, and regional psychological associations.

## Preparation for Licensure

One factor that will significantly increase your employment potential, particularly in the nonacademic job market, is professional licensure or accreditation. Most states require 1,500 hours of postdoctoral training to be eligible for licensure, and graduating doctorates are usually not eligible right away. There are several things you can do during the internship year to expedite your licensure process. Investigate the requirements for licensure of the state where you intend to work. Note any areas of training that may be required for licensure that you can fill in before leaving the internship. For example, in California, courses in human sexuality and ethics are required before a person is eligible for licensure. Sometimes required training experiences can be obtained at your internship site more easily and less expensively than after graduation.

Many new psychologists preparing for licensure or accreditation are surprised at the heavy emphasis on risk management and ethical issues in the national and state exams. Despite the best efforts of talented professors, ethical and legal issues are often of theoretical interest only during one's academic training. The application of legal and ethical standards becomes more of a practical reality during the internship. Some internship sites require trainees to read and sign an ethical guidelines form (Baird, 1999). Interns should be thoroughly familiar with the ethical principles of psychologists as well as the legal standards within the particular state. It is also necessary to regularly update yourself on current laws, which are revised as new cases are adjudicated. Having discussions of ethical issues with supervisors and classmates can be an invaluable resource for honing your professional judgment as well as preparing for the licensure examinations.

## The Internship Year as a Springboard to Your Post-Graduate Position

The relative pressure and timing of your job search will vary depending on your career goals. Notices for academic positions begin to appear in the *APA Monitor*, the *APS Observer*, and other sources soon after the beginning of training. If you plan on applying for these types of positions immediately on completion of the internship training, you will probably be on the job market before the end of your first rotation. For nonacademic positions, administrative and clinical experience accumulated during the internship year provide a foundation for your job applications. Although opportunities may arise earlier, the job search for these positions usually becomes more intense in the spring of the internship year.

The internship can provide a wealth of resources for assisting in your job search. Attend any available seminars on developing your curriculum vitae and on job seeking. Some sites also arrange for representatives from a myriad of professional jobs to lead discussions on the practical realities of postdoctoral employment. If a seminar format is not available, you can visit various agencies to interview clinicians and the team about the likelihood of available employment. Talking with a community mental health center director, university selection committee chair, VA psychologist, or private practitioners about the relevant factors for getting a foothold in their particular system can be invaluable. If you are particularly interested in an agency or group, become acquainted with the facilities, resources, and personnel. You may also wish to volunteer to give a talk or present an in-service training, which will both benefit the facility and give you an opportunity to hone your speaking abilities.

Networking within your internship can mean enlisting the aid of your supervisors, program consultants, fellow interns, and other contacts. Referrals through friends and colleagues may be as likely to help you find out about a position, particularly those that are advertised in house and not posted in national listings, such as the *APA Monitor*. Let your internship director, supervisors, and faculty at your doctoral granting institution know very early about your long-range interests with respect to job types, locations, and institutions. If they know of anyone whom you should contact in the area, consider asking them to contact the source or provide you with a letter of introduction.

The competition for postgraduate positions and training hours for licensure can be intense, and the most desirable positions are quickly flooded with applicants. A key recommendation from one or more supervisors during your internship can help your application stand out from the pack. Even if you are not immediately entering the professional job market, it is best to ask for a letter when that person's experience of you is fresh. Your graduate program professors may seem part of another world, especially if you have completed your dissertation and are geographically remote. In truth, they may know you better than your internship supervisors, and can therefore write a much stronger letter. Baird (1999) offered the following guidelines for soliciting letters from supervisors: Always provide advance notice when requesting a letter, complete any specific forms necessary, and provide clear instructions regarding special requests. It is also helpful to provide your supervisor with a brief summary of your academic achievements, internship or practicum experience, and any specific accomplishments.

When conducting a job search outside of your internship and graduate school's geographic areas, you would do well to set aside time early in the year to attend national conventions to use job placement services. If you are interested in a particular geographical area, be sure to attend that area's regional or state convention. Similarly, plan on attending conferences and utilizing placement services relevant to your specific practice areas of interest. Plante (1996, 1998) offered principles of success and guidelines for obtaining employment for psychology interns. He suggested that trainees often underestimate the ways in which their skills can be applied to an array of settings in industry, educational, and clinical areas. New opportunities may be created for the recent graduate by thinking more broadly about one's skills and considering piecing together different jobs, such as a half-time job at a university or mental health service clinic with a part-time psychological assistantship in a private practice.

## Passages

The process of terminating the internship is complex and often not addressed. Early awareness about termination may occur midway through the internship year, if not sooner (Guinee, 1998). Yet some interns experience denial and resistance to the termination process (Lamb et al., 1982). To ensure a therapeutic termination with patients, Baird (1999) recommended using a structured format to help address critical issues. This may be especially helpful when therapy is terminated or transferred because of schedule demands rather than the achievement of prearranged goals. Interns may seek assistance from supervisors in terminating therapeutic and staff relationships, although it is also important to allow time to conclude supervisory relationships. Often a shift in the supervisory relationship occurs as the intern desires more collegial supervision, independence, and autonomy. All too often, neither the intern nor the supervisor brings up termination issues in the context of the supervisory relationship (Baird, 1999). Saying good-bye can be difficult for both supervisor and trainee. However, given that the supervisory relationship is a model for learning about therapeutic relationships, feelings about termination should be addressed at this time.

There rarely seems to be a definite rite of passage out of the internship year. Friends and colleagues often drift off to new jobs and concerns. Taking on new roles requires letting go of old roles. Individuals may experience a loss of the role of the student or trainee, coupled with an incomplete assumption of a new identity. This feeling of loss may be exacerbated by having dreams and expectations confronted with reality. Indeed, for many graduates seeking licensure, it can be quite a disappointment to face another year or so of required supervised training before most states will allow you to sit for the license examinations. Finally, after working for the better part of a decade to graduate, the reality of a shifting and competitive professional job market can be felt as an insufficient reward for your efforts. There is often an unspoken expectation that the completion of the internship and conferring of the degree will dramatically change a candidate's self-image and life setting. This is, of course, unrealistic. An awareness of your feelings about these changes, and their related issues of dependency and self-definition, can assist you in moving toward an integration of your personal and professional development.

Interns may wish to plan activities to facilitate the transition out of the internship and provide further opportunities to say goodbye. Guinee (1998) suggested informal gatherings such as a farewell dinner, party, or a retreat to allow interns to look back on and process the year. It can also help solidify relationships that may last a lifetime. Baird (1999) encouraged interns to write thank-you letters after the internship to supervisors, the training director, staff, and other individuals who may have provided assistance during the year. Providing staff with an intern group picture is also a way of expressing appreciation.

Olson, Downing, Heppner, and Pinkney (1986) found that most training programs do not prepare students for entry into a professional setting, the role demands of professional life, and the personal adjustments required. These authors suggested a number of activities that trainees could pursue to mitigate this "emotional roller coaster," including interviewing supervisors about professional transitions they have experienced, inquiring about the availability of mentors during job interviews, making specific plans to maintain contact with graduate-program peers, and making plans to strengthen resources for handling tasks or roles that have been difficult during training.

Personally, as well as professionally, the completion of the internship is a chance to develop a new, but by no means final, sense of one's professional self. It may signal the start of a time of change, exciting and positive in some respects but most likely full of quandaries and reassessment. Levinson (1978) called this stage of one's life "a remarkable gift and burden." The end of the internship signals not an end to learning or development, but a shift in roles as you continue to learn and develop professionally.

## ACKNOWLEDGMENTS

The authors express their appreciation to Hal Dickman and David Wexler for their contributions in creating an enriching and stimulating internship experience and for their wisdom and friendship.

## REFERENCES

American Psychological Association. (1992). Ethical principles of psychologists and code of conduct. *American Psychologist, 47*, 1597–1611.

Baird, B. N. (1999). *The internship, practicum, and field placement handbook: A guide for the helping professions* (2nd ed.), Englewood Cliffs, NJ: Prentice Hall.

Biaggio, M., Paget, T., & Chenoweth, M. (1997). A model for ethical management of faculty-student dual relationships. *Professional Psychology Research and Practice, 28*,184–189.

Cole, M., Kolko, D., & Craddick, R. (1981). The quality and process of the internship experience. *Professional Psychology: Research and Practice, 12*, 570–577.

Constantine, M., & Gloria, A. (1998). The impact of managed health care on predoctoral internships sites: A national survey. *Professional Psychology Research and Practice, 29*, 195–199.

Dana, R., Gilliam, M., & Dana, J. (1976). Adequacy of academic clinical preparation for internship. *Professional Psychology, 7,* 112–116.

Foster, L. (1976). Truth in advertising psychology internship programs. *Professional Psychology, 7,* 120–124.

Gold, J., Meltzer, R., & Sherr, R. (1982). Professional transition: Psychology internships in rehabilitation settings. *Professional Psychology: Research and Practice, 13,* 397–403.

Guinee, J. P. (1998). Erikson's life span theory: A metaphor for conceptualizing the internship year. *Professional Psychology: Research and Practice, 29,* 615–620.

Hafner, A. (1973). Innovations in clinical psychology internship training. *Professional Psychology, 4,* 111–118.

Hammel, G., Olkin, R., & Taube, D. (1996). Student-educator sex in clinical and counseling psychology doctoral training. *Professional Psychology: Research and Practice, 27,* 93–97.

Harrar, W., VandeCreek, L., & Knapp, S. (1990). Ethical and legal aspects of clinical supervision. *Professional Psychology: Research and Practice., 21,* 37–41.

Heine, R. (1973). The clinical internship in medical and non-medical settings: A report of student opinion. *Professional Psychology, 1,* 104–106.

Holroyd, J. (1973). Problems implementing an elective internship program. *Professional Psychology, 4,* 478–480.

Kaslow, N., & Rice, D. (1985). Developmental stresses of psychology internship training: What training staff can do to help. *Professional Psychology: Research and Practice, 16,* 253–261.

Kurtz, R. (1974). Emerging issues in accreditation of training programs in school psychology. *Journal of School Psychology, 12,* 114–120.

Lamb, D., Baker, J., Jennings, M., & Yarris, E. (1982). Passages of an internship in professional psychology. *Professional Psychology, 13,* 661–669.

Levinson, D. (1978). *The seasons of a man's life.* New York: Ballantine.

Malouf, J., Hass, L., & Farah, M. (1983). Issues in the preparation of interns: Views of trainers and trainees. *Professional Psychology & Research and Practice, 14,* 624–631.

Moskowitz, S., & Rupert, P. (1983). Conflict resolution within the supervisory relationship. *Professional Psychology: Research and Practice, 14,* 632–641.

Oehlert, M., Sumerall, S., & Lopez, S. (1998) *Internship selection in professional psychology: A comprehensive guide for student, faculty and training directors.* Springfield, IL: Charles Thomas.

Olson, S., Downing, N., Heppner, P., & Pinkney, J. (1986). Is there life after graduate school? Coping with the transition to postdoctoral employment. *Professional Psychology: Research and Practice, 17,* 415–419.

Petzel, T., & Bemdt, D. (1980). APA internship selection criteria: Relative importance of academic and clinical preparation. *Professional Psychology, 11,* 792–796.

Plante, T. G. (1996). Ten principles for success for psychology trainees embarking on their careers. *Professional Psychology: Research and Practice, 27,* 303–307.

Plante, T. G. (1998). How to find a first job in professional psychology: Ten principles for finding employment for psychology interns and postdoctoral fellows. *Professional Psychology: Research and Practice, 29,* 508–511.

Rice, D., & Gurman, A. (1973). Unresolved issues in the clinical psychology internship. *Professional Psychology, 4,* 403–408.

Sheinberg, K., & Keeley, S. (1974). Training practices and satisfaction with pre-internship preparation. *Professional Psychology, 5,* 98–105.

Sheinberg, K., & Leventhal, D. (1981). Attitudes of internship directors toward pre-internship training and clinical training models. *Professional Psychology, 12,* 639–646.

Shows, W. (1976). Problems of training psychology interns in medical schools: A case of trying to change the leopard's spots. *Professional Psychology, 7,* 205–208.

Snyder, C., & Ray, W. (1972). Applying for a predoctoral internship in clinical psychology. *Professional Psychology, 3*, 385–386.

Solway, K. S. (1985). Transition from graduate school to internship: A potential crisis. *Professional Psychology: Research and Practice, 16*, 50–54.

Stedman, J. (1997). What we know about predoctoral internship training: A review. *Profession Psychology: Research and Practice, 28*, 475–485.

Sturgis, D., Verstegen, J., Randolph, D,, & Garvin, R. (1980). Professional psychology internships. *Professional Psychology, 11*, 567–573.

Tedesco, J. (1979). Factors involved in the selection of doctoral internships in clinical psychology. *Professional Psychology, 10*, 852–858.

Tipton, R., Watkins, C., & Ritz, S. (1991). Selection, training, and career preparation of predoctoral interns in psychology. *Professional Psychology: Research and Practice, 22*, 60–67.

Weiss, S. (1975). The clinical psychology intern evaluates the training experience. *Professional Psychology, 6*, 435–441.

Zammit, G. K., & Hull, J. W. (1995). *Guidebook for clinical psychology interns.* New York: Plenum Press.

# V

# Becoming A Professional

# 25

# Coping with Licensing, Credentialing, and Lifelong Learning

*Bruce R. Fretz*

The information and advice in this chapter are primarily for those readers planning careers as practicing psychologists, as opposed to teachers on researchers. However, because even the latter sometimes wish to engage in part-time practice, they too may find it useful. Psychologists who work in clinics, hospitals, managed care companies, or in their own practices are required to have licenses and/or other professional credentials, which must be renewed throughout their entire careers. These credentials are often, at least initially, based on what has been studied in graduate programs; therefore, even though licensing may seem an issue far in the distant future, students should begin to pay attention to licensing requirements as they begin thinking about choosing a graduate program.

The first section of this chapter focuses on licensing as a psychologist: why it is needed and what kinds of licenses are available, as well as what implications different kinds of licenses have for choices of graduate programs, internships, and first career positions. The second section of this chapter reviews the key requirements for increasingly important additional professional credentials. These credentials have always been valuable for informing the public about the special expertise of psychologists; now they have become almost essential to have if a practicing psychologist wishes to be a paid provider for a managed care company. The last sections of this chapter focus on the importance of, and requirements for, effective continuing professional education. Emerging technology brings new opportunities for making lifelong learning not only a part of professional credentialing but also of value to the effectiveness of your career as a psychologist.

# WHO NEEDS LICENSING AND WHY?

All practicing psychologists are now required to have some sort of professional license. The exact nature and title of these licenses will vary from state to state and may also vary according to graduate degree. The primary reason for such requirements is the protection of the consumer. Although it may seem acceptable to take the attitude "let the buyer beware" for those purchasing refrigerators or used cars, our society has long felt that when persons (a) are "purchasing" or "consuming" services that they may not know much about or (b) may be in especially vulnerable times in their lives, such consumers should have some assurance that the service providers (e.g., doctors, dentists, lawyers, psychologists) have met acceptable standards of training and ethical practice.

The licensing of psychologists first began in the late 1940s; however, it was not until the 1990s that licensing became essential for all practicing psychologists. As Fretz and Mills (1980) described, licensing did not become at all widespread until the emergence, in the 1960s, of health insurance coverage for psychological services. Even then, licensure was required only for those in independent practice; psychologists working in nonprofit clinics and hospitals did not need licensure. The industrialization of health care in the 1990s (managed care, preferred providers organizations, etc.) changed all this; there are now few, if any, opportunities for any mental health professional to practice without some sort of licensure. (See Gelso and Fretz, 2001, for a fuller exploration of the emergence and impact of industrialized health care on the practice of psychology.)

## Who Sets and Monitors Licensing Requirements?

Each state in the United States and each province in Canada determines what kinds of licenses to provide and what requirements must be met. Moreover, each state and province has a board that monitors psychologists' fulfillment of training and ethical practice requirements. Because states and provinces have different legislatures, there is considerable variance in requirements, and one can never be assured that meeting the requirements for licensure in one state or province will allow for licensure in another. Helping states and provinces work as collaboratively as possible is the primary purpose of the Association of State and Provincial Psychology Boards (ASPPB) (Box 4389, Montgomery, AL 36103; 334-832-4580).[1] ASPPB can always provide addresses of state boards as well as information on reciprocity between boards, that is, which states will accept licensure in one state as meeting the qualifications for licensure in another. (ASPPB recently developed the Certificate of Professional Qualification in Psychology to help psychologists cope with varying state licensing requirements. This certificate is not a credential for professional competence or specialization but may be helpful for psychologists moving from one state to another.)

---

[1]As each national licensing or credentialing organization is first mentioned in this chapter, its address and phone number are given. Although many of these organizations are developing electronic web sites, many of their URLs are still in flux and are therefore not listed. Those interested in accessing any available electronic information and application forms should enter the organization's name into a browser or call the phone number provided and ask if a web address is available.

## What is Looked at by Licensing Boards and What are the Implications?

*Degree Labels, Courses, Practica, Internships, and Supervised Experience.*    Licensing boards look first, and primarily, at the label of the degree obtained. To become licensed as a psychologist, the most critical factor is that the graduate program completed be a program in psychology. The degree may be obtained from a College of Education, of Business, of Human Development, and so forth, but must be clearly indicated on the transcript as a program of study in psychology. All doctoral programs that are accredited by the American Psychological Association (APA, 750 First St. NE, Washington, DC 20002, 202-336-5500) automatically meet this requirement; some programs that are not so accredited have achieved designation status in Doctoral Psychology Programs Meeting Designation Criteria, prepared by the ASPPB and the National Register of Health Service Providers in Psychology (1120 G St. NW, Suite 330, Washington, DC 20005, 202-783-7663). Doctoral degrees that are from neither APA-accredited nor designated doctoral psychology programs will rarely qualify a candidate for licensure as a psychologist; therefore, the first question an applicant to a psychology doctoral program should consider is whether the program is accredited or designated as a psychology program.

For students who wish to be licensed at the master's level, there may be much more flexibility about degree program, depending on what kinds of licensure is available at the master's level (see later discussion of types of licenses). If licensure at the master's level is being considered, then applicants to a master's-level program should ascertain whether the state in which they wish to practice requires that an applicant's graduate program have a particular degree title, such as master's degree in mental health counseling, master's degree in clinical social work, or master's degree in marriage and family counseling.

Beyond the title of the degree, state and provincial boards will next consider both the courses and practica that the applicant completed. Coursework will often be examined even if the degree is from an APA-accredited program. For doctoral-level psychologists, most states adopted standards established in the late 1970s mandating courses in four basic areas of psychology (biological bases, cognitive-affective bases, social bases, individual differences), as well as coursework and practica in the areas of psychological assessment and intervention. At the master's level, the various kinds of licenses may have less specific and extensive requirements, but will still often include basic knowledge requirements as well as practicum requirements. Students should always ascertain how the programs in which they plan to enroll meet the course and practicum requirements for licensure in the state in which they plan to practice.

Licensure at the doctoral-level of psychology always requires completion of an internship and supervised postdoctoral experience. The amount of time required at each of these levels varies from state to state (see Stewart & Stewart, 1998), but is most typically a 1 year internship (may be predoctoral or postdoctoral) and at least 1 year of supervised experience after the doctoral degree is received. There is also much variation among states as to the level of organization required in the internship and postdoctoral experience. Some states prefer that applicants have APA-accredited internships and APA-accredited postdoctoral residencies to meet supervised experience requirements. At the other extreme, in some states all that is required is that a licensed psychologist indicates that he or she has received the number of required hours of supervision. Most critically, the supervisor in all of these settings must usually be a licensed psychologist.

***Examination for Professional Practice in Psychology.***    For anyone who wants to be licensed as a psychologist at either the master's level or doctoral-level, most states and provinces now require the candidate to take the Examination for Professional Practice in Psychology (EPPP). This multiple-choice examination is prepared and administered twice each year by ASPPB. It covers all the basic knowledge areas of psychology as well as assessment, intervention, and ethics. Ryan and Chan (1999) provided provocative data on misperceptions many examinees have about the EPPP. The examinees—that is, recently graduated psychologists—assume the test assesses practice competence, whereas it is really only an assessment of one's knowledge of psychology. Such knowledge is seen as a necessary, but not sufficient, foundation for competent practice. Ryan and Chan argued that the ASPPB should provide more information about both the contents and purpose of the exam, and data on its validity, to advanced graduate students in psychology, well before they actually face the exam. Currently, examinees receive only limited information a few months before taking the exam, and specific validity data are available only by paying additional fees.

Each state and province sets its own passing score for EPPP examinees. Because these standards vary, a passing score in one state may not be acceptable in another state or province. Therefore, psychologists who move may be required, later in their careers, to retake the EPPP and earn a higher score. Obviously, it is therefore best to take this exam as soon as one is eligible after completing graduate work and to prepare for the exam. The *APA Monitor* regularly advertises workshops and home study courses that familiarize candidates with the exam and identify areas that need to be studied. Candidates who have a strong background in basic psychology often nonetheless find it useful to review a basic introductory text, reacquainting themselves with basic learning, perceptual, biological, and social psychological phenomena, and updating their knowledge.

In addition to passing the EPPP, in some states candidates for licensure are also required to complete an oral examination. Novy, Kopel, and Swank (1996) provided an extensive description of one state's (Texas) oral examination as well as suggestions for how to enhance the effectiveness and fairness of oral examinations. These oral exams often include questions specific to the state's psychology licensing law; therefore, applicants should always include study of the licensing law in the state in which they are taking any oral or written exam beyond the EPPP.

For students who are planning to pursue licensure at the master's level in programs other than psychology (e.g., mental health counseling, social work, marriage and family therapy), there are other examinations to be considered. Because this chapter is written primarily for those considering careers in psychology, the examinations for these types of licensing are not described here. An excellent resource for further information on master's-level licensing/certification exams is Wallace and Lewis (1998).

## TYPES OF LICENSES

### Doctoral-Level Psychologists

It should already be clear to the reader that there are various levels of licensure available for those wishing to practice psychology. In this section, three types of licenses are discussed. All three are often obtained by students who want to practice "psychology," yet each requires differing levels of commitment to years and type of study and each has limitations. In most cases, if one wants to be called a "psychologist," and have an independent practice, it is necessary to be licensed as a doctoral-level psychologist. In many states and provinces, to advertise as a "psychologist," licensing at the doctoral-level is mandatory. As will be explored in subsequent paragraphs, other kinds of licenses are available that may permit someone to advertise and provide counseling and psychotherapy, but the title on the license is something other than psychologist, such as psychological assistant or licensed mental health counselor. Moreover, in some states, certain titles like "psychotherapist" are not licensed or certified, and anyone, without any special training, can set up a practice as a psychotherapist, psychic counselor, and so forth. Such practices, of course, can be dangerously misleading to consumers and to the practitioners themselves because neither legal nor liability protection can be provided for untrained, unlicensed practitioners.

Two unique features about doctoral-level psychology licensing need to be briefly noted. First, although the term *licensing* is used throughout this chapter, in some states and provinces the term *certification* is used instead. Although there are some fine points of law that make this distinction meaningful for some interprofessional relationships, for students planning a career in psychology, the differences between "licensing" acts and "certification" acts have no real practical implications. Second, doctoral-level psychology licensing is, in most states and provinces, "generic"; that is, no matter what one majors in during graduate study in psychology, the procedures for licensing are the same. The person who studies social or biological psychology and wishes to become licensed will have to meet the same degree and course requirements as the one who studies counseling or clinical psychology. "Generic" psychology licensing has created some special issues that are further discussed later in this chapter.

There are now over 60,000 doctoral-level licensed psychologists in the United States. The basic components of such licensure were described in the preceding section. Psychologists who hold such licenses are able to set up their own independent or group practices, become part of hospital staffs, or join panels of providers for managed care companies. The Practice Directorate of the APA has, as its primary mission, advocacy and support for practicing psychologists. Doctoral-level licensing provides the greatest number of, and broadest range of, opportunities for practice as a psychologist.

***Specialty Licensing Issues.*** In the early years of development of licensing for psychologists, the primary goal was to distinguish psychologists from a wide range of other practitioners who were offering mental health services, such as social workers, guidance counselors, psychotherapists, and marriage counselors. The emphasis in early laws was on "generic" psychology training. Such laws permitted licensing of those who, in their graduate study in psychology, focused on areas such as sensation and perception, biological psychology, and so forth, and therefore perhaps never completed any courses in psychological assessment or therapeutic interventions. By the late 1960s, when insurance companies began to reimburse psychologists for therapeutic services, these companies (and later, managed care companies) wanted assurance that those who were licensed as psychologists had indeed been appropriately trained to make psychological diagnoses and therapeutic interventions. Some states, in the past few decades, attempted to set up different licenses for those with such training as compared to those with only more basic "generic" training in psychology. However, because of a high degree of overlap in training in various specializations within psychology (e.g., social, personality, clinical, organizational, school, counseling), these attempts to differentiate for licensing have proved extraordinarily difficult to justify and maintain. At any one time in recent years, there have never been more than two or three states that have offered specialty licensing; moreover, the states offering such specialized licenses keep changing because of the difficulties in maintaining distinctions. As explained in the later section on the National Register of Health Service Providers in Psychology, there are credentials that can be obtained that make specialized licensing unnecessary.

*Provisional Licensure for Initial Postdoctoral Years.*     In the earlier section in this chapter describing the basic requirements for psychology licensing, it was noted that most states require 1 or 2 years of postdoctoral supervised experience before one is eligible for licensing. Until the emergence of managed care companies, this stipulation had never proved troublesome for reimbursement of interns or postdoctoral supervisees because a supervising psychologist or psychiatrist certified that competent services had been provided. However, in this age of industrialized health care, most managed care companies will pay only for services provided by *licensed* practitioners, regardless of the kind of practitioner. Because many of the clinics and hospitals that have long trained interns and new postdoctoral psychologists are now being privatized, it has become difficult, if not impossible, to support such trainees if no reimbursements can be obtained for their services. Therefore, there has been a call for developing provisional licenses for the initial postdoctoral years so that reimbursements could be obtained for services provided by psychology interns and residents. As of this writing, it is still too early to tell whether provisional licensing will become prevalent. Nothing in the call for such licensing has changed the substance of preparation for licensing as a psychologist. Therefore, students planning careers in psychology do not need to alter plans, but merely be aware that, just as some states have provisional driving licenses for the first few years one is driving, so too may psychologists have provisional licenses for their first years of practice.

## Master's-Level Psychologists

As already noted in the preceding section on doctoral-level licenses, in most states and provinces, the *independent practice of psychology* (that is, supervision by another professional is not mandatory) requires a doctoral-level license in psychology. Prior to the 1980s, a fair number of states had master's level licensing of psychologists for independent practice; it is still possible to meet some older psychologists who are practicing independently with only a master's degree psychology license. However, in recent decades there have been fewer than 5 states offering master's-level licenses that allow for independent practice within that state. On the other hand, about 25 states have maintained some sort of master's-level licensing in psychology. These licenses typically require that the licensee practice *only* with supervision from a doctoral-level licensed psychologist. The title of the license in most states is not simply psychologist, but rather something like psychological assistant, or psychological technician. Such licenses continue to provide career opportunities for those with master's degrees in psychology in clinics, hospitals, and practices where there is at least one licensed doctoral-level psychologist who can provide supervision. In this age of industrialized health care, where the least expensive provider is often given preference, such opportunities for practice, under the supervision of a doctoral-level professional, may well continue or even expand.

The requirements for obtaining a master's level psychology license, in those state that offer such licenses, typically include completion of a master's degree in psychology. A master's-degree in counseling or family therapy, for example, will often not be acceptable for meeting the educational requirements for master's degree psychology licensure. Because there has never been an accreditation or national designation system for master's-level programs in psychology, there is no assurance that any one program will qualify a graduate for master's level licensure.

It should be apparent that psychologists have long preferred to see the doctoral-level as the only fully acceptable level for licensing in psychology. Consequently, a "terminal" master's degree (that is, not pursuing education beyond the master's level) has been considered by many psychologists as "second-class" status. Indeed, one cannot be a full member of the American Psychological Association (APA) unless a doctoral degree is obtained. Even though there is an organization dedicated to addressing concerns related to master's-level licensure in psychology (North American Association for Masters in Psychology, 400 Boulder Court, Norman, OK 73072, 405-329-3030), the long history of resistance from the APA to accrediting master's degree programs, or licensing graduates of such programs for the independent practice of psychology, has caused many students to consider pursuing master's-degree licenses of the types described in later section on master's-level counselors/licensed professional counselors.

*Master's-Level School Psychologists.* All of the preceding material on limitations of a master's degree in psychology is somewhat attenuated by obtaining a master's degree in *school psychology*. Because each state has its own requirements for certifying school psychologists, that are different from the licensing of psychologists, there are numerous opportunities for those who complete a master's degree in school psychology to work for school systems. It should be noted, however, that the independent practice of psychology outside of the employing school system is not allowed by certification as a school psychologist. For those who would like to specialize in school psychology and practice outside of schools, as well as within schools, the *doctoral* degree in school psychology is the appropriate degree to obtain. The APA accredits doctoral-level programs and internships in school psychology; those programs are always listed in *Graduate Study in Psychology* (APA, 1999). Information on training, career, and credentialing opportunities for school psychologists, at either the master's-degree or doctoral-degree level, may be obtained from the National Association of School Psychologists (4340 East West Highway, Suite 401, Bethesda, MD 20814, 301-657-0270).

## Master's-Level Counselors/Licensed Professional Counselors

The continued resistance of the profession of psychology to licensing at the master's level gave impetus to the development of licensure for master's-level counselors. Almost all states now have some form of certification or licensure for counselors, with the most frequent title being *licensed professional counselors*. The second most frequent title is *certified marriage and family therapist*. By the 1990s, there were over 130,000 licensed professional counselors, a number greater than all licensed psychologists and psychiatrists combined. Each year now, there are approximately three times as many new counselors who become licensed as there are new psychologists who become licensed (Cummings, 1995).

In recent years, as managed health care plans have sought to obtain the services of the least expensive licensed mental health professionals, great strides have been made by advocates of licensed professional counselors for rights to engage in fully independent practice and to perform some diagnostic and psychotherapeutic procedures. Although such persons may not call themselves psychologists nor advertise their services as psychological, they are able to provide many of the therapeutic counseling services that were previously the primary purview of doctoral-level psychologists and psychiatrists.

The American Mental Health Counselors Association (801 N. Fairfax, Suite 304, Alexandria VA 22314, 703-548-6002) has been the most active advocacy group and provided the leadership in developing program accreditation, certification examinations, and standards for licensure. Hollis and Wantz (1994) described hundreds of master's-level graduate programs for counselors. Wallace and Lewis (1998) provided an excellent resource for understanding the prerequisites for becoming a licensed professional counselor. For states such as California, where the number of master's level programs in marriage and family therapy exceeds those in mental health counseling, the accreditation and certification procedures of the American Association for Marriage and Family Therapy may be more relevant (1133 15th St. NW, Suite 300, Washington, DC 20005, 202-452-0109). Students interested in licensing at the master's degree level should clearly obtain information from one or both those sources regarding both the kinds of master's-degree programs in which to enroll and the kinds of supervised experiences that must be obtained to qualify for licensure. In most cases, the master's-level coursework and training involves 2 full years, followed by a specified period of supervised experience.

Before leaving the topic of master's-level counselors, brief mention should also be made of opportunities in clinical social work. Although social work has been a major profession for over a century, it was only in recent decades that the more focused specialty of licensed clinical social work emerged. Those who complete master's-level degree programs in clinical social work and go on to obtain the necessary supervised experience to become an LCSW (licensed clinical social worker) will often have therapy practices similar to those of licensed professional counselors and even licensed psychologists. Information on the broad diversity of careers in traditional social work may be obtained from the National Association of Social Workers (750 First St. NE, Washington, DC 20002, 202-408-8600). Information specific to degree programs and licensing procedures for the LCSW may be obtained from the National Federation of Societies for Clinical Social Work (Box 3740, Arlington VA 22203, 703-522-3866).

## PROFESSIONAL CREDENTIALS: WHAT ARE THEY AND WHY ARE THEY VALUABLE?

Over the past 50 years a number of professional credentials have been developed to provide the public with more information about advanced levels of training, experience, and competence of psychologists. Drum and Hall (1993) described how these developments have helped set high standards for the profession. Now in the age of industrialized health care, all of these credentials have become even more valuable in helping psychologists qualify for provider panels, that is, to be approved as a psychologist who can be reimbursed for services for clients of a managed care company.

In this section, five different kinds of credentials for doctoral-level psychologists are described, as well as the basic requirements for each. The credentials are described in the approximate order in which one would obtain them after completing a doctoral degree in psychology, although the order can be highly variable. Obtaining either of the first two credentials described will greatly facilitate acquiring all of the others in this section.

For those who pursue licensing as master's-level counselors, there are other kinds of specialized credentials too diverse to be covered within this chapter. Information on such credentials may be obtained from the national organizations listed in the preceding section on master's level counselors/licensed professional counselors.

## Accredited Postdoctoral Residencies

This section describes a relatively new credential. It was only in 1999 that the American Psychological Association began accrediting postdoctoral residencies in psychology. These residencies are entered following the completion of the predoctoral internship and completion of the doctoral degree. Postdoctoral residencies not only provide for the fulfillment of most states' postdoctoral supervised experience requirements, but they also facilitate qualifying for other credentials described in this section, especially if they are APA-accredited residencies.

As of this writing, only a small percentage of new doctoral-level psychologists enter residencies (most are not yet APA accredited because of the newness of the procedures, and many residencies are still called postdoctoral fellowships). It is expected that many more residencies will be created in coming years, both at the general postdoctoral-level and in specialized areas such as neuropsychology, psychoanalysis, and clinical health psychology. Acceptance into any one of these accredited residencies will require a high level of performance in the course work, practica, and internship parts of the predoctoral degree. Students who wish to enter a postdoctoral residency should begin to look at the requirements of the kind of residency they wish to enter no later than the third year of their predoctoral program; this will allow for completion of any essential coursework or practica that would help them meet a residency's requirements.

## National Register of Health Service Providers in Psychology

Because of the problems related to generic licensing, described earlier in this chapter, the National Register of Health Service Providers in Psychology (1120 G St. NW, Suite 330, Washington, DC 20005, 202-783-7663) was created in 1974. This register identifies licensed psychologists who have been trained and supervised in the delivery of direct, preventive, assessment and therapeutic intervention services. These psychologists are then called health service providers, as compared to, for example, psychology professors or researchers or organizational consultants. States that have requirements that a psychologist be a health service provider in order to become licensed recognize listing in the National Register (NR) as fully meeting this requirement. A number of managed health care companies have explicit policies of giving preference to those psychologists listed in the NR for becoming part of their provider panels (e.g. Pacific Care Behavioral Health). Magellan, a major health care corporation, uses the NR for verification of credentials of psychologists who apply to be providers.

To become listed in the NR, first a psychologist must obtain a doctoral-level license from at least one state. Then, an applicant's degree, coursework, and supervised experience (minimum of 3000 hours) are carefully examined to determine if all NR educational and supervised experience criteria are met. These criteria are explicit; you may request them from the NR while you are still a graduate student in order to ensure that your training program, internship, and postdoctoral supervised experience meet NR requirements.

## American Board of Professional Psychology: Specialty Certification

Established in 1947, the American Board of Professional Psychology (ABPP; 2100 E. Broadway, Suite 313, Columbia, MO 65201, 573-875-1267) was created to recognize high levels of attainment in a specialty within psychology. In earlier years, a psychologist could not apply for ABPP certification until 5 years of postdoctoral experience had been completed. That requirement was changed in the 1990s to 2 years of supervised experience; therefore, doctoral-level psychologists may now become applicants for ABPP certification almost as soon as they have become licensed. Bent, Packard, and Goldberg (1999) provided an informative brief history of the development of ABPP procedures. These procedures have typically included a review of a work sample from the applicant as well as a 4- to 5-hour competence examination covering the areas of psychological assessment and intervention skills, ethical sensitivity, and utilization of research and theory in practice.

Psychologists who successfully complete ABPP requirements can identify themselves as "board certified" and as having received the diplomate in their specialty. Although ABPP specialty certification was initially limited to the 3 specialties of clinical, counseling, and industrial/organizational, in recent decades the number of specialties in which an ABPP diploma may be obtained has expanded to 12, ranging from behavioral to school psychology. Each specialty has its own examination procedures; information can be obtained from the ABPP at the address already given.

## APA College of Professional Psychology Certificate of Proficiency

One of the newest credentials available to psychologists is the Certificate of Proficiency. As of this writing, the only certificate available is in the "Treatment of Alcohol and Other Psychoactive Substance Use Disorders." Additional certificates of proficiency will be established in areas much more focused than those specialties recognized by ABPP (described earlier), but for which there are highly specific knowledge and skills. If prescription privileges for psychologists become, as expected, more broadly established (Guterriez & Silk, 1998), it is likely that there will be a Certificate of Proficiency created for prescription privileges. These certificates are useful to psychologists in demonstrating both to potential clients and to potential employers that they are well qualified in a particular kind of treatment procedure. It is often a unique intervention skill that makes a psychologist attractive to employers such as hospitals and managed care companies.

Only licensed psychologists may apply for these certificates; applicants must show at least 1 year of experience in the area of the certificate and pass a certification exam specifically created for the certificate of proficiency. Information on procedures for applying for certificates of proficiency may be obtained from the APA College of Professional Psychology (750 First St. NE, Washington, DC 20002, 202-336-6100).

## Hospital Privileges

This last credential to be described is somewhat different from all others in that it is not granted by any national organization. Each individual hospital decides on which professionals it will grant hospital privileges to—that is, the privilege of treating patients within a hospital even when not an employee of the hospital. Beginning in the 1980s, a number of state legislatures mandated that qualified psychologists must be eligible for hospital privileges in appropriate treatment units, such as psychiatric inpatient units, and drug and substance abuse units. As industrialized health care becomes more integrated—that is, as hospitals merge with clinics and group practices—hospital privileges are becoming more important to psychologists. With such privileges, a psychologist, who has clients who at some time require hospitalization, will be able to continue treatment of the client in the hospital, rather than having to transfer the care of the client to another professional caregiver. The National Register of Health Service Providers provides the only national listing of those who have hospital staff privileges (listees must also meet the qualifications of, and be listed in, the NR).

Each hospital has its own criteria and credential review procedures for granting hospital privileges to licensed professionals. Each of the first four credentials described in this section greatly facilitates psychologists obtaining hospital privileges. However, just as important are the recommendations of physicians and other health care providers in the community concerning how effective an applicant psychologist has been in helping patients they have referred to him or her for psychological services.

## CONTINUING PROFESSIONAL EDUCATION: LIFELONG LEARNING

In a study of what makes counselors and therapists pleased and satisfied with their careers, Skovholt and Ronnestad (1992) found a key component was what they called "continuous professional reflection." It consisted of "ongoing professional and personal experiences, a searching process with others within an open and supportive environment, and active reflection about one's experiences" (p. 141). Their findings provide empirical evidence for the tried and worn graduation speech cliché: Graduation is not the end, but rather the beginning. Somewhat ironically, just at the time "students" complete a graduate degree, they are often most keenly aware of how little they really know! In this section, both traditional and exciting new opportunities for lifelong learning are explored.

### Traditional Continuing Education: A Checkered History

In many regulated professions, such as medicine, law, and psychology, the renewal of licenses has often required that professionals provided evidence of "continuing education." Why is completing an MD, a law degree, or a doctoral degree in psychology not enough education? Traditionally, there have been two public responses and one covert response to this question. The public ones are that (a) as professionals gain experience they find certain areas in which they want to receive more specialized training than they had in their original degree, and (b) as new technologies or new bodies of knowledge develop, professionals need to learn about them. They are no longer "in school," so how will they learn this material unless they take continuing education seminars or courses? The covert reason for supporting continuing education comes from an awareness that professionals, especially those who are in full-time practice and not teaching or supervising other professionals, often pay little attention to journals and emerging new information in their field and become more and more stagnant. As Skovholt and Ronnestad (1992) found, stagnation frequently leads to feeling "burned out" and to a desire to leave the profession.

With these three perspectives on the values of continuing education (CE), it can certainly be understood that many states have, with all good intentions, required various amount and forms of continuing education. Some states require completion of specific courses on topics such as child abuse, ethics, and human sexuality. Most states specify only that a professional must provide evidence of having participated in $x$ hours (with $x$ being a varying variable!) of seminars, workshops, or courses that have been approved by a state or national organization. At its best, this approach can be effective if a professional carefully considers what kind of continuing education he or she truly needs and is able to find good offerings of this type, completes the CE offering, and receives feedback as to how much progress he or she has made in pertinent knowledge and skills. At its worst, professionals simply choose CE offerings only if they are given in attractive resort settings and then attend as few hours as possible, often receiving no assessment as to whether any new knowledge or skills have been learned. Fortunately, such negative perspectives on CE have led psychologists to look carefully at how to turn the unanticipated bureaucratic outcomes of required CE into the kinds of ongoing professional experiences that Skovholt and Ronnested (1992) found lead to truly satisfying careers. VandeCreek, Knapp, and Brace (1990) prepared an excellent description of how CE programs can be designed to obtain positive outcomes for professionals as well as enhanced services for their patients. Soon after their paper was published, the APA sponsored a major national conference on CE in psychology, laying the groundwork for new perspectives and technologies in "education and training beyond the doctoral degree" (APA, 1995).

## Emerging Forms of Continuing Professional Education

Emerging forms of continuing professional education now often reflect a broader educational perspective, as well as incorporating new technologies. The broader perspective is found in the second part of the title of this entire section: Continuing Professional Education: Lifelong Learning. Degrees and credentials are only steps along the way in a life of learning. Graduate school itself provides not only the courses and training experiences necessary to obtain a degree, but also many opportunities for personal and ongoing professional development. Gelso and Fretz (2001) provided specific suggestions on how to take advantage of such opportunities through elective courses, professional readings, professional conventions, "externships," internships, the dissertation, and initial postdoctoral career choices. As Gelso and Fretz explained, the key to turning graduate school into professional development—and later, any required CE into meaningful personal and professional development—is to change the "means to an end" attitude into an attitude of professional development. Rather than simply meeting a graduate school or licensing requirement, ask how it can be done in a way that meets your own professional needs.

Combining this broader perspective on CE with what psychologists know about good pedagogical techniques helped the participants in the APA conference on postdoctoral education and training identify four needs: (a) strategies for psychologists' self-assessment of their own professional strengths and weaknesses, (b) strategies for psychologists to review the range of interventions available to address their own weaknesses, (c) multiple ways of arranging for an appropriate intervention and evaluating personal progress, and then finally (d) strategies for reiterating these steps so that next CE efforts are chosen after a new assessment to determine what is the next weakness to be addressed. As Gelso and Fretz (2001) pointed out, emerging electronic technology provides a way of responding to all four of these needs. Simply by going online, psychologists can make self-assessments, identify available options of various intensity and style, then complete appropriate CE offered via teleconferencing or online services. At the completion of the CE offering, the psychologist can complete an online assessment to determine if he or she has attained an adequate level of knowledge and skills or whether further work is needed. Future CE seems likely, therefore, to be much more "user-friendly" and intrinsically satisfying than the CE of past years.

## TECHNOLOGY AND SEAMLESS CREDENTIALING

The same electronic technology that can enhance CE can also greatly facilitate applying for and obtaining all the kinds of credentials described in this chapter. Until now, for almost every new credential applied for, psychologists had to begin anew the process of completing a multipage application form, requesting transcripts, confirming supervision received, and obtaining certificates indicating earned credits of CE. In recent years, national leaders of psychology credentialing organizations have begun to look at ways of using electronic technology to reduce redundant application requirements. In the final paragraphs of this chapter, suggestions are given for kinds of information to accumulate in a personal electronic file that may, in subsequent years throughout one's career in psychology, be called up and simply inserted into application forms. It is expected that, in the reasonable near future, all credentialing agencies will follow the lead of the National Register and provide for online applications, thereby allowing an applicant simply to download accumulated required information from a personal electronic file onto the application form.

### Building a Professional Portfolio

From the first semester in graduate training in either a master's degree or doctoral degree program, there are numerous bits and pieces of information that students often fail to save. "The course is over, throw out all that 'stuff.'" Yet, in later applications for professional credentials, one may well be asked for (a) a course syllabus and (b) the name of text used; for practica, requests may be made additionally for (c) number and type of clients seen, (d) number and types of psychological assessments made, (e) name and professional discipline of supervisor and (f) copy of the written evaluation provided by the supervisor. Obviously, all of this information can easily be scanned into one's personal electronic portfolio at the end of each course. Whenever professional development opportunities are pursued through volunteer research or services, attending professional conventions, and so forth, they also should be documented in the portfolio, along with the names of any faculty members or supervisors who could attest to these activities.

Pertinent to the establishment of electronic files, in 1999, the National Register of Health Service Providers (address given earlier) established the National Psychology Trainee Register, designed to allow psychology interns and postdoctoral residents to file, electronically, information on their graduate training and supervised experience. For psychologists planning to enter health service positions, using this register allows for an early determination of acceptability of these training and experience. Moreover, with this information already on file in the National Psychology Trainee Register, later applications for credentials (after licensure is obtained), such as listing in the NR, an APA Certificate of Proficiency, or the ABPP diploma, will be a much briefer and surer process than the current ones.

## Virtues of Carefulness and Thoroughness

All the advancements in electronic technology have not overcome the need for two virtues in the real world of credentialing: carefulness and thoroughness. The writer of this chapter has more than 25 years of service as a reviewer and board member of credentialing organizations; it is from that experience that this last section has emerged. Although spell-check will catch spelling errors, it will not catch errors like writing the current date in the space that asks for one's birth date, or dates of the internship being shown as taking place before one entered graduate school. What is a reviewer to conclude when an applicant does not provide requested confirmation of supervision received, or indicates he or she graduated from an APA-approved internship when there is no official listing of such an internship? Or if an applicant indicates his or her degree is in psychology when the transcript says "Family Studies"? Sometimes these are simply errors of carelessness; at other times they are misrepresentations caused by misunderstandings, such as believing an internship was APA approved because the faculty in the APA-approved doctoral program said it was OK to accept that internship.

Although many of these errors or misrepresentations can be clarified by contacting the applicant, the credentialing process is then delayed, often for months. Moreover, reviewers, when faced with such errors, often then question the professional qualities of the applicant: If the application is completed carelessly or thoughtlessly, does this say something about how the psychologist keeps progress notes or communicates psychological assessment results to schools or courts? Hopefully, these few sentences say enough about the virtues of carefulness and thoroughness.

To sum up this chapter, there are highly effective strategies, from graduate school through to the age of retirement, for developing successful and deeply satisfying careers as fully credentialed professional psychologists. I hope that you as readers will make frequent use of them.

## REFERENCES

American Psychological Association (1995). *Education and training beyond the doctoral degree.* Madison, CT: International Universities Press.

American Psychological Association (1999). *Graduate study in psychology.* Washington, DC: Author.

Bent, R. J., Packard, R. E., & Goldberg, R. W. (1999). The American Board of Professional Psychology, 1947–1997: A historical perspective. *Professional Psychology: Research and Practice, 30,* 65–73.

Cummings, N. A. (1995). Impact of managed care on employment and training: A primer for survival. *Professional Psychology: Research and Practice, 26*, 10–15.

Drum, D. J., & Hall, J. E. (1993). Psychology's self-regulation and the setting of professional standards. *Applied & Preventive Psychology, 2*, 151–161.

Fretz, B. R., & Mills, D. H. (1980). *Licensing and certification of psychologists and counselors.* San Francisco: Jossey-Bass.

Gelso, C. J., & Fretz, B. R. (2001). *Counseling psychology* (2nd ed.). Fort Worth, TX: Harcourt Brace.

Gutierrez, P. M., & Silk, K. R. (1998). Prescription privileges for psychologists: A review of psychological literature. *Professional Psychology: Research and Practice, 29*, 213–222.

Hollis, J. W., & Wantz, R. A. (1994). *Counselor preparation* (8th ed.). Muncie, IN: Accelerated Development.

Novy, D. M., Kopel, K. F., & Swank, P. R. (1996). Psychometrics of oral examinations for psychology licensure: The Texas examination as an example. *Professional Psychology: Research and Practice, 27*, 415–417.

Ryan, A. M., & Chan, D. (1999). Perceptions of the EPPP: How do licensure candidates view the process? *Professional Psychology: Research and Practice, 30*, 519–530.

Skovholt, T. M., & Ronnestad, M. H. (1992). *The evolving professional self.* New York: Wiley.

Stewart, A. E., & Stewart, E. A. (1998). Trends in postdoctoral education: Requirements for licensure and training opportunities. *Professional Psychology: Research and Practice, 29*, 273–283.

VanderCreek, L., Knapp, S., & Brace, K. (1990). Mandatory continuing education for licensed psychologists: Its rationale and current implementation. *Professional Psychology: Research and Practice, 21*, 135–140.

Wallace, S. A., & Lewis, M. D. (1998). *Becoming a professional counselor* (2nd ed.). Thousand Oaks, CA: Sage.

# 26

# Community Intervention: Applying Psychological Skills in the Real World

*Raymond P. Lorion*

*A. Dirk Hightower*

This chapter describes a generic skill that we have come to appreciate increasingly over our careers. The skill complements our clinical, diagnostic, and therapeutic techniques as well as our conceptual, methodological, and statistical abilities. In fact, we see the capacity to relate to the world outside of the clinic, the hospital, the campus, and the laboratory as essential for the effective application of these other skills. Many professionals need to acquire that skill on entry into the professional ranks; for some, it needs to be refreshed periodically thereafter. Years of higher education, especially at the graduate level, distance far too many of us from the communities, agencies, services, providers, and residents of settings in which we conduct our clinical and scientific activities. Many of us return to those settings and people with the assumption that our professional responsibility is to do "to them" rather than "with them." Thus, we have come to view ourselves as different from before and hence from those we serve or study. As careers advance and success is achieved in professional settings, the gap may (re)open or even widen, especially if academic and professional standing and their attributed expertise are not balanced with understanding and empathy for the lives of everyday folks.

Sarason (1985) provided valuable insights into the costs of such off-putting and distancing behavior by professionals. He offered the term *professional preciousness* to convey the sense that professional knowledge, experience, and perspectives are always superior to those of lay individuals. Effectively, what began as the pursuit of a career in the service of others becomes detached from those whom we seek to serve! This chapter examines that perspective, its implications for clinical and research activities, and ways that this gap may be reduced.

We remember vividly our initial attempts to "serve" the community. Local agencies were approached to recruit *them* into *our* efforts to assess *their* needs and design and implement *our* interventions. We were unprepared for the skepticism, suspicion, and resistance from individuals and agencies that followed. Our responses to *their* reaction varied from initially questioning *our* skills, to defending the virtue of *our* intentions, to assuming self-righteously that *our* concern for the needs of *their* residents exceeded *their* concern. Not understanding their unwillingness to accept gratefully and without question *our* offer to help *them* led us to rely on *our* professional standing and the presumed infallibility of *Doctor* or *Professor* to justify *our* cause. Predictably, this strategy met with little success; inevitably it made explicit the "us versus them" quality of the interaction and heightened each party's discomfort with and questioning of the other. Fortunately, the experience and wisdom of mentors and community colleagues helped us distinguish professional skills per se from the professional role.

With reflection, it became apparent that, good intentions notwithstanding, we triggered a number of land mines. To undo the damage, steps had to be retraced before tasks were accomplished or before assistance, albeit needed and even desired, was accepted. Mutually beneficial opportunities were jeopardized because of communications distorted by assumptions whose validity remained unexamined by either party. With the unerring perceptiveness of hindsight, it is evident that prior to graduate school, the first author received a hint of dangers ahead. The warning came not from a mentor or supervisor, but from a construction coworker. The master carpenter under whom I had apprenticed described mixed emotions about my decision to pursue a career in clinical psychology. The carpenter's support for the decision was mingled with a sense of loss. In his words, "they [i.e., professionals generally and "shrinks" particularly] don't think, act, or talk like 'us' [i.e., working-class people] and they sure don't mix with us." The carpenter was convinced that a change would occur and that graduate training would separate me like all professionals, from "real" people. He doubted that our friendship would last or that I would retain or appreciate what he had taught me.

The master carpenter's concern reflected a serious obstacle for many professionals: acceptance by professionals and those they serve of an assumed difference between the professional and "real" people. This obstacle is especially serious for the mental health professions, including those in the applied psychological fields, because of popular stereotypes about our capacity to "read minds," that is, to know how someone really feels, and our continual analysis of the subtleties of interpersonal situations. For many (and unfortunately, too many of us), the mental health professional seems constantly to be judging, evaluating, and analyzing others. This image is reinforced by laypersons who share personal experiences and concerns when meeting a psychologist and by psychologists who encourage such informal disclosures. As noted later, *professional* distance is appropriate under certain conditions. It must not, however, generalize to *personal* distance. Some protection against that outcome can be found in the definition of a profession:

A calling requiring specialized knowledge and often long and intensive preparation, including instruction in skills and methods as well as in the scientific, historical, or scholarly principles underlying such skills and methods, maintaining by force of organization or concerted opinion high standards of achievement and conduct, and *committing its members to continued study and to a kind of work which has for its prime purpose the rendering of public service.* (emphasis added; *Webster's*, 1967)

Careful attention to that definition, in particular to the emphasized components, can be useful as one begins interacting with a community's residents or agencies. By remaining aware that "public service" represents the purpose of professional skills, the mental health professional can avoid at least some pitfalls (Lorion, 1991). Ironically, the motive that led most of us to become mental health professionals—to understand and help others— too often is lost in the initial excitement and anxiety of undertaking at least that pursuit. In struggling to "do well", some forget that the real goal is to "do good," or, at least, "do no harm" (Lorion & Iscoe, 1996).

## OBSTACLES TO INTERVENTION

Many errors may interfere with attempts to initiate clinical, consultative or research efforts in a community. Although few professionals stumble over more than one or two of these at a time, even one or two can undermine the effectiveness of the most refined professional skills. Rather than attempt to prioritize them in terms of potential damage, we simply present them here alphabetically. In reviewing these, the reader should pay heed to the old adage, "if the shoe fits…. " Given the authors' shared involvement in the development of a long-lasting, seemingly well-fitting community-based prevention project, we invite readers to review an initial (Cowen et al., 1975) and updated (Cowen et al., 1996) description of the Primary Mental Health Project for concrete examples of how one might successfully proceed from conceptualizing to implementing a program.

### Arrogance

Simply stated, professional training, with its emphasis on scholarship, technical skills, and professional excellence, sometimes deludes one into assuming that the lack of professional credentials or a lack of familiarity with professional jargon renders others devoid of wisdom, knowledge, understanding, and experience. So misguided, a professional's interactions with others become elitist, and unidirectional, and, consequently, little real exchange occurs between the service provider and service recipients. Nonprofessional colleagues who are not appreciated for the perceptiveness of their insights or the effectiveness of their activities may begin to feel devalued and come to resent the professional. Professional opinions and activities may be presented and perceived as the only ones of value. In response, a community agency may ignore a professional's requests to implement a program because it refuses to respond with the expected self-deprecation. At times, the contact is simply discontinued, or it lasts long enough to highlight the professional's inadequacies.

### Carelessness

Completion of professional training for some is accompanied by the assumption that one's "homework" is over and professional skills are complete. From this erroneous position, one enters a situation with inadequate knowledge of its history, its present state, its political realities, or its multiple agenda. Most professionals eventually recognize that their doctoral education prepares them to ask the questions and find answers, rather than providing the answers a priori. It is unprofessional to enter any situation, clinical, consultative, or research, without preparation and without an appreciation of what one does not know. Simply realizing the need to visit the setting in which one intends to deliver service is important. Where are its boundaries? What is its history? Who inhabits it and what are their patterns of comings and goings? Are the setting's occupants there by choice? If a research question is to be asked, it is important to know whose question it is and how different members of the community, agency, or setting will interpret and/or benefit from the findings. If a clinical referral has been made, it is important to understand the contextual parameters of the focal problem.

If, for example, one is intent on consulting to a school district's special education unit, it is imperative that one understand that unit's administrative structure and its place within the district's organizational schema. A consultant and a researcher who intend to solicit a community agency's cooperation in data collection should not contact the setting without preparing a working draft of the responsibilities, expectations, and commitment of each party, a proposed scheduling of events, and expected limits of respective involvements. Without such starting points, ambiguities can arise whose subsequent clarification may undermine from the outset a working relationship. If so, commitments may subsequently have to be retracted, eroding the professional's credibility.

In essence, it is critical that in the excitement of starting one's career, one temper one's enthusiasm lest commitments exceed capacity and haste leads to many marginal products rather than a few selected excellent ones. Many a career has been crippled early, and sometimes late, by the reputation of not carrying through on one's promises and disappointing consumers of one's services. Credibility is initially assumed, but once lost it is difficult, sometimes impossible, to regain.

### Distance

As noted, a professional may have the self-perception or may be perceived by others as somehow "different" from others in a community and therefore feel required by all concerned to assume a preordained role (e.g., as an impartial expert; as an "objective" evaluator) in interactions. To the extent that being a professional reflects the possession of a defined body of knowledge and specific skills (cf. the definition of "profession" cited earlier), the assumption of unique roles and responsibilities is appropriate. It should not, however, lead to the misconception that "different" skills and knowledge are equivalent to "better" or "more important" skills and knowledge. If the latter perspective is adopted by the professional, he or she may insist on an artificial distance that leads to an inability to appreciate the unique skills and knowledge of "lay persons" and even members of other professions as resources in problem solving.

A mental health professional, for example, may enter a school to assist with a problem child or to study a new instructional strategy and fail to respect and take advantage of the expertise of those involved in the educational process, such as the teacher whose front-line insights can both facilitate and improve the professional's work. Sensitized to the professional's insistence on his expertise, the front-liners may hesitate to offer unsolicited (albeit critically important) comments or to respond positively to offered suggestions. Distance begets distance and elicits rejection or passive-aggressiveness rather than cooperation.

Recently, the first author moved to a new university and began, once again in his career, to collaborate with a local school system. Without an intervention program or specific study in hand, he approached a local school, explained his recent arrival in the city, and requested an opportunity to discuss his interests and background with the principal. That meeting led to an open discussion with teachers about his interests in the prevention of factors that place youth at risk for emotional problems generally and violence and substance involvement specifically. With the intent of becoming familiar with the local school system, the specific setting, and local educators, he offered to assist teachers however he could. Over the next few months, he met regularly with six to eight teachers to discuss their concerns about "behavior" and strategies for responding to disruptive children. Those meetings culminated in the formation of a team of university researchers, graduate students, and teachers who plan to meet over the summer to formulate a proposal for "enriching the school climate." That proposal will be presented to the faculty of the school for their review, revision, and, hopefully, approval in the fall. What is important to note is that the proposal will justifiably be viewed as *their* proposal rather than as the first author's. It is also important to point out that the initial contact and exploratory meetings were not undertaken simply as a means to "get in." If the years have taught us anything about working in communities, it is to respect and gain from the wisdom of those in the trenches who confront the issues of concern daily with limited resources and multiple competing demands for their time and attention. False humility is not the key; an appreciation of one's limitations and of the absolute necessity of collaboration leads to the expression of genuine respect.

Ideally, implementation of some version of the proposal resulting from months of informal contact will lead to a pilot study of a combined school–family approach to reducing disruptive behaviors in the classroom. Ultimately, in close collaboration with that school and others nearby, a formal funding proposal will be prepared for submission to federal, state, local, and foundation sources. That submission will include both the first author and representatives from the schools as coinvestigators and coapplicants. In all likelihood, the school system will receive the bulk of funds to cover service costs, with that portion needed for evaluation and other scientific components of the work subcontracted to the university. Within such a structure, schools typically feel both empowered and partnered.

## Frailty

Even though the meek will ultimately inherit the earth, their immediate success as professionals can be difficult. Under most circumstances, community interventions carry with them a cost related primarily to the capacity to "hang in there" and gain credibility by demonstrating one's commitment to the task at hand (e.g., a research project) and related willingness to overcome obstacles that impede attainment of desired goals. Commonly referred to as "paying one's dues," this aspect of professional life reflects the testing of one's professional qualifications, abilities, and persistence by those whose cooperation is sought (Lorion & Iscoe, 1996). As discussed later, entrance into a community often requires an initiation period during which one's credentials, resolve, and self-confidence are scrutinized. Refusal to complete this "rite of passage" and to "show one's stuff" can quickly undermine one's acceptance into a community agency whose staff has worked long and hard to gain credence with a skeptical clientele. In contrast, responding to the initiation phase with openness and a demonstrated determination to accomplish one's goal will serve as valuable currency that can subsequently be translated into cooperation and true collaboration. As one person who gave us a particularly difficult time in becoming involved with a school once said, "I had to find out if it was important enough to you to fight for before I'd let it become important to me."

## Grandiosity

Bigger is not always better, and complexity is *not* a sign of professional competence. Rather, "start small and go slow" and "keep it simple, stupid—KISS" are rules that have served us well. Whenever possible, start small, especially when you are working with a new effort or a foreign system or agency. Starting small allows for more careful scrutiny of your efforts, a better focus on quality control, and an improved chance to thoughtfully address the inevitable "brush fires" associated with "new" interventions. A small successful "pilot" will provide a solid foundation from which to build the necessary relationships for larger more risky efforts. Starting small is less expensive, permits you to prudently address inevitable missteps, reduces administrative worries, provides valuable experiences working within a system, and affords a chance to test an intervention's merits before widespread implementation. A series of small successes builds credibility and capacity; a single large failure is rarely ignored or dismissed (Cowen et al., 1975, 1996; Lorion, 1983).

Another errant tendency for many professionals is to think complex thoughts and then try to incorporate everything into the initial study or intervention. Graduate training may be partially at fault for this tendency. For example, how many times have graduate students created a "new" intervention and attempted to conduct a randomized trial to test its validity at the same time? Too many times to count. Grandiosity is not limited to the neophyte, however. Recently, a multidisciplinary group of seasoned professionals was planning an intervention for preschool children with asthma in the preschool setting. Each professional group contributed to the plan: the physicians wanted to test different medications, the mental health professionals an intervention for the parents, the educators wanted training for teachers, and all the researchers together wanted a randomized design with a control group. All these components are arguably important, but if all were included at once, the complexity of the effort would have been its death. Wiser heads prevailed and priority was given to that effort that was simplest, most well developed, and predicted to account for the greatest amount of variance. Each of the other components was to be developed, piloted, and refined before being added to the mix.

Frequently, to work in the community, complex issues must be approached simply. It is acceptable, and usually better, to develop an intervention without conducting a randomized trial the first time it is piloted. Even when we know most mental health issues have multiple causes, it remains acceptable to work with one independent variable or one issue at a time. If one has a choice between complexity and simplicity, always choose simplicity; it will usually be more professionally elegant.

## Impatience

Somewhere in Murphy's encyclopedia of laws there must be one that states that "everything takes longer than it does." Professional time and real-world time are not the same, because those asked to cooperate with a professional have numerous, equally important demands on their time. The professional must accept the reality of such competing demands and resist the temptation to insist that his or her needs be given priority. If nothing else, community intervention is an extremely time-consuming life event in which multiple compromises must be made. As noted, with respect to carelessness, it is important that anticipated goals, activities, and schedules be communicated as early as possible with a community agency as a point of discussion and deliberation. Most proposals require modification (invariably in terms of extending rather than decreasing the time commitment). Negotiation of a mutually acceptable schedule often serves both as a vehicle for the initiation trials and for the development of reciprocal appreciations of the demands encountered by all involved.

In the absence of careful discussion about issues of timing, the potential for disaster is very high. It is likely that insistence on a rigid timetable will result in its immediate rejection and significantly reduce the likelihood of subsequent interaction with that setting. In the event of the immediate acceptance of the proposed timetable, caution should be the watchword. Typically, the setting's realities (even when good intentions motivated the acceptance of the project) will result in unavoidable delays throughout the period of agreement. Thus, time must be invested early in order to develop a truly acceptable timetable that respects the occurrence of foreseeable and unforeseeable delays. In the majority of instances, patience and flexibility serve one well. When time is truly "of the essence," a record of prior flexibility may provide the necessary chits to meet mandatory deadlines.

## Naiveté

Most professionals approach community settings with misunderstandings about a setting's functions and operations. Limited direct experience with new work settings explains one's initial naiveté. Its continuation, however, is neither justifiable nor wise. Initial admissions of ignorance may be graciously accepted and even allay somewhat the setting's suspiciousness. Quickly, however, continued naiveté can be interpreted as disinterest in the setting or criticism of its procedures. Strategies for efficiently learning about a setting are discussed later.

One issue about which professionals seem most naive is their failure to recognize that information is exchanged within and across community settings, agencies, and systems. As a professional seeks to learn about settings and agencies within a community, the agencies through their staff, in turn, learn about the professional. An agency's staff uses its contacts in academia, in funding sources, in the professional community, and in the community generally to learn as much as possible about their potential collaborator. Prior contacts with the local or state service agencies or schools by the professional are identified and assessed. One's "reputation" is based on attitude, interpersonal style, and, especially, productivity—that is, were previous promises kept and "deliverables" complete and timely? Early involvements with a community, in response to clinical referrals, requests for evaluation assistance from a setting, or recruitment of participants for one's research, should be carried out with maximum care, openness, and professionalism. It is frequently difficult to overcome early disappointments. The guiding principle is that one gets only a single opportunity to make a first impression.

Consider the example provided earlier, describing the first author's initial contacts with a local school. He has since learned from colleagues at the university of calls that they received in order for the school's personnel to "find out about this guy." In fact, a colleague from another state described a call received from a teacher who knew someone who was married to someone who knew of the distant colleague's work on a topic similar to that of the author's.

The call was to determine if the author's work was known and if the field had any negative views of his manner of relating to local schools. Finally, it is clear that the local school made calls to other school settings in which the author has worked (identified by his prior university affiliations). Readers should assume that their work occurs within a relatively small world that has become even smaller with increasing access to the Internet.

### Suspicion

Seemingly forewarned, some professionals approach community settings anticipating that the setting will respond with hostility, disinterest, and skepticism. Within this assumption lies the seed of a negative self-fulfilling prophecy. Concerned that a setting will not accept a study's protocol or an intervention in its entirety, a mental health professional may initially present only elements presumed to be acceptable; this is a mistake! Once approval is obtained, the scientist may hope to introduce the additional components gradually, perhaps even without further discussion; this is inevitably a bigger mistake! Some settings will feel deceived and terminate their cooperation. Others may honor their initial commitment but express their displeasure by refusing further involvements or approaching them with skepticism and distrust.

A majority of community settings that have cooperated with professionals in research, programmatic, or consultative activities have shared the fate of not receiving promised final reports, feedback, or follow-up. Their individual and combined experience in this area represents perhaps a primary obstacle to continued participation with professionals generally, and academics particularly. When a referral of any type is made, its outcome often remains totally unknown. Hence the community agent has no way of knowing whether the referral was appropriate and whether his or her interactions should change in any way to support the intervention.

These examples suggest that a setting's reluctance to participate or cooperate may be justified by past experience and may reflect the general tendency to tar all professionals with the same brush. In our experiences, the most effective response to that possibility is to acknowledge its existence, discuss specific concerns, and create a specific set of agreements that will operationalize the collaborative involvements of each party and provide a vehicle for the review of actual or presumed shortcomings.

## INTERVENTION STRATEGIES

In preparing this chapter, we reminded ourselves repeatedly that its focus was to be sufficiently general to serve many applied mental health fields. We assumed that the reader is not a native of the community in which professional skills will be used and is a stranger to the agencies and settings with which cooperation is sought. Given those assumptions, the process of developing or applying community intervention skills can be divided into the following components:

1. The community: a first glimpse.

2. The setting/agency: preliminary considerations.

3. Gaining entry: negotiations and contracts.

4. Collaboration: translating words into actions.

5. Feedback and follow-up.

## The Community: A First Glimpse

Graduate training in mental health teaches much about understanding people as individuals and relatively little about the communities in which they live, work, and play. By definition, however, the latter are centrally relevant to the application of acquired skills. So, how does one "work up" the community?

A reasonable first step is to learn something about its geography. What are its boundaries? Who are its neighbors? Where do people—live? receive services? go to school? shop? work? and play? Plotting such facts on a city or county map teaches one much about the community's structure and its resources, and can also identify some of its needs. If surface public transportation is available, riding on its major routes can provide a useful overview of the community: people, architecture, shops, and such. Additional information can be gained by visiting major shopping areas throughout the community, and by dropping into neighborhood restaurants, community centers, and even bars.

Depending on one's specific interest, a more focused examination can be made of the community's medical, mental health, educational, industrial, or vocational resources. For any of these categories it is useful to identify their location within the community, their diversity, their working hours, their funding base, and, finally, their organizational structure. How are the various components of these community segments linked to each other in formal and informal ways? Which individual, group of individuals, or governing bodies oversee the functions and interactions of these components? How does the selected segment of the community (e.g., the schools) interface with its other segments (e.g., mental health)? What, if any, important local, state, regional, or national events have impacted on that segment during the past year? Finally, what are the major political factions and issues that influence the operation of that segment of the community?

Similar attention should be paid to the community's residents. If the setting in which one intends to practice professionally represents a major geographic change (e.g., East to West, North to South, urban to rural, etc.), differences in customs, speech, and food preferences may be marked. Time should be invested in meeting its people and learning from them what the community is like. Valuable resources for such information include the retired population, shopkeepers, clergy, school principals, directors of human resources from both profit and not-for-profit organizations, and neighborhood newspapers. A student whose dissertation involved a survey of adolescent girls' parenting in low-income urban neighborhoods marked by violence spent months "just" visiting the community, talking with residents, eating meals with those who frequented local eateries, and chatting with shopkeepers. Her efforts enabled her to design and conduct a valuable ethnographic study.

Finally, it is important to understand a community's political, fiscal, and demographic base. Who are the community's elected leaders? Who are its most influential and/or respected citizens? Which individuals are perceived negatively; which are on the rise? What are the major political issues in the community and who are their advocates and opponents? However devoted one might be to the *New York Times*, the *Washington Post*, or any other major newspaper, the real information will be found in local and even neighborhood newspapers. Newcomers to an area should spend considerable time talking and, especially, listening to the issues that fill coffee-shop conversations, local talk radio, local television news reports, and public hearings.

As part of his effort to learn about the local schools, the first author has attended neighborhood association meetings, met with clergy, and spoken to health care providers, trolley drivers and riders, and parent volunteers in the schools. He has chatted with students in hallways, classrooms, and recreational areas of the school. What he has learned over many years is that much information can be acquired from a university library and from reviewing relevant scientific literature. What information is gained from those sources, however, must be balanced with that which is gained through community reconnaissance.

Other questions can and should be asked about the sources of the community's fiscal resources. What is its tax base? Which industries contribute most to the economic and cultural quality of the community? Which budgetary issues arouse the most and least debate? A review of the community's line-item budget may reveal support for one human service program (e.g., a recreational program for the elderly) and disproportionate reductions in another (e.g., Meals on Wheels). Another aspect of a community's economic base is the nature and structure of its charitable organizations (United Way), local foundations, and volunteer organizations. Newcomers should identify which services the community values, which services are underfunded, and insofar as possible, attempt to understand the factors that determine the distribution of resources.

A third set of questions needs to be asked regarding the community's demographics. Does the community have racial/ethnic boundaries? What are the birth rates? How many births are to teenagers? What are the arrest rates? What percentages of arrests are for drugs? How well are the schools performing? What are the income levels of the community residents? What proportion of the population qualifies for public assistance? What faith communities are present? Which specific denominations are active and influential within the community? Similar to plotting geographic features, overlaying pertinent statistics on a community map highlights potential strengths and needs of the community.

Some readers will question the value of investing considerable time to learn about a community. After all, with luck, opportunities for carrying out one's professional activities will appear without much delay; then the information gained would seem irrelevant. Yet learning about one's community is not primarily about generating business (although, admittedly the contacts gained should contribute to that outcome). Rather, the purpose of this "homework" (quite literally) is to optimize one's professional functioning by minimizing the level of carelessness and naiveté manifested in one's professional activities. Moreover, knowledge of a community generates credibility and enables one to function more quickly within the community. Thus, when recommendations are made, they are likely to reflect an appreciation of the global environment in which they are to be carried out. Few residents will share an equal store of this knowledge about the community. Hence, the "newcomer" can represent a valuable resource for the identification of a community's needs and the resolution of its problems.

## The Setting/Agency: Preliminary Considerations

On a smaller scale, similar information should be acquired about any agency or setting with which the new professional intends to invest time in research, clinical, or consultative activities. It is important to understand an agency's organizational structure, personnel makeup and practices, funding base, and administrative policies. Documenting the setting's history and major developmental stages can tell one much about its initial purposes and the forces which shaped its current form and function. In the coming months, the first author will engage a group of 7th and 11th graders to work with graduate students on a history of their schools' neighborhoods. The resulting profile will be included within early attempts to facilitate student and parent adoption of a code of conduct under development by a team of teachers and parents.

It is especially important for an investigator who intends to conduct research or evaluate a community program or agency to spend time in the setting merely observing its actors and actions. For example, if the research is to be conducted in a school, we recommend that researcher's initial request be for permission to spend several days observing what occurs in the building, how people interact, and how they spend their time. If a high school is the target setting, knowledge of its layout is important because such a significant portion of the student's time is spent moving from one point to another. Understanding movement patterns can be extremely useful to the design of a study that must collect data without interfering with the setting's carefully choreographed traffic flow. It is quite likely that such observations will inform the evaluation design presented to the school. At the least, one would have shown respect for the setting by acknowledging one's ignorance of its patterns and appreciation of their importance. Similarly, for a clinical setting, it may be important to understand the client's steps from initial contact, to first visit, through the paperwork, to actually seeing someone, and to appreciate the service provider's need to balance the numerous hours of service with the need for record-keeping, completion of forms, phone calls, meetings, and unanticipated (yet inevitable) crises.

When training professionals as consultants to educational settings, we have assigned them initially as silent observers of the teacher's school day prior to engaging in consultation. Our rationale is quite simple. The potential consultant is not qualified to advise a teacher without having an appreciation that a classroom teacher may attend simultaneously to the needs of up to 35 children, teach 1 or 2 while remaining sensitive to the behavioral or psychological needs of 3 others, and keep all students enthusiastic about learning. Until a consultant appreciates the disruptive capacity of a single overactive child and the difficulty of individualizing the curriculum for 1 or 2 students in a class of 35 unique individuals, he or she is not ready to propose a viable solution.

If the setting of interest involves social services, there is similar value in following a case worker for several days. Before considering research strategies or interventions, it is useful to appreciate the demands of attempting to attend to the multiple needs of destitute families, of enforcing regulations that seem at times inequitable, at times too lenient, and at times too slow, and, most importantly, of wanting to change something immediately, only to be confronted by a seemingly endless series of regulatory steps. In our experience, an ideal way in which to obtain an appreciation of a caseworker's ordeal is to observe one or two sessions of the local foster care review board. Within a few hours, 20 to 30 families with multiple difficulties will be discussed. What is quickly evident is the scarcity of options available to meet simultaneously the needs of the children and of their parents (who themselves are often children). Also evident is the extent to which the typical caseworker cares deeply about the clients and the professionalism with which complex problems are identified, analyzed, and resolved.

Therein lies the essential purpose of this exercise—the development of a sincere appreciation of the demands and limitations that characterize the settings in which one intends to apply one's professional skills. If successful, the exercise can contribute significantly to the avoidance of many of the obstacles discussed earlier, especially distance and arrogance. After more than two decades of meeting and working with individuals who spend each day in educational, welfare, or correctional facilities, the authors continue to be impressed by the complexities of the problems that are confronted and the persistence and competence of the efforts to respond to them.

### Gaining Entrance: Negotiating Contracts

A probable outcome of completing these two preliminary strategies is that there will be requests for the professional's services as clinician, consultant, or researcher. Alternatively, these preliminary steps can identify "gatekeepers" who can facilitate the conduct of planned investigations by introducing one into a setting and by encouraging other relevant community agents and agencies to participate. Thus the preliminary steps of getting to know the community and the setting(s) represent an important ingredient in gaining entrance.

Once involved with a setting, the professional will discover that the easy part may be over. Thus far no demands have been made of, or by, the professional. An invitation to provide service or a request to conduct research in a setting alters that fact. Once contact is made and an outcome is targeted, the professional is responsible for ensuring that expectations are made explicit and that the criteria for accountability are defined. Regardless of who initiated contact, the mental health professional cannot abdicate that responsibility. Insofar as an essential characteristic of professional functioning is that one's actions are deliberate, one cannot avoid the process of negotiation and contracting.

In spite of expertise in human behavior and human interaction, many mental health professionals (especially relatively new ones) seem quite uncomfortable negotiating the specifics of what they will do, when, under what conditions (including, of course, the amount of reimbursement, if any), and what is expected of the other party. General expressions of interest or commitment by either party can be problematic. Without explicit review of specific expectations on both sides, the potential for misunderstanding, frustration, and dissatisfaction is high. Anxious to begin their careers and afraid that early expressions of caution or requests for clarification may jeopardize an initial offer, novice professionals may withhold questions. Unprepared or unwilling to detail expectations for those in a setting and specific benefits of participation, a new researcher may choose to take the "yes" and run with it. The incorrect assumption is that all are better off if the details are left ambiguous, which is rarely confirmed with experience.

The alternative to ambiguity is clarity developed through negotiation and detailed in letters of agreements or contracts exchanged by all involved. This process is especially important for the consultant and researcher. In either case, the following should be discussed and agreed to in writing: (a) the respective roles of all parties involved; (b) time frames for the initiation, conduct, and completion of responsibilities; (c) the mechanisms whereby modifications of (a) or (b) can be negotiated; (d) costs associated with the various aspects of the collaboration and identification of the party responsible for each cost; (e) the deliverables, product(s), or goal(s) to be accomplished in the collaboration as well as the specific means by which their completion is to be assessed, and the person(s) responsible for assessing the acceptability of the product(s) or goal(s); (f) if research is involved, clarification of data ownership and requisite procedures for determining authorship, publication format, and other public or professional dissemination of findings; and finally, (g) mechanisms for the termination, revision, or renewal of the agreement.

Admittedly, few of us involved regularly with community interventions began by engaging in such specific and arduous negotiations. Hindsight and scars, however, have made most of us wish we had examined gift horses closely. What seemed amicably understood initially, frequently did not remain so. Resulting disagreements were always inconvenient, frustrating, occasionally bitter, and, at times, disastrous. We suggest that the aforementioned issues be reviewed, those that a reader deems unimportant to completion of the task be discarded (but only after thoughtful deliberation), and those that remain be addressed.

## Collaboration: Translating Words into Actions

The most critical aspect of a community intervention process is, of course, its actual conduct. Negotiated agreements should serve as a blueprint for the activities of those involved. If feasible, the project should be reviewed within a reasonable amount of time after its inception to assess its "fit" within the agency. Necessary modifications can be made at that time, and, ideally, procedures can be set for the remainder of the contractual period. This step is particularly important for the applied researcher whose experimental conditions must be standardized to insure replicability. For a consultant, a review of the initial sessions provides an opportunity for (a) identifying misunderstandings and concerns, (b) considering alternative strategies for maximizing the agency's benefit from the interaction, and (c) clarifying misperceptions about respective expectations and roles. Agencies, which make clinical referrals, appreciate meeting with a clinician after one or two referrals to review the appropriateness of the referral, the adequacy of information provided as part of the referral, and the kinds of feedback about referred cases they can expect. Community agencies understand the demands of confidentiality. They also often have legitimate needs for information about a client's progress. Balancing these concerns—client confidentiality and agency needs—is a complex professional task that should be addressed during the early review.

As noted initially, this chapter will not address the specific skills and activities that define the professional's community involvement. It is assumed that requisite skills were developed as part of graduate education or learned on the job. Obviously, the professional will have been involved in the "practice" of such skills since graduate education. As noted, however, such preparation provides rudimentary abilities, to be shaped and refined with experience. The need for such preparation is recognized by experienced community agents. What many find a problem is its denial! In fact, community agents can contribute in significant ways to the improvement and sophistication of one's professional expertise if allowed the opportunity to do so. Early feedback can be an important part of this process.

Should additional skills be necessary in order to engage in a desired form of community involvement, such skills should be acquired through formalized continuing education, postdoctoral opportunities, or collaboration with a colleague who has expertise in that subject matter. Needless to say, the community is *not* necessarily the best place to acquire new skills through on-the-job training, unless that goal is clearly understood and accepted by all involved. Typically, such arrangements require the supervision of an experienced mentor and the negotiation of a specific set of expectations and responsibilities for supervisor, trainer, and agency. The agency's right to expect something (e.g., free service) from the trainee in return for its cooperation in the training process should be recognized and, as possible, honored.

Underlying the points made in this chapter is the basic assumption that community intervention should not be "me versus them" but "us." In our opinion, effective community intervention, clinical consultation, or research requires mutual understanding, respect, and involvement between the professional and the community. A recent review of the early history of the mental health disciplines' involvement in community consultation and prevention interventions made evident the centrality of true collaboration in program success (Lorion, 1998). For that reason, we recommend that *all* intervention activities be defined a priori as collaborative and that one of the professional's privacy goals be to insure that ownership of the activities and of its products be perceived jointly by those involved. On the office walls of both authors are posters that read:

> Give me a fish and I eat for a day,
> Teach me to fish and I eat for a lifetime.

If a portion of one's professional time is committed to communicating one's expertise to those in the community, a by-product of the involvement will be an increment in the agency's staff's skills. By attempting to leave some of oneself in the agency, the professional has lost none of his or her skills, knowledge, or expertise, and the value of the intervention to the agency increases, as does, we believe, its involvement in a commitment to the intervention.

By way of illustration, the authors collaborated some years ago on research involving the development and evaluation of a program to prevent learning disorders and emotional disturbance in primary-grade children. Rather than request the school district's permission to run "our" research in their primary grades, we asked for a series of meetings to discuss the general issue of prevention and relate our prior experience with school-based prevention programs. From the outset, our goals were explicit. If research were to be conducted in the district, it would be collaborative research with school personnel involved in all stages of planning, implementation, evaluation, and dissemination of findings. It was agreed that school district personnel would serve as co-principal investigators on funding applications. If materials were prepared and effective procedures identified, they would be made available to the district's personnel through requisite training and supervision. If scientific papers were prepared or professional presentations scheduled, appropriate district personnel were to be involved and to receive full credit for their collaboration.

As we entered our fourth year of research, we were pleased that the "marriage" was going well. The research design differed positively from its original conceptualization because of the district's input. Not only did we ask our questions; we discovered that the design informed the district's ability to plan and monitor special education services. The project's demands exceeded expectation, as did its payoffs! Cooperation levels among teachers, parents, and central administrators were excellent. A more comprehensive investigation of a prevention effort developed that provided all parties with more and better data than would have been obtained otherwise. Equally important, we learned from the collaborative effort and, hopefully, removed some of the stigma previously associated with seeking to conduct research in the schools.

### Feedback and Follow-Up

This section is brief, for its message is simple—*all* community interventions must include predefined formal mechanisms for feedback and follow-up. The most frequent and legitimate complaint of community settings toward professional involvements is that promised or implied feedback is never received or is submitted in a form (e.g., the manuscript of a scientific report) that is difficult to understand and of little use to the setting. As noted, primary negotiations should address the issue of feedback. It is recommended that those directly involved in the intervention—such as parents, teachers, and caseworkers—be consulted about the preferred design of the feedback mechanism. In many instances, use of multiple modalities is preferred. Thus, senior administrators may receive a comprehensive report, managerial personnel a more problem-oriented report, agency personnel one or more staff development sessions, and consumers a brief flyer describing the program, its goals, and its findings.

The frequency of feedback should reflect both the duration of the intervention and, if experimental procedures are involved, its potential reactivity. Assuming that the intervention is ongoing, regular reports to those involved should be considered. Particularly in those instances in which research procedures will not be compromised, quarterly feedback might even serve as a "newsletter," which both informs readers about the intervention's continued existence and progress, and serves as a medium for exchanging relevant ideas, concerns, questions, and so on.

Whatever its form, feedback should be accompanied by planned follow-up sessions. These should clarify questions arising from feedback, resolve incomplete details, and ensure that the agency's expectations relevant to the intervention were addressed. This step also serves as an appropriate vehicle for reviewing a project, assessing its successes and failures, identifying unanticipated obstacles, and clarifying ways to optimize future collaborative efforts.

To summarize, involvement in the development, implementation, and/or evaluation of community interventions, be they clinical, consultative, or research, represents an exciting and challenging career choice. The professional who chooses to follow that path must, however, be prepared to forego many of the protections of the office or campus-based professional and rely on professional skills and personnel qualities without the entrapments of titles. Community interventions require openness to alternative roles, collaborative activities with colleagues from multiple disciplines, and constant examination of one's functioning by the consumers of one's services. Community intervention requires the flexibility to adopt one's skills to problems and situations not anticipated in textbooks and the humility to recognize and admit the need to pause, reflect, and, at times, acknowledge one's limitations. Most of the time, however, it requires the willingness to approach a problem as a member of a team and to use creatively the talents and experiences of all members of the team to identify an innovative solution to the problem at hand. When the team "gels" and the collaborative effort is successful, the results are exciting and gratifying. The payoff is that goals are accomplished, community systems are made to work responsively and effectively, and those responsible have learned much in the process. To reach that goal, the professional might consider the following guidelines:

Be yourself.

Be respectful.

Be responsible.

Be open.

Be honest.

Be persistent.

Be trustworthy.

Be trusting.

Work like hell.

## REFERENCES

Cowen, E. L., Trost, M. A., Lorion, R. P., Door, D., Izzo, L. D., & Isaccson, R. (1975). *New ways in school mental health: Early detection and prevention of school maladaptation.* New York: Behavioral Publications.

Cowen, E. L., Hightower, A. D., Pedro-Carroll, J. L., Work, W. C., Wyman, P. A., & Haffey, W. G. (1996). *School-based prevention for children at risk: The Primary Mental Health Project.* Washington, DC: American Psychological Association.

Lorion, R. P. (1983) Evaluating preventive interventions: Guidelines for the serious social change agent. In R. D. Felner, L. Jason, J. Moritsugu, and S.S. Farber (Eds.) *Preventive psychology: theory, research and practice in community interventions.* (pp. 251–272). New York: Pergamon Press.

Lorion, R. P. (1991). Prevention and pubic health: Psychology's response to the nation's health care crisis. *American Psychologist, 46,* 516–519.

Lorion, R. P. (1998). Prevention goals and indirect/consultation strategies: Meeting current needs through a re-commitment to underused means and ends. In A. S. Bellack & M. Hersen (Eds.), *Comprehensive clinical psychology, #6* (pp. 277–300). New York: Pergamon Press.

Lorion, R. P., & Iscoe, I. (1996). Reshaping our view of our field. In R. P. Lorion, I. Iscoe, P. H. DeLeon, & G. VandenBos (Eds.), *Psychology and public policy: Balancing public service and professional need.* (pp. 1–21) Washington, DC: American Psychological Association.

Sarason, S. B. (1985). *Caring and compassion in clinical practice.* San Francisco: Jossey-Bass.

*Webster's: Third international dictionary of the English language.* (1967). Unabridged. Springfield, MA: G. & C. Merriam.

# 27

# Developing a Career in Psychology

*Steven Walfish*

Whether I originally conceptualized this chapter I thought the focus would be on the multitude of opportunities available to new psychologists. I quickly realized that this would be a challenging task for an entire book. So, my focus for this chapter is the personal and practical issues involved in developing a career in psychology. How can emerging professionals match their own interests and needs to a workable career in either academia or independent practice?

## ISSUES FOR THE NEW GRADUATE ENTERING THE JOB MARKET

Plante (1998) noted that recent market changes have increased the level of worry among psychology interns and postdoctoral fellows embarking on careers. He described a section of a professional issues seminar that he teaches that focuses on the job search process, and offered advice on such basics as completing one's degree, preparing appropriate vitae, and the importance of networking and contacting possible employers. Three topics he presented are of paramount importance.

- *The need to be realistic.* Finding the ideal job immediately on completion of training is not common. However, your first professional position is also unlikely to be your last. Benefits can be gleaned from all positions in terms of providing useful experience, further training opportunities, and future career opportunities.

- *The need to expand the window of opportunities beyond the traditional roles demonstrated during graduate training.* New professionals often underestimate their job skills and how they can be applied in a wide variety of jobs in business and industry, schools, hospitals, the media, and other agencies. The chapter by Ware earlier in this book stressed that students with a degree in psychology at the baccalaureate level have skills that are marketable in a number of settings. This is even more valid for those with degrees at the master's or doctoral level. However, students must be willing to take a perspective different from the one presented in the typical graduate program. For example, when I was a first-year graduate student, my office was in a laboratory directed by a professor who conducted memory research. That year one of the professor's students received his doctorate in experimental psychology and he took a position doing market research for a major wine company. I did not understand this choice at the time. However, given the dearth of positions in academia, the ever-present difficulty in obtaining grant funding, and the relative low pay in a college or university (compared to the potential in the private sector), I now better understand it. He was able to recognize the value of his research training and how it could be applied outside of the basement of the psychology building. Similarly, in a study of master's degree recipients in community psychology, Paelet (1978) found that two-thirds of these graduates became employed as human service administrators. What is of interest is that the job titles for these graduates, for the most part, did not include the designation "psychologist."

- *The need to be open-minded.* Trainees with only one career path in mind run the risk of becoming disillusioned by the unforeseen negative aspects of that path. Plante offered the reminder that it is impossible to know if one will like a particular job or career path without actually having done it for a while, and that job interests, needs, and requirements are likely to change over the course of a lifetime. Change is natural.

Mesh (1989) observed that the typical student spends little time developing employment strategies, and that professors may unintentionally collude with students by focusing almost exclusively on academics. Even if students choose to let professors know they intend to take a job outside of academia, both groups may still avoid focusing on the "outside world."

Olson, Downing, Heppner, and Pinkney (1986) attempted to demystify the transition from graduate school to new employee. They suggested that being aware of the differences between expectations and realities may help to ease the transition to employment. Although much time and effort are given to obtaining employment, little, if any, time is spent on anticipating adjustment to the new work environment.

## CONDUCTING A SELF-ASSESSMENT REGARDING CHOICE OF A CAREER PATH

A self-assessment is a process in which individuals begin to acknowledge their own particular blend of education, experiences, values, needs, and goals (DeGalan & Lambert, 1995). All too often, new graduates follow a career path that has been outlined for them by say, professors who may want their students to become academics and follow in their footsteps, much like parents who has always wanted children to grow up to be "professionals." Family friends may urge you to go into industry because "that's where the money can be found." Older relatives may hold the value, "Get a job in government, that's safe and secure, and you'll have good benefits."

It is important to take into consideration the wise counsel of all those in your support system when considering a career path. Given that most new graduates have little experience in "the real world," it could be naive, or even arrogant, to completely discount their input. However, the decision of which road to choose is solely yours. DeGalan and Lambert's (1995) out-line for conducting a self-assessment may prove valuable in this decision-making process. Their seven steps include: (a) understanding your personal traits; (b) identifying your per-sonal values; (c) calculating your economic needs; (d) exploring your longer term goals; (e) enumerating your skill base; (f) recognizing your preferred skills; and (g) assessing skills needing further development.

Each student should conduct a thorough and honest self-assessment. Too often students are driven by one question: "Where can I get a job?" More personally satisfying and constructive would be the question, "What job and what path is right for me?" Pesmen (1996) pointed to the importance of carefully examining personal goals along with professional goals in order to determine where you really want to be—and what you want to be doing—for the greatest num-ber of hours per day. Super and Super (1995) suggested that those in an occupation are often somewhat reluctant to look at it objectively, for under careful analysis some aspects may be less favorable. Educate yourself about all aspects of your career alternatives, both good sides and bad. For example, there are truly wonderful aspects of an independent clinical practice, but there are risks and negative aspects as well (Connerty, 1990; Freudenberger & Kurtz, 1990; Walfish & Coovert, 1990)

One important distinction Messmer (1995) urged new graduates to consider is the question of job search versus career search. If you are committed to staying on a particular career path, the available positions to seek will be narrower than if you are primarily interested in gaining new experiences. But a job search may yield more flexibility in terms of type of position or company considered for employment and geographical location.

Too often, people expect new graduates to have their careers "take off" after receiving their degrees. However, choosing an all-consuming career often requires a sacrifice of balance in your life. One of my mentors once told me, "While it does happen, it is extremely unusual to find examples in life of individuals who have great careers, great marriages, and great rela-tionships with their kids. One usually fails miserably." Unfortunately, observation has led me to share this same belief. I urge you to keep this in mind as you make personal value decisions concerning your career.

## SOURCES OF INFORMATION REGARDING JOB AVAILABILITY

As already mentioned, an important first step for new graduates is to conduct a self-assess-ment. Ettinger (1996) further pointed out the need to relate the self-knowledge you gain in this process to the available work opportunities. You will need to be able to locate, access, evalu-ate, and use career and labor market information that outlines options and opportunities. The more self-knowledge that you obtain combined with your increased knowledge of available opportunities, the more likely you are to make a better career choice.

The most traditional source for jobs for psychologists is in the APA *Monitor on Psychology* (www.apa.org). In an early study, Gottfredson and Swatko (1979) found that almost two-thirds of doctoral-level and one-half of master's-level unemployed psychologists re-ported having responded to ads placed in this publication. A mid-1980s study of 2,914 of these ads reported that 1,229 (42%) were for academic positions and the remaining were for human services, business, government, and other nonacademic settings (Yoder & Crumpton, 1987). Another source is in the *APS Observer* (online at the APS web site Psychologicalscience.org). The vast majority of these positions are faculty jobs at colleges and university and postdoctoral research fellowships.

A third significant source is *The Chronicle of Higher Education* (www.chronicle.com). The most obvious heading is under Social Sciences—Psychology. However, limiting your search to this department will eliminate a large number of positions for potential employment. In an online edition of this periodical, positions of interest to psychologists could be found under various headings, including criminal justice, education, ethnic studies, women's studies, public administration, social work, public health, communications, counseling, human resources, educational administration, student affairs, health and medical services administration, minority affairs and affirmative action, residence life, health sciences, consultants, foundations, publishers, research facilities, and nonprofit organizations. In addition to the college and university positions, also search under "community colleges" to see what possibilities may exist for you in those settings.

A fourth source of job listings is the local newspaper. One strategy is to order a subscription to the Sunday edition of the paper in the city, to which you would like to relocate. A more efficient method is to utilize the Internet.

Most newspapers have an online edition that includes their classified ads. An amazing job-searching web site may be found at www.careerpath.com, where classified sections of 88 separate newspapers may be searched in a very brief time for positions of interest to psychologists. The newspapers listed are from all over the country and range in size from the *Los Angeles Times* to the *Elmira Star Gazette*.

A fifth source is the newsletters of state psychological associations. These associations permit out-of-state memberships. One benefit is each group's newsletter, which lists employment opportunities. Such a listing is how I found the practice that ultimately led to my relocation to Washington State. In some cases it is possible to order the newsletter without joining the organization.

Finally, explore connections via the Internet. Many agencies and institutions allow you to apply for a position directly online by answering some questions and e-mailing a copy of your vitae. One job information site is monster.com., where a recent search under the word *psychologist* yielded 69 separate positions all over the country. These included direct service clinical positions in clinics and hospitals, government positions, and corporate industrial/organizational positions. Mentalhelp.net is a general mental health web site that also includes an employment link. In a recent month, it listed 82 direct service mental health positions.

Most professional organizations now also have a web site, which lists positions. Through your training, become familiar with these organizations, join them if you have the funds (many have low-cost student memberships), or just read their newsletters online. You also may not be familiar with all sites that may be relevant to your job search. A cruise on the Net recently revealed a site for the Society of Industrial and Organizational Psychology (www.siop.org), listing more than 60 positions. There were also numerous positions on a site for Social Psychologists (www.socialpsychology.org).

Kohout (1999) presented data on job search methods for new doctoral-level psychologists collected. For health service providers, the most successful job search methods were: (a) informal channels; (b) newspaper ads; (c) meeting of employers through former jobs; (d) sending in an unsolicited vitae; and (e) receiving an unsolicited offer. For research positions, the most successful job search methods were: (a) informal channels; (b) the APA *Monitor*; (c) faculty advisor; (d) newspaper ads; and (e) *The Chronicle of Higher Education*. She suggested that for both groups of job seekers, "it can be who you know" that will facilitate finding a job. So let those in your support system, both professional and personal, know that you are "in the market." Almost two-thirds of the new psychology doctorates responding to the survey said that the position obtained was their first choice.

## SOURCES OF ADVICE IN CAREER DEVELOPMENT

There is much to be learned about career possibilities from your mentors and practicing psychologists. Speak to them about opportunities in the field in general and how opportunities may match your professional skills and personal desires. When completing practicum requirements, speak with your supervisors about the type of work they do in that setting and about interesting things their colleagues are doing in that and in similar settings. Ask how they went about a job search and how they decided to take this particular position. Mentors and supervisors often like to share this type of information with budding professionals.

The web site of *The Chronicle Of Higher Education* (www.chronicle.com) is a rich resource of information related to career development both inside and outside of academia. Each week it features columns of interest to graduate students grappling with concerns about their professional lives. Table 27.1 presents four of these column titles relevant to career issues and sample of their topics. These particular articles may not be available (although you may be able to search the archives), but these kinds of discussions may be useful at all stages of your career. Other employment-related web sites typically have sections related to career development. At the APA web site (www.apa.org) there is a section called PsychCareers that

**TABLE 27.1**

Columns and Sample Titles from the Chronicle of Higher Education

| Column | Titles |
| --- | --- |
| Beyond the Ivory Tower | "Networking your way to a new job" |
| | "How to use graduate school strategically" |
| | "Deprogramming from the academic cult" |
| | "Making the transition to a nonacademic career" |
| | "How to transfer your skills to the real world" |
| Career Talk | "How to show you are a good teacher" |
| | "Getting ready to go on the job market" |
| | "You've got the job, now what?" |
| | "When you get the job offer" |
| | "How to handle interview curveballs" |
| Catalyst | "Is the tenure path the best route for you?" |
| | "When faculty consulting helps and when it hurts your career" |
| Moving Up | "True tales from the job search front" |
| | "The worst mistakes you can make" |
| | "Mastering the interview for an academic job" |
| | "Strategies for making big changes in your career path" |
| | "How to prepare yourself for a higher level job in administration" |

currently includes an advice column as well as a message board for individuals to post a question and receive feedback from other psychologists.

## POSTDOCTORAL EMPLOYMENT AND FELLOWSHIPS

For those seeking a career in research, doing a postdoctoral internship can be an important stepping-stone to developing a specific area of future study. Glenwick, Mroczek, and MacDonall describe this in their chapter in this book. These positions are usually grant-funded opportunities with faculty members who already have an established research program. The new doctorate typically joins the research team and collaborates with team members, while being mentored by the senior faculty member. Often the postdoctoral fellow is encouraged to stake out one piece of the research project to develop and spearhead as the primary pursuer of knowledge in this aspect of the work. In this way he or she can mark out and develop an interest area. This can lead to publications as senior author, as well as the groundwork for grants proposals to support the new line of research. Announcements of postdoctoral fellowships are usually found in the *APS Observer* and the *Monitor of Psychology.*

In clinical areas, postdoctoral fellowships allow the new doctorate to specialize in one particular area of work. Although predoctoral internships tend to be generalized (inpatient and outpatient, child and adult, assessment and therapy), postdoctoral fellowships tend to be extremely focused. For example, there may be a concentrated year devoted to completing neuropsychological assessment, forensic assessment, or cognitive therapy for depression and anxiety. The fellowships tend not to pay much and are very intensive. However, the intensity of the learning experience can lead to the development of specialized and marketable skills, which may pay rich dividends for a long time to come.

Fretz's chapter in this book discusses issues related to postdoctoral training experience and subsequent licensure. Stewart, Stewart, and Vogel (2000) examined interns' plans regarding postdoctoral training. Surprisingly, significant percentages of these interns were not aware of the details of the postdoctoral requirements for licensure (especially supervisory requirements) within the state where they intended to become licensed as a psychologist. The top five influences affecting choice of postdoctoral work were: match with professional interests, proximity to partner and family, geographical location, the fact that the opportunity was "a job," and amount of salary or stipend. The most highly preferred activity primarily focused on clinical work with some applied research for graduates of PhD programs. Child psychotherapy and long-term therapy with adults were the preferred clinical activities for graduates of PsyD programs.

Cuts in the number of postdoctoral positions constitute a problem for new graduates, especially because 1 year of supervised work experience is required by most states in order to be able to sit for the licensure examination. Thomas (2000) reported that APA has appointed a task force to address this issue, and noted the existence of a movement to remove the requirements and allow new graduates to practice immediately. However, he pointed out, insurance companies, managed care companies, and Medicare and Medicaid do not support such changes. Therefore, it may be some time before the current requirements are replaced.

I also suggest that emerging professionals be proactive in seeking third-party reimbursement. Not only does this have the potential to create further income for an individual in the context of independent practice, but its success may also make them more attractive applicants for potential employers. For example, in my clinical practice I am currently supervising for licensure as a psychologist an individual who recently received her doctorate in clinical psychology. Due to the way licensure laws are written, she is not eligible to become licensed as a psychologist until she has completed the experience requirement of 2,000 postdoctoral hours, taken and passed the national examination, and then passed an oral examination given in our state. This entire process will take her well over a year. However, she was savvy enough to become a certified mental health counselor (available in our state for master's-level therapists) just as she was completing her predoctoral internship. She became eligible for insurance reimbursement through a few of the panels that were open to new providers. Due to the combination of the referral contacts of our practice and her high level of professional and interpersonal skill, she will have a full private practice in less than 15 months after receiving her doctorate. This would not be possible had she not had the foresight to obtain this certification. (I want to mention, though, that one prominent academic told me that he was opposed to a person developing a practice in this manner before the doctorate was received. His view is that students should not be in the position of being able to do independent practice).

## INTERVIEWING FOR A NEW JOB

Heppner and Downing (1982) depicted the "emotional roller coaster" of new psychologists interviewing for jobs. In this excellent paper, the authors described relevant activities that take place before, during, and after the interview, as well as the psychological processes associated with the interview experience. They discussed practical issues regarding making the arrangements to visit the site, finding out information about the position and/or institution, and postulating interview questions and answers beforehand. During the interview, prospective employers evaluate not only the content of your answers to questions but your interpersonal style as well. During most interviews you will be invited out to lunch or dinner. This is not a recreational process but also a component of the interview. Prospective employers are considering asking you to become their colleague. Only in rare circumstances do great credentials outweigh a poor interpersonal style.

Heppner and Downing (1982) also reminded interviewees that it is their job to collect sufficient information to make a determination about whether or not to accept the job if it is offered. Too often, for new graduates the interview is viewed as a "one-way street," going into the process feeling lucky if they get the job—"any job." Coming from a stance of "desperation and begging" will not allow you to fully evaluate whether or not you actually want this job. You could be spending many of your hours devoted to this organization and committing your career pathway to the people with whom you are interviewing. It is important to be centered in your own thoughts, values, and ideals, which once again points to the need to conduct a thorough self-assessment prior to the beginning of the interview.

## NEGOTIATING FOR THE NEW POSITION

There are some jobs where the pay and benefits being offered to the applicant are "carved in stone" with little flexibility available. These are most likely to be positions in government, schools, human service agencies, or postdoctoral fellowships. If you have been offered a position in the private sector (e.g., corporations, group clinical practices, consulting firms), there may be some leeway to negotiate for higher levels of income and benefit packages (e.g., stock options, profit sharing, amount of vacation being offered), as well as lifestyle issues (e.g., flexibility of hours, ability to telecommute).

Most people are uncomfortable with the negotiation process. In order to be able to negotiate from a position of strength, you have to be willing to say "no thank you" and walk away from the offer. The more desperate your need to have this particular position, the less likely it is that you will be able to ask for something that is in your best interest. If the person negotiating with you knows that you can walk away at any moment, and the corporation or practice really wants you because of your talents, then it may be willing to increase the attractiveness of the package being offered. However, be realistic in what you are asking for in the negotiation process. Rarely do employers "give away the store."

In university positions, unless you are a "superstar," there is typically little room to negotiate a higher base salary than is being offered. However, many other important issues can be discussed. This can include teaching course load, seed money to set up a laboratory or purchase equipment, assignment of graduate student assistants, availability of summer teaching, travel funds for attending conferences or visiting grant agencies, and amount of time available to do outside consulting or clinical practice. Most universities want their professors to be involved in outside service activities in order for them to be active in the profession, be current in their skills, and to do community outreach. However, they do not want this to become a primary focus such that teaching, research, and service to the university suffer. I once interviewed for a position in which the faculty member who was leaving was considered to be too involved in his clinical practice. The message to me was loud and clear: "We want you to practice, but not too much."

Negotiations should eventually be put on paper. As a new professional I was uncomfortable with putting agreements in writing. I viewed myself as an informal person who had good working relationships with the people to whom I consulted. Unfortunately, a few occasions of unpleasant effects convinced me that there are times a signed contract can better protect my interests. Bernstein (1978) pointed out:

> The myriad of understandings, implications, and agreements that are mutually understood during the interview can vanish with the resignation, transfer, or forgetfulness of the interviewer. Therefore, clarity concerning all understandings and agreements is critical. (p. 341)

## SALARY INFORMATION

The APA Research Office provides an excellent source of salary information for psychologists. These data are often published in *The American Psychologist*, offered for free at the APA web site, or are available from reports that may be purchased directly from the Research Office. Data are presented on positions in academic departments, educational administration, research and research administration, direct human services (clinical, counseling, school), administration, industrial and organizational psychology, and applied psychology. Data are presented for both doctoral- and master's-level professionals as well. Remember that these data are from a self-reported salary survey of APA members and may not represent the salaries of all psychologists.

These data are invaluable when applying for academic jobs. For example, one report focuses on median salaries for professors at all levels, presented in terms of geographic location and public or private status of the institution. Such information can be helpful in gauging what range of starting salary could be expected in negotiations. Also, public universities are required to make available the salaries of each of their employees. This information is often found in the library of the institution. Armed with this information, job applicants can be aware of what salaries are being paid in the particular department and what salaries they could reasonably request. This is also a way to assess the honesty level of the individual negotiating on behalf of the university (usually the department chair). For example, I am aware of one faculty member who interviewed at another institution for a position and was told it was offering him a salary above that of the other associate professors. However, he had already checked the budget on file in the library and found that he was being offered a salary below all the other associate professors. The candidate thus knew the chair was lying to him. This knowledge helped him decide not to take the position.

## GENDER ISSUES

The "Guidelines For Conditions of Employment" (APA, 1987) stated:

> APA supports efforts of psychologists to eliminate the effects of past discrimination in professional training and employment and urges all employed psychologists to take an active part in promoting affirmative action by their employers whenever possible. (p. 728)

Despite this declaration, the profession of psychology is not immune from the gender discrimination that is seen in our culture. In a fascinating study, Steinpreis, Anders, and Ritzke (1999) asked academic psychologists to critique the curricula vitae (CVs) of job candidates. The content of the curricula vitae remained the same, but the gender of the candidate was changed for half of the reviewers. Under review, the "male" applicants received higher suggested salaries, an increased likelihood of being offered a job and being granted tenure, and a greater respect for their teaching, research, and service records. What is astonishing is that both male and female reviewers were more likely to vote to hire a male applicant than a female applicant with an identical record. That is, the gender bias found in this study could not be solely ascribed to "male chauvinism" or to efforts by a "good old boys network" to keep women out of the university. Male and female reviewers were equally biased. These results suggest that both men and women need to receive a great deal of education and consciousness raising if women are to be viewed as equals in academia and are to achieve the goals set out in the "Guidelines for Conditions of Employment described above.

The researchers in the Steinpreis et al. (1909) study asked reviewers to rate the credentials of potential job applicants, but there is additional evidence of gender inequity in pay in actual settings for psychologists employed in medical school settings. Despite no differences in productivity or years of employment, male faculty members are better paid than their female counterparts (Black & Holden, 1998; Williams & Wedding, 1999). A study of school psychologists yielded a similar picture. Levinson, Rafoth, and Sanders (1994) found male school psychologists working longer contract lengths and making more money than their female counterparts. When monthly salaries were compared, differences remained. These results were not a function of differences in age, experience, employer, psychologist-to-student ratio, or number of schools served. Thomas and Witte (1996) also found gender differences in their study of school psychologists. Clearly, more needs to be done to achieve gender equality in our profession.

## DEVELOPING A CAREER IN ACADEMIA

When most individuals think about a career in academia, they think about the type of setting in which they received their own training. For example, when I was in graduate school, the ideal position to obtain was an assistant professorship in an APA-approved clinical psychology training program. Two things are clear: There are just not enough faculty openings in these settings for many students to realize this ideal fantasy, and there are many other ways to have a career in academia besides the familiar model in which one was trained. These positions should not be considered less satisfying, as rewarding careers in academia can come in all shapes and sizes and locales. Assistant professorships and lecturer appointments in departments of counselor education, social work, public health, psychiatry, applied psychology, family studies, marriage and family counseling, and addiction studies are just as prestigious and may be more rewarding than those in a department of psychology. Keller (1994) edited a fascinating volume in which 14 academic psychologists described their career paths in a variety of academic settings.

Yocom, Bruce, Cochenour, and Box (1999) presented their experiences of applying for and obtaining faculty positions in departments of counselor education. They discussed issues of timing the job search, sources of information about available positions, completion of the application packet, preparation for and dealing with the interview process, and negotiation and acceptance issues. Keep in mind that each step requires preparation. When Brems, Lampman, and Johnson (1995) reviewed academic job applications for an entry-level faculty position in experimental psychology, they found "a grave problem with regard to the appropriateness and completeness of academic job applications."

Sheehan, McDevitt, and Ross (1998) presented data from 98 chairs of academic search committees regarding the criteria used to hire faculty. The "fit" between the candidate's research and teaching experience and the particular needs of the department was emphasized. Letters of recommendation emerged as the most important factor in evaluating applicants' written dossiers. Interestingly enough, number and quality of publications were important, but not the most important. Performance at the interview with the search committee emerged as the deciding factor for those candidates that were interviewed. These authors also cited examples of "what not to do" during the interview, which is useful information for those seeking academic positions to examine. Yocom et al. (1999) offered a sample list of questions for the interview committee, as well as a list of questions likely to be asked of the applicant by the interview committee members.

Students see the lives of their professors typically after the professors have become established in their field. They have already secured positions at the university, published enough to get tenure, taught the same course enough times for it to be polished, supervised several theses and dissertations, and received grant funding for their research. Zanna and Darley (1987) presented a collection of chapters by leading academics on how to develop a successful academic career, "must reading" for anyone considering a career in the academic world.

Salancik's chapter in Zanna and Darley (1987) entitled "Power and Politics in Academic Departments," should prove articularly helpful. Rheingold (1994) brought together a wider variety of shorter articles on developing an academic career and on spending effective time in academic settings.

## ISSUES RELATED TO DEVELOPING AN INDEPENDENT PRACTICE

Independent practice (more commonly referred to as private practice) offers the opportunity for psychologists skilled in assessment and psychotherapy to own their own business. It allows greater flexibility in scheduling, control over one's business activities, and potentially greater financial rewards than work in a public setting. Simono and Wachiowiak (1983) found that psychologists left university-counseling centers for independent practice for personal growth and change, and for better pay.

However, independent practice is not for everyone, just as owning a business is not for everyone. Nash, Norcross, and Prochaska (1984) identified time pressures, economic uncertainty, caseload uncertainty, and business management demands as the main stressors in owning a practice. Their study was conducted before the advent of managed care, which reduced fees and restricted the practice of assessment and therapy. In general, supervising support staff who are the gatekeepers to your business, purchasing and maintaining expensive telephone and computer systems, or turning a client's account over to a collection agency for failure to pay a fee for services that you rendered may not seem rewarding.

Young and Weishaar (1997) described services provided by independent practitioners during a typical day. Volumes have been written about developing an independent practice (Beigel & Earle, 1990; Browning & Browning, 1986; Kolt, 1999; Lawless, 1997; Margenau, 1990); there are also books related to business, ethical, and legal issues in such an endeavor (Woody, 1988a, 1988b, 1989; Woody & Robertson, 1997). Walfish and Coovert (1990) pointed out that independent practice is a nice way to help human beings and earn a living at the same time. They suggested these prerequisites: (a) being willing to work long and hard hours, (b) having excellent communication skills, (c) having the spirit of an entrepreneur, (d) having strong professional skills, (e) being fair and ethical, (f) knowing the right people (or being willing to meet the right people), and (g) being lucky! In a separate study Walfish and Coovert (1989) conducted a Delphi Poll of a panel of experts for the best strategies for beginning and maintaining an independent practice. They also solicited tips for graduate students considering this as a career path. Commitments to excellence, to the clients, to the community, and to one's personal and professional development emerged as key factors. For graduate students they suggested becoming competent, being patient with one's progress, and paying attention to practical considerations. Let me stress the importance of patience. It is extraordinarily unusual for someone to go into independent practice and to have a full schedule within a short period of time, just as someone opening a local hardware store can't reasonably expect wall-to-wall customers the first day or the first week. Even after having building a successful practice in Tampa, Florida, when I opted to relocate to the Pacific Northwest, it took approximately 2 years to rebuild my practice.

Because of market forces and changes in public policy at the macroeconomic level, practices and types of services delivered by individual clinicians in their own practices can change at the micro level. Failure to recognize these trends leads to anger, resentment, disillusionment, burnout, and dissatisfaction with the endeavor and profession. Psychologists in independent practice may also have a sense of entitlement, believing they should be able to hang out their shingle, practice long-term individual psychotherapy, and to be reimbursed at their full fee for these services. They need to be flexible in their thinking and to evolve in response to market forces and policy changes, or else they will be unhappy clinicians and businesspeople.

I have been in independent practice on a full-time basis for eighteen years, starting after having a 1-year postdoctoral fellowship. During that year I did begin a part-time practice in the evenings. My daily activities 18 years ago when I started, 10 years ago when my first practice was established and on "cruise-control," and now in my current practice are very different. Due to my experience in working with substance abusers in the early days of my first practice, I received many referrals to treat people who had been convicted of driving while intoxicated (DWI) and assessed as having a drinking problem. It would be safe to estimate that 90% of these people did not want to be in therapy. As my practice evolved into a fuller schedule, I decided that I would only see people who were in therapy on a voluntary basis. My traditional assessment skills and background in substance abuse enabled me to develop a relationship with inpatient substance abuse treatment centers and to complete evaluations with their patients in a Twelve-Step context. These evaluations became the focal point of my practice activities, and psychotherapy was a secondary activity. But with the advent of managed care, funds for traditional psychological testing in these settings dwindled to a trickle. However, my early therapy training was in crisis intervention and brief therapy models. I completed a formal brief therapy-training module with a large managed care company. Because I was successful in this, I received large numbers of referrals from them. As managed care companies value clinicians with a brief cognitive therapy focus, I have been fortunate to have been reinforced for this work with a large volume of referrals. My point is that it is important to be able to recognize the public policy and market forces and be willing to change, rather than resist and become stagnant and bitter. I would not suggest that one conduct therapy that is not enjoyable or felt to be against one's values. However, we are not entitled to specify exactly how we make a living (and often a very good living). As working psychologists, we are no different from the loggers in the Pacific Northwest who have had to adapt their vocational life due to changes in macroenvironmental policy changes or auto workers in Michigan who adapt to the introduction of robotics.

Finally, I would like to reiterate the need to be flexible and entrepreneurial It is important to continue your intellectual and professional development. There is no lack of articles on how clinical skills can be translated into developing services for those in need.

The new field of behavioral medicine illustrates the process of translation. Clinical and counseling psychology is becoming more integrated with medicine (Haley et al., 1998; Pruitt, Klapow, Epping-Jordan, & Dresselhaus, 1998), as clinical research explores the multiple connections of mind and body. It is difficult to pick up an issue of *The Journal of Consulting and Clinical Psychology*, *Professional Psychology: Research and Practice*, *The Monitor on Psychology*, *The Journal of Counseling Psychology*, or *The Journal of Clinical Child Psychology* and not see an excellent research study that has implications for offering behavioral health services (usually cognitive-behavioral in nature) for clients with medical problems. These are general journals; there are also specific behavioral journals in psychology, such as *Health Psychology* and *Journal of Clinical Psychology in Medical Settings, Pediatric Psychology*, and in medicine, such as *Pain* or *Headache*. Become a voracious reader and explorer of such sources of ideas, and utilize your skills to make life better for people and earn a living at the same time.

## THE PSYCHOLOGIST IN A PLETHORA OF ROLES

Several books describe career opportunities and career paths for those entering psychology and the human services field in general. An important early contribution was presented by Woods (1976). More recently, Sternberg (1997) highlighted the experiences of individuals who chose 14 different paths, primarily at the doctoral level. Baxter (1990) focused primarily on counselors employed at the master's level. Collison and Garfield (1990) presented a wide variety of possibilities for mental health professionals. Consult these books and others like them. Mental health professionals work in all walks of society. Finding employment may be a function of knowing what might be available and how one's training and skills can fit into these positions.

There will always be jobs available in the traditional positions where psychologists have found themselves: in academia, college counseling centers, schools, government, and large corporations. They fit the mold of what trainee expectations developed during the course of graduate school and internship, but they are highly competitive. Consider other possibilities as shifts in the economy occur, along with changes in population demographics; there will always be a need for graduates of psychology training programs to be innovative in their thinking. Recall Paelet's (1978) description of the study in which in which graduates of community psychology programs found meaningful work with job titles that did not include the word "psychologist." In the last chapter of Woods (1976), "Potpourri: Jobs of psychologists in nontraditional and innovative roles," there is a sampling of such positions, including work in a public defender's office, as a childhood development specialist in television programming, as an aide in a U.S. Senator's office, conducting environmental research, as a warden for a juvenile correctional center, as a guidance specialist with foreign students, as an overseas industrial consultant, evaluating pharmaceutical interventions, as a museum consultant, and as a psychologist in a medical publishing company. Within the APA there is an acute awareness that there are not enough faculty positions available for those graduating with degrees in the more basic and experimental fields of psychology. These graduates can benefit from consulting the section of the APA web site focusing on nonacademic careers in psychology to better understand how research skills can transfer outside of the world of traditional experimental design.

In summary, consider the suggestion of Woody and Robertson (1997) that unknown and unpredictable conditions mean that predicting employment opportunities is always speculative. Both clinical and academic organizations are facing downsizing, and with the emergence of managed care, independent practice may not sustain itself as the outstanding growth industry it has been in the past. Making these points, Norcross, Karg, and Prochaska (1997) asked, "Where will the solid employment opportunities be created for our next generation of clinical psychologists?"

On a more optimistic note, the U.S. Department of Labor forecast of growing employment opportunities for psychologists through 2008 is a positive indicator for readers. If you seek and obtain appropriate training, develop your skills, conduct a self-assessment of your values and goals, and remain willing to be flexible and innovative in your thinking, you may build a wonderful career for yourself as a professional psychologist.

# REFERENCES

American Psychological Association. (1987). Guidelines for conditions of employment of psychologists. *American Psychologist, 42*, 724–729.

Baxter, N. (1990). *Opportunities in counseling and development careers*. Lincolnwood, IL: VGM Career Horizons.

Beigel, J., & Earle, R. (1990). *Successful private practice in the 1990's*. New York: Bruner Mazel.

Bernstein, B. (1978). Points to ponder when seeking a new professional position. *Professional Psychology, 9*, 341–349.

Black, M., & Holden, E. W. (1998). The impact of gender and productivity and satisfaction among medical school psychologists. *Journal of Clinical Psychology in Medical Settings, 5*, 117–131.

Brems, C., Lampman, C., & Johnson, M. (1995). Preparation of applications for academic positions in psychology, *American Psychologist, 50*, 533–537.

Browning, C., & Browning, B. (1986). *Private practice handbook*. Los Angeles: Duncliffs.

Collison, B., & Garfield, N. (1990). *Careers in counseling and human development*. Alexandria, VA: American Association for Counseling and Development.

Connerty, S. (1990). Private practice: Promise and reality. In E. Margenau (Ed.), *The encyclopedic handbook of private practice* (p. 453–460). New York: Gardner Press.

DeGalan, J., & Lambert, S. (1995). *Great jobs for psychology majors*. Lincolnwood, IL: VGM Career Horizons.

Ettinger, J. (1996). *Improved career decision making in a changing world*. Garrett Park, MD: Garrett Park Press.

Freudenberger, H., & Kurtz, T. (1990). Risks and rewards of independent practice. In E. Margenau (Ed.), *The encyclopedic handbook of private practice*. New York: Gardner Press.

Gottfredson, G., & Swatko, M. (1979). Employment, unemployment, and the job search in psychology. *American Psychologist, 34*, 1047–1060.

Haley, W., McDaniel, S., Bray, J., Frank, R., Heldring, M., Johnson, S., Lu, E., Reed, G., & Wiggins, J. (1998). Psychological practice in primary care settings: Practical tips for clinicians. *Professional Psychology: Research and Practice, 29*, 237–244.

Heppner, P., & Downing, N. (1982). Job interviewing for new psychologists: Riding the emotional roller coaster. *Professional Psychology, 13*, 334–341.

Keller, P. (1994). *Academic paths: Career decisions and experiences of psychologists*. Mahwah, NJ: Lawrence Erlbaum Associates.

Kohout, J. (1999, August). *Employment of new psychology doctorates in the 1980's and 1990's*. Paper presented at the Meetings of the American Psychological Association, Boston.

Kolt, L. (1999). *How to build a thriving fee-for-services practice: Integrating the healing side with the business side of psychotherapy*. New York: Academic Press.

Lawless, L. (1997). *How to build and market your mental health practice*. New York: John Wiley and Sons.

Levinson, E., Rafoth, M., & Sanders, P. (1994). Employment-related differences between male and female school psychologists. *Psychology in the Schools, 31*, 201–207.

Margenau, E. (1990). *The encyclopedic handbook of private practice*. New York: Gardner Press.

Mesh, S. (1989, August). *Developing employment strategies: Fears and fantasies influencing students' perspectives*. Paper presented at the Meetings of the American Psychological Association, New Orleans, Louisiana.

Messmer, M. (1995). *Job hunting for dummies*. Foster City, CA: IDG Books.

Nash, J., Norcross, J., & Prochaska, J. (1984). Satisfactions and stresses of independent practice. *Psychotherapy in Private Practice, 2*, 39–48.

Norcross, J., Karg, R., & Prochaska, J. (1997). Clinical psychologists in the 1990's: II. *Clinical Psychologist, 50,* 4–11.

Olson, S., Downing, N., Heppner, P., & Pinkney, J. (1986). Is there life after graduate school? Coping with the transition to postdoctoral employment. *Professional Psychology: Research and Practice, 17,* 415–419.

Paelet, D. (1978).The MA postgraduate marketplace in community psychology: A case study. *Journal of Community Psychology, 6,* 175–178.

Pesmen, S. (1996). *Dr. Job's complete career guide.* Lincolnwood, IL: VGM Career Horizons.

Plante, T. (1998). How to find a first job in professional psychology: Ten principles for finding employment for psychology interns and postdoctoral fellows. *Professional Psychology: Research and Practice, 29,* 508–511.

Pruitt, S., Klapow, J., Epping-Jordan, J., & Dresselhaus, T. (1998). Moving behavioral medicine to the front line: A model for the integration of behavioral and medical sciences in primary care. *Professional Psychology: Research and Practice, 29,* 230–236.

Rheingold, H. (1994). *The psychologist's guide to an academic career.* Washington DC: American Psychological Association.

Sheehan, E., McDevitt, T., & Ross, H. (1998). Looking for a job as a psychology professor? Factors affecting applicant success. *Teaching of Psychology, 25,* 8–11.

Simono, R., & Wachiowiak, D. (1983). Career patterns in college counseling centers: Counseling psychologists report on their past, present and future. *Professional Psychology: Research and Practice, 14,* 142–148.

Steinpreis, R., Anders, K., & Ritzke, D. (1999). The impact of gender on the review of the curricula vitae of job applicants and tenure candidates: A national empirical study. *Sex Roles, 41,* 509–528.

Sternberg, R. (1997). *Career paths in psychology: Where your degree can take you.* Washington, DC: American Psychological Association.

Stewart, A., Stewart, E., & Vogel, D. (2000). A study of intern's plans and preferences for postdoctoral training. *Professional psychology: Research and practice, 34,* 435–441.

Super, C., & Super, C. (1995). *Opportunities in psychology careers.* Lincolnwood, IL: VGM Career Horizons.

Thomas, J. (2000). Helping postdocs find jobs early is among goals of new APA panel. *National Psychologist, 9*(2), 1–3.

Thomas, A., & Witte, R. (1996). A study of gender differences among school psychologists. *Psychology in the Schools, 33,* 351.

Walfish, S., & Coovert, D. (1989). Developing and maintaining an independent practice: A Delphi Poll. *Professional Psychology: Research and Practice, 20,* 54–55.

Walfish, S., & Coovert, D. (1990). Career as business. In *The encyclopedic handbook of private practice* (pp. 431–441). New York: Gardner Press.

Williams, S., & Wedding, D. (1999). Employment characteristics and salaries of psychologists in United States medical schools: Past and current trends. *Journal of Clinical Psychology in Medical Settings, 6,* 221–238.

Woods, P. (1976). *Career opportunities for psychologists.* Washington, DC: American Psychological Association.

Woody, R. (1988a). *Fifty ways to avoid malpractice.* Sarasota, FL: Professional Resource Exchange.

Woody, R. (1988b). *Protecting your mental health practice.* San Francisco: Jossey-Bass.

Woody, R. (1989). *Business success in mental health practice.* San Francisco: Jossey-Bass.

Woody, R., & Robertson, M. (1997). *A career in clinical psychology: From training to employment.* Madison, CT: International University Press.

Yocom, D., Bruce, M., Cochenour, J., & Box, C. (1999). Stalking the academic appointment. *Counselor Education and Supervision, 38,* 260–269.

Yoder, J., & Crumpton, P. (1987). Some characteristics of jobs announced in the APA *Monitor. Professional Psychology: Research and Practice, 18,* 399–401.

Young, J., & Weishaar, M. (1997). Psychologists in private practice. In R. Sternberg (Ed.), *Career paths in psychology: Where your degree can take you* (pp. 71–91). Washington, DC: American Psychological Association.

Zanna, M., & Darley, J. (1987). *The compleat academic: A practical guide for the beginning social scientist.* Mahwah, NJ: Lawrence Erlbaum Associates.